the cinema of DAVID CRONENBERG

DIRECTORS' CUTS

Other titles in the Directors' Cuts series:

the cinema of EMIR KUSTURICA: *notes from the underground*
GORAN GOCIC

the cinema of KEN LOACH: *art in the service of the people*
JACOB LEIGH

the cinema of WIM WENDERS: *the celluloid highway*
ALEXANDER GRAF

the cinema of KATHRYN BIGELOW: *hollywood transgressor*
edited by DEBORAH JERMYN & SEAN REDMOND

the cinema of ROBERT LEPAGE: *the poetics of memory*
ALEKSANDAR DUNDJEROVIC

the cinema of GEORGE A. ROMERO: *knight of the living dead*
TONY WILLIAMS

the cinema of ANDRZEJ WAJDA: *the art of irony and defiance*
edited by JOHN ORR & ELZBIETA OSTROWSKA

the cinema of KRZYSZTOF KIEŚLOWSKI: *variations on destiny and chance*
MAREK HALTOF

the cinema of DAVID LYNCH: *american dreams, nightmare visions*
edited by ERICA SHEEN & ANNETTE DAVISON

the cinema of NANNI MORETTI: *dreams and diaries*
EWA MAZIERSKA & LAURA RASCAROLI

the cinema of MIKE LEIGH: *a sense of the real*
GARRY WATSON

the cinema of JOHN CARPENTER: *the technique of terror*
edited by IAN CONRICH & DAVID WOODS

the cinema of ROMAN POLANSKI: *dark spaces of the world*
edited by JOHN ORR & ELZBIETA OSTROWSKA

the cinema of TODD HAYNES: *all that heaven allows*
edited by JAMES MORRISON

the cinema of STEVEN SPIELBERG: *empire of light*
NIGEL MORRIS

the cinema of ANG LEE: *the other side of the screen*
WHITNEY CROTHERS DILLEY

the cinema of TERRENCE MALICK: *poetic visions of america (second edition)*
edited by HANNAH PATTERSON

the cinema of WERNER HERZOG: *aesthetic ecstasy and truth*
BRAD PRAGER

the cinema of LARS VON TRIER: *authenticity and artifice*
CAROLINE BAINBRIDGE

the cinema of NEIL JORDAN: *dark carnival*
CAROLE ZUCKER

the cinema of JAN ŠVANKMAJER: *dark alchemy*
edited by PETER HAMES

the cinema of JOHN SAYLES: *a lone star*
MARK BOULD

the cinema of SALLY POTTER: *the poetics of performance*
SOPHIE MAYER

the cinema of
DAVID CRONENBERG

from baron of blood to cultural hero

ernest mathijs

 **WALLFLOWER PRESS** LONDON & NEW YORK

First published in Great Britain
in 2008 by

Wallflower Press
6 Market Place, London W1W 8AF
www.wallflowerpress.co.uk

A catalogue record for this book is available from the British Library

ISBN 978-1-905674-65-7 (paperback)
      978-1-905674-66-4 (hardback)

Series design by Rob Bowden Design

CONTENTS

Acknowledgements   vii

Introduction: Cinema, Reality and What to Make of It   1

1   Exploration and Experimentation: *Stereo* and *Crimes of the Future*   9

2   Revolution and Rage: *Shivers* and *Rabid*   28

3   Cars and Races: *Fast Company* and *The Italian Machine*   53

4   Cult Curio: *The Brood* and *Scanners*   72

5   Politics and Paranoia: *Videodrome* and *The Dead Zone*   102

6   Science and Progress: *The Fly* and *Dead Ringers*   129

7   Muses and Machos: *Naked Lunch* and *M. Butterfly*   156

8   Scars and Wrecks: *Crash*   180

9   Cues and Clues: *eXistenZ* and *Spider*   196

10 Family Affairs: *A History of Violence* and *Eastern Promises*   225

Notes   257

Filmography   276

Bibliography   284

Index   306

ACKNOWLEDGEMENTS

This book has been in the making, in one form or another, since 1993. Its topic has survived mutations of many shapes, including academic dissertations, essays, reviews, presentations, classes, courses and bar talk. Like offspring, it has turned out completely different from what it was supposed to be yet it could not be closer to what it needed to be.

Many minds and hearts had a hand in helping to bring this project to fruition. I owe gratitude to the Department of Communication Studies at the Free University of Brussels and the Department of Theatre, Film and Television at Aberystwyth University, which invested in the start of this project, and the Department of Theatre and Film at the University of British Columbia, which allowed me time to complete it. I thank the Fund for Scientific Research of Flanders and the UK's Arts and Humanities Research Council for grants to support part of the research, and the Belgian Royal Film Archive for providing me access to the troves of information they hold on Cronenberg. Particular thanks go to Professors Martin Barker, Mark Jancovich and Brian McIlroy for stimulating feedback and encouragement. I also want to express my thanks to a range of colleagues and students who aided me with their expert knowledge, inside views and good advice: William Beard, Patricia Canino, Nicholas Campbell, Wouter Hessels, Russ Hunter, John Landis, Tatiana Maslany, Xavier Mendik, Bert Mosselmans, Kim Newman, Matthew Ross, Jamie Sexton, Katherine Spring and the MA class of 2005–06 at the University of British Columbia.

I am hugely indebted to Yoram Allon of Wallflower Press, who believed in this from the start and kept a close watch on proceedings – always with the right encouragement at hand. Thanks must also go to Ian Cooper and Jacqueline Downs for taking charge of the editing process.

Finally, my sincerest thanks to my wife Emily, my children, and the entire family for granting me time to plough away in the depths and darkness that is film analysis. I could not have completed this without their generosity and patience.

This book is dedicated to four free spirits who taught me to think: Hubert Dethier, Dina Hellemans, Sylvain Keuleers and Ernest Mandel.

Vancouver, July 2008

Just because you're paranoid doesn't mean they're not after you.

Catch-22 (Mike Nichols, 1970)

If you're a wonderful paranoid, you believe that someone is in control, and to me that's optimistic. You think that someone somewhere has figured it out, has managed to control it, and has a vision of how things should be. To me, that's optimistic. So, I'm not even allowing myself the optimism of paranoia.

David Cronenberg (in Breskin 1992: 232)

INTRODUCTION: CINEMA, REALITY AND WHAT TO MAKE OF IT

Our own perception of reality is the only one we'll accept, it's all we have to go on, and, if you're going mad, that is still your reality.

— David Cronenberg (in Lucas 1983a: 151)

Reality is what you make of it. It's almost as though you choose one and you cling to it. We see that politically. I see that in Mr. Bush. You see these people living out a different reality and they're acting on it. And they're not compatible realities, but they are ferociously devoted to these realities. It's kind of interesting, when it's not terrifying. And you realise that they will kill people to maintain the level of realness of those realities. That's a scary thing, but it's a very human thing. No other creatures in the universe do that.

— David Cronenberg (in Kaufman 2003 n. p.)

Baby, life's what you make it.

— Talk Talk, 'Life's What You Make It'

The Public Presence of David Cronenberg

It is impossible to write about film and not discuss culture. No film exists in isolation. Apart from its evident place in culture as an artefact, as a product with economic, social and political implications as part of an industry, craft or policy, each film also has a content, structure and style that relates to the world we live in. I agree with film scholars who urge that film studies should separate itself from attempts to use cinema as a vehicle to illustrate theories, philosophies, opinions, interventions, or

– heaven help us – prophecies of doom or glory. Cinema is not a tool designed to support either science or the other arts, but an expression in itself.

This does not mean cinema is only about the screen. Many films actually attempt to make claims about the world with their stories, images, metaphors, characters, settings or other techniques (together *with* them, not *via* them – note the distinction between companionship and channel). David Cronenberg's are such films. They offer insights into the human condition. They also remark, sometimes in passing but invariably with eloquence, on 'the times' they, and we, live in. That observation forms the backbone of this book, and it recurs in each chapter.

While firmly rooted within the then-fashionable underground scene *Stereo* (1969) and *Crimes of the Future* (1970) carried within them reflections on the 1960s counterculture as well as criticisms of how it was undermined. *Shivers* (1975) and *Rabid* (1977) speculated on the monstrosity inside each of us, and how humans face their mortality and morality – especially in the face of death and lust – while being haunted for their 'abnormalities' and their 'Baron of Blood' director chased from his home. *Fast Company* (1979) reflected on adaptability, dedication and teamwork as Cronenberg was finding his professional grit. *The Brood* (1979) and *Scanners* (1981) exposed cults at the same time as they became cults of the flourishing horror genre. *Videodrome* (1983) and *The Dead Zone* (1983) commented on the politics of paranoia even as they, and Cronenberg, became entangled in censorship. *The Fly* (1986) and *Dead Ringers* (1988) unpacked the industries of science and medicine at a time when curing people was developing into a greedy business. The adaptations from literature and drama – *Naked Lunch* (1991) and *M. Butterfly* (1993) – while also being about writing and staging the self, represented Cronenberg's breakthrough as a 'cultural hero' with the elitist and exotic cultural spheres they investigated. *Crash* (1996) was as much about incompleteness and deformation as it was about controversy, largely by being ripped out of context. The search-and-destroy narratives *eXistenZ* (1999) and *Spider* (2002) showcased failed interventions in actions, private lives and history, exactly at a time when Cronenberg seemed to be interfering with the reception of his films more stubbornly than before. *A History of Violence* (2005) and *Eastern Promises* (2007), finally, examined the violent foundations of that nucleus of culture called family while being produced against the background of warfare, religious zeal, ruthless competitiveness, human trafficking and diasporic immigration that obstruct family happiness worldwide.

There, that is the book in a nutshell. Each chapter in this study tackles two issues simultaneously: the films, and how they are inspired by, negotiate with, and impact on the cultures they originate from. At times, these 'cultures' are microscopic: a local underground scene, a subculture, a few critics, or one's family. Often however, these cultures are large. They can encompass territories (Toronto, Ontario, Montreal, Québec, Canada, 'middle-America', North America, London, Western civilisation, the Orient…), timeframes (the permissive 1970s, the tax shelter system, the greedy 1980s, the disengagement of the 1990s, post-9/11 civil anxiety) or events (1970 martial law in Québec, the 'Video-Nasties' controversy, the AIDS awareness campaigns of the mid-1980s, Canadian pro- and anti-censorship campaigns in the 1980s, the fatwa against

Salman Rushdie, the war in Iraq...). At their broadest, the themes and concepts that link Cronenberg's films to their surroundings involve crucial concepts of the world we (want to) live in: the role of family in modern times, the rhetoric of the American Dream, the influence of government policies on individual freedom, the role of the artist, the quest for the meaning of existence. To assume Cronenberg's films remain mute amidst the cultural commotion these concepts provoke would be to do injustice to them.

Cues and quotes
The methodology used in this book is best described as a combination of reception studies and textual analysis. The theoretical background against which this method plays is one that asserts, as David Bordwell does in his dissection of critical interpretation, *Making Meaning* (1989), that films are 'made to mean' by audiences discussing the cues and clues the films offer. Occasionally, such meanings are fairly self-explanatory, coming from texts pregnant with allusions just waiting to be harvested. At other times, audiences need their sharpest sophistication in order to grasp any meaning at all. Easy or difficult, most films' cues are there to capture. To complicate matters, Cronenberg's films often contain both levels of meaning within one sample – frequently disguising themselves as one easy type (a horror movie about experiments gone wrong has the lesson 'do not mess with nature') while also inhabiting the traits of the more difficult variation (the lesson might also be that 'science is a pursuit that constructs a reality to fit the cultural needs of its time').

Audiences not only cognitively construct meaning, they are sometimes also bombarded with it – hit in their guts, their instincts and moral beliefs, shocked and shaken beyond comprehension. Then, the puzzle-solving intellect struggles to maintain dominance over the offended sensitivity. Cronenberg's films are masterful in such bombardments, asking us to consent to imagery of exploding heads, ripped torsos, sexual violence, abused women, torture, suicide, decay and unbridled sexuality we would not otherwise, perhaps, consider watching. And once in a while audiences just cannot take it and resist. *Shivers, The Brood* and *Crash* are just a few examples of the uproar Cronenberg's films have caused internationally.

The meaning of films is not a one-way street with cues and clues from the film translated by audiences into cultural value; bits and pieces of public culture and private concern, what I would like to call 'quotes' (quotes from the world, as it were), are stuck onto the film. Some of these quotes are inconspicuous and have no permanent impact on meaning (a distraction during a screening, or a wandering thought about daily niggles); others create a framework that forces meaning upon the film (your first ever nude scene, or watching a film at a festival amidst a boisterous audience); yet others offer tools for interpretation (the unexpected connection with a book recently read, or another film). The first Cronenberg movie I was consciously aware of – indeed enthralled by – was *Scanners*. Biking my way to a small-town library in northeast Belgium I made a habit of passing by what was to my limited knowledge the biggest video store on earth. Outside hung a poster for *Scanners*, and next to it some lobby cards with the exploding head prominently visible. The promise of an exploding head was probably too much to keep the mind of an impressionable boy from racing and though it took me years to actually see the film, because of the quick turnover in that store and it not being the kind of film state television would broadcast (though Belgium's public network did show *Videodrome* once when regular programming was suspended due to a strike), I memorised the name of the director. When *The Dead Zone* and *The Fly* came around I was ready to be converted, with the former becoming my first Cronenberg video rental; the latter my first theatrical Cronenberg. Later, as a student looking for a 'cool' topic for a dissertation the private passion I held for Cronenberg's films also turned out to have educational currency. In what I perceived to be a futile act I wrote Cronenberg a letter asking if he would send me some information for my research. The fact he actually wrote back terrified me! Small as these 'quotes' may be they have undeniably informed my positioning of *Scanners* as a cult film, *The Dead Zone* as an accessible mainstream film, *The Fly* as a box-office hit, *Videodrome* as a hidden gem and *Naked Lunch* as high art – and I seem not to be alone in that. In general, quotes floating around the film, pressed into the viewing situation, are as significant as cues buried inside it.[1]

Public presence, active auteur

Critical and academic attention for the cinema of David Cronenberg has traditionally seen his films as a certain set of production qualities and inspirations (clues and cues in other words), most of them amounting to something 'kind of offbeat, kind of weird, kind of strange' that makes a Cronenberg film. I would like to balance that by offering an account that also, not exclusively but in addition, recognises the cultural situations and practices that preoccupy Cronenberg's audiences, be they fans watching his films in cultish congregations such as genre festivals, critics challenged by the literary references scattered around the narratives, or students, buffs and cinephiles curious to see where Cronenberg got his peculiar reputation of Baron-of-Blood-turned-cultural-hero from. Each of those conditions and practices generates its own discourse and references, and observing how they fit or resist the stuff oozing out of Cronenberg's films outranks discussing them as if they exist in a vacuum.[2]

Prevalent throughout this book is the understanding that Cronenberg's films have a place in public culture. That presence is mostly researched in a direct way: assessing the public life of the films as commodities and cultural artefacts. There is however also an indirect component: ancillary materials and discourses such as the critical reception, publicity materials, distribution circles, debates in interviews, biographical information, sequels (even when Cronenberg had nothing to do with them), or the previous and subsequent professional affiliations of the films' personnel (doesn't it make a difference when an actor like Nicholas Campbell pops up in no less than four Cronenberg films?) all have their own places in the cultural industry and art of cinema. Yet they influence the way audiences access and assess them. Together, the direct and indirect presences lead to a frame of reference: a complex network of nodes and connections, 'degrees of separation' as playwright John Guare would call them, which make up the reputation and cultural status of the oeuvre.[3] One thing these connections never are is just private. This book is only interested in the receptions of Cronenberg's films inasmuch as these are shared on public platforms; it does not care about 'private pleasures' if these do not enter the official sphere of culture.[4]

A filmmaker as clever as Cronenberg is aware of these processes and frameworks. There is a natural impulse to intervene in the reception of one's own films that typifies the beginning of a career, and Cronenberg's activities to assert his authorship have been no different, writing letters to papers, reacting to hostile reviews and granting interviews to information-hungry fanzines to get his own views known to his audiences. In that regard I would like to call Cronenberg an *active auteur*.[5] Perhaps more than most other filmmakers, however, Cronenberg's efforts have paid off, partly because of his insistence, partly because his opinions are indeed insightful intellectual exercises in sophisticated interpretation – if nothing else, Cronenberg is certainly the most learned and astute of filmmakers in terms of intelligence. There is a general consensus among critics that Cronenberg's opinions on his own films are to be accepted and trusted – that they are the *nec plus ultra* of their meaning – a situation the indispensability of the extremely popular *Cronenberg on Cronenberg* interview book is a symptom of (Rodley 1997). This position has given Cronenberg almost full ownership over the debates of his films, and whenever there are attempts to tear that ownership away from him (as was the case with the *Crash* controversy) he acts in frustration. Thankfully, Cronenberg has not retreated into an ivory tower. Even today, he shares his insights generously. Literally all one needs to know about him is available as a source. Yet he continues to be accessible and gentle, radiating the confidence of an active auteur, erudite, articulate and comfortable with intellectualising his films.

The Cronenberg project

Mark Irwin, for a decade Cronenberg's director of photography, once famously said that Cronenberg remade the same movie every time, as if it was one long project (in Lucas 1983a: 149). Irwin has a valid point. Cronenberg's oeuvre is nothing if not consistent. When his films are watched back-to-back the similarities are striking. Cronenberg's style is characterised by wide-angle lens compositions (separating individuals from each other but also foregrounding the protagonist's subjectivity), smooth tracking shots, sparse use of music and a resistance to parallel cutting, slow motion and jittery handheld camera work (though the early films do contain some of these). Cronenberg's formal arrangements construct a sense of desolation and detachment. Set designs are similar throughout his oeuvre, with a flair for low-key, Spartan, slightly underlit scenes (cold and cool but not flashy or shiny), earthy tones of colour and a peculiar preference for old-fashioned wallpaper (especially in *The Brood, The Dead Zone* and *Spider*). Cronenberg's films hardly ever deviate significantly from the 90-minute length the horror genre accustomed him to. The stories are straightforward in their fixation on a minimum of protagonists and supporting characters (there are seldom big crowd scenes), and any external aids to storytelling are kept to the bare essentials (few voice-overs, usually no framings by narrators external to the story). Generally, the focus is on one character and their struggle to break out of a reality they are convinced they are trapped in.

Thematically, Cronenberg's films are about subjective interpretations of reality that are seen as (or become) objectively real – either in the conviction of the characters or in their experiences. Much, then, is in the eye of the beholder. As the quotes at the beginning of this introduction infer, Cronenberg believes our perception of reality is not necessarily the ontologically truest one, but it is essential we hang on to it for dear life because it is the only thing we have. That makes for isolated, lonely, abandoned and disillusioned characters – often brought to suicide or death by their existential dread of being alone. In that sense, Cronenberg is, as he has often indicated, a true existentialist.[6] A convinced atheist, he sees no reality outside our own mundane life; no greater scheme besides biological evolution and no general path mankind follows besides the one we carve out for ourselves (including the mistakes we make while trying).

What distinguishes Cronenberg in his existentialism is his appreciation of the human body. In an effort to 'mend the Cartesian rift' between Mind and Body (as he himself has repeatedly put it (see Drew 1984: 17), Cronenberg's films equip the human body with a will of its own. Amoral in the most literal sense, there is no 'good' or 'bad' body. Cronenberg asks viewers to accept a tumour, a wound, a deficiency not as a fault or flaw but a companion to the rest of the body. Cronenberg once used the metaphor of colonialism to describe the relationship between the 'normal' body and its outgrowths; the growths are first seen as a rebellion by the 'normal' body, then their desire for independent existence is resisted, and finally some arrangement is found in which the two are forced to live together. As one character in *The Brood* says of his tumour: 'I have a revolution on my hands and I am not very good in putting it down.' The parasites in *Shivers*, the armpit penis in *Rabid*, the flesh-gun in *Videodrome* or the mutating Brundle-Fly in *The Fly* do not get the chance to come to full and functional fruition. Visually Cronenberg's interest translates in so-called 'money shots' fitting the genre of the horror film in which much of his oeuvre has found an ideal niche. Close-ups of mutated and disfigured bodies abound in those films, from root-like nerves extending from a man's nostrils in *Crimes of the Future* to the mashed-up blood-squirting nose of a villain in *A History of Violence*; from the razor slicing a girl's abdomen in *Shivers* to a knife puncturing an eye in *Eastern Promises*. Each Cronenberg film seems to contain such shocking images. Beyond immediate shock value these shots offer a way into understanding Cronenberg's fascination for the accidental composition and contingency of the human body and how it is 'supposed' to look.

Cronenberg is not a propagandist in forwarding this observation. He usually pitches his existentialist characters against (or amidst) cults: firm and fanatic flocks of believers. The scientists and revolutionaries who lead such cults are zealous but not entirely unconvincing – it is not so much comforting to believe their ideas about sexuality, science, progress and the meaning of life, as it is exciting and intellectually stimulating. Doctors Stringfellow, Rouge, Hobbes, Keloid, Raglan, Ruth, O'Blivion, Weizak, Brundle, Mantle, Benway and the underground figures Vaughan and Vinokur are among the most credible film prophets of doom and glory. They invariably corral then command a troupe of dedicated followers who worship them as cult idols, even gods. The cultist dedication and conspiratorial secrecy of congregations and corporations is not only frightening but also appealing in its efficiency and ruthlessness. These organisations include the Academy of Erotic Inquiry, the Institute of Neo-Venereal Disease, the Starliner Towers inhabitants, the Keloid clinic's cosmetic surgery addicts, the Somafree Institute's Psychoplasmics patients, Consec's Scanners (but also the defected Scanners), the Cathode Ray Mission and Spectacular Optical, Bartok Industries, Mantle Inc, Interzone, Vaughan's Car Crash disciples, Antenna Research, Cortical Systematics (but also the revolutionary Realists), the East Coast Irish mafia, and the Russian crime syndicate Vory V Zakone.

The list above also shows a development: the earlier examples stress voluntary collaboration – in the name of science or self-improvement – whereas the latter examples tend to stress family relationships. Cronenberg's position towards the family unit is an ambivalent one. As early as 1983, Tim Lucas observed Cronenberg's 'abiding concern with family' (1983a: 149). Subsequently, Philip Nutman (1992) and Serge Grünberg (1992: 131–5) noted how most films up to and including *Dead Ringers* see family bonds destroyed, 'doomed to failure'. Since the beginning of the twenty-first century, however, the nuclear family has been portrayed more sympathetically. It is still largely a mess, but at least it is a failure to be cared for rather than just horrified by. There are brief moments of family happiness in Cronenberg's later work, a significant change from the early days. The 'family' theme is also one that extends into the production process. Cronenberg is known for establishing familial relationships with his cast and crew, often hiring them time and again. If one ties all the family metaphors together (Cronenberg's family, the cult as family, the crew as family, the family of critics and fans) the impression emerges that Cronenberg presents 'family' as a constructive element in our culture – the most instinctive expression of the need to unite forces to ensure one's individual survival.

The conflict between the frightened, abandoned individual and the tightly-knit cultist community or family is one that is never fully resolved in Cronenberg's films. Nor can it be. The clash between the distorted perception of reality of the anxious individual in its unreliable body, and the formally organised, objectifying perception of reality advocated by supposedly rational communities is incommensurable – paradigmatically different. As such, then, Cronenberg's films are explorations of the tension between the One and the Whole, the unique entity and the collective, both destined to be restricted by what they are prepared to accept as real.

My discussion of the public presence of Cronenberg's oeuvre is not limited to his feature films. I have also included discussions of his short films, his acting work and some other activities he has been involved in (chairing juries, public speaking, patronage and so on). Hence, this book offers discussions of *Transfer* (1966), *From the Drain* (1967), *Secret Weapons* (1972), *The Lie Chair* (1975), *The Italian Machine* (1976), *Nightbreed* (Clive Barker, 1990), *Last Night* (Don McKellar, 1998), *Jason X* (James Isaac, 2001), *Camera* (2000) and *At the Suicide of the Last Jew in the World in the Last Cinema in the World* (2007). There are also passages on aborted projects such as *Total Recall* (Paul Verhoeven, 1990) and *Red Cars* and additional acting work in *Into the Night* (John Landis, 1985), *Trial By Jury* (Heywood Gould, 1994), *To Die For* (Gus Van Sant, 1995) and *Resurrection* (Russell Mulcahy, 1999), which hardly ever get recognised as even part of the oeuvre. For the overall picture of the public presence of Cronenberg such materials are crucial. They complete the portrait of a career, an attitude and a reputation – not just Cronenberg's, but equally that of an industry or an audience.

Beyond the materials Cronenberg himself has been involved with, films and trends he has helped shape also demand scrutiny. The sequels to *The Fly* and *Scanners*, and the *Dead Zone* television series are obviously influenced by the originals. Conversely, the materials Cronenberg claims to have been inspired by help determine his public presence. Famously original, Cronenberg only associates himself with a few literary figures: Vladimir Nabokov, William Burroughs, Samuel Beckett, Franz Kafka and Fyodor Dostoyevsky. In the margin of those mentions, there is the cultural status of writers whose work he has adapted for screen, such as Stephen King, J. G. Ballard, David Henry Hwang (as well as Puccini's *Madame Butterfly*) and Patrick McGrath. More indirectly, the horror fan press (*Fangoria* and *Cinefantastique* in particular); the film festivals of Toronto and Cannes; his acquaintances with John Landis, Martin Scorsese, Salman Rushdie, Clive Barker; occasional affiliations with critics such as Tim Lucas or special effects artists like Chris Walas; his endorsements of numerous forms of art and entertainment; his feud with the British conservative press; and a deft letter to the leader of his country ... all of those nodes help map a network of connections that complete a picture of one of the most influential filmmakers of the last three decades.[7] Cronenberg's esteem extends beyond cinema into the essence of culture.

Reality – and what to make of it

Films are never just films. They are also about the lives they touch, the cultures they come from and are released into, the people who make them and see them. Film studies should not be blind to the ways in which films operate as cultural artefacts that help shape reality as well as represent it. Cronenberg's films create trouble, raise consciousness and provoke strong feelings; they give people the chance to make demarcations, take up positions and form alliances. These complex, stimulating, shocking stories of exploding heads and gristle guns, car crashes and talking type-writer bugs, can thrill, disgust and even help us to make sense of reality.

CHAPTER ONE

Exploration and Experimentation:
Stereo and *Crimes of the Future*

Everything you think do and say is in the pill you took today.
> – Zager & Evans, 'In the Year 2525'

Abandon every hope, ye who enter here.
> – Dante, *The Divine Comedy*, Canto III, 7

The Artist as a Young Man

David Cronenberg was destined for a profession in the arts. He was born on 15 March 1943 into a Jewish middle-class family in the Crawford Street neighbourhood of Toronto; at the age of 15 the family moved to a residential area north of Eglinton Avenue. His mother Esther was an accompanist and rehearsal pianist, and father Milton a freelance writer – editing the magazine *True Canadian Stories*, writing the stamp column for the *Toronto Telegram* and contributing to *Reader's Digest*. David's older sister Denise was a ballet dancer. She would later be wardrobe mistress and costume designer for his films, from *Videodrome* onwards. In such a milieu, the young Cronenberg's explorations of and experimentations with the arts and intellect were stimulated. According to Peter Morris, Cronenberg's parents would indulge his enthusiasms, whether they were for playing guitar, veterinary medicine or racing technology – one passion that would not wane (1994: 15). Cronenberg went to Kent Senior School, and then to Harbord Collegiate Institute; he then spent the last years before he went to University at North Toronto Collegiate Institute.[1]

Both Morris and Chris Rodley observe the 'lack' of trauma or repression in Cronenberg's childhood, offering the death of his cat as the most terrible event throughout his formative years. That is, until the illness and untimely death of his father touched the family profoundly:

> He [his father] resented my mother because he was dying and she wasn't, and she resented having to take care of him. I remember him saying to me that he didn't see why he should have to die and I should live. His body was sick; he said he wanted to have my body.[2]

But that was not to happen until 1973, when Cronenberg was thirty years old, had already made two avant-garde features, and he found his first wife Margaret Hindson becoming gradually estranged from him and their daughter Cassandra. Still, even if there is no 'classical' trauma, from his teens onwards Cronenberg fits the model of the liberal intellectual. He performed well at school, did not espouse any dominant religious views, enjoyed watching films indiscriminately (one of his favourites being *Forbidden Planet*), read widely, and tried his hand at story writing. He submitted a short story to the *Magazine of Fantasy and Science Fiction* at the age of 16. Unfortunately it was rejected (see Sammon 1981: 22). All these explorations and experimentations led Cronenberg to see science and art as equally important intellectual endeavours, which he observed as if from a distance. The entry for the 1960–61 Harbord Yearbook, which he wrote himself, says:

> David is a writer and a perceptive genius as well. As such, he is an observer. These, being his own terms, are thus indisputable. This is how he explains the fact that he has done nothing in his five years at Harbord. He merely observes. His future is quite indefinite. All we can say is 'good luck!'[3]

Cronenberg graduated from Harbord with an average of 80% (an excellent score in the days before inflated marks), which meant his name was 'forever walled' at the school, as writer and co-alumnus Ashley Allinson puts it.[4]

In 1963, Cronenberg enrolled as a Science Major in the University of Toronto, then Canada's most established university. But he dropped out within a few months because he found the courses lacked the 'excitement, discovery, creativity … the infinite possibility that you get with the study of literature, and which you should get with the study of science' (in Rodley 1997: 7). To put it in the terms of the then-topical philosopher of science Thomas Kuhn, Cronenberg sought paradigm-shifts, not 'normal science' (Kuhn 1962). Cronenberg's attitude was that of the person for whom the question is more interesting than any finite answer – not the preacher but the philosopher. As philosopher, Cronenberg loves understatement, like many of the characters in his films, especially the scientists. With the exception of *Videodrome's* Brian O'Blivion perhaps – who is quite brash – Cronenberg's scientists try to let their work speak for itself. But that does not mean they are estranged from the world, reclusive and solitary. No, they seek contact, as did Cronenberg in his formative years, and they love to hang out. Seth Brundle in *The Fly*, Elliot Mantle in *Dead Ringers* and Allegra Geller in *eXistenZ* appreciate human interaction, and seek it even if they are a tad awkward in their manners, otherwise they would never attend the social functions that set off their adventures. This profile of marginal belonging fitted Cronenberg as a university student perfectly. He quit the science programme and enrolled in English, finishing first in his class after his first year. He began to be a 'dilettante aesthete', as Morris calls it, growing his hair and developing an aesthetic attitude towards life. Amidst a developing cultural framework that gradually highlighted political stances, this meant Cronenberg would still be the relative outsider, his appreciation of the Beats, Nabokov and Burroughs slightly off-centre with the prevailing mood amongst English students.

Cronenberg completed two more years of his English degree, then decided he needed a break, and travelled throughout Europe for nearly a year. He lived mainly in Copenhagen which, along with Amsterdam, was probably one of the cities most in tune with the hippie culture of the time – and one where his aesthetic interests would fit well with local 'provos', students whose political actions were essentially aesthetic and intended, like the surrealists, to shock the bourgeoisie. He returned to his English degree and eventually graduated in 1967 (see Sammon 1981: 22).

The Toronto Underground: Cinethon, Transfer and From the Drain

When he returned to Toronto, Cronenberg became engulfed in its thriving underground film culture, one whose ascendance and frame of reference is worth some elaboration if we are to understand Cronenberg's beginnings in film.

On a national level, Canadian cinema itself had finally begun to get noticed. The market of theatres was relatively large (roughly 1,500 theatres and drive-ins), and in 1967 the government initiated the Canadian Film Development Corporation, designed to support feature fiction production. Besides a highly respected series of documentaries, the most significant achievements were the independent efforts of Larry Kent, Don Owen and David Secter. Kent started indie film production in the west of Canada with his infamous *The Bitter Ash* (1963), a film about rebellious youths that was screened at campuses in Vancouver and Montreal before it was banned (see Anon. 1963: 1; Douglas 1996). Kent went on to explore themes of sexuality and drug-taking in subsequent films such as *Sweet Substitute* (1964) and *High* (1967), and though his exposure never stretched beyond intermittent screenings in Canada's main cities, he remained an important exponent of a newly emerging cultural trend. Similarly, Don Owen's *Nobody Waved Goodbye* (1964) put youthful rebellion at the centre of its narrative. It too became notorious, mainly because it was funded by the National Film Board and was hence supposed to be a documentary, but also because it exposed a gap in appreciation between Canada's critics (who hated it) and New York's reviewers, who saw the rebellious attitude as one relevant to the times (see Murphy 2006). This dichotomy between critical appreciation in Canada and the United States would also become visible in the reception of Cronenberg's films. Finally, David Secter's *Winter Kept Us Warm* (1965) too explored youthful rebellion, this time with a gay relationship forming part of the narrative. Filmed on location at the University of Toronto, Secter's film made a huge impact on Cronenberg, who cites it regularly as a film that pushed him towards film practice himself – it also featured Iain Ewing and Jack Messinger, who would appear in Cronenberg's own films. But while these three films shared with Cronenberg's early work a spirit of rebellion, their philosophical grounding and challenging of morality is far removed from his own. Their characters explore freedom but get tangled up in the moral maze that is created – it is no coincidence that the films end on a dubious note, either unable to advance the newly-won freedom fully or by having the old social forces break up newly-formed relationships. Cronenberg's films would avoid this trap by obliterating that maze. For him, the inspiration did not lie with the search for a new order, but rather with the dismissal of all systems of order, a true 'counter milieu'.[5] It would not shield Cronenberg from disdain and controversy, but it did give his films an entirely different set of qualities. So while Cronenberg's introduction to film came at a time of heightened activity, a re-birth as Jim Leach calls it (2006: 24–35), they could never be compared to traditions in Canadian cinema (see also Melnyk 2004: 100–7).

Next to this national re-birth, much of the impetus of the Toronto underground film culture came from the United States, especially New York. The screenings of *New York Eye and Ear Control* (1964) by Torontonian Michael Snow (residing in New York at the time) were pretty well publicised, even leading to headlines. Soon, venues such as the Bohemian Embassy and the Film Societies of the University of Toronto and McMaster University in nearby Hamilton became kernels of underground film activity, instigating production as well as exhibition.[6] Morris details how the McMaster Film Board, set up in 1965 by Peter Rowe, Ivan Reitman, Dan Goldberg, Eugene Levy and John Hofsess produced and distributed films, one of which, Hofsess's *Black Zero* (1967), has Cronenberg in a brief nude scene (1994: 36–7). In Toronto, Cronenberg became involved in the founding of a similar society, the Film Makers Co-operative of Canada, together with Bob Fothergill and Iain Ewing. A theatre called Cinecity, operated by Willem Poolman, became the centre of all activity.

In this exciting atmosphere of underground cinema, Cronenberg started his own career. After having prepared himself for shooting by reading copies of *American Cinematographer*, Cronenberg rented a 16mm camera and helped by his then fiancée (and later wife) Margaret and a few friends he shot *Transfer* and *From the Drain*. *Transfer* tells the story of a psychiatrist sitting at a table in the snow (a typical Canadian landscape), listening to the complaints of his patient, who has been obsessively following him. Seven minutes in total, *Transfer* is a short meditation on the interaction between a subject investigating (the psychiatrist) and an object investigated (the patient), a traditional scientific relationship, but offered here with a twist – after all the object is not supposed to talk back. *From the Drain* also contains two men, both in a bathtub, who appear to discuss biological warfare. Some sort of plant comes out of the drain, and strangles one of the men. In an eerie, yet also Chaplinesque gesture, the other man disposes of his shoes in a cupboard already filled with shoes. While described by Cronenberg as a Beckettian absurd sketch, *From the Drain* also covers a conspiracy, of trying to rid the world of war-veterans – in this sense it parallels Beckett's *End Game* (1957). Of course, at the time, the war referred to could not be anything else but Vietnam, a topic particularly relevant in Canada, which had just opened its doors to American draft dodgers.

Making two shorts was one thing; getting them noticed another. Cronenberg profited from a major event in the Toronto underground scene in the summer of 1967 called Cinethon – a two-day marathon at Cinecity of experimental and avant-garde cinema covering the best and newest from North America, including established American underground films by Kenneth Anger (*Eaux D'Artifice*, 1953; *Inauguration of the Pleasure Dome*, 1954), Andy Warhol (*Vinyl*, 1965) and Bruce Conner (*A Movie*, 1958), and premieres from Ed Emshwiller (*Relativity*, 1966), Michael Snow's wife Joyce Wieland (*Bill's Hat*, 1967) and George Kuchar (*Hold Me While I'm Naked*, 1966). Among the most lauded films were Robert Nelson's hilarious allegory of racial equality *Oh Dem Watermelons* (1965), Richard Preston's *Son of Dada* (1967), and Gunvar Nelson and Dorothy Wiley's messy criticism of the obsession of beauty *Schmeergunz* (1967) – a film preoccupied with 'garbage, vomit and excretement'. Amidst all that *Transfer* was also shown. In a review in Toronto's *Globe and Mail*, it was called 'a pathetic effort by Toronto's David Croonenberg [sic]. Horribly acted and scarcely directed, it didn't have the decency to be original: it was stolen from a Nichols and May sketch' (Kareda 1967: 14). If one ever wonders where Cronenberg's occasional dissatisfaction with the critical reception of his films originated, here it is. An indignant Cronenberg sent a letter to the newspaper, replying he had 'never in any medium come across the sketch'. Moreover, Cronenberg asserted in 1967:

> *Transfer*, within the context of Cinethon, was totally original. It was heavily dependent on dialogue and was the only film in the festival using lip-synchro-nized sound exclusively. One can only pretend to critical omniscience for so long before a lack of true comprehension of the intricacies involved in one medium or the other shows through. (1967: n. p.)

In spite of having his name misspelled and his work thrashed in this first ever review, Cronenberg had no real reason to feel aggravated. Cinethon was a success, and the wide coverage it enjoyed gave the Toronto underground scene, and hence Cronen-berg's career, a real boost (see Delaney 1967). Still, at a time when filmmakers were experimenting with multiple reel projection (in Hofsess's *Palace of Pleasure* (1966), or Warhol's *Chelsea Girls* (1966)), or exploring visual richness, Cronenberg had to up the ante and move further on from 16mm shorts if he wanted to be considered a serious filmmaker. After having received a $3,500 grant to write a novel, Cronenberg rented a 35mm camera and started work on *Stereo*.

There is no easy way to summarise *Stereo*. As with so many other experimental films of the time it is as much an experience as it is a story in which voice-over and image conflict with each other. What follows is kept intentionally descriptive to give an impression of the kind of experience it was.

The film opens with a long and static black and white shot of what looks like a campus ground, featuring a concrete building in a park with a sculpture. A helicopter approaches. A man (Ron Mlodzik) dressed in a caped outfit (he looks like a cross between a lord, a highwayman and a rock star) exits the helicopter. As he looks around, in extreme slow motion, a voice-over tells us that we are about to witness an experiment: eight 'highly unique individuals' underwent brain surgery in order to give them telepathic capabilities, 'extra-sensory perception, or ESP'. What we are to witness is the first meeting of all subjects, at the Sanatorium of the Academy of Erotic Inquiry.

Once our caped protagonist has entered the Sanatorium, the voice-over tells us that the experiment relies on the interdependency of the 'organic' relationship between the researcher and the subject. Meanwhile, our protagonist is shown his quarters. A quick montage of the interior reveals props and furniture matching the outfit of the guest (velvet pillows, ornate decorations, religious icons, glass cases with antique plates), clashing with the hyper-modernist architecture of the Sanatorium (long corridors with sparsely decorated, concrete walls and floor-to-ceiling windows). As our protagonist flirts with a blonde woman, the voice-over proceeds to tell us that the researchers selected for the experiment are what the leader of the experiment, 'theorist of the socio-chemistry of the erotic', Doctor Luther Stringfellow calls Category A subjects: people likely to display some degree of intensity in how they deal with others, including a willingness to take the erotic elements of that relationship to the farthest possible extremes – including physical love between researcher and subject. After all, it is only thus that the researcher can assign to that subject his or her proper place in the 'research mosaic'. By the time the voice-over has finished its explanation of this part of the methodology, the man, now strolling the gardens, is flirting with another inmate – male this time.

In an abrupt change of rhythm and style, the idyllic, sunlit scenery of the gardens is suddenly intercut with jerky, blurry, dark and almost 'sneaky' imagery from the control room of the experiment, where we see on close-circuit monitors how a researcher and subject prepare to have sex. Some subjects, the voice-over informs us, have had their larynx removed, in an attempt to investigate non-language-based forms of telepathic communication. As a researcher caresses an anatomy dummy (with its innards exposed), a blindfolded woman sits nearby. After a while, they start making love. In the garden, our protagonist is still flirting with the other male – actually the very same person who is making love to the woman inside. 'If there can be no love between researcher and subject, there can be no experimentation,' the voice-over proceeds. Since all psychological experiments are unique, non-uniform and non-repeatable, and inextricably mixed with the personalities conducting and conditions governing the act of research, all research is, in fact, 'an act of faith, of love' – 'amor vincit omnia', reads the label on a bottle filled with drugs our protagonist receives in exchange for a transistor radio. When the main character shows the bottle to another person, they decide to take the pills. As he has a harsh hallucination, the voice-over tells us that telepathists' minds can merge, synthesise and become communal. There are two ways to fence off such blending, we are told. The first is physical distance. The second is 'schizophrenetic partition' (first explored by a female subject), which is the development of two selves, a false one that functions as a decoy, and a true one that remains shielded. However, the true self defends itself through eruptions of morbid images (vampirism, necrophilia) in order to maintain its existence.

Darkness has fallen at the Sanatorium. Stringfellow's hypothesis, we are told, is that there can only be telepathic communication when there is an emotional relationship, reinforced by erotic attraction. Between strangers, there is only noise. A blonde, big-breasted woman walks along a corridor with a virile-looking man. Soon after they are making love on an operation table, as the camera pans around them to get up close, really close. In another corner of the Sanatorium, our protagonist, a companion and a dark-haired woman stand around, looking quite bored. If the telepathic struggles between individuals are extrapolated to larger groups of people, they form a map for the evolution of social contact between humans, a female voice-over tells us. We witness the woman being excluded from social interaction; her companion leaves her and walks away with two others. In a warehouse filled with drugs, our protagonist is administered another pill. 'Telepathic communes' we are told, are an advancement of the earlier mentioned conglomerate. The commune replaces the 'obsolescent' family unit, and can fulfill the function of a community, a system of willing, mutual reciprocation. However, as the voice-over explains, telepathy can also reduce sensorial activity to its most mundane operations. As if to emphasise this, we see a minute-and-a-half-long close-up of a subject staring at his finger, which slowly reaches the tip of his nose then descends to his lips before he absently stares out of the window. And we find our protagonist sitting at a table, doodling away, snacking on chocolate bars. He toys with them, but the moment he touches a pacifier, he collapses in extreme anguish. As he writhes on the floor in pain, we also see him chased by his dominant opponent – in some astoundingly fast tracking shots.

On the level of sexuality, our voice-over postulates, the experiment in telepathy demonstrates that there is no reason to differentiate between heterosexuality and homosexuality when it comes to degrees of 'perversion' or pleasure. Omnisexuality is the norm in a world of 'three-dimensional men'. In the ensuing bacchanalian threesome, they fondle and grope each other passionately, clearly enjoying themselves. As the group cuddle continues in extreme slow motion, the voice-over warns us to remain cautious of the positive effects: in a rehearsal of the meeting of all subjects, five of them retreated into catatonic isolation. Two of them committed suicide and one pierced his skull with an electric drill – an 'act of considerable symbolic significance' the voice-over calls it. As if to underline the dangers, our protagonist violently slaps the brunette after she bares her breasts at what first seems a cozy, traditional cup of tea, with pills of course. And moments later, the virile man brutally pushes aside, then slaps, the blonde woman – an outburst punctuated by the fact it occurs several times in an overlapping editing sequence. The voice-over adds that subjects were equipped with transmission receivers through which Stringfellow conveyed messages, first to appease the subjects' initial dependency on him, but gradually decreasing their doses so they could achieve communal cohesion by sharing the few that would still be received. Upon breaking contact all together, Stringfellow suffers a severe depression, suggesting he was as much dependent on the subjects as they were on him. The subjects too were becoming exhausted and delusional. In slow motion, the woman picks up the cape in which our protagonist arrived at the Sanatorium, straightens her head (reasserting her false self perhaps?), and leaves. 'It will be some time before the data will be fully evaluated,' the voice-over concludes.

Omnivorous dedication

From the first seconds *Stereo* is clearly an avant-garde film. The nonsensical front credits ignore convention. Peter Morris sees them as mocking the Canadian National Film Board's documentary tradition, where quasi-technical info often preceded the film itself (1994: 47). There is no direct sound and the three academic voice-overs are the only sounds we hear. Because Cronenberg wanted to shoot in 35mm and there was no budget for post-synchronisation, the one-track voice-over appeared to be the only possible option (see Morris 1994; Rodley 1997). Still, the austere soundscape fits well with the modernist setting of the University of Toronto's Scarborough campus, which had opened a few years earlier. Several rooms in the building are high-tech, such as the control room and the operation theatre. In contrast with that high modernism, the characters wear vintage outfits, often recalling historical dresses; our protagonist's initial outfit curiously resembles that of Hutter/Harker in F. W. Murnau's *Nosferatu* (1922), which set a standard for all vampire stories since. *Stereo*'s explicit reference to vampirism aside, there is something of *Dracula*'s Jonathan Harker in the main character. He is both victim and hero, flustered by what happens yet unfazed. His arrival at the Institute is exactly like that of Harker arriving at Dracula's castle (and who could resist comparing the University of Toronto's new campus to the Count's castle?). True to vampire genre conventions, *Stereo* ends with a blonde woman who was first seduced by the protagonist now donning the cape and continuing the prowl.[7]

The lush black and white photography is supported by an array of stylistic interventions. Taking full advantage of the architecture, Cronenberg seems to try every trick in the book: elaborate pans, jittery handheld shots, fast tracks, low and high angles, parallel editing, overlapping and elliptical montage, slow motion, long static close-ups and extreme long shots all appear frequently. While this may give the impression that he is just trying things, the unity of place and the episodic nature of the narrative do support this wide variety quite well. It gives the film a dynamic flow that counters the rigid structure of the 'research report'. *Stereo* shares that style with Michael Snow's films. Its eerie overtones, the casual violence, the sexualised encounters, the fetishism, and the erratic drug-taking also bring it close to *Les Yeux sans visage* (*Eyes Without a Face*, Georges Franju, 1958), the films of Kenneth Anger and the surrealist legacy.

The story has a complex chronological arrangement. As it turns out, the images we see are those of the first meeting of all (surviving) subjects in the experiment, which the entire voice-over narration actually precedes. As such, then, the images often contradict, punctuate, demonstrate or elaborate the voice-overs' lectures about what the experiment is supposed to do, and how the meeting is prepared. By all measures, the experiment must be deemed a failure: two of the eight subjects die, one is severely injured, two get beaten and there is obvious distress among the others. The basic story of the lead-up to the meeting is told by three voices, of which the third (the female) only comes in after 33 minutes – exactly halfway. Though it seems that the images are ordered in episodic chronological succession, there is no real assurance for that as Cronenberg is using a variety of formal systems. For the most part, the narrative is categorical: as a research report it is structured according to the methodologies and observations of the experiment. But if we see how the images function in relation to the voice-overs, there is also an associational and rhetorical system at work: some scenes appear to elaborate on the voice-over's suggestions (the slaps confirm the warnings about the experiment's weaknesses; the long close-up confirms the argument about mundane actions), while others bluntly contradict them (as we hear of the two suicides we are still seeing the passionate, orgiastic hugs). It seems Cronenberg wanted to try to combine all possible aspects of film form at once, in a personal way.

Thematically, *Stereo* is as omnivorous as it claims its telepathic characters are. In an effort perhaps typical of the graduating student, all the knowledge, ideas and jargon amassed during years of immersion in an intellectual environment are regurgitated. We find references to virtually every academic topic, from contemporary philosophy (existentialism), through clinical and social psychology, neuro-linguistics, cybernetics and interpersonal communication theories, to sociology, bio-chemistry and – of course – aesthetics. As an exposé, *Stereo* comments on the state of knowledge of the human condition. By using the metaphor of telepathic communication, *Stereo* asks pertinent questions about how humans use communication to build their worlds. It has that in common with the contemporary work of Canadian communications scholar Marshall McLuhan, who saw technology as determining our ways of living together. His famous dictum 'the medium is the message' is here applied to telepathy, where, as the voice-over remarks, the form and style of communication is indeed determining what is said (see McLuhan 1964; McLuhan, with Fiore 1967). The link with McLuhan is almost a personal one: McLuhan was director of the University of Toronto's Centre for Culture and Technology during Cronenberg's time there (several websites claim he actually taught Cronenberg).[8] But unlike many of the contemporary philosophies whose ideas are echoed in *Stereo*, the film itself is less pessimistic about the future. Yes, the experiment may have gone wrong, but the liberation of sexual and social energy is surely a hopeful development. Against Herbert Marcuse's then-popular one-dimensional-man theory (man reduced to couch-potato consumer) (1964), *Stereo* proposes a three-dimensional sexual omnivore: unbridled, active sex as a saviour from capitalism's passive consumption. *Stereo* proposes the couch be used not to watch television but to have sex.

But the core motive must be 'dedication'. Not only is there the obvious dedication of Cronenberg the debutante filmmaker to his craft and art, *Stereo* also contains proposals for three realms of human enquiry: art, science and sex – the triumvirate that covers all human actions leading to insight, enlightenment, embellishment or ecstasy. In all cases, the enquirer's dedication is translated into a direct involvement with the process of the action. This seems obvious for sex. If you want to know about it you have to do it. Similarly, art begs practice as well as reflection. But in the case of science, interference is to be avoided as it would block true understanding. As Cronenberg puts it: 'It was like having to murder an amazing creature in order to dissect it. Unfortunately, when you've dissected it, it's dead. All its colours fade. All the things that attracted you in the first place are gone' (in Rodley 1997: 7).

Stereo objects to such distancing and urges science to get involved with its subjects – literally so. One of the major difficulties of scientific research in an academic environment ruled by 'scientistic' procedures of reducibility and reproducibility is that it is designed to withhold the researcher from participation. As in *Stereo*, the researcher should fall in love and get involved with his/her subject, make active love to it. This theory of dedication, of love, prevails throughout *Stereo*.

Crimes of the Future

Crimes of the Future, Cronenberg's second feature, went into production before *Stereo* received its official release in Ottawa. Most of the shooting took place in the autumn of 1969, in and around Massey College, also part of the University of Toronto, and as with *Stereo*, Cronenberg kept a relaxed, informal working schedule, calling mostly on his friends in the underground scene for assistance (for an insightful personal description, see actor Jon Lidolt's essay on shooting the film (2007)). Willem Poolman, Don Owen, Iain Ewing, Kaspars Dzeguze, Norman Snider and several other colleagues appear in the film. It was completed with an advance from the New York-based distributor International Film Archives (who had picked up *Stereo* for screenings in New York), and the newly formed Canadian Film Development Corporation. Though the title is self-explanatory – it refers to crimes that might happen after the narrative ends – it is also a reference to the Norwegian writer Knut Hamsun, whose novel *Hunger* includes a character writing a novel called *Crimes of the Future*.[9]

In content, *Crimes of the Future* is very similar to *Stereo*. Again we open at an institution, framed not in black and white this time but in full colour, and not to silence but to indistinguishable noise, what William Beard calls 'buzzing, chirping and clicking' (2005: 15). Three researchers of the House of Skin clinic, one of them wearing red nail polish, are staring at a crawling patient. A voice-over introduces himself as one of the three, Adrian Tripod; the other two are interns. The clinic, founded by Doctor Antoine Rouge 'treats severely pathological skin conditions caused by contemporary cosmetics'. As the two interns chase the unruly patient around the clinic's yard, Tripod watches from the shadows, pensive, lamenting the loss of the House's prominence and the disappearance of his mentor, Rouge. The patient appears to be the only one left at the House, and as Tripod describes it, the foam emerging from his ears signals he is dying. This goo seems attractive to many, and we see one of the interns and Tripod lick it from their fingers with gusto. Soon blood flows from his mouth and he dies as Tripod kisses him passionately. Tripod and his associates spread his ashes, and we are told that the disease that caused his demise, Rouge's Malady, has had a devastating impact on the world's population. Initially, we learn, the malady only appeared in post-pubertal females, of which there are now hardly any left, but it has since spread to the population at large.

After the patient's death and the closure of the clinic, Tripod visits the Institute of Neo-Venereal Disease, with which Rouge had previously collaborated. But the former colleague he meets there has contracted the disease himself and has started to develop new organs – unique and fascinating but without function, a form of 'creative cancer' his nurse calls it. When they are removed and stored in coloured jars, he becomes nostalgic about them. Unable to make himself useful, or feel welcome, Tripod leaves. He finds a job as a physician at the Oceanic Podiatry Group Therapy Programme, where Rouge's philosophy influences practice. Having demonstrated how he would use an esoteric form of foot massage to treat patients, he proceeds to treat a clearly distressed person, until that person's nail-polished foot repels him. Another person intervenes, drags the patient away violently behind a wall (to loud cracking and bubbling sounds, like a radio tuned to a dead channel), and when he re-appears he defiantly spits out what looks like the patient's heart at the feet of Tripod. Considerably more anxious now, Tripod starts with his next patient, one with 'webbed toes' but this one shoves him away and leaves, after throwing him a card, and tasting the blood from the heart of the previous patient – yet another reference to vampirism *Crimes of the Future* shares with *Stereo*.

After these altercations Tripod leaves the programme for another job, as a courier for Metaphysical Import/Export. He delivers goods (socks and underwear wrapped in plastic) to candidates for management positions. Tripod's voice-over muses that his mentor Rouge, to whom he describes himself as 'preternaturally close', contracted the disease as well, even though he had always claimed he was immune to it, and his death was only confirmed by those who had wished him dead all along. 'I feel sure that he no longer exists', Tripod nevertheless concludes. While he observes one of the candidates exercising ballet poses in a very long, static shot, he tells us he studied the card the web-toed client threw at him and discovered it was an invitation. Soon after, we see Tripod at a gathering of conspirators – 'heterosexual paedophiles' in what looks like an expressionistically-lit art gallery filled with large glass spheres. Here he meets the web-toed man again, and the group's leader, Tiomkin, who postulates there must now evolve a new sort of sexuality 'for a new species of man'.

The voice-over shifts address. No longer speaking in the first- but in the third-person, it informs us that 'Adrian Tripod has been accepted by the board of directors of the Gynecological Research Foundation', a shady corporation with its own armed guard, which has acquired a new 'research import', a young girl of about five years old, who is to be induced prematurely to puberty, and who may or may not already be exposed to Rouge's Malady. In a scene reminiscent of depictions of early 1970s terrorism, Tripod and his two accomplices kill the guard, and kidnap the girl. Hiding in a hotel (the same one Rouge may have stayed in near the end of his life), the trio sets about impregnating the girl. Wearing gloves, the first man approaches, but even as the girl sits alluringly he cannot do it and leaves the room. Tripod is next. As he slowly undresses, the voice-over informs us 'Adrian Tripod senses the presence of Antoine Rouge'. He sits down. The girl puts white goo in her mouth. Tripod too has some. In slow motion, a blue tear rolls from his eye. The girl smiles, at the camera.

Total institutions

Locking up sick people in confinement, administering specially-designed care to what turn out to be violent criminals, and kidnapping innocent children for the good of humankind, Crimes of the Future has all the characteristics of a popular sociology thought experiment. Whereas Stereo also considered such situations, there remained a prevailing sense that communication or a sophisticated use of signs, or transmission procedures, would trigger true understanding, and bring out the best in people. Dedication would lead to love, and all would be well. The experiment in Stereo failed, but hope remained. In the not-too-distant future of Crimes of the Future such hope seems gone: Tripod is filled with despair. He no longer believes dedication and love will help, and though he makes several attempts, first with the last clinic patient, then with Rouge's former associate, and even with the disturbed patients of the therapy programme, he fails to achieve any progress. The dedication he himself shows is not met with reciprocal effort – a refusal that was also showing at the end of Stereo. In that film absent theorist Stringfellow falls into a depression after having broken with his subjects. Crimes of the Future's absent theorist Rouge commits suicide.

Above all, it seems the institutions themselves block any chance for success. The institution in Stereo is ominous, like Dracula's dark castle, but at least remained largely neutral in the experiment. In Crimes of the Future there is no such neutrality. Its seven institutions mirror the classical structure of heaven and hell in being either good or bad: the House of Skin clinic, the Institute for Neo-Venereal Disease (a sort of clinic as well), the Oceanic Podiatry Group Therapy Programme (again a type of clinic, though the telephone wires above its high concrete fences also give it the look of a barbed-wired concentration camp – maybe the foot massage is a form of torture?), the secretive Metaphysical Import/Export corporation, the hide-out of the paedophiles (which resembles a cult's temple), and the vault-like Gynecological Research Foundation. All of these seem to have agendas of their own, and with the presumable exception of the paedophile terrorists, none of them show any interest in curing the disease. Instead, they are all caught up in keeping their inmates and employees busy with ridiculous procedures like sorting underwear or sampling organs, or even just walking vast corridors (something the liaison officer of the Gynecological Research Foundation fears will kill him, which is why he refuses to walk when he is alone). In the seventh location, as in Dante's seventh circle, an apparently intermediate location (infernal for the girl, potentially heavenly for the paedophiles), all action seems futile: nothing happens, and the film just ends.

A logical reaction against such totalitarian environments would be to start a revolution: to instigate a sudden, violent disruption against the suffocating continuity of 'business as usual'. But in contrast to *Stereo*, revolutions in *Crimes of the Future* have lost their credit. The apotheosis, with Tripod and his accomplices gunning down a guard and kidnapping the girl, appears unlikely to change anything, because the actions towards 'cure' are as despicable as the 'disease'. In this, *Crimes of the Future* reflects some of the signs of the 1960s counter-culture's sudden collapse. With the smearing of blood and references to cults, *Crimes of the Future*'s ending is an uncanny reference to the then-topical Manson Family killings and their ideas of 'revolution' as they publicly expressed them (all of which took place in the months preceding and during shooting[10]). Cronenberg would later acknowledge this influence:

> We were now in a sort of half-life, the afterglow of the 1960s. Charles Manson and Woodstock had happened [Cronenberg is probably confusing Woodstock with Altamont here]. Bobby Kennedy had been shot. It was another era. It was well and truly getting to be the 1970s. (In Rodley 1997: 35)

Still, while the nihilistic consequences of the ending seem obvious the story itself does not go the whole way. We are left to ponder whether Tripod will be able to overcome his moral objections (overcome his love too) and rape the girl/Rouge – and become as nasty as the thing he wants to change. 'I was trying to come to terms with the balance between the two of them', Cronenberg comments:

> If you're a Red Brigade terrorist I suppose it would be very cathartic to say that and to believe it – that you must tear down all the old order and live in eternal chaos – but I never believed that and still don't. On the other hand there is something stifling about a certain kind of monolithic order and established social structure. (In Beard & Handling 1983: 169).

This ambiguity was to become a staple in Cronenberg's oeuvre. In *Shivers* and *Rabid*, but also in *Videodrome* and *The Dead Zone*, he would ask similar questions, offering different perspectives and suggestions each time. From *The Fly* onwards those issues increasingly became personal ones, internalised in the dilemma's of characters, though they never fully disappeared. I will return to this in subsequent chapters.

One major reason why any uprising or revolution against the institutions in *Crimes of the Future* seems unlikely to succeed is because there is no alternative: nothing exists outside those monolithic organisations. In that sense the film is about the oppression of choice by what Canadian sociologist Erving Goffman (1961) has called 'total institutions', and what French philosopher Michel Foucault (1991) saw as 'complete and austere institutions': organisations which maintain strict control over a number of like-situated individuals cut off from society for a considerable period of time, forced to lead an enclosed and formally governed life, with sometimes a total loss of privacy. At the time of *Stereo* and *Crimes of the Future*, Goffman's theories were discussed widely, certainly in and around his alma mater, the University of Toronto. Goffman's case studies concerned asylums and mental hospitals, and his focus was on individuality and behaviour. For Foucault, who researched prisons, the focus was on mass control over the human body, more than its mind. Whereas Goffman did not question how and why people ended up in care or imprisonment, Foucault did, and offered a reason: institutions' ability to put away those who behave and act differently is a demonstration of their power to police, not in the name of any greater good, but because they *can*. Ultimately, only institutions, preferably of an incorporated nature, remain; individual freedom disappears.

For Cronenberg, the human body is the last possible site of resistance against such oppression. Even total institutions cannot control the innards of a body – much as they would want to and try to through torture. Hence that inside becomes a safe haven from interference. But in *Crimes of the Future* that last resort is in danger. Rouge's Malady, like other inconveniencies (incontinence, blushing, excessive sweating, blisters...) appears to break down the ability of the human body to keep itself to itself. When it starts to involuntarily or prematurely shed its contents, it indicates loss of individual control and surrender to the care of institutions – much like we admit our sick to care centres. In *Stereo*, the human body was a bastion in resisting control, or a stimulator for communication, especially when its sensuality was activated. In *Crimes of the Future*, there is no more sensuality, no bastion. The last protective borders are broken down; the film abounds with body parts and excrement. The foam oozing from ears, the syrupy blood, the heart ripped out of a chest or the hotel's concierge's 'root-like excrescence growing from his nostrils' (which he believes to be extensions of cerebral nerve cells) signal the demolition of the border between the inside and outside of the body, the personal and the public, between the private and the regulated. The degradation of the human body's dignity, especially in the violent and denigrating behaviour towards inmates (the clinic's patient, the client at the therapy programme, the girl), make *Crimes of the Future* a grim reflection on how far individuals who feel empowered by their authority will push their powers of total control, predating in a sense the infamous 1970s Stanford Prison Experiment.[11]

Formally, *Crimes of the Future* shares a lot with *Stereo*. There are some little differences, such as the use of colour. The use of the wide-angle lens is more prevalent than before, and slow motion has diminished drastically. In that sense, *Crimes of the Future* is closer to Cronenberg's overall visual style, which contains a high degree of wide-lensing (typical of course for filming in confined quarters of which there are so many in Cronenberg's films). But there is still a multitude of striking angles (high and low, straight and tilted), which in combination with the architecture of Massey College creates framings and compositions similar to *Stereo*. Perhaps the biggest change is that there is one voice-over instead of three. It is possible to see this as another indication of the presence of total institutions: in *Stereo* there is a diversity of voices within the same institution, whereas in *Crimes of the Future* all institutions speak with the same voice. In the end Tripod's first-person narration is even replaced by a third-person address – another sign of institutionalisation. The rapport between voice-over and imagery is tighter than in *Stereo* (what we hear backs what we see), and there is a logical progression of time and space, again an indication of control. By and large, the two films are closely related, and stylistically quite separate from the rest of Cronenberg's work.

The Reception of Stereo and Crimes of the Future

As is often the case with underground cinema, the release and reception of *Stereo* and *Crimes of the Future* occurred step by step, each screening at a time, slowly building towards a reputation. *Stereo* had its first screening on 26 February 1969 in the Cinecity theatre in Toronto, to considerable success. In *Take One*, Joe Medjuck raved about its technical brilliance, and suggested its aesthetics 'clean out your mind' (1969: 22). Similarly, the *Globe and Mail*'s long review called *Stereo* 'really weird' but also 'formidable', concluding Cronenberg deserves 'three cheers'. '[Cronenberg] went ahead and did what most people just have hypotheses about' (M. McM 1969: 22). On 23 June 1969 it had its official premiere at the National Arts Centre in Ottawa, where it was shown in a series of screenings that also included work by Snow and Wieland. It also played in Montreal, again to favourable reviews that called it 'fresh and unconventional' (Hofsess 1977: 278), or an 'elegant dream' (Delaney 1970a: 34).

This first reception wave acknowledged Cronenberg's uniqueness. Uncommon for reviews, there were hardly any references to other films (Warhol's *Vinyl* being the exception). Cronenberg was considered a case in his own right. Even the inclusion of *Stereo* in a New York programme of science fiction films at the Museum of Modern Art (quite a coup for Cronenberg), did not change that. While *Stereo* was listed alongside *2001: A Space Odyssey* (Stanley Kubrick, 1968), *Metropolis* (Fritz Lang, 1927), *La Jetée* (Chris Marker, 1963), *Invasion of the Body Snatchers* (Don Siegel, 1956) and *Forbidden Planet* (Fred M. Wilcox, 1956) it was not compared to them. Each review isolated it in a separate paragraph (see Weiler 1969: 32; Arnold 1969: B8). The series gave *Stereo* such a solid reputation in New York it was later granted a two-night rerun at the Film Forum movie society (see Shepard 1969: 32).

Stereo's acclaim paved the way for *Crimes of the Future*. Even before its release, it had been noted in the Toronto press, sometimes by some of the people in it, who mentioned scenes which would not make it to the final version – especially one involving streetsweepers and a municipal health officer, a trope Cronenberg would later include in *Rabid* (see Dzeguze 1969: 4; Martin 1969: 29). And when it was released it too received a share of good reviews, though almost exclusively in the periodic press such as *Artscanada* and *Take One* (see Anon. 1970; Pringle 1970; Brigg 1971). Then, within a matter of weeks, the buzz died. Cronenberg would only find his name in the paper as the slide-projectionist for music artist Udo Kassemets, and *Crimes of the Future* received far less bookings than *Stereo* (see Kraglund 1970).

Both films, however, faired reasonably well outside North America. *Stereo* had successful screenings at festivals in Edinburgh (August 1969) and Adelaide (September 1969 for *Stereo* and April 1970 for *Crimes of the Future*). Both films attracted sizeable audiences for screenings at the Belgian Film Archive, in December 1969 and April 1971 respectively.[12] In France and the United Kingdom in particular, they received much praise. Critics of *Le Monde* and the British Film Institute's *Monthly Film Bulletin* published highly appreciative reviews, again without making any references to other cinema of the time, though there is one mention of Von Sternberg, and also a telling comparison to one of Cronenberg's literary heroes, Vladimir Nabokov (see Rayns 1971a; 1971b).

Such isolation from other cinema is understandable if the scope of comparisons is limited to other avant-garde and underground cinema. While they have a cool, clinical style and an intellectual cachet common to experimental cinema of the time, their narrative drive sets *Stereo* and *Crimes of the Future* apart from the structural and abstract cinema of filmmakers such as Wieland, Snow, Malcolm Le Grice, Hollis Frampton and Stan Brakhage. But if we take the lead from the MOMA series and place them among commercial genre films, there are several stylistic and thematic links. The similarity with *2001: A Space Odyssey*, which is frequently mentioned, is obvious, though mainly based on the viewing experience rather than any similarity in narrative or structure – both are far-out adventures. The films which, in consequence, motifs and metaphors *Stereo* and *Crimes of the Future* really share a cultural sensibility and concern with are those whose plots revolve around secretive conspiracies, often featuring medical experiments, total institutions and a sense of imminent doom, and whose characters have to cope with, and overcome, claustrophobic confinement and social isolation. This preoccupation connects them with Roman Polanski's *Repulsion* (1965) and *Rosemary's Baby* (1968), with which they also share an interest in cults (which at the time also informed other Canadian cinema; see chapter two). Other examples are *La Jetée* (which only really started to penetrate North America's market by the late 1960s), the Italian science fiction film *Omicron* (Ugo Gregoretti, 1963), *Night of the Living Dead* (George A. Romero, 1968), *Eden and After* (Alain Robbe-Grillet, 1970), *THX 1138* (George Lucas, 1971), *Solaris* (Andrei Tarkovsky, 1972), even *Dark Star* (John Carpenter, 1974). Each of these films displays the same economy of production values, striking wide-angle shots, often from a low angle (a solution for shooting in enclosed interiors), and austere compositions. A little bit bigger in production values, but equally obsessed with dystopia, paranoia, conspiracies and medical experiments is *The Omega Man* (Boris Sagal, 1971), a movie version of Richard Matheson's *I Am Legend*, a film, much like *Crimes of the Future*, about problems of fertility and the end of the human race. *Crimes of the Future* avoids *The Omega Man*'s messianic figure who through sacrifice saves the world, and that avoidance makes it a more atheist film, based not on belief but on 'emergent evolutionism', a variant of Darwin's evolutionary theory that argued evolutionary processes could also include sudden leaps and changes, such as Rouge's Malady's extermination of women (see Morris 1994: 24).

From Experimentation to Exploitation: Secret Weapons and the Dissolution of the Underground

After these initial encouraging beginnings, Cronenberg's career slowed down. *Stereo* and *Crimes of the Future* got occasional additional screenings here and there (several in New York), but their public presence ended rather abruptly. At the end of 1970, Cronenberg left Toronto for the French Provence town of Tourettes-sur-Loup, in between Nice and Cannes, where he lived for a year. While there, he made three fillers for the Canadian Broadcasting Corporation (CBC), *Jim Ritchie Sculptor*, *Letter From Michelangelo* and *Tourettes*. After his return to Canada, Cronenberg directed a few more fillers, and his company Emergent Films was also commissioned to direct an episode of the CBC late night series *Programme X*, called *Secret Weapons* (1972).

This episode proved to be a pivotal juncture. Scripted by his close friend Norman Snider, with old buddies Mlodzik, Bruce Martin and CFDC director Michael Spencer acting, and featuring a futuristic story involving a total institution (a pharmaceutical corporation) that meets with resistance from rebellious bikers, *Secret Weapons* appeared a return to the kind of films Cronenberg had been making before.[13] Certainly Cronenberg approached the episode as a personal exploration of private obsessions. The appearance of the motorcycle gang was not so much an innovation as the first occurrence of a motif that would recur throughout his career (see chapters three and eight). But the fact that this time he was working for a commercial fee, within the constraints of regular production structures (even though he enjoyed lots of freedom from the CBC, who were very hands-off) made a huge difference. Cronenberg has often commented that he needed to convince himself to start thinking about his films as 'movies' not 'cinema'. With that he refers to a distinction in the economic framing of film: 'movies' refers to an economy in which films are part of an industry, meeting commercial needs while satisfying artistic ones, whereas the term 'cinema' implies a model in which the sole emphasis on the artistic endeavour limits the exposure and reception of the product. Cronenberg's visit to the 1971 Cannes Film Festival had taught him there was mileage in the 'movie' model. He commented 'yes, I was willing to do what was necessary to make commercial movies' (in Beard & Handling 1983: 171).

Cronenberg's change in attitude fitted a more general shift in film culture: from experimentation and exploration to exploitation. Partly this was a conscious move away from highbrow culture, with its modernist taste hierarchies and pretensions. Underground filmmakers pushing their explorations to the limits of bourgeois taste tolerance increasingly found that the established networks of reception (such as film societies, museums, government-funded art centres and festivals) for their films would resist their efforts. *Stereo* and *Crimes of the Future* may not have rattled the censor's chains, but several of Cronenberg's friends did find their films banned and/or confiscated. The most infamous case was the trial over *Columbus of Sex* (1969), a film directed by John Hofsess, and produced by Ivan Reitman and Daniel Golberg, which was seized by the police during a preview screening at McMaster University, and charged with obscenity. To everyone's surprise the charges were upheld and after a phony trial in which the prosecution plucked five people from the street, invited them to see the film and presented them as witnesses (one of them said a film that shows no relation between the so-called story on the soundtrack and the pictures would be an obscene film; another asserted that even Picasso's paintings were obscene so surely this film had to be as well), Hofsess, Reitman and Goldberg were found guilty and fined. The film remained banned.[14] The notoriously prudish Ontario Board of Censors ensured other films easily received 'X' certificates, effectively banning them from the networks of exhibition they were intended for. As a result, veterans of the underground such as Kenneth Anger and George Kuchar or art-house directors like Alain Robbe-Grillet, Harry Kümel and Paul Morrissey, who had noticed that their more risqué materials did better in more commercial circuits, started to cater to this new market and embraced genre conventions, often stretching them a bit to fit their own visions. Films like *Invocation of My Demon Brother* (Kenneth Anger, 1969), *Daughters of Darkness* (Harry Kümel, 1971), *Flesh For Frankenstein* (Paul Morrissey, 1973), *Blood for Dracula* (Paul Morrissey, 1974) and *Successive Slidings of Pleasure* (Alain Robbe-Grillet, 1974), found themselves successful in commercial markets, together with films from outlaw directors such as Alejandro Jodorwosky's *El Topo* (*The Mole*, 1970) or Stan Brakhage's *The Act of Seeing With One's Own Eyes* (1971) that happened to contain the 'right ingredients': sex and violence.

All this certainly gave the commercial indie market a new impetus. But the market itself also underwent a transformation. Answering to an explosion in student numbers, changes in downtown demographics and new distribution channels, the art-house and film society network of exhibition which had catered to the middle-class was being replaced by midnight movies, college screenings and grindhouses, whose punters would be younger, curious, movie savvy and infected with a taste for mixing popular and lowbrow tastes.[15] The effect was a strange confluence between the experimental and the exploitative, which saw the soft-porn of Russ Meyer and Radley Metzger shoulder to shoulder with the experimental cinema of Brakhage, the new horror film associated with Warhol and Anger, and even crossovers between emergent feminist filmmaking and macho biker movies – actually *Secret Weapons*' biker gang is led by a woman who believes in rebellion only.

This evolution affected the long-term reception of *Stereo* and *Crimes of the Future*. In an exploitation market they stood no chance, and with the real avant-garde retreating into the enclosed world of galleries and museums, where possibilities to project 35mm were extremely limited, both films had to wait for about a decade before they resurfaced. Following the success of *The Dead Zone* and the acclaim of *Videodrome*, Cronenberg's early works were also fêted in several retrospectives in London, Toronto and Los Angeles. Benefiting from this interest, *Stereo* and *Crimes of the Future* even enjoyed an official re-release, together with the television episode *The Italian Machine*, in August 1984. *Variety* wrote: 'In now-beginning premiere revivals, pic will be of interest to hardcore Cronenberg cultists for the appearance of numerous of the director's themes and fetishes in embryonic form' (Anon. 1984a: 17).

Fitting their underground reputations, *Stereo* and *Crimes of the Future* never got proper video releases. Although there was a Japanese edition of *Crimes of the Future*, and the film was also included on the laserdisc edition of *Dead Ringers*, exposure remained insignificant – if you wanted to see them you had to catch a scarce screening at a film museum, or access a pirated version (I fondly remember my own second-generation tape of a 16mm screening in a film museum – appropriately underground). Further retrospectives did not do much to change that. Finally, in 2004 both films appeared as extras on the DVD of *Fast Company*, which was itself a seldom-seen Cronenberg film. While still not a release in their own right, the DVD edition did re-introduce *Stereo* and *Crimes of the Future* to the world, and since then numerous Internet reviews and comments have at least given them some sort of permanent public presence. As the once-bible of the New York underground *Village Voice* put it, they 'scan as crystal-clear sonograms of Cronenberg's obsessions in utero' (Lim 2002).

The term uterus is ominous here. Cronenberg's subsequent offerings would place his interest in the ability of the human body to mutate and generate life in the context of the bloodiest of genres: the horror film.

CHAPTER TWO

Revolution and Rage: *Shivers* and *Rabid*

As any citizen in the streets can tell you, martial law has come to Montreal.

– A news reporter in *Rabid*

40,000 men and women everyday ... Redefine happiness
Another 40,000 coming everyday ... We can be like they are
Come on baby ... don't fear the reaper.

– Blue Oyster Cult, 'Don't Fear the Reaper'

Somewhere in the mid-1970s, in a cinema theatre near you...
'If you think you're not afraid of the dark' ... a man rips a woman's clothes, *'If you think you have a strong stomach'* ... a man vomits, *'If you feel nothing can shock you'* ... a woman stabs a man in the neck with a large knife, *'If you say you don't scare easily'* ... a man's face is attacked by a creature, *'If you believe you've seen everything'* ... a glass falls on a bathroom floor, a woman in a bathtub screams as she is pulled down, *'Then prepare yourself for'* ... *Shivers*!

As people lurk behind an open fridge, strangled or attacked in their car, assaulted in elevators, a deep voice-over announces: *'The motion picture that takes you beyond fear. Beyond your wildest nightmare. And brings you face to face with terror. Beyond the powers of priests or science to exorcise.'* A woman, her face dripping with blood, her mouth wide open and her eyes held upward makes a loud gasping noise as if possessed by a demon. *'What are they?'* asks the voice-over, as we see an uncanny version of a very hungry caterpillar crawl through the grass. *'Raging demons from another world? Blood thirsty creatures that must be killed? Or incarnations of absolute evil?'* A woman turns in slow motion towards the camera (Barbara Steele! horror fans will exclaim). Children batter an elderly man in a corridor, men collapse from agonising chest pains, girls pull on leashes like mad dogs, a mob thrashes down an apartment door. The voice-over continues, *'They possess men. Women. And children. Drive them to acts of unbelievable horror. No one is safe. The only escape is death.'* A car crashes, a slow-moving crowd (zombies?) closes in, a camera races down the stairs into a dark basement, a deep red shape in a dark pit jumps up and a hand slides off the side of a washing machine... *'If this picture doesn't make you scream and squirm you'd better see a psychiatrist, quick.'*

Fifteen to eighteen months later, in the same theatre...
A terrified woman jumps up in a hospital bed and screams at the top of her lungs. Nurses and patients run in panic through the corridors of the hospital as a man collapses, covered in blood. *'All around people are dying, and only Rose knows why.'* Rose calls for help. As a car approaches the hospital, pandemonium has broken out. All over town people attack each other, biting, hitting, clubbing each other to death. A radio reporter announces *'an outbreak of a new strain of rabies that is potentially the worst of this century'*. A car falls from an overpass and is rammed by a truck. *'Don't worry'* says the voice-over, *'he's dead, and the dead can't hurt the living.'* We see military personnel guiding garbage trucks carrying men in chemical protection suits through nightly city traffic. A news anchor reads: *'The prime minister was reluctant to officially declare the state of emergency, but as any citizen in the streets can tell you, martial law has come to Montreal.'* We see civilians lined up by armed police, a man pulled out of a queue and separated from his wife. *'Shooting down the victims is as good a way of handling them as we have got,'* declares an impatient official to reporters. In a crowded shopping mall a security guard guns down a suspect, wounding bystanders and killing the mall's Santa Claus. In a jail, one guard kills another with multiple shots in the chest. In a subway train, a woman foaming with rage assaults a man as the other passengers trample each other in a stampede. *'You can't trust your mother. Your best friend. Your neighbour next door. One minute, they're perfectly normal. The next ... Rabid.'* Rose screams again. In slow motion, city workers in protective suits throw a body (Rose?) into a garbage truck. *'Pray it doesn't happen to you,'* says the voice-over.

Body Horror: Mimetic Violence, Abjection and Repression

These are the trailers for *Shivers* and *Rabid*, Cronenberg's first two commercial feature films. They contain a curious mix of the common and the horrific. The *Shivers* trailer is a cross between between a daily tabloid television news report chronicling the ways the world is going berserk and how society is crumbling, a shopping channel's weekend overview of deals on household appliances such as fridges, washing machines, bedroom furniture and electronic toothbrushes, and a smart horror flick filled with winks and nudges to everything from *Invasion of the Body Snatchers* (Don Siegel, 1956), *Black Sunday* (Mario Bava, 1960), and *Night of the Living Dead*, to *The Exorcist* (William Friedkin, 1973). Likewise, *Rabid's* trailer promises an experience of terror that comes from close to home. It infects our loved ones, perhaps even yourself, and it inhabits places modern citizens regard as secure and safely guarded sites of care: a shopping mall, a hospital or a jail. Moreover, battling that terror apparently brings out the worst in the upholders of law and order, as they dispose of suspects indiscriminately, pull people out of line-ups, and gun down the symbol of peace and goodwill, Santa Claus.

In more than one sense *Shivers* and *Rabid* continue where *Stereo* and *Crimes of the Future* left off. They consider the body as a site of revolution, awash with lustful, vampiric desires to suck blood and infect insanity upon innocents, and countered by attempts to rein it by totalitarian systems of control. The context within which *Shivers* and *Rabid* are produced and released, however, are radically different. The constraints and expectations of the horror genre regulate their forms, and the 1970s film culture of pessimism and permissiveness determine their cultural impact. Therefore, this chapter pays particular attention to the theoretical grounding that informed, and accompanied, body horror, and to the networks of distribution and reception that received *Shivers* and *Rabid*.

It is with a consideration of the human body we should start. It informs not just *Shivers* and *Rabid* but also *Stereo* and *Crimes of the Future*, as well as all of Cronenberg's later films. It is also a core characteristic of modern horror cinema. The monster comes from within ourselves, bursting out of our bodies; it is everywhere, in all walks of life, in what we hold familiar, as well as in our own families. Its terror is total, it is random and indiscriminate, and all resistance is futile. It features full and explicit body-to-body attacks, straight and direct, with no sophistication, driven only by animal instinct and a determination to seek and destroy. Since *Shivers* and *Rabid*, this particular strand of horror films became known as 'body horror' and Cronenberg is regarded as its best representative, credited with inventing and developing it into one of the horror genre's most exciting and disturbing sub-genres.

Body horror's inspirations are diverse. To see where Cronenberg's body horror is coming from it is necessary to elaborate on the cultural regulation of human desire. As is evident from the trailers of *Shivers* and *Rabid*, people at their most basic, stripped from all social and cultural mechanisms of control, act purely out of desire: they want what other people have, and they want other people. French philosopher René Girard defines the first desire as 'mimetic desire' (1977; 1986; 1987; Mathijs & Mosselmans 2000). According to Girard, all humans are intrinsically equal and subjectively empty (void of meaning and property). But when a model is held up to them they will want it, they will try and take it, and they will engage who has it. 'Mimetic desire' thus leads to mimetic violence, to individual warfare to acquire properties. In this warfare, the property itself is less important than the want, for even when the property is obtained the desire remains, leading to more mimetic violence. For Girard, cultures are attempts to regulate mimetic desire. Individuals successfully joining forces (on an opportunistic basis only) against one person with a property will want to celebrate the moment of 'union' between humans this joint effort instigated, so they will commemorate the defeated as a scapegoat (the one who caused the violence) but also as a god (the one who, inadvertently, facilitated the unity). After a while, argues Girard, the physical defeat (the sacrifice) of the scapegoat/god is no longer necessary. Instead rituals representing the act symbolically will replace the actual violence.

The concept of mimetic desire and violence as explained by Girard, is usually understood to be concerned with real physical objects as the properties that are at stake, but it easily includes sexual desires as well – people wanting to 'have' other people. This forms the main concern of the work of Herbert Marcuse (1966), who sees the regulation of sexual impulses and instincts, the regulation of *access* to human bodies, as the key to establishing civilisation and culture. The tools through which this happens are abjection and repression. Abjection is the tool that regulates actual access. According to anthropologist Mary Douglas (1966), all cultures have common taboos that involve safeguarding the human body from 'impurity' and 'danger' by protecting it from physical harm and violation. Incest, murder and basic hygiene (ritual cleanliness) form some of the most basic examples, but they can become as idiosyncratic as a culture will allow them to become. For Douglas, the best way to ensure the protection of the body is to draw a fine line between the interior of the body (its private aspect which no one should be able to penetrate, and which no one should control except the owner of the body), and its exterior appearance (which is subject to social functions), and establish a sense of uncleanliness and disgust, of abjection, around whatever transverses the border between the inner and outer of the human body. Hence the common unease with blood, sperm, vaginal fluids, urine, spit... or the gooey earwax from *Crimes of the Future*. In more sophisticated degrees, pimples, pus, cysts, abscesses, foam, and tears or sweat can also be evidence of a transgression of the border between the private interior and social exterior of the body – of lack of control over the body. For Julia Kristeva (1982), a culture's attempt to hide the bodily abject, is often revealed in its attitudes and prudishness towards certain groups of people – women, the disabled, children and so forth.

Regulating access, through abjection, to prevent unbridled desire is one thing, but what is the compensation? Repression is the tool that compensates for the lack of access. According to Marcuse, repressing our desires inflicts a suffering upon humans, but it produces the benefits of culture. 'The sacrifice has paid off well,' he adds, 'in the technically advanced areas of civilisation, the conquest of nature is practically complete, and more needs of a greater number of people are fulfilled than ever before' (1966: 3). Yet Marcuse sees a danger in over-regulating repression (and thus abjection and desire), because it can lead to 'surplus repression': the repression in a society that is beyond what is needed to maintain order and that exists only to protect the power and privilege of the establishment (1966: 37). Marcuse's fear is that this may lead to what he calls a 'onedimensional man', an uncritical and conformist acceptance of structures, norms and behaviours – like the shooting of Santa in an attempt to do 'good' (Marcuse 1964).

What we see in body horror is an exploration of the ultimate consequence of Marcuse's fear: if bodies are overly regulated and restrained by society's structures, will they not resist control and revolt? And will the revolt not result in the chasing of previously forbidden desires? In *Night of the Living Dead* and *Dawn of the Dead* (George A. Romero, 1979), that is exactly what happens. In *The Texas Chainsaw Massacre* (Tobe Hooper, 1974) the family of Leatherface is pushed so far out of their livelihood and traditions, and ridiculed for their backwardness and looks, that they discard culture and resort to primitive mimetic violence. The locations where such outbreaks occur are often sanitised and sterile sites like labs and observation stations. Medical or military experiments are the superlative step in creating the most extreme conditions to which bodies can be subjected, and that is why hospitals and medicine often form a background for body horror. In films such as *Shivers* and *Rabid*, and the earlier *Stereo* and *Crimes of the Future*, as well as in Cronenberg's later films, characters and stories explore submission to extreme conformist acceptance and observe surplus repression, but they also explore the obliteration of the system by letting desires take over from needs (often through triggers like a drug, virus or parasite). What makes Cronenberg's body horror unique is that he takes the position of the philosopher: he does not take sides, but lets his stories and characters check the consequences of the possibilities; sometimes abandonment to desire seems worth the sacrifice, and sometimes not.

Shivers: Revolution

Let us turn to *Shivers* first. Once Cronenberg had decided to make commercial features, he tried to sell his new script to several producers. Cinépix, a Montreal-based production company active in the softcore market with films such as *Valérie* (Denis Heroux, 1969), and *Pile ou face* (*A Very Private Party*, Roger Fournier, 1971), declared an interest because they saw the soft-porn market slowing down and wanted to invest in horror films.[1] But they were reluctant to enter a deal that would involve Cronenberg as a director. It took them a few years to decide, and unbeknownst to Cronenberg they even tried to sell the project to other directors. During a trip to Los Angeles with his friend Norman Snider, Cronenberg met with Barbara Steele, who he was hoping to cast, and was introduced to Jonathan Demme, who had just directed Steele in *Caged Heat* (1974).[2] When Demme told him John Dunning and André Link of Cinépix had shown him the script and asked him to direct, Cronenberg was understandably furious. He went back to confront them but found a message waiting for him confirming the project was a go-ahead, with him as director, and support from the Canadian Film Development Corporation on top of it. Michael Spencer of the CFDC admitted their first reaction to the script in 1972 was one of 'revulsion and confusion' (in Vatsndal 2004: 97). But a few years later they decided to fund it anyway.

Unsure of Cronenberg's stamina Cinépix surrounded him with a string of habitués. Executive producers Dunning and Link appointed Cronenberg's old buddy Ivan Reitman, who had since made *Foxy Lady* (1971) and *Cannibal Girls* (1973), as line producer (he also ended up doing the musical soundtrack). Reitman brought in *Cannibal Girls'* co-writer Daniel Goldberg and director of photography Robert Saad.

The special effects job was given to Joe Blasco, of *The Lawrence Welk Show*. Cronenberg himself cast Ron Mlodzik again. The total budget was $180,000 and the shooting schedule was 15 days.

As male leads Cronenberg cast Paul Hampton, who had appeared in *Women of the Prehistoric Planet* (Arthur C. Peirce, 1966), the fake blaxploitation heist film *Hit!* (Sidney J. Furie, 1973), and the exploitation film *Private Duty Nurses* (George Armitage, 1971), and veteran television actor Joe Silver, who had just been in the Montreal-set *The Apprenticeship of Duddy Kravitz* (Ted Kotcheff, 1974). Allan Migicovsky also joined *Shivers* from that film. Cronenberg made a big impression with his female leads, casting three solid cult queens. Susan Petrie's fame was mainly limited to Canada, where she enjoyed minor celebrity status for her roles as an object of desire in Québec sex farce, and Cinépix production, *Loving and Laughing* (John Sole, 1971), the coming-of-age drama *Rip-Off* (Donald Shebib, 1971), and the revenge film *Vengeance is Mine* (John Trent, 1974). Lynn Lowry was 'hot property' to genre and B-movie fans for her parts in the horror film *The Crazies* (George A. Romero, 1973), and the satanic-cult movie *I Drink Your Blood* (David E. Durston, 1971), the porn-chic *Score* (Radley Metzger, 1973), and two of production company Troma's earliest films *Sugar Cookies* (Theodore Gershuny, 1973) and *The Battle of Love's Return* (Lloyd Kaufman, 1971). The coup-de-grace was the casting of scream queen extraordinaire Barbara Steele, famous for her roles in *La Maschera del demonio* (*Black Sunday*, Mario Bava, 1960), *The Pit and the Pendulum* (Roger Corman, 1961), *8½* (Federico Fellini, 1963) and *Danza macabra* (*Castle of Blood*, Antonio Margheriti, 1964). Together with the aforementioned *Caged Heat*, *Shivers* started a second phase in Steele's career, in which she played smaller cameo roles that built on her reputation established in the 1960s – a clear sign of her rapport with audiences. This niche-appeal proved essential for the film's perception in a genre market. The presence of Lowry and Steele created considerable credibility with potential buyers, distributors and exhibitors – and the critics may have been the only ones unaware of their appeal.

The 15-day schedule made for a tense shoot. In hindsight, Cronenberg endearingly and somewhat embarrassedly recalls his anxiety when confronted with the nuts and bolts of commercial filmmaking: 'They [Cinépix] knew, better than I did, how little I knew about professional filmmaking […] you're watching me learn how to make movies.'[3] The routines of his experienced crew helped Cronenberg through the first few days and after that he quickly found his own feet. The entire production was set up on location, on Îles-des-Soeurs (or Nun's Island), just outside Montreal, and the confines of the location created a suffocating atmosphere of narrow corridors, window-less corners, impersonal interiors, flat, shadowless lights and plain colours the film eventually benefited from. Blasco's effects were largely improvised on-set, and besides being surprisingly innovative for someone without previous feature-film experience, their rough immediacy added to the film's sense of claustrophobia. Some of the stories of the *Shivers* shoot have since entered popular film folklore: how Cronenberg stayed overnight in the room where the effects-creatures were being prepared and almost asphyxiated because of rubber fumes; how the lack of space got on some of the extra's nerves and how this influenced their on-screen actions of rage (Cronenberg recalls:

'We all wanted to rip that place apart and run, naked, screaming through the halls'); probably the best-known piece of trivia is the slapping of Petrie – apparently a form of preparation she and Cronenberg had rehearsed to help her cry, but one that affronted Steele so much she pinned him to the wall threatening to punch him in the face.[4]

All of this gives the impression that *Shivers* breathes a sense of revolution, and revolution is exactly what the story offers. The film chronicles the breakdown of law and order and its replacement by a new order – animalistic but no less organised. The interaction between the inhabitants of Starliner Towers at the beginning is one of courteous restraint and civilised control. At the end they are an uncontrolled mob, with only one desire: to throw themselves into a never-ending Dionysian orgy. From the first scene we know something is awry. While sales manager Merrick (Ron Mlodzik) entertains a young couple interested in purchasing a flat we also see a young girl (Kathy Graham) dressed in a school uniform wrestling with a middle-aged man (Fred Doederlein). The man overpowers and strangles her – lifting her skirt and shirt in the act, giving the struggle a weird sexualised element. He then tapes the girls' mouth and rips off her clothes, baring her breasts. He cuts open the girl's body with a scalpel, and pours detergent in the wound, burning her innards. Looking satisfied, he cuts his own throat...

When the bodies are discovered it is revealed they were Annabelle Brown and Doctor Emil Hobbes. The police face a mystery. But Starliner's own medical doctor, Doctor Roger St Luc (Paul Hampton) gets a call from Hobbes' former partner Rollo Linsky (Joe Silver) who tells him Hobbes was trying to breed a parasite that could nest in a human's body and take over the functions of failing organs. He also reveals Hobbes had been having an affair with the girl since she was twelve. Not knowing what to make of it all, St Luc goes to his practice, where he sees Janine Tudor (Susan Petrie) who tells him about her husband Nicholas (Alan Migicovsky) and his abdominal problems. Nicholas, who also had an affair with Annabelle, has been having increasingly violent convulsions and cramps so bad he had to come home from work. He is throwing up heavily – blood but also something else, which is being released in the toilet, the bathroom and off the balcony. When a distressed Janine finds Nicholas at home something in his stomach is clearly working its way up.

St Luc's suspicions start to grow when another patient, also 'acquainted' to Annabelle, tells him about some similar 'lumps' in his abdomen. Then, as his fiancé, nurse Forsythe (Lynn Lowry), tries to attract his attention by changing, slowly and teasingly, from her nurse's uniform into a sexy black dress and boots in his practice, he receives another call from Linsky who has discovered papers in which Hobbes details his ideas about mankind's 'overrational body that's lost touch with its instincts, too much brain and not enough guts'. Hobbes wanted to develop a parasite that is a combination of aphrodisiac and venereal disease to turn people back to sex – by using the willing Annabelle as a guinea pig and implanting a parasite. When St Luc tells Linsky Annabelle was a 'pretty popular girl' at Starliner Towers and he has several patients he now believes may have been 'infected' by Annabelle, they agree to attack the parasite, and start with Nicholas.

But it is too late. The parasites Nicholas coughed up have crawled into the basement, and up the water pipes. Among the people they infect is Janine's best friend, the free spirited Betts (Barbara Steele) who is violated as she is taking a relaxing bath. Pandemonium follows, as children, women and men of all ages are infected and turned into sex-crazed animals making love to each other wildly, indiscriminately and without any taboos. Nicholas too, is suddenly very fond of his wife. With the parasite visibly moving underneath his skin and in his throat, he gropes her and forces her into sex. She resists and runs to Betts, who comforts her, kisses her passionately ... and passes on her own parasite to Janine. When Linsky arrives he finds Nicholas, whose parasites jump into his face. He pulls them off with pliers, and smashes them in the sink but Nicholas stuffs them back into both their faces. As she attempts to escape by car, nurse Forsythe is infected as well. Seductively, she tells St Luc she's had a bad dream in which she had sex with an old, badly smelling, repulsive man, who tells her that 'everything is erotic, everything is sexual, that even old flesh is erotic flesh, that disease is the love of two alien kinds of creatures for each other, that even dying is an act of eroticism ... that to physically exist is sexual. And we make love beautifully.' When he sees a parasite rising from her throat, St Luc punches her unconscious. Her mouth taped, he tries to make his way out of Starliner Towers, but to no avail. A mob grabs nurse Forsythe, and she joins them. After a chase, St Luc is cornered in the swimming pool. In a wild orgy, Betts, Janine and nurse Forsythe pass him the parasite.

That same night, a convoy of cars leaves Starliner Towers, on its way to Montreal. A radio broadcast informs us 'there is still no confirmation by Montreal city police concerning alleged reports of a city-wide plague of violent sexual assaults. The assaults, believed to have originated in the vicinity of Starliner Island, began late last night and have spread with increased frequency this morning. The reports have been termed irresponsible and hysterical by a Montreal city police spokesman...' It is less than 24 hours after Hobbes chased Annabelle.

The most common interpretation of *Shivers* is of a film dubiously torn between a sense of repulsion for the actions, an unease with the discarding of taste, reason, conventions and cultural boundaries, and a sense of exhilaration for the liberating potential portrayed. For Murray Smith (2000), *Shivers'* quality lies in the fact it does not ask the audience to see the infected as victims, even though they lose all human complexity. William Beard argues *Shivers* inhabits two contradictions: he puts the anguish and discomfort felt by (mainly) female characters against exploitative sex scenes which seem composed to gratify male viewers; and he posits the cleanliness of the antiseptic environment against the messiness and visceral nature of the parasite infections (1983: 19–23; 2005: 37–41). It is an ambiguity common to Cronenberg's films, but one that is etched here in far more crude dichotomies. For Smith and Beard, the line along which the dichotomy runs is a moral one – we are invited to ask ourselves 'what is good?' and 'what does good mean?' Does it mean liberation, or does it mean restraint and repression?

I believe *Shivers* is less concerned with morality than with survival. It asks not what is 'good' or 'wrong' but what works and what is effective. It represents a revolution not in its effects or goals – for that would still invite a moral question – but its pragmatics: what succeeds in overthrowing an order, and who benefits? It is an attitude encapsulated in the moniker 'Hobbes', which our mad scientist shares with the English seventeenth-century philosopher Thomas Hobbes, famously known for his *homo homini lupus* (man is a wolf to men) – stressing self-interest and survival as the key motivators to human actions.[5] Richard Slotkin (1973) used such considerations to study the role of violence in the establishment of the cultural myth of the American frontier.[6] According to Adam Lowenstein, a similar concern was at the heart of debates about culture in Canada at the time of *Shivers'* release, especially through Margaret Atwood's proposal to suggest 'survival' (not 'who made it' but 'who made it back') as the key theme in Canadian art (2005: 148). In the case of *Shivers*, survival first means surviving at Starliner Towers, and then setting out from that Arc to colonise the world.[7]

Judged by its pragmatics, *Shivers* is the story of a successful revolution, the breakthrough of unrestrained sexual liberation within the most mundane and reserved environment possible: a high-rise apartment building that is the symbol of cultural regulation, with its own guards, its own clinics, its own laundry service, everything in abundant supply to keep it clean. As Reynold Humphries remarks, even walking around at Starliner Towers is subject to strict control; as in a hotel, lifts and lobbies function as locks (2002: 174–5). Residents are kept in quarantine, separate from each other, ushered and guided along by the building's staff, and even sounds are channeled carefully (when a couple complains about the noise in the corridors Merrick assures them he will deal with it instantly). With such self-imposed constraints on bodily movement Starliner Towers is a site of total sexual repression. The marriage of Janine and Nicholas is on the verge of collapse – she is uptight and anxious, he is not interested in anything. Free-minded Betts is bored stiff, and St Luc is immune to the advances of nurse Forsythe. As if to punctuate Hobbes' point about people's 'over-rational body', we see St Luc passively watch her undress in front of him without answering her advances; a very strange juxtaposition of body (hers) and mind (his) as he takes in Linsky's information that Hobbes wanted to 'turn the world into one beautiful mindless orgy'. The parasite inserted into Annabelle is the trigger that upsets that frail order. It is perhaps telling it has to be a girl who has just come of age (Annabelle is 19 when she goes around infecting everyone), the embodiment of sexual fertility and desire. The charms of 'Parasite Annabelle' are such that all cultural taboos are shed, and a very real and physical sexual revolution is the result.

Infiltrative actions instigate the revolution. The entry of Nicholas's parasites into the overly ordered and quarantined world of Starliner Towers occurs through the nooks and cracks in the building's system: through the rather shabby looking laundry room (always on the threshold between messy and clean) and the water pipes (coming up into the clean bathrooms instead of flowing out of them). The most pointed activity of transfer is that of kissing: wet, moist and sensual. The kisses illustrate the indiscriminate nature of desire: kisses passing on the parasites are frequently emphasised by the use of slow motion (a rather unusual device for Cronenberg), especially when they brush taboos: Bett's lesbian kiss with her friend Janine, a young girl's French kiss of an elderly man (in the presence of her mother) and nurse Forsythe's kiss of St Luc amidst a polygamous pool orgy. Like orgasms, these slow motion kisses prolong and celebrate one single moment: that of the revolution itself, the exhilaration and adrenaline of its practice, not its morals.

Once instigated, collaborations propel the revolution. Characters possessed by the parasite are portrayed as active and enterprising, and the ones resisting it are for the most part passive, placid and immobile – literally so in the case of Nicholas. St Luc and Linsky, as medics heavily invested in keeping the body in rein, are the only ones who really try; Linsky is killed by Nicholas's parasites, and all St Luc does is run until he too is cornered and infected. There is no concerted attempt to fight the revolution. In fact, the only forms of collaboration occur on the side of the infected. In acts that mirror Girard's theory of opportunistic alliances to obtain objects of desire, those infected appear to be able to briefly interrupt their sex-activities to gang up on, or even trick, not-yet-infected humans. That rudimentary form of cooperation gives the revolution they start some appeal, as if it is not based on egoistic fulfillment of needs, but on some sort of solidarity, of units working together. Everyone is equal in the eyes of the infected – equally sexual, equally attractive, 'even old flesh is erotic flesh' as nurse Forsythe proclaims.

On the other hand, one cannot help think that the sheer violence and distress involved in the infections – the forceful rape-like penetrations of others' bodies – acts against the effectiveness of the revolution. Even if its procedures are effective, its methods may destroy what is supposed to be rescued. In the interest of physical well-being, maybe some taboos about how human bodies can be approached, touched, groped, violated, need to remain. At the very least, they uphold the impression that sex and love are something that has to be agreed upon between two partners. That is far from the case in *Shivers*. Consenting love occurs once, when Betts comforts and then kisses Janine. It may have occurred when Annabelle did her round of men too, but her predatory appearance in a flashback leads to believe there was at least some force involved. All other cases start as rapes and indecent assaults, with Betts' bathtub rape one of the most powerful – a scene reminiscent of Steele's previous bath scene in *Terror Creatures* (Massimo Pupillo, 1965), but also a horizontal version of the shower scene from *Psycho* (Alfred Hitchcock, 1960).

The destructive force guarantees the success of the revolution: in the end everyone is infected. But it also obliterates all remains of the previous order, and any vision of a new future. No one is left to represent the old, there is nothing to come back to, and what was before is now gone forever. No continuity, no tradition, no survival, no future, and no one saying that is a bad thing – maybe that is why Canadian critics fulminated against *Shivers* so much.

Rabid: Contra-Revolution

With the same intensity as *Shivers*, *Rabid* investigates the opposite possibility: what if the revolution fails? What if the revolution's pragmatics lead to nowhere? According to Cronenberg:

> Revolution brings with it death, pain, anguish and disease: often nothing positive to replace what was destroyed. Also, revolutions are always betrayed. To be so intent only on the event itself, and not to have any thought to what

happens after, means you're not being a serious, pragmatic revolutionary [...]
There aren't many people who have achieved it: Castro, yes; Che Guevara, no.
(In Rodley 1997: 66–7)

The production process of *Rabid* is far less of a juicy tale than *Shivers*. Upon the box office success of *Shivers*, Cinépix commissioned a new script from Cronenberg, who offered them *Rabid*. The CFDC reluctantly co-funded it. Reitman produced it, and brought in cinematographer René Verzier (*The Pyx* (Harvey Hart, 1974)), and editor Jean LaFleur (*Death Weekend* (William Fruet, 1976)), a crew familiar with both Cinépix's back catalogue and the horror genre. Joe Blasco did the special effects again, this time assisted by Byrd Holland (*Lemora* (Richard Blackburn, 1973) and *The Baby* (Ted Post, 1973)). Cronenberg asked if he could cast Sissy Spacek in the lead role (he had admired her in Terrence Malick's 1973 film *Badlands*), but he was offered, and upon the advice of Reitman settled for porn star Marilyn Chambers (*Behind the Green Door* (Mitchell Brothers, 1972)), a choice for the exploitation market: 'Why does a distributor from Spain (say) want to see *Rabid*? He'll go see it if Marilyn Chambers is in it' (in Rodley 1997: 54). Frank Moore, with whom Cronenberg had just collaborated on *The Italian Machine* (see chapter three), became the male lead. Joe Silver reprised his role of the supportive scientist from *Shivers*. Also from *Shivers*, Vlasta Vrana and Ron Mlodzik were given small parts in *Rabid*. The budget totalled about $500,000, and shooting took place in and around Montreal in November and December 1976.

Rabid tells the story of Rose (Marilyn Chambers), who, while on a motorcycle trip with her husband Hart (Frank Moore), has a near fatal crash. Patients from the nearby Keloid clinic, specialising in cosmetic surgery, witness the crash and the couple is brought in for treatment. Hart is only bruised, but Rose's condition is critical. She needs a skin transplant. Instead of giving her a normal skin graft, however, surgeon Doctor Dan.Keloid (Howard Ryshpan), treats the removed skin tissue and erases its genetic specificity so it becomes 'morphogenetically neutral', ready for another type of genetic job.

One month later, with a loud scream, Rose suddenly regains consciousness. Fellow patient Lloyd (Roger Peliard) comforts her. They hug and caress, Rose breathing heavily as if she is reaching an orgasm, and then he collapses, bleeding profusely, shouting something's stung him. Lloyd manages to get away, but is too embarrassed to tell the doctors what happened; they think he tried to molest the still unconscious Rose. But it soon becomes clear Rose has developed an insatiable lust for blood. With a sting-like protrusion from underneath her armpit, which like a penis erects when Rose is feeling 'hungry' for blood, she stings her victims, then sucks their blood. It has to be human blood too: when Rose wanders outside the clinic, to a shabby farm where she hugs and caresses a cow, attempting to suck its blood, it just makes her sick. What kind of human blood she gets is not important. She first seduces then assaults the drunken old farmer (Terence G. Ross), and later the same night, a young female patient (Terry Schonblum) in a hot tub inside the clinic. Still that same night, Keloid examines Rose and sees some sort of penis-like proboscis protruding from underneath her armpit, but before he can reach any conclusions he too is impaled by it.

Rose's victims don't die from their wounds either. Instead, they develop some sort of rabies that sets them on a rampage throughout the surrounding countryside: Lloyd attacks a cab driver, the disfigured farmer assaults customers and staff at a diner, and Keloid goes beserk during an operation. By the time Hart and Keloid's partner Murray Cypher (Joe Silver) arrive at the hospital to visit Rose, the entire place is in uproar, and a foaming Keloid is contained by the police. But Rose is nowhere to be found. She is hitching rides to Montreal, first with Smooth Eddy (Gary McKeehan), then with a nice old lady. Frank tries to track her down from a police station that sees the full effects of her rampage when a police officer inoculated against Keloid's bites still goes mad and has to be gunned down. Meanwhile, the Québec Bureau of Health is taking measures to contain what they see as an epidemic of a rare strain of rabies. 'Don't let anybody bite you' is their advice to the public.

When Rose reaches Montreal she stays with her friend Mindy (Susan Roman). Prowling the dodgy quarters of town, she lets men seduce her in sleazy theatres and then sucks their blood. Soon, Montreal is awash with rabid crazies, and a state of emergency is declared, wherein people are issued with vaccination cards (in effect, a form of ID card). Anyone without such a card can be pulled aside and detained indefinitely. Soldiers are ordered to shoot victims on sight. Rose experiences the scope of what she has set off when she witnesses an outburst of rage at a shopping mall: a guard guns down a rabid on the run, killing the mall's Santa and injuring several bystanders in the melee. Cypher too is killed, at home, by his wife. Frank narrowly escapes the same fate when a rabid attempts to get in his car, but a soldier shoots him, and men in quarantine suits clean the contaminated blood off his windshield. He finds Rose, who has just infected Mindy, and tries to contain her. She escapes, but can no longer bear the fact she is responsible for the mayhem in the city. In a heroic act of self-sacrifice, she picks up a stranger (future Hollywood director Allan Moyle), infects him, then waits in his art-filled apartment until he regains consciousness and turns on her. Against a background of wailing sirens and gunshots, her body, picked away at by a street dog in a backstreet dump, is found by military personnel in protective suits. Just more rubbish to them, they pick her up and throw her in a garbage truck. With a last look at the now harmless armpit, she is mauled by the truck's grinders.

There are several ways in which *Rabid* is more sophisticated than *Shivers*. The camera direction is much smoother. The narration is innovative in its consistent use of technological appliances to convey essential story elements: instead of dialogue or monologues we have phone conversations (at least a dozen), radio reports and television news broadcasts that tell us – and the characters – what is going on. In a break from dramatic tradition, the intense farewell conversation between Rose and Hart happens over the phone, not face-to-face. There are filmic references and winks that testify to Cronenberg's familiarity with popular culture: before Rose approaches Judy in the hospital's hot tub, we see Judy toting a biography of Sigmund Freud; a poster for *Easy Rider* adorns Hart's workshop; and when Rose prowls the streets of Montreal's bustling entertainment district,[8] she enters a porn theatre named Eve (the title of one of Marilyn Chambers' porn films was *The Resurrection of Eve* (Jon Fontana/Artie Mitchell, 1973)), where a Cinépix film is playing. After she has consumed the sleazebag who seduces her there, she wanders the streets again, and passes a poster of *Carrie* (Brian De Palma, 1976) – a film that contains, like her, a female lead in a modern horror film that is monstrous and heroic. If nothing else, these asides enrich *Rabid*'s intertextual appeal, and entrench its significance for fans and genre audiences.

Because of its setting in Montreal, *Rabid* also manages to integrate small details of Canadian culture. They are evident in the forthright operations of the provincial health authority, but also in the quintessentially Québecois farm, the snow on the road, the drunken natives in the police station, the television broadcast of *Across the Land with Stompin' Tom Connors* (a maritime folk singer), the middle-class shopping mall (which Canadians invented) and of course the siege of Montreal and its connection to the so-called 'October Crisis' of 1970. The Crisis was a hot political topic in Canada in the 1970s. Following several bomb explosions and the kidnapping of a British diplomat and a provincial minister by a movement called the Front for the Liberation of Québec (the FLQ), the then-prime minister Pierre Trudeau evoked the War Measures Act to declare a state of emergency in the province of Québec in October 1970. It brought tanks and armed soldiers onto the streets of Montreal and it gave local police far-reaching powers, effectively suspending civil rights. By the end of December most of the FLQ had been arrested or found exile in Cuba, but the news about the local politician found dead in the trunk of a car, televised sights of military power, several hundred arrests and the fear of a Québec uprising had left a big impression on Canadian citizens, one that is marvellously captured in Michel Brault's 1974 docudrama *Les Ordres*. The story of *Rabid* provided a unique opportunity to revisit that atmosphere and Cronenberg and the producers seized it, inserting in the narrative soldiers on the streets, police searches and a spokesperson as combative and outspoken as Pierre Trudeau. In *Rabid*, his alter ego bluntly declares 'shooting down the victims' is a good way of handling them. As Cronenberg recognises, the resonance of the October Crisis made sure that 'no one in Canada seeing this movie would not make the connection'.[9]

No matter how overt the link with the October Crisis is, however, it is not what *Rabid* really is about. Thematically, *Rabid* is a companion piece to *Shivers*, and on the basis of the story it is obvious how: a medical experiment creates an out-of-control contagious disease that causes the human body to develop an insatiable lust for sex. Its first thirty minutes also portray, just like *Shivers* (and *Stereo* and *Crimes of the Future* for that matter) a bubble-society: a confined retreat that separates sequestered people from culture-at-large. Once the initial infection is accomplished, the story moves away from the quarantine environment. *Rabid*'s rage, like rabies, seems to thrive better in increasingly messy and dirty settings. The hospital is left behind for locations such as a muddy, earthy cattle stable ('Rembrandt in a barn', Cronenberg calls it in a reference to the Dutch painter's unpolished realism),[10] the stained seats of a sleazy porn theatre, broken-up roads, messed-up windshields and, finally, the backstreet waste dump where Rose's body is found. Whenever a more controlled, cleaner environment presents itself – the jail or the shopping mall – it is ruptured by excessive violence: multiple shots in the chest kill a veteran police officer in the jail; and none less than Santa is a casualty in the mall shooting (a death Cronenberg describes as 'cathartic').[11] As in *Shivers*, bathrooms act as crucial sites of transgression, with Rose infecting Judy in a hot tub, and

Revolution and rage: David Cronenberg as an extra – on the attack, in *Shivers* (left); dead, in *Rabid* (right)

several of her nightly prowls starting from her friend's bathroom, where she writhes on the floor in torment in a wet T-shirt.

But where the revolution in *Shivers* appears to succeed, in *Rabid* it fails. One reason may be that even though the infection and the infected rabids desire uncontrolled, messy surroundings, they can really only survive in secluded conditions; once they hit the streets they are not as tough as they thought they were. Metaphorically speaking, real life culture, hardened by centuries of survival, is too strong to be toppled by a few bites and foams, and whenever it feels threatened it bites back, with a vengeance. In that sense, *Rabid* appeals to Nietzschean philosophies of survival and evolution (see Bruno 1989; Ramasse 1989; Garofalo 1993; Cristalli 1995). But the real reason why the revolution in *Rabid* fails lies in what Rose symbolises. Her actions resemble what Girard calls the scapegoat model. She is *maléfique* (bad) because she has caused the outbreak of rage, even though it was beyond her reasonable control. But she is also *bénéfique* (good) because her actions unite the rest of the population in an effort to set their differences aside and cast out the evil threatening their cultural order. As such, she is an ambiguous scapegoat, one that deserves to be commemorated as much as cast out. On top of that, Rose's guilt and self-sacrifice makes her a martyr. By offering herself for the greater good she demonstrates a moral concern – quite the opposite of the amoral characters in *Shivers*. For Girard, the self-sacrificing scapegoat is definite proof of cultural achievement. It is testimony of a set of values superseding individual desires and needs, of repression and surplus repression being successful. It is also an attitude quite familiar to the province of Québec, with its Catholic legacy. In his personal history of Francophone settlers in North America, Philip Marchand (2005) writes that the violence underpinning this particular form of colonisation, and its preoccupation with failures, martyrs and doomed futures fits Girard's scapegoat theory remarkably well, which he paraphrases as: 'it is better that one man should die than that the whole nation should perish'.[12] Whether inspired by Montreal's heritage or by Cronenberg's personal vision, the despaired ending of *Rabid* is a total opposite of *Shivers*': instead of survival, we find suicide.

Old Horror, New Horror: The Context of Release of Shivers and Rabid

With more than thirty years of hindsight blurring the view it is difficult to grasp how far apart *Shivers* and *Rabid*, and body horror, stood from the generic traditions and routines of the time. Suggesting they made an impact on the mainstream is overstretching their reach. The horror films mainstream audiences were familiar with were *The Exorcist* and *Jaws* (Steven Spielberg, 1975). Next to this, European horror was characterised by haunted house or gothic horror movies, such as Paul Naschy's Spanish werewolf movies and Jean Rollin's French vampire films, the deliberately artistic horror of Harry Kümel, Werner Herzog or *Die Zärtlichkeit der Wölfe* (*Tenderness of the Wolves*, Ulli Lommel, 1973), the folklore horror of *The Wicker Man* (Robin Hardy, 1973), and the rapidly imploding British Hammer horror series, which all researched old evils instead of new threats.

Underneath this mainstream and art-house surface however, a myriad of exploitation and underground cinema was brewing. Blaxploitation films such as *Foxy Brown* (Jack Hill, 1974), *porn chic* such as *Deep Throat* (Gerard Damiano, 1973) and *Behind the Green Door*, excessively violent vigilante films such as *Death Wish* (Michael Winner, 1974), lush soft-porn (*Score*), women-in-prison films (*Caged Heat*), or nunsploitation (*Flavia the Heretic* (Gianfranco Mingozzi, 1974)), testified to an attitude with industry and audiences alike that was permissive towards films testing the boundaries of taste and decency. Both *Shivers* and *Rabid* fitted such a sensibility perfectly, and by using actresses like Lynn Lowry (from *Score*) and Marilyn Chambers (from *Behind the Green Door*), they invited comparisons and associations.

If we look only to the horror genre, *Shivers* and *Rabid* came at a time when the genre was showing the first signs of a profound paradigm shift that was about to change it forever. The most important facets of that 'revolution' involve: (1) an increasing popularity of the genre that is not met with critical acclaim, turning horror films into a sort of popular resistance against dictated taste; (2) a perception of 'independence' in means of production and access to audiences – a situation that would ensure the genre's themes and motifs would not be watered down by studio executives or voluntarily cut by their makers to suit market segments; (3) a network of reception with a reputation for indiscriminate support and an opportunistic knack for exploitative profit: inner-city cinemas looking to expand into more lucrative markets of exploitation cinema, drive-ins, repertory theatres that would rely on packaged screenings (double or triple bills), cinematheques and college theatres would form the centre of the market;[13] (4) a tendency towards realism that highlights the difference between the fantastic horror film, whose distance from reality reduces its relevance to an allegorical one, and the realistic horror film, which claims direct cultural relevance; (5) a stylistic ambiguity in devoting much of the story and screen time to building a close attachment to the monster (and its values of unrepressed desire and sexuality), and then showing in precise detail its destruction – the hero who defeats the monster seems accidental and so are his values; (6) the apparent need for explicit imagery of death and flesh wounds, which, aided by special effects, emphasise the necessity to detail the violent abuse of the human body, and the literal violation of bodily integrity (the last frontier of humanity) – thus blurring the border between good and evil, man and monster: how many limbs does one need to lose before one is no longer a human being?; (7) the turning and twisting of the formulaic relationship between the 'normal' hero and the 'evil' monster by placing the source, and actions, of evil so close to that of the hero and his surroundings that if affects him too – in other words, the horror formula is no longer about defending normality (in most cases this means white, middle-class, individualist, capitalist, patriarchal, monogamous, society encapsulated in the nuclear family) against an outside threat (usually a seductive, egalitarian, heredi-tary, communal collective, such as a sect, a coven, a mad house, an orgy, or socialism), but about trying to defend oneself against the threat within, often leading to the sacri-ficial death or suicide of the hero; (8) the assumption that the source of evil is directly connected to historical and contemporary forms of waste, such as warfare, pollution, excess, over-consumption, gluttony and greed – combatting the idea of progress; (9) an overall tone of pessimism, cynicism and despair about the possibility of humans surviving the odds stacked against them – often leading to unhappy, or open endings in which nothing is restored and only traumas persist; (10) and finally, a tendency to provide audiences with inside jokes and references to other examples of the genre, as homage or critique, and to real life events, historical or topical (the real life of serial killers, the Vietnam War, Watergate, race riots, martial law, protests, terrorism) – thus stressing their interest in intervening in society with an active voice of dissidence.[14] Put together, these characteristics pulled horror cinema out of its juvenile innocence (and its juvenile markets) and positioned it as a grown-up exploitation product, still to be consumed by the young, but with more serious pretension than before. *Shivers* and *Rabid* became, through their visions and public presence, forerunners of that shift.

At the time of *Shivers'* and *Rabid's* release, this sensibility was still an anomaly in the genre. Only a small number of films, such as *Night of the Living Dead*, *Last House on the Left* (Wes Craven, 1972), *Raw Meat* (aka *Death Line*, Gary Sherman, 1972), *It's Alive* (Larry Cohen, 1974), *The Texas Chainsaw Massacre*, *Frightmare* (Pete Walker, 1974), *Carrie*, *Squirm* (Jeff Lieberman, 1976), *Suspiria* (Dario Argento, 1977) and a few other European films – many of them from debuting directors – were regarded as its representatives, as were a few genre-crossovers, like *Flesh For Frankenstein* (Paul Morrissey, 1973), *The Rocky Horror Picture Show* (Jim Sharman, 1975), *Thundercrack!* (Curt McDowell, 1975) and *Assault on Precinct 13* (John Carpenter, 1976). Their reception histories stress their initial 'outside' position before they became the centre of the new wave (see Staiger 2000: 179–87; Weinstock 2007).

When compared to their national competition, *Shivers* and *Rabid* were exceptional by default: Canadian horror films were few and far between, and several never found a nationwide audience. The secret sect story *Le Diable est parmi nous* (*The Sensual Sorceress*, Jean Beaudin, 1972), Cinépix's pre-Cronenberg dip into horror, a film that was typical of a 'short burst of early-Seventies Canadian devil-cult thrillers' (Vatnsdal 2004: 67) mostly inspired by *Rosemary's Baby*, was hardly screened outside Québec. Zombie movie *The Corpse Eaters* (Donald R. Passmore/Klaus Vetter, 1974) only played in and around Sudbury Ontario, before it was bought and shelved as a tax write-off, a fate that also befell Oliver Stone's debut *Seizure* (1974). Only five Canadian horror films received some wider visibility and success in the few years before the release of *Shivers*.[15] Among the most acclaimed was the Julian Roffman production *The Pyx* (aka *The Hooker Cult Murders*), about a prostitute murdered by a Satanic cult (see Vatnsdal 2004: 67). While successful, it faded from public view quite quickly, sidelined by the massive success of *The Exorcist*. Ivan Reitman's *Cannibal Girls* (1973) enjoyed the public's attention for a somewhat longer period, mostly because it catered well to grindhouse and college crowd audiences. In terms of appeal, critical attention and aesthetic impact the only real Canadian competition for *Shivers* came from American immigrants Bob Clark and Allan Ormsby. Clark's *Dead of Night* (1974) became the second zombie picture from Canada, and was a moderate success. Ormsby's *Deranged* (1974) gained notoriety as an early serial killer film; and *Black Christmas* (Bob Clark, 1974) quickly became a trendsetter for the slasher sub-genre (Cronenberg would later use John Saxon, Leslie Carlson and Art Hindle from this film's cast). While attracting some recognition, they did not really cause the kind of uproar *Shivers* and *Rabid* elicited, nor did they invite associations with the larger framework of dissenting independent cinema.

Perhaps the best possible illustration of the clash between the sensibility inhabited by *Shivers* and *Rabid* and the more mainstream horrors of the mid-1970s is to consider Cronenberg's own brief attempt at a Gothic haunted house film of the time, the television episode *The Lie Chair* (1975/76).[16] As a style exercise, *The Lie Chair* is decent but 'predictably scripted' (Rodley 1997: 51), and if one takes exception to curiously returning references to cars (see chapter three), it is a symptom of an entrenched, exhausted tradition. Even for contemporary television audiences its staple opening scene, with its pouring rain, thunder and lightning and a soaked couple with car trouble knocking on the door of a heritage house, asking to use the phone to call a garage, was an overused trope. The fact that the same year saw two decidedly disrespectful and unruly parodies of that style – *Thundercrack* and *The Rocky Horror Picture Show* – both containing similar scenes, but this time as part of a total deconstruction of the genre, proves how over-ripe it had become. It just *had* to be parodied. According to Rodley, Cronenberg accepted the television work because he was uncertain about his future in cinema: should he continue to push his own vision or just comply and accept the established clichés and become proficient in their use? (ibid.). *Thundercrack* and *The Rocky Horror Picture Show*'s ruthless dismantling of the 'old horror style' showed he made the right choice to push a new vision.

Controversy: the release and reception of Shivers
Cronenberg was fully aware of how the horror genre was changing at the time of *Shivers*' release; it is one of the reasons why the title of the film was changed from *Orgy of the Blood Parasites*, which Cronenberg and the Cinépix people felt sounded too much like a film from the 1950s. It became *The Parasite Murders*, and that was the title under which it was released in English Canada. AIP, which handled the American distribution, changed it to *They Came From Within*, a decision which invoked references to 1950s Cold War science fiction, pigeonholing it not as the revolutionary break from traditional horror it was, but as a continuation of the old style. *Frissons*

(the title for Francophone Canada and France) proved so successful that it was translated back into *Shivers*, which subsequently became the international title, later to be adopted around the world.

The title issue offers a good view of the distribution challenges *Shivers* faced. In Canada, it had to penetrate two virtually separated markets: the Francophone and the Anglophone, the first hermetic through its language barrier, and the second elusive because of its geographical size. In the United States, AIP was putting *Shivers* out in the B-movie market which was still largely dominated by a tendency to promote to children and teenagers: matinees, double bills with rude comedies, suspense thrillers or chase films, or coupled with an alternative to a regular mainstream movie, so that parent and child alike would be able to get a pleasurable night or afternoon out. *Shivers* was too edgy for this audience. The midnight movie market it would have done so much better in (and which it would have ended up in had it been released unrated or X-rated) was still only a marginal economic force, and not one AIP wanted to get involved with. Finally, the European market was a very unpredictable one, relying largely on festival exposure and exhaustive deal-making for separate territories.

Still titled *The Parasite Murders*, *Shivers* was first presented at the film market of the Cannes Festival in May 1975, a choice no doubt inspired by Cinépix's good grounding in the French market (as a Montreal company specialised in Francophone softcore movies). It received considerable attention from critics as a 'subtle parable on sexual taboos', and attracted several European buyers for a 1976 release (see Schlockoff 1975; Viviani 1975). *Shivers* was also screened at the Edinburgh International Film Festival in August 1975. At the time, this festival managed to combine an interest in film theory and avant-garde cinema with a fascination for exploitation movies. The year *Shivers* was screened it hosted a seminar on 'Brecht and Cinema', organised by the editors of the academic journal *Screen*, and premiered Michel Brault's October-crisis film *Les Ordres* and Jean-Marie Straub and Danièlle Huillet's *Moses und Aaron* (1975). But it also screened *Boxcar Bertha* (Martin Scorsese, 1972), *Death Race 2000* (Paul Bartel, 1975), and *Crazy Mama* (Jonathan Demme, 1975). *Shivers* received a cool reception at Edinburgh, especially at the hand of critic Robin Wood, who wrote that:

> The most striking of this year's batch of exploitation movies, by virtue of its detestability, was David Cronenberg's *The Parasite Murders*. Its derivation is from *Invasion of the Body Snatchers* via *Night of the Living Dead*, but the source of its intensity is quite distinct: all the horror is based on extreme sexual disgust. (1975: 25–9)

Though Wood called *Shivers* clumsy and indifferent, his references to *Night of the Living Dead* and *Invasion of the Body Snatchers* equipped it with authoritative associations and placed it, involuntarily, within the vanguard of a 'new kind of horror', with a huge potential for revolution and controversy.[17]

Controversy was indeed what *Shivers* caused upon its release in Canada in autumn 1975. About a month prior to its release it gained instant notoriety through one review by Marshall Delaney (a pseudonym for Robert Fulford), who had seen a preview of the film. This preview was an initiative of Cronenberg and Cinépix, who had hoped to create a climate of goodwill for the film's release. After all, Delaney (1970b) had written positively about *Stereo*, and seemed lenient towards films whose tastes could offend. Delaney's opinion was, however, extremely negative. Raging against what he called a Roger Corman 'school of filmmaking and film connoisseurship [that sees] schlock movies, horror films, porno films and old biker films as a vital part of cinema' he argued it was 'impossible to convey just how bad' *Shivers* was, concluding 'things can't get worse' now. As its title – 'You Should Know How Bad This Film Is. After All, You Paid For It' – suggests, Delaney saw the film not just as 'depraved' and 'worse than junk', but also as a product that should not have been granted government funding. Most of the article was in fact devoted to dismantling the funding practices of the CFDC. That was also the aspect *Saturday Night* seized upon for its sensational cover header: 'If this is the only way to have a film industry in English Canada then perhaps we should forget about the whole thing' (1975: 83–5).

Because of *Saturday Night*'s impact with cultural policy-makers the story created a huge controversy, one that pitched two views on Canadian cinema against each other. On one side stood politicians like Judy LaMarsh and established critics like Martin Knelman, Peter Harcourt and Robert Fulford who defended the tradition of National Film Board documentaries and European art cinema (auteurist, issue-driven, highbrow, understated, modernist), asking how films like *Shivers* could possibly help advance culture in Canada. On the other stood CFDC executive Michael Spenser and a new generation of filmmakers, like Cronenberg and Reitman, who acknowledged the power and appeal of genre and popular, even exploitation, cinema – were the bare-knuckle fist-fights and the blood on the ice in Canada's national game, hockey, not also exploitative? Spenser (1975) wrote a letter in defence of the CFDC to *Saturday Night*, as did Cronenberg, who called Delaney 'hysterical', 'paranoid' and 'ignorant' (1975b: 6). Several other letter-writers supported him (no letters in support of Delaney were published). But soon the controversy was no longer limited to the pages of the magazine. *Saturday Night* theatre critic Martin Knelman (1975) repeated the attack on *Shivers* and the CFDC in Canada's major paper, the *Globe and Mail*, and also used a review of *The Rocky Horror Picture Show* to remark on *Shivers*' inferiority and witlessness. Again Cronenberg riposted in a letter, but to no avail (1975a). Comments in virtually all major newspapers added fuel to the fire, as did negative reviews in the film magazines *Séquences* and *Motion*; before long MPs were asking questions about it in the House of Commons and *Shivers* was denied a screening at the Canadian Film Awards.[18]

The controversy did not deter audiences, however, and *Shivers* quickly became a huge success in Ontario and Québec (less so in the west of Canada) (see Martin 1976; Portman 1976). Within a year it had made $3 million, at that point the biggest profit ratio of any English-Canadian film ever, and it went on to gross in excess of $5 million (see Hofsess 1977). Nor was the film unanimously panned, either. In the popular weekly *Maclean's* Cronenberg's old partner-in-crime John Hofsess speculated that the commotion reflected more on battles over taste hierarchies in Canada than on the film itself (1975: 90). Of particular significance is the outspoken support *Shivers* received from *Cinema Canada*, a magazine founded by the Canadian Society of Cinematographers in 1972 that had been trying to become both a trade paper and a critical reflection on the business, establishing itself as a promoter of innovative film form and content (including genre film). The initial negative reports on the film probably only intensified the urge to defend it, and in consecutive reviews (and a guest article by producer André Link) it was lauded as a contemporary masterpiece of horror. Responding to what they perceived as a typical 'attitude of super criticism of all things Canadian', *Cinema Canada* instead highlighted Cronenberg's artistic concerns ('death and anticipation of death'), the topicality of his vision ('the question of man as body as opposed to man as spirit') and the way in which he revolutionised the horror genre (Chesley 1975; Edwards 1975; Link 1975).

That emphasis on genre revolution also typified the international reception, which was mainly negative, with some significant exceptions. In the US, where *Shivers* got a patchy town-by-town, theatre-by-theatre release (often as part of a double bill), most critics denounced the film as terrible, tacky and of poor cinematic quality, while also recognising it as funny and effective. It did good business in Chicago and New York, but was less visible, and hence less successful, outside the metropolitan areas (see Canby 1976; Sachs 1976). In Europe, three festival screenings were instrumental to its reception. The Edinburgh International Film Festival became the point of reference for most British reviewers, who judged the film in slightly more positive terms than the Americans. While some critics deemed it 'degrading' or 'diseased', others felt its 'most explicit and stomach-turning' grisliness was 'witty' and 'subversive'. Together with some appreciative comparisons to *The Towering Inferno* (John Guillermin/Irwin Allen, 1974) and *All the President's Men* (Alan J. Pakula, 1975), to boost its seriousness and sense of cultural anxiety, it earned enough credits from British reviewers to become a surprising, moderate success.[19] Most Belgian and French reviewers based their evaluations on the January 1976 screening at the festival of Avoriaz, which had a distinct flavour for horror and the fantastic, screening in the same year *The Texas Chainsaw Massacre, Race With the Devil* (Jack Starret, 1975), *The Premonition* (Robert Allen Schnitzer, 1975) and *The Rocky Horror Picture Show*. No wonder, then, that several reviews included references to *Night of the Living Dead* and *Invasion of the Body Snatchers* again, as well as a lament that these new horror films pre-empted the 'horrible end of the world'. Lastly, the October 1976 screening at the festival of Sitges, where it won the award for Best Direction, exposed *Shivers* to the Mediterranean market, framing it, as in Avoriaz, as a breakaway from the traditions of the horror genre. As British novelist and horror film critic Kim Newman put it: 'the poster of the UK release [the 1976 release which saw *Shivers* playing on a double bill with *Cannibal Girls*] pointed out *Shivers* had won first prize at the Sitges festival of horror films. The idea that a horror film would win a prize and there *was* a festival for horror films was kind of radical.'[20] In all cases, *Shivers* still presented something new, something through which reviewers could point to new trends and possibilities. One Belgian critic put it thus:

A regular horror film confronts us with horrible alien creatures … our horror is justified, because the monster is invariably 'a bad object'. Cronenberg has cleverly exploited this rule, and has turned its values around ... our horror concerns positively a monster, but a very dubious one, since it represents our sexuality. (Holthof 1976: 37)[21]

The fan press too reacted ambiguously to *Shivers*. Charles Leayman wrote in *Cinefantastique* that the film could be regarded as a trip through 'the historical evolution of the horror film genre as an art form' (1976: 23). Like Wood, Leayman referenced the structural similarities between *Shivers*, *Invasion of the Body Snatchers* and *Night of the Living Dead*, along with *Repulsion* and *Le Boucher* (*The Butcher*, Claude Chabrol, 1970), in praising it as true horror art. But in the same magazine Frank Jackson dismissed it as 'gross' – despite the efforts of subcultural magazines such as *Mad Movies* or *Vampirella*, grossness was obviously not yet the revolutionary production value of body horror it would become a few years later (see Petit 1975; Gressard 1976).

Continuity: the reception of Rabid
Whereas the revolutionary potential of *Shivers*, in its story or in its capacity to offend the established order of film culture appreciation, was a constant theme in its reception, *Rabid*'s public presence was less dominated by it.

Rabid rarely caused cultural commotion upon its release; when it did, it was of a smaller scale, and there would be a firm connection with *Shivers*' reputation. *Rabid* premiered in Canada in April 1977. Before it was released, *Cinema Canada* made sure its readers were reminded of *Rabid*'s predecessor via an article that unabashedly celebrated it as an absolute masterpiece, lambasting critics who had denounced it:

> Cronenberg's film has suffered the same critical disdain that was accorded *Psycho*, *Night of the Living Dead*, *Invasion of the Body Snatchers*. Perhaps serious art in the horror genre must expect to be reviled before it is understood. *Shivers* (by whatever name) will join those classics. If Cronenberg continues to grow this film will rank with *Psycho* as a personal statement. At the very least it will rank with those other two films, as a powerful expression of an anxiety of its day, so deep it hurts. (Yacowar 1977: 55)

Cinema Canada ensured it was among the first to set the tone for the reception of *Rabid* with a glowing review. Typifying most subsequent reviews, the 'unashamed similarity' with *Shivers* inevitably noted in the article was balanced by an observation of a 'move' in its style (more ambitious in its direction) and scope of the subject matter (more ambitious in its settings) (Irving 1977: 57). Designed perhaps to advance comparisons with *Shivers*, the 'move' argument allowed *Rabid* to be dealt with more as a film artefact than as a cultural phenomenon. Gone were the references to the CFDC, politics and disgust – as the *Cinema Canada* review noted, '*Rabid* rouses not our disgust, but curiosity' (ibid.). Cronenberg himself, though, was on his guard; as he explained in several interviews, the *Shivers* controversy had made him apprehensive about Canadian critics (see Hookey 1977). As if to prove this, he experienced a personal embarrassment when his Toronto landlady, who had misread one of the *Rabid* reviews and thought she had been sheltering someone her 'good friend' Robert Fulford called a 'pornographer', ordered him out of his apartment and set a city-zoning inspector upon him. Cronenberg got his revenge by buying a house in the same street, and he vented his frustration in a long letter published in the *Globe and Mail* in which he lashed out at Fulford's 'despicable hysteria', which threatened to take away his livelihood and the roof over his head. Comparing his predicament to that of 'the seer, the prophet, the Jew, the alien', he admitted he now feared 'the knock on the door in the middle of the night [when] the living dead take you away' (Cronenberg 1977: 6). Humiliating as the situation may have been it was much less of a storm than the one *Shivers* had caused. Overall, the Canadian reception of *Rabid* confirmed Cronenberg as a consistent director – not yet praised or respected but noted nationally nevertheless. The explicit Montreal setting gave *Rabid* a resonance for the entire country and even though hardly any reviews made reference to the 'October Crisis', it still gave the film enough leverage to receive attention nationwide, gradually penetrating a wider part of popular culture.

Rabid also displayed consistency in consolidating Cronenberg's market success. Backed by a better US distribution deal, with Corman's New World Pictures, and by a highly successful sales pitch at the market at the Cannes Film Festival, *Rabid* grossed about $7 million, making Cronenberg the most bankable director in Canada at the time (see Hofsess 1977). The distribution deals meant that *Rabid* was shown more widely than *Shivers*, and enjoyed a broader and more diverse critical reception. In France and Belgium in particular the film enjoyed some notable acclaim, either for its thematic similarity with *Shivers* or its unpretentious celebration of gore – undoubtedly influenced by the fact that some Belgian and French critics gradually started appreciating some of the facets of body horror. In most other countries critics were rather harsh on the film, while also recognising its potential for 'tongue-in-cheek camp' (Schreger 1977: 28).

An exception was the fan press reception. By 1977 Cronenberg had started to become one of the horror fans' new heroes, a status that, by the time of *The Brood* and *Scanners*, would turn him into a cult hero (see chapter four). Lining up *Rabid* next to *Shivers*, the fan press emphasised both the continuation of Cronenberg's vision and his consistent success, labelling him a future king of horror. *L'Écran fantastique* published an eight-page interview with Cronenberg to accompany their review of *Rabid*, and *Cinefantastique* published a career overview and a very positive review (written by Mick Garris who, as a distributor and director/producer, would become a major supporter of the new wave of horror). There is an excitement in these pieces about Cronenberg's work that stands in some contrast to the blasé receptions of films about possession such as *The Omen* (Richard Donner, 1976), *The Exorcist 2: The Heretic* (John Boorman, 1977) or *Ruby* (Curtis Harrington, 1977), and is found only in the admiration for other 'new horror', such as *Suspiria* or *The Hills Have Eyes* (Wes Craven, 1977).[22]

Midnight movies: The long-term receptions of Shivers and Rabid
The small but committed and dedicated fan following for Cronenberg's films gave *Shivers* and *Rabid* a long-standing presence in the public domain. That presence was always at the fringes of popular culture; decidedly outside the mainstream. But if we

bear in mind it occurred in a pre-home viewing era it constitutes a peculiar prominence for two films that were initially, according to critics and opinion formers, better forgotten as soon as they were released.

The long-term public presence of *Shivers* and *Rabid* was such that it gradually raised the esteem of the films until they were almost regarded as underground avant-garde – quite distinct from the box office successes and low culture grindhouse appeal of their immediate release. Several factors played a role in this turn: the cult reputation of *The Brood* and *Scanners* was significant in dragging Cronenberg's earlier efforts into the limelight, as was the fact that the critics and press who had celebrated the thematic sophistication of *Shivers* and *Rabid* became more authoritative (see chapter four). But the key element was the adoption of *Shivers* and *Rabid* into the midnight movie circuit. This circuit originated as a network of exhibition and distribution concentrated around late-night screenings in urban centres and college towns of films that had missed out on a 'proper' distribution – by accident, incompetence or reluctance, because they were too edgy and sophisticated for the drive-in circuit, too hard for the matinee circuit and often unsuited for the double bill. In the midnight movie circuit such films would be programmed for weeks and months in a row, gradually acquiring a cult following (see Hoberman & Rosenbaum 1983). The phenomenon of midnight movies took off at the beginning of the 1970s, when films such as *Invocation of my Demon Brother* (Kenneth Anger, 1969), *El Topo* and *Night of the Living Dead* were screened, at midnight, for months on end at theatres like the Elgin or the Waverley in New York; San Francisco, Paris, Brussels, London and Toronto also quickly developed thriving midnight movie cultures. The circuit contained a peculiar mix of modern horror, the underground and the avant-garde (see Hawkins 2000; Betz 2003). One thing most of these films had in common was a preoccupation with putting the human body in precarious situations – ready for mutilation, violent penetration or abuse. By the late 1970s a canon of midnight movies had been formed, with alongside the above-mentioned pictures, *Freaks* (Tod Browning, 1932), *Equinox* (Jack Woods/ Dennis Muren, 1970), *Pink Flamingos* (John Waters, 1972), *The Harder They Come* (Perry Henzell, 1972), *Emmanuelle* (Just Jaeckin, 1973), *The Texas Chainsaw Massacre*, *The Rocky Horror Picture Show* and *Eraserhead* (David Lynch, 1977) at its core.

When *Shivers* and *Rabid* hit the midnight movie circuit, in the late 1970s and early 1980s, it was in a state of transformation, moving away from once-a-night screenings in individual theatres. Without other networks to take the vacant spot in the United States, this equalled a decline. But on the European scene – which most writers on midnight movie culture ignore – event screenings such as once-a-month triple or quadruple bills of 'all-nighters', or one-night festivals, filled the gap. *Shivers* and *Rabid* featured prominently in this changing constellation. For instance, if we look at the Belgian market, we see how *Shivers* and *Rabid* first enjoyed late-night screenings and re-releases in grindhouses and also in adventurous programmes at the Royal Film Museum.[23] But subsequent programming occurred at mini-festivals, like the screening of *Shivers* at the Monty in Antwerp, alongside *Tout va bien* (*Everything's Fine*, Jean-Luc Godard, 1972), *Lenny* (Bob Fosse, 1974), *Medea* (Pier Paolo Pasolini, 1969 – a staple of the European midnight circuit) and the ubiquitous *Night of the*

Living Dead and *Eraserhead*, on 23 March 1979.[24] In the autumn of 1983 *Shivers* and *Rabid* toured a number of Belgian cities as part of a 'Night of the Demons' quadruple-bill late-night festival, organised by the programmers behind the illustrious Knokke-le-Zoute festivals that had introduced Jack Smith and Kenneth Anger to European audiences. In Germany and Italy there were similar trajectories. In France, the success of *Naked Lunch* and *M. Butterfly* led to the re-release of *Shivers* and *Rabid* as a double bill in theatres in Paris in December 1994. Together, these screenings helped maintain a permanent presence. Moreover, the other films in whose company they appeared – often deemed as subversive – helped solidify their reputation as films flirting with ideas of revolution.

In North America, *Shivers* and *Rabid* were less frequently re-released or screened. Instead, *Shivers* especially continued to cause furor in debates about taste and criticism. Cronenberg's appearance in a panel at the Toronto International Film Festival in 1979 was accompanied by a screening of *Shivers*, and in 1983 the festival honoured him with a full retrospective of his films, covered widely in the national press. Such laudations frequently reignited old feuds over the revolutionary or reactionary agendas of the films. Until the mid-1980s the unrepentant Fulford (1978) and Wood (1983) kept repeating their disgust of Cronenberg, and Hofsess (1978) and *Cinema Canada* (see Macmillan 1981; Scott 1983) kept defending him.

If taken outside their theatrical contexts, however, the revolutionary framework disappears. The video and DVD releases of *Shivers* and *Rabid* did not change their reputations much: while both were reasonably successful they did not become typical video hits (at least not when compared to *Scanners* or *The Fly*), and while most DVD-reviews on the Internet are fairly positive they are also non-committed. Nor are there significant regional differences, beyond a small variance in tone between the North American DVD presentation ('going mad is just the beginning') and the European ones ('the infectious high-rise nightmare shocker'). Instead of arguments on the politics of body horror and theories of revolution, evolution and contra-revolution, or even acknowledgements of the references to politics and terrorism in the films, the weight of subsequent Cronenberg films has obviously drawn reviewers to comparisons with immediate successors. In sum, there is a lot of respect for the films, but only in the shade of other works by Cronenberg, as niche films with historical value, testifying perhaps to a decade revolutionary enough to spawn body horror, but not in the same league as the tractates *Videodrome* or *Crash*.[25]

Conclusion

The receptions of *Shivers* and *Rabid* had several effects. Firstly, they turned Cronenberg into a local celebrity (for a time, public enemy number one), with some resonance outside Canada. As the body horror genre grew, so did his reputation, and *Shivers* and *Rabid* subsequently became key points of reference for a sizeable part of the body horror canon, especially for European gore films such as *Buio Omega* (*Beyond the Darkness*, Joe D'Amato, 1979), *Demons* (Mario Bava, 1985), *Schramm* (Jörg Buttgereit, 1993), and *Trouble Every Day* (Claire Denis, 2001).[26] Secondly, the decision to 'go commercial' had drilled Cronenberg in the harshest possible aspects of the film business in Canada: getting funding, defending your film against critics, doing the long tours of festivals, setting up an alliance with the fan press and, above all, persisting in the belief of his practices. Finally, the controversies and praise that followed the release of *Shivers* had allowed Cronenberg to carve out a space for his work. By the end of 1977 he was still far away from acceptance as an artist, but he was no longer the gifted but inconsequential amateur from before: instead he had shown how his films could strike a cultural nerve, and he had conquered a corner of the Canadian cinema market that was now distinctly his. Even if the establishment did not approve of his obsessions and visions, at the very least it acknowledged them. Dangling the frightful idea of bodily revolution in front of critics and audiences, Cronenberg had moved from novice to notice to notorious. Now he had to become normal.

CHAPTER THREE

Cars and Races: *Fast Company* and *The Italian Machine*

In the electronic age, the machine becomes a work of art.
And in the age of automation human beings become works of art.
– Edward and Lana in The Italian Machine

For Ferrari's, red.
– David Cronenberg, asked about his favourite colour
(in Harkness 1981: 17)

Unseen, Unwanted, Impossible to Place

Every oeuvre has to have its renegade, its *opus maudit*; every class its misfit. Without it, careers would be too perfect, too easily channelled into a model interpretation. In the case of Cronenberg's oeuvre that film is his drag racing movie *Fast Company*. The film does not appear in most overviews of Cronenberg's work, and when it does it is easily dismissed.

There are several reasons for this dismissal: *Fast Company* is not a horror film, it does not have the same single-minded focus on mutating bodies. Indeed when, at the end of the film, three 'bad' characters die the deaths are spectacular rather than horrific: a driver perishes in a car explosion, a mechanic accidentally sets himself on fire and a manager crashes his plane into a truck – it is purgatory, but without the horror. In a review of the film, Martha Jones mentioned that 'to Cronenberg this is more of an action element than any vestige of his interest in horror' (1978: 19). But there is no sexual violence, no monster and no medical experiment. Even Cronenberg himself acknowledges that the film stands apart from all the other films he has made: while he holds the film dear ('It's all coming from me' he says, 'it was a labour of love'), he also admits it 'doesn't seem to fit with the rest of my work now' (in Rodley 1997: 70). It is also the first film Cronenberg did not write himself, though he received co-writer credit for his changes to the script; he only became involved in the project when it was already well into development. Because of its isolation from the rest of the oeuvre, critics usually sideline *Fast Company*.

The second reason for a dismissal of the film is an aesthetic one. *Fast Company* is not generally considered a great film. William Beard, who completely ignores the film in his book on Cronenberg, but who was one of the only critics to review it when it was released, wrote that 'under ordinary circumstances one wouldn't even notice it' (1979: 32). While he immediately added that in the hands of Cronenberg nothing is ordinary, he asserts 'I can't in good conscience recommend *Fast Company* [because of] the banality of the scenario' (1979: 33). Serge Grünberg sees it as Cronenberg's 'only Hollywood attempt', and recognises that Cronenberg sees *Fast Company* as an integral part of his oeuvre but nevertheless dismisses the film as 'without ambition and not of great interest' (1992: 70). Similarly, Géraldine Pompon and Pierre Véronneau acknowledge that Cronenberg continues to stand by his film, though they too claim it is 'not a very memorable piece' (2003: 59–61).

The third reason is a logistical one. *Fast Company* was made under the tax shelter regime that allowed entrepreneurs and companies to fully deduct their investments in film from their tax returns. The system was set up as an attempt to allow Canadian films to attract commercial funding that could be comparable to that of American films. Because it was constructed around a fairly loose procedure of 'promises' to invest, a lot of the tax shelter films never got their full funding and if they did there was often no guaranteed distribution, because that was of no concern to the financers. *Fast Company* became embroiled in this system from the very beginning. It had a fairly rushed shooting schedule (during the summer of 1978), and had a quota number of Canadian actors in the cast; there could only be two American actors for the bigger parts, which meant that Claudia Jennings had to receive special permission from the actors' union ACTRA to take the female lead (see Jones 1978: 18). As it turned out, *Fast Company* hardly got released at all. It premiered in Cannes on 16 May 1979, but it never got distributed outside a few areas of Canada and the US. Immediately after the Cannes screening distributor Danton Films announced openings in Edmonton and Toronto, but added that 'we don't care if it ever opens in New York or Chicago' (see Scott 1979a). As Peter Morris relays in Cronenberg's biography, the American distributor almost immediately went bankrupt, and the film got tangled up in litigation and was withdrawn from screenings (1994: 86).

Unseen, unwanted and impossible to place: with such odds against it, it is no surprise that *Fast Company* hardly features in overviews of Cronenberg's work. But if we lift the film out of the framework of pre-constituted concerns and narrow aesthetic evaluations and instead place Cronenberg's oeuvre in a broader context of film culture and its socio-political landscape, then a reconsideration of the film's achievements becomes necessary. The themes of motor racing and racing technology are chief among these, next to motifs about rebellion and professionalism. Equally interesting are non-textual facets such as the pervasive presence of race-film culture (a genre that seems to linger persistently in the discourse on Cronenberg's work) and the degree of 'professionalism' that entered his career, one which found itself expressed in his attitude towards the filmmaking process, and the logistics of the shooting – with particular significance for the interaction with crew and cast. Finally, there is the longer-term presence of the film, especially its DVD release, which has re-introduced it to the public eye and sparked new interest. In such light I would argue that *Fast Company* is less a failure than an intriguing outing addressing and prefiguring characteristics of Cronenberg's oeuvre.

Professionalism and rebellion

Fast Company tells the story of veteran race champion Lonnie 'Lucky Man' Johnson (William Smith), fading star of the FastCo race team. Other members of the team are the old, trusted mechanic Elder (Don Francks), the young hot shot second driver Billy 'the kid' Brooker (Nicholas Campbell), factotum and truck driver PJ (Robert Haley) and the team's new bunny/mascot Candy (Judy Foster). Opposite the team stands the manager, and the representative of sponsor FastCo, Phil Adamson (John Saxon), who is not so much interested in winning races as in sticking to the budget and selling FastCo oil cans – 'winning is too expensive' he says. It suits him that Lonnie is becoming more and more complacent – a situation reinforced by his long absences from his girlfriend Sammy (Claudia Jennings), who he mostly only gets to speak to over the phone. Things come to a head when Lonnie blows up the engine of the top-fuel dragster of the team, leaving only the funny car to race (the funny car is a separate class of racing car); Adamson threatens to pull all funding and Lonnie is forced to take the seat in the funny car (at the expense of a disgruntled Billy) to meet the sponsor's demands. But even then Adamson does not arrange for a replacement engine for the top-fuel dragster. When Lonnie discovers this he kicks Adamson off the team (quite literally), and decides to continue as an independent. With the support of Sammy and Candy he steals back the funny car Adamson had confiscated and enters a final, deciding race against their eternal rivals, Gary Black's Blacksmith team – who have now received the funds Adamson denied Lonnie's team. Adamson also has Blacksmith's mechanics sabotage the track, but in spite of that Billy (who has received the blessing of Lonnie to run the final race) wins the race. Black becomes the victim of the sabotage and dies; his mechanic also dies in a fire and when Adamson tries to escape in his private plane Lonnie chases him in the dragster down the track, until Adamson crashes into a truck and he too dies. Having settled the score, Lonnie retires with Sammy.

Within this straightforward narrative three themes stand out. The first two, rebellion and professionalism, occur on the level of the film's explicit theme – as morals of the story – and are closely intertwined. At the beginning of the film few of the characters behave as professionals: Lonnie is complacent, unfocused and does not care enough about the material he is responsible for. He seems to have lost interest in reaching the top or wanting to win, he is uncomfortable with his popularity and prefers to spend time alone in the truck.[1] Billy is too hotheadeded – he still has to learn to be disciplined. PJ even forgets to bring spare tyres and Elder may keep up a tough façade when he claims he is 'trying to win' but he nevertheless complies with Adamson's corporate vision: selling oil cans is more important than winning races. Adamson, obviously, has no interest in the sport but at least he has clear professional reasons for his actions – certainly at the start of the narrative. In his words, winning is too expensive if it means it will 'bust the budget'. 'If I don't eat, you don't eat, nobody eats!' he adds. And with the ultimate professionalist credo, 'it's showbiz', he shuts down all discussion.

This situation changes completely in the second half of the film, when Adamson becomes so maniacally obsessed with sabotaging Lonnie that he loses his professionalism and pays for it with his life. Lonnie and his team, however, become the ultimate professionals, displaying textbook collaboration, team spirit and skill. Billy accepts Lonnie as the better driver and Lonnie ultimately accepts his role as mentor to Billy. Their professionalism even helps them to overcome rigged competition. The unprofessional mechanic of the Blacksmith team dies, as does Black himself (though his death is redeemed as a sacrifice – perhaps a nod to his earlier chivalry, another professional value). As such, professionalism is posited as a survival strategy – become good at the job or be gone. As I will argue later, it was a strategy also very relevant to Cronenberg's career at this point.

Lonnie and his team find their professionalism when they rebel against the corporate pressures of Adamson. This small, organic community-versus-corporation theme is not without precedent in Cronenberg's oeuvre. It permeates *Stereo* and *Crimes of the Future*, even though rebellion is not endorsed there, and it is present in *Shivers*, in which it is actively encouraged (see Handling 1983: 106). It also appears in *The Italian Machine* (see below). In the case of *Fast Company*, it is not so much the kind of rebellion but its *moment* and direct aftermath that are significant. After Lonnie throws Adamson off the truck Adamson has the funny car confiscated. A little while later Billy and PJ discover it on display at an 'Autorama' car show; when they relay this to a boozing, depressed Lonnie, the idea of the car – the beloved, living and breathing technology – 'roped off' and locked away drives him into action, activating his dormant professionalism. 'Is it hurt?' Elder asks, before Lonnie finally asserts himself: 'Let's go get *her*'. A few minutes later we see that the gang have stolen the car back and are working in their repair shop to clean and fix it. Accompanied by a sexy song sung in a hoarse, hushed voice we see them go through an elaborate foreplay: they replace parts, caress the car's bodywork, they lubricate, oil and smear it, they fill its tubes. Through their professional care they are putting the car on heat, literally and metaphorically, prepping it for an ultimate performance.

Racing, technology and sex

It is at this point that the link between professionalism and the most important theme of the film, its fetishistic passion for technology, becomes too evident to ignore. In a sense, even before that point it is clear that the film clearly loves the cars more than the stars or the story. For most critics, the story and characters are the weaker points of the film. I will elaborate on Cronenberg's use of actors below but it is worth noting how, in a rare review of *Fast Company*, Kim Newman complained that the experience and cachet of William Smith, Claudia Jennings and John Saxon were 'sadly wasted' (1984: 47). Narrative unity and continuity too are left underdeveloped. Beard argued 'that on the script level *Fast Company* is without any important redeeming qualities' (1979: 32). It is true that in foregrounding the characters and narrative *Fast Company* does not generate much aesthetic insight. That is because it is a film that is genuinely about races and cars and the culture of drag racing – the story is only a vehicle to explore that particular culture.

For the trained observer this is clear from the beginning and, indeed, throughout the film. Many of the extras and passers-by are part of the drag race culture. Fans of the sport may recognise some of them, like Gordie Bonin or Bob Papirnick who drove the 'FastCo' cars – involved here as expert consultants – as professionals. They may recognise the Edmonton racetrack, the second largest in the country at the time, with a notorious reputation of its own. Or they may simply see a familiar set of characters: a driver, bunnies, fans, mechanics, managers and announcers. Beyond doubt they will pick up on the many references to the drag race culture, encapsulated not only in the brand names of props that are used (Valvoline and Goodyear prominent among them), but also, of course, in the car brands. Next to the top-drag makes, for instance, *Fast Company* allows ample screen time for a typical amateur race between a Pontiac and a Plymouth (with the Plymouth not advancing more than a yard). In what must have been a deliberate attempt to push this kind of referencing up a notch a key narrative scene in the film – a discussion between Lonnie and Adamson about who will drive which car – takes place in a for-sale secondhand Cadillac.

But the most compelling aspects of *Fast Company* as a drag race film lie outside characterisation or narrative. As director of photography Mark Irwin explains, in an interview in the DVD documentary, there was a distinction between shooting the narrative scenes (which were all more or less tailored to give the feel of an American, automotive western – including an emphasis on the colours red, white and blue, which became the team colours of FastCo) and the race scenes, which were given a much more documentary presentation; a '*vérité*' look' he calls it. This is evident from the many close-ups and medium-close shots of cars being prepped on the track, towed to the starting line, slicking their tyres, getting fired up. This footage is among the most attractive of the entire film because it features actual professionals, not actors, people who see racing as their job and their way of life. Irwin explains how getting close to the action felt like he was intruding on a semi-private sphere, and he had to gain these mechanics' and drivers' trust in order to be allowed so close to the machines. There is even the odd courteous acknowledgement of the camera, a brief nod here and there, as one would only find in documentaries. Similarly, the races themselves are filmed in a style much more akin to documentary and even sports reports than fiction cinema. The moment the drivers get in their cars the film seems to lose all interest in the characters, and the dynamics of the race preparations dictate the flow of events.

In all, there are eight races. The first three are grouped together in the first ten minutes, and in the last five minutes there are another two. All of these scenes make excellent use of cinematography, with crane shots, panning cameras, low wide-angle shots in the middle of the track, driver point-of-view shots and cabin shots. Tellingly, there is no use of slow motion: the best impression of the blasting speed of the race cars is not achieved by slowing the image down. The preparation and aftermath of the races also receive ample attention, especially the tense moments when the cars line up on the grid and spin their wheels, and the post-race minutes when the drivers climb out of their cars and, in absolute silence, await the crew to tow them back. These moments are void of narrative relevance. One montage of the preparation and aftermath would have given sufficient information to the viewer. But in showing, race after race, the almost ritualistic obsession with detail typical of the drag race culture (and showing them through a style equally obsessed with ritual), *Fast Company* actually shifts its focus to become not a story but a *document* about car racing and technology. It is in those minute moments right before, after and during the races that the film lays down a lot of its characterisation – moments of adrenaline-packed concentration and peaceful inner reflection respectively.

One race in particular stands out. It has no relevance to the development of the narrative: it is a race in which Billy drives the funny car before he is told Lonnie will replace him henceforth. But we never see Billy until the race is over and the funny car is parked in the pit lane again; what we do see is a short montage of the preparation (with the same rituals as before: spinning the wheels, gearing up, getting the best touch on the starting line). The entire race itself is filmed from a fixed camera inside the car, through a wide-angle lens; the lack of stability of the dragster is literally visible through the camera's vibrations. In a highly unusual extra-diegetic intervention, pulled directly from sports report conventions, a chronometer appears on the right side of the frame clocking the time the car needs to bridge the quarter of a mile (6.45 seconds).

Even more remarkable is the sound of the entire scene. By the time of the race the viewer is accustomed to the roars, sputters and thundering of the race engines, often draining out the actors' and lane crew's voices – the replacing of dialogue by noise is another indication of how *Fast Company* privileges documentary observation over conventional narrative. But in this scene we do not just get the technological sounds; we hear the impact the eruption of power has on the driver. Once the quarter-mile is run the camera stays in the car – in a continuation of the same shot. We *hear* the driver shut off the engine, followed by the squeaking of the brakes, the flapping of the brake parachute and, clearly audible, the gasping, heavy breathing of the driver. It almost sounds like a sigh of relief, of post-orgasmic satisfaction. In this auditory counterpoint to the noise that preceded it *Fast Company* achieves more empathy for the driver character, and more appreciation for his professionalism, than in any of the dialogue.[2]

This relationship between car and driver, between technology and humans, is *Fast Company's* most important theme. It is evidenced in the races, in the heavy sighing of the driver after the race, but also in the professional care, the almost loving obses-sion, with which Lonnie and his team prep the recaptured funny car for its ultimate performance. The insinuation that there is something sexual in this relationship is punctuated more explicitly when in one of the few sexy scenes of the film the moment of ejaculation is replaced by an act of fetishism: at the height of a sex romp with two hitchhiker girls Billy has one of them pour motor oil over her breasts. Even this moment has a professionalist tenor, when we hear Billy brag that 'there is a lot of junk you can pour down your pipes, but you gotta take care of your babies so I suggest you go like the *pros* and go FastCo if you want that power, performance and potential'. It is amusing to hear Cronenberg's audible surprise on the DVD commentary track when he discovers that this scene – which he was convinced had been cut – was included in the final version after all. His amazement is such that he calls it a 'great moment in the history of cinema'. As a reference to the scene in the *Variety* review of *Fast Company* confirms, it was certainly included in the version shown at Cannes. For the *Variety* reviewer it is even a key scene, one which affirms the film as a true racing movie. In fact, he laments there is 'only one scene [that] has car bunnies getting motor oil poured down their naked breasts' (Adilman 1979: 24).

As a final point here, it is necessary to note how the sexual innuendo of the rela-tionship of the drivers does not translate itself into a sleazy style that equals drivers' and crews' treatment of their cars and equipment to 'making out'. For that, Cronen-berg's and Irwin's styles are too detached. While they put cars and racing technology centre-stage, the attitude they maintain is one of observation rather than fan-like adoration. The detachment also translates itself in prudence. Even in Billy's sex scene and in the funny car preparation scene there is some sagacity in the way any sexual tension is framed. Throughout, the professionalism of the characters, and their focus on skills and attention to detail, replaces most desire with *care*. That care might be called fetishist and obsessive, but only rarely does it cross over into an unruly frenzy – a professional impression of control is maintained.[3] In that sense, *Fast Company* is very different from *Shivers* and *Rabid*.

The Italian Machine

Yet *Fast Company* does have a nice thematic fit with Cronenberg's oeuvre at that time. Even for those only aware of Cronenberg's immediate feature-length predecessor, *Rabid*, there is a nice little point of connection in that the entire narrative of that film is triggered by a motorcycle accident, the result of Rose and Hart racing down the roads.

A much stronger link is found in the theme and motifs of a half-hour television episode of the CBC series *Teleplay* Cronenberg had directed two years before, called *The Italian Machine*.[4] Its interest in motor racing is evident from the very opening. While tuned-up car engines roar in the background, an off-screen narrator informs us we are on 'the Isle of Man, the finest road racing circuit in the world, with a history that goes back to 1911, and which has bred the world's finest riders'. It turns out the voice comes from a disc on a record player, recounting the 1958 Isle of Man race.[5]

Lionel (Gary McKeehan) is a bike fanatic and the owner of a local motorcycle repair shop. When he hears from one of his friends, Bug (Hardee Lineham), that a local dealer has managed to obtain a Ducati 900 Desmo Super Sport, of which there were reportedly only forty made, he visits the dealer, Reinhardt (Chuck Shamata), who tells him he has sold the machine to a wealthy art collector, Edward Mouette (Louis Negin), someone with a keen interest in 'techno-art' and very liberal ideas about sex. Determined to 'liberate' the Ducati, Lionel, Bug and another friend, Fred (Frank Moore), talk their way into the house of Mouette, posing as art photographers. They meet Mouette's wife Lana (Toby Tarnow), and their kept man, Ricardo (Géza Kovács), a handsome gigolo who claims his role is that of resident living artwork – so gorgeous he is paid for just sitting around. The three friends blackmail Ricardo (who has a cocaine addiction) into convincing Mouette that if he sells the Ducati to him he will go into history as the first person who has sold one *objet d'art* to another. Mouette takes the bait, but insists Ricardo leaves the house with the Ducati. He is offered a new residence in Lionel's garage.

It is not difficult to see the parallels between *The Italian Machine* and *Fast Company*, and much of Cronenberg's oeuvre for that matter. There is an obvious focus on technology at the core of the narrative, accentuated by the many technological props and motifs in the film. There is also the sexualised relationship between man and machine, and the dependence on professionals: Lionel is obsessed by the Ducati and once he sets eyes on it he just *has* to touch it, caress it, grope it. And while Ricardo himself does not seem attracted to the Ducati, his development is strikingly similar to it: he is fetishised but he also needs professional care. In much the same way the Ducati is withering away in the collector's house, without proper care Ricardo's health deteriorates as soon as he is pulled out of the art collector's environment – maybe he 'will break' asks Fred's girlfriend. Only when they both receive the professional care their sophisticated, fragile constitutions demand will the Ducati machine and the Ricardo human/artwork be fine, feel satisfied.[6]

As is the case with *Fast Company*, much of the core theme in *The Italian Machine* is revealed via the careful attention for locations, props, sounds and references rather than through characters. The garages of *The Italian Machine* and *Fast Company* are uncannily similar: littered with tools and spare parts yet not untidy or sloppy – there is a method at work here. Lionel and his friends wield motorcycle spare parts or tools as totems. While there are no races in *The Italian Machine* there is an abundance of engine sounds, audible via Lionel's records of the Isle of Man races; when planning the attempt to lure the Ducati out of the hands of Mouette, Lionel becomes so agitated only the engine records can calm him down. And just like the many real-life drag racing references add to *Fast Company*'s weight, *The Italian Machine* carries a large number of references to technological brands such as Canadian Tire, Ferrari, Norton, Honda, Lambretta, Yamaha and the Ducati of course. In fact, in one of the most poignant exchanges Ricardo compares the world of car care to that of the art world when he replies to the Mouettes' observation that 'in the electronic age, the machine becomes a work of art' and 'in the age of automation human beings become works of art' by asserting that 'the art world becomes just another branch of Canadian Tire. So simple.'[7]

Fast Company and Race-Film Culture

If one puts *Fast Company* and *The Italian Machine* together a fascinating theme emerges: the sexualised link between racing technology and human bodies, one that has a tendency towards the objectification of humans, is preferably approached from a detached perspective, is best managed professionally. Beyond coincidence or karma, this theme also informs a wider framework. There is a remarkable parallel, an intricate bond, between the themes of professional care and car technology present in *Fast Company*, Cronenberg's personal career trajectory and the wider cultural presence within which the film was produced and released.

To begin with, there is a moral neutrality that fits Cronenberg's previous films. The race car and drag racing culture, like the virus in *Shivers*, or the world of plastic surgery in *Rabid*, are topics of ambiguous fascination, consisting of appealing as well as undesirable properties and impacts. While the overall view of the race cars is certainly a sympathetic one, there are also telling moments of implied criticism. Perhaps the most important one is the ending when, after their victory over Adamson and the Blacksmith team, Lonnie's team does break up: Lonnie retires to stay with Sammy, PJ and Elder roam the road looking for new materials and Billy and Candy head for an uncertain life as race-pros. The tenor of the scene is a far cry from the glory such happy endings are usually accorded (although, of course, by Cronenberg standards it is still one of the most joyful in his oeuvre). The logical consequence of this observation is that *Fast Company* does not make an ethical judgement on its subject.

There is a cultural consideration to the moral ambiguity, one that links exceptionally well to a contemporary trend in genre cinema. Movies with races as a significant motif had been a staple feature in cinema since the 1950s. By the mid-1960s, such movies began to veer away from the black-and-white contrast between good and evil racers in favour of more complex portrayals of car-race culture, spawning a veritable genre of race movies. Often, especially in the case of the biker movie, racing was pushed into the realm of subculture, as was the case with *The Wild Angels* (Roger Corman, 1966), *Hell's Angels on Wheels* (Richard Rush, 1967) or even the outrageous *She-Devils On Wheels* (Herschell Gordon Lewis, 1968), culminating in *Easy Rider* (Dennis Hopper, 1969). In these narratives, moral judgements became less and less of a concern, often only present to appease censors.[8] Simultaneously, characters became less central to the stories, and cars, bikes and races became the main attractions. This was particularly true for films about professional racing – first broached by Roger Corman in *The Young Racers* (1964) and subsequently propelled into popularity by James Garner in *Grand Prix* (John Frankenheimer, 1966), Paul Newman in *Winning* (James Goldstone, 1969) and Steve McQueen in *Le Mans* (Lee H. Katzin, 1971). These films formed a firm counterbalance to road movies, which may have relied upon amateurish reckless driving and which were often also of a morally ambiguous nature, but in whose stories the cars themselves stayed mere vehicles. Drag racing movies, always a less visible minority among this pack of films, positioned themselves in the middle between the poles of grand prix racing and road movies. As *Two-Lane Blacktop* (Monte Hellman, 1971), *Drag Racer* (John Cardos, 1971) and *Fury on Wheels* aka

Jump (Joseph Manduke, 1971) testify they found a way to marry the spirit of liberty so essential for road movies with the professionalism of the grand prix films. Combine that with the ethical ambivalence of virtually all car racing movies since the mid-1960s, the near-objective documentary style with much attention to accuracy, detail and life-like stunt work, and it becomes evident how the detached professionalism in *Fast Company* is not a stand-alone feature, but rather the exponent of a well-established sub-genre, entrenched in the ethos of its times.

Indeed, the cultural ramifications of car racing films are well tied to the era. The 1970s are often said to be the decade in which core cornerstones of the American value system were questioned. The car, and the glorification of car racing with it, became implicated in that process. The beginning of the 1970s could still endure George Lucas's unabashed worshipping of car culture in *American Graffiti* (1973), but after the oil shocks of 1973, the first car-free weekends in Europe and a surge in traffic casualties, combined with incidents like the spectacular crashes of Formula One drivers Niki Lauder and Ronnie Peterson, such uncritical devotion was no longer possible.[9] Cars became devils as well as gods – their image equally good *and* evil. The competitive aspect of racing gradually moved away from the racetrack onto the highway, and from subculture into illegality. A new breed of driving characters entered cinema history, combining horror and racing with a critique of the cultural and legal role of the car in society. It was again Roger Corman who stood at its cradle, with *Death Race 2000* (Paul Bartel, 1975), soon followed by more zany films like *Canonball* (Paul Bartel, 1976), *The Gumball Rally* (Charles Bail, 1976), *Convoy* (Sam Peckinpah, 1977), *Grand Theft Auto* (Ron Howard, 1977), *Smokey and the Bandit* (Hal Needham, 1977) and *The Canonball Run* (Hal Needham, 1981), or the demonic *The Car* (Elliot Silverstein, 1977) and the dystopian *Deathsport* (Allan Arkush/Henry Suso, 1978), with Jennings as its female lead, as well as the first *Mad Max* film (George Miller, 1980).[10] The atmosphere of moral ambivalence these films share with *Fast Company* is clearly no longer a stylistic intervention, but rather a cultural imperative – right for the times.

If it ever seems there are miles between the freeway antics of Smokey's Pontiac TransAm and the racetrack dragsters in *Fast Company*, one need only think of the en route scenes in the latter (complete with trucks, bunnies and flat tyre), or the simply splendid escape scene in which the funny car, finding itself outside its normal habitat, almost immediately indulges in a road race,[11] to see how *Fast Company* too takes its issues to the streets – turning the competitive element into one of economic and social survival. Also, the way in which *all* these films represent gender relations hardly needs illustrating: women are objectified into props and cars are fetishised into super sexual creatures. The kind of male professional has stayed the same: rebellious, stubborn, fast and furious, but also careful and caring: in that respect Lonnie Johnson's William Smith surely equals Steve McQueen's Michael Delaney.

Cronenberg the Professional

The major themes in *Fast Company* also seem to have relevance for Cronenberg's career at this point. In fact, there is an intriguing parallel between the professionalism in *Fast Company* and Cronenberg's own move towards becoming a 'professional'. Until *Fast Company* he had only made films from his gut, instinctively, helped by his deep knowledge of literature and art, but isolated from the routines and practices of the industry. This is not to suggest Cronenberg had been deliberately amateurish; his collaborations with Ivan Reitman, Joe Blasco and others had been, if nothing else, mutually respectful, efficient, task-driven and achievement-led. But they happened at a time when Cronenberg was still anxious about his own merits. Via *Fast Company* he became a guild member, a full part of the craft; he entered normalised practice.

For one, Cronenberg was becoming a professional filmmaker by allowing his aesthetic and philosophical obsessions to become balanced by standardised routines. To many, Cronenberg was some sort of freak or madman, fearfully intelligent, equally possessed by muses and demons. The story of how Martin Scorsese was terrified to meet him after having seen *Shivers* has entered popular folklore, but it showcases how much Cronenberg was considered an outsider even to his colleagues. Nicholas Campbell recalls being blown away by *Shivers* and *Rabid* (which he viewed prior to being cast in *Fast Company*). Similarly, John Landis tells with fondness, but also some caution, how on each panel of 'young horror filmmakers' he and Cronenberg found himself on, 'David would impress and silence everyone with his erudition – I mean he would scare people because we were all just movie makers and he clearly had a philosophy'.[12] In his personal life, Cronenberg was isolated too. He was now living separately from his wife,[13] embroiled in a bitter divorce and a custody battle, and on one occasion his reputation of a 'pornographer' had even led him to be evicted from an apartment he had rented (see chapter two). He still felt vilified by a large segment of the cultural establishment for the shocks *Shivers* and *Rabid* had caused. There was no certainty he would ever direct another film – in fact, after the shooting of *Rabid*, he had not been behind a camera for nearly two years.

Fast Company proved to be the way out of this isolation. Cronenberg relates how much of a relief it was when he was invited to attend the Motion Picture Institute convention in Banff, Alberta, in January 1978, where he found his work was not rejected as 'bad' or 'unacceptable' but his professional skills, his contribution to the craft were praised. 'They reacted to it as a film,' Cronenberg said (in Govier 1979: 50); his work was treated as a legitimate piece of filmmaking. *Fast Company* was a project already well in development when Cronenberg joined. But that is not a reason to dismiss its place in his oeuvre. In fact, it may have been a necessary, urgent leap towards his personal development – or there might not have been any further oeuvre at all. The project had originated as a story by Alan Treen, and was adapted for the screen by two Vancouver-based writers, Courtney Smith and Phil Savath. Smith went on to produce the film, with Michael Lebowitz and Peter O'Brian. Cronenberg was asked to direct *Fast Company* by Lebowitz, a first-time producer who had been looking for a director with an affinity with cars and motor racing. *The Italian Machine* made Cronenberg eligible, but Lebowitz was more charmed by Cronenberg's recreational interest in race cars. With regard to cinema that passion was still in its infancy, especially when compared to the obsession it has become since (see chapter eight). But, as Martha Jones explains of Cronenberg:

an interest in fast machines comes naturally to him. He has raced cars, bikes and go-carts just as a hobby, and himself owns a Ferrari and a Lancia ... 'I didn't want David only for his reputation as a director, but because I know he knows cars, as well' explains Michael Lebowitz.[14] (1978: 18)

Regardless of that personal interest, the most meaningful aspect of the offer to direct *Fast Company* was that it showed Cronenberg he was starting to be seen as a professional. *Fast Company* was the chance to prove he was indeed not only an artist making films, but an acutely proficient, versatile and skilled filmmaker.

To begin with, the location was in western Canada. It may seem a trite point, but for someone whose career up until then was deeply anchored in Ontario or Québec, shooting in the western province of Alberta was proof of a changing cultural reach. Previous chapters in this study have indicated how Cronenberg's films always had an international appeal, but within Canada his reach had been largely confined to the provinces of Ontario and Québec. It was in these two provinces that Cronenberg was 'placed' by critics, and it was here too that he was followed, as it were. To move west, to another province – especially as far west as Alberta – was to move up; to substitute a provincial for a fully national level. In a country as big as Canada it also meant Cronenberg could handle the logistics of a shoot outside his own backyard, thus achieving a reach only true professionals can obtain. On the level of the film's aesthetics, the explicit setting of Edmonton gives *Fast Company* a radically different atmosphere to Cronenberg's previous films. Instead of the interior images of apartments, malls and hospitals, with their sense of clinical claustrophobia, we see wide open spaces, endless skies, breathtaking vistas and – quite unique for a Cronenberg film – clear horizons: we actually see the sky meet the earth.

A second way in which *Fast Company* showcased Cronenberg's move to full professionalism was in his directing of actors. This chapter has already hinted at the criticism the film received for its lack of sophistication in characterisation. However, if we read Newman's complaint about the acting in full, it reveals how Cronenberg himself is kept free from blame:

> The real disappointment of *Fast Company* lies in the film's indifferent use of William Smith, Claudia Jennings and John Saxon, a trio who bring to an exploitation film the kind of cachet that Jack Nicholson, Jane Fonda and Jason Robards would lend a mainstream feature. In his handling of Barbara Steele, Marilyn Chambers, Oliver Reed, Samantha Eggar, Patrick MacGoohan and Deborah Harry, Cronenberg has shown himself capable of giving a cult performer the scenery on which to chew, but the leads of *Fast Company* are sadly wasted. (1984: 47)

The implication here is that it is the material that prevents quality acting and characterisation, not the direction. Cronenberg himself recalls the shooting of *Fast Company* as the first time he became aware that his self-invented method of actor's direction was akin to a professional one – a 'normal way of directing' he calls it. In her on-set report, Jones describes that method as 'earnest' and 'meticulous', with 'Cronenberg's voice a soft, constant flow as he almost hypnotically encourages the actors', almost 'Zen-like' (1978: 18). If nothing else, it earned Cronenberg a lot of professional respect, with John Saxon singling him out as an 'awfully good-natured director' (see Rodley 1997: 72). When talking to actors like Nicholas Campbell, for whom *Fast Company* was the first of four collaborations, there is a palpable sense of camaraderie and deep engagement – and not just the kind one finds among film crews and casts as long as they are on the same project, but something that seems a combination of the intimate and professional. There is 'tremendous focus', recounts Campbell when discussing Cronenberg's methods of directing:

> He would always be right there with you, with what you were trying to do, but he also always makes sure that you got what he wanted. He's serious, quiet fun [...] He would also give you the feeling what you did mattered, even if it was already quite clear in his mind where he was going with your scene. He would rehearse it with you and then go back behind his monitor but he would make sure there was no one else there – just you and him. Very professional.[15]

In a similar endorsement, *Variety* calls attention to Cronenberg's tight 'hunkered down direction', especially of Smith and Jennings (ironically, *Fast Company* was the last film of this B-movie queen before she died in a car crash, aged 29 (see Peary 1991: 272–3)).

A third way in which *Fast Company* established Cronenberg as a 'pro' concerns the crews he works with. Cronenberg obviously enjoys working with the same personnel again and again: the make-up of his crew is consistent across films and even decades, giving the impression of some sort of 'professional family' – once you are inside the family, he will stick with you through thick and thin.[16] Previous chapters have demonstrated how Ron Mlodzik and Ivan Reitman, for instance, were instrumental in earlier periods in Cronenberg's career. *Fast Company* was crucial in bringing Cronenberg together with a number of important collaborators that helped determine his unique style: it was the first time he worked with director of photography Mark Irwin, editor Ron Sanders, production designer Carol Spier and sound engineer Bryan Day. Each of them would stay with Cronenberg for at least a decade, playing an essential role in the development of his career to become Canada's most renowned filmmaker.

The music, too, played a role. *Fast Company* is the first time Cronenberg had a professional soundtrack – not the one-track sound of *Stereo* and *Crimes of the Future*, and not the merely functional filler tunes of *Shivers* and *Rabid* (which only support the emotion and action but do not create an encompassing atmosphere). Lebowitz originally wanted Bruce Springsteen for the soundtrack and had to settle for Fred Mollin, but from the first seconds of the film, with the title song 'Fast Company', Mollin's arrangements hit the right atmosphere – one of buddies, beers and burgers – that is maintained throughout the film. With *Fast Company*, the soundtrack, and soundscape, of Cronenberg's films became central to creating the overarching tenor of the story – and his subsequent collaboration with Howard Shore would prove this beyond any doubt.

The long-term economy of Fast Company: tax shelter and DVDs
As a film that offered Cronenberg the opportunity to showcase how much of a professional he was, it was also an opportunistic film for opportunistic times – another
take on professionalism. The newly-installed Canadian tax shelter laws, which made
it possible for individuals and companies to invest in local cinema and get a nice
tax break made him, as he put it, 'hot property' (in Rodley 1997: 69), not so much
because he had themes they cared for, but because Cronenberg had shown he could
make a profit and was reliable. In that sense, the long-term resonances of *Shivers*
and *Rabid* kept Cronenberg on the radar of producers and audiences; kept him in
demand.

Many critics look back at the tax shelter years in horror and decry the 'lack of
quality' produced during its existence – films like *Meatballs* (Ivan Reitman, 1979),
The Changeling (Peter Medak, 1980) or *Prom Night* (Paul Lynch, 1980) whose adher-
ence to genre and formula was seen as a shortcoming rather than an asset. George
Melnyk called it a 'source of cultural embarrassment' (2004: 121), and Geoff Pevere
and Greig Dymond write that:

> A host of producers from around the world flocked to Canada to cash in on
> the bonanza by making movies that were Canadian only in the checklist sense.
> As they were usually the result of doctors, lawyers, dentists and other upper-
> income *professionals* less concerned with art than a tax dodge, a number of
> commercially, not to mention culturally, hopeless productions were rushed
> into production which otherwise would rightly never have seen the light of
> script development … It meant a lot of Canadian-made movies pretending to
> take place in other, more universally appealing (read 'American') places than
> Toronto or Vancouver, but it also meant making movies with stars who had
> international appeal. (1996: 216; emphasis added)[17]

All of this is certainly true of *Fast Company*. The film is supposed to pass for an
American movie, hence the American B-movie stars, the red-white-blue colours
everywhere and the references to America as centre of power. The characters always
seem to go 'stateside' whenever they leave the FastCo team for even the shortest time,
and most of the decisions that impact on the team are made from the US: that is
where the order comes from to shut the team down, that is where the new top-fuel
dragster is supposed to come from and that is from where Sammy is calling to ease
Lucky Johnson's mind. In a curious way it is almost a parallel of the power relations
between Hollywood and the Canadian film industry – a neat location governed from
elsewhere. The Edmonton racetrack could keep its own name as its (American) reputation was big enough to function as an attraction in itself.

The criticism that the tax shelter films never really established the broad popularity and appeal they were supposed to create (upon which a truly Canadian cinema
of cultural esteem could be based) is also true in the case of *Fast Company*. The film
was hardly released and never quite profitable. But, both in the general case of the
tax shelter films and in the singular case of *Fast Company*, there is another side to this

argument, one that lies in the longer-term value of films and film culture. As Melnyk admits, the tax shelter films did establish a 'vast training ground' (2004: 121), and Pevere and Dymond balance their criticism by acknowledging that

> the tax shelter system was not without its benefits. The fact is, the careers of David Cronenberg and Ivan Reitman were kick-started by the tax shelter production boom, and the sheer volume of movies made transformed Canada from a production backwater to a seasoned *pro* almost overnight. (1996: 217; emphasis added)[18]

Some of the films did reasonably well, like the aforementioned *Meatballs* and *Porky's* (Bob Clark, 1981). What is usually overlooked is how much money several of the tax shelter period films made outside their cinematic releases. *Prom Night* and *My Bloody Valentine* (George Mihalka, 1981) became huge video hits, *Atlantic City* (Louis Malle, 1980) was an enduring television success (especially on European television), as was the tail-end tax shelter film *Christmas Story* (Bob Clark, 1983), which became a huge seasonal favourite; also there simply would not have been an industry called Hollywood North, with films like *First Blood* (Ted Kotcheff, 1983) as part of it, without the tax shelter (see Gasher 2002).

Beyond that, the tax shelter system allowed, and sometimes forced, Canadian filmmakers to confront the issue of genre, something they had been avoiding for too long. As Jim Leach explains, many of the tax shelter films were genre films because formulas were thought to have universal appeal, so they could draw audiences from all walks of life. But 'formulas are a basic feature of popular cinema and not necessarily as restrictive [as] implied ... Popular cinema depends on a creative play with formulas' (2006: 47). It is exactly this flexibility in working with genres that the tax shelter system prevented for many, but facilitated for some. Leach continues, arguing that the tax shelter system discouraged such 'creativity', and that the attempt to look American gave these films a sense of 'placelessness'. However, if we look again at the longer-term reception, and allow ourselves to include some of the most visible interpretations of the tax shelter films (especially on the Internet),[19] then it is striking to see how many of these films are recognised, and discussed, as Canadian – not American – and how audiences are at pains to stress just how Canadian these films are to them. In their views, 'creativity' and 'Canadianness' become synonyms for how these films deviate from the trodden paths; and 'Canadianness' becomes a sign of quality, or, at least, oddity with the potential to be quality.

The long-term reception of *Fast Company*, and especially its post-DVD release appreciation, shows notable similarities. On *Canuxploitation*, the film is reviewed as distinctly Canadian, within a context of genre cinema, without even so much as a mention of America (save the ubiquitous 'red, white and blue imagery'). Instead, it is regarded as a genre film in the tradition of National Film Board documentaries – thereby slotting it straight into the mainstream of Canadian film historiography.[20] *DVD Maniacs* makes explicit mention of the tax shelter system in its discussion of Cronenberg's audio commentary, stating that it enlightens any understanding of the film as Canadian.[21] *DVDVerdict* goes even further. It acknowledges the tax shelter system as one that forced Cronenberg to combine his visions (they call them 'disparate' in the experimental films, and 'rough' in the case of *Shivers* and *Rabid*) 'creatively' within the limits of a genre framework.[22] In other words, it forced Cronenberg to be a pro. These three reviews are indicative of the dozens available. They demonstrate how the long-term reception of *Fast Company* appreciated how the tax shelter system instigated a more hard-nosed approach in Cronenberg's filmmaking. This is not just the benefit of hindsight. It is also an indication of how both the aesthetics and the economy of film extend beyond a film's immediate release.

In that respect it is essential to note how the DVD release of *Fast Company* has an economic significance as a collector's item. It is not important that *Fast Company* is not Cronenberg's best film, or indeed not good at all. It is presented to an audience quite happy to purchase and acclaim it as part of an oeuvre whose other accomplishments will give it value as the missing piece. As if to reinforce that strategy in the package, Blue Underground's release contains a series of extras that lift it well beyond its merits as a presentation of a film previously inaccessible. The inclusion of a Cronenberg commentary adds much to the historical value. It also reclaims the film as his project, that of the professional auteur Cronenberg. The documentary interview with Mark Irwin – who also discusses his other collaborations with Cronenberg – confirms that reclamation. But by far the most lauded extras are *Stereo* and *Crimes of the Future*. As every single review observes, the presence of Cronenberg's two early avant-garde efforts are a sales argument in themselves: if you don't like *Fast Company*, buy the DVD for *Stereo* and *Crimes of the Future*. Next to that, they drive home the argument that Cronenberg's oeuvre should be seen as one whole, a trajectory covering such a range that it is worthy of celebration for that reason alone. Ultimately, it demonstrates how, in the longer term, the momentary difficulties and differences in achievement at the time of the making of *Fast Company* (and *Stereo* and *Crimes of the Future* for that matter) become part of a larger tale – that of the cultural presence of Cronenberg – giving them new meaning.

Red Cars and Other Cars

It was the intention of this chapter to demonstrate a crucial evolution in Cronenberg's film practice, a move towards professionalism that made him a filmmaker able to successfully negotiate his concerns within an industry notorious for its sensitivity to economic fluctuations, aesthetic volatility and a dogged rigidity when it comes to day-to-day routines. If Cronenberg was ever going to continue making films professionally, if he was going to make a living as an artist as well as building an oeuvre, a back-catalogue and a team of trusted co-workers, then taking the driver's seat as he did in *Fast Company* was a phase he needed to go through.

In itself, *Fast Company* is not art. It was not meant to be and it could not be. Similarly, *The Italian Machine* never attracted much critical acclaim, probably because of its relative inaccessibility. At their best, the two pieces function as missing links of evolution between Cronenberg's avant-garde work, his early horror shockers and his later work. If one substitutes professionalism for science – that ultimate professionalisation of expertise where obsession and fetishism become dedication and methodic research – it is not much of a stretch to make links between *Fast Company, The Italian Machine* and the later, more mature films that made him a cultural hero.

It would be a while before cars and races would retake centre-stage in Cronenberg's films. But they would not disappear altogether. In fact, their sparse use might even give them a more significant function, before *and* after *Fast Company*. At the end of *Shivers*, the plague/revolution spreads out of Starliner Towers via a car convoy – technology carrying the parasite further. At the beginning of Rose's infection and rage lies a motorcycle crash – technology causing the rage.[23] A car breakdown forces Neil and Carol to knock on the door of a strange house in *The Lie Chair*. These are all telling narrative impulses. Post-*Fast Company*, the final scene in *The Brood*, when Frank wrongly believes he has saved Candy, is set in a car. The car chase and crash in *Scanners* gives Cameron the opportunity to catch one of his pursuers and turn the dynamic from hunted to hunter. Likewise, *Videodrome's* Max receives crucial information on a television in the back of a limousine. In *The Dead Zone*, Johnny's coma and strange abilities to foresee the future develop after a car crash. In *The Fly*, it was Seth's car sickness that gave him the idea to experiment with teleportation. In later films, cars become more symbolic movers than actual carriers: reality has shifted well beyond the point of credibility at the end of *Naked Lunch*, but Bill nevertheless kills his wife in a car – again a car as a last location. Switching from cars to motorcycles, in *M. Butterfly*, Gallimard is exposed as a spy right after he has delivered documents with his vintage BMW. Chapters eight and nine will elaborate on the use of car technology in *Crash*, and on the motif of the chase, as well as that peculiar garage in *eXistenZ*. In *A History of Violence*, it is worth noting the vehicles of Tom and Edie as indications of their desire to be all-American, and the symbolic value of Tom's night ride to Philadelphia, where he meets and kills his brother – a drive into hell. Anna's Ural motorcycle in *Eastern Promises* is not just an extension of her assertiveness and cultural roots, but also a key means through which she and Nikolai become 'attached' to each other. What points can be made, as well, of the complete lack of cars in *Stereo, Crimes of the Future, Dead Ringers* and *Spider*, also the most dark (and darkly-lit) of Cronenberg's films?

Rumours concerning attempts to make a film about Ferrari surfaced from time to time and ultimately culminated in the publication of a book about the unfinished project, filled with images, ideas and thoughts about what was to become a film about the Jim Hill/Wolfgang Trips rivalry in the 1961 Formula One championship. In the introduction to the book Cronenberg makes explicit mention of his fascination for the *professional* aspects of the rivalry, and a few lines on he mentions how the script included in the book, too, is one that indicates *professionalism* ('professional moviemakers'). Cronenberg is too clever a fellow not to know scholars would pick up that thread.

Red Cars also provides the best possible first-hand account of how Cronenberg saw cars and engines relate to the rest of his oeuvre, and to the times when it was made. He writes in the preface: 'Take apart an engine and you look into the brain of the man [sic] who designed it. Take apart an engine, and you look deeply into the culture that produced it.'[24]

Things that go: motorcycles and cars set off plots – left to right, top to bottom: the virus is spread by car in *Shivers*; a stranded car traps a couple in *The Lie Chair*; craving for a Ducati in *The Italian Machine*; Rose's blood lust is instigated after a motorcycle crash in *Rabid*; a funny car breaks free for revenge in *Fast Company*; Candy's abduction by the brood in *The Brood*; after causing a car crash, Revok escapes in *Scanners*; a paranoid plot is revealed in the back of a car in *Videodrome*; a car crash sets off Johnny's visions in *The Dead Zone*; car sickness as a reason to experiment with teleportation in *The Fly*; an ambulance races Bev to hospital in *Dead Ringers*; during a ride, Bill is sucked into the paranoid world of Interzone in *Naked Lunch*; Gallimard works as a motorcycle courier before he is arrested in *M. Butterfly*; the staging of James Dean's fatal crash in *Crash*; escape into the countryside by Land Rover in *eXistenZ*; a car brings Dennis back to the asylum in *Spider*; gansters in a Cadillac bring trouble in *A History of Violence*; East meets West via the Ural motorcycle in *Eastern Promises*

That is essentially what *Fast Company* delivers – a look into the micro-culture of genre cinema at the end of the drive-in the era right before video would change spectators' viewing habits forever, and the car's relevance for cinemagoing would be demoted from promising leisure instrument to functionalist commuter vehicle – drop offs instead of pick-ups. *Fast Company* also gives a peek into the peculiarities of Canadian filmmaking at the end of the 1970s, and into Cronenberg's own development into a professional filmmaker, granting him the opportunity to 'break stride, take time out' (see Jones 1978: 17) so he could prepare to literally blow minds.

CHAPTER FOUR

Cult Curio: *The Brood* and *Scanners*

Show me your anger. Then I can understand it.
                                                    – Doctor Raglan to his patient, Mike

Ever see that scene in *Scanners* when that dude's head blew up?
                                                    – *Wayne's World* (Penelope Spheeris, 1992)

I'm into exploding heads just like any other young, normal North American boy.
                                                    – David Cronenberg in *Cinefantastique* (1980: 35)

Fade in...

Raglan: You're not looking at me, Mike. You're not looking at me in the eyes. That's weak. Only weak people do that.

Mike: I could look you in the eye if I wanted to, Daddy. I just ... I just don't wanna look you in the eye.

Raglan: I guess you're just a weak person. You must have got that from your mother. It probably would have been better for you to have been born a girl. Then we could have named you Michelle. You see, weakness is more acceptable in a girl, Michelle. I'm sorry, I mean, Mike. I keep forgetting...

This scene opens *The Brood*. Its two minutes contain only long-held medium close-ups of Doctor Hal Raglan (Oliver Reed) and Mike (Gary McKeehan). Facing each other, against a black background, they seem to be playing out some sort of ritual – Raglan provoking Mike by questioning his masculinity. 'Wait a minute,' he continues, 'Why don't I call you Michelle all the time? Then I wouldn't have to be so goddamn ashamed of you and your weaknesses.' At that point the perspective switches to a shot from the back of an auditorium, and we see that their confrontation is played out on a stage, in front of an audience, cloaked in darkness. That audience appears curious and attentive – when a latecomer sits down no one looks disturbed. Yet they are not completely enthralled, they maintain an expectant posture, in patient anticipation.

What they are waiting for happens soon after. When the camera resumes its position near Raglan and Mike, and pans around them (thus acknowledging both their intense closeness and the audience), the debate heats up. Raglan taunts Mike to speak up, to 'show his anger'. An enraged, emotional Mike tears off his shirt and exposes a series of boils and spots on his body. As the audience shift in their seats, adjusting to the shock, the boils seem to grow bigger, into scabs and scars covering his entire body. 'This is what you do to me inside,' he cries exhausted. The stage lights go out. 'Wow,' whispers someone in the audience, 'that man is a genius.' An assistant (Nicholas Campbell) enters the stage: 'Doctor Raglan would like to thank you all for coming this afternoon.' The show is over, the audience shuffle to the exit…

Cut to…

'I would like to scan all of you in this room, one at a time. I … I must remind you that the … er … scanning experiences used here … are painful. Sometimes resulting in nosebleeds, earaches, stomach cramps, nausea, sometimes other symptoms of a similar nature … There's a doctor present, Doctor Gatineau … I know that you've all been prepared for this but I thought I'd just remind you just the same … And here is one other thing: no one is to leave this room once the demonstration has begun … At this point I'd like to call for volunteers.'

This scene comes ten minutes and 24 seconds into *Scanners*. At the point when the scanner character (Louis Del Grande) utters these words the audience has settled in, made themselves comfortable. It is a new scene, not connected to the events in the previous two scenes, and the character is new to us. His entire speech, all thirty seconds, is filmed in frontal close-up, against a black background – there is nothing to distract our attention but that talking head, obviously addressing someone behind the position of the camera – as if he is looking for an audience. After the statement the perspective switches to a point-of-view shot from the back of that room: an audience in a half-filled, slightly sloped auditorium, with red seating. A volunteer steps up, sits next to the demonstrator, asks if he should 'close his eyes', and they start the 'scanning', a trance-like concentration in which it appears they try to get into each other's minds. It soon becomes clear the volunteer is more experienced at the mind-

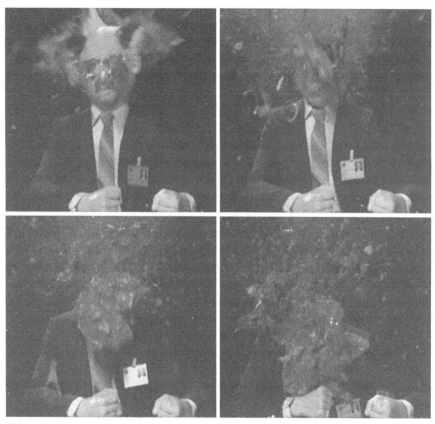

'Kaboom! The finest exploding head of all time' in *Scanners*

game than the 'scanner'. As he concentrates his powers, his opponent's wriggles and squirms become increasingly desperate until, in 47 frames of gushing splatter gore, his head explodes on-screen in a fountain of blood and flesh, literally filling every corner of the frame.

Needless to say these scenes have attracted quite some attention. *Scanners'* exploding head is considered the ultimate horror special effects shot supreme, the genre's most infamous 'money shot'. A variety of reviews devoted up to half of their precious space to it.[1] The scene has since claimed a top spot in virtually every poll of special effects efforts. To give one example, in the words of Jason Arnopp, editor of *SFX's Horror Special Collector's Edition* of 2004, it is simply captioned as 'Kaboom! The finest exploding head of all time.' No further explanation warranted. It is ranked number one in the 'most gruesome money shots in horror history' (the prize for second-best exploding head goes to Tom Savini for *Maniac* – he blows up his own head).[2]

Similarly, the opening scene of *The Brood* was widely noticed. Danny Peary wrote elaborately about the 'open sores, lesions, bumps and bruises', employing a vocabulary – part medical, part 'yukkie' – that became typical in descriptions of the shocking imagery of the film (1981: 36). William Beard too gives full attention to the 'startling and powerful' scene (2005: 75). Reviews from 1979 to 2007 may hold differing appreciations of the film, but many agree that when it comes to the hideous display of 'red welts erupting all over the skin' in its opening, *The Brood* does 'not dawdle, nor pussyfoot; if you came for tomato ketchup, you will get it'.[3]

Cult

The Brood and *Scanners* are frequently referred to as cult films, more so than other Cronenberg films. As the discussion of the reception of *Shivers* confirmed, cults usually take a few years to develop.[4] But in the case of *The Brood* and *Scanners* it developed almost instantaneously. From the earliest reviews *The Brood* was framed in terms of Cronenberg's 'cult following' (*Variety*), 'cult-potential' (*Globe and Mail*) or 'cult status' (*Maclean's*).[5] It features prominently in Stephen King's anthology *Danse Macabre* (1981: 101–2, 130–1). Similarly, no opportunities were wasted to call *Scanners* a cult. *Maclean's* otherwise negative evaluation singled out Cronenberg's 'cult reputation' ('on a par with George Romero and *Dawn of the Dead*') to explain his appeal across cultural platforms, as did numerous other publications at the time; *Cahiers du cinéma* used the occasion of an essay on the cult of *Eraserhead* to label *Scanners* 'un film culte'.[6] The term 'cult' reappears throughout the reception trajectories of both films. *The Brood* was one of only three films to have an entry in Peary's *Cult Movies* (1981: 36–9), Welch Everman's *Cult Horror Films* (1993: 47–9) and Karl and Philip French's *Cult Movies* (1999: 51–2) – the other two were *Freaks* and *Plan 9 From Outer Space* (Edward D. Wood Jr, 1959), considered amongst the best in any cult canon. Since then, references to the 'cult following' of the two Cronenberg films recurred whenever they were discussed, in user comments, message boards or on secluded fan and blog sites.[7]

There are multiple reasons for the instant cult reputation of *The Brood* and *Scanners*. For one, they display an acute awareness of their potential for shock and outrage with a particular segment of the moviegoing audience that appreciates the splatter and gore. By embedding the most horrific shots into scenes that occur in auditoriums, on a stage with an audience in attendance, the films seem to suggest a relationship between the spectators *in* and the viewers *of* the films – implying that the conspiring curiosity and interests of the people watching these demonstrations is similar to that of those watching these films. And there is something very peculiar about those audiences. In both *The Brood* and *Scanners* the auditoriums are only half-filled, with people seemingly only mildly interested in what is supposed to happen. They sit with a polite, partly expectant look on their face. They are there, obviously, because there is the anticipation that something spectacular might occur; they may have been promised some sort of shock or revelation. Probably nothing extraordinary will happen because usually nothing does at these kinds of occasions – but you never know. Their posture also seems to reveal they are seasoned veterans. When the boils appear or the head explodes, there is no hysteria. No one is too traumatised by what happens, and if they are, they are not going to show it. In short, both scenes seem to be asking: how tough are you?

This posture strongly resembles that of college crowd midnight movie audiences, late at night, readying themselves, half-excited, half-disappointed in anticipation of what some trailer, word of mouth or fanzine has promised will be an eventful evening.[8] The set-up of the auditorium invokes that of a movie theatre, and the auditorium audience's behaviour is similar to the attitude of 'toughness' Mark Kermode describes:

> Going to see these movies was essentially a lonely pursuit since no one at school shared my enduring enthusiasm ... [At best it was] considered something to be endured, a test of machismo, an instantaneous thrill (and often a great way to cop off) but nothing more. Only at the late-nighters would I find myself surrounded by other loners who, like me, weren't there to impress anybody but themselves. (2001: 129)

The attitude expresses a desire to like what is disliked by other audiences, a partisan desperation, like a cabal, to distinguish oneself from other moviegoers. 'Are there really people who want to see reprehensible trash like this?' asks Roger Ebert in his review (1979). Obviously, there are. As another critic suggests: 'Cronenberg knows his audience does not flock to his films in search of a message or a great performance. They come seeking thrills and chills, and he obliges by getting under their skin and making their flesh crawl' (James 1979: 4). That audience is a sizeable one. As the *Times* remarks: if audiences retain 'their craving to feel their flesh creep and their stomachs turn, [t]his new film should prove a commercial hit' (Robinson 1980).

Apparently, then, the shocks sustained by the aforementioned scenes hit a cultural nerve. Here lies another explanation for the cult reputation: the reception of *The Brood* and *Scanners* occurred within an emerging wave, a 'cult of horror' that first challenged, and then determined, the ideological and aesthetic norms of the genre, and of popular culture in general. This emergent trend will be sketched further on in the chapter, when we come to the reception *The Brood* and *Scanners* received in North America, the United Kingdom and Europe. Special consideration will go to the kinds of public debates that embraced or opposed Cronenberg's films, to the impact of the use of special effects in the films (and the significance of those effects in the new horror culture) and to the contribution of the films to new strategies of viewing and fandom of horror cinema.

The Brood and *Scanners* are also seen as cult because they are very personal films with vested interests. They derive much of their meaning through the ways in which they display and create affiliations or discomfort. *The Brood* and *Scanners* are not easy to like, and they are certainly not the critics' darlings. Much like cults, they offend the uninitiated. In an upfront, unsettling manner they unequivocally press their core themes hard into the faces of viewers, forcing them to confront the films' implications with their own personal and moral principles. Liking, and defending, *The Brood* and *Scanners* discloses something about one's attitude towards life; hating them profoundly is equally revealing.

Finally, issues of appreciation aside, on a purely textual level their narratives revolve around cultist issues: they tell stories of varying degrees of devotion, intimacy, reclusiveness, affiliation, community and partisanship between siblings, families, sects and underground movements. As such, they adhere to the meaning of cult as confessional and congregational, and it is there that our discussion should start.

The Brood ·

The Brood tells the story of the aftermath of a failed marriage and its effects on the children. Like so many failed marriages its tale is complicated not so much because of the narrative and the actual actions but due to the secrets and inferences buried in them.

The film starts with a demonstration of a new technique in psychotherapy, called Psychoplasmics, developed by Doctor Hal Raglan. He encourages his patients at the Somafree Institute to give real, tangibly physical shape to their anger, and to go 'all the way through it to the end'. The demonstration is witnessed by Frank Carveth (Art Hindle), whose wife Nola (Samantha Eggar) is one of Raglan's interned patients. Frank is kept away from her; only their daughter Candice (Cindy Hinds) is allowed to see her sporadically. But when Frank discovers bruises and scratches on Candice's back after a visit to Nola he is convinced she may be abusing her, and tries to confront his wife. Raglan refuses to allow him access, and Frank's lawyer advises him that he could lose custody of Candice if he refuses to let her see her sick mother. Still uncertain whether Candice should visit Nola on the weekend, Frank leaves her with Juliana (Nuala Fitzgerald), Nola's mother, while he goes to work. As Candice and an incessantly drinking Juliana reminisce over old photos and Candice hears how her mother would frequently be covered in bumps as a child, Raglan confronts Nola in a therapy session and she confesses she was abused by Juliana. Immediately after that revelation, Juliana is attacked and beaten to death by a small creature dressed in a winter suit. Frank has to collect a terrified but placid Candice from the care of the police, whose psychologist warns him a deep trauma may be building up in Candice. It expresses itself in introverted behaviour and silence – in fact Candice only speaks again twice, once when she asks her father to invite her school teacher over for dinner, and once to tell him about a 'very bad dream'.

Meanwhile, during a session with Raglan and his assistant Chris (Nicholas Campbell), Nola expresses the fear that Frank might take Candice away from her because he is not willing to wait until she gets well. Nola also implicates her father Barton (Henry Beckman), who has since divorced Juliana, for doing nothing to protect her from the abuse by her mother. Determined to expose Raglan, Frank visits one of his former patients, the strange Jan Hartog (Robert Silverman), who shows him the scars of the Psychoplasmics therapy (a cancerous lump dangling from his neck) and claims he suffers from cancer as the result of Raglan's 'encouragement of his body to revolt' against him. Still, Frank hesitates to go through with the lawsuit. Barton, meanwhile, accosts Raglan and threatens to get his daughter out of his custody if she is not told of the death of her mother (something Raglan wants to keep from her to prevent any upset in her therapy). Later that night, Barton, drunk and depressed, calls Frank from the house where Juliana was murdered. Reluctantly Frank, who has Candice's school teacher Ruth (Susan Hogan) over for dinner (the two are developing a liking to each other: 'We could talk after Candice goes to bed,' suggests Frank), goes over to make sure the old man is fine.

He isn't. Drunk as hell, awash with self-pity, Barton takes refuge in the bedroom of his former house. As he sobs on the bed, the creature appears from under it. It grabs a glass bowl, jumps on the bed and bludgeons Barton to death. This time we get to see its face: young, childlike, but so distorted with anger it looks like it is wearing a mask. Frank is also attacked when he enters the house and discovers Barton's body. But as he tries to free himself from the creature's strangling hold, it suddenly loosens its grip, gasps for air and dies. While Frank alerts the police Ruth, still babysitting at his home and flicking through a copy of Raglan's book, 'Shape of Rage', receives a threatening phone call from Nola. The same night the police conduct an autopsy on the creature: it turns out it has 'irises but no retinas', carries a yolk sac (a kind of gas tank) on its back, lacks sexual organs and has no bellybutton, which means it 'has never really been born'. 'Jesus,' sighs the cop. At Somafree, Nola rages against Ruth, and what she perceives as her attempts to steal her family. When Frank gets home Ruth hurries away and he has to console a terrified Candice who has had 'a very bad dream'.

As it dawns on Raglan that Nola might have some involvement in the murders, he orders Chris to expel all other patients from the institute. As Raglan prepares himself to confront Nola (whom he has separated in a shed), Frank brings Candice to school. But as Candice enters her class she is stopped by what look like two other children (in winter suits). They usher her out of the room, and then attack and kill Ruth. Upon a pupil's screams Frank rushes in and finds the dead Ruth. Candice is missing. Desperate, Frank and the police search for her in an apartment where Nola kept Candice 'for nine months', but there is no Candice. Instead we see her, hand in hand with the creatures that killed Ruth, walking along a snowy highway – on their way to Somafree.

A day later, a despairing Frank finds Raglan's patient Mike lingering at his front door. He tells him Raglan has been experimenting with 'the kids your wife is taking care of'. An alarmed Frank races to Somafree. He finds Raglan, who tells him the creatures are 'the children of the rage' of Nola, 'motivated by her anger'. Repentant, he proposes to save Candice from 'the brood' if Frank appeases Nola – for that will keep them mellow. 'Be nice to her' he warns Frank. At first, Nola remains calm towards Frank. She lifts her gown and reveals to him how she produces the brood. They grow as pulsating foetuses in a womb-like sack on the outside of her body. She rips open the sack to liberate them and then licks the blood and birth fluids off their tiny bodies. Frank's reaction of disgust sets off Nola's anger. It awakens the creatures precisely when Raglan is rescuing Candice. They attack him, kill him and go after Candice, whom Nola says she would 'kill before I let you take her'. As the brood turn towards Candice and grab her Frank strangles his wife, who is still holding her new-born creature. He rescues Candice, and drives away. On the arms of a traumatised Candice bumps start to appear. Her eyes widen in terror...

Confession: the public expression of a private inspiration
At its most direct, *The Brood* is a confessional autobiography, an account of the divorce
and custody battle Cronenberg had gone through when shooting *Fast Company*. *The
Brood* was not supposed to be the film it became. With the tax shelter system in full
swing, and his credentials as a professional filmmaker supporting him, Cronenberg
was approached for a script that could be made into a genre film, and the story, as
he put it, 'pushed its way right up the typewriter ... I really don't think I had any
choice. It was like automatic writing ... It's my most autobiographical script, and I
was very compulsive about writing it' (in Rodley 1997: 75).[9] But once the screenplay
was completed Cronenberg decided to stick with it. Nor did he pretend it was not
related to his life; he made his confession public: 'I could have shut up about *The
Brood* and not said it had anything to do with my private life, but I obviously felt
the need to mention that it did. So the consequences are there' (in Rodley 1997: 79).
When casting Samantha Eggar and Art Hindle he looked for actors who resembled
his former wife and himself. According to Cronenberg, they were a 'reasonable movie
facsimile' (in Rodley 1997: 76).

The personal connection also established itself in terms reviewers could
directly relate to through an explanation of *The Brood* as Cronenberg's version of
Kramer vs. Kramer (Robert Benton, 1979). *Kramer vs. Kramer* was released amidst
wide publicity in December 1979. At that time *The Brood* had only been released in
the US, Canada and France, and some US cities were still publishing reviews of the
film.[10] More comparisons appeared in March 1980 when *The Brood* and *Kramer vs.
Kramer* were released across Europe, and Cronenberg reiterated the connection in
numerous interviews, gladly adding how much he loathed the niceties in *Kramer vs.
Kramer*.

> It is my version of *Kramer*, and for my money, it's a much more realistic
> version, emotionally ... Where is that anger, that rage, that desire to kill?
> Everyone's so sweet, so compassionate, so understanding. She's on the witness
> stand and he's saying 'No don't say that about yourself, you're too wonderful'.
> That's bullshit. After only eighteen months with his father, the kid seems to
> have no interest in the possibility of living with his mother. Now that is a
> fiction. The ambivalence of the kid is not portrayed. The reversal at the end,
> so sweet, that's supposed to be a happy ending in some way, and obviously
> isn't. (in Harkness 1981: 16)

It is important to acknowledge this reference, as it is one of the ways in which *The
Brood* became an antagonising tool. Because it pertained to counter the seriousness and moralism associated with social problem films, *The Brood* became, in some
instances, a welcome substitute for 'mon oncle Kramer' – one good example was its
celebration by critics eager to counter the 'tendencious and fashionable middle-brow
base' of mainstream film criticism.[11] In other words, Cronenberg's decision to allow its
personal impulse to become public knowledge, and his insistence on taking a stand on
it, equipped *The Brood* with an unexpected political significance. It split critics along

ideological lines the same way it divided them along aesthetic lines, and it forced them to confess which partisan principles of 'good cinema' they subscribed to.

Kramer vs. Kramer is not the only personal comparison Cronenberg invited reviewers to relate *The Brood* to. By naming Candice's school the 'Krell School' he solicited comparisons with *Forbidden Planet*, which he confessed knocked him out as a kid (see Rodley 1997: 84). Cronenberg also commented on how the secluded location of the Somafree Institute, Raglan's methods and the acting postures of Eggar were designed to provoke associations with the practices and attitudes of the religious cult his former wife joined (see Rodley 1997: 76) Nola does not move throughout the entire film. She sits and kneels, in a position in between devotion and command, between disciple and priestess. With Cronenberg going public with his private life, small details like Juliana's remarks to Frank that he 'now knows what it feels like. Being a parent. Being blamed for everything. To have the past distorted, so you don't even recognise yourself anymore' become implications of the tactics of cults: to erase one's past to bring them to a new birth as a new being – a parent, or a disciple. It encapsulates Cronenberg's frustration.

Contentions, confusions and complications of The Brood

No one has to accept Cronenberg's intention as the ultimate meaning of *The Brood*. One can indeed question whether many viewers were even aware of its personal origins. Often, *The Brood* was dismissed as an example of bad storytelling regardless of its personal relevance. Several early reviews saw the film as 'muddled' or 'inconsequential', lacking coherence or relying too much on 'drawn-out expository scenes'.[12]

In some cases *The Brood* elicited explications opposing Cronenberg's claims: the film is not about a man saving his daughter, but about a man violently suppressing his wife and her rights within the family. This stance most famously caught the public's attention when it became a point of contention at the 1979 Toronto International Film Festival. Robin Wood and Richard Lippe, the programmers of the festival's American Nightmare section, which presented a thorough overview of the horror genre through a series of screenings (including *Shivers* and *The Brood*) and a panel discussion with contemporary directors in the genre. Cronenberg's films were 'last-minute additions' to the programme, which wanted to show them as a representative of the 'most reactionary element at work in the genre'. Cronenberg was 'warned of the attitude of the programmers, was invited to appear at a seminar, and accepted' (Scott 1979c: n. p.).

Since his dismissal of *Shivers*, Wood's position towards Cronenberg's films had not changed. In *The American Nightmare*, the collection of essays accompanying the seminars and screenings, Wood accused *Shivers* and *The Brood* of repressing the inherent drive towards sexual and social liberation that characterised the more liberal films in the horror genre (1979a: 24). For Wood, *The Brood* was a misogynistic pamphlet, a typical example of the horror genre's treatment of women. Nola's character, and that of her abusing mother, were not so much a source of evil that needed to be contained or terminated because it threatened family life, but victims of a society ruled by men whose fear of women is expressed through violent suppression – it is only evil because it is female in a patriarchal society. Male weaknesses, noted Wood, were not punished.

Unsurprisingly, Cronenberg took issue with Wood's contentions. In Wood's own account of the seminar discussions, published in *Film Comment*, he described Cronenberg's response as one 'resisting any social analysis ... in favour of a meta-physical reading' (1980: 28). It did not do much to alleviate Wood's criticisms. In fact, his dismissals became even stronger, and in the same essay he confessed to a 'hatred of Cronenberg's films' (ibid.). Through his wide acclaim as a critic and scholar Wood's perspective became very influential. *The American Nightmare* became a favourite textbook in film classes; essays from it are often reprinted in anthologies. His disposition towards Cronenberg, however, has since been nuanced considerably. Barbara Creed (1986; 1993) is equally harsh on the film but lets Cronenberg off the hook – as a man he is incapable of escaping his culture's patriarchal foundations. Creed sees *The Brood's* depictions of women as evidence of men's fear of them, and their submission is an inevitable expression of cultural history. For her, the monster in *The Brood* is not what Nola *becomes* in the hands of men, but what she always *was* – a woman. In particular, Frank's (and by extension every male's) anxiety for women expresses itself through Nola's (and by extension every woman's) power to create life. Frank is disgusted by Nola's womb not because it is monstrous; rather he sees it as monstrous because it is something he – as a male – cannot control or subject to his powers. His, and Raglan's, efforts to contain Nola's 'hysteria' are ways of rational-ising her reaction against their attempts to 'treat' her as a sign of her madness – they confuse her reaction to their treatment as the cause of the disease she is suffering from. Every woman who has her child taken away would react that way. For Creed, Nola is even more dangerous than 'normal' women because she has managed to find a way to give birth 'without the agency of a male'. Her offspring are hideous because they exist independently from men – remember how the autopsy showed they were 'not really born at all'?

William Beard (1983; 2005), taking issue with the psychoanalytic perspective of Creed's interpretation, points to *The Brood's* confused depictions of masculinity and the male characters' failures to suggest the film is far from uncritical about their positions and actions. Juliana may have been the one with the drinking problem and the 'long series of lovers' (as Frank puts it), but her ex-husband Barton is not inno-cent – he let the abuse happen. Frank is increasingly unwilling to help his wife; in fact he tries to avoid any involvement with Nola, Ruth, Barton, even with Hartog. Ruth reveals he has missed a parent/teacher meeting, and he is always late to pick up Candice from school. He never carries out his threat to sue Raglan, and he is unwilling to fully side with Hartog. Similarly, Raglan fails miserably in his duty towards his other patients. In Beard's account, the collective failures to keep the family on track resemble a melodrama, in which family units are in constant turmoil and disorder. As a horror-melodrama, *The Brood* finds a repulsive bodily expression for that turmoil: it manifests itself, at its most acute, as messy fluids (blood, sweat, tears), and Frank's repulsed reaction and his unwillingness to get his hands dirty to save his wife and his family have far-reaching consequences: they affect the future of his daughter.[13]

Together, Beard's and Creed's analyses depict *The Brood* as a film that is far more ambiguous than Cronenberg's autobiographical admission and Wood's linear interpretation suggest. This ambiguity puts Nola's madness in a different perspective. She may indeed be going mad and causing havoc, but the world around her is not doing much to help. I believe *The Brood's* essence lies not in how the confusions obstruct the film's meaning, but rather that its essence is captured in its complications. Compared to Cronenberg's previous films, *The Brood* has a less clear distinction between essential and supporting characters, and it is only through taking *all* of them into account and only by charting *all* of their mutual relationships that a full picture emerges.

Consider Frank: he may be presenting himself as an assertive, responsible, caring person, but when we look at his relationships with the people around him we see that emotionally he seems shallow, socially he is isolated and, as Beard points out, he never really achieves anything. Why does he not contact his own family? There is no sign of his parents, or any other siblings whom one would expect to help out at family crises like these. Has he alienated himself from them? If we exclude people he knows through Nola or in connection to Raglan, there are only two people acquainted to Frank: the contractor of the building he is restoring, and Ruth Mayer, the school teacher. The acquaintance with the contractor is strictly professional, and judging by the delays on the restoration it is not a very prosperous one. The relationship with Ruth first appears to be professional as well; she reminds him of his duties as a parent. Then it gradually develops into a potential friendship. After Candice's overture to Ruth, Frank even seems willing to date her (while his wife is still in therapy!), but any chance of a romance is cut short by Frank's clumsy response to Barton's call, and Nola's telephone threat. Without further ado Ruth tells Frank his life is 'a bit too complicated now' and disappears. She is killed shortly after. Even in the shortest of meetings and conversations Frank finds himself antagonising people: he is bored with Juliana, annoyed with Barton, yells at his lawyer, is frustrated with Ruth's rejection, disgusted with Nola, rude to the police psychologist, curt with his contractor, embarrassed with Mike and Hartog, angry at Raglan – and in the end the bumps on Candice's arm warn us that she, too, is cross with him. For Frank, Nola is to blame for all of this, but he seems unable to question himself. At one point he confides to Ruth that he sometimes tells himself 'you got involved with a woman who married you for your sanity hoping it would rub off ... Instead it started to work the other way around.' In the light of how he treats people it is a revealing remark. Contrary to his lawyer's suggestion, he is not a 'mensch' with anyone, and 'sometimes' he blames Nola for it. But are we also allowed to think there is shared blame? After all, we never really get to know why he married Nola. 'Thirty seconds after you're born you have a past, and sixty seconds after that you start to lie to yourself about it,' Juliana says to Frank. She might not be talking about herself, but about him.

This interpretation does not disprove Cronenberg's, Wood's, Creed's or Beard's analyses. Instead it shows how the complications of *The Brood* allow for multiple readings. A number of other readings are still possible: the relationship of Raglan towards his male patients Hartog and Mike, and his assistant Chris, deserves scrutiny, as does the trope of alcohol (whoever drinks gets killed in *The Brood*), or the unworldly surnames given to the characters – as Peary points out Carveth, Raglan, Mrazek, Trellan and Desborough are certainly not common phone directory names (1981: 39). *The Brood's* contentions, confusions and complications may remain muddled forever – and that may well be the point. At the end of his essay Peary laments: 'Why can't contemporary filmmakers ever let us leave the theatre thinking it's all over and all is well?' (1981: 38).[14]

The cult of horror

At this point it is imperative to bring into view the wider cultural framework within which *The Brood* was being adopted. It extended well beyond the boundaries of the tax shelter, film reviewing and Cronenberg's private sphere. These factors may have influenced how audiences and critics appreciated or rejected *The Brood*, but they do not explain how it reached, and fit into, the midnight movie culture described at the beginning of this chapter. According to Canadian film critic Lawrence O'Toole *The Brood* became a cult movie because it appeared at a time when North America was 'hell-bent for horror' (1979b: 46). The popularity of the scary movie genre reached gigantic proportions: everything from *Halloween* (John Carpenter, 1978) through *Dawn of the Dead* and *Invasion of the Body Snatchers* (Philip Kaufman, 1978) to *Alien* (Ridley Scott, 1979) seemed not only a big success but also appeared to touch a cultural nerve, especially with a younger generations of avid moviegoers, devouring them with insatiable appetite. And it was not just movies: comic books, heavy metal music, gothic new wave, punk rock, Stephen King, Anne Rice, Kiss, even Meat Loaf – they all relied on horror imagery such as devils, skulls, vampire teeth, snake tongues, pale faces and blood red eyes, and they all attracted wide fandom. O'Toole connected the cultist adoration for horror with contemporary religious cults (like the People's Temple in Jonestown, which ended in a mass suicide) and threats of real horror (Skylab falling from the sky, nuclear meltdown, cancer, acid rain), inferring that they were signs of a society looking for certainties where there were none. For O'Toole, that fear explains much of the appeal of horror. He quotes George A. Romero: 'the rationale is, since this is the way we're going why not celebrate it?' O'Toole used *Alien*, *The Brood* and *Love at First Bite* (Stan Dragoti, 1979) as examples to track the themes and metaphors of this new wave. Its main components were the emphasis on body horror (the monster comes from inside, or near you), the refusal to provide a comforting ending (either everyone dies or there is a 'big question mark') and the exposition of fanaticism (not just in the portrayal of characters, but also in the relentless drive of horrific events happening on the screen – there are no more rest points). For O'Toole, the origin of the cult reception of these films lay in the college crowd midnight screenings of the mid-1970s, which had brought films like *Night of the Living Dead*, *The Rocky Horror Picture Show* and *The Texas Chainsaw Massacre* to notoriety (2008: 257). The momentum these films generated was now carried over into a wide cultural phenomenon, one to which Colonel Kurtz's 'the horror ... the horror' from *Apocalypse Now* (Francis Ford Coppola, 1979) seemed an appropriate accompaniment.

O'Toole did not have to look far for inspiration for his article on the outrageous popularity of horror in the late 1970s: *The Brood* was released in his hometown Toronto, where entrepreneurs like Garth Drabinsky were producing films like *The Changeling* which also became a cult film, and – as noted above – even the Toronto International Film Festival was preparing its special nights on horror (with Wood inviting George A. Romero, Larry Cohen, Brian De Palma, Wes Craven, John Carpenter, Stephanie Rothman, Bob Clark and David Cronenberg – all exponents of the brave new wave of horror). Nor was O'Toole the only one to notice the cult. The French-Canadian magazine *Séquences* observed it as well. Patrick Schupp (1979) counted no less than 37 horror film releases in less than two years – among them films by Lucio Fulci, Don Coscarelli, Mario Bava, Carpenter, Romero, Cohen – and *The Brood*, on whose 'anthropophageous children' he elaborates. Schupp explains the cult of horror through its appropriateness for the uncertainty of the times: isn't it normal that audiences are drawn to films featuring ecological disasters, technological dangers and the breakdown of the nuclear family when that reflects their real-life anxieties? It is a question Wood poses as well, in his essays for *Film Comment*. Even though he rejects Cronenberg's views, he nevertheless sees them as relevant for the times. Outside North America, French, Belgian, German, British and Italian commentators were noticing similar correlations between the cult of horror and cultures' anxieties.[15]

Before *The Brood*'s reception had any time to further calibrate, *Scanners* intervened, and intensified Cronenberg's affiliation with the cult of horror. The earliest mentions of *Scanners* came ahead of most of the reception of *The Brood*, in August 1979, before the Wood controversy, and at a time when even reviews of *Fast Company* were still appearing (see Anon. 1979a; Scott 1979d) – indications of the vitality of tax shelter-propelled Canadian film production and the industrious activity of 'Canada's one-man horror industry' David Cronenberg, but also manifestations of the fractured distribution it suffered. *The Brood* fared better than *Fast Company*, and was distributed smoothly in Canada and most of western Europe (though only French audiences got to see it before 1980).[16] But the American distribution was less well orchestrated. Financial difficulties at New World interrupted the flow of release considerably and while *The Brood* did well financially, its exposure remained underneath its potential.[17] Even before it was wrapped and post-production completed, *Scanners* was enjoying much wider coverage. Better business choices played an important part in this: Vision 4, which had been in charge of *The Brood*'s production, was dissolved and regrouped as Filmplan, a company with a better financial structure and promotional strengths. The American distribution was moved from New World to Avco-Embassy, where Cronenberg was reunited with Bob Rehme (who had overseen New World's distribution of *Rabid*). Avco-Embassy bought *Scanners* in first draft, and Filmplan inserted it into its press releases more than a year before it premiered. Obviously, they felt Cronenberg's brand name was developing positively and they were willing to give the new project maximum exposure (see Anon. 1979b; Anon. 1979c).

Scanners profited massively from *The Brood*'s association with the cult of horror. It allowed audiences and critics to pre-establish an alliance to the film, use it as a tool in their formation of its (and their) place, aesthetics and principles. One outcome was that Cronenberg's name and *Scanners* were inserted more easily into writings on popular culture. The *Globe and Mail* included Cronenberg in its overview of 'new wave popular culture', and argued that its 'rudeness' was a key quality: 'As in the horror films of John Carpenter and David Cronenberg, underneath the new wave's obsessive use of the Old Guard pop clichés is a nagging worry that something very rude is at large in the neighbourhood' (Testa 1980). According to writer and essayist Norman Snider (1980), Cronenberg (and Chris Stein of pop group Blondie, whom he compares him to), 'takes popular culture very seriously'. That is why he appealed to the cult of horror, and to reviewers who took it equally seriously.

A symptomatic example of this pre-release alignment was David Chute's celebration of Cronenberg (and by extension of the cult of horror) in *Film Comment*, in March 1980, predating the release of *Scanners* by almost a year. Chute's essay opened with the assertion that:

> *The Brood* is the scariest, smartest, most original horror movie of the Seventies, and the richest emotionally – but you've probably never heard of it. For all the media attention lavished on horror last year, in the midst of the genre's marked commercial resurgence, scarcely a word was written anywhere about *The Brood*. (1980: 42)

Chute promised *Scanners* would be better, and better noticed. The essay featured a still from *Scanners* prominently on its title page, and ended with an extensive description of the film, which included a prediction that it would become Cronenberg's 'first box-office smash'. Chute's essay was a landmark endorsement for Cronenberg, not just in pre-empting *Scanners*, but also in countering negative receptions. It contained a remarkable rebuttal by Cronenberg of Wood:

> Wood struck me as an academic in the most rigid sense: a man with a thesis to protect. He seemed quite taken aback when I told him that I thought *They Came From Within* was a positive film. [It] seemed to shake his interpretations of my films, and I can only hope that he'll acknowledge that in print someday. (in Chute 1980: 37)

In a funny and ironic editorial intervention the editors of *Film Comment* added a footnote to Cronenberg's statement, which said: 'Not bloody likely', referencing Wood's essay in the same issue in which he lashed out at Cronenberg once more (see Chute 1980: 38). Chute's long laudation of Cronenberg's films included recurrent references to fan and genre press (he cites *Halls of Horror* and *Cinefantastique*) as legitimate sources of authoritative information, equal to news wires and press releases. This is an important element in understanding the source of the alignment. It means Chute credited Cronenberg's films with a pressing cultural relevance *because* the director is championed by the cult of horror. It made *Scanners* a key instrument in that cult *before* it was even released.

The trope of cult and congregation also runs through the story of *Scanners*. The film opens with a derelict man, Cameron Vale (Stephen Lack), wandering through that most North American of ritualised social spaces: a shopping mall. As he scavenges for leftovers he sets his eyes on two women giving him a disapproving look. He concentrates; he can hear their thoughts as voices in his head. As he does, one of the women starts shaking uncontrollably. Frightened, Cameron interrupts his activity and runs away, chased by two men in long coats who shoot an arrow into his wrist; he passes out. As he wakes up he is in the custody of Doctor Paul Ruth (Patrick McGoohan) of Consec, a company specialised in international intelligence, security and weaponry, who tells him he is a 'scanner': his thoughts can penetrate people's minds and – if used in a certain way – his scanning powers can be used to control and kill other people. Ruth gives him a sedative, the drug Ephemerol, which suppresses the extremely stressful side effects – such as the voices – of being a scanner. Meanwhile, a 'scanning' demonstration at Consec runs out of control, when the company's scanner is upstaged by Darryl Revok (Michael Ironside), a rival scanner who explodes the Consec man's head. He is apprehended by security, but avoids sedation, brutally kills off his escorts (one of whom he makes kill his colleagues and commit suicide) and escapes.

At an emergency board meeting Ruth reveals that Consec has now lost control over all of its own scanners (236 of them), and they are being threatened by what appears to be an underground counter-movement of scanners led by Revok that is set to destroy a society that sees them as freaks, 'telepathic curiosities'. Ruth unfolds a plan to use Cameron – who is unknown to Revok – to infiltrate the movement and terminate Revok's command. The danger is that scanners are notoriously unreliable, and Ruth has to turn Cameron into a faithful follower of Consec. During Cameron's training, Ruth tries to convince him of the need to rescue his 'brothers and sisters' for the benefit of mankind. At a secret 'psychic gymnasium' Ruth introduces Cameron to yoga master Dieter Tautz (Fred Doederlein), who will help him control his powers. Cameron quickly outclasses Tautz. Ruth next brings Cameron to Benjamin Pierce (Robert Silverman), a scanner who killed his entire family. Released from prison, Pierce has since become sculptor of deformed, grotesque heads. Cameron poses as an art dealer to gain access to Pierce. When he scans Pierce's agent to extract the location of Pierce's whereabouts another scanner notices him. When Cameron finds Pierce he refuses to give him any information. As he exits his workshop (and the giant head sculpture in which they conversed), Pierce is gunned down. Enraged, Cameron kills all four assailants. He scans the dying Pierce for information, and 'detects' Kim Obrist (Jennifer O'Neill), who leads a community of defectors from Revok's army.

Alerted by Consec's own head of security, Braedon Keller (Lawrence Dane), Revok tracks Cameron and Obrist down. One of his hit squads raids their hideout and they kill most of their friends during a séance. Cameron captures one of Revok's men and learns that Revok is producing a drug called Ephemerol in vast quantities, on an industrial scale. He infiltrates Revok's factory, Biocarbon Amalgamate, and gathers evidence that Consec is also involved in these plans. Cameron and Kim warn Ruth and reveal Consec's involvement in Revok's activities. Before Ruth can give them more information Keller kills him, but Cameron and Kim manage to escape. They access the computer program (called Ripe) from a remote location, using Cameron's scanning powers, and before Keller can have the files destroyed they gather a list of names of doctors prescribing Ephemerol. Upon visiting one of the doctors Kim is scanned by a pregnant patient's unborn foetus, and they deduce the drug is administered to pregnant women in the hope it will create a super race of scanners. A moment later, Cameron and Kim are shot with sedating arrows. When Cameron wakes up he is a captive of Revok, who discloses not only that Ruth was his father, but was also Cameron's, and they are brothers. Because Ruth had experimented on his unborn children, Cameron and Revok are more powerful than all the other scanners, and Revok urges Cameron to join forces. Furious, Cameron attacks Revok and the two engage in a scanning duel, getting more violent until both are bleeding and burning, from multiple wounds. As Kim comes by she enters the room where the brothers' duel took place; she finds a burnt corpse. From behind a couch Cameron assures her he is fine. When he appears the voice has Revok's body. 'We've won,' he says.

Community and conspiracy: cults in Scanners

The stories of *The Brood* and *Scanners* both reference cults. In *The Brood* Raglan's Psychoplasmics is run like a sectarian community from which one cannot escape unscathed, as Hartog and Mike discover. In *Scanners*, we have Consec, a company so secretive, displaying such a permanent fear of the outside world and a siege mentality, it immediately evokes comparison with sects and religions with tight membership control, though it also bears resemblance to fictional cults led by an evil genius, made famous in James Bond movies. Opposite Consec, we find another cult-like congregation: the smaller, more peaceable self-help community of meditating scanners called 'Scanners Anonymous' who have broken with Revok. Headed by Kim, they spend most of their time trying to find the positive elements of their scanning abilities. Serge Grünberg describes their activity as an 'orgy in which Kim Obrist, Cameron, and other scanners commune mentally – a communion that holds the middle between the communal "good vibrations" of hippies and transcendental meditation' (1992: 102).

Further references to hippies and meditation are invited by yoga master Tautz and the Psychic Gymnasium. Then there is the figure of Doctor Ruth: at the same time the ring leader of Consec and the divine father of the scanners. His long hair and beard make him look like a West Coast hippie cultist. He seems more aloof than dangerous – a bit 'zoned out'. The fact that his role is played by Patrick McGoohan, whose screen fame relies on the cult series *The Prisoner* (1967–68) is a case of clever casting. Like Frank in *The Brood*, Cameron does not seem to have much patience with these cult-like communities and their activities: he is aggravated by their unwillingness to see the truth of the conspiracy – one that he himself only gradually becomes aware of – and undertake action against Consec. This cult trope can also be seen in Philip Kaufman's remake of *Invasion of the Body Snatchers*, to which *The Brood* had also been compared in reviews (and with which it shares Art Hindle) (see Schiff 1984: 30), and *One Flew*

Over The Cuckoo's Nest (Milos Forman, 1975). Michael Ironside's Revok looks a bit like Jack Nicholson's Randall McMurphy, and in one scene a tape of a young Revok shown to Cameron also calls into mind the imagery of the Stanford Prison Experiment.[18] If nothing else, the similarity between the sectarian madness at the heart of *Invasion of the Body Snatchers* and *One Flew Over The Cuckoo's Nest*, and the narratives of *The Brood* and *Scanners* demonstrates the closeness in their aspiration to problematise the tensions between formal and informal ties within close-knit communities.

It also invokes a sense of paranoia. In Frank's case the conflict remains at a small-scale level: the paranoia only occasionally exceeds the secrets and distrust of the family circle. Cameron's terrain of action is much wider. His family are the 236 other scanners, and his quarrel with Consec concerns not so much Doctor Ruth but the entire corporation and an underground movement. That also shifts *Scanners'* generic allegiance. If *The Brood* is a horror-melodrama, *Scanners* relies much more on the conventions of the conspiracy thriller – a genre Cronenberg would return to with his two subsequent films, *Videodrome* and *The Dead Zone*. The association of *Scanners* with the cult of horror prevented anyone from remarking on its qualities as a conspiracy thriller – as we will see other elements were stressed instead. But I believe that it is worth some elaboration. In the late 1970s the conspiracy thriller developed an aesthetic of its own, almost like a sub-genre, which *Scanners* borrowed from, and contributed to. In the wake of Watergate, and under the influence of films such as *The Conversation* (Francis Ford Coppola, 1974), *The Parallax View* (Alan J. Pakula, 1974), *All the President's Men* (Alan J. Pakula, 1975) and *Three Days of the Condor* (Sydney Pollack, 1975), conspiracy thrillers had been imbued with a political subtext, which articulated itself in a sense of paranoia: one is always watched, and no truth can be trusted except one's own – and even 'oneself' is unreliable (see chapter five). In *Scanners*, the political subtext is largely absent, but many of its visual motifs are present. There is the doppelganger, not so much in the duplication of the protagonist, but in the form of clone-like multiple opponents, such as the collective identities several scanners seem to have. It reminds us of cloning experiments, thought-control and a film such as *The Boys from Brazil* (Franklin J. Schaffner, 1978). There are secret communication systems such as telepathy, extremely close to paranoia (in both cases featuring 'voices in heads' foreboding danger); and there is an abundance of surveillance imagery such as grainy security camera recordings, close-ups of recording equipment, and monitoring systems. The style of the scene in which Cameron retracts information from Consec's computer mainframe via the phone calls into mind the scene in *Three Days of the Condor* in which Joseph Turner (Robert Redford) links all of New York's phone networks to hide his caller identity; and in tone it resembles the menacing calls Nikolai Dalchimsky (Donald Pleasence) makes in *Telefon* (Don Siegel, 1977) that activate undercover spies by reciting poetry that pulls them into a trance – a sort of scanning *avant-la-lettre*.

Both *The Brood* and *Scanners* also influenced later films, such as *Brainstorm* (Douglas Trumbull, 1983) and *Strange Days* (Kathryn Bigelow, 1995), or the *X-Files* television series (1993–2002), which combined the traits of 'family', 'cult' and 'paranoia'. Whoever thinks such links are far-fetched should just look at the autopsy scene on one of the brood or the burnt out corpse (Cameron's body) in *Scanners*.

Cronenberg's heads: the style of the cult

The Brood and *Scanners* have a stylistic core that is also appealing to unaligned cultists. There are obvious differences between both films. Shot on a bigger budget, with a rushed script (often rewritten during shooting), *Scanners* is far less of a personal story for Cronenberg. It swaps intimacy for spectacle, the story of a broken marriage for that of a nationwide conspiracy. Where *The Brood* carried its meanings in the nooks and cracks and details, implied instead of explicated, *Scanners* advocates its meaning loudly. *The Brood*'s bodily deformations implode, those in *Scanners* explode. In both cases there is a family bond between the story's protagonists and antagonists (the spouses in *The Brood*, brothers in *Scanners*), but in the latter that family significance for the development of the narrative shifts from causal to casual. Instead of household details, *Scanners* has car chases, crashes, explosions, fires, gun battles (at least twenty people get killed on-screen), helicopters and swift location switches – there is no 'home' in the entire film.

To the similarities next: apart from a striking correspondence in acting styles (underplayed as always in Cronenberg films) the music stands out. From the credit sequences on, both soundtracks resemble a Hitchcockian score – menacing, mesmerising and expectant, with a slight leitmotif running through. They sound a lot like Bernard Herrmann's compositions for *Vertigo* (Alfred Hitchcock, 1958) and *North by Northwest* (Alfred Hitchcock, 1959), but also for *Taxi Driver* (Martin Scorsese, 1976), with which they have a sense of foreboding, paranoia and psychological distress in common – suspense of an apocalyptic kind. At crucial moments the musical sounds are punctuated by the silences of the characters, especially in the cases of Candice in *The Brood* and Pierce in *Scanners*.

This brings us to the depictions of characters. *The Brood* and *Scanners* share a cold, detached style that stands apart from the baroque atmosphere of Fulci's and Dario Argento's movies, or the 'in-your-face' frankness of Landis's films, or the dazzling flows and rushes of De Palma's and Carpenter's films. In spite of their storylines' suggestions of immediacy and emergency there aren't even many chases and runs. Nor do they possess the primitiveness and naturalism that typified Romero's and Craven's films (at least back then). Instead, they consist of mostly fixed, static shots, without too much fanciful cutting between them. Occasional match-cut dissolves (of the faces of assassins in *Scanners*) or elaborate pan shots (Raglan's on-stage experiment in *The Brood*) are kept to a functional minimum, suggesting the collective identity of Revok's scanned henchmen and the developing bond between Mike and Raglan respectively. The contents of the shots are austere: rooms only contain the most essential furniture, and exteriors are void of busy, buzzing crowds or any lively vibrancy. As Danny Peary remarks, Cronenberg's pictures depict 'cold, snowy weather (everyone wears coats and scarves, and walks under grey skies) to suit their icy dispositions and give us chills' (1981: 39). Many reviewers have remarked on the presence of snow in Canadian genre cinema: why film something so typically Canadian as snow if you want your film to pass for – or compete with – American genre films? Cronenberg provides an explanation:

Psychoanalysis and Freud: in *Rabid* (top) and *The Brood* (above) – Cronenberg pre-empts the critical reception of his films

If the principal photography wasn't complete by the end of the year (31 December), then all these guys who were totally dependent on their tax write-off from you didn't get it. So there was a lot of hanky-panky, doing two months of second-unit photography after the New Year, and so on. On the other hand, can you see *Scanners* shot in the lushness of summer? It was meant to be very deadly – a cold, harsh, nasty film. It was perfect. And for *The Brood* too. (In Rodley 1997: 87)

Within the icy frames, characters remain immobile – they stand, sit, kneel, stare – the dynamic is certainly not coming from any athletic movement of their bodies. In an otherwise sparsely decorated *mise-en-scène* most shots contain medium or close-up shots of heads talking, thinking, looking. Such shots make sense, as much of the cause and motive for the narrative lies in the scanning, brooding 'heads' of the characters.

His fondness for isolated shots with heads also gives Cronenberg the opportunity to play with the juxtaposition of these heads within the frame – characters' heads will frequently find themselves surrounded by pictures or posters (more heads) that tell stories in their own right. In one such framing in *The Brood* we find pictures and books of famous psychoanalysts and artists (Raglan prominent among them, but also Sigmund Freud, Jacques Lacan, R. D. Laing, Arnold Newman and Alberto Giacometti) together with religious icons in a room shaped like a coffin – Nola's hideout. Not only does this imply Nola sees Raglan as a guru, whose cult she voluntarily joined, but the presence of Freud, Lacan and Laing suggests that the entire science of psychoanalysis is a kind of sect. In the light of the criticism the film would subsequently receive from Wood, Creed and others it is tempting to see this as a pre-emption of the academic reception of the film – let us not forget the neat close-up of Ernest Jones' biography of Freud in *Rabid*, with a frowning face on the cover.

Likewise, when one of Revok's scanners wanders through the debris of a record shop trashed by a van that crashed into it he finds himself backed by a poster of rock singer Herman Brood in a shot reminiscent of the way Norman Bates' figure is framed against a wall covered with dead, stuffed birds. This is more than just a nod to *Psycho* or a pun on the title of Cronenberg's previous film. Brood was emblematic of the new wave of music the cult of horror praised so much: tough as nails, provocative, rebellious and embroiled in scandals, especially with his then-wife, German punk singer Nina Hagen. Similarly, sculptor-scanner Ben Pierce holds a collection of giant heads, prominent in most of the scenes with his character (and actually also very visible in the trailer, promotional materials and illustrations for reviews). In short, it is heads all around in *The Brood* and *Scanners*.

Still, filmed heads makes for rather dull imagery. That is, until you take the early shocking scenes (detailed at the beginning of this chapter) into account: the initial shocks of these scenes demonstrate how nasty things can get whenever heads are on display. By inviting viewers to link each closely viewed head with the head-on shocks of the beginning and, hence, the possibility of another terrorised mind, another explosion, Cronenberg maintains suspense in scenes where there would otherwise be no visual tension. It enshrines the pivotal position of the exploding head shot. It *is* the access to any understanding of the film, and of its appeal, especially for cult audiences.

Exploitation and exploding heads: the reception of Scanners
At the time, few commentators attempted a detailed discussion of *Scanners'* theme of conspiratorial cults, and not too much space was spent analysing its framing. Instead, most efforts concentrated on the exploitation aspect of *Scanners*. Heads were all around in those discussions as well, but in a distinctly different fashion. Let us start with the promotion. Evidently, the exploding head shot featured prominently in the trailer for *Scanners'* release. The final shot of the trailer actually shows the head blowing up, but cuts away right before we see the major splatter in which it results. During the trailer it is revealed that there are 237 scanners in the world (the 236 Ruth mentions plus Cameron) who can read and destroy people with their minds, and that

there is a conspiracy by them to seize control; they need to be stopped. The images from the exploding head scene that intersperse with this narrative almost seem to tell a different parallel story, one of thrills and kicks in seeing a duel between two people until the head of one of them explodes – much more childlike in entertainment value than what appears to be a sophisticated conspiracy narrative, but probably also a lot more fun. This mode of presentation – as a film that offers audiences a good shock to the system in a nasty, fun way – is one that audiences of the time were certainly likely to pick up on. As if to press that point, audiences in selected territories also had the chance to be exposed to a 'sensational TV ad campaign which features shots of a test audience chewing its nails', thus ramming home the association between the audience in the auditorium and the intended audience for *Scanners*, and in the UK 'explicit promotional promises' were created through a poster campaign containing – you guessed it – the exploding head shot (Testa 1981: 51).

The prevalence of the exploitation element also rings through in other aspects of the promotion and reception of *Scanners* at the time of its release. Ian Conrich, in his excellent overview of *Scanners'* British release, and its crucial place in what he calls 'neo-horror film culture', quotes from the Canadian press release, in which producer Pierre David heralded the film as 'the most spectacular ... ever produced in Canada ... we're using the services of six top special effects men from Canada and the US and the results of their efforts will be extraordinary, thrilling action sequences' (in Conrich 2000: 43).

Coming from a producer interested in as broad an audience as possible, the statement exemplifies *Scanners'* self-presentation to a wider public, not just as a wink to its fans. Conrich goes on to show how reviewers picked up on this aspect, and on the shot's impact, in their evaluations of *Scanners*. While most British reviewers expressed a deep distaste for *Scanners*, they all acknowledged the impact of the exploding head shot (see Conrich 2000: 35–49).[19] As Paul Taylor wrote in *Monthly Film Bulletin*, the promises created through the promotional campaign were 'trustily delivered, though unexpectedly early' (1981: 79). France, Spain and Italy received *Scanners* more warmly than the UK, with very positive appreciations in the general press and film press alike (see Tesson 1981: 57–8). The Netherlands and Belgium, while also largely displaying negative responses, were nevertheless milder in their rejections than the British press. In Germany, the film received mixed responses.[20] It seemed as if it was on the verge of acceptability, and it made Cronenberg a name that drew wide attention inviting connections between his themes and images (the head shot predominantly among them), and contemporary culture.

The best way in which this is exemplified is in the critical reception of the film in North America. Upon its release on 450 screens in mid-January 1981 *Scanners* did extremely well. It actually made it to the top of the US box office intake for a few days, no doubt helped by a highly visible promotional campaign and much press attention – which included reports of the surprise success of this Canadian from out of town, and an urban legend-like incident of gun-firing during a screening of *Scanners* in New York.[21] In Canada, where it opened a week later, it was also a big hit, partly as a result of its widely reported New York and Los Angeles successes (see Cloutier 1981; Scott 1981). The popularity of *Scanners* is reflected in a number of positive reviews in prominent publications which, without exception, extensively referenced the exploding head shot.[22] *Variety*'s review opened with:

> The trick with horror flicks at this stage in the game is to conjure up something audiences haven't seen before, and on this score *Scanners* offers at least one literally eye-popping moment and another that can only be called mind-blowing. (McCarthy 1981: 26)

There were hostile reviews too. David Sterrit wrote that 'the total IQ of this dopey movie remains perilously close to zero' (1981: 18). A *Washington Post* review added:

> *Scanners* gets off to a slow start with an epileptic fit, a heart attack and some nosebleeds. Then a person's head is blown apart, spraying blood and bits of brain all over the place. The filmmaker, David Cronenberg ... says, however, that the climax is *really* violent. This reviewer did not stay to see it. (Martin 1981: 23)

But even these reviews acknowledged the exploding head shot and audiences looking for thrills knew where to go. In terms of combining a positive judgement with an appreciation of the imagery, Jack Kroll's (1981) article in *Newsweek* went perhaps the furthest, suggesting not only a relationship between *Scanners'* head shot and passages from Homer, but putting the special effects in general at the centre of the story, and making them culturally iconic.[23] In short, the North American reception solidified the cult reputation of Cronenberg as a filmmaker very much in tune with the cultural edge of his times, and it used the exploding head shot, and not the story or its themes, to do so.[24]

The Baron of Blood and the legend of special effects

The Brood and *Scanners* quickly became canonical; crowbars through which the cult of horror forced its breakthrough from subculture to 'cool'. In a sense, other films, and other directors besides Cronenberg could have fulfilled that function. There was room enough for multiple kings of schlock and princes of darkness: John Landis's *Schlock* (1973) and *An American Werewolf in London* (1981), George A. Romero's *Martin* (1977) and *Dawn of the Dead* (1978), Larry Cohen's *It's Alive* and *It Lives Again* (1978), Wes Craven's *The Last House on the Left* and *The Hills Have Eyes*, John Carpenter's *Halloween* and *The Fog* (1980), Lucio Fulci's *The Psychic* (1977, with *Scanners'* Jennifer O'Neill) and *City of the Living Dead* (1980), Brian De Palma's *Carrie* and *The Fury* (1978), Joe Dante's *Piranha* (1978) and *The Howling* (1981), and Dario Argento's *Suspiria* and *Inferno* (1980) were also part of the canon. But *The Brood* and *Scanners* had two advantages that set them apart from most other contenders: a director who did not shy away from claiming artistic merit while touting the label of gory horror, and a legend surrounding the special effects.

Both advantages were first carried forward by the fan press. I have already mentioned their significance in promoting *Rabid*. At the time of *Scanners*, this fan press generated a constant stream of information on Cronenberg that more mainstream outlets gladly used for their own writing. This situation catapulted the fan press out of its subcultural confines. Their circulation skyrocketed and former amateur fan reviewers now found themselves writing for non-fan audiences without having to compromise their aesthetic pretensions. An amalgamation occurred which saw the fan press become more professional and the regular press more agreeable towards fannish interests, all of which helped shape the public discourse on Cronenberg, and his reputation. Simultaneously, that press – especially *Fangoria* and *Cinefantastique*, arguably the two top fan magazines for horror at the time, but also the usually more sci-fi oriented *Starlog* – generated a lot of attention as a subject of interest on their own accord. The surge was not limited to North America either. The French leading fan magazine, *L'Écran fantastique*, published the very first European preview of *Scanners* (beating every other publication to it) and returned to discuss the film several more times during the year. Other fan publications such as *Future Life, Starlog, Cinemagic, Gorezone, Fear, Starbust, Mad Movies, Vampir* and *Halls of Horror* quickly followed suit and became acknowledged sources for legitimate information. Until *The Brood* Cronenberg was a name only known to die-hard fans, industry professionals and to a small group of reviewers for publications in the margin of the public sphere. The cult of horror propelled them, and him, into full public view as the champion of a new generation – the only true 'Baron of Blood', and *Scanners* the spearpoint of its canon.[25]

As Robin Wood had discovered during the Toronto International Film Festival debates, Cronenberg insisted on seeing his own films as art as much as anything else. This became abundantly clear during the reception of *Scanners* when Cronenberg was regularly prompted to give his comments on his films' artistic inspirations.[26] An indicative – and widely acknowledged – example of this is *Cinefantastique*'s career overview of Cronenberg. The magazine put Cronenberg's head (in a design which makes it look as if it is exploding) on the cover of its tenth anniversary issue, and published an extensive overview article/interview on the director. In the anniversary editorial *Cinefantastique* editor Frederick Clarke mused:

> We saw the trend coming, back in 1972 when it was just getting underway. … And grow it did. Some would say like a weed, considering the glut of *Halloween* imitators which sprang up this year, all seemingly starring Jamie Lee Curtis. That kind of unimaginative repetition normally spells the death of a cycle … But the genre seems healthy enough to survive the hack work … One segment may become overexposed, but the field is here to stay, and will remain in the forefront. Stick with us in the '80s, and watch the genre as it grows. (1981: 3)

It was highly significant that Cronenberg was *Cinefantastique*'s cover boy of the moment. It was an endorsement of his leading position in the cult of horror that also made him human to those who feared him to be an ethically deplorable madman. Next to a summary of his most gruesome imagery (several inserts zoomed in on the special effects of *Scanners* and *The Brood*) the issue also recounted how several

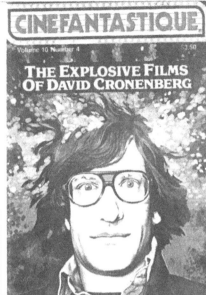

The Baron of Blood: David Cronenberg on the cover of the fan press in the early 1980s

personal stories, like his divorce or the death of his father, had inspired his writing, and it cemented his nickname 'The Baron of Blood':

> 'More Blood!' was Cronenberg's first remark on seeing the tableau at left, designed for his photo session. The remark triggered a round of laughter from observers present in the office of Avco project director Mick Garris. Cronenberg's wife had predicted exactly what he would say. During filming of *The Brood*, actor Art Hindle gave Cronenberg a T-shirt that read 'More blood!' Admitted the director, 'Yeah, I do that sometimes.' (Sammon 1981: 21)

The title 'Baron of Blood' was now no longer an ironic label of self-defence but a distinguished honour for a veteran of horror, and the label through which *Cinefantastique* crowned Cronenberg the king of the cult.[27] Having Cronenberg drop references to Nabokov, Warhol, Anger, Descartes, Breton, Dali and Burroughs helped to give the cult some sort of historical grounding and sediment it into longer-term cultural developments – as did having him say 'I think of horror films as art' and declare himself an 'artist' while discussing his work in public forums (as he did in a panel at the time, in the company of Landis and Carpenter – 'their mouths were hanging open' he recalls).[28] It mattered that critics were able to write that Cronenberg, like Romero and others, had been misrecognised artists for almost a decade. It also mattered that they could write about these directors as people – with families, emotions, ambitions, responsibilities and doubts.

The legend of *Scanners'* special effects was also closely aligned with the agendas of the fan press. It is the result of the cult of horror's preoccupation with explicit gore, and its infatuation with the craftsmanship and authorship of on-screen explosions, creature make-up and animation. Dissecting the production of special effects became a primordial means through which the cult of horror achieved an aesthetic grounding – explaining how sophisticated these shots and scenes are creates admiration for the craft and labour involved in its technical accomplishments. It also helped defuse concerns about the unmitigated violence and gore the special effects were usually asked to support. Explaining how an exploding head works makes blowing it up more tolerable – less a sign of moral decadence and more one of technological progress. It helped make the cult of horror in its entirety acceptable. One major consequence was an auteurist approach to special effects supervisors. Acknowledging special effects creators as artists had become something the genre press, specialist magazines and, gradually, film magazines began to do increasingly, and cult audiences/fan audiences had started paying attention to. Special effects makers became markers of the integrity of the genre.

In a field with stiff competition from *An American Werewolf in London, Dawn of the Dead, Alien* and *The Fury, Scanners'* effects team topped that of every other horror film of the time. To find, on the opening credits of *Scanners,* 'consultant for special make-up effects' Dick Smith, with 'special effects' Gary Zeller and 'micro effects' Dennis Pike side by side, meant that what followed had to contain some *tour de force.* Smith was the godfather of modern horror effects, with his groundbreaking work on *The Exorcist;* Zeller had achieved wide recognition for his collaborations with Tom Savini on *Dawn of the Dead;* and Pike had of course worked on *The Brood.* Their cultural currency at the time should not be underestimated, and was certainly worthy of opening-credit acknowledgement. Mark Kermode makes a convincing argument for their importance by asserting that 'the movies themselves seemed acutely aware of their audience. More than any other genre, horror movies play to and feed upon the knowledgeability of their fans … Special effects men became recognisable to devotees who provide the hardcore fan-base for the genre' (2001: 129). Even if not many reports at the time added the names of Chris Walas, Stephan Dupuis and Tom Schwartz – totalling the 'six specialists' producer David mentioned in the press book – it was still a dream team for every fan.[29]

Not only was this collaboration very well publicised, it was also discussed as a 'historical accomplishment' in the history of special effects – a legendary opportunity and a mythical, sublime moment. *Film Comment* eagerly reproduced Cronenberg's reference to the achievement: 'Gary Zeller, who did the explosive effects for *Dawn of the Dead,* rigged up an exploding head for us that was so good we probably won't be able to use it' (Chute 1980: 42).

As Conrich points out, *Fangoria* put the exploding head on its cover, 'exploited dramatic images of the special effects', and devoted several articles to the film (they had previously also pictured *The Brood* on their cover) (2000: 40). *Cinema Canada* published a long feature article on the work of Gary Zeller. Accompanied by half a dozen pictures of half-completed props, and preceded by a large photo of Zeller in his army cap ('for good luck'), it chronicled several stages of the effects production. The tone was one of admiration and professional respect for 'artists of illusion' from a trade paper published by colleagues in the Society of Canadian Cinematographers (see Siegel 1980). Similar articles appeared at numerous other places. Mike Child and Alan Jones' preview in *Cinefantastique* not only featured a large picture of the exploding head, but also a lengthy discussion of its techniques and aesthetics, with details of the use of alginade, plaster, rubber moulds, gelatin and resin glue, to achieve as much gore as possible:

> The required gore included various gashes, bruises, bleedings and burnings. But the main challenge was to blow up a human head realistically enough to withstand the camera's close stare. How do you destroy a head? (1980: 35)

With much folklore surrounding it, its auteurs, its aesthetic pretensions and its allegiance to the genre's fans all confirmed, the exploding head shot helped *The Brood* and *Scanners* become huge cults. It slotted in perfectly with the prevailing zeitgeist, while still maintaining enough of an edge as a trendsetter to not become a trend-follower. That is why *The Brood* and *Scanners* are not just fannish, but public cult films. And the exploding head shot's two seconds encapsulate the sensibility of an era. Kaboom indeed.

Long-Term Receptions: VCR Aesthetics

After their immediate reception *The Brood* and *Scanners* remained in the public eye, although they were not always mentioned in the same breath. To some extent *The Brood*'s cult mainly survived because of its closeness to *Scanners*, functioning as a key association to it. But once in a while it attracted attention on its own merit, especially in debates about censorship (such as the censors' refusal to allow an uncut screening during the Cronenberg retrospective at the 1983 Toronto International Film Festival – see chapter five), or in discussions of films that warranted 'another look', especially on television, where Stephen King was among the first to note its appearance (1981: 211).[30] That of the hundreds of films screened and broadcast at any time *The Brood* invariably attracts commentators' curiosity explains a bit about the film's enduring cult appeal.

Both *Scanners* and *The Brood* were released on video in 1982, with considerable success given the relatively small size of the video market.[31] In 1984, by the time video rentals first reached a noticeable peak and had penetrated teenage popular culture, *Scanners* became one of the films most discussed, together with the movies of Bruce Lee and Terrence Hill, *The Texas Chainsaw Massacre*, *Faces of Death* (Conan Le Cilaire, 1979), *Poltergeist* (Tobe Hooper, 1982), *The Thing* (John Carpenter, 1982) and *The Evil Dead* (Sam Raimi, 1983). School playground talk would be about swirling nunchakas, drawn-out revolver duels, ultra-fast face slaps, roaring chainsaws and exploding heads – features you could use the pause and rewind buttons of the VCR remote effectively for.

The era of video and the pause button intensified the discussion of the 'authorship' of the exploding head shot. During the first half of the 1980s the shrewdness and inventiveness of the creatures and tricks in box office hits such as *Gremlins* (Joe

Dante, 1984), *A Nightmare on Elm Street* (Wes Craven, 1984) and *Indiana Jones and the Temple of Doom* (Steven Spielberg, 1984) had equipped special effects with a reputation as a production value integral to the development of cinema. At the same time, a curious dichotomy was developing between the different kinds of respect special effects received. On one side stood the 'Special Effects Entrepreneur', who had incorporated his craft into an industry (Chris Walas's CWI was a prime example). While highly admired, their accomplishments were also seen as offering lip service to Hollywood – supporting narratives and illustrating entertainment. Even if the effects were executed by the best in the business they were still seen as part of the *business*, not the art. On the other side of the spectrum stood the 'Special Effects Auteur', a rogue, streetwise aesthete with a rock 'n' roll attitude, who produced messy, gutsy effects. Tom Savini was the prime example of this breed. The dichotomy drove a wedge between the horror culture community and, for instance, separated *Cinefantastique* readers from *Fangoria* readers.

Because *Scanners* spanned both ends of the dichotomy, this position actually enhanced its mythical status: it possessed in Dick Smith a father figure accepted across the industry but still regarded as 'legit' by fans; in Gary Zeller it had a colourful member of the independent scene, who favoured the risky and artistic side of the craft, especially where it concerned pyrotechnics (he ended up working on low-budget features such as *The Capture of Bigfoot* (Bill Rebane, 1979) and *The Last Dragon* (Michael Schultz, 1985)).[32] In the innovative and industrious Walas, who had received acclaim for contributing to *Raiders of the Lost Ark*, *Dragonslayer* (Matthew Robbins, 1981), *Return of the Jedi* (Richard Marquand, 1983) and *Gremlins*, it included one of the most celebrated effects artists of the time; and in Dupuis it had a genre specialist who had become renowned for his work on *Amityville II: The Possession* (Damiano Damiani, 1982), *Strange Invaders* (Michael Laughlin, 1983) and *Spasms* (William Fruet, 1983) – perhaps not the greatest of films but, like the above-mentioned, bursting with street credibility. With such 'cultural capital' ready to be discovered in the credits – and VHS-viewers *would* use the pause button not just to review the shot but also to peruse the credits – the line-up of the exploding head team became somewhat of a 'legend', a unique moment in the development of the cult of horror that gave it an edge over the competition.

And then there was the texture of the shot itself. Pause-button in hand it invited a frame-by-frame appreciation that required a new sort of aesthetic sensibility, one that would exhaust virtually all possible synonyms for 'spray', 'splash', 'splatter', 'slush', 'gush' and 'sprinkle'. Katherine Monk describes the shot as 'talking heads explode like so much pus between a pair of tweezers' (2001: 235). Geoff Pevere and Greig Dymond describe it as a 'watermelon left in a microwave: the kind of scene where you go "yuck!" and then play it over, in slow motion, about six times' (1996: 39). By all accounts it stood up to close scrutiny, and the fact that several books on Cronenberg carry frame-by-frame illustrations of the shot attests to its credibility.[33] The shot's realism also rang true to the cult of horror's DIY attitude. The shot was not real in any ontological sense, but compared with the 'tongue-in-cheek', 'mannerist' and 'fantastic' special effects that were being unleashed around 1984 it stood out as *authentic*. It ripped you apart instead of seamlessly slipping you into a dream mode, and in that sense it mirrored the cult of horror's preference for hard electric dissonant sounds over the smooth synthesised symphonics of the early 1980s rock scene. The exploding head created the impression that it related to the same gritty, messy world audiences would find in everyday life.

The authenticity is also where today's value of the shot lies: as a touchstone for 'handcrafted' (not digitally enhanced) special effects mastery. Especially since the advent of the 'digital era' and the Internet, audiences rediscovering the film on DVD have been emphasising its 'genuine' effects. But by now the matter was no longer only one of authenticity (though numerous DVD reviewers called the shot 'still astonishingly convincing'),[34] but one that allowed debates about *kinds* of realism. And here, again, *Scanners* drew battle lines. As one fan-reviewer wrote after a paragraph-long exposé of the shot's mechanics: 'Nowhere in that paragraph will you find the word "computer" or the term CGI. Do you know why? CGI sucks. Hard.'[35] Combined then, the fact that several of the most noteworthy and visible special effects wizards of the 1980s first collaborated on a new cultural trend's most infamous 'money shot' (more realistic and authentic than others), and the wide debate around its creation and reputation, equipped the exploding head shot with a 'legend', essential for any cult film's enduring public presence.

The exploding head shot is the cult of horror's equivalent of *Psycho*'s shower scene. It became a marker for the new sensibility of a subculture graduating into the public sphere. And it is not just the graphic texture of the shower scene that the exploding head shot shares, but its place in the narrative – 'unexpectedly early' for unseasoned audiences – and its place in the activity of 'moviegoing routines' as well.[36] The ways in which *Psycho* changed movie-attending practices have been well documented (see Williams 1994). *Scanners* deserves a similar status. It is an exemplar for exploring VHS-movie watching (remote in hand, finger on the pause button) and setting the habit of 'knowing laughs' at screenings (or cheers at conventions and festivals) (see Van Extergem 2004), maybe on a smaller scale than *Psycho*, but undeniably present. The exploding head shot, like the shower scene, asks the audience to adapt to a new viewing position. As the scanner himself says: 'I know you've all been prepared for this, but I thought I'd just remind you just the same: no one is to leave this room once the demonstration has begun.' The exploding head shot is the shower scene inside out.[37] A legend.

Conclusion: Cronenberg's Crew

Cults have long tails. After *The Brood* and *Scanners* were accompanied in the Cronenberg canon by other films, they remained popular with a niche audience that treasured the cult of horror of the late 1970s, early 1980s, even when the fan press started championing more 'tongue-in-cheek horror' like *Return of the Living Dead* (Dan O'Bannon, 1985) or *Aliens* (James Cameron, 1986), and special effects were no longer a sign of rebellion (see chapter six). By then, *Scanners* had sunk in as 'the exploding head movie, need we say more?' (Pevere & Dymond 1996: 36), ready to be franchised just like *A Nightmare on Elm Street* or *Halloween*.

Only three Cronenberg films, *Scanners*, *The Dead Zone* and *The Fly*, were ever serialised and/or remade, a sign of his strong control over his materials. Two of the three were not his creations to begin with. *The Dead Zone* (Lionsgate/CBS-Paramount, 2002–07) developed into a television series far removed from the film. Beyond Chris Walas's somewhat underrated *The Fly II* (1990), *The Fly* never materialised into a full-blown series (though rumours abound about another remake, especially in the wake of Cronenberg's own opera version of the film, which premiered in Paris in June 2008 to lukewarm reviews). In the case of *Scanners*, Cronenberg remembers that 'Pierre David came to see if I was interested in being involved in *Scanners II*. I wasn't, but said, "Am I going to get any money on the sequel based on my original characters and idea?" He said, "No. You didn't have a lawyer then"' (in Rodley 1997: 92).

Cronenberg did receive credit for the sequels to *Scanners* that David produced: *Scanners II: The New Order* (Christian Duguay, 1991), *Scanners III: The Take Over* (aka *Scanner Force*, Christian Duguay, 1992), *Scanner Cop* (which Pierre David himself directed in 1994) and *Scanner Cop II* (Steve Barnett, 1995). Releases of the original in packages with the sequels have kept the film in the public domain, as has Jake West's *Inside Scan* (an extra for the Anchor Bay DVD release). Rumours concerning a remake of the original *Scanners*, under the wings of, according to the source, Lionsgate and directed by James Wan (*Saw*, 2004), or Dimension Films, and directed by Darren Lyn Bouseman (*Saw II* (2005) and *Saw III* (2006)) or David S. Goyer (*Blade: Trinity*, 2004) have also helped to maintain public awareness of the film. On top of this, persistent rumours circulate about an imminent remake of *The Brood*. As the streams of interest and speculation indicate, the cult mileage of *The Brood* and *Scanners* is far from over.

As cult films, *The Brood* and *Scanners* manoeuvred Cronenberg out of the shadows of subculture, into popular culture's limelight and a genre's canon. Compared to his previous films they demonstrated a 'directorial maturity' while still enjoying some 'juvenile pleasure' in jolting viewers out of their seats (Peary 1981: 36). That maturity was partly the result of Cronenberg's personal progress, as *The Brood*'s development from a personal frustration into an artistic enterprise testifies, and of the sedimentation of themes recurrent throughout his work, such as the Cartesian divide between body and mind, and the ambiguities between good and evil – no one is merely reactionary or revolutionary in *The Brood* or *Scanners*. But it also meant that budgets were bigger, and production procedures were smoother than before, even if the tax shelter system complicated them.[38]

Cronenberg's crew – his own congregation of devoted personnel – played an essential part in that achievement. *The Brood* and *Scanners* are the first Cronenberg films that carry his name above the title, a clear indication of his authorial command over them. But Cronenberg also relied on a troupe of experts that he could trust, and with whom he had worked with before. The films were backed by veteran associates Pierre David, Victor Solnicki and Claude Heroux (first as Vision 4, then as Filmplan), and most of the team from *Fast Company* was on duty again for one or both of the films: director of photography Marc Irwin, designer Carol Spier, editor Ronald Sanders and sound recordist Bryan Day. Dennis Pike did special effects make-up for both films. New additions to the Cronenberg 'family' were assistant director John Board, effects designers Stephan Dupuis and Chris Walas, gaffer Jock Brandis and composer Howard Shore.

Actors reappeared as well. As an assassin in *Scanners*, Géza Kovács is even more menacing than as art-object Ricardo in *The Italian Machine*. After *Fast Company*, Nicholas Campbell was hired again for *The Brood* (where he plays a small part that is nevertheless essential in supporting the narrative). Robert Silverman, who had appeared in *Rabid*, has key appearances in *The Brood* and *Scanners*; as Jan Hartog and Ben Pierce he provides alternative insights into the protagonists. To audiences, his characters offer a thrill (through the spectacles of his cancerous growth in *The Brood* and his giant sculpted head collection that gets blown to bits in *Scanners*) and a puzzle, adding to the films' ambiguities. Kovács, Campbell and Silverman would return in future Cronenberg projects, as would Cindy Hinds, who would play a girl in *The Dead Zone*; Stephen Lack, who earned a small part in *Dead Ringers*; and Reiner Schwarz (*The Brood*'s Doctor Birkin), who would appear again in *Videodrome*. Gary McKeehan's character Mike in *The Brood* exudes the same intensity as his Lionel in *The Italian Machine* and Smooth Eddy in *Rabid*, providing much of the tone of the story. Susan Hogan's character of teacher Ruth in *The Brood* parallels the anxious young woman she played in *The Lie Chair*. As Dieter Tautz in *Scanners*, Fred Doederlein reprises his role of radical scientist Emil Hobbes from *Shivers*. Also from *Shivers*, Sonny Forbes has a small part in *Scanners*, as did Victor Desy from *Rabid*. Cronenberg called these players his 'informal repertory company', in an endorsement that fittingly evokes the image of a close-knit family (see Braun 1981).

CHAPTER FIVE

Politics and Paranoia: *Videodrome* and *The Dead Zone*

Over our lives preside the great twin leitmotifs of the 20th century – sex and paranoia.

> – J. G. Ballard, Introduction to *Crash*

Yeah, there's a storm on the loose, sirens in my head
Wrapped up in silence, all circuits are dead
Cannot decode – my whole life spins into a frenzy...
Soon you will come to know ... When the bullet hits the bone.

> – Golden Earring, 'Twilight Zone'

Are we living in a land
Where sex and horror are the new Gods?
When two tribes go to war, a point is all you can score.

> – Frankie Goes to Hollywood, 'Two Tribes'

From Cult to Subculture to Culture: The Horror Industry in the 1980s

Synthesizers and electro-pop, big hair and tight jeans, the VCR and MTV, Ronald Reagan and Margaret Thatcher, the Cold War, nuclear missiles and 'Star Wars', Lebanon and Nicaragua, unemployment and corporate greed, AIDS and famine, *Pac Man* and the Walkman, series, serials, sequels, remakes, sampling and franchises,

Friday the 13th and *Cats*, and the general commodification of past tastes through persiflage and pastiche: the 1980s have a bad reputation. For many, the decade signals a return to political and aesthetic conservatism and prudence, displaying a lack of genuinely original ideas and an obsession with recycling in the one area of our existence where it would never be environmentally wise to do so, the area that thrives on novelty and exploration: the arts and culture.

While taste hierarchies of today allow the celebration of many horror films of the 1980s that were initially not considered masterpieces, only a handful of horror auteurs and oeuvres that had taken off in the 1970s withstood scrutiny within the 1980s and beyond. A lot of careers that seemed so promising in the 1970s lapsed, or even came to a grinding halt. Joe Dante and John Landis became more interested in other genres. Tobe Hooper's collaboration with Steven Spielberg on *Poltergeist* (1982) saw him achieve box office success but also lose his edge. George A. Romero branched out with *Knightriders* (1981), then delivered a mediocre third installment to his zombie franchise with *Day of the Dead* (1985), and only partly recovered with the undervalued *Monkey Shines* (1988). Larry Cohen directed an underappreciated little cult gem with *Q, the Winged Serpent* (1982), and then gradually saw his career dwindle, with *It's Alive III* (1985) not able to stop the spiral (although he continued to do well as a screenwriter). Stephanie Rothman stopped making films altogether, and by the end of the 1980s even champions such as John Carpenter and Wes Craven were thought to have lost their momentum, with some of their excellent work, such as Carpenter's *They Live* (1988) or Craven's *The Serpent and the Rainbow* (1987) virtually ignored in favour of their programmatic involvements in the *Halloween* and *A Nightmare on Elm Street* franchises. While European horror became more diverse than ever, with fascinating developments in Belgium, the Netherlands, Germany and Austria, the auteurs of the 1970s withered away: Mario Bava and Lucio Fulci died, Harry Kümel had difficulties finding investors and the careers of Jean Rollin and Dario Argento became too chequered to be consistent.[1]

Ironically enough, at the same time the horror film became more visible and popular than ever. The raise in revenue from franchises made the genre highly profitable, and the increase in diversity at the expense of auteur horror turned it into a market-based culture of hits and misses. There was a surge in channels and networks of reception: a veritable explosion in genre film festivals (the European fantasy festivals of Rome, Brussels, Porto and Avoriaz chief among them); new local distributors specialising in the genre (especially in the video market: examples included Vipco and Redemption); an increasingly professional fan press (with *Heavy Metal*, *Cinefantastique*, *Fangoria*, *Starlog* and *L'Écran fantastique* achieving far-reaching circulations); more horror specials on cable television; and an abundance of massively popular fan conventions of which Stephen King, one of the decade's definitive horror icons, wrote:

> Horror movie-fans communicate their likes to each other by a kind of grapevine which is part word of mouth, part fanzine reviews, part convention-hall chatter at such meetings as the World Fantasy Convention, the Kubla Khan Ate, the IguanaCon. Word gets around. (1981: 210)

King compared the horror cult fan with a 'working miner', who is 'not looking for the big strike, which may come tomorrow or the day after or never [but is] only looking for a livin' wage, something to keep him going yet a while longer' (ibid.). The apt 'living wage' metaphor indicates how much the cult of horror was becoming a self-sustaining industry, how it had moved from the midnight movie circuit to legitimate platforms of exhibition. Many festivals and conventions had grown out of late-night screening venues, which now became more closely entangled with distribution and promotion networks or video distribution. These events not only functioned as showcases for the films they programmed, but also attracted considerable public attention in their own right. They evolved from 'private' affairs (with selective and limited access) into official events with commercial or even government funding, under full legal and public scrutiny, far removed from the 'form of fandom' where Janet Staiger claims it remained, a sign of the move out of the underground of the new loud horror subculture and into a professional industry.[2] By the second half of the 1980s, horror cinema was one of the healthiest parts of global film culture, and an investor-friendly, profit-guaranteed business.

Politics and science: Cronenberg's reputation and the anxieties of a decade
Cronenberg is one of the only members of the cult of horror whose reputation and reception remained untouched throughout this development, as a director whose work would be regarded as emblematic for the horror genre in the 1980s. His oeuvre's move away from the formulaic constraints of a genre that had allowed him to make his mark and become a fully-fledged professional seemed to coincide with addressing some of the decade's most pressing anxieties, and Cronenberg's foray into the wider realms of film culture paralleled what some critics called the dilution of the horror genre across other cinematic styles and themes.[3]

That development occurred in two steps, each containing two of the four films Cronenberg directed in between *Scanners* and *Naked Lunch*. Separating them into two distinct chapters highlights several themes and tropes that would otherwise remain undetected.[4] This chapter will concentrate on *Videodrome* and *The Dead Zone*, and their treatment of politics and paranoia. The prevalence of these two themes at the surface level of the films, but also underlying some more implicit motifs, illustrates how Cronenberg's oeuvre remained acutely aware of the areas of media technology and political culture of the 1980s (censorship debates, the Cold War and North American politics in particular), while still paying lip service to the widening popularity of the horror genre (for instance in riding the wave of Stephen King adaptations in the early 1980s).

The next chapter will discuss Cronenberg's role in the film culture of the second half of the 1980s, one said to shed its desire to intervene in, or to retrace, cultural progress in favour of mannerist reflections upon progress's most coveted currency – capital. In particular, the analysis there will demonstrate how *The Fly* and *Dead Ringers* take up pressing issues of health and science such as AIDS, fertility and cosmetic surgery but are less occupied with the functions of science and more with its corporate exploitation and human failure to put science to benevolent use.

With the first step, Cronenberg demonstrated that he stood at the top of the horror genre and was indeed one of the most original, talented and uncompromisingly accomplished horror filmmakers in the world, broaching relevant issues at a time when many others abandoned them. It won him recognition as a 'master of horror', high praise, attention from beyond his peer group, festival retrospectives and concern about his portrayal of, and influence on, society – it meant Cronenberg moved from being a symptom to an instigator of cultural progress. With the second step, he became the person most likely to show how to use the traits of the genre to establish a new canon, one that surpassed horror – artistically, culturally, commercially *and* in terms of gore – pushing its themes and motifs into academies of esteem and debate it had not been able to enter before: the academia of scholarship and the academy of Hollywood, to be precise.[5] By the end of the 1980s, Cronenberg would be the single most important filmmaker working *with* the genre (not just *in* the genre), applying it to explore cinema's role in culture; a determined step in becoming a cultural hero.

Long Live the New Flesh: Special Effects and the Prefiguration of Videodrome

Videodrome is the quintessential, comprehensive Cronenberg – the crux to cracking the code of the 'Cronenberg Project'. Every motif and metaphor explored in any Cronenberg film originates or resonates in this film: science, technology (both shiny and fleshy), body horror, gore, isolation, hallucination, medicine, paranoia, family dysfunctions, physical sexuality, male and female sado-masochism – they all resound in *Videodrome*. Yet, *Videodrome* is an elusive and reclusive piece of work. As a 'first first-person film', as Cronenberg called it (in McGreal 1984: 9), it requires the viewer to assess all information through an unreliable main character, whose understanding of the narrative and its consequences is, to say the least, muddied (does he even know what is going on?). For some, *Videodrome* is incomprehensible by default; for others it is a secret map to the Cronenberg universe; in each case it is not an easy movie.

Even before its release, *Videodrome* was announced as complex and challenging. The pre-production process was straightforward enough – a script Cronenberg had steered through a few drafts, and a by now seasoned team of collaborators: producers Victor Solnicki, Claude Heroux and Pierre David (now under the mantle of Filmplan II, still supported by the tax shelter system),[6] and largely the same crew as *Scanners*; the main difference being the employment of renowned special effects and make-up artist Rick Baker (who had just won an Academy Award for his work on *An American Werewolf in London*), make-up artist Mark Shostrom (who goes uncredited) and consultant Michael Lennick (a champion of the use of video effects in film).[7] Shooting went relatively smoothly, with delays causing it to extend beyond Christmas 1981.

From quite an early stage in the production, *Videodrome* became a highly anticipated project within the specialist press, partly thanks to the success of *Scanners*, but also as a result of the shoot being shrouded in secrecy. Reports on the creation of '*outré* interactions of men and machines' and rumours about 'a hand that takes the shape of a gun, a man who inserts a videocassette into his stomach, TV sets becoming fleshy, living things…', or shots of a naked Deborah Harry (popular singer of the New York new wave band Blondie) involved in kinky situations, found their way into print frequently.[8] Throughout 1982, the popular fan magazine *Cinefantastique* added to the buzz by devoting a stream of articles (see Lucas 1982a; 1982b; 1982c) to what it called a 'tremendously exciting' project. It quoted Baker as saying 'I'm not supposed to talk about it, but I'll tell you something – it's *weird* ... There are a lot of strange things'. And it cited Cronenberg: 'it is very *au courant* and hip and new wave and trendy'.[9] Among these articles, the ones chronicling the production of the special effects fuelled expectations even further. Writer Tim Lucas's precise descriptions of the devices and his mention of the involvement of the legendary make-up artist Dick Smith fitted a contemporary preoccupation with the urge for novelties of the special effects industry (and of audiences). His asides about how other journalists violated the secrecy and revealed some of the sado-masochistic elements of the effects outside its context generated even more curiosity (see Lucas 1982b). As the *Washington Post* reported in a feature article about the accelerated professionalism of visual effects, the stakes were high those days:

> If there's going to be gore, it has to be clever gore ... One reason *Friday the 13th* did well was that somebody was lying in bed, and an arrow was shoved up through him. People hadn't seen that before. It was different. And the arm in *Cat People* [an arm ripped off by a giant cat] helps bring them in. (Williams 1982: D1)

In the words of Cronenberg:

> There are really only a limited number of fabulously good effects people, and a lot of films and producers who are clamouring for these people, so the chances that you will get to work with somebody like Dick Smith or Rick Baker depend very much on how interesting and what kind of challenge it is you're presenting them with. If you ask them to do something they did ten years ago, obviously it is not going to excite them as much as when it is something that they know their own colleagues are going to phone them up and say how did you do that?[10]

More than just indicating the popularity of the newest of production values, this interest in special effects fulfilled an important function in the storytelling and use of metaphors in 1980s horror and science fiction: it helped to sustain moods and atmospheres that can carry a film, and hence construct, rather than merely support, the story. The forms of these constructions became more important than the stories themselves. Philip Brophy called this shift in attention 'horrality':

> 'Horrality' involves the construction, deployment and manipulation of horror – in all its various guises – as a textual mode. The effect of its fiction is not unlike a death-defying carnival ride: the subject is a willing target that both constructs the terror and is terrorised by its construction. 'Horrality' is too blunt to bother with psychology – traditionally the voice of articulation behind horror

– because what is of prime importance is the textual effect, the game that one plays *with* the text, a game that is impervious to any knowledge of its workings. The contemporary horror film *knows* that you've seen it before; it *knows* that you know what is about to happen; and it knows that you know it knows you know. And none of it means a thing, as the cheapest trick in the book will still tense your muscles, quicken your heart and jangle your nerves. (1986: 5)

Brophy's concept explains why horror films of the early 1980s no longer tried to tell original stories but instead tried to deliver avid, knowing audiences the thrills they were seeking without bothering too much with 'realism' and 'psychology', two paradigms for narrative conventions which, in Brophy's view, were 'belching plug-holes', in which a lot of thrills actually disappeared. For Brophy, the masterworks of horror of the 1970s were those films that delivered short-cut thrills: *The Exorcist, Carrie, Dawn of the Dead* and *Alien*, with their very shallow psychological realism, and lots of special effects. Instead of experiencing fear through psychological realism, Brophy argued, viewers engage – through the visual effects – with numerous thrills they know already but which will, delivered in the right way, still startle them and produce the thrill they were looking for. Never mind that the 'effect' is a construction, that it is 'the cheapest trick in the book'. If it is done well, it will work.

The general press quickly picked up on the flood of gory effects in horror films, and *Videodrome* was linked to topical concerns associated with it: fears of watching television, the downgrading of public culture (concerns that journalists also saw reflected in *Poltergeist*; see Shale 1982), and especially debates about the influences of the popularity of the horror genre on other forms of culture and on vulnerable viewers (a debate that would intensify with the 'Video Nasties' controversy, discussed below). For some, horror films were 'going too far', and *Videodrome* was frequently mentioned as a warning of just how far they could and would go, alongside films opening in the months preceding its release, such as *Cat People* (Paul Schrader, 1982), *Halloween III* (Tommy Lee Wallace, 1982) and *The Thing* (John Carpenter, 1982) – each of them a remake or a sequel (see Stein 1982). Amidst this speculation a quote from Pop Art guru Andy Warhol emerged that called *Videodrome* the '*Clockwork Orange* of the 1980s'.[11]

On top of all that came Universal's insistence on last-minute changes to the film, in response to test screenings in Boston, upon which Cronenberg commented:

There was a transit strike in Boston that day, so we got about half the audience we wanted. I remember being shocked to see black ladies coming with their two-year-old kids, because it was a free movie and they didn't have a babysitter. One baby screamed all the way through. I realised that I was in trouble. (In Rodley 1997: 101)

Cronenberg took the test screenings to heart, appropriated them into his auteurist vision (note in the quote below how he claims it helped *him* understand the film better) and changed *Videodrome* around, to make it more comprehensible and less confrontational. The whole process added another five months to the production, which was now scheduled for release in early 1983, the longest wait for a Cronenberg film since *Shivers*. As Cronenberg explained:

> I used to think the idea of having previews for films was a bizarre cop-out of the industry. ... I used to think: a poet doesn't preview his poetry, but I was wrong about that. Because poets always used to go out and read their poetry to audiences and they would refine it afterwards. And for the very same reason: because you get so close to it ... that you begin to lose some kind of contact with the audience. And you have to vicariously experience it again through an audience so that you can really see what *it* is.[12]

First person shooter: Videodrome
It is a film of astounding vision, in its complexity and clutter. *Videodrome* starts with a flickering television screen, one that is alternating between the kind of noise William Gibson, in the contemporary novel *Neuromancer* (1983) would describe as '*the color of television, tuned to a dead channel*', and a sort of breakfast television channel-cum-alarm clock which announces, through the kind, soothing voice and face of personal secretary Bridey James (Julie Khaner), another day in the life of Max Renn (James Woods), executive in charge of Civic TV, a small cable channel dealing in cheap thrills and kicks. As Max prepares breakfast in his cluttered, messy apartment, and helps himself to some leftover pizza, he checks production stills in advance of a meeting with Japanese producers who are trying to sell a soft-porn series called *Samurai Dreams* to Civic TV. Looking at a still of a nude Japanese woman masturbating Max inadvertently smears pizza tomato sauce on it, then licks his fingers. He meets the producers in a room at the Classic Hotel, its corridors filled with sounds of crying babies and adults arguing at the top of their voices. Inside the room, there is more clutter to wade through (a half-empty bottle of booze, crackers and crisps, loose newspaper pages) and sleazy sales talk to be rebuked before Max gets his tapes. At his office he watches an episode, with two of his vice-presidents, in which a naked, masturbating geisha is ganged up on by two samurai in warfare outfits.[13] 'What do you think?' he asks them. 'Oriental sex is a natural. It will get us an audience we never had before,' says Moses (*The Brood*'s Reiner Schwarz, a real-life broadcaster of cult status in Toronto – first as a riotous radio talk show host of the late 1960s, then as a rebel of the early MTV years (see Dale 1982)). Rafael (David Bolt) disagrees: 'Not tacky enough. Not tacky enough to turn me on. Too much class. Bad for sex.' 'Its too soft,' agrees Max, 'I'm looking for something that will break through. Something tough.'

According to Fredric Jameson, *Videodrome* 'triumphantly evades all high cultural qualities, from technical perfection to the discriminations of taste and the organon of beauty' (1992: 22). Besides its stress on the lower depths of culture (porn, illegal trafficking, cheap liquor, takeaway food, piracy, belly dancing), Jameson also refers to the clutter, dirt, tackiness, noise and flickers that abound in *Videodrome*. They give an acute impression of untidiness, near-chaos and unfinishedness that heightens the sense of paranoia, conspiracy and anxiety: where are we (the characters as well as the audience) to find the real clues, a guide or a sense of direction amidst this trash and filth? How to detect, like Max, what will make the right impact? So much stuff lying around gives every location Max finds himself in a feeling of exasperation and exhaustion. For Jameson, cluttered environments challenge capitalism's reliance on 'perfect ordering' (exemplified in glossiness, shiny technology, clean and sterile interiors, austere exteriors and so forth), because they challenge standardised routines which are used to make sense of the world. If too much stuff is always on display – as it is all the time in *Videodrome* – then too many things mean too many things, and all meaning evaporates. Jameson makes the comparison with the novels of Thomas Pynchon, and his use of 'entropic hyperboles' and 'endless interconnectedness' that give as prominent a place to details, asides and irrelevant bits and pieces of observation as they do to the core of the narrative.[14] Pynchon's novels are filled with clutter, through which a story is woven that is so hard to detect that the texture of the clutter frequently replaces it. For Pynchon, and for Jameson (who celebrates this technique as revolutionary) and apparently also for *Videodrome*, which visualises it in practically every shot, the 'texture of clutter' is not a burden of which the narrative needs to be cleansed, but a quality, for in its obscuring of true meaning (true taste, true enlightenment) it frees up all alternative kinds of meaning. At first, Max seems at home in this messy maze – he feels in charge of it, ready to look in its nooks and crannies for even dirtier stuff. So, soon after his unsuccessful meetings we find him in the shadows of gleaming skyscrapers, in a decrepit brick building with plaster peeling from the walls, in the company of the ragged Harlan (Peter Dvorsky), a DIY video pirate who clandestinely tapes shows for Max. Harlan shows him a raw excerpt of video material taped presumably from Malaysia in which two hooded men dressed in leather throw a screaming woman against an electrified clay wall, rip off her clothes and beat her. 'Grotesque, as promised,' smiles Harlan. Max's next stop is Rena King's (Lally Cadau) talk show, where he is placed opposite Nicki Brand (Deborah Harry), the host of the radio talk show 'Emotional Rescue', and media prophet Professor Brian O'Blivion (Jack Creley) – who only appears on a remote monitor (he explains he 'refuses to appear on television, except *on* television'). Asked if he cares about concerns that his station contributes to a 'social climate of violence and sexual malaise', Max responds: 'I care enough in fact to give my viewers a harmless outlet for their fantasies and their frustrations, and as far as I'm concerned that's a socially positive act.' Nicki disagrees, and argues that the 'overstimulated times' of today lead to 'craving stimulation for its own sake'. Max challenges Nicki's red dress – 'You know what Freud would have said about that dress' – and she welcomes the innuendo. Max shifts in his chair and leans towards her, about to make out. As Max makes his move, and the show's careful direction of classic TV-style medium-close shots disintegrates, Rena turns to O'Blivion on the monitor. But he ignores her prompt and prophesises idly about contemporary media and the special names, like O'Blivion, that everyone will soon have.

Max's television performance, and his cheeky upstaging of the talk show format, turning it into a dating show on the spot, is indicative of a formal arrangement of *Videodrome* that adds to the texture of clutter. Besides lots of stuff, dirt and props creating an 'overstimulation' for those seeking clear meanings and metaphors, the whole set-up of Rena King's show, and of numerous other scenes, displays a multitude of communication platforms through which such overstimulation can be mediated and amplified. When Max first talks to Nicki, we see her reply on the monitor of the camera that will capture her during the airing of the show. O'Blivion appears *only* on television. And by physically moving closer to Nicki (and out of the frame of his own 'camera view') Max upsets the neat triangle of shots (and triangle of meanings) the debate had attempted to carve. In the end, Rena is lost for words, and lost for meaning.

Such multiple platforms and channels complicate the confusion that the texture of clutter had already instigated – not just more stuff to deal with, but more ways through which it is presented. Moreover, a third factor conflates any process of meaning even further: when Max returns to Harlan and asks him, while watching another static-heavy episode of the torture show, which is called 'Videodrome', 'when the plot starts to unravel', a series of references kicks off that help position 'Videodrome' – and *Videodrome* – in the contemporary media landscape. 'There is no plot,' Harlan explains, 'it just goes on like that … It's a real sicko.' Max is in awe. 'Brilliant. It has almost no production costs and you can't take your eyes off it' – an almost prophetic reference to reality television. When Harlan also reveals it is US-made, from Pittsburgh no less, Max's interest increases.[15] But before he pursues 'Videodrome' any further, he pursues Nicki. She, too, is fascinated by 'Videodrome'. 'It ain't exactly sex,' warns Max when Nicki puts a tape in the VCR, expecting porn. 'Says who?' asks Nicki. As the flickering, distorted, noisy tape plays, Max and Nicki get comfortable. 'I like it,' Nicki confesses. They make passionate love on the floor as the torture and mayhem unfolds on the screen behind them. Max gently pierces Nicki's earlobes and licks the blood from the needles – the nearest Cronenberg has come to a vampire metaphor since Rose in *Rabid*. In slow motion, as if intoxicated, he blinks his eyes. As the camera travels back, the room appears strangely similar to the one in 'Videodrome', the clay wall looming over them. For the first time, there is a sense that hallucination is mixing with reality.

The next morning Max meets Masha (Lynne Gorman), one of his regular providers of soft porn. She shows him a pilot of her new show, 'Apollo and Dionysus'; it looks a lot like Tinto Brass's *Caligula* (1979). When Max informs her he wants to programme 'Videodrome', Masha offers to be his agent, 'to sell subterranean everywhere'. And Masha is not the only one interested. So is Nicki, who tells Max she is going to Pittsburgh to audition for 'Videodrome', even after he rudely warns her to stay away from these 'mondo weirdo video guys' – the next media reference, this time to the ilk of *Mondo Cane* (Gualtiero Jiacopetti/Paolo Cavara/Franco E. Prosperi, 1962) and *Cannibal Holocaust* (Ruggero Deodato, 1979). Nicki's response is to burn her breast with a cigarette and let a reluctant Max smoke it. Masha has also become reluctant. She alerts Max to the fact that 'Videodrome' is 'snuff TV' – a reference to the urban legend of snuff movies (films in which people appear to get killed on camera, *for* the camera), a legend several cheap exploitation movies, such as *Snuff* (Michael Findlay/ Roberta Findlay, 1976), successfully cashed in on. Masha also has a name for Max: Professor Brian O'Blivion.

The reference tour across plotless reality TV, porn, BDSM, porn chic, mondo cinema and snuff exploitation has made it clear that 'Videodrome' is to be ranked among the media's most notoriously controversial and outlawed exploitation. And Max wants it. Back amidst clutter, he walks from a littered street in the slums, filled with hastily applied leaflets, among a crowd of bums, with shouts of 'piss', 'shit' and 'fuck' audible in the background, into a building called the Cathode Ray Mission (a sort of mix between a Catholic church, a methadone clinic and a Salvation Army safe house for TV addicts, with flickering screens tuned to all kinds of stations). He searches for O'Blivion and finds his daughter Bianca (Sonja Smits), who informs him her father will contact Max to send him a message.

Gradually Max loses control over the messy maze. Increasingly intoxicated by the episodes of 'Videodrome' he keeps playing, he starts hallucinating. When Bridey walks by to drop off cassettes, and in passing tells him Nicki has gone missing, he hits her when she touches the VCR – what *we* see, from his point of view, is Max hitting Nicki. When he snaps out of his daze and apologises, Bridey claims he did not hit her at all. One of the tapes, she tells him before leaving, is from Brian O'Blivion. When Max touches the tape it breathes heavily, a sigh. For the first time in the film the music comes to the foreground, a heavy electronic organ sound. Max starts the tape and O'Blivion's face fills the screen. He tells Max that his 'reality is already half video hallucination'. He confides to Max, in direct address, that the visions he had caused a tumour that killed him. As he says this, he is violently strangled by a hooded person who turns out to be Nicki. 'I want you Max,' she says. Nicki's sweet, sensual voice lures Max closer to the television set on which the tape plays, until he puts his head against the screen, filled with Nicki's lips, and the set moans and groans heavily, bulging and bending under Max's caresses, until finally Max moves his head *into* the set, *into* Nicki's mouth.

The next day, Max brings the tape to Bianca. She discloses that it was her idea to give him the tape, knowing it would induce hallucinations. She also reveals that the 'Videodrome' signal was designed by O'Blivion to create tumours, initially in an attempt to turn mankind into an ameliorated technological animal. But O'Blivion's partners betrayed him, and he became the first victim. Now Bianca is dedicated to keeping her father's legacy (and good name) intact. Looking to know more, Max watches more O'Blivion tapes. But as the professor tells him 'there is nothing real outside our perception of reality' and Max, bored, scratches the gun he has started wearing against his abdomen, he suddenly notices his body has developed a huge vaginal slit there. Max feels compelled to put the gun inside it, virtually fist-fucking himself. When he pulls out, the gun is gone and so is the slit. In panic, Max trashes his flat, but the gun is presumably still in his newly-created womb.

As the clutter and multiple platforms increase – and the number of possible meanings with them – so do the hallucinations. As the lines between reality and distorted perception fade the number of meanings multiply, but it becomes more difficult to determine which ones can be trusted. Even the attempt of Barry Convex (Les Carlson), chief of special operations at the global corporation Spectacular Optical, the company now behind 'Videodrome', to answer all questions cannot change the nagging doubts that have entered Max's mind. After all, the garbage outside the Spectacular Optical office is piled visibly high, the door sticks a bit, loose-fitting flyers cover a wall, so many visors and sunglasses to try on ... there is just too much stuff around to narrow it all down to just a few meanings. Convex is convincing though, and Max lets himself be talked into having one of his hallucinations recorded while wearing a virtual-reality helmet (another new media reference; another additional channel of communication). But soon Max finds himself with a whip in his hands lashing at what he thinks is a television set embodying (or 'capturing') Nicki, whereas it turns out to be Masha. He wakes up and finds Masha's body next to him in bed, dead. His hallucinations are rampant now.

For the first time, Max switches off a channel – eliminating the static coming from the television set in his flat. But it is too late. When he calls Harlan for help, Harlan brings in Convex. They reveal that Max, as the owner of 'cesspool' Civic TV, was a target in their 'war' against the softness of North America. They forcibly insert a pulsating video tape into the slit in Max's belly, programming him into their cause. As Max crawls across the dusty, cracked, littered basement of Civic TV, in agony, he reaches into his stomach and pulls out the gun. It fixes itself into his hand and arm, becoming his own phallic fleshgun. An assassin for 'Videodrome' now, Max's first victims are Moses and Rafael; next up is Bianca. Max announces himself menacingly as he stands in the shadows of the Mission, but then he waivers. When Bianca says, 'It was to be you after all, you've come to kill me', he steps into the light and answers, 'No, I don't kill people'. As he retreats into the shadows again Bianca tricks him into a room with a television set, on which he watches Nicki being strangled on 'Videodrome'. The television turns to static and a gun protrudes from it. It shoots Max but he does not die. Reprogrammed now as a crusader for the 'video word made flesh', Bianca orders Max to turn on 'Videodrome' with the command 'Long live the new flesh'.

In what is arguably the most overstimulated and cluttered sequence in *Videodrome*, Max does exactly that. After having waited for the right moment across the street, next to a shabby homeless person trying to get passers-by to pay to 'see the monkey play' (the monkey being the small television set he has set up – another platform, another channel, more clutter), Max first confronts Harlan and kills him with a grenade he has Harlan pull out of his stomach slit (more clutter, obviously). He then crashes a Spectacular Optical convention, disrupts Convex's rallying speech and shoots him. As Convex writhes on the floor his head and chest split open and his intestines and brains spill onto the stage (the sounds of the eruptions appropriately amplified via yet another communication channel: the convention's intercom).

Max flees into the most desolate and decrepit shelter: an unused barge in the harbour. Amidst empty bottles, shreds of newspaper and garbage, he sees Nicki appear on a television set. She urges him to go on 'to the next phase', beyond death, 'to destroy his old flesh, and become the new flesh'. The set shows Max, amidst the rubble on the barge, walking towards a burning fire. He kneels down, puts the fleshgun against his head and as he declares 'Long live the new flesh' he pulls the trigger. The set explodes and its intestines spread across the floor of the barge. In a repeat of what he has seen on the set Max kneels down next to the fire, puts the fleshgun against his head and as he declares 'Long live the new flesh' he pulls the trigger – the only way out of the multi-meaning nightmare of multi-channel cable television clutter he had become.

From the Past to the Future: The Dead Zone

From a first-person story to another person's story: *The Dead Zone* was the first film Cronenberg based on other source material. It was a Stephen King novel published in 1979, adapted for the screen by Jeffrey Boam, under the aegis of producers Dino De Laurentiis and Debra Hill. From a macroscopic point of view *The Dead Zone* can easily be seen as an attempt to cash in on what was at the time fast becoming a Stephen King mania, at least judged by the rush with which his novels and stories were being developed into films and television series. Films such as *Carrie* and *The Shining* (Stanley Kubrick, 1980) had demonstrated there was mileage, commercially and aesthetically, in adapting King material for the screen, and the writer's popularity as a chief representative of the widening cult of horror (reinforced by his confessional personal history of the horror film, *Danse Macabre*, 1981) made eager producers grab every opportunity to exploit the momentum. By the time *The Dead Zone* was being released, in 1983–84, at least six other King films were unleashed upon film and video audiences globally. All of these were well embedded in the cult of horror, and came with good credentials. *Creepshow* (1982) was an omnibus of five short monster stories that did reasonably well on video, mostly because George A. Romero directed it; *Cujo* (1983), directed by Lewis Teague (who had made *Alligator* in 1980), had a fairly wide release and did well before finding an audience among avid fans of video horror (and receiving scorn from those expecting a *Howling*-like werewolf tale); *Christine* (1983) was the first in a series of lesser John Carpenter films and while it did well at festivals (especially in Avoriaz in 1984, where *The Dead Zone* was screened as well) it was seen as a sign of fatigue in the director; *Firestarter* (Mark L. Lester, 1984), with Drew Barrymore, was very well received on video and cable but its reach remained limited; *Children of the Corn* (Fritz Kiersch, 1984) never really got much visibility beyond the US (where it did not do too badly) and a few chequered festival screenings.[16]

Intended as a Hollywood project, Cronenberg was only brought on board well into the planning of *The Dead Zone* (see Lucas 1982d); that did not prevent him from having considerable input. The entire project was shot in Ontario, and with the exception of composer Howard Shore, who was replaced by Michael Kamen, Cronenberg could rely on his trusted team of collaborators. Troupe veterans Jack Messinger, Géza Kovács, Peter Dvorsky and Leslie Carlson were cast in supporting parts. Two-time Cronenberg actor Nicholas Campbell was initially promised the lead role, but was ultimately moved to a smaller (yet essentially Cronenbergian) part in favour of Hollywood star Christopher Walken – the laconic attitude Walken and Campbell display in *The Dead Zone* adds much to the film's melancholic and near somnambulistic atmosphere, a feat often credited to Walken for which Campbell deserves equal credit. The genre pedigrees of Walken (*Brainstorm*; *Last Embrace* (Jonathan Demme, 1979)) and co-stars Brooke Adams (*Invasion of the Body Snatchers*), Tom Skerritt

(*Alien*) and Herbert Lom (*Mark of the Devil* (Michael Armstrong, 1970), among many others), and producers De Laurentiis (*King Kong* (John Guillermin, 1976); *Conan the Barbarian* (John Milius, 1982)) and Hill (the *Halloween* franchise), gave the project an additional edge, upon which the fan press happily started speculating. All of this meant that in contrast with *Videodrome*, *The Dead Zone* would above all be judged by comparison: as a horror film, as a King adaptation, as another famous horror director's take on King and as a Cronenberg project.

The Dead Zone opens with images of a rustic, idyllic countryside with wooden houses, swirling empty roads lined with telegraph poles, white picket fences and rolling hills dotted with majestic, old oak trees – images more in tune with slasher films' devious impressions of tranquility in tiny towns forgotten by time than with Cronenberg's usual urban and hypermodern pulsating nervousness. After the title credit music, a school bell is the first sound we hear: a reassuring sound of civilisation, order and steady progress. It is a few days before Halloween. Teacher Johnny Smith (Christopher Walken) is reading to his class from Edgar Allen Poe's *The Raven*. Everything breathes an air of serenity: the map of North America on the wall, the tweed jacket, corduroy trousers and glasses worn by Johnny, the books in order on the shelves, even the sombre conclusion of *The Raven* ('*and my soul, from out that shadow, that lies floating on the floor, shall be lifted nevermore*'), which Johnny quotes out loud, seems subdued, reduced to nothing more than nostalgia and melancholy.

The tone of the opening minutes slips *The Dead Zone* into a mood prevailing in a lot of films of the time, one that reaches far outside the generic frame of reference of horror and King: early 1980s film culture, exhausted by the experiments and revolutions of the 1960s and 1970s, and no doubt encouraged by a political turn towards conservatism (embodied by President Ronald Reagan) is characterised by a desire to represent an idealised past from before all the attempts to construct a better world. This attitude involves an interest in fixing the past instead of the future, as it were, partly because many of the paths towards the future had fast become blocked (cluttered, in the case of *Videodrome*) dead end streets. Films expressed this nostalgia in two major ways: a tone of melancholy, and literal attempts to return to the past in order to undo, or redo, it – usually by enlisting special effects to suggest actual time travel.[17] *The Dead Zone*'s opening minutes are emblematic of the first expression, and much of that tone is kept alive throughout the film in terms of acting style, music and locations – not just the unnamed town which hosts the opening segments, but also subsequent towns such as Castle Rock and Ridgeway, all of which are at one time or another home to Johnny.

The reason Johnny becomes such a wanderer lies in a tragic accident and its aftermath. After assigning *The Legend of Sleepy Hollow*, which Johnny recommends to his pupils as a story about 'a teacher who gets chased by a headless demon', he takes his fiancée Sarah Bracknell (Brooke Adams) to the local theme park for a rollercoaster ride. Johnny does not enjoy the ride. Dizziness and a headache overcome him. He declines the invitation to come inside Sarah's house with a gallant 'some things are worth waiting for' and drives off. On the way home he has a terrible car accident that throws him into a five-year-long coma. When he regains consciousness, Sarah is married to someone else, and Johnny's mother (Jackie Burroughs) has become a religious devotee – clinging to faith has obviously helped her to cope. Under the guidance of Doctor Sam Weizak (Herbert Lom) Johnny begins his recovery. But then strange things happen: when he touches the hand of a nurse he 'sees' her daughter inside their burning house, screaming for help and rescued by firemen. Later, when he touches Weizak's hand, he 'sees' into his past, into the hell of World War Two, how he got separated from his parents during the German invasion of Poland. Johnny also 'sees' that Weizak's parents did not perish, but are alive and well, and living in California. Weizak soon discovers Johnny speaks the truth, yet he does not re-acquaint with his parents. 'It wasn't meant to be,' he says.

Johnny's new talents trouble him as much as they help others. They keep him on guard, reluctant – unable to reconnect to Sarah when she visits him, unable to help his mother after she has a heart attack – and they also give him increasingly bad headaches whenever he uses them, for instance when a journalist (Peter Dvorsky) challenges him to a demonstration. He grows frustrated. When Sheriff Bannerman (Tom Skerritt) of nearby Castle Rock asks Johnny if he is willing to help find a serial killer, Johnny is – again – reluctant to help, dismissing the Sheriff's appeal to help in God's name. 'God threw a truck at me,' Johnny replies bitterly, in a jibe at religion not uncommon to many of Cronenberg's films, and one which recurs poignantly in *A History of Violence*, which *The Dead Zone* bears much resemblance to (see chapter ten, note 4). Johnny seems to want to live according to his favourite line from *Sleepy Hollow*: '*As he was a bachelor and in nobody's debt, nobody troubled their head about him anymore.*'

But then Sarah visits again, around Christmas time, with her baby son Denny, and they warm to each other. Over dinner, Johnny's father (Sean Sullivan) remarks how good it is 'to have a family eating around this table again'. It is an image hitherto unseen in a Cronenberg film; although it is only a resemblance of a family, and Johnny and Sarah do not push their feelings for each other any further, the dinner scene is at the same time testament to the nostalgia for security and melancholy so overly present in many other early 1980s films, and a sign of how Cronenberg's oeuvre itself is warming, ever so slightly, to the idea of family happiness – a sharp contrast to Max's meals in *Videodrome*, always eaten on the go, always alone. The short happy family congregation makes Johnny decide to help Sheriff Bannerman after all. When he is given the opportunity to touch the hand of yet another victim, a young girl, he 'sees' the murder happen. He is unable to intervene but he does recognise the perpetrator: Bannerman's deputy Frank Dodd (Nicholas Campbell). Bannerman and Johnny hurry to Dodd's house, where his mother (Colleen Dewhurst) holds them up long enough for Dodd to act out a meticulously prepared and chillingly executed suicide ritual. Dressed in a long rubber oil slicker, he plants the pair of scissors used to kill the girl upwards on the bathroom sink. He kneels in front of them, with his hands folded behind his head and with his eyes and mouth wide open as in a trance, and pushes his head onto the sharp scissor blades slamming them into the hard palate of his mouth. Bannerman and Johnny find Dodd dead, the scissors sticking out of his mouth, his body still quivering. In a film with so few explicitly shocking images

Suicide with style: Nicholas Campbell in *The Dead Zone*

the scene stands out as a truly flinch-inducing Cronenbergian touch. As he backs away, Johnny is shot and wounded by Dodd's mother. The incident puts Johnny off using his talents again. He moves to another town, where he tries to cope with the headaches (and a worsening limp) that are slowly destroying his body. He resumes private tutoring. In a lesson we notice *Sleeping Beauty* appears to have been added to the curriculum – another melancholic story about the 'passing of time'.

But that mood changes when Johnny is drawn out once more, like a retired, reluctant gunfighter, and this time something has changed – there is a blank spot in the visions he has, a 'dead zone', which means he can alter the course of events. This is where *The Dead Zone* starts toying with the second expression of altering the passing of time: 'fixing it'. In most films from the 1980s that tinker with time it is the past that is fixed, not the future, but fitting the forward-looking oeuvre of Cronenberg *The Dead Zone* aims to intervene into the future. Again it is winter. Johnny runs into Greg Stillson (Martin Sheen), a God-invoking, brashly campaigning conservative candidate for the Senate displaying a fanatic optimism ('My God, what a glorious day!' he shouts). According to the father of a child Johnny is tutoring (and whose life he saves a little later), Stillson is a dangerous populist. His curiosity piqued by the fact Sarah is one of Stillson's volunteers, Johnny attends a rally. He shakes Stillson's hand and 'sees' the candidate will, once elected president, cause a nuclear holocaust. Determined to prevent this he gets out an old rifle, travels to another Stillson rally, hides in the wings and when Stillson starts his speech, aims over the balcony to shoot him. Sarah, who is present with her husband and baby Denny, sees him and screams. For a second, Johnny is distracted; his first shot misses. Stillson grabs Sarah's baby and uses it as a shield. His bodyguard shoots Johnny straight through the heart. As Johnny lies dying he touches the hand of an outraged Stillson. He 'sees' a picture of Stillson hiding behind the baby on the cover of *Newsweek*. The scandal will end Stillson's career, and save the world. 'It's finished' Johnny sighs. He dies in Sarah's arms.

'You are either in possession of a very new human ability, or a very old one' Doctor Weizak says at one point to Johnny. He means it can be used towards the past as well as towards the future. For the most part *The Dead Zone* points towards Johnny's past, and his nostalgia for the happy times with Sarah he was supposed to have. That is why for many the film is romantic, typical for the 1980s. But in its last segments *The Dead Zone* substitutes its yearning for a past that never existed for an intervention into the present, aimed at the future. At that point it becomes a typical Cronenberg film.

The wolf is loose: surveillance and assassination

'We make inexpensive glasses for the Third World, and missile guidance systems for NATO,' touts Barry Convex of Spectacular Optical in *Videodrome*. With the same glee, and a bit more fanaticism, Stillson announces 'the missiles are flying' in *The Dead Zone*.

Missiles were everywhere in the early 1980s, so it is no surprise the cult of horror fared extremely well at the time. But beyond fear was a sensibility broader than horror, that seemed less tangible and controllable, yet more menacing: paranoia. Rampant technology was seen to pose a firm threat to mankind when put into the hands of the military, bureaucracies and corporations, either by facilitating around-the-clock surveillance to keep citizens in check, or by handing them the means to obliterate whoever opposed them. Paranoia became a term that expressed a fear more worrying than monsters from wherever. The fact that computer-guided sound barrier-breaking nuclear missiles could just annihilate entire communities without so much as an air siren or a whizzing wind announcing the destruction created a constant feeling of anxiety – comparable in tension, though not in magnitude, with the memory of the evacuation and deportation that was buried deep inside Doctor Weizak in *The Dead Zone*. 'The wolf is loose,' Johnny whispers when he recalls Weizak's separation from his mother when German soldiers invaded the ghetto. It is an expression that means that danger is – always – imminent and one can never relax or assume it is over. It is no wonder Weizak does not want to call his mother after all those years. He does not want to revive those traumas again; the wolf is not to be let loose again.

Videodrome and *The Dead Zone* are obsessed with paranoid anxiety. It puts them in check with the paranoia embedded in the suspicion of new social movements towards the high-tech arms race, nuclear missiles, nuclear energy, computer controls for weapons systems, military technocracy, mass communications technologies and mass media corporations (and its concentrations and convergences), much of it encapsulated in the assassination attempt of American president Ronald Reagan in 1981, and at that same president's megalomaniacal 'Star Wars' project – in itself an expression of paranoia.[18] The two films are not alone in that fascination. In fact, they share their paranoia with many other films of the time, such as most of the King adaptations mentioned earlier, the first two *Mad Max* films (George Miller, 1979; 1981), *Blow Out* (Brian De Palma, 1981), *Blade Runner* (Ridley Scott, 1982), *Dune*

(David Lynch, 1984), *1984* (Michael Radford, 1984), *Brazil* (Terry Gilliam, 1984) and *Body Double* (Brian De Palma, 1984).[19] It is also present in the highly influential novels of Thomas Pynchon, whose collection *Slow Learner* (1984) appeared around the time (and who would later write the definitive 1980s paranoia novel, *Vineland* (1990), a sort of Californian version of *Videodrome*), and in a movement more or less inspired by Pynchon (especially his *The Crying of Lot 49* (1966) and *Gravity's Rainbow*, (1973)), the so-called cyberpunk wave of new literature, of which William Gibson's *Neuromancer* was the epitome. Cyberpunk's obsession with paranoia and conspiracies became a tag for narratives about threats posed by technology in frequently bleak and dystopic social settings, with ambiguous endings.[20]

In *Videodrome* and *The Dead Zone*, Max and Johnny are clearly distrustful of any representations of technology they encounter – they are both psychologically tainted. Max scolds practically every form of technology he encounters, and though Johnny encounters far fewer and far less spectacular forms of technology, he also profoundly distrusts any he comes across, most visibly the 'science' Doctor Weizak represents and the 'politics and missiles' Stillson stands for. But it is in two of paranoia's most visible pathologies, surveillance and assassination, that both films really explore how the state of mind of their main characters also leads to actions and events that alter the lives of other characters and, hence, the world they live in. After all, everyone can be paranoid, but only through actions of surveillance and assassination might it affect the rest of us.

Let us start with *Videodrome*. At its most basic level, Max's paranoia is part of his narcissism. Everything in the film, and in Max's world, is about him, or so he believes and perceives it. So, naturally, he is paranoid about what everything means, and only his reluctance to become engaged – in relationships, conversations (he cuts off several people in the film) and people (observe how disrespectfully he treats Bridey or Masha for instance) – saves him from becoming so obsessed with everything it would incapacitate him. At the same time, his disengagement is also a symptom of his paranoia, making him steer clear of traps, set-ups and pitfalls. The 'Videodrome' show challenges that fragile equilibrium, because it gives Max the impression that getting involved (in the illegal taping, the watching, the participating) adds another level of excitement to life. This is drug-seeking behaviour or, as Nicki has it, 'craving stimulation for its own sake'; something Max's drinking and chain smoking leads us to believe he is prone to anyway. If we see *Videodrome* purely from Max's perspective, what happens next is only the hallucination of an addict unable to differentiate between fiction and reality.

But there is a bigger scope, and that is where technology really matters. *Videodrome* also asks us to assume that what is happening to Max can, and indeed *will*, happen to anyone. There are powers that *make* us addicted; powers, as in George Orwell's *1984* (1949), that look over us to make sure we comply (the surveillance); and that intervene if we don't (the assassination). Throughout the film runs the impression, made explicit in so many anxious news reports of the time, that 'things have gone too far'; that because of the fast progress in technology society has entered a stage where anyone exposed, even without the predisposition Max has (or, one could argue, without the inoculation Max's history as a sleaze-pro has given him), will be hooked to 'violence' and 'sex' and, especially, the combination of both (some of these anxieties will be detailed below).[21] Moreover, beyond that contemporary concern, *Videodrome* also adds the impression that someone is in charge of it all. There are numerous clues that point to this bigger scope, all of them hinting that there is 'something more', like an 'underlying structure' (if there is more, what does it look like?), and a conspiracy (who controls it?): there are Max's references to 'political prisoners'; there is Harlan's appearance, a cross between a Sandinista guerrilla and a terrorist; there is his not-to-be-misunderstood party programme: 'North America is getting soft, patrón,' he says, 'and the rest of the world is getting tough, very tough. We're entering savage new times'; there are, also, the posters in the background of *Videodrome*: Max's office has posters of fictitious films called *Something* and *Up from the Depths*; those in his flat, of static (it *could* also be a really elaborate maze), of the moon landing (a long-standing, popular subject of paranoid and conspiratorial speculation), of a big eye (like the one present in virtually every poster and title sequence for reality television), of 1970s pop culture's most chameleonic narcissistic paranoiac, David Bowie – all of these clues lead us to believe there is more 'out there', controlling us.

The surveillance is represented by two competing organisations in *Videodrome*: the Cathode Ray Tube Mission of the O'Blivions and Spectacular Optical. Both are primarily associated with 'eyes' and 'watching', and with the period in Western history that highlights those activities for the first time through technology: the Renaissance.[22] Spectacular Optical's slogan is 'keeping an eye on the world', and their cover is an optical fashion design company – Max tries on several pairs of their glasses before he is made to put on the VR-helmet that will survey his hallucinations. Spectacular Optical's most elaborate show is their annual convention, which has 'Medici' (one of the benefactors of the Italian Renaissance) as a theme. Dancers choreograph a Renaissance play, with a painting of Michelangelo in the background and 'love comes in at the eye' and 'the eye is the window of the soul' as eye-catching tag lines on display around it. At the Mission, Bianca's office is decorated, in contrast with the design of the other locations, in a very elaborate Renaissance style: busts, torsos, books, etchings and drawings, figurines, chess boards, wooden furniture, elaborate tapestries, statuettes, candles, a stained glass window with an armoured saint, a beautifully illustrated handwritten book on a cathedra, all representing the O'Blivions' belief that the world only exists if it is represented through observation and reproduction. What differentiates the Renaissance obsession of the O'Blivions from that of Spectacular Optical is their emphasis on representations outside the system of mass-technological reproduction. In that sense, they are purists, believers of some sort, in what Walter Benjamin (1969) has called the aura of uniqueness of a representation – the fact there is only one original representation.

The assassination element of *Videodrome* is only briefly explored, through Max's role as a hired hand/gun. First, he is programmed to assassinate on behalf of Spectacular Optical and, after his conversion by Bianca O'Blivion, he turns on them on behalf of the O'Blivions. In each case, Max is pretty lethal. In fact, the only time he falters, when Bianca overturns him, is when he has a rare moment of clarity and steps out of the shadows, literally, to announce he is no killer. Still, Max's actions do not seem to change much. Not only does the film end before we are to find out if he was effective, and not only would there be no way of checking that effectiveness objectively because we only see events from Max's subjective perspective (he might not even have shot anyone at all; O'Blivion pointedly reminds him, and us, 'there is nothing outside our perception of reality'), the last sequence leads us to believe Max, and the rest of us, are now so beyond assassinations as a means to win the battle that we might as well just move on 'to the next phase'. Whatever that may be.

We should now consider *The Dead Zone*. Max's hallucinations are wholesome; they do not have many breaks and lapses that pull him out of his daze (the brief moment described above is an exception). Johnny Smith, on the other hand, only has a few moments in which 'real' reality is interrupted in favour of visions, and those moments are really the only instances of surveillance in *The Dead Zone*. The main difference is that Johnny is not too narcissistic but too altruistic; he is not after gain for himself – all he wants is to be left alone – but he does care for others: the girl in the burning house, the girls of Castle Rock, the pupil in danger of falling through the ice, the fate of the world, and Sarah, of course. His altruism is so well developed that he cannot help but help, unless he creates a 'controlled environment' in which he can avoid that urge. After the Castle Rock incident he has learned not to touch others anymore, not to open their letters, so he does not get to know their problems and does not have to act.

But then Stillson appears. At first he just seems brash, not dangerous. One reason for that is that Stillson's supporters are more sympathetic characters than the ones backing Spectacular Optical or the O'Blivions: Sarah is a good woman, as is Roger Stuart (Anthony Zerbe), the father of one of Johnny's pupils, who puts him in touch with Stillson – he even calls the politician a 'turkey', saying that he only supports him because it is dangerous not to be Stillson's friend. In fact, if we distrust Johnny's visions as much as we distrust Max's, there is only one scene that really shows us Stillson is a menace. In a short scene after the character of Stillson is introduced an event occurs whose sole purpose is to demonstrate to the audience that Stillson is indeed *bad*. Stillson and his henchman Sonny (Géza Kovács) blackmail a newspaper editor, Brenner (Les Carlson), whose paper is ready to spill the dirt on Stillson's background. Brenner is silenced by the threat that if he publishes his evidence pictures of him frolicking with prostitutes will be made public too; he backs off and Stillson continues his campaign. The fact that Johnny is not present in the scene (and indeed never finds out about it) makes it objectively real, and it gives the audience an understanding of why Johnny's hunch about Stillson is correct, and he needs to be eliminated.

When Johnny does act, and turns to assassination, he is even less effective than Max: he does not even kill Stillson. It is only fate that makes Stillson hold a baby as a shield and end his career. At least Johnny's actions did indeed really take place. There is no doubt, as there is in the case of Max, that he did shoot. Actually, it is *because* Johnny's actions exist objectively that they are less effective than Max's, and that they come across as 'unfinished' (or, as Johnny calls it, they have 'a dead zone'), less perfect than the fiction Max dreams up. It almost points to another one of O'Blivion's aphorisms: 'reality is less than television'. But the outcome of his actions, though we are made privy to them, is not to be measured. We will never really know what would have happened had he not shot, and had Stillson not used the baby as a shield.

If they are both ineffective, equally the result of the psychological obsessions of the main characters (Max is too narcissistic, Johnny too altruistic), then what makes *The Dead Zone*'s assassination attempt look so much more reasonable than the ones in *Videodrome*? The reason that makes Johnny's actions seem sensible lies in an understanding the audience has about Stillson's true nature as a crook. The blackmail scene gives that proof objectively, at least on the level of the narrative. Another scene confirms that this warrants attention. Johnny asks Doctor Weizak if 'knowing what you know now, if you had the chance to kill Hitler, would you?'. Weizak first resists the question, then adds that as a scientist, concerned with the well-being of mankind, he certainly would; just cause, in other words. But on a wider level this just cause is also provided by the awkward similarities between real-life politicians and politics, and Stillson. Audiences are more likely to agree that Stillson is a menace because of the frame of reference of political corruption, assassination attempts on politicians, sleaze politics, gung-ho conservatives, Christian fanaticism and muscle-rolling gun-boat politics betraying diplomatic negotiations with the kind of threats to 'nuke everyone' (that certainly did it for me), that they have been able to observe in real life. The scene in which a power-mad Stillson, dressed in bathrobes like a decadent Roman emperor, high on religious zeal, uses *The Dead Zone*'s most sophisticated piece of technology (a handscanner that checks the identity of those pressing the red button) to start a war in the name of biblical 'destiny' was very close to reality in the 1980s (and still is). 'Hallelujah. Hallelujah,' says Stillson as he sends the missiles on their way. Because of the paranoia rippling through the last stretches of the Cold War such a scene seemed real enough. Hence Johnny's cause was more sympathetic than Max's, even if both of them were ineffective.

'Halfway to Real Respect': The Reception of Videodrome and The Dead Zone

In 1981 John McCarty published *Splatter Movies*, a book documenting the 'brave new wave' of gore-filled horror films causing a furore at the end of the 1970s and early 1980s. In an interview, McCarty asked Cronenberg about his status. Cronenberg replied: 'I'm half way to real respect, I suppose, though still not totally there at all' (1981: 108). *Videodrome* and *The Dead Zone* added considerably to Cronenberg's overall reputation, especially since they could act as a double feature. The reception of *Videodrome* stretched almost across half a decade, from the anticipation of the film in 1981 to the last releases in 1985. That of *The Dead Zone* was more concentrated, encompassing less than two years (1983 and 1984). In several territories, especially in Europe, they virtually coincided .

In North America, *Videodrome* and *The Dead Zone* were released about nine months apart. Universal granted *Videodrome* a fairly wide release in major theatres but, in a change from previous releases, did not give it the chance to garner momentum, and instead pulled it fairly quickly. Cronenberg recalls feeling 'it had been a mistake to release the film wide; ... it should have been handled as an art film, and been given slow, deliberate promotion, using critical response to promote it' (in Rodley 1997: 101). *Videodrome* did not do as well as *Scanners*, but reviewers agreed it was an intriguing, rewarding experience. Most of the fan press seemed to like it, especially *Cinefantastique* and *L'Écran fantastique* which raved about it. *Starlog* and *Heavy Metal* found the film almost incomprehensible but published positively-inclined interviews.[23] The professional film press was enthusiastic, and gave it high marks,[24] as did the nationwide North American press and the international press (the exceptions were the *Washington Post* and the *Christian Science Monitor*).[25] The Canadian press linked the film to contemporary debates about censorship and the levels of sex and violence on pay- and cable TV, and even to representations of AIDS, but that did not prevent eminent outlets from liking *Videodrome*.[26] Apart from a few grumbling local voices it appeared adversity towards the film was limited, perhaps more the result of high-profile critics wanting to demarcate themselves from the 'Cronenberg-haters' and align themselves with someone who was seen as one of the most intelligent horror filmmakers.

In the UK, the only other country in which *Videodrome* was released before *The Dead Zone*, in November 1983, it was less favourably received, but that was no exception from Cronenberg's usual reception there until the mid-1980s.[27] Those countries seeing *Videodrome* only after *The Dead Zone*, gave it an even more positive reception than in North America: in France, Belgium, Italy and Germany reviewers agreed *Videodrome* had become a key work in Cronenberg's oeuvre. The box office success and unanimously glowing reception of *The Dead Zone* worldwide, and especially its high praise at the Fantasy Festivals of Avoriaz (where it won an award) and Brussels (where it screened together with *Videodrome*, which Cronenberg had brought along with him), surely helped *Videodrome* get a better press – all the more so because it could be pitched as a 'pure' Cronenberg untainted by the Hollywood and King 'compromises' that *The Dead Zone* had to endure.[28] *The Dead Zone*'s success unlocked new platforms of exposure for Cronenberg, attracting press attention for *Videodrome* which came tagging along in its wake. In return, *Videodrome*'s sense of an incomplete experiment, with its seriousness, its loose ends and angles and its chequered, almost sneaky release gave it the feel of a true 'discovery' – a brilliant failure misunderstood by the world. It had the Francophone and Italian press raving, and it created a whole new platform of appreciation for Cronenberg, who had now become an 'auteur' in his own right.[29]

Besides the higher quantity of public presence caused by the double reception of *Videodrome* and *The Dead Zone*, there was also an increase in quality. Not only, as indicated above, did more and more reviewers sway towards appreciating Cronenberg, and not only did audiences come to see *The Dead Zone* in bigger numbers than any previous Cronenberg film, the endorsements became also, gradually, more precious. Andy Warhol famously called *Videodrome* the *Clockwork Orange* of the 1980s; John Carpenter called Cronenberg the 'only real artist' in the horror genre; and Martin Scorsese endorsed Cronenberg on several occasions, pitching him as a director whose films were 'so good you can only see them once' on the *The Late Show* with David

Letterman (see Lucas 1982a). Heavyweight critics like Andrew Sarris also moved to the defence of Cronenberg, dismissing old adversaries like Robin Wood as outdated (see 1983: 43). But by far the biggest endorsement came from academia. In 1983, the Academy of Canadian Cinema dedicated a full volume to the films of Cronenberg, entitled *The Shape of Rage* (a reference to a book title in *The Brood*) with scores of praise for his work – the only exception being an essay by Robin Wood in which he repeated his attack on Cronenberg from 1979 (see chapter four). The book was tied to a double retrospective at the Toronto International Film Festival: all of Cronenberg's films were screened, including the elusive *Stereo* and *Crimes of the Future* (they would also be screened in Los Angeles a few months later) and he was allowed to select an idiosyncratic canon of science fiction cinema that would also be screened (the list included *Un chien andalou* (*An Andalusian Dog*, Luis Buñuel/Salvador Dalí, 1929), *Zéro de conduite* (*Zero for Conduct*, Jean Vigo, 1933) and *Taxi Driver*).[30] The Shape of Rage received good reviews and Cronenberg's reputation, and that of his 'sturdy cult' (Testa 1983), was certainly lifted a few steps up the cultural ladder by it. Also in 1983, the first English-language PhD dissertation featuring more than a passing mention of Cronenberg was successfully defended (Sharrett 1983). In 1984, the British Film Institute (BFI) devoted a full dossier to Cronenberg – one in which Scorsese repeated his glowing endorsement (1984: 54). Like *The Shape of Rage*, the BFI dossier was constructed around a retrospective. It also featured an interview with Cronenberg, and added interesting essays on his television work. The inclusion of an essay on Cronenberg in Barry Keith Grant's reader on the horror genre, also published in 1984, further cemented Cronenberg's status as key to understanding contemporary popular cinema. For the first time, critics started using the term 'thematic consistency' without a shred of irony – probably the last to use it jokingly was James Woods on the set of *Videodrome*, after he had been reading some reviews of Cronenberg's films. Cronenberg happily played along. No doubt he enjoyed Woods' critical praise in the form of a joke more than Robin Wood's (1983) politically inspired resistance.

The nascent academic appreciation of Cronenberg did not really politicise his reputation (though Wood certainly tried in his chapter in *The Shape of Rage*) so much as made it more philosophical, tying it to a wide range of thinkers on the functions of technology, sexual repression and violence in society. Christopher Sharrett's observation, for instance, that Cronenberg 'recapitulates René Girard's notion that "violence, if left unappeased, will accumulate until it overflows and contaminates the surrounding area"' (1983: 106), notes the link with violence but then moves on to see this as a theoretical and philosophical issue, rather than one that pertains to have an immediate function (as a warning or promotion). Other cherished references used across academia and the press included René Descartes, Kenneth Anger, William Burroughs, Paul Klee, Jean Baudrillard, Vladimir Nabokov and Marshall McLuhan – more weight than the label 'Baron of Blood' could bear.

The long-term reception of *Videodrome* has only added admiration for the film, up to the point where it has now become indeed a key to Cronenberg's work, the discriminator between the 'early' and 'mature' Cronenberg. Since the mid-1980s, the film did increasingly well, at art-house screenings, on video and on cable TV – quite fitting for its theme. The film's status within Cronenberg's oeuvre is unsurpassed. At this juncture in time it is the only Cronenberg film to which an entire book is devoted, and its DVD edition, through the highly acclaimed Criterion Collection, is the most elaborate of all his films.[31] Though not of a cult status comparable to *The Brood* and *Scanners* – it is probably *too* serious for that – it easily features on many cult canon lists.[32] *The Dead Zone* has also done well, but less so as a Cronenberg piece. It is still popular as a Stephen King adaptation (regarded as one of the best ever), but most of its thematic preoccupations are now sidelined in favour of a nostalgic appreciation – exactly the kind the second half of the film resisted. More important than their separate long-term receptions, however, is the fact that when put together *Videodrome* and *The Dead Zone* signalled how Cronenberg had successfully bridged the gap between fandom and academia and moved towards universal admiration.[33]

'Video Nasties' and censorship: politics by proxy
One aspect of the reception of *Videodrome* and *The Dead Zone* that did become highly politicised was its affiliation with controversies and scandals involving censorship. Strictly speaking, it had nothing to do with the films themselves, but meant a lot for the public profile of Cronenberg in countries such as Canada and the UK, and it greatly affected the long-term reputation of Cronenberg as a liberal filmmaker. Cronenberg was no stranger to censorship (see chapters two and four). Even when his films were uninvolved, parallels would be drawn that would politicise his work beyond his intentions.[34] With *Videodrome*, the issue started even before the film was released, in 1982, and in 1984 it exploded.

Spooked by the excessive use of special effects in horror movies, and by ancillary factors, reports started appearing about the 'worrying signs' of what all that excessive imagery would do to audiences. Some of these ancillary factors included random information, such as the fact that John Hinckley, who tried to assassinate Ronald Reagan in 1981 claimed to have been influenced by *Taxi Driver*. Others were the result of campaigns that singled out titles, such as the feminist attack on pornography (which started out as a civil rights issue but soon spun out of control in the hands of zealous pressure groups), or the actions of some overly ardent local authorities – the police of Antwerp confiscating a print of *The Texas Chainsaw Massacre* from a theatre, the Brussels justice department seizing copies of *Faces of Death* or German and Manchester police raiding video stores. Most of these actions stemmed from insecurity: about the rapid expansion of the video porn industry, mondo cinema and sensationalist documentaries (like *The Killing of America* (Sheldon Renan, 1981)); about labour relations in the ever-changing media industries (regularly combined with worries over health and safety regulations); about unfamiliarity with the aggressive marketing techniques of new distribution companies such as Vipco (distributor of *Driller Killer* (Abel Ferrara, 1979)), Go Video (distributor of *Cannibal Holocaust*), Wizard Video (distributor of *Terminal Island* (Stephanie Rothman, 1979) and *The Boogeyman*) or New Line Cinema (which released *The Evil Dead*); about inadequate regulation guidelines for new carriers (such as cable TV or video); and about laws ill-equipped to prosecute and/or protect consumers, employees and the interests of the industry. Before long, these ancillary factors became so intertwined a politically volatile climate emerged that allowed politicians and self-proclaimed moral crusaders to lump actual and simulated, real and fictional, implicit and explicit, representations of sex and violence together as an 'issue' that needed tackling, and action taken against. The tone also became more aggressive and accusatory. Many reports featured Cronenberg's name, often in the vicinity of films such as *The Evil Dead*, *Bloodsucking Freaks* (Joel Reed, 1980) and *Incubus* (John Hough, 1981) (see Stein 1982). As one report claimed:

> Nobody who pays to see *Bloodsucking Freaks* ('Scenes of nude women guillo-tined, drilled in the head and otherwise mistreated will turn off most viewers' – *Variety*) is likely to expect Julie Andrews among the flowers. And those who ventured to David Cronenberg's *Scanners* ('10 seconds: the pain begins; 15 seconds: you can't breathe; 20 seconds: your head explodes') were anticipating not intelligence, but brains. (Williams 1982: D1)

If nothing else, it made Cronenberg wary of the possibilities of censorship; and it made him acutely sensitive to the differences in rating and censorship systems between the United States and Ontario, Canada (a complaint he insisted hampered Canadian film culture).[35]

Throughout 1983 and 1984 Cronenberg was forced to position himself, and his work, against several implications and conjectures. The first was the so-called 'Video Nasties' controversy in the United Kingdom. Acting upon a request to provide video retailers with a list of titles likely to be impounded or seized if stocked (to save them from random raids such as the ones by Manchester police, but also to make retailers aware of their rights and duties), in 1982 the Director of Public Prosecutions published a list of 74 film titles, dubbed 'Video Nasties' by the press, that had at one point or another been investigated; not one of them was a Cronenberg film. It took until 1984 before a new law gave the British Board of Film Classification (BBFC) the authority to regulate and censor videos – which led to the prosecution of 39 titles. Consumer and moral campaigning groups (such as Mary Whitehouse's National Viewers' and Listeners' Association) and the British press (most notably the *Sunday Times* and *Daily Mail*) gave the 'Video Nasties' list a lot of publicity and created a national media hysteria around the 'issue'.[36] In the course of their campaign many titles were implicated, including *The Brood*, *Scanners* and *Videodrome*, whose video release was postponed, even after receiving three crucial cuts.

At the same time, in his native Canada Cronenberg had to cross swords with the Ontario Censorship Board; a board that had banned films such as Bernardo Bertoluc-ci's *Luna* (1979), Michael Snow's *Rameau's Nephew* (1981) and Volker Schlöndorff's *Die Blechtrommel* (*The Tin Drum*, winner of the Academy Award for Best Foreign Language Film in 1981). At first, Cronenberg was only associated with the issue by proxy. Upon the release of *Videodrome* several publications were quick to make the link between the film and censorship. In the widely-read *Maclean's*, the article discussing *Videodrome* started with:

The timing was perfect. As women's groups across Canada protested that soft-core sex movies on pay TV would inexorably become more explicit, David Cronenberg's *Videodrome* opened last week in more than 600 theatres across North America. Its subject: how a sadomasochistic video snuff show drives a viewer to hallucination and finally suicide. (Czarnecki 1983: 61)

The connection made was one that recurred throughout the reception trajectory of *Videodrome*, and though it was merely an inference it did implicate Cronenberg.[37] Soon, however, the issue became personal. When the Toronto International Film Festival proposed to screen *The Brood* as part of its Cronenberg retrospective in September 1983 the organisers were informed they could not show the uncut version, a blunt reminder of the censorship Cronenberg had to endure in previous years. Moreover, in the spring of 1984 Cronenberg, together with, among others, Jackie Burroughs (Johnny Smith's hyper-religious mother in *The Dead Zone*), opposed the hastily-made decision of the Alliance of Canadian Cinema, Television and Radio Artists (ACTRA), the Canadian film industry's union (of which he was a 'high-profile member'), to forbid their members to work on films that would condone or encourage deviant sexual behaviour and sexual violence, to 'practise stringent self-censorship' and to lobby for the outlawing of 'proscribed conduct', meaning certain specific representations of sex and violence.[38] A few days later, 62 actors signed up to Cronenberg's protest, urging ACTRA to 'spend more energy to become an effective negotiating board, and stop trying to decide what is morally acceptable for its membership' (see Scott 1984b). When the Ontario Censorship Board also raided art galleries and confiscated artworks, prevented the screening of Dusan Makaveyev's *Sweet Movie* (1974) at the 1984 Toronto International Film Festival and even banned Jean Genet's *Un chant d'amour* (*A Song of Love*, 1950) from the provocative Forbidden Film Festival (with Cronenberg scheduled to appear on one of its panels), causing Jack Smith to withdraw his two films (*Flaming Creatures* (1963) and *Exotic Landlordism of Crab Lagoon*[39]), the entire dispute started to become more principled: whose authority is it to decide on the appropriateness of the public presence of art? In the end, two Ontario High Court decisions ruled that the activities of the Ontario Censorship Board were illegal, executed beyond their authority.[40]

Although Cronenberg's own involvement usually remained minimal, the enveloping debate about the regulation of depictions of sex and violence, and the effects of their fictional representations in film, on video, television and in print would, from now on, frequently include his name as a reference. When Cronenberg would occasionally speak out against censorship his comments would be bracketed as coming from a 'liberal'. That was for instance the case in 1987–89, when Cronenberg, in the company of Margaret Atwood, supported the opposition, which included a Canadian librarian's strike, against the Progressive Conservative government bill that attempted to outlaw pornography (the so-called C-54 bill, that would only make an 'exemption' to the ban for works of art, hence leaving it to the justice system to determine what 'art' is and opening artists up to prosecution for their expressions).[41] By the end of 1989 the debate about censorship and pornography had descended into paranoia instead of politics, with each side being painted as intolerant and conniving by the opposing camp. One example was the attempt, in December 1989, to implicate Cronenberg in concerns about how media harm or influence vulnerable citizens, when his name was carelessly joined together with that of Hitler, in an article that tried to blame an entire culture for a heinous college massacre in Montreal.[42] No wonder Cronenberg started reacting defensively to this politicised, paranoid public presence.[43] It seemed Cronenberg's exit from the dungeons of horror into the full and public artistic limelight would also mean his name and his films would have to tolerate being misrepresented beyond belief.

It is a typical characteristic of censorship attempts that they return cyclically. So, in the early spring of 2008, Cronenberg was forced on the barricades once again, this time to protest bill C-10, which proposed to grant the Canadian government the power to take away funding from films it deemed offensive. The proposed bill was the result of right-wing religious lobbying, that singled out Cronenberg's films together with Lynne Stopkevitch's *Kissed* (1996), *Ginger Snaps* (John Fawcett, 2000) and several Atom Egoyan features. At the time of writing, Cronenberg was leading the protest against the bill; probably not for the last time.[44]

Conclusion: Allusions, the Paranoia of Interpretation and the Active Auteur

Whatever debates Cronenberg and his films found themselves in, they coincided with a boost in the appreciation of his work. In 1983, he was awarded the Genie for Best Director for *Videodrome* at Canada's annual film awards, and a few months later *The Dead Zone* won three top prizes at the Fantasy Film Festival in Avoriaz. Cronenberg's personal appearance amidst the reception of his work, his availability for interviews, his insistence on setting the record straight and his interventions into what he saw as 'wrong' interpretations of his films – with a penchant for resisting overly political read-ings – made him a very active figure, a bit like a public intellectual.[45] In chapter nine I will elaborate on this active presence, proposing to see it as a form of 'active auteur-ship'. But it is necessary to puncture the topic already a little bit here, to grasp fully the kind of 'untouchable' status Cronenberg would later obtain as one of the most intelligent filmmakers of his time – always a step ahead of his critics. In the beginning of the 1980s, many reviewers, be they writing for the fan press (like Tim Lucas), or academically (like Robin Wood), started to take notice of what Noël Carroll (1982) has called the use of allusions in cinema since the 1970s – winks, nudges, asides, quotes, clues and cues to film history, popular culture and art and politics. Allusions provide clever audiences with additional viewing pleasure; not just in-crowd cult fans inducted into the secrets of the cult, but also on a broader level – one that assumes a college-educated, informed audience willing and able to recognise these references and use them in their enjoyment of a film. In a sense, the popularity of allusions is indicative of how the cult of horror's viewing strategies became normalised practice.

For David Bordwell, the looking for allusions by critics and audiences is an activity that can derail proper film interpretation, leading to excessive inferences and rhetorical freewheeling that does not help understand films better at all, and only showcases the cleverness of critics. In Bordwell's words, 'film criticism takes it as its goal to understand the author better than he understands himself' (1989: 210). This comment is mirrored perfectly by remarks such as Susan Ayscough's, who paraphrases Scorsese when she suggests that: 'David himself doesn't know what his films are about' (1983: 15). I would like to suggest that Cronenberg resists such a process profoundly. Bordwell rightly observes 'two can play this game. The flexibility of the ask-the-artist topos gives filmmakers a chance to manipulate the interpretive institution' (ibid.). The two examples Bordwell gives are 'the director of *In a Lonely Place*' (cult figure Nicholas Ray) and Cronenberg: 'David Cronenberg acknowledges that in *Videodrome* he deliberately entices critics with a tension between medieval and Renaissance thought, as well as quotations from Yeats and Leonardo' (ibid.). The critic Bordwell refers to is Tim Lucas, who chronicled the production of *Videodrome* for the fan magazine *Cinefantastique*. Parts of Lucas's materials were reprinted in the academic book *The Shape of Rage* that set the tone for the scholarly reception of Cronenberg's films.[46]

Given the motif of paranoia, is it too much to suggest that Cronenberg 'planted' the seeds for appraisal of his films by academics by carefully feeding them piecemeal information he knows they will eagerly pick up to show how clever they are? Maybe. But, like with paranoia itself, it becomes impossible to distinguish between what is planted into the interpretation and what is actually present *in* the film – what is a construction and what is content? And that ambiguity fits the theme of paranoia so well it confounds attempts to unravel it.

At the time of *Videodrome* and *The Dead Zone*, such considerations remained limited to the core of Cronenberg's audience. The majority of cinemagoers, while aware of his name now, still saw him as a cultist filmmaker, and an exponent of the horror genre. That is why I reserve the term 'active auteur' for almost twenty years later, when indeed the majority of Cronenberg's audience seem to have grown accustomed to his interventions, and accepts them for the sincere and clever signs of depth they are.

CHAPTER SIX

Science and Progress: *The Fly* and *Dead Ringers*

Timortis Conturbat Mea
(The fear of death disturbs me)

      – David Cronenberg (in Rodley 1997: 58)

A little learning is a dang'rous thing;
drink deep, or taste not the Pierian Spring:
Their shallow draughts intoxicate the brain,
and drinking largely sobers us again.

      – Alexander Pope, *Essay on Criticism* (1711)

I–I'm a human fly
A–and I don't know why
I got 96 tears and 96 eyes.

      – The Cramps, 'Human Fly'

Greed is Good: Science and Commerce

It may be a tiny detail in itself but it encapsulates the attitude of an era: the first glimpse of Cronenberg in a film other than his own is a shot of his index finger pointing at a slide displaying complicated electrical circuits. It is also the first time his voice is heard. 'They're claiming we've got a synchronisation problem,' he says.

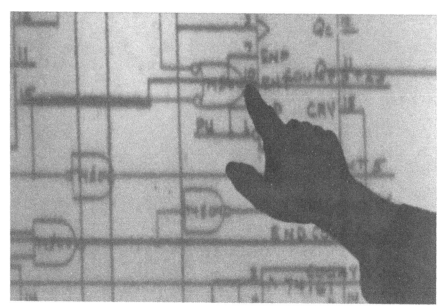

The Baron of Blood ventures beyond his own films: David Cronenberg's hand enters the frame in *Into the Night*

The occasion is *Into the Night*, an LA-set somnambulistic neo-noir noted mostly for its B. B. King soundtrack, breezy mood and numerous cameos, one of which is by Cronenberg.[1]

Cronenberg plays the supervisor of a group of aerospace engineers, and heads a meeting where his team is trying to solve a problem a partner/rival company has alerted them to. In itself, the part is perfect. The combination of the biological (the limb) and the technological (the circuits) confirms a fascination with science that is omnipresent in the films of Cronenberg, so it is only right he should play such a role. But the kind of scientist Cronenberg gives a voice, and body, to in *Into the Night* is markedly different from the regular type so common to horror films. He is employed by a modern private corporation, one that does not tout its achievements unless for profit, and sees competition more than innovation as the motor for scientific progress. Cronenberg's character is not indifferent to the pressures of commerce. The meeting is about addressing clients/competitors' needs, and as a team leader Cronenberg is ruthless, scolding insomniac employee Ed Okin (Jeff Goldblum) for still sticking to an industry standard abandoned as long as two weeks ago.

Apart from the fact that *Into the Night* brought Cronenberg into contact with Goldblum, whom he would cast in *The Fly*, Cronenberg's small part in it announces a new sensibility for the main characters of his next films: scientists would move from playing supporting roles to becoming the protagonists in both *The Fly* and *Dead Ringers*, and besides their fanaticism and stubborn belief in 'bettering' the world, sometimes against better judgement, they would display a topical characteristic: greed – they are in it for the money, and for themselves.

Greed meant a lot more than money in the 1980s. It was an all-engrossing discourse of excess, an exhaustive drive towards accumulation, accompanied by a demonstrative display of the power such a drive would bring – just to see if one 'can get away with it' as Max says in *Videodrome*. If we look further than the purely economic meaning of the desire to accumulate wealth, the concept of greed validated actions that defied the logics of efficiency (beyond rationality, progress or growth), defied morality and embraced discursive unreliability (its liberal handling of fact and truth). In *Wall Street* (Oliver Stone, 1987), an emblematic film about corporate raiders and their attitudes; super-trader Gordon Gekko (Michael Douglas) makes a speech about greed that gives some hints of the defiance of efficiency:

> Greed, for lack of a better word, is good. Greed is right; greed works. Greed clarifies, cuts through and captures the essence of the evolutionary spirit. Greed, in all of its forms, greed for life, for money, for love, knowledge – has marked the upward surge of mankind.

The extension of greed into pure thirst and desire for something 'upward', yet insisting on its link with human evolution, lies very close to what motivates Max in *Video-drome* or Stillson in *The Dead Zone*. It is also essential to the acts of the lead characters in Cronenberg's other films of the 1980s, *The Fly* and *Dead Ringers*. At one point in *The Fly* scientist Seth Brundle (Jeff Goldblum) berates his girlfriend Veronica (Geena Davis) for not wanting to go through with an experiment that he claims sends a 'power surging inside'. Annoyed with her caution he runs off, shouting: 'Drink deep, or taste not!' The similarities in speed of talking and verbosity, the rhetoric of destiny, the gluttony and the sense of urgency and intensity between Seth and Gekko are striking. Once they go off at a tangent they do not hold back. In *Dead Ringers* Doctor Elliot Mantle (Jeremy Irons) is all set to woo the wife of the chairman of a fundraising board over a fancy dinner until his twin brother Beverly (Jeremy Irons) alerts him to the medical condition of the famous movie star Claire Niveau (Geneviève Bujold), waiting to be examined in their treatment room. Without a second thought, Elliot rushes off towards the new 'challenge' – one that is both medical (her condition is curiously rare) and personal (he seduces many of their patients).

Never are Cronenberg's scientists interested in progress or in bettering the world. They are in it for themselves, in the first instance to satisfy their own curiosity and appease their own fears. In *The Fly*, Seth develops an experiment because he wants to cure his own motion sickness; in *Dead Ringers*, the specialist gynaecologist twins Elliot and Beverly Mantle treat infertile women both because they are fascinated by women's physiognomy, and to get laid. Then they move beyond that, in search of extensions of the rush the possession and control over human bodies gives them, into abuse and manipulation.

In *The Fly* and *Dead Ringers* these actions of greed beyond the logic of rationality and progress signal the beginning of the end for the scientists. It also highlights their twisted morality: egocentrism and an inability to refuse to act on their greedy impulses cause wilful and desperate wrongdoing. This attitude is again perfectly encapsulated by *Wall Street*, in a scene in which Gekko argues with his junior colleague Bud Fox (Charlie Sheen) about why he 'wrecked' the airline company Bluestar by dismantling and selling its assets: 'Because it is wreckable,' Gekko shouts out in anger, unable to see why that would be wrong. This is not so much immorality that wilfully seeks to do evil, as amorality that is blinded by the narcissistic belief that the actions of people as brilliant as Gekko, Seth or the Mantle Twins should not be questioned, and do not need to be held to moral standards because they are working towards something 'upward'. Seth and Elliot in particular are convinced they are still doing the right thing, even if they are smart enough to see how unconventional their actions are. Like most scientists in Cronenberg's films they exempt themselves from regular morality to achieve immortality. Whenever they are cautious it is not for ethical reasons, but because it might not be 'safe'.

On top of the defiance of efficiency and the immorality comes unreliability and unaccountability. Seth and the Mantle twins construct a web of deceit around their actions by pretending they serve other purposes. Moreover, Seth's perception of reality is seriously distorted by the condition he acquires through the experiment (both in its manic and depressed stages), and Elliot and Beverly's drug abuse causes their sense of reality to become twisted too. A sense of paranoia is common to this understanding of greed: it suspects competitors and rivals behind every corner. Seth becomes increasingly distrustful of anyone who might want to help him; the Mantle twins become so paranoid they are even afraid to venture outside their home.[2]

In both *The Fly* and *Dead Ringers*, as in *Wall Street*, the environment in which all this happens is an unabashedly commercial one. In *The Fly*, Seth operates privately, seeking funding and financers outside the regular channels that subsidise and sponsor health care and scientific research. In *Dead Ringers*, the Mantle twins have their own privately sponsored, commercially run, clinic. They treat rich people, patients who can afford their services. This atmosphere of the commercialisation of science fits, of course, the neo-liberal economics and politics of the 1980s. But in showing how the scientific careers and lives of Seth and the Mantle twins evolve, become corrupt and end disastrously, *The Fly* and *Dead Ringers* might also act as warnings against such unbridled commercial greed.

The paths that the scientists follow, and their encounters with love, destroys them. Their demise is linked to the mess and excesses accompanying greed in the health sector – expressed in both films through the use of technology, in the changes in design of interiors, and via metaphors of degeneration, disease and the consequences of the commodification of health care. On a larger level, the reception of *The Fly* and *Dead Ringers*, especially their commercial and prestige success, and the way these were linked to hot issues such as AIDS or fertility treatments, gave these metaphors of science a pressing topical relevance – and turned them into cautionary tales.

The Fly

The metaphor of science pushes itself to the fore from the very beginning of *The Fly*. The credit sequence is decorated with little red drops flickering on the screen, like blood cells in full swing or, as Seth Brundle will later refer to it, 'general cellular chaos'. As ominous orchestral music swells, the red drops are complemented with blue and green, together making up the primary colours of light (and of the television screen). Gradually the drops come into focus and we discover we are in fact at a fundraising party for Bartok Science Industries, where journalists mingle with academics, scientists and philanthropists – the sort of commercial environment quite fitting for the 1980s urge to replace the public funding of science with private and corporate sponsoring.[3]

The Fly does not waste any time setting itself up as a horror story. 'I am working on something that will change the world and human life as we know it,' announces reclusive scientist Seth Brundle to *Particle Magazine* journalist Veronica Quaife at the party. Initially, she is just looking for a way out of the conversation. But something about Seth tells her there may be a scoop here, and she decides to let him take her to his lab – the horror cliché here is not so much avoided as pipped at the post when the scientist lures the damsel to his lab within the first three minutes of the film. During the drive, Seth confesses his chronic motion sickness. They arrive at a derelict, seemingly abandoned warehouse, where Seth has his lab installed away from prying eyes. Sweeping aside another horror cliché he accompanies Veronica's entrance with a dramatic tune on the piano, and when she makes a move to leave he jokes: 'It's too late. You've already seen them. Can't let you leave here alive.'

The horror clichés summarily dismissed, the commerce of science takes over the story. Seth demonstrates how he can transfer objects (Veronica's stocking) from one pod to another. Fascinated, Veronica asks for more information, and as Seth explains how he sees himself as some 'manager', who 'farms out pieces' and then 'assembles' them (another nice reference to a 1980s commercial obsession, 'outsourcing'), she secretly tapes the conversation and takes her tape to her editor (and ex-boyfriend), the slick yuppie Stathis Borans (John Getz). He is not impressed but Seth manages to cut a win-win deal with Veronica: she gets full access to his work and can author a book on the project, as long as she waits for him to be ready to demonstrate the teleportation of living matter (himself). At first, progress is slow, and experiments with monkeys fail. The bloody, squealing and shivering ugly mess one baboon disintegrates into reminds the viewer this could still turn nasty. The setback forces Seth to teach his system how to assemble human flesh properly – he needs to 'learn about the flesh'.

Quite appropriately, at that moment, love intervenes. Interrupting a discussion about what kind of meat they should have for dinner (cheeseburger or steak) Seth and Veronica's own fleshy desires set them ablaze. The sex inspires Seth, and still naked he cuts up the raw steak and teleports one half. That half turns out to be inedible; the computer is 'interpreting, translating, rethinking' the flesh, rather than reproducing it – something only humans can do. According to Seth, the 'computer should go crazy about the flesh, like old ladies pinching babies', and he sets about doing just that. But as love intervenes, so do its complications. At the same time as Seth succeeds in successfully teleporting another baboon, Stathis, paranoid with jealousy (and appearing to be high on cocaine), threatens Veronica with revealing the story prematurely unless she keeps him informed. As she arranges this, Seth too is jealous. Drunk on champagne, he teleports himself – just to demonstrate *he* is the brilliant one.

When Seth teleports himself, the camera shows us he is not alone in the pod. A fly has snuck in with him. Initially, the effects are fabulous. The rearrangement of Seth's flesh appears to have reinvigorated him (like an extreme makeover massage). He feels great, fit and energetic, with astounding reflexes and balance – Olympic gold material. He claims it 'purified and cleansed him'. It has also given him a manic drive (not cocaine- but sugar-fuelled), and high on his own ego and achievements (which he calls 'messianic'), he becomes impatient with those who cannot keep up. Seth, now perpetually craving sugar, has an exhausting sex marathon with Veronica, before telling her that she only knows 'society's straight line about the flesh', that she 'cannot penetrate beyond society's sick, grey fear of the flesh', before leaving her behind. He goes out on the town, in a scene inviting comparisons to so many others that show well-to-do businessmen slumming it. He enters a sleazy bar and challenges the local muscleman, breaking his wrist in an arm-wrestle match and leaving with the bar's trophy lady, Tawny (Joy Boushel). After another night of extensive sex with Tawny, during which Seth teleports himself again, Veronica shows up unexpectedly: 'Be afraid, be very afraid,' she warns Tawny.

From there on the horror increases by increments, turning *The Fly* into an excessive medical horror exhibit. Upon inspection of the teleportation process Seth discovers his body has been fused with that of the fly. And with that the narrative changes; it is all about the body of Seth now. Instead of dialogue and interaction, Seth's monologues and his gradual disintegration become the main means through which the story is told (a process Cronenberg would later revisit in *Crash*, with much more controversial reactions). His means of communication become impeded: he loses his finger nails, so it becomes more difficult to type on the computer. Scabs have appeared on his face. Thick insect hairs start growing all over his body. He warns Veronica his 'bizarre form of cancer' is accelerating relentlessly, and it might be infectious so she spends less time with him. As his powers wane, with crawling across walls and ceiling and regurgitating being the only 'impressive' things he can still do, his monologues become more macabre. He claims to be 'stricken by a disease with a purpose, maybe not such a bad disease after all'. Almost crippled now, he stumbles around his lab, vomits on his food and loses one of his ears (equally repulsive is that Veronica still presses a hug against the bloodied, gaping wound on that side of his face). He loses his teeth and his voice changes, making voice-recognition impossible – in short he is turning into 'something else'.[4]

Yet no matter how disgusting and freakish Seth becomes he keeps four core human characteristics functioning until the very end: his scientific inquisitiveness, his humour, his sense of cultural and political distinction and his ability to love and care. When Veronica comes to tell Seth how much she cares for him and to inform him she is pregnant with their baby, he first introduces her to his 'Brundle Museum of Natural History', a collection of lost limbs and organs he has kept for posterity. Invoking a reference to Franz Kafka's *Metamorphosis* (1912), in which a man wakes from a nightmare to find himself transformed into a giant insect, he then tells her to leave. 'I'm an insect who dreamt he was a man and loved it, but now that dream is over and the insect is awake,' he says. 'Insects don't have politics,' he adds. 'They're very brutal. No compassion.' 'I will hurt you if you stay,' he claims; so they must say goodbye. As Veronica turns away, Seth sobs in sadness, accompanied by melodramatic music.

In the last ten minutes, as many of the horror clichés return and science is abandoned in favour of the fantastic, *The Fly* turns into a melodrama – the kind where love does not conquer adversity. When Veronica decides to abort Seth's baby (subsequent to a horrible dream she had about giving birth to a giant larvae – Cronenberg himself plays the delivering doctor with glee), he follows her into the abortion clinic, kidnaps her and carries her to his lair. He asks why she will not bear the last that is left of him. Stathis follows them with a shotgun, but he is overpowered by the Brundlefly monster, who regurgitates over his arm and Gucci-loafered foot with his liquid acid spit, burning right through them. Seth wants to fuse with Veronica and the unborn baby in order to form 'the ultimate family, more human than I am alone', but she resists. As Seth's body rapidly decomposes, and whole chunks of flesh drop from his body, he drags her into one of the pods. As he locks himself into another one, Stathis, with an extreme effort, destroys the connection between the pods. The fusion still takes place, but with Brundlefly and the pod. A mass of flesh slumps out of the pod, with only its eyes resembling anything faintly human. The creature crawls towards Veronica, who grabs the gun but cannot make herself shoot what was once her true love. In a final humane gesture, the creature puts the gun against it own head, begging her to put it out of its misery. In tears, Veronica pulls the trigger. Fade to black; two lights resembling the creature's eyes are the last to die away.

Dead Ringers

Dead Ringers' story arc is very similar to that of *The Fly*. It, too, is mostly set in interiors that get increasingly messy as the science disintegrates. But *Dead Ringers* is more muted and restrained in its presentation, with more elegiac music, and a more chic, resolutely upper middle-class setting.

The topic of science is again announced from the first images of the film. But whereas it took *The Fly* quite a while to figure out that along with science comes the crucial issue of sex, *Dead Ringers* acknowledges it immediately: the credits are illustrated with etchings and drawings of medical surgery, delivery instruments and human innards from the Middle Ages and Renaissance, against a blood-red background – depicting hooks, retractors, wombs, foetuses and conjoined twins. The story starts in Toronto, 1954. Ten-year-old twins Beverly and Elliot Mantle (Jonathan and Nicholas Haley) stroll across their street, discussing the science of human sex. They agree that 'because humans don't live underwater', they need to touch each other in order to achieve fertilisation. They offer to test their hypothesis on a neighbour, Rafaella (Marsha Moreau), and ask her to have sex with them in a bathtub. 'It's an experiment,' they explain. Offended, Rafaella tells the twins to 'fuck off', adding they don't even know 'what the word fuck means'. Disappointed, but not offended, the twins retreat. 'They are so different from us,' they sigh, 'and all because we don't live underwater'. True to their scientific obsessions, the twins (now played by Jeremy

Irons) attend Harvard Medical School, where, before they graduate, they develop a new gynaecological instrument – the Mantle retractor – that becomes the industry standard. After graduation they return to Toronto to practise gynaecology in their private fertility clinic. Though they share the same job and home, and are close to each other in every respect, the twins do have differences: Beverly (Bev) is more the reclusive researcher and diligent practitioner, and Elliot (Elly) more the manager and hustler, the one who gets the grants and goes to ceremonies.

We move to the 1980s. One day, famous actress Claire Niveau visits the clinic, with a view to ascertaining how she might become fertile. Bev discovers her uterus has an anomaly, shares the news with his brother (who is instantly fascinated) and for once they change roles: Bev woos a Contessa over dinner to get a grant and Elly has the medical consultation with Claire, a consultation which soon turns very sensual. When, later that evening, Elly gleefully reports to Bev that Claire will be waiting for him the next day, they bear a cunning smile – they have shared women before.

Before long, Claire is dating who she believes to be Bev, but in fact both twins are dating her; Bev taking advantage of Elly's smoothness, and Elly using Bev's softness. But something is different from previous occasions. For one, Claire has a quite particular sexual appetite. She claims to have been 'extremely promiscuous, and never used contraceptive devices, never even thought contraceptive thoughts', supposedly to increase her chances of getting pregnant but also, it transpires, because she is 'bad', and needs to be 'punished'; because she desires, as Elly puts it, 'a little slap on the ass'. He adds that 'she's an actress, she plays games all the time; you never know who she really is'. So, medical instruments become tools for the enhancement of Claire's pleasure. Claire is also a heavy user of prescription drugs that ease what she calls her 'psychosexual' problems. She uses the drugs to become euphoric and to have – as Elly puts it – 'sex like Nagasaki'. Beyond the specifics of her sexual pleasures, however, Claire hides a deep need to become pregnant in order to finally become what she sees as 'a real woman'. Claire's longing touches Bev profoundly, and for the first time he refuses to share intimate details with Elly, even when the latter claims 'you haven't fucked Claire Niveau until you tell me about it'. A subtle schism develops between the brothers as they move into what Elly labels 'unknown territory'. Claire, too, feels something is up. She asks Bev why he has a female name, why he resists playing games and impersonations, and suggests he is schizophrenic. Shortly after, she finds out she has been dating both twins, and confronts them. She leaves; Bev is devastated.

All the psychoanalysis, drug-taking, role-playing and sexual explorations take their toll on Bev. His scientific work falters, and he becomes curt and impatient with clients. He starts having anxiety attacks, fearful that Elly (who has accepted an associate professorship) will no longer support him, yet at the same time he seems determined to loosen the ties between them and stand on his own feet and stop some of the sharing. One evening, a drunken Bev stumbles in on an award ceremony where Elly is giving an acceptance speech for a prestigious award, and embarrasses himself and his brother in front of their peers, revealing *he* is the one doing all the hard work. When Elly starts bringing his mistress Cary (Heidi von Palleske) to their home Bev even makes plans to move out. And he starts seeing Claire again. As his anxieties and pill-popping worsen, the thought of being separated from Elly becomes both an obsession and an unbearable burden, one in which he imagines Claire to play a crucial role. In a dream he witnesses her biting a phallic umbilical cord that connects him and Elly – she rips a bloody root-like piece of flesh out of their bodies, as if she is aborting the one brother from the womb of the other. Elly also suffers from the separation as he jets across the country on a lecture tour. He copes by ordering twin escort girls for relaxation; he commands one of them to call him Elly and the other to call him Bev.

It is again paranoia that drives science out and twists what could have become true love into obsessive insecurity, and as in *The Fly* the downward spiral cannot be stopped. When Claire leaves to shoot a film, Bev collapses; afraid she will have an affair with someone else, he sinks into a depression. With the practice, and their business, in danger, and their commitment to practising medicine almost completely abandoned, Elly decides to leave the glamour and gloss of the public recognition and step in to make amends with his brother. He takes him back into their apartment, and attempts to have them share women again, Cary first among them. But Bev's mind and body become increasingly erratic and he ends up in hospital; he not only starts making medical mistakes, but also leaves any caution behind and experiments with novel methods of examination, up to the point where he commissions a new set of instruments from a medical artist (Stephen Lack) so he can 'work on mutant women'; and he almost kills a patient. In Bev's mind more and more women's bodies are 'all wrong'. Unable to appease patients and the hospital board any longer, the brothers are told they have to forsake their practice. Powerless to change anything, Elly tightens his control over the abuse. Challenged by Bev, he also comes clean about his real reasons to help, through the medical rhyme to the death of the original Siamese twins, Chang and Eng, which he asks Bev to recount:

Chang died of a stroke in the middle of the night. He was always the sickly one. He was always the one who drank too much. When Eng woke up beside him, and found that his brother was dead … he died of fright, right there in the bed.

Poetry has replaced diagnosis, the weird surgical instruments Bev had made are exhibited as art sculptures, objectivity is now discarded. Convinced he too will perish if Bev does not get better, Elly tries to get synchronised with his brother, and then reverse the downfall. He too takes to drugs. As their lives descend into madness, their once clean and sterile apartment turns into a mess, as does their clinic. Even Claire's love can no longer help Bev. It also becomes difficult to tell them apart; soon, the two are completely drug-addled, shuffling around in identical filthy clothing in the rubble and garbage, dishevelled and unkempt, inseparable in every sense. On their birthday, a dazed Bev operates on an equally insensible Elly with the recovered mutant instruments, trying to surgically detach himself from his brother. He cuts him open, then falls asleep. When he wakes up he leaves the clinic, and tries to call Claire. But he cannot make himself talk to her. Her question, 'who is this?' is the last sentence spoken in *Dead Ringers*. It remains unanswered. Bev goes back inside, and crawls up next to the dead body of Elly, where he lies motionless, his eyes wide open – as if he died from fright.

The commodification of health care

The endings of *The Fly* and *Dead Ringers* single out the main characters' eyes, the organ *Videodrome* asked us to see as 'the windows of the soul'. Much as that latter film is about watching, *The Fly* and *Dead Ringers* are about being watched, and about arranging one's look accordingly – about perception. Seth watches himself change into a bug in countless shots that show him looking into the mirror, and for the Mantle twins too, perception is crucial. 'We are always perceived as one person', explains an otherwise egotistical Elly, when asked why he insists on helping Bev.

For many critics, *The Fly* and *Dead Ringers* are about the perception of women by men. Both films are not only widely discussed academically, but also seen as highly contentious. Much of that has to do with the films' portrayal of what Pete Boss (1986) has called 'bad medicine' – the abuse of the medical profession as a tool to exercise men's power over women. For Tania Modleski (1986) and Barbara Creed (1986; 1990), such films express what they call womb envy: the inability of men to come to terms with the superior reproductive abilities of women. Frustration over this inability manifests itself in extreme explorations of the human body (especially the female one), and attempts to assert control over, or alter, them at will, in the hope that this will yield power. That is what Seth tries to do with Veronica – and when she resists his jealousy it turns him into a destructive force for himself, her and their unborn child. Similarly, the inability of Bev and Elly to 'master' the unusual biological make-up of Claire drives them into addiction, madness and death. In both cases the women are, at least in the eyes of the men, the ones that initiate the bad medicine and science, the ones that prevent the world from making sense, and that pushes them over the edge – it makes men 'careless', 'anxious', 'impure', 'jealous'. In short, for these critics, *The Fly* and *Dead Ringers* allege women cause bad science and disaster because they are so different. I will return to the connection between gender and science when discussing the reception of *The Fly* and *Dead Ringers*. Now I want to expand this observation with a new initiator, one that explains Cronenberg's male characters' distrust of women not so much psychologically but through the political economy of science and health care.

It is the bad practice of science that causes Seth and the Mantle twins to perceive women as 'others', regarding them with paranoia and anxiety. At one level, they have learned to cope with that anxiety, by developing rationing techniques to minimalise emotional involvement (such as detachment through sharing sex, clinical examination, insulation, reclusion). Such tactics of disengagement are also often in operation in the routines of health science or health care (which is, after all, the kind of science Seth and the Mantle twins are in). But besides being an activity facilitating 'coping', this science, and its approaches and procedures, equally embed and intensify the anxieties they are meant to cure – a bit like the pills Elly starts taking to help Bev: while they are designed to enable him to help, they also prevent him from helping because they create dependability. Only when confronted with strong women – women who choose their partners freely, women who are independent financially – do those flaws become evident; it causes the *already* flawed and bad science to escalate.

The main reason why the approaches and procedures of this *kind* of health science, or health care, are bad lies in the kind of greed mentioned above, one that serves as the *modus operandus* of the main characters of *The Fly* and *Dead Ringers*. Greed is often expressed through the compartmentalisation of items and assets that can be traded off separately (a company's pension funds, its shares, its copyright, its archives and so forth). Commercial science and its administration also depend on this process, on the ability to separate an item – be it a product or a human being – into isolated pieces (or causes) and manufacturing or treating them piece by piece, trading those treatments (and the labour of study and research it involves), and then assembling them into the finalised item (which can again be traded). The health science in both *The Fly* and *Dead Ringers* relies on this segmentation and specialisation, to the point where any view of the *whole* becomes undesirable. Consider Seth's explanation of how he works:

I don't work alone. There's stuff in there I don't understand. I'm really a system's manager man, I farm out pieces to guys that are much more brilliant than I am. I say, 'Design me a molecular analyzer', and they do. I just assemble it. None of them knows what the project really is. [Bartok Industries] leave me alone because I'm not really expensive. And they know they'll be owning all of this.

And consider the Mantle twins' business when confronted with Arlene (Lynne Cormack), a desperate, persistent patient:

Bev: There's no point to this discussion Arlene.
Arlene (sobbing): There is a point. There definitely is a point. You started with me and now you won't carry through. W-we have a relationship.
Bev: But you test out fine. It's your husband that's the problem. And all he probably needs is a good sperm wash.
Arlene: If it's only a matter of laundry, why are you so opposed to doing it?
Bev: We don't do husbands. We do female infertility. We do women; that's our specialty.
Arlene: But I *am* a woman. And I want you to take care of me. I trust you. It's hard enough these days to find someone in the medical profession that you can trust.
Bev: Arlene, that's wonderful. That's – I mean, it's really wonderful. But we don't do husbands. We don't deliver babies, either. We make women fertile, and that's all we do [pause]. To achieve anything in life, one has to keep life simple [pause]. Don't you think?

The look on Bev's face as he says this indicates even he has difficulties justifying what he tells Arlene. He finds himself defending a system of care that refuses to offer a treatment outside its commercial specialisation and would rather leave Arlene infertile than help. 'Keeping life simple' equals cutting care into pieces, cheap or expensive, and then outsourcing and trading them.

If seen through this perspective, health science is interested in two actions only: the procedures to separate then assemble, and the manners through which these actions are *performed*. Only the impression of efficiency counts, not the actual effectiveness: as long as it looks as if elements and factors are isolated pieces and can be separated, it will look like a solution, and a diagnosis is arrived at (and can be sold). In the case of *The Fly*, Seth still makes the effort to assemble the pieces of his project (and he even takes on some labour outside his expertise, such as 'learning about the flesh'); there is still a move towards completion. This is evidenced by the type of special effects the film contains: they demonstrate aspects of separation (the baboon that gets turned inside out), but even more spectacularly they showcase instances of fusion and assembly: putting Seth and the fly into Brundlefly, and later merging Brundlefly with the pod. The completion turns out to be wrong, but the intent was nevertheless there. In *Dead Ringers* such a project is absent; there is nothing to assemble, only individual treatments. Fittingly, the instances of special effects we find are of separation only. The only fusion occurs between Bev and Elly, not any of their patients. The best example of this is the acclaimed motion control technique that allowed director of photography Peter Suschitzky to capture Elly and Bev in one frame with a moving camera. At several points in the film the camera follows one Mantle coming into a room, to have the other one join him in the frame a little later, and one of the two leave it as the camera keeps moving. The technique enhances the impression of interaction between the two. It makes them seem close to each other. Any other moments of assembly in *Dead Ringers* are purely performative, and look staged. The surgery in which a woman gets some additional organs implanted to help her get pregnant is one such example. Conducted in what is after all called an operating theatre, it is cloaked in dramatic overtones, with the surgeons wearing red ceremonial robes, observed by an eager audience of students, and accompanied by Elly's expert commentary. William Beard compares the set-up to a church (2005: 253); I believe it is more like another type of cult: that of a sales presentation, one selling a dream of happiness. 'I'm into the art of glamour' Elly tells Claire at one point, when he visits her trailer on the set of a movie and observes the fake bruises put on her face by the make-up artists. He loves the performance, and Claire loves exposing it.

The science in *The Fly* fails to provide care, and in spite of its high aspirations towards 'social responsibility' (Elly's words in a lecture) the science in *Dead Ringers* does not even try to hide the fact that it does not administer care, or cure. Nothing gets fixed, only separated and traded. This type of commodified, segmented, performative science is unmasked by the strong women Veronica and Claire, and it is because they expose its fraud and pretentiousness that they are disliked, opposed and abused. Not because they are women, but because as independent and intelligent people they probe beyond the gloss and rhetoric into the economy of the science, and confront Seth and the Mantle twins with their underlying intentions: Icarian greed for recognition and messianic power – power over women, power over themselves and power to create life.

If this is 'womb envy', then in *The Fly* and *Dead Ringers* its origin is economic, not psychological.

Mess and excess

Once unsettled by Veronica and Claire, the obsessions of the doctors of *The Fly* and *Dead Ringers* lead them beyond science, into what Elly calls 'unknown territory', areas of speculation, and as their professionalism is replaced by dangerous experiments that invariably have dire implications, the look of the characters changes – the impression they leave upon others as well as their physical shape. That change is paralleled by a gradual increase in the degree of debris and messiness in the interiors, which turn into cesspools and filthy caves within which the characters retreat and, inevitably, perish.

At the beginning of *The Fly*, Seth's loft in a warehouse (a setting quite similar to the artist's loft in Martin Scorsese's *After Hours* (1985) – a film with which *The Fly* shares a male anxiety about the loss of control) is clean and meticulously organised. At the end, it is a complete mess, littered with wrappings, the remnants of half-eaten food, rubble, clutter, blood, limbs, twisted metal and smouldering remains. In *Dead Ringers*, a similar process takes place. At first, Bev and Elly's fancy apartment looks like the cold and sterile flat of Wall Street businessman John (Mickey Rourke) in *Nine and a Half Weeks* (Adrian Lyne, 1986), yet another critique of the excessive greed of the 1980s. There is shiny furniture, expensive decor, designer cutlery, state-of-the-art minimalism and a breathtaking view of the skyline. The clinic also looks crisp, clean and pure – sculpted, with lots of empty surfaces. But as the brothers lose their tight grip on reality, fast food leftovers, wrappings, paper and bottles remain on shelves and the floor. In the end the apartment and clinic are littered with half-eaten cakes, used needles, stains and burns, candle wax, worn and dirty clothes, unopened mail, melted ice-cream, ripped tissue and paper towels, blood and surgical instruments. No clear mind works or lives there. If you do not look after yourself properly and keep things tidy, no pills will clear your head and no treatment will cleanse your body, and you will die.

These deteriorations are emphasised by the fact that all other indoor settings, with the exception of Claire's and Veronica's apartments, are either public places or private property of utmost formality and cleanliness – chic restaurants, lecture auditoria, expensive hotel rooms, operating theatres, consultation rooms, offices and graduation halls – places for formal exchanges, treatments and sales. All of these interiors assume care is a for-profit service; all of them regard health as a commodity. The outdoor world is dangerous, both in *Dead Ringers* and *The Fly*. The only places Seth visits (apart from a short holiday with Veronica) are the seedy red light district and dirty rooftops. There are only four outdoor shots in *Dead Ringers*, all of them featuring Bev in distress: the first shows an ambulance rushing him to the hospital after he collapses; the second shows him wandering the streets in search of someone who can design instruments for operating on mutant women (he ends up in an art gallery); the third sees him vomiting in the street and trying to steal those very instruments; and in the fourth he stumbles to a phone booth, only to quickly retreat back inside. Elly is never seen outside at all.

Projects, Funds, Awards, Ceremonies: Cronenberg and Hollywood

The two cleanest and most social locations in *The Fly* and *Dead Ringers* are the Bartok Science Industries party where journalists and scientists mingle with industry people (and Seth meets Veronica), and a venue where Elly accepts an award, in which every single mirror and piece of glass is so clean it looks like a mirror palace; too much glitter to be considered truthful. They are places of social rituals and ceremonies, of subtle manners and subtle padding, places where one is supposed to show off one's qualities without seeming too desperate or eager – a thin line both Seth and Bev (who walks into his brother's acceptance speech and disturbs it, making a fool of himself) have difficulty finding and sticking to.

Coincidentally or not, Cronenberg's own career in the mid- and late-1980s showed considerable resemblance to the situation Seth and the Mantle twins find themselves in. The successes of *Scanners* and *The Dead Zone*, the respect for *Videodrome*, the commercial failure of which Cronenberg dismissed ('it wasn't like *Heaven's Gate*' he says in Rodley 1997: 119), as well as the efforts of his then-agent Mike Marcus and producer Pierre David, had made Cronenberg a desired name in Hollywood. He was considered an expert filmmaker in whom a company could safely invest money and expect a profit. Moreover, his mannerisms and eccentricities had also become bankable: gruesome effects attracted audiences; critics had started to appreciate the validity of explorations of body mutations as metaphors; approaching films as projects and packages (with the stages for screenplay commissioning and development increasingly separated from the actual production, as Cronenberg had experienced with *The Dead Zone* and *The Fly*), became routine practice; and shooting films in Canada, or Hollywood North, became more common (not just for Canadian filmmakers but also for Hollywood producers looking for cheap labour because of a favourable currency exchange rate) – in short, Cronenberg's work was increasingly seen as fitting the model of film practice, and he had become acceptable to 1980s Hollywood.

In 1983 Cronenberg completed a script for Universal, entitled 'Six Legs', which was never developed any further, although part of it resurfaced in *Naked Lunch* (see chapter seven). He was then offered the chance to direct *Beverly Hills Cop* (Martin Brest, 1984), *Witness* (Peter Weir, 1985) and *Top Gun* (Tony Scott, 1986). He also got the chance to direct the script from fellow Canadian Tom Hedley for *Flashdance* (Adrian Lyne, 1984) and, later, the Brian Moore adaptation *Black Robe* (Bruce Beresford, 1991) (see Snider 1984; Allemang 1989). In what was possibly the closest to Hollywood jetsetting he would ever get, in 1984 Cronenberg visited Rome, and De Laurentiis's studio, and later Tunis, to scout locations for a project he became firmly involved in for a brief period: an adaptation of Philip K. Dick's story 'We Can Remember It For You Wholesale' (1966) under the title *Total Recall* (see Anon. 1984b). Cronenberg spent about a year preparing the project. He rewrote several script drafts by horror genre veterans Ron Shusett and Dan O'Bannon, contacted actor Richard Dreyfuss to play the lead role, set up an art department in Rome and even had some preliminary creature effects and costume designs developed. Eventually De Laurentiis, upon the instigation of distributor MGM, dropped him from the

Corporate science and ceremonial gatherings: *The Fly* (top); *Dead Ringers* (bottom)

project. A few of his ideas and creatures survived subsequent production changes: it was Cronenberg's idea to make the character more human than heroic, and the head housed in a character's chest is a decidedly Cronenbergian touch (even though it also appeared in the original script). In the end, De Laurentiis's company went bankrupt and Carolco took over, with Paul Verhoeven and Arnold Schwarzenegger teaming up to complete the film in Mexico. But it is a telling sign of Cronenberg's appeal to the fan press that it would continue to treat *Total Recall* as a Cronenberg-related project, and touted his contributions above those of the others involved (see Florence 1991).

The list of offers and near-projects Cronenberg was associated with reads as a micro-canon of mid-1980s Hollywood cinema. Yet, while Cronenberg enjoyed the appreciation of Hollywood's elite, in the way Seth and the Mantle twins enjoyed their day in the sun, he remained cautious: the hospitability the mainstream film industry extended towards him was not to be mistaken for genuine friendship. Like Seth and the Mantle twins he would remain a bit of an odd figure, best to be formal with and only approached on a case-by-case basis. When *Total Recall* fell through, Cronenberg was practical enough to accept Mel Brooks' offer to direct a remake of *The Fly*, under the aegis of Stuart Cornfeld. The fact that *The Fly* was to be a remake of a tale that had gone through several adaptations – a story by George Langelaan, a script by James Clavell, a movie by Kurt Neumann, a new script by Charles Edward Pogue and rewrites by Cronenberg – only seemed to fit the Hollywood business of packaging and franchising.[5]

As it turned out, *The Fly* quickly became Cronenberg's most successful feature. It was distributed by 20th Century Fox worldwide (the first time Cronenberg had a worldwide distributor), and was accompanied by a clever promotion campaign that used Veronica's warning to Tawny – 'be afraid, be very afraid' – as a key slogan that resonated with general audiences (announcing it as a special kind of horror film) as well as with Cronenberg's core fans (assuring them the film had not been toned down for the mainstream market, and was a step up from *The Dead Zone*). It had an opening across almost two thousand theatres in North America in the summer of 1986, eventually making about $60 million in theatre revenues.[6] About one-third of that sum came from the European market, where the film was released in January 1987 at the Fantasy Film Festival of Avoriaz, where it won the Special Prize of the Jury. In the following months, *The Fly* won the Academy Award for best make-up effects (Chris Walas and Stephan Dupuis), three Saturn awards (including best horror film), the award for cinematography from the Canadian Society of Cinematographers (Mark Irwin) and nominations at the Fantasporto festival in Portugal and the BAFTA awards in the United Kingdom. *The Fly*'s outstanding special effects also attracted laudations from prominent industry journals such as *Cinefex* and *American Cinematographer* (one more sign of how accepted Cronenberg had become in Hollywood) (see Lucas 1986a; 1896b; Magid 1986). Much like Elly Mantle, lifting an award and receiving recognition from peers at ceremonies was fast becoming a regular occurrence for Cronenberg and his team, evidence of the director's emergence on a global public platform where his actions would be deemed newsworthy – for instance in the steady stream of mentions of his previous films, whenever they were screened or broadcast, in far-from-home territories such as the Netherlands, Italy, Belgium or France.

With such acclaim behind him Cronenberg decided to take the step to become his own producer with *Dead Ringers*, a project whose origins push the similarity between the films' portrayals of science and commerce even further. The story of *Dead Ringers* was initiated by the real-life case of the Marcus twins, two upper-class gynaecologists who were found dead in their fancy East 63rd Street apartment in New York, apparently from drug withdrawal. Cronenberg wrote the script with his long-time friend Norman Snider, initially under the title 'Twins'.[7] Much like a scientist trying to sell his brilliant idea to funders and backers, Cronenberg struggled to get the project off the ground for more than five years with Lorimar, ABC and De Laurentiis, until he had to take on the financial responsibility himself. As Chris Rodley put it: 'suddenly, David Cronenberg Productions became landlords overnight and Cronenberg himself, in collaboration with Marc Boyman, became a producer' (1997: 143). Long-time Cronenberg collaborator John Board eventually became a co-producer, and all of Cronenberg's regular crew were also on board. The only one missing from the 'family chain' was Mark Irwin.[8] He was replaced by the already legendary Polish-British cinematographer Peter Suschitzky, who had worked on *It Happened Here* (Kevin Brownlow, 1965), *The War Game* (Peter Watkins, 1965), *The Rocky Horror Picture Show* and *The Empire Strikes Back* (Irvin Kershner, 1981).

The film was first screened at the Toronto International Film Festival – oddly enough for someone who had taken the stage at the festival a few times, and who had had a retrospective of his films there, *Dead Ringers* was Cronenberg's first actual Toronto world premiere. Combined with the fact he had produced it, it gave the event the feeling that he had succeeded in turning his small business into a self-owned industry. The Toronto reception was a big success; subsequent release proved to be a moderately lucrative business venture. Without the support of a global distributor such as 20th Century Fox, *Dead Ringers* had to be sold territory by territory, which limited exposure somewhat, but it still made about $16 million worldwide – half of which was earned overseas (where it was backed by screenings at the Fantasporto and Avoriaz festivals – the last time Cronenberg went to the latter). As important as the money it made, however, was the fact that *Dead Ringers* received numerous critical accolades: prizes at Fantasporto and Avoriaz, a record number of Canadian Genie Awards (eleven wins out of 13 nominations), and Best Direction and Best Actor awards from the critics' circles of Los Angeles and New York respectively. Many critics felt the ultimate recognition by Hollywood – the Academy Award – was the missing jewel in *Dead Ringers*' crown, a concern that was voiced by Jeremy Irons in his acceptance speech for his 1990 Academy Award for Best Actor in a Leading Role (for Barbet Schroeder's *Reversal of Fortune*), when he explicitly thanked Cronenberg.

The commercial success of *The Fly* and the awards showered on *Dead Ringers* were recognition of the fact Cronenberg was no longer a figure limited to a genre, or a wave. He had become his own (family) business force, a brand name claiming its own shelf in the store with characteristics unlike any other – odd but marketable.

Health, Gender and AIDS: The Critical Reception of The Fly and Dead Ringers

Amidst all this acclaim and praise the critical reception of *The Fly* and *Dead Ringers* requires some special attention, as it gives an explanation of how and why Cronenberg's success was accompanied by a steep increase in respect for his artistic and intellectual achievements.

Much of that change in attitude towards Cronenberg was the result of contingencies, events and developments outside the control of the director and his productions, which nevertheless informed the way they were received. For one, in spite of the gore present in *The Fly*, Cronenberg was now seen less and less as the most outrageous exponent of the cult of horror, and even as the Baron of Blood he was being surpassed and upstaged in goriness and splatter. It no longer had quite the same impact when reviewers mentioned that *The Fly*'s second half made them throw up, or that Brundlefly 'makes the monster in *Aliens* look like Grandma in a Norman Rockwell painting'.[9] Comparable and even more extreme claims could be found in the receptions of *The Hunger* (Tony Scott, 1984), *Return of the Living Dead, Re-Animator*

(Stuart Gordon, 1985), *From Beyond* (Stuart Gordon, 1986), *Hellraiser* (Clive Barker, 1987) and *Brain Damage* (Frank Henenlotter, 1988); in the video clips and cover art for heavy metal bands like Anthrax (*Spreading the Disease*, 1985) or Slayer (*Reign in Blood*, 1987); or the sequels to *Halloween*, *Friday the 13th* or *A Nightmare on Elm Street*, films that were seen as exercises in gore only, mannerisms of new horror and the 'sebaceous school of special effects ... pioneered by Cronenberg' (Canby 1986: C18). Of course, *The Fly* reminded everyone that Cronenberg could exchange blows with the newcomers any time, but the film also demonstrated that he was fast moving beyond the cult of horror.[10] The fan press for instance, gradually moved away from reporting on Cronenberg as a 'hot' or 'cool' item; instead, reports in *Fangoria*, *Starlog*, *Cinefantastique*, *Starfix* or *L'Écran fantastique* on the production and reception of *The Fly* carried a tone that was appropriately reverent for a veteran master, yet also distanced enough (gently accusing Cronenberg of being too smart and serious, or too satirical) to suggest they were now more attracted to the newer generations.[11] By the time of the release of *Dead Ringers*, most of the fan press had quietly started abandoning Cronenberg, judging him no longer relevant to their interests, and downsizing their coverage of his work from production reports and feature articles to – at best – mid-sized reviews.[12]

Alongside the discourse that elevated Cronenberg's gore onto a level where it became a canonical exemplar for subsequent waves of horror cinema, a more significant evolution took place whereby the themes, metaphors and indeed the aforementioned 'thematic consistency' of Cronenberg's films became a topic of immediate and wide cultural relevance – no longer the frivolous and freewheeling philosophical speculations of a lone individual, but wider social questions. Much of that had to do with how the commodification of care, and the attention towards the management of health and well-being, became pressing issues of public policy and academic research in the 1980s. The rise of cultural studies had given researchers the opportunity to link representations of popular culture (film, music, television, literature and so forth) to current affairs. Feminist critics Tania Modleski (1986) and Barbara Creed (1986; 1987) speculated on how popular culture represented changes in society along gender lines. Special issues on horror and science fiction appeared in *Camera Obscura* and *Screen*, and critics began to devote more attention to the connection between a text and its contextual resonance[13]. Science, the human body in crisis, dysfunctionality and sexuality rapidly became prime interests, and Cronenberg's films found themselves becoming points of reference in those discussions.

One debate that crystallised such concerns was that of the privatisation of health care, which took place along parallel lines in Europe and North America. Inspired by neo-liberal and conservative views on care (and promoted by the administrations of Ronald Reagan in the US and Margaret Thatcher in the UK), proposals were made to replace and augment the services offered by what were seen as overly bureaucratic institutions such as the National Health Service (in the UK), or the provincial health care plans in Canada, or even such inclusive bastions of public health care as the Netherlands and Belgium, by private services. This debate occurred against a background that saw changes in labour (more women sought to become active in the workforce in ways similar to men's careers), in gender roles in parenting and the place of the family in society (against a background of dropping birth rates in Western countries, discussions over unwanted pregnancy, and the state's role in baby and child care) and health science (treatments for cancer drew a lot of attention, concerns over pollution increased, the term *stress* entered the health discourse). Naturally, cinema explored these issues, or used them as backdrops, in films such as *Weird Science* (John Hughes, 1986), *Peggy Sue Got Married* (Francis Ford Coppola, 1986), *Mauvais sang* (*Bad Blood*, Leos Carax, 1986), *Three Men and a Baby* (Leonard Nimoy, 1987), *She's Having a Baby* (John Hughes, 1988), *Working Girl* (Mike Nichols, 1988) and numerous others. However, none of these films addressed the intricate connections between sex roles, health and commerce as well as Cronenberg's.

The problem that most critics and reviewers had in combining an obvious desire to enter topical cultural debates and relate them to individual films was the lack of an appropriate case study. That case finally presented itself in the form of the global anxiety concerning AIDS. With its clear-cut connection between bodily mutation, science and sexuality, and encompassing, through awareness campaigns, the inference of certain types of leisurely behaviour, and the struggle for funding and 'patents' for treatments, symptom combating or diagnostic procedures, AIDS managed to synthesise the above sketched discourse within one single word. Moreover, the topicality of AIDS and its ideological implications, such as the impact on liberal and emancipative movements coinciding with the worldwide 'return to traditional values', made it culturally emblematic.

It did not take long for AIDS to become a referential tool in the reception of the films of Cronenberg.[14] The first to make the link was John Harkness, in 1983. Harkness referred to 'AIDS and Kaposi's Sarcoma (known as "gay cancer")' to show how films like *Shivers* 'ironically' addressed recent threats to sexual liberation. Importantly, Harkness also connected the AIDS reference to a criticism of the ideological tone of Robin Wood's criticism of Cronenberg (see chapters two, four and five). It led Harkness to state that 'Wood was a better critic when he was repressing his homosexuality' (1983: 23), inviting the reader to think Wood's aversion of Cronenberg was not so much a critical mistake as a deliberate attempt to ignore the cultural relevance of his work.[15] Harkness's essay was reprinted in *The Shape of Rage* and in the same book an essay by Wood appeared criticising Cronenberg's films. Evidently, Harkness's reference to AIDS formed one of the points addressed by Wood. Wood claimed that to suggest '*Shivers* is some kind of anticipatory film about an actual human tragedy can only make it appear even more distasteful than it already is' (1983: 129).

Until the release of *The Fly* in August 1986, AIDS references remained marginal in Cronenberg discourse. By that point, the AIDS epidemic had generated worldwide media attention, and its cultural implications had begun to take shape, making references to AIDS legitimate and even necessary in writings on culture[16]. It comes as no surprise then that many reviews of *The Fly* refer to AIDS and its implications when trying to make sense of the physical decay of scientist Seth Brundle, and the obvious sexual implications the narrative attributes to his disease.[17] The first to do so were Jay Scott, Andrew Sarris, Brian Johnson and Pauline Kael in the *Globe and Mail*, the

Village Voice, Macleans and the *New Yorker* respectively. Scott observed *The Fly* as a 'strong, if subliminal dollop of AIDS panic' (1986: n. p.). Sarris saw it as a movie full of subtexts addressing the 'speed-and-drugs horrors of our time' such as 'addiction, paranoia, and … the widespread fear of AIDS and AIDS victims' (1986: 47). Johnson wrote that Cronenberg had 'found a metaphor to explore contemporary phobias of cancer, AIDS, senility and schizophrenia' (1986: 41). Kael, who was less positive about the film than the others, still acknowledged its significance as a 'metaphor for AIDS or cancer' (1986: 210). No doubt 'infected' by these four, dozens of other references to AIDS followed, representing a wide range of texts across platforms, types of press and in different countries (the US, Canada, the UK, France, Belgium, the Netherlands, Italy, Australia). Typically, many of the references to AIDS in reviews of *The Fly* were not limited to publications with selective readerships, but instead appeared in high profile, 'quality' broadsheets and magazines. The *Globe and Mail*, the *Village Voice*, the *New Yorker* and *Macleans* have already been mentioned, but also the *Financial Times, Knack Magazine, NRC Handelsblad, Libération* and *Time Out* included references to AIDS in their reviews, as did reputable, well-established film periodicals like *Segnocinema, Cahiers du cinéma, Film Quarterly* and even *Cinefantastique*.

There was not just the quantity of references to AIDS. The central position of references to it in reviews of *The Fly* also pointed to the fact that for understanding this film AIDS was a major tool – a *necessary* observation. Most of the references were used in support of crucial arguments on the meaning of *The Fly*, enhancing the impression that most (if not all) cues from *The Fly* could be related to AIDS, and inviting the conclusion that arguments on science and its role in society, infectious diseases, promiscuity, bodily mutations and dysfunctions, the social isolation of the sick, and the dangers and morals of sexuality, could all easily be collapsed into the AIDS problematic. Whereas Harkness in 1983 merely suggested a possible connection between AIDS and the metaphors used in Cronenberg's films, many reviews of *The Fly* proposed that the film *itself* was an AIDS metaphor. Thus, references to it moved to the centre of the critical reception of Cronenberg.

Apart from being topical, AIDS references in relation to *The Fly* also fulfilled a rhetorical function. The social consensus on the importance of AIDS allowed for a convergence between different opinions on Cronenberg, and transcended differences in ideology – of the reviewer and of the publication. The first two American reviews that refer to AIDS can serve as an example here: Kael's review in the *New Yorker* used the AIDS reference to make a negative point about *The Fly*, while Sarris's review in the *Village Voice* employed it to support a positive evaluation.[18] Both the *New Yorker* and the *Village Voice* have different interests, the former belonging to 'establishment writing', with much attention given to 'high culture', the latter presenting itself as 'left wing', devoting much space to 'underground and popular culture'. By both mentioning AIDS and attributing significance to it as a metaphor, the Kael and Sarris reviews seemed to suggest that while the value of *The Fly* could still be subject to debate, its significance was undisputed. An excellent example of this was *Film Quarterly*'s review, which argued that the AIDS subtext equipped not just *The Fly*, but Cronenberg's entire oeuvre with a cultural relevance:

As has been widely noted, the film's harrowing subtext is the AIDS epidemic, a visitation whose symptoms and spread seem uncomfortably in synch with long-time Cronenbergian forebodings ... one cannot today watch *They Came From Within* or *Rabid* without a sense that these two sexual plague films have caught up with the sexual plague years, that Cronenberg's antennae were indeed tuned in to some early warning system ... Though *The Fly* (wisely) foregoes any direct reference to its obvious real-life analogue, the presence of AIDS – that is, the presence of AIDS victims – lends a depth and tone more profound ... on his perennial theme. (Doherty 1987: 40)

The point about the 'prophetic power' of Cronenberg's earlier films fitted perfectly within the expansion of references to art and literature with regard to the director – within one paragraph his reputation moved from 'venereal horror director' to 'artist'. Above all, with the AIDS metaphor well established it had become possible to fully appreciate the cultural relevance of Cronenberg's films. They could now be regarded as progressive, no longer limited to what Harkness (1983) called 'alternative social structures based on our world' but addressing 'obvious real-life' reality.

Even after *The Fly* had disappeared from theatres references to AIDS continued to play an important role in public debates about Cronenberg, and about contemporary culture (within which Cronenberg had become a regular presence). There are several reasons for this; an obvious one is that AIDS did not lose its topicality. As Douglas Crimp (1988), Susan Sontag (1988) and Judith Pastore (1993) observe, its large-scale implications put it constantly in the middle of cultural attention. Apart from that, AIDS references carried a considerable cultural weight. Unlike other cultural references (and much like the disease itself) AIDS references were prominent in almost every layer of society, crossing boundaries of class, race and gender. In fact, it could be argued that this made AIDS references not just cultural, but also cross-cultural, affecting virtually every cultural 'niche'. On top of that came the awkward concurrence – a coincidence so striking it invited critics to notice it – that the AIDS epidemic fitted the moral and economic policies of the Reagan and Thatcher administrations only too well. It allowed right-wing campaigners such as Anita Bryant and Mary Whitehouse to draw parallels between the culture of 'permissiveness' and 'moral laxity' they claimed existed and view AIDS, the disease, as a punishment from God. As Kenneth MacKinnon described it in his overview of representations of medicine in 1980s cinema: 'It is almost as if the Western world, and with it its mass entertainment, were gearing itself up for the arrival of AIDS ... into a world where the very governments have geared themselves up to fight their perceptions of decadence, to draw clear lines between accepted and unacceptable lifestyles, to seek out "the enemy within"' (2005: 43). Put simply, AIDS was too important a reference to be dropped.

Cronenberg himself initially resisted the AIDS metaphor. John Costello wrote: 'Cronenberg took great pains to distance the film [*The Fly*] from being read as an AIDS allegory' (2000: 64). When explicitly asked whether he liked the AIDS references, Cronenberg answered that:

AIDS is a metaphor for something else ... [*The Fly*] is about death as most horror films are, and the transformation that happens to the main character. He could be dying of cancer or sure it could be AIDS. It's really what happens when what we take to be our normal bodily state begins to disintegrate but I'm really thinking of it as growing old. (In Lewis 1987:17)

With this statement Cronenberg pointedly summarised the issue: references to AIDS in the reception of *The Fly* did not necessarily refer to the content of the film text, but rather fitted a then-topical concern as well as critical discourse which was as much concerned with its subject as with its perceived role as social commentator.[19]

The reception of *Dead Ringers* added to that relevance a hitherto missing ingredient: class and distinction as artistic achievement – 'Cronenberg chic', as one reviewer put it (Temmerman 1989: 19). The film received ample attention across the world. In the eyes of those already favouring Cronenberg's work *Dead Ringers* was a step up from previous films (see Jaehne 1988; Taubin 1988). The absence of special effects and multiple gross-out moments was invariably seen as a quality, as was the sombre, elegiac and detached tone of the film – Cronenberg wielding a scalpel cutting away excess in favour of substance was a popular metaphor in reviews. However, with the horror genre no longer readily available as a framework for these metaphors and arguments, reviewers turned to a different frame of reference, one that recognised artistic attempts. As such, then, *Dead Ringers* quickly became an art-house favourite, on a par with, and compared to, European art-house films such as *Wings of Desire* (Wim Wenders, 1987), *Dekalog* (Krzysztof Kieślowski, 1987–89) and *Un monde sans pitié* (*A World Without Pity*, Eric Rochant, 1989) or films highlighting issues of gender, sexuality and the body such as those by Peter Greenaway and Pedro Almodóvar – esteemed company by any measure. In turn, the comparisons facilitated references and arguments about literature and art (one example is the art of Joel Peter Witkin).[20] The art-house trajectory also gave *Dead Ringers* a relatively long shelf life, with sporadic screenings in second-run theatres until the beginning of 1990.

An essential part of the reputation of *Dead Ringers* as Cronenberg's most accomplished work of art is its reception in what I will call the elitist film press: publications whose very selection of what they are reviewing presents their preference. Practically each territory has such an outlet: *Mediafilm*, *Andere Sinema* and *Grand Angle* in Belgium; *Skrien* in the Netherlands; *Filmdienst* in Germany; *Sight and Sound* in the United Kingdom (at least until the early 1990s, when it became much more inclusive); *Cahiers du cinéma* and *Positif* in France; *Segnocinema* in Italy; *Cineaste*, *Film Quarterly* and *Film Comment* in the United States. Cronenberg's films had sporadically been reviewed in these publications before, and several had shown temporary interest in his oeuvre (see chapter four). But with *Dead Ringers* all of them, without exception, felt compelled to state their allegiance and (re-)claim Cronenberg as auteur. Long interviews, lengthy essays and speculations on how *Dead Ringers* evoked a 'postmodern' or 'modern' sense of anxiety were typical techniques employed to that effect.[21]

For good measure some influential resistance remained, especially from a feminist perspective. For Canadian journal *CineAction* (run by a collective with Robin Wood as prominent representative) the praise for *Dead Ringers* was 'astonishing' because it ignored the 'arcane nihilism' and the 'barbaric underside of medicine' that were part of 'a social crisis triggered by the real fears of AIDS'. Instead, the reviewers urged, *Dead Ringers* remained 'complicit with the system of oppression' (Jacobowitz & Lippe 1989: 64–8). Barbara Creed (1990) too, repeated *Dead Ringers* was essentially misogynistic: an expression of male hysteria, of what she calls 'phallic panic'. Even as reruns of the adverse reactions Cronenberg had had since the mid-1970s (apparently still unresolved) these isolated criticisms bore signs of the topicality of Cronenberg in the second half of the 1980s, with their references to how his films, here called 'theoretical chic' pushed the right buttons of 'complex social and cultural issues' – AIDS listed among them (Jacobowitz & Lippe 1989: 64–8).

From Hollywood to Hollywood North: reception of The Fly and Dead Ringers
In the years following the release and immediate reception of *The Fly* and *Dead Ringers*, AIDS kept recurring as a prominent reference that had clearly been cemented into the overall opinion of Cronenberg's work. It popped up in interviews related to his other films, in textbooks about the horror genre and in re-considerations of Cronenberg's representations of homosexuality, to suggest 'queerness [could] in no way be seen to be on the margins of Cronenberg's oeuvre' (Ramsay 1999: 53).[22] The term even started appearing in essay titles: Edward Guerrero's (1990) essay on 'AIDS as a monster in science fiction and horror cinema' focused on Cronenberg's *The Fly* and Carpenter's *The Thing* as films that best expressed the 1980s anxieties about disease, contamination and sexuality in a commercial environment. For Andrew Parker, Cronenberg's films were already 'expectant' of these motifs, even before they became topically relevant (1993: 217). In the end, mentioning AIDS became a rhetorical instrument of newly emerging protocols to pigeonhole Cronenberg's films. When Cynthia Freeland (1996) wrote about critics using references to AIDS from a feminist viewpoint, she treated the term as a critical tool rather than a topical fact. Since then, the capitalised denominator AIDS has appeared in even the briefest considerations of both *The Fly* and Cronenberg, as shorthand for a way of solidifying the oeuvre's status as in tune with the times and, hence, urgent and relevant: in capsule DVD reviews, Best-Of overviews and even on websites promoting his later films.[23]

The artistic achievement that was *Dead Ringers*, and the praise it received, also crystallised in the long-term reception. The film received a lush laserdisc release (by Janus/Criterion), and it was highlighted in television listings whenever it was broadcast.[24] More significantly, it pulled Cronenberg criticism – which was now fast becoming a viable sub-industry within academia – out of the stranglehold of genre reviewing, to the point where it no longer became necessary to even mention the director's horror antecedents. In some cases (and most ironically in the Netherlands, where he had hardly received any good press at all), reviewers even lamented the fact he was now no longer a 'rebel'.[25]

The persistence of the AIDS metaphor and the continued appeal of *Dead Ringers* not only put Cronenberg in the international spotlight as a cultural hero, it also pulled him away from Hollywood. Only a few years after he had been embraced by it, he found himself at odds with it again, this time as a more revered filmmaker than before, but nevertheless still on the outside. What came instead was Canadian acclaim. According to Toronto critic Jay Scott even *The Fly* was already 'a movie that is a battle between Cronenberg the Canadian artist and Cronenberg the Hollywood entertainer. In the end, the Canadian wins' (1986: n. p.). As Canada's most recognisable and best-known film export product, Cronenberg had involuntarily become its spokesperson, and that meant he was less a part of Hollywood than an alternative to it. He became a sort of veteran inspiration for what seemed to be emerging as a new wave of Canadian cinema, characterised by the debut features of Atom Egoyan (*Family Viewing*, 1987), former assistant director on *The Fly* Patricia Rozema (*I've Heard the Mermaids Singing*, 1987) and Bruce McDonald (*Roadkill*, 1989). With the tax shelter days long behind them, this new generation sought achievement not in genre cinema but in quirky and stubbornly personal projects, and Cronenberg's *Dead Ringers* fulfilled the role as a model in this respect (with its worldwide acclaim and record number of Genie awards). At the same time, the appeal of Toronto, Vancouver and Montreal as centres for Hollywood productions looking for cheap but reliable (and English-speaking) labour – many of which had had training in Cronenberg's films – turned Canada into Hollywood North (see Denton 1987). Here, too, Cronenberg was becoming a keystone reference as someone who had proven that Hollywood-financed, commercial productions could be completed successfully in Canada. In other words, Hollywood was substituted for Hollywood North. At the end of the trajectory, it was Cronenberg the Canadian artist, former Baron of Blood, who emerged from the melee. In that sense, Cronenberg's reputation developed in the opposite direction to that of the Mantle twins in *Dead Ringers*. Their engagement with art, through the design of operating instruments, accelerated their downfall and their loss of sanity. In the case of Cronenberg, his status as Canadian artist cured him from Hollywood, and helped him keep his mind.

Beyond Greed? Family in Cronenberg's Films

For the most part, this chapter has treated the love of Seth Brundle and the genetic bond between the Mantle twins as causes for disaster and bodily harm, as obstacles to their greed rather than facilitators for happiness. As instances of family, and embryonic longing for family happiness in the case of Seth, they are under-researched, probably because the limited number of characters in both films, and their microscopic cultural lens – they look no further than the four walls in which they operate – do not invite much elaboration on family groupings. Yet, the stories of both *The Fly* and *Dead Ringers* hinge upon one premise the audience needs to accept in order to stay with the plot: that what they are watching is 'believable'. In order for that to happen, audiences need to acknowledge, however implicitly, that the bond between Seth and Veronica, and between Elly and Bev, runs so deep they stick it out together. As Geena Davis put it: 'establishing how much we love each other before the accident became very important, because if you didn't believe that we really love each other more than any couple ever has, why would Veronica stick around?'[26] Of course, the publicity around the real-life relationship she had with Goldblum helped drive that message home (they really *do* love each other). But besides that, Seth and Veronica have family plans, which lead to Veronica's pregnancy. When Seth's transfiguration makes Veronica change her mind, and she wants an abortion, his solution is to fuse all of them together, into 'the ultimate family. A family of three united in one body.' Jill Nelmes implies a link between depictions of family and portrayals of the body in Cronenberg's films when moving from a discussion of the 'familiarisation' of men in *Three Men and a Baby* to *The Fly* and *Dead Ringers* (2003: 271–2). The only difference is one of tactics – with the men in *Three Men and a Baby* obviously better at accepting and adapting to the family situation they find themselves in. But regardless of the male characters' suitability in *The Fly* and *Dead Ringers*, both films testify to the importance of family as the strongest possible commitment a human can make, based on true love and caring – not the commodified care of health science, but the wholesome one of personal care. In the light of these, and other, family-like congregations populating Cronenberg's earlier films, and the familial longings expressed in his work, the trope of family deserves a brief discussion at this point (one that will be returned to in more detail in chapter ten).

Family happiness is rare in Cronenberg's films. To begin with, there is the seeming incompatibility between horror and family happiness. According to David Hogan (1986), the family in the horror film is not so much a safe haven but rather a vehicle for bringing about evil. Countless husband/wife, parent/child and other family relations harbour evil. This means that the violence needed to defend the family from evil needs to be directed inwards – to their own family, to the loved ones. From Frankenstein's monster (his symbolic child), through Dracula's brides, the alien children of *Village of the Damned* (Wolf Rilla, 1960) and the deranged psychopath son of *Psycho*, to the possessed spouses of *Rosemary's Baby*, the family in the horror film is subject to internal struggles, generating evil from within. For Wood (1979a) and Creed (1993) these struggles are sexual of nature. The habits and rituals at the core of family life are the effects of a nasty sexual struggle, a battle between masculine and feminine forces, tearing the bond between lovers to pieces. For Tony Williams (1996), such struggles also rip apart the idea of a coherent family unit. Moreover, the powers at large in the world (politics, nature, war and so forth) are also reflected as tensions within the family, threatening that bond from yet another angle, bending its habits in yet another tense twist.

Hogan, Wood, Creed and Williams identify Cronenberg's films as a key example of the way in which families in horror films are replaced by a relentless combat between what are supposed to be partners. Instead of families, Cronenberg usually offers romances and relationships overshadowed by domestic violence, lethal technology and social obstacles. In *Stereo* and *Crimes of the Future* institutions make families impossible; in *Shivers* family becomes superfluous as everyone turns on each other (including siblings) in an omnivorous orgy of lust and violence; in *Videodrome* the VHS-inspired sado-masochist play between lovers escalates well before any romantic routine enters the story; *The Fly* suggests that the reason for Seth Brundle's demise into a mutated Brundlefly lies in his inability to respect the arrangement he has with

Veronica (his betrayal of her coincides with, and actually fuels, the angry, self-centred experiments that lead to his death); in *Dead Ringers* the Mantle twins' sharing of lovers leads to suicide through surgery, effectively breaking the only family bond present in the film; in *Naked Lunch* Bill's struggle with his wife ends with him apparently accidentally killing her (or is Bill's wife only a figment of his drug-induced hallucination?); in *M. Butterfly* the love struggle between loners is hindered (yet also instigated) by ethnic routines of gender performance, and marred by a battle of political espionage; in *Crash*, crushes are expressed through car crashes and casual sex; and in *eXistenZ*, any hint of romantic routine is contained within the protocols of a computer game. In most of these films the male protagonist ends up dead, and women are traumatised and victimised.

This list of affairs and abruptly aborted relationships, topped by the spectacular failures to make a family in *The Fly* and *Dead Ringers*, does not mean Cronenberg ignores the topic of family altogether. Several of his films do portray (yearnings for) traditional family life. Sadly, such happiness remains a utopia or a distant past. The epitome of this is *The Brood*, which chronicles the breakdown of trust and love between Nola and Frank Carveth in gory detail. At least Frank and Nola *had* a family at one point. In *The Dead Zone*, poor Johnny Smith's accident prevents him from marrying his beloved Sarah, and the freakish talent of foresight he gains precludes all hope of further involvement. Johnny's newfound ability is one he – as his doctor puts it – has an obligation to put to use for the world, but in so doing Johnny is forced to commit suicide, bit by bit; a cruel fate. Finally, *Spider* might be seen to foreground the family as a locus for romantic love (in that sense it precedes *A History of Violence* and *Eastern Promises*), but any happiness is thwarted by Dennis Cleg's killing of his mother. In dissecting the conditions that undermine families, these films lay bare the patriarchal, misogynistic, ethnocentric, xenophobic, protect-ionist and inherently violent foundations of 'family' – best encapsulated perhaps in the man's seizing or conquering of the woman.

Children are frequently represented as obstacles and as problematic to family happiness, rather than the welcome results of its consumption: the girl in *Crimes of the Future* is perceived as a clear threat; those in *Shivers* are equipped with as much of a ferocious sexual appetite as the adults (and let us not forget it was a minor who started the infections); the small creatures in *The Brood* act out horrible revenges and kill family members; while Johnny in *The Dead Zone* loves children, it is ironically a baby (the symbol of family, and the one thing Johnny and Sarah always longed for) that makes Johnny hesitate, and he is gunned down by security; Veronica's wish for a baby in *The Fly*, expressed in her dream, turns out to be a mutant maggot; the desire to become pregnant drives Claire into the arms of the twins in *Dead Ringers*; and the Cleg family's happiness in *Spider* is undermined by their schizophrenic and psychopathic son Dennis. It is clear, then, that children do not bode well in Cronenberg films.

The few happy families in the director's work are mostly culturally constructed ones, rather than biological ones – and as such they indicate allegiances pooled by need and choice instead of genes. The best example occurs in *Scanners*, where the congregation of renegade scanners led by Kim Obrist functions like a large household that shares practical responsibilities as well as offering emotional shelter. Their community is obliterated before it has the chance to develop any further, but the brief display of relief and support it offers Cameron (idealised through the 'integrated scanning' during the séance) gives it a strong sense of cohesion and belonging – certainly the kind of refuge and powerhouse a family could be. By extension, that is also what the conspirators in *Crimes of the Future*, the infected inhabitants of Starliner Towers in *Shivers*, the family of professionals in *Fast Company*, Doctor Raglan's patients in *The Brood*, the revolutionaries in *eXistenZ* and the followers of Vaughn in *Crash* seek, mostly in vain. The convictions of these family-like communities are modestly liberal, occasionally libertine, apparently granting equality between genders and generally less prejudiced than the outside world they are fencing off. Similar to underground movements and cults, they exist in semi-legality. To preserve their secretive make-up, they have developed cult-like rituals of membership and hierarchy. That does not protect them though: they are under constant threat of dissolution – in fact in most Cronenberg films they seldom survive attacks. Survivors of such assaults are left abandoned or betrayed – lonely.

CHAPTER SEVEN

Muses And Machos: *Naked Lunch* and *M. Butterfly*

I stumble into town, just like a sacred cow
Visions of swastikas in my head, plans for everyone.

> – David Bowie, 'China Girl'

Give me absolute control over every living soul
And lie beside me, baby, that's an order!

> – Leonard Cohen, 'The Future'

C'mon you little eastern girl
Welcome to the occident world!

> – Mano Negra, 'Letter to the Censors'

Globalised Hedonism: 'Interzone' and the 'Orient'

Welcome to the 1990s, the end of communism, the end of apartheid, the end of the millennium, the end of ideology and certitudes, the end of history – the era that turned the global village into a globalised marketplace of hedonism and consumption.[1] It was a decade that kicked off with Brian De Palma's adaptation of the 1987 Tom Wolfe novel *Bonfire of the Vanities* (1990), and Brett Easton Ellis's *American Psycho*

(1991), two texts showcasing decadence as the consequence of greed. Throughout the 1990s, explosions in global communication, transport and travel were accompanied by increased civil and sexual liberties (being gay and lesbian almost became 'chic') and moral relaxation, all of it encapsulated by the lax and leisurely attitude of the job-hopping, globe-trotting, sexually casual, frivolous yet bored Generation X.[2] Simultaneously, the political establishment in the UK, US and several European countries became upset by sex scandals (real or hyped) that seemed to confirm the old guard's inability to manage their own desires – if it was not a decade of decadence as so many neo-conservatives tried to paint it, it was at least one in which the pursuit of leisure and pleasure around the globe took up a prominent place. But taboos remained. Amidst all the libertarianism, sex between people of different ethnic backgrounds was still rarely accepted in mainstream cinema. The abolition of the old X-rating of the Motion Picture Association of America's Classification and Rating Administration, and its replacement with the NC-17 rating, saw acclaimed art-house films such as *The Cook, the Thief, His Wife and Her Lover* (Peter Greenaway, 1989), *Henry and June* (Philip Kaufman, 1990; the first title to receive the new rating) and *Atame!* (*Tie Me Up! Tie Me Down!*, Pedro Almodóvar, 1990) – films whose sex scenes derive part of their appeal from foreign locations and exotic flavours – vilified. In spite of efforts such as *Jungle Fever* (Spike Lee, 1991), *The Wedding Banquet* (Ang Lee, 1993) or *Higher Learning* (John Singleton, 1995), the combination of intercourse and intercultural relations was perhaps too uncomfortable for North American taste administrators.

Cronenberg's first two films of the 1990s fit these discourses neatly. Consider these scenes from *Naked Lunch* and *M. Butterfly*, respectively. The first takes place in Interzone, a sunny, dusty and exotic borough in a market town in North Africa, in the 1950s. In a rustic bar, American expatriate writer Bill Lee (Peter Weller) notices two other American writers, one of them strongly resembling his deceased wife Joan. He asks his companion, the slightly sinister German secret agent Hans (Cronenberg veteran Robert Silverman), who the two are and if he can talk to them. Hans sighs, and waves over local pretty boy Kiki (Joseph Scorsiani) from the bar.

> Hans: Kiki, Mr Lee is curious about the Frost couple. He'd like to meet them.
> Kiki: I think the woman would have sex with you, Mr Lee. But the man, he only likes Interzone boys.
> Bill: I don't wanna fuck 'em. I just wanna talk to them.
> Hans: You know how Americans are, Kiki. They love to travel and then they only want to meet other Americans and talk about how hard it is to get a decent hamburger.

Ignoring Hans' comments, Kiki invites Bill to come to a party the Frosts are attending later that night. Kiki and his friends accompany Bill. When they arrive, Joan Frost (Judy Davis) commends Bill on the 'hot threesome' he arrived with. 'They're very cheap, and they're really a lot of fun,' she adds, as she takes a swig from a flask of booze.

The second scene, from *M. Butterfly*, moves the action to the Orient, Beijing, 1964. In the garden of the Swedish Embassy in China, French diplomat René Galli-mard (Jeremy Irons) reluctantly sits down for an opera performance. 'Is there some diva passing through town?' he asks his German companion, Frau Baden (Annabel Leventon – a Transylvanian from *The Rocky Horror Picture Show*). She explains they are about to see excerpts from Puccini's *Madame Butterfly* by a local singer. René cheekily admits he has never seen the opera, but he asks her to keep it quiet as he wants everyone to think he is 'profoundly cultural'. As the show unfolds René asks why the singer seems so sad. Frau Baden explains: 'She will fall in love with an Amer-ican sailor. Big mistake … He will marry her, but he's not serious.' René gives an understanding nod. As the singing becomes more dramatic, Frau Baden continues: 'Her American sailor has now left. He is not coming back.' René sits up straight; he becomes intrigued.

These two scenes have more in common than neocolonial Germans badmouthing the rudeness of Americans abroad. While set in the 1950s and 1960s they exhibit a cultural attitude that is also decidedly of the 1990s. *Naked Lunch* and *M. Butterfly* centre on expatriate intellectuals, one a writer who is asked to become a secret agent, and the other a diplomat who is seduced by a secret agent, who become infatuated (albeit to different degrees) with local sexuality. It unwittingly implicates them in various plots, and before long they find themselves in a downward spiral of compul-sive passion, substance abuse and paranoia, until their personalities become unhinged and they lose their grip on reality. The scenes mentioned above initiate the protag-onists' fascination through allusions to sexuality they had not yet experienced, or denied themselves to explore – they get interested enough to start experimenting. It is essential to the films that such infatuation occurs amidst a range of nationalities and cultures (German, French, American, North African, Chinese, Japanese) that stress the artificiality of the locations' exoticism, and shows them as arenas of discourse rather than real places. As Jim Leach wrote with regard to *M. Butterfly*:

> The casting of an unmistakably English actor as a French diplomat – in a film by a Canadian director based on the work of an American playwright set in China alluding to an opera set in Japan by an Italian composer – only serves to heighten the sense of unreality. (2006: 72–3)

More than a sense of unreality, such a range heightens the impression of *construct-edness* that pervades the perception of reality of Bill and René. Pulled out of their habitual surroundings, exiled from their roots, they find that the customs they are used to no longer apply, that the world has become an incomprehensible place, and that they have to fake understanding it. It makes them not only utterly paranoid but also insensible. They become stereotypes of an offensively colonial attitude they seem unable to shrug off, part of a way of perceiving whatever lies outside the West as a place where morality no longer holds and where they, as Westerners, can feel entitled to try and get away with murder, adultery and abuse. Eventually, they are made fools of, and the local cultures they feel so superior to bite back with a vengeance.

This chapter will put the themes of sexuality and intercultural relations in the framework of 'queer politics' and 'orientalism', two concepts that link sex to power. *Naked Lunch* and *M. Butterfly* embody that link in the persons of the macho and muse: the woman as the passive muse, 'represented' or 'looked upon', and the male as the macho presenter or creator, the 'bearer of the look', bending the world to his will.[3] In painting this dichotomy, the two films also sketch a distinction within the act of creation of cultural meaning: in *Naked Lunch* the active male creates meaning by shaping words into reality without considering their reception (indeed, it almost seems Bill does not care who will read his work). In *M. Butterfly*, reception is everything, as René is an interpretive audience to what is staged for him. In both cases, gender politics and orientalism help determine the outcome of their creative acts.

Nabokov, Kafka, Burroughs: Cronenberg and Literary Culture

The fact that *Naked Lunch* and *M. Butterfly* have a well-respected status as artworks, based on highly esteemed source materials, received within an increasingly eclectic and highbrow arena of reception – a far cry from the more popular and crude 'cult of horror' surroundings Cronenberg had found himself a part of just a decade before – is an essential condition for understanding their appeal. Whether regarded as counterpoint to, or part of, the newly invigorated independent cinema scene of North America, or of a small wave of postmodern literary adaptations, *Naked Lunch* and *M. Butterfly* terminated Cronenberg's association with the genre of the horror film, the connection now surviving solely in the eye of the beholder, with occasional explicit gore shots giving succour to the hardcore horror fans.

Chapter five alluded to Cronenberg's nascent reputation as an 'active auteur': a filmmaker seen as the single most important creative force in the composition of his oeuvre, and also one directly concerned with the reception of his work. While this reputation did not come to its fullest fruition until later (see chapter nine), *Naked Lunch* and *M. Butterfly* are determined steps in the direction of that reputation, especially since they, for the first time in Cronenberg's oeuvre, consolidate a connection with highbrow culture – in the form of literature, drama and opera.[4] As such, the films opened up a new reception framework for Cronenberg, one of young adult and college niche audiences looking for alternativity and auteurs –the kind of audiences Cronenberg had to some extent already been getting with *Videodrome* and *Dead Ringers*. It was an audience smaller than the one attracted by *The Dead Zone* and *The Fly*, full of attitude and pretension, savvy and more difficult to impress. But it was also one that once conquered would be more resilient, loyal and active in the 'word of mouth' promotion of objects of admiration. When compared to the horror fans Cronenberg had drawn a decade earlier, this 'market' would regard him perhaps less as an auteur and more as an author: more on his own terms and less as part of a 'genre', 'cinema' or even 'popular culture'. For these audiences, Cronenberg was a fellow intellectual who happened to make films instead of write and/or compose.

One clear example of this change in perception is the reception of Cronenberg at the very beginning of the 1990s, prior to the release of *Naked Lunch*. The Cinémathèque

Québécoise published a dossier on him in 1990 that was also published as a book in France (Handling & Véronneau 1990). Though mostly a translation of the 1983 *The Shape of Rage* book it nevertheless signalled Cronenberg's acceptance into the higher echelons of film art. Also in 1990, the Rotterdam International Film Festival mounted a retrospective of Cronenberg's films that was accompanied by a dossier that (again) reprinted part of *The Shape of Rage*, but also included a lengthy introduction by esteemed novelist and screenwriter Jan Blokker. The same year, the Belgian art-house centre Stuc (in the college town Leuven) had its own retrospective, programming Cronenberg's films alongside a celebration of Stanley Kubrick's (see Lauwaert 1990; Temmerman 1990). Encouraged by these recurrent appearances on the public stage, and by associations with other cultural heroes (and indeed by frequent television broadcasts of Cronenberg's films), much of the European film press dedicated special issues or lengthy overview articles to Cronenberg. This interest was particularly visible in France, where the very fact that the illustrious *Cahiers du cinéma, Positif, Revue du cinéma* and other outlets found a filmmaker whose value they could agree upon, marked Cronenberg's ascendance into the canon of 'cool'.[5] References to the William Burroughs/Bob Wilson/Tom Waits rock opera *Black Rider* (based on Carl-Maria Von Weber's opera *Der Freischütz*) and the work of David Lynch (*Wild at Heart* (1990); the television series *Twin Peaks* (1990)) provided excellent opportunities for speculation on the future projects of Cronenberg within an art-house and highbrow context. As if to solidify that status, in the autumn of 1990 Cronenberg was named Chevalier in the Order of Arts and Letters of France, in recognition of his contribution to the art world.

Across the ocean, in the US and Canada, Cronenberg seemed to acquire a cross-over status, remaining much more an outsider from any kind of framework, or, as one journalist put it, 'a gifted nut case', rather than experiencing a determined elevation towards highbrow culture (Clark 1990: 4D). News about Cronenberg ranged from the very popular to the elitist and academic. He received much attention for his first significant acting role, as the evil Doctor Decker in Clive Barker's horror movie *Nightbreed*. The fact he got to play a 'monster' (who *had* to be a doctor of course) was an indication of how he had become some sort of totemic icon whose very name and presence in a horror film would link it to the genre's heyday – in much the same vein as his earlier direction of an episode of the *Friday the 13th* television series ('Faith Healer', 1988). Added to that was some recognition for his work on two episodes of a Canadian 'true crime' series *Scales of Justice* ('Regina vs Horvath' and 'Regina vs Logan' – the former featuring *Videodrome* and *The Dead Zone*'s Les Carlson), both broadcast in 1990. In perhaps his least acclaimed efforts, Cronenberg also tried his hand at commercials, for Ontario Hydro (1989), Caramilk (1990) and one episode in a 'director's collection' of commercials for sports equipment multinational Nike. This last commercial, with the Cronenbergian title *Transformation*, actually functions as a neat and tight summary of some of Cronenberg's favourite themes, and their grounding in the history of horror cinema: a slimy bug-like alien life form with claws, living inside a pod, is fed a giant larva, inside of which is a Nike Air 180 shoe. The bug tries the shoe on and breaks from the pod as a fit, skilled, human athlete.[6]

In addition, Cronenberg's name increasingly became a point of reference in ancillary debates. In his hometown of Toronto everything film-related was being measured against the name, or involvement of 'Cronenberg', from car race reports, through his public presence in Toronto and his appearance at various rallies, to his cameos.[7] In 1990 and part of 1991, with none of his films on release, his name was nevertheless mentioned every few days in local papers the *Toronto Star* and/or the *Globe and Mail*. Outside Toronto, reviewers found it necessary to refer to him in relation to the work of Jeremy Irons, James Woods, Jeff Goldblum or Christopher Walken (after they had acted for Cronenberg), or in reviews of the films of David Lynch or Peter Greenaway (as some sort of reinforcement of their 'value'). Even music critics started using his name as a point of comparison. Simultaneously, but on the other side of the cultural spectrum, Cronenberg continued to attract the attention of academics in the arts and literature, his oeuvre entering scholarly debates and theories.[8] That commentators assumed Cronenberg's name was well-known enough to be mentioned without explanation, or that he was worthy of unqualified academic analysis, meant it had entered the public consciousness of popular culture and contemporary art.

A key element in the gradual acceptance of Cronenberg into these spheres was the escalation of references to literature. Interviews, reviews and discussions of his work had always been spiked with references to literature. When we make exceptions for the writings Cronenberg had been using as sources (Stephen King for *The Dead Zone*, Bari Wood and Jack Geasland for *Dead Ringers* or George Langelaan and James Clavell for *The Fly*),[9] most of which are part of the more popular realm of literature, many of these references are decidedly highbrow. As early as 1971, Tony Rayns invoked comparisons with Vladimir Nabokov and Jorge Luis Borges in his review of *Crimes of the Future*. Nabokov quickly became a set point of reference for discussions of Cronenberg, one reinforced by Cronenberg's own frequent mentions of Nabokov as his 'mentor'.[10] Since *Videodrome*, the Nabokov-Cronenberg connection has become an almost self-standing point of interest for writers on Cronenberg. Next to Nabokov, Franz Kafka also occupied a key position as a preferred reference point in the criticism of Cronenberg.[11] Until and through the 1990s, journalists mentioned the name of Kafka about as often as that of Roger Corman, Martin Scorsese or *Alien*; all vehicles of considerable importance in giving Cronenberg's work a noticeable public presence, and promoting it.[12] It is in that sense that references to Nabokov and Kafka need to be seen as well: besides offering a critical tool for the intrinsic understanding of the preoccupations of the films, they provide readers and audiences with instant pointers for cultural placement – extrinsic tools for connections as it were. This does not imply that Cronenberg's audiences invariably consisted of avid Nabokov or Kafka readers; instead it means the public reputation of these names would give audiences a hint as to how, where and why they should approach these films. The Kafkaesque element in *The Fly*, for instance, evident in the reference to *Metamorphosis* (where a man wakes up to find he has been turned into a bug overnight – see chapter six), would provoke reviewers to mention the name of Kafka, thus inviting readers and audiences to see the film as not just a run-of-the-mill horror picture, but a smart piece of cinema that was both accessible and fully able to satisfy their intellect. Around the beginning of the 1990s, after *Dead Ringers* had shown audiences Cronenberg at his most art-house, such references began to take on a more central place in the changing cultural reputation of Cronenberg – as that reputation moved from Baron of Blood to cultural hero, Scorsese and Corman disappeared and Nabokov and Kafka took over.

Cronenberg himself played a prominent part in that change, by offering interviewers numerous references. In fact, he did so with such frequency it occasionally annoyed reviewers to have such heavyweight references thrown at them – perhaps because it prevented them from finding a safe pigeonhole for Cronenberg. As one reviewer remarked in a lengthy interview article in the *Washington Post* upon the release of *Scanners*: 'Cronenberg, who writes as well as directs his own films, litters his conversation with references to Descartes, Nabokov, Burroughs, Freud and McLuhan' (Harrington 1981: H1). Acknowledging literary antecedents might seem a strategy in contrast with Cronenberg's insistence on his originality, but – as the Kafka references demonstrate – there was an elegant way out of that contradiction. Isolated mentions of Kafka had appeared in several interviews, but it was in the winter of 1983/84 that the reference began to occur frequently in the discourse of Cronenberg, in two related ways: as an indication of literary inspiration that still stressed true originality, and as a defence against politicised readings of Cronenberg's films. In the latter case, Cronenberg employed Kafka, and the bureaucratic 'Kafka hell' in an argument against overly active censorship initiatives that would lay down laws about the regulation of art. The reference was made in connection to the then-topical debates about censorship in Canada; a debate that saw Cronenberg's name associated with that of revered Canadian author Margaret Atwood and, again, Nabokov – whose books critics claimed would fall foul of censorship laws (see chapter five; see also Ayscough 1983; Downey 1987). In the former case, Cronenberg mentioned Kafka, together with Fellini and Borges, as an example of an author who (like him, it is implied) 'actually creates his own precursors, linking together strings of writers not seen to be connected before Kafka's emergence. His work modifies our conception of the past, as it will modify the future' (1984: 57). Not only does this argument link Cronenberg's work to Kafka's, it also embeds it in the same frame of understanding: unique yet widely connected to respected achievements in the arts and literature.

By the early 1990s the references to literature had moved beyond Kafka and Nabokov. Authors as varied as Gustave Flaubert, Thomas Pynchon, J. G. Ballard (before *Crash* had emerged as a Cronenberg project), Edgar Allan Poe (not just in relation to the quotes in *The Dead Zone*), Samuel Beckett (see chapter nine) and, almost inevitably once any literary canon is invoked, William Shakespeare also appeared. Then, just when it seemed virtually any 'cool' writer would qualify as an exemplar for Cronenberg's esteem, the *Naked Lunch* project forwarded William Burroughs as the quintessential reference. That reference did not come out of the blue. According to Cronenberg, he was 'possessed' by Burroughs even at a stage before it had become clear he was going to become a filmmaker, and he mentioned his interest in a Burroughs adaptation as early as 1981 (in Rodley 1997: 157). Critics picked up the connection as well: the interview from the *Washington Post* quoted above listed Burroughs alongside Nabokov; and in a long review of his films in the *Globe and Mail*, also in the early

1980s, Burroughs was again invoked, together with Nabokov, Sartre and McLuhan, as a key influence, one that Cronenberg felt compelled to tear himself away from because 'Burroughs and Nabokov were suffocating me' – note again the technique of referencing while preserving originality (in Scott 1983). Around the same time, future *Dead Ringers* screenwriter Norman Snider felt it safe to proclaim, in an essay on the long-lasting influence of the Beat writers, there could be 'no David Cronenberg without William Burroughs' (1983: n. p.).

Once *Naked Lunch* was announced as 'the next Cronenberg', Burroughs became absolutely pivotal.[13] After all, *Naked Lunch* marked Cronenberg's first 'proper' adaptation: a project he instigated rather than inherited (which had been the case with *The Dead Zone* and *The Fly*), and one based on a book with a span beyond topical popular culture (which had been the case with Wood and Geasland's *Twins*, the source for *Dead Ringers*). Burroughs' novel combined high critical esteem with an enduring cult reputation that resonated well in literary circles that crossed over with art-house audiences. Because of that immense resonance, the sheer mention of Burroughs in discussions of Cronenberg lifted them into a literary frame of reference.

The pervasive persistence of this frame became particularly evident during the reception of *Naked Lunch*, which coincided with its inclusion in a small wave of high-profile literary adaptations noted for their interest in the act of writing, as well as with a rise in academic publications on Cronenberg – both adding flesh to the literary bone. This evolved into a fully-fledged acceptance of Cronenberg as a respected cultural icon by the time of the release and reception of *M. Butterfly* – in the wake of which Joan Dupont of the *International Herald Tribune* became the first to openly declare Cronenberg a 'Cultural Hero' (1993: 18).

Naked Lunch: words and writing

Let us start with *Naked Lunch*. Cronenberg first considered the idea of adapting the novel in 1984, when he met producer Jeremy Thomas. Cronenberg, Thomas and Burroughs visited Tangiers in 1985, but nothing materialised. After Thomas secured the financing for *Naked Lunch* in 1988, Cronenberg spent most of 1989 writing a draft screenplay. It was during this drafting that it became clear *Naked Lunch* would be about the act of writing and creation as much as it would be an adaptation of the book. As Cronenberg put it:

> I had to abandon the project of a direct translation, knowing it to be impossible, in order to be faithful to it. I had to fuse myself with Burroughs in order to bring something of *Naked Lunch* to the screen. I can hear some crude producer/director saying that, but really meaning that he wanted to dominate it and impose his own will on the material because he was too insecure to be faithful. But you can't. (In Rodley 1997: 161)

As well as reinforcing the fact that any Cronenberg adaptation would also be considered his own creation, this decision also enabled him to incorporate other work from Burroughs, such as the more autobiographical *Exterminator!* (1973) and *Queer*

(1985). Cronenberg spent most of 1990 rewriting the script and re-planning the production; the entire operation was initially to be shot in Algeria but because of Iraq's invasion of Kuwait, and the political volatility of the region, plans had to be changed. The entire shoot was rescheduled for Toronto. The delay this caused led to some speculation about whether the production would actually still go ahead at all. In hindsight, having the production stay in Toronto was an advantage. Instead of being bound by demands of realistic representation, Cronenberg and his crew could now re-create Burroughs' world from scratch. Shooting in Toronto's studios highlighted the 'constructedness' and artificiality of *Naked Lunch*, and fitted Cronenberg's intention to 'reshape' Burroughs' work rather than sticking to the text. It also made it possible to put the very act of 'creation' forward, and advance the trope of 'discovery' and 'invention' – one that would meet very well the main characters' prime obsessions (see Levin 2003).

As it turned out, *Naked Lunch* was not only an adaptation of a book; it is itself structured as a manifesto about writing and the power of words. The opening titles show bright colours in sharp shapes (squares, triangles, lines) sliding across the black screen, in a leisurely, frivolous fashion reminiscent of the credit scene of Billy Wilder's sex comedy *The Seven Year Itch* (1955). Sex is indeed not far away when one observes the shapes slide back and forth, as pieces of a rudimentary puzzle looking for the hole they match. A saxophone (played by Ornette Coleman) improvises wild jazz sounds, very much in the free jazz mode that had become associated with Beat literature. The coloured puzzle pieces appear to improvise too. Whenever they overlap, new colours come about – and not just the ones that logically follow from mixing colours: a lot of the combinations seem to result in pink, a colour associated with homosexuality, a key theme in Burroughs' work, and one that was pushing itself to the foreground in Cronenberg's films as well. After the titles come two dedication quotes. The first is 'nothing is true, everything is permitted' by Hassan I Sabbah. The phrase confirms the tone of creation and freedom the titles had already suggested. It is followed by a quote from Burroughs: 'Hustlers of the world, there is one Mark you cannot beat: The Mark inside…'. If the first quote gave an impression of liberation and irresponsibility, the second assumes a more predetermined perspective on the world: one of paranoia, fate and destiny. With such weighty openings, audiences are warned: this is a film that demands a degree of knowledge, and it asks to be worked at, not just passively consumed. It requires effort to interpret its subtexts.

The opening shots reaffirm the demand: in tested film noir fashion the shadow of the fedora of Bill Lee (Peter Weller) slides over the door of an apartment. His fist knocks on the door. 'Exterminator', his voice announces. It takes thirty seconds before we see anything else but Bill's shadow (his face, warped in concentration as he exterminates bugs in the apartment), and a full minute before he utters another word. 'I ran out,' he explains to his boss (Claude Aflalo), when he asks for another ration of bug powder, over and above his regular doses. 'Do you want me to spit it right into your face? … What do you? Eat the stuff?' his boss angrily shouts. Frustrated, Bill withdraws from the conversation, and storms out.

The inferences to sex (the spitting), drugs (eating the stuff) and paranoia (Bill's reaction of suspicion and frustration) in these early scenes form a triangle of metaphors that runs throughout the film as a constant menace to Bill, hindering him in every step he takes, obstructing his 'true calling' – to be a writer. In fact, they become more and more explicit as the film progresses. Exactly what kind of writer Bill is, or how good he is, remains unclear, even though the film will show him writing quite a lot. But any writing and words about writing are constantly loaded – to the point of obfuscation – with references to the sex, drugs and paranoia that are pushing their way up from Bill's subconscious into every conversation or action. As the deep frown on Bill's face in the opening scene (and in fact in most of the film) constantly reminds us, it is his troubled mind that is his most important obstacle: his doubts about his sexual identity, his proneness to addiction and drug-induced delusions (in itself of course an expression of his sexual insecurity) and his paranoia (the result of the realisation that he cannot trust himself because of his hallucinations). Like *Videodrome*, *Naked Lunch* is a first-person narrative, showing every action and utterance through Bill's perception. That means that any obstructions to Bill that are presented as exterior causes need to be understood as having an interior source as well. Unlike *Videodrome*'s Max Renn, Bill is aware of how his preoccupations skew his perception of reality, and at times he appears even amused by how his drug-induced mind bends whatever happens into sex/drugs/paranoia-coloured metaphors – as if he stimulates it as some sort of creative act of thinking. At other times, however, the inferences and hallucinations seem to take him by surprise, and frustrate or confuse him. His way of coping with the latter is, initially at least, to do exactly what he does after his boss lashes out at him: to try and pretend he is alien to it all, and feign non-involvement.

The scene immediately following the confrontation with his boss is a perfect example of these complex processes. It shows Bill resisting getting drawn into a conversation about writing with his buddies, professional authors Hank and Martin (Cronenberg veteran Nicholas Campbell and Michael Zelniker, as thinly-disguised versions of Jack Kerouac and Allen Ginsberg respectively), because of the sexual and narcotic innuendo in their words (which are of course his own thoughts as much as what is actually being said):

Hank: You see, you can't rewrite. 'Cos to rewrite is to deceive and lie, and you betray your own thoughts. To rethink the flow and the rhythm and the tumbling of the words is a betrayal. It's a sin, Martin.
Martin: I don't accept your Catholic interpretation of my compulsive necessity to rewrite every single word at least a hundred times. Guilt is the key, not sin. Guilt for me not writing the best that I can; guilt for me not considering everything from every possible angle, balancing everything.
Hank: Well how about guilt for censoring your best thoughts? Your most honest primitive, real, thoughts. 'Cos that's what your laborious rewriting amounts to, Marty.
Martin: Is rewriting really censorship, Bill? 'Cos I'm completely fucked if it is.

Bill (stone-faced): Exterminate all rational thought ... That is the conclusion I have come to.

Martin: What is the man talking about? I'm being serious.

Hank: So is he ... So, how is the extermination business going there, Bill?

Bill: Somebody's stealing my roach powder. Somebody's got it in for me.

Hank: Hmm, well, maybe you should take it as a sign. Maybe you should try your hand at writing pornography.

Martin: Yeah, a novel a week at 120 bucks. It's serious money. I could connect you with a guy (points at Hank). We're thinking about collaborating on one ourselves.

Bill (shakes his head): I gave up writing when I was ten. Too dangerous.

Hank: Only if someone reads what you write. So far, we haven't had that problem.

Bill: I found my profession. I'm an exterminator.

Martin: Of course, Bill, that's just what the world needs. More literate exterminators.

Hank (leans back and lights a cigarette): Of course, then, you know, you're gonna have trouble if you can't keep track of your roach powder.

This conversation has been quoted at length because it demonstrates how *Naked Lunch* works the metaphors of sex, drugs and paranoia into any talk about the act of writing, in every possible sentence, nuance and phrase. To anyone slightly familiar with the subtexts of the works of both Burroughs and Cronenberg, it should be clear the above conversation is not just about writing, but equally, and increasingly explicitly so, about sex, drugs and paranoia. At Hank's last remark, he and Martin burst into laughter, revealing more overtly than before to the audience, and to Bill (who asks them, 'do you boys know something about this?'), they have been talking in code – Bill's bored, dissatisfied wife Joan (Judy Davis) is using the powder to inject into her breasts as a potent, heroin-like narcotic (an image recalling that of Nicki burning her breast with a cigarette in *Videodrome*).

Everything in *Naked Lunch* is thus coded, and sexuality, addiction and suspicion form the keys to understanding the narrative, and the meaning of writing. When Bill confronts Joan, she claims shooting up the bug powder is a 'very literary high': 'It's a Kafka high. You feel like a bug.' Intrigued, Bill accepts Joan's invitation to try the stuff. Soon after, in a narrative move straight out of the *noir* genre, Bill is approached by two narcotics agents who take him 'downtown' to interrogate him. During the interrogation, the agents pull out a box from which a giant bug emerges; it throws itself at Bill's confiscated powder. After the agents exit the room, the bug addresses Bill, talking through an anus-shaped orifice at the top of its torso. It introduces itself as Bill's 'case officer' – read, his subconscious homosexual libido. The bug asks Bill to rub some powder on the lips of the orifice, and when Bill obliges it moans and sighs in orgasmic satisfaction. The bug then instructs Bill to get rid of his wife, whom it identifies as an agent from Interzone – an organisation the bug describes, in a reference to *Casablanca* (Michael Curtiz, 1942), as a 'notorious free port on the North

African coast; a haven for the scum of the earth, an engorged parasite of the under-belly of the West'. As if temporarily regaining control over himself, Bill smashes the bug with his shoe and rushes to his wife, who, in a state of total dependency, asks him to rub some powder on her lips. Again, Bill obliges, and they make passionate love. Desperate to kick his habit, Bill visits Doctor Benway (Roy Scheider), who supplies him with a black counter-powder, from the Brazilian centipede, that is guaranteed to seize the addiction – 'like an agent that has come to believe his own cover' (the agent here being Bill's latent homosexuality). Back home, he walks in on Hank having sex with Joan, with Martin sitting next to them, reading from Bill's writings. Martin asks Bill if they should join in the orgy. Only slightly annoyed, Bill shoots up some powder, mixed with the antidote, injects some into his wife's leg and grabs a gun. Pretending to play a game of 'William Tell', he asks his wife to put a glass on top of her head. He aims, fires and kills her – in exactly the same way Burroughs had in real life killed his wife Joan Vollmer (Bill's wife's maiden name is Rohmer), in an incident said to be a drunken accident.

Section Two: Interzone. On the run, Bill first seeks refuge in a bar, where a beaut-iful boy asks if he is 'a faggot'. 'Not by nature,' replies Bill, though he admits circum-stances force him to consider it. The boy introduces Bill to a friend, 'specialised in sexual ambivalence'. That friend turns out to be a giant alien bug, a mugwump. The mugwump instructs Bill to buy a Clark-Nova typewriter and seek exile in Interzone, from where he is to file a report on the killing of Joan. In exotic, dusty Interzone, Bill diligently sets about typing the report of Joan's murder. But after getting acquainted with Hans, who asks Bill if he can put him in touch with Doctor Benway to sell a 'large stash of black meat', Bill becomes embroiled again in a complex scheme of sex, drugs and paranoia. Hans turns out to be an underground supplier of centi-pede drugs. Bill becomes an addict again, suffers from hallucinations and the bug reappears – this time fused with Bill's typewriter. It orders Bill to change the strict, factual writing of his report and to adopt a more reflexive tone, including sentences such as 'homosexuality is the best all-around cover an agent ever has', which, as Bill types them, arouse the bug/typewriter to the point of orgasm. As Bill's resistance to homosexuality fades, his writing moves away from reality – away from non-writing, reporting and even pornography, into the realm of imagination. From now on, Bill is, as Hans observes, ' a writer of fiction'.

The next step is to apply that fiction and push it onto reality. At another meeting with Hans, Bill notices a couple of American expatriate writers, Tom (Ian Holm) and Joan Frost. Joan is the spitting image of Bill's dead wife; he becomes instantly infatu-ated with her, and seeks the Frosts' company, getting himself invited to a party through young, gay Kiki (as outlined in the description at the beginning of this chapter). At the party, Tom and Bill talk about writing, a conversation that slips flawlessly into the murdering of Joan (Bill's *and* Tom's), until Tom reminds Bill how conversations about writing are code, to be employed while the real, telepathic conversation is about muses and how to kill them. Typewriters, Tom suggests, help to achieve that task, and he offers Bill his Martinelli. The morning after the party Bill also meets Yves Cloquet (Julian Sands), an aristocratic Swiss gentleman who flirts with Bill, forcing him to admit his homosexuality – albeit in a veiled fashion, via a story. As Bill's drug habit gets worse, and his hallucinations increase (they now feature large centipedes as well), his obsession with Joan grows too. Accepting Tom's offer to use his Martinelli, he writes a letter to Hank, begging for help. But Bill's own Clark-Nova bug attacks and destroys it, warning Bill to be on his guard with the Frosts. Bill visits Joan, and they share a writing session on Tom's other typewriter, an Arabic Mujahaddin. As their typing gets saucier, the Mujahaddin opens up like a vagina, and a protruding penis extends from it. While Bill and Joan have passionate sex the Mujahaddin transforms into a giant winged bug that feverishly joins in the sex. The action is interrupted by the Frosts' lesbian housekeeper, Fadela (Monique Mercure), who holds a strange, compelling sexual power over Joan. She throws the Mujahaddin out of the window where it is smashed to pieces.

All of this and more is dutifully logged by Bill on his Clark-Nova bug typewriter, though the writing becomes more and more obscure and impenetrable, and the entire story is rapidly taking on the form and structure of an espionage novel, in which the big power blocks opposing each other are men (gay men) and women (who are not even human at all, as Bill's typewriter has it). Indoctrinated into that game, Bill continues to gather information on various conspiracies even after Tom confiscates the Clark-Nova at gunpoint, in revenge for the destroyed Martinelli. Bill goes underground. When Hank and Martin visit him, he is almost completely paranoid and delusional; he does not even remember having sent portions of his writing to them, and is surprised when his friends tell him a publisher is actually interested in his *Naked Lunch* manuscript, a title that is foreign to him. He tells his friends it is probably all an elaborate and well-prepared conspiracy. In spite of his reluctance, Hank and Martin diligently edit the shards and fragments of Bill's manuscript, and fawn over its quality. After they leave Bill manages, with the help of his now-lover Kiki, to get the typewriter repaired. Shaped as the mugwump's head, with its open mouth as the keyboard and its many antennae oozing slime and drool, the mugwump takes over as Bill's new case officer, setting him on the trail of Doctor Benway, who is supposedly leading Interzone's major drug emporium. With Kiki, Bill seeks out Cloquet for more information, but he is only willing to trade it for sex with Kiki. Bill agrees, and Cloquet tells him Fadela is the person who will lead him to Benway. Cloquet then turns into a giant bug that rapes Kiki and drills his skull until he dies. Penetrating Fadela's lair, Bill discovers she operates an elaborate drug den where the antenna juices of enslaved mugwumps are sucked by desperate addicts (Hans and Joan among them). Putting on his hard-boiled *noir* detective act, Bill confronts Fadela and tells her her game is over. In reply, Fadela rips open her torso, to reveal … Benway. The doctor tells Bill he wishes to recruit him to his operation, and lead its expansion into neighbouring Annexia. Bill agrees, but asks if Joan can join him. 'Without her I cannot write,' he says.

The conspiracy unravelled, Bill's book is finished. He and Joan drive to the border with Annexia. Asked by the border guards to prove he is indeed the writer he claims to be and to 'write something', he grabs his gun, turns to Joan, tells her it is time for the William Tell routine, aims and shoots her through the head. Bill has thus finally managed to kill off the obstacles to him becoming a true writer: he is clean of drugs, he has uncovered all the conspiracies that made him so paranoid and he has shed himself of women. He is a liberated writer. Impressed, the guards welcome Bill to Annexia.

The reception of Naked Lunch: independent cinema and the cult of cool literature
Strange as it may seem, given all its weirdness, *Naked Lunch* was not considered an isolated or unique effort in the early 1990s. It was one of several independently-produced North American films about writers and writing appearing at the tail end of a veritable wave of literary cinema. Many of these films had themes very similar to Cronenberg's film. Before *Naked Lunch*, Bernardo Bertolucci had already released *The Sheltering Sky* (1990), based on an autobiographical novel by Paul Bowles (the real-life alter ego of *Naked Lunch*'s Tom Frost), and set, like Cronenberg's film, in North Africa. Also in 1990, *Henry and June* chronicled the steamy love affair of writers Henry Miller and Anaïs Nin in interbellum Paris. Gus Van Sant drew international attention with his adaptation of the unpublished novel about drug addiction *Drugstore Cowboy* (1990), in which Burroughs had a small part as a priest (Burroughs also acted for Van Sant in the short film *Thanksgiving Prayer*, 1991). A year later, Van Sant adapted Shakespeare's *Henry IV*, and turned it into the gay drug fable *My Own Private Idaho*. At the same time, Peter Greenaway directed *Prospero's Books* (1991), an adaptation of Shakespeare's *The Tempest*, in a fashion highlighting its constructedness. Just prior to *Naked Lunch*, the Coen brothers released *Barton Fink* (1991), a tale of literary talent absorbed by Hollywood (modelled on the experiences of Clifford Odets and William Faulkner); the film featured Judy Davis again acting as the muse. *Barton Fink* ran rife with metaphors of paranoia, as did Steven Soderbergh's *Kafka* (1991), which featured Jeremy Irons, whom Cronenberg had introduced to Soderbergh (see Goddard 1990). Curiously, all of these films had in common a certain view of women (as muses) by male writers (whether queer or macho, or both), painting them as 'necessary evils' in the creative process – a view both reverent of female qualities and denigrating towards any attempts made by women to escape the roles ascribed to them by male writers. Since *M. Butterfly*, and the culture of its reception, pushed this observation even further, it will be expanded on below.

The connection between *Naked Lunch* and other literary films did not go unnoticed; it set the tone for much of the critical reception. *Naked Lunch* premiered in North America in late December 1991, and was immediately compared to literature. *USA Today* opened its review asking 'Newspaper ads once asked it of Stanley Kubrick's *Lolita*, and now the question is back: How did they make a movie out of *Naked Lunch*, William S. Burroughs' once-banned and beyond non-linear 1959 novel?' (see Clark 1991: 4D). The review praised the film as a 'gutsy', 'warped', 'bent *Casablanca*', before awarding it 1.5 points out of 4 (ibid.). That combination of respect and dismissal summed up the overall response in North America. For once, being Canadian did not seem to help much; in his home country *Naked Lunch* was admired yet deemed not for regular consumption. Compared to *Dead Ringers* and *The Fly* the film did rather poorly at the box office, garnering little over $2 million in North America, and about double that in the rest of the world. Quite fittingly, the *New York Times* suggested that never had Cronenberg 'offered his audience a more debonair invitation to go to hell' (Maslin 1991: C1). Still, when the right attitude and company was assumed, as suggested by the *Globe and Mail*'s reviewer, who went to see it 'with a literate friend', *Naked Lunch* was considered a major achievement, not just for pulling off filming the unfilmable, but for giving Burroughs' nightmare a matching cinematic equivalent (see Scott 1992: n. p.).

If looked at across the entire year – 1992 – there is little doubt that Cronenberg still managed to reach the audiences he had made this film for. The cult following of Burroughs and 'cool literature' certainly found their way to the theatres. In North America, the film press was also sympathetic. *Cinefantastique* and *Cinefex* lauded it for its elaborate special effects, and its rebellious and reflexive tone linked it to horror cinema of the time, such as *Gremlins II* (Joe Dante, 1990), *Alien³* (David Fincher, 1992) or *Braindead* (Peter Jackson, 1992) – films in which splatter gore was combined with dry humour, an anarchic spirit and a tongue-in-cheek reflexivity. Chris Walas's CWI produced the special effects, and that inevit-ably drew attention from the fan and trade press of the genre, which briefly seemed to regain interest in Cronenberg.[14] But the interest remained limited to the special effects only – while there were many references to the 'horrific' aspects of Burroughs' writing, it was not seen as corresponding with the tradition of horror cinema. For the American film press, and also the more literary press, *Naked Lunch*'s focus on the macho and/or gay romantic *maudit* writer, and the fatal muse he is inspired by, was an invitation to discuss the process of 'creativity', and its implications – especially its misogyny. It cemented comparisons with the literary films mentioned above, while providing a link with Cronenberg's earlier work.[15]

But the real impact was in Europe, where Cronenberg had been elevated into a cult in his own right (see the section on the European pre-*Naked Lunch* reception above). The collaboration with the even bigger cult figure of Burroughs, and the possibility of discussing an adaptation that was as much about Burroughs as about the act and process of writing, gave many reviewers the opportunity to launch themselves into full literary mode, as if they had become book critics.[16] The place where *Naked Lunch* premiered in Europe, at the prestigious Berlin International Film Festival (the Berlinale), meant it was presented within a context of art and art-house cinema. Though it did not receive any major awards, the very fact it made it onto the programme pulled the German-speaking press, which had already developed a keen interested, ever closer to Cronenberg.[17] In neighbouring regions Italy, France and Belgium *Naked Lunch* had long runs at art-house theatres and cheap second-run student theatres, sometimes for up to nine months. The film also had smaller successful screenings at those genre festivals with a keen interest in the more artistic and daring (and less formulaic) horror pictures, such as Fantasporto in Porto and the Brussels International Festival of Fantastic Film (BIFFF) (both in March 1992). In the latter case, the Belgian Royal Cinematheque staged a near-complete retrospective of Cronenberg's films. After the hesitant overture towards *Dead Ringers*, the UK's reception of *Naked Lunch* was one of the most positive Cronenberg had enjoyed – as with the North American press, it garnered respect and admiration, especially in the film press and more liberal newspapers, and particularly directed at producer Jeremy Thomas.[18]

It is easy to dismiss *Naked Lunch*'s lack of popular success as a failure, and judged by the measures of *Dead Ringers* and its award appeal, and the massive box office hit that *The Fly* had been, it was certainly less successful. But *Naked Lunch* hit a deeper note. The way it settled Cronenberg's name with a core audience that *Variety* described as 'buffs' and 'highbrow audiences in general', and the manner in which it found a hardcore cult of 'cool literature' and chic post-horror in Europe added more depth and substance – more flesh – to Cronenberg's reputation as a respected cultural force.

M. Butterfly: 'Oriental sex is a natural'[19]

If the reception of *Naked Lunch* confirmed Cronenberg's reputation as an artist, *M. Butterfly* reinforced this, solidifying it into esteem. Moreover, it did so in a fashion that kept links with previous Cronenberg materials well-established, so that the label of 'cultural hero' did not come at the expense of integrity or consistency – quite the opposite: *M. Butterfly* was as concerned with ambiguity, perception and the creation of reality as had been *Naked Lunch* or its antecedents.

At first glance, *M. Butterfly* is the most uncharacteristic Cronenberg film next to *Fast Company*. Shot on location in China and Central Europe, on a studio-financed budget larger than any of the previous productions (and the largest until *A History of Violence*) it was a break from his regular procedures. Adapted from a successful Broadway play, which was itself inspired by a true event *and* by an almost century-old legendary opera, *Madame Butterfly* (which in turn was inspired by a tale even older than that), it had a genealogy that made it more difficult than ever to claim 'active authorship' over.[20] Shot in a highly dramatic and epic, yet largely naturalistic, style with picture-postcard views, at magnificent locations – not just the Great Wall of China (which is effectively reduced to a wallpaper backdrop through the peculiar framing of the scenes set there) but the old innercity architecture of Paris as well as various elaborate stage designs – it is far removed from the sparsely decorated sets of Cronenberg's previous films. Even the recurrence of a lead actor (Jeremy Irons) was a novelty, at least in Cronenberg's commercial career.

But if compared to the themes that inhabit *Naked Lunch*, *M. Butterfly* was a logical next step in Cronenberg's career. It shares with the Burroughs adaptation an interest in exploring the processes of the creation of art, beauty and aesthetic pleasure – in this instance not literature but drama, performance and theatricality. Like *Naked Lunch*, its storyline arcs from the postwar past to the present, albeit in a more historically accurate and less imaginary fashion than that film. It has the same obsession with exoticism and gender roles that *Naked Lunch* had; it takes a similar position towards the portrayal and function of women (as muses) and men (as machos) in the creation of art, as roles inscribed onto people without much of an opening, or understanding, for resistance. Finally, *M. Butterfly* and *Naked Lunch* both present themselves as detective and espionage stories that are eventually unmasked as tales of paranoia: the outside enemy ultimately turns out to be the inner one – oneself. The main difference, perhaps, is that whereas *Naked Lunch* ultimately remains unapologetic in its machismo (Bill kills Joan again, just to prove he is a writer), *M. Butterfly* has room for a wider, more complex, perspective that takes into consideration the cultural and social conditions under which artworks are encountered. Put simply, *M. Butterfly* takes the audience's perspective on the same theme as *Naked Lunch* – this time the centre of attention is not the person creating, but the person perceiving the creation, the culpable witness.

That was also the position Cronenberg assumed from the start of the project. He instructed his agent to find him a project with a big studio that would not require much personal involvement in terms of financing (which had cost him much effort and anxiety with *Dead Ringers*), planning and scriptwriting (which had delayed *Naked Lunch*). He read the script of *M. Butterfly*, adapted by the playwright David Henry Hwang from his Tony-award winning 1988 Broadway play of the same name. Cronenberg reached a deal with Geffen Pictures to produce it for just under $20 million, with shooting to take place in China, Budapest (with second unit photography in Paris) and Toronto (for studio interiors). Being able to rely on his regular crew allowed Cronenberg to keep the costs acceptable (at least to Geffen Pictures' standards). Cronenberg's major involvement in the screenplay was to tone down what he called the rather declamatory stand against stereotyping, which had been very important to Hwang – a descendant of Chinese Americans – and make the main character of René Gallimard, who was based on the real-life example of French diplomat Bernard Boursicot, more ambiguous. The theatricality of the language was kept intact. Hwang and Cronenberg felt it demonstrated just how much Gallimard was constructing his favourite reality, as diplomat, secret agent and lover. Hwang remained the screenplay's only author. It was the first time since *The Dead Zone* Cronenberg did not share a writing credit. All in all, the smoothness with which the entire project moved ahead was an indication that, if he was willing to sit back and let the subject, or the studio, have some say in the organisation and execution of it, his craftsmanship and talent was well-recognised in Hollywood.

M. Butterfly announces itself like an Academy Award-aspiring David Lean meets James Bond film. A symphonic orchestral soundtrack with a catchy tune embellishes a credit sequence that lets all the exotic clichés of the Orient flutter across the screen: a painted mask, orchids, bonsai trees, paper screens, a fan, a yin-yang sign, tapestry and kimonos, a parasol, a bamboo stick, terracotta dishes, a cherry tree and, of course, a beautiful butterfly. Instead of flapping its wings, however, it remains immobile – a first sign of its shackles. The title scene closes with the announcement 'this film was inspired by a true story'. Next, we move straight into the world of diplomats and spies of the West stationed in the Far East. In a soft-focus sunlit room French envoy René Gallimard mulls over some classified materials that the French secret service might be interested in. As he strolls across the streets of Beijing, discussing his 'licence to kill', René makes an assured impression. Here is a well-educated, well-bred, Western man brought up in the belief he is in command, in control and entitled to whatever he wants. Even the cheeky admission to the woman sitting next to him at an embassy garden party that he has never seen Puccini's *Madame Butterfly* is part of that casual arrogance – why should he have? By the time the garden party's excerpt show of *Madame Butterfly* draws to a close, however, René has changed. He has become enthralled by the spectacle of true, tragic love that the Butterfly character represents. He attributes his fascination to the performance of the actress Song Liling (John Lone). But when he compliments her for the 'beauty' of the show, she replies curtly:

> Well, yes, to a Westerner ... It's one of your favourite fantasies isn't it? The submissive Oriental woman and the cruel white man ... what would you say if a blonde cheerleader fell in love with a short Japanese businessman? He marries her and then goes home for three years during which time she prays to his picture and turns down marriage from a young Kennedy. Then, when she learns her husband has remarried she kills herself. Now, I believe you would consider this girl to be a deranged idiot, correct? But because it's an Oriental who kills herself for a Westerner, you find her beautiful.

René smiles and admits she has a point, but later, to his wife, Jeanne (Barbara Sukowa), he complains about the arrogance of the Chinese. His wife shrugs it off. Citing the example of different nose-blowing practices, she professes: 'East is East, and West is West, and never the twain shall meet.' René obviously dislikes having his presumptions pushed into his face, to be dismissed as ignorant and self-centred. But it also spikes his interest, and for the rest of the film he continues to willingly, almost incomprehensibly, let himself be fooled by Song Liling, assuming the position of the passive audience that almost masochistically has its prejudices exposed then frowned upon.

Whereas *Naked Lunch* put the writer as creator of the story forward, *M. Butterfly* advances the audience as an equal partner in that game. The remainder of *M. Butterfly* abounds with situations in which René sits in an audience. The first instance of this comes right after the dinner party, in René's bedroom, when his wife mockingly performs a Chinese singer 'doing' *Madame Butterfly*, holding her fashion magazine as a fan. René, again, is fascinated. Next, we see him wandering through night-time Beijing, an audience to its culture. Then, he visits the Beijing Opera, and sits in rapture as he watches a performance. After the show, he walks Song home, and they discuss imperialism. She leaves him in front of her home – abruptly shutting the door to him. Still an audience, René walks home and sees an elderly man catching dragon-flies (a neat continuation of the bug trope from *Naked Lunch*, and one Cronenberg would revisit with *eXistenZ*'s mutant insects). He takes one, and observes it flicker its wings on his hand, as if he is controlling it and it is pleasing him. Soon, Song and René are having an affair, described as 'dangerous' by Song. René visibly enjoys the fact Song keeps describing to him, spelling out explicitly, how she longs for him. He consciously keeps her at some distance, and wallows in her begging to see him more. It makes him feel strong and powerful. For a while he becomes proactive. It even leads to a promotion to a sensitive intelligence position. Song's self-declared inexperience at 'pleasing a man' in a Western fashion, spurs his confidence even further as he faces a nasty power struggle inside the embassy. René becomes privy to highly classified information about Vietnam, and starts preaching 'understanding' and even proph-esising about the 'submissive Oriental soul'.

But René is soon returned to the state of audience. It turns out Song is an agent for the Chinese government. Her 'Western decadence' is a cover. As her power over him grows (he longingly calls her 'butterfly' now), it is her turn to keep her distance. Claiming pregnancy, she retreats to the countryside to 'have the baby'. In her absence, the Cultural Revolution forces René and all Westerners to keep a low profile. When Song returns with a son, she is arrested and sent to a labour camp, and René is devastated. His analyses unmasked as posture, he is demoted and sent home. Back in Paris amidst the May 1968 student revolts (to which he is more an audience than a witness), René sinks into a depression. Even attending, and repeatedly listening to, *Madame Butterfly* does not lift his spirits. Then, when Song suddenly shows up at his doorstep, he once more tries to become an active force – even if it is only as a diplomatic courier. Again, he is betrayed. He is arrested for espionage, and at a trial, which he passively undergoes, he sees what everyone else apparently knew all along: that Song is a man. René does not seem all too surprised. A faint smile slides across his face. Had he not known all along as well? Still, René has difficulty acknowledging the truth in the face of Song. It is only after he is, one last time, reduced to an audience – the forced audience to Song's masculine nudity (the 'naked truth') in the police vehicle that drives both of them to prison – that he realises how his reality has been a construction, a lie he loved to live: 'I'm a man who loved a woman created by a man. Everything else simply falls short.'

Only in the very last stage setting does he abandon being an audience and become an actor – literally so. In an elegiac prison performance of *Madame Butterfly*, with himself as both a celebrity and the tragic Oriental (which of course he has *de facto* become), lamenting the true love he felt, he commits suicide – for real this time, the 'biggest performance of his career', as Madame Butterfly.

The reception of M. Butterfly

M. Butterfly premiered as the gala opening film at the Toronto International Film Festival in September 1993, home turf for Cronenberg. It was preceded by an exhibition of his special effects in the Royal Ontario Museum (yet another highbrow territory Cronenberg was becoming comfortable with). It also came in the wake of several more retrospectives of his oeuvre – the largest being 'The Strange Objects of David Cronenberg's Desire', a 300-piece exhibition accompanied by a full retrospective of all his work, including the television dramas and commercials, staged in Tokyo in the spring of 1993. All this attention generated massive press coverage, but it did not guarantee a smashing reception. In monetary terms, *M. Butterfly* matched the box office performance of *Naked Lunch*, but given the wide release it received through Warner Bros., and the significantly higher budget it had enjoyed, it was generally perceived as a commercial failure. Even Cronenberg himself admitted that it did not do well (in Rodley 1997: 180). Early reviews in particular seemed to have difficulty accepting *M. Butterfly*. For once, critics were not prepared to accept Cronenberg's view, and they objected to the premise that Gallimard would be blinded enough by his love for Song Liling to never realise she is a man (see McCarthy 1993). There was also a struggle to accept this as a 'Cronenberg film', a first, and rare, sign of Cronenberg's 'auteur' status being used against him – as if reviewers had arrived at a model of what a Cronenberg film should be, and were berating him for not living up to it (see MacInnis 1993). Remarkable in these criticisms was that the same constructedness that was seen as a feature quality of *Naked Lunch*, was now derided as 'unconvincing' – especially with regard to the figure of John Lone's Song Liling (see Clark 1993). Amidst these struggles, the fan and genre press also abandoned Cronenberg; there were no special effects or bloody and horrific moments to warrant their attention – an attention that was increasingly leaning towards cult television such as *The X-Files* (1993–2002) anyway.[21]

One important reason for this lack of enthusiasm for *M. Butterfly*, besides the faults reviewers found in its make-up, was that critics and audiences found it difficult to attach the film to something bigger – a trend, a wave, a cause or a topical interest. I will argue below the film does indeed have such a larger alignment, in the form of its ambiguous attitude towards orientalism and gender politics (and queer politics in particular), but at the time of its release in North America it was certainly not perceived as such. Much of this refusal to connect *M. Butterfly* to a larger context had to do with the lack of comparable films that were highly visible on the public's radar. Unlike the films *Naked Lunch* had been compared with (which had definitely been identified as the same class), any films that were noted alongside *M. Butterfly* were mostly considered incidental points of reference. The two films mentioned the most were *The Crying Game* (Neil Jordan, 1993) and, to a lesser extent, *Basic Instinct* (Paul Verhoeven, 1992). *The Crying Game* had exposed the same 'trick' (the substitution of male and female and its shock revelation) a few months before the release of *M. Butterfly*; it became a logical point of comparison. But such comparisons hardly ever went beyond simply noting that Jaye Davidson was a more 'realistic' or 'beaut-iful' female figure than John Lone – a strange observation given *M. Butterfly*'s criticism of exactly such culturally coloured perceptions. The fact *The Crying Game* not only predated *M. Butterfly*, but had also been a surprise box office success in North America added to the importance it was accorded, pushing the comparison in its advantage.[22]

These negative sounds were not uncontested; in fact they were often matched by expressions of admiration for Cronenberg's efforts and daring (see Maslin 1993; Murphy & Jameson 1993). Moreover, as *M. Butterfly* was released in other territories across the world, general opinion swayed in its favour. Much of that was the result that its European reception did find a wider anchor point: that of the rise of Asian cinema – not just films *from* Asia, but *about* Asia as well. Preceded by *Indochine* (Régis Warg-nier, 1992) and *L'Amant* (*The Lover*, Jean-Jacques Annaud, 1992), 1993 saw European festivals welcome *The Wedding Banquet*, *Farewell My Concubine* (Chen Kaige) and *The Puppetmaster* (Hsiao-Hsien Hou) to much acclaim. All of these films found their way into the North American market via the Toronto International Film Festival – which added *M. Butterfly* and *The Joy Luck Club* (Wayne Wang) as new premieres. While for North American reviewers all of these films were brand new, and hence difficult to string together, European critics and audiences had had the time to see the connections that bound them. As a result, *M. Butterfly* received a much more sympathetic reception in Europe, especially in Italy, Belgium, Germany and France, and in Eastern Asia – where Cronenberg had become the new 'cool' Westerner, together with David Lynch.[23]

Queer politics and orientalism

The distinction between the North American and European receptions of *M. Butterfly*, and especially their use of different points of comparison, pushes the theme of cultural environment to the fore of the Cronenberg discourse. It is a new theme in the reception trajectory of his work. Until *M. Butterfly* Cronenberg's films had been kept safely within the range of Western culture. There were hardly any intercultural encounters to be witnessed. Up until *The Fly* all of his subjects had been fiction (albeit with a speculative application to reality). But *Dead Ringers, Naked Lunch* and *M. Butterfly* had their source material in historical reality, based upon true events. The last two also included 'foreign' locations – outside North America, in Africa and the Orient.

As was pointed out in the introduction to this chapter, if we look at the themes of these films three elements stand out: the sense of the *constructedness* of reality (as something made up by humans, though not necessarily constantly under their conscious control), sexuality and immigration. The conflation of these themes (enabling as much as hindering each other) anchors them into the tenuous cultural debate of gender politics across cultural borders. Besides the two conversations with neocolonial Germans quoted at the opening of the chapter, numerous moments in *Naked Lunch* and *M. Butterfly* address these politics. When Hank and Martin visit Bill in Interzone, and Hank explains why he has to go back to the United States (because his own book is 'too American'), Bill replies: 'America is not a young land. It is old, and dirty, and evil. Before the settlers. Before the Indians. The evil was there, waiting.' As if to emphasise the same point, Tom remarks, in a scene not connected to Bill and Hank: 'No American should find himself in a foreign land without a pistol.' It is inviting to read criticisms of American foreign and colonial policy into these comments – and perhaps we should. But I believe a topic more general is addressed here: that of crossing the boundaries of one's existence as a cultural human being – on a personal as well as social level – and the complexities those crossings bring to the mindsets of people already confused. As Cronenberg put it in relation to *M. Butterfly*:

> Gallimard is about being dissatisfied with your own culture and then throwing yourself bodily into another culture to abandon your own culture. It's a kind of self-hatred to do that; people who learn another language and marry a woman or a man of that other language and become completely consumed by that other culture and abandon their own culture and their own friends and their parents and their own paths and themselves. It's an illusion because the culture that you're taking on is not your culture, you're always an outsider, especially in a culture like that of the Chinese or Japanese. There's no melting pot mentality; they don't want you to be Chinese. (In Rodley 1997: 182)

Cronenberg refuses to distinguish between the small-scale personal situation of one individual and the general concerns of large groups of people. He collapses them into each other. The personal is always collective, and vice versa, and both are constructions.

The theoretical concept that best explains that complication is 'orientalism', proposed by Lebanese literary critic Edward Said (1978). At its simplest, orientalism refers to the way representations of the landscapes and inhabitants of the Orient (which historically included North Africa, the Middle East, Persia and regions further East) answers to a view of what the Orient *should be* in Western eyes, not what it effectively *is*. Said researched representations of the Orient in numerous novels and narratives and concluded orientalism is not only a *constructed* image of reality, but also one that allows little or no room for alternatives. As Caribbean scholar Stuart Hall explained:

> Not only, in Said's 'orientalist' sense, were we constructed as different and other within the categories of knowledge of the West by [colonial] regimes. They had the power to make us see and experience *ourselves* as 'Other' ... It is one thing to position a subject or a set of peoples as the Other of a dominant discourse. It is quite another thing to subject them to that 'knowledge', not only as a matter of imposed will and domination, but by the power of inner compulsion and subjective conformation to the norm. (1990: 223)

Once the constructedness of the representation is achieved, any possibility for the represented Oriental (or any 'other') to regain control over it, becomes impossible without accepting the rules of the representation – many of them confirmations of stereotyping. Moreover, since this robs Orientals of any chance to resist their representation by Western governed media (film chief among them), the question could be asked whether the concept of orientalism is actually limited to representations such as film and literature. Or, as Lawrence Grossberg put it, 'does the Oriental exist apart from orientalism?' (1996: 95).

That is certainly the case in *Naked Lunch* and *M. Butterfly*, where nothing exists outside the identities Bill and René construct. Bill's perception of Interzone is as much his construction as it is a reality. In fact, there is no distinguishing between them. The Doctor Benway and the Joan he encounters in Interzone may well be fabrications entirely, the results of him pushing certain characteristics onto people. With regard to Joan, Bill lets himself be inspired by what he feels a macho man should want from a woman. She should be his muse – his Song Liling. When he becomes more comfortable as a homosexual (even if he convinces himself it is just a part), he relegates the image he constructs of her to 'lesbianism'. She stops being a muse to the macho when both images no longer suit him.

Similarly, René constructs Song according to his presuppositions of what an Asian woman should be. He lets himself be inspired by other fictions, such as Puccini's opera. The fact Song reminds him that that is what he is doing does not stop him. He feels compelled to construct a representation of Song, and that will – by definition – be an orientalist one. This is exactly Hall's and Grossberg's point; René *cannot* stop himself. Once he goes down the path of constructing, he is forced to represent her this way. René's long speech at the end of the film, just before he commits suicide, admits this: that the representation is more compelling than reality, easier to believe in and more convincing. Ironically, Song is doing the exact same thing as René. S/he too is constructing an image of René easy enough to believe in. *M. Butterfly* does not spend enough time with Song to allow audiences to make up their minds whether this counter-construction is an act of resistance, of compliance with Song's commanders or of reciprocity (loving René the way he does). Judged by the stripping naked of Song in the police vehicle after the trial, it is understood Song's construction was much more in response to René's than one in its own right, less a case of action than reaction.

If we look at both *Naked Lunch* and *M. Butterfly* as social comments, beyond the obsessions of their characters, they seem to assume a most Cronenbergian standpoint, one he had put forward since his earliest films: that true contact and understanding is impossible. According to Hwang, the force of stereotypes in intercultural contact makes such understanding even more difficult:

> The myths of the East, the myths of the West, the myths of men and the myths of women – these have so saturated our consciousness that truthful contact between nations and lovers can only be the result of heroic effort. Those who bypass the work involved will remain in a world of surfaces, misperceptions running rampant. (2003: 1406)

Clearly, neither René nor Bill made such heroic efforts. While they paint themselves romantically (in the case of René) or stoically (in the case of Bill) as machos treating their muses appropriately, free from guilt, they do not attempt to reach beyond the comfort of their constructed representations. If, as Linda Ruth Williams claims, both films are about masculinity in crisis, about 'masculinity inside out', then this crisis is unbeknownst to the protagonists (1999: 30).

The long-term impact of Naked Lunch and M. Butterfly

The most significant long-term impact of *Naked Lunch* and *M. Butterfly* are the avenues they opened up for Cronenberg's films to become part of the higher and more respected (one could say more eclectic and elitist) circles of appreciation. The literary link Burroughs provided, and the connection with classical music, opera and theatre enabled through the adaptation of Hwang's work, gave Cronenberg perhaps not the widest possible popular success, but they made his work and his name more acceptable beyond film. After 1993, it was expected that an intellectual or a 'connoisseur of cool' would be familiar with the name Cronenberg. To that extent he had become a true cultural hero – far removed from the 'Baron of Blood' label he had been carrying.

In the years to follow, Cronenberg would continue to make overtures to the art world outside cinema. In 2003, *Naked Lunch* was the first of his films to get a prestigious Criterion DVD release. In 2006, Cronenberg curated an exhibition on Andy Warhol at the Art Gallery of Ontario. A year later it was announced he had signed a contract with Penguin to write a novel. In 2008, Cronenberg ventured further into opera, when he directed a version of *The Fly* (with libretto by Hwang and music by his long-time composer Howard Shore) at the Théâtre du Châtelet in Paris, to mixed critical acclaim (see Anon. 2008a; 2008b). Anytime soon, a DVD release of *M.*

Butterfly is to be expected that will possibly change the tenor of its long-term reception by attracting new reviews that will likely re-evaluate the film and place it in the context of the films Cronenberg has made since. In 1993, much of that still lay in the future, and Cronenberg would not be Cronenberg if his career did not first steer away from that path to arrive at it via a detour.

At one point in *M. Butterfly*, René drives around in Paris on a vintage BMW motorcycle – an inconspicuous detail to the regular audience, but a mark for the Cronenberg devotee as significant as a Hitchcock cameo. For a few moments, this motorcycle reminds the viewer of the presence of Cronenberg-the-auteur. Admittedly, of all Cronenberg's films, *M. Butterfly* has the fewest such signature marks. But when Cronenberg would return to the issue of immigration and exile, and of intercultural understanding (or, rather, the lack of it), the vehicle of the motorcycle reappeared. In *Eastern Promises*, Cronenberg used an equally vintage Russian Ural motorcycle to ignite a tale of inverted orientalism, of people seeking refuge not from the West in the East, but from the East into the West, looking for a better life and instead experiencing displacement. The Ural bike plays a much more prominent role as vehicle for communication and understanding in *Eastern Promises* than the BMW in *M. Butterfly*, and similarly *Eastern Promises* presented a more pressing plea for understanding of cross-cultural communication and immigration than *M. Butterfly* had. It is perhaps an indication of how in between the two films motor fanatic Cronenberg had found a new perspective regarding gender and intercultural politics and had come to realise it was not just a topic that burdened the communication between East and West but between cultures and subcultures in closer proximity to each other as well. His first film after *M. Butterfly*, which put vehicles very much at the forefront narratively and thematically, and would largely reinvent Cronenberg to the world, was already a step in that direction. That film would be *Crash*.

CHAPTER EIGHT

Scars and Wrecks: *Crash*

Do you see Kennedy's assassination as a special kind of car crash?
— James Ballard (James Spader) in *Crash*

Drive away and it's the same
Everywhere death row, everyone's a victim
Your joys are counterfeit. This happiness political shit …
Under neon loneliness, motorcycle emptiness.
— Manic Street Preachers, 'Motorcycle Emptiness'

Cars and Sex

'We're about ready to go here,' says a crew member as he checks the harness of the Steadicam operator on the set of a car commercial shoot. It is the first line of dialogue in *Crash*. We, the audience, are about ready to go too. After all, the film has started a few minutes ago and there is no clue about what is going on. All we have seen is a strange sex scene in an airplane hangar in which an attractive blonde woman presses her naked breast against the shiny steel of a plane's wing as she is approached from behind by a man who lifts her skirt and kisses her bottom before making love to her. Cut to the car commercial set, where everyone is gearing up to shoot. Upon the cue of the camera crew, the assistant director shouts out: 'OK, has anybody seen James Ballard? You know who I mean, the producer of this epic?' But James (James Spader) is unavailable right now. He is in an adjacent room having sex with the camera girl (Alice Poon), quite graphically depicted. That is sex scene number two. Immediately after, we see the blonde woman, Catherine (Deborah Unger), and James on the balcony of their apartment, high above Toronto's highways. It turns out they are husband and wife, and while discussing their day (he asks her about the sex in the hangar, she asks him about the sex with the camera girl) they have sex on the balcony, him standing behind her as she watches the traffic on the streets. That is sex scene number three, all in the span of the first four minutes of the film.

Cronenberg famously commented on the sex scenes in *Crash* as a deliberate statement of aims:

> The film begins with three sex scenes. For most people that means it is a pornographic film; they've never seen a movie that began with three sex scenes before. And instead of watching to see what I'm really doing with that, they just react the way they normally do – which is to switch off and wait for the movie to get going – but it doesn't get going because the sex scenes *are* the movie so if they resist watching them for narrative, for character development, for the texture, for other things which are there – they don't get the movie. I had little screenings of the film – my version of the Hollywood test screening … I just showed it to some friends and people; and I got a card that said 'a series of sex scenes is not a plot', and my reaction to that was 'why not'? (In Barker, Arthurs & Harindranath 2001: 5; emphasis added)

Crash tells the story of James Ballard, a director of commercials, and his wife Catherine, a trainee pilot – so the sex scenes that opened the film were work-related. A couple in their thirties living in Toronto they have, as those scenes exemplified, a marriage in which extramarital affairs are openly discussed, and even promoted. 'Poor darling', Catherine offers solace, as James complains his partner of the day did not come. 'Maybe the next one,' she whispers as they make love high above the traffic of the highway.

One day, James loses control over his car and slams into the vehicle of Helen Remington (Holly Hunter), a doctor at the immigration department of the airport, whose husband, a chemical engineer for a food company, is instantly killed. While recovering in hospital, James bumps into Helen again, who is accompanied by former specialist in international computerised traffic systems, Vaughan (Elias Koteas), a scarfaced man who shows great interest in his scars and wounds – as he scans James' body he almost sniffs them. After he has left the hospital, and amazed at the traffic volume he now notices to be heavier than ever before, James visits the lot where his wreck is impounded. There he meets Helen again, looking for her car. He gives her a ride to the airport. As they drive, a mutual sensuality envelops them – her red gloves against her cigarette, stockings and white trench coat ('a fucking kimono' she calls it) slowly arouse James, who keeps fiddling with his seatbelt until, in frustration, he takes it off. Helen, too, has noticed the increase in traffic: 'They seem to be gathering for some special reason I do not understand. There seems to be ten times as much traffic.' Their languid ride comes to an abrupt end as James' car is cut off. With Helen's help he narrowly avoids an accident and he makes it to the airport parking lot. There, Helen and James make passionate, rushed love to each other. Once home, James also has sex with Catherine.

Days later, James joins Helen at a strange, illegal spectacle: Vaughan and stunt pilot Colin Seagrave (Peter MacNeill) dramatically restage the car crash that killed film star James Dean (yet another James). Driving the same sports car as Dean, a Porsche Spyder, Vaughan and Seagrave refuse to wear any prophylactic protection – no helmets, belts or padding, nothing between the soft flesh of men and the hard body of the vehicle. As he and the camera sensually caress the silver chromed curves of the Porsche, Vaughan whisperingly announces the stunt:

> Don't worry, that guy's gotta see us. These were the confident last words of the brilliant young Hollywood star James Dean as he piloted his Porsche 550 Spyder race car toward a date with death along a lonely stretch of a California two-lane blacktop, Route 466. Don't worry, that guy's gotta see us. The year: 1955. The day: September 30. The time: now.

During his speech, as Vaughan gets more agitated with each breath, the camera also reveals an audience for the stunt: a stand filled with half-interested, half-detached voyeurs and thrill-seekers (not unlike the one waiting for the demonstration in *Scanners*). Like a stripclub audience, they applaud politely so as not to betray their excitement. Vaughan and Seagrave drive the Porsche at the exact speed Dean and his German factory mechanic Rolf Vudrich were driving that night into the oncoming car of student Colin Turnipseed. They smash into each other. With minor injuries, but generally unhurt, Vaughan and the stuntmen survive the collision. As the camera lingers over the post-coital wrecks, Vaughan closes the performance: 'James Dean died of a broken neck and became immortal.' At that point howling sirens herald the arrival of what is assumed to be the police, and the crowd disperses ('It's not the police, it's the Department of Transport' corrects Helen). Vaughan, James and Helen, who puts Vaughan's hand between her legs, drive the still fuzzy Seagrave home. Vaughan introduces James to his wife, Gabrielle (Rosanna Arquette), a woman whose legs and lower torso are supported by a metal and leather harness (the result of a crash), and to his new project: 'The reshaping of the human by modern technology.'

James ponders over the encounter with Vaughan, as he and Catherine drive home from work, in separate cars. As they stand still in front of a red light James observes Vaughan backing his car behind Catherine's Porsche. Vaughan chases Catherine, nearly rear-ending her a few times, before she pulls over, distressed. Vaughan races away. That night, as Catherine and James have sex, she asks him to describe to her what it would be like to sodomise and fellate Vaughan. When Vaughan later takes

James for a night ride, he explains he always wanted to drive a 'crash car with history', like Albert Camus' Vega, Grace Kelly's Rover 3500 or the car he is driving, a Lincoln similar to the one in which John F. Kennedy was assassinated – a special kind of car crash. Vaughan explains the more dangerous philosophy beneath the 'crude sci-fic concept' that the 'reshaping of the human body by technology' is: to introduce car crashes as a form of (pro)creation. They pick up a prostitute with whom Vaughan has sex in the back of the car while James drives.

One night, Catherine is also invited into Vaughan's car. They drive by the site of a huge accident – it actually looks like a night-time movie set. Vaughan is exalted, taking pictures of the bewildered victims and the firemen cutting loose trapped bodies as he declares the site a 'work of art'. He directs a mesmerised Catherine to pose amidst the burning wrecks, then discovers that one of the victims lying dead in a mangled wreck is Seagrave – who had gone ahead and restaged a project he and Vaughan had been meaning to plan: the Jayne Mansfield crash. They drive to a car wash to clean some of the crash's blood off the car. The moment the steaming water sprays over the car and it becomes engulfed with semen-like soap Vaughan and Catherine start having sex, first cautiously, then rougher, until a bruised Catherine catches Vaughan's semen in her hand and spreads it over the back of the leather driver's seat – from where James has watched everything. At home, James caresses Catherine's bruised body, and they make love gently.

The next day, James accompanies Gabrielle as she struts with her cane and harness through a car showroom. While a salesman helps Gabrielle fit into a Mercedes, she puts her hand in James' lap. Soon after, we see the two in a parking lot with the Mercedes, having sex: James struggling to untie and deconstruct Gabrielle's straps, then exploring her deep scars, kissing and licking them and even trying to fuck them. Increasingly dazed, and less and less interested in his work as director, James is summoned again by Vaughan, who is getting a series of sketchily-designed tattoos inked onto his body; 'prophecies' he calls them. He convinces James to get one too, on his inner thigh. The Lincoln parked on the side of the road, Vaughan and James examine each others tattoos and bodies, and have rough sex. When James wanders from the car into a junkyard, and sinks down in a wreck, Vaughan crashes the Lincoln into it, twice, as if to punctuate the penetration and ejaculation their bodies had experienced only just before. Back home, Catherine tells James someone has scraped her car. 'It is Vaughan' concludes James. With Vaughan increasingly elusive, Catherine and James decide to look for him on the roads – which are now eerily empty. Instead, he finds them, and furiously, as if driven by rage and jealousy, chases their Porsche with the Lincoln until, unable to control the wheel any longer, he careens off a bridge into a bus. The car in flames, Vaughan is dead. At the car impound, the Lincoln is visited, as if at a wake, by Gabrielle and Helen. They solemnly open the car and make love inside it.

James and Catherine pay to have the Lincoln released. On a rainy day, James drives it in a chase with Catherine's Porsche. He pushes her off the road, and the Porsche crashes and topples over. Catherine is thrown beside it. As she slowly recovers James slides behind her and starts having sex with her. 'Maybe the next one, darling,' James says. 'Maybe the next one.'

Love, interruption and deformation

'We were interrupted,' says James, early on in *Crash*, when asked if his camera girl came when they had sex. 'Maybe the next one,' he sighs at the end when his collision with Catherine fails to hurt her. It testifies to a major theme in *Crash*: the necessary incompleteness of any attempt to meet desires to full satisfaction. *Crash* deals with cars and sex, but also with the concept of incompleteness and deformation, the actions that turn cars into wrecks and sex into scars.

A closer look at the narrative of *Crash* from the point of view of the crashes and sex scenes – the penetrations so to speak – reveals a tight structure.

Sex scene 1: Catherine and a stranger (her instructor?) in an airport hangar
Sex scene 2: James and his camera assistant on set
Sex scene 3: Catherine and James on their balcony
Car crash 1: James and Helen in the car in the parking lot
Sex scene 4: Catherine gives James a handjob in the hospital
Sex scene 5: James and Helen in the car in the parking lot
Sex scene 6: Catherine and James at home
Car crash 2: the restaging of James Dean's fatal crash
Sex scene 7: Catherine and James at home
Sex scene 8: Vaughan and the prostitute in the Lincoln (with James watching)
Car crash 3: the restaging of Jayne Mansfield's fatal crash
Sex scene 9: Vaughan and Catherine in the Lincoln in the car wash (with James watching)
Sex scene 10: Catherine and James at home
Sex scene 11: James and Gabrielle in the Mercedes in the parking lot
Sex scene 12: James and Vaughan in the Lincoln
Car crash 4: James and Vaughan in the junkyard
Car crash 5: James and Catherine in the Porsche, and Vaughan in the Lincoln
Sex scene 13: Gabrielle and Helen in the Lincoln
Car crash 6: James in the Lincoln and Catherine in the Porsche
Sex scene 14: Catherine and James at the side of the road

If penetration and/or ejaculation define the acts of sex and crashing, the film consists of six crashes and 14 sex scenes (one such act every four-and-a-half minutes if we add them up). That is, by any standards, a lot.

In contrast to traditional sex scenes in mainstream cinema, *Crash*'s sex scenes are always either abruptly cut into or away from. As Chris Rodley observes, they are also frequently grouped together (1997: 197–200). The groupings reveal much about Catherine and James' relationship. The first three sex scenes demonstrate the kind of open marriage Catherine and James have. It is, however, not loveless; neither James nor Catherine look for love outside their marriage, only for thrills and kicks. In fact, if we look at the three sex scenes between them that occur at home, right after acts of infidelity (James' sex with Helen, James' very arousing encounter with Vaughan at the Dean restaging, and Catherine's rough sex with Vaughan), they are among the most tender and gentle in the film. Catherine and James actually love each other very much, and they share their experiences not so much in order to escape or repair their relationship, but to take it to the next level of satisfaction which, of course, they fail to reach. James seems unable to reach a climax, twice remarking that he did not come. Catherine's pleasure seems entirely interiorised. Maybe they will reach culmination with the 'next one'.[1]

Vaughan interrupts their marital happiness and plans for transcendence. James and later Catherine are intrigued by the new concept Vaughan introduces, namely to see car crashes 'as a fertilising rather than destructive·event, a liberation of sexual energy, mediating the sexuality of those who·have died with an intensity that's impossible in any other form'. Maybe it is the stimulant they have been looking for that proves there is indeed a next level to their love. But Vaughan's concept does not hold up. It becomes deformed along the route. Not only does it change from 'reshaping the human body by technology' to something more sinister, he also loses sight of it as he becomes more and more infatuated with James. When having sex with the prostitute, he is really seducing James through her. But James stays loyal to Catherine, siding with her whenever needed. It irritates Vaughan to the point where he chases Catherine's Porsche and almost pushes her off the road, then hurts her deliberately when he has sex with her in front of James, and finally sneakily scrapes her car. She is a rival in his desire for James. Only once does Vaughan get James to himself, after they have their tattoos and have sex in the Lincoln. When James wanders off afterwards and relaxes in a wreck in the junkyard, the still unsatisfied Vaughan is so frustrated he rams him, twice. For James it is a sign Vaughan is not the 'next one' he and Catherine are looking for, but a liability instead. So they let him find them and cause his fatal car crash. With the human body of Vaughan·out of the way, James and Catherine try to see if the Lincoln, with which Vaughan has 'merged', can elevate them onto the next stage of fulfillment. It can't. They are still left to look for the 'next one'.

While Catherine and James' search remains incomplete, and its procedures constantly interrupted·and deformed, *Crash* does show that there is no story, no project, more important than that of love. That is what Cronenberg is arguing in the first three scenes: a mutual love between Catherine and James so profound that it leads them, together, wanting more – like an addiction. Vaughan too becomes addicted to love (his love for James) and it leads him to abandon his project in favour of pure adrenaline chases. Ultimately, James' love for Catherine is bigger than his love for Vaughan. So he dies and she lives.

'Prophecies are ragged and dirty': the fetishism and fantasy of technology
Occasionally, people are unable to cope with not having their desires and cravings met. In *Crash*, Catherine and James are in danger of substituting their search for their aims: their looking for the 'next one' might replace the actual finding of it – if ever there was anything to find at all. In the hospital we can still assume James is aroused by Catherine more than by her talk of car wrecks that stink of body and machine fluids, but his arousal at the end is undoubtedly connected as much to the twisted,

smouldering wreck as to the 'immaculate cleanliness' of icy blonde Catherine (the high-tech of womanhood).[2]

One way of channelling such increased desires is repression. William Beard sees the 'super cool' look of Crash as representing a frozen repression – an impression of extreme control and tightness that is reflected in the post-industrial, techno-cultural landscapes of concrete and metal, with streams of cars lining up on highways and people disciplined into high-rise apartments and interiors of plastic and shiny aluminium that are spotlessly clean, with the sole purpose of not allowing the tiniest bit of abject desire to break through (see 2005: 388–90). Whilst agreeing fully with Beard, I would highlight another aspect of channelling desire, one more rooted in what Cronenberg sees as the fetishism for the technological vehicle for desire and sexuality that is the car.[3] Crash contains several perfect examples of car fetishism.[4] Helen and Gabrielle, for instance, only have sex in cars. 'Only in cars?' asks James at one point. 'I didn't plan it that way,' replies Helen. Helen and Gabrielle watch car crash safety videos together while sensually caressing each other, and they make passionate love in the Lincoln. When they have sex with James it is in the driver's seat. Their attire adds to the fetishism: Helen's leather gloves, nylon stockings and shiny grey metallic bra (from which she twice exposes her breast), and Gabrielle's fishnet stockings and leather and metal harness increase their fusion with car technology, rubbing, scraping and caressing the chrome, metal and leather. Gabrielle is only too pleased when her wrapped leg gets stuck in the car seat coating of the Mercedes – it is as if the car gropes her.

Seagrave's fetishism goes further than sex: he aims to relive moments when car and body fuse in the act of the car crash. He ignores his wife and anyone else, and only thinks about planning car crashes. The only reason he wants 'big tits' is so they can explode into his head when crashing into the steering wheel. The two crashes Seagrave is involved in are also the most elaborately fetishistic ones, requiring minute preparation and meticulous execution – a narrow-minded sense of detail fitting the profile of the fetishist. They are filmed differently too. In contrast with the traditional cinematic car crash, there is no use of slow motion, multiple overlapping montage or replays. Each impact is shown only once, in real time. Blink and it is over. In that respect the crashes are similar to the races pictured in Fast Company. The camera is often positioned on the right or left side of the hood, excluding the driver from the shot and highlighting the streamlined machinery and the opposing car (not its driver). In the Dean restaging, much attention is devoted to the backing up of the cars on the racetrack, and the 'post-coital' squeaking and clunking of the car as it comes to a stop (mirroring scenes from Fast Company almost perfectly). At the exact moment of impact it is possible to see Seagrave's red jacket (a homage to Dean) appear amidst the fray of broken metal parts, flakes and splinters flying from the cars – almost like a splatter of blood at the centre of the mayhem. Impatiently, Seagrave does not even wait for his partner Vaughan to execute the Mansfield crash as an orgiastic explosion that is, as Vaughan comments repeatedly, perfect in its design.

As fetishist supreme, Vaughan goes the furthest, almost substituting gratification in favour of a fanatic belief in the prophetic possibilities of his project. Vaughan does not live in the present anymore. 'This is the future, Ballard,' he says. Most importantly, it is an imperfect future. 'Prophecies are ragged and dirty,' he insists. The utopia he sees is filled with things unfinished and messy: greasy, sticky, twisted, thwarted, warped, perverse and crippled. As I will detail below, several critics commented negatively upon *Crash*'s display of 'perverted' or 'abnormal' sexuality: homosexuality, lesbianism, sodomy, infidelity, orgy, rape or coercion, prostitution, 'sex with cripples'. Their concern comes from a reflex reaction. Much like the films François Truffaut and André Bazin singled out as 'cinéma de la cruauté' *Crash* is a film that does not readily accept norms and measures of normality. Instead, by offering alternatives, it exposes and challenges those norms, *de facto* becoming a plea for amorality. It touched several critics and public opinion formers deep in their sensitivities.[5]

Beyond being fetishistic or prophetic, however, Vaughan's views are also fantastic. In fact the entire film can be seen as a succession of fantasies by the main characters. After all, the preface of the novel states that:

> in the past we have always assumed that the external world around us has represented reality, however confusing or uncertain, and that the inner world of our minds, its dreams, hopes, ambitions, represented the realm of fantasy and the imagination. These roles, it seems to me, have been reversed. The most prudent and effective method of dealing with the world is to assume that it is a complete fiction – conversely, the one small node of reality left to us is inside our own heads. (Ballard 1995: 5)

As a film, *Crash* only has the flimsiest of causal time and place successions. As Ballard argued in its defence: 'There are no conventions *Crash* is relying on' (1997: 97). The slow, deliberate tempo, the stretched, metallic sounding guitar music, the air of disengagement of the characters who look so distanced as if nothing touches them, as if they are merely chasing cars and having sex in their dreams just like everyone else, might all point to a fantasy. 'Are we imagining it?' asks James at one point, when he and Helen notice the increase in traffic. Maybe they are. Maybe the entire post-crash world of James only exists in his imagination, the result of the trauma of his collision. Gabrielle's harness is strikingly similar to that of a Steadicam operator (his camera girl's?), and the Mansfield crash site certainly resembles a movie set, the kind a car commercials director like James would dream about after having been in a crash. In that sense, *Crash* is certainly 'beyond depravity', as Cronenberg cheekily adopted a phrase meant to criticise the film: it is only imagining it, just pretending.

The Crash Controversy: Cool and Depraved

Upon its release, *Crash* caused upheaval and polarised opinions. In a field that features strong competition from *Shivers*, *The Brood* and *Scanners*, it quickly became the most notorious of Cronenberg's films. A decade later it *still* divides audiences.[6] It is exactly the thought that it is equally possible that the whole range of alternative moralities and actions offered in *Crash* are only playful stagings, and that nothing is real, that offended so many critics, who condemned the lack of 'seriousness' with which it knocked about paradigms.

One component of the controversy is the shock impact *Crash* had in particular territories. Given the streams of pre-release publicity, comments and anticipation that characterise film reviewing in the twenty-first century it almost seems impossible to imagine *Crash* hit regional reviewers, distributors and local censors virtually unprepared. In the years leading up to the worldwide premiere, Cronenberg had been in the news repeatedly. Fitting his increasing recognition as Canadian cultural hero and cinematic icon, there was a surge of academic publications on Cronenberg, including the first PhD exclusively devoted to his work.[7] But that did not lead to significant speculation about the dynamite material *Crash* was to become. Instead, the press seemed more preoccupied with reporting on Cronenberg's few acting jobs such as *Blood and Donuts* (Holly Dale, 1995), late releases of *Nightbreed*, a cameo in *Moonshine Highway* (Andy Armstrong, 1996) (the first signs of his active auteurship spreading beyond his own films; see chapter nine); with television broadcasts of *The Fly* and video releases of *Shivers* and *Rabid*; and with his relationship with the Cinespace Studio complex that filed for bankruptcy (part of a then-general concern about the economic instability of the nation's film industry in times of crisis). Notices of the shooting of *Crash* in the autumn of 1995 were published without much annotation. If and when J. G. Ballard was referenced it was usually in the form of a mention of *Empire of the Sun* (1987), Steven Spielberg's adaptation of Ballard's novel about his childhood years in World War Two. It truly seemed that with making *Crash*, Cronenberg was going underground again, an impression that was intensified by the lower budget (around $8 million, significantly less than the $22 million of *M. Butterfly*) and the scaled-down logistics – a small crew working close to home.

When *Crash* premiered, the initial shock was limited. The film was accepted for the May 1996 Cannes Film Festival, where it was one of a number of Canadian entries. Even then the Canadian and international press had more interest in reporting how the 'Canadians were crashing Cannes' than in *Crash*. There was even talk of a small surge in Canadian cinema, with international recognition for the films of Patricia Rozema, Atom Egoyan (who was part of the Cannes jury), Robert Lepage and Cronenberg, and several more up-and-coming, such as Srinivas Krishna's *Masala* and Pierre Gang's *Sous-Sol* – two films that also testify to the chequered and multilingual colourfulness of Canada's film culture. After the screening on 17 May that all changed drastically. *Crash* got a sharply divided reception and eventually scooped the award for 'originality, daring and audacity' – a category made up by a 'passionately divided' jury led by Francis Coppola, in order to acknowledge *Crash* without awarding it a regular prize.[8] Even at the ceremony there was a mixture of boos and cheers. The immediate critical reception around the world was varied too. *Variety* called it 'utterly cool' and 'frostily sensual' but also 'irrelevant' and 'risible'. On the American East coast it was seen as 'strange and risky' by the *New York Times*. The *Guardian* said it was 'too cool to be apocalyptic'. To the *Irish Times* it was 'cool and clinical' and also 'morbid'. The Australian *Sydney Morning Herald* said it invited 'steely reactions'. The French reception was moderately positive, with *Libération* declaring *Crash* 'magnifique', *Les Echos* seeing it as 'no more than a succession of cool and pretentious scenes' and *Le Monde* finding it 'feverish' and 'clean, for such a dirty subject'. The Belgian *De Standaard* thought it was 'bizarre'. The Italian press seemed more interested in linking *Crash* to what was to become Cronenberg's new project: the Ferrari film *Red Cars* – which many anticipated excitedly. The Canadian press even expressed a sort of national pride in the face of aversion: '*Crash* is bearing the flag for Canadian film here and it's got more sex, nudity and kinkiness than all the European and Scandinavian pictures combined. Kinda makes a Canadian feel downright cool', wrote the *Toronto Star*. In short, enough variation in opinion and plenty of references to how this 'cool' film was a festival controversy, but nothing that would announce an upheaval like the one that was to come.[9]

The term 'cool' and what was meant by it became one pillar of the evaluation of *Crash*. The other was 'depravity'. And it is the association between the two terms that provoked a full-scale controversy, particularly in the UK. The connection was first made by Geoff Brown in the *Times*, who noted the film's 'cold and clinical' atmosphere towards acts of sex he 'could not possibly describe in a respectable newspaper' would invite commentators 'with axes to grind, to grind away' (Brown 1996: n. p.). Sure enough, before long someone did, and it led to a fully orchestrated campaign to ban *Crash* in the United Kingdom.[10] The first to oppose *Crash* was the *Evening Standard*'s veteran critic Alexander Walker, who described it as containing

> some of the most perverted acts and theories of sexual deviance I have ever seen propagated in main-line cinema. [*Crash*] is vulnerable on almost every level: taste, seriousness, even the public safety risk of promulgating such a perverted creed. (1996: n. p.)

More than its actual content it was the subheading that accompanied the review that drew attention: 'a movie beyond the bounds of depravity'. Initially, Walker's view did not cause too much concern; his views as a critic had been perceived as eccentric before. But, as Barker and his team rightly observe, *Crash* got gradually caught up in a maelstrom of articles that positioned it as a symptom of moral decadence, two indications of which were its 'depravity' and 'coolness'. The most active voice in the debate became the *Daily Mail*. Between November 1996, following *Crash*'s screening at the London Film Festival (that Cronenberg attended in an attempt to support the distribution of the film), and its official submission to the British Board of Film Classification (BBFC) to receive a certificate, and June 1997, when it finally went on general release the *Daily Mail* campaigned actively to have *Crash* banned. It published reviews, called for the boycott of Sony (parent company of distributor Columbia TriStar), harassed censorship examiners, producer Jeremy Thomas and the London Film Festival, and pushed the then-cabinet minister for Heritage, Virginia Bottomley, to urge local councils to 'use their powers to ban the film'. The most active voice in the *Daily Mail*'s campaign was Christopher Tookey, their regular film reviewer, who on this occasion stepped up as public opinion former, the most contentious example of which was a front-page article titled 'Ban This Car Crash Sex Film', from November 1996, followed by a review entitled 'Morality Dies in the Twisted Wreckage' in which Tookey asserted that *Crash* promoted 'the morality of the satyr, the nymphomaniac, the rapist, the paedophile, the danger to society' (1996b: 6).[11] Tookey's serial hysteria, littered with factual errors, created an atmosphere of moral panic that made it virtually impossible for other reviewers to avoid it. The result was that nearly every local and regional outlet in the UK felt compelled to address the perceived 'depravity', either in efforts to dismiss it (of which there were very few[12]) or in attempts to signal its irrelevance (of which there hardly more[13]).

Cronenberg saw himself confronted with a critical discourse that ignored the parameters he had set for the reception. At a press conference at the London Film Festival he wryly noted that beyond depravity means 'my movie is not depraved, because if you're "beyond the bounds of depravity" then you are by definition someplace else, and I certainly thought the film was someplace else' (in Kermode & Petley 1997: 16). Cronenberg's voice did not seem to matter much to the debate; the *Daily Mail* had moved it beyond the individual qualities of *Crash*, onto the cultural sphere it accused it of being a symptom of: the 'liberal', 'anything goes', 'endless downward spiral' of 'relativism' and 'moral vacuum' the 'intellectual establishment' had pushed the good citizens of England's middle class towards. By the end of November Westminster City Council banned the film from screens in its jurisdiction, which included the many cinemas of London's West End. When, in December, the BBFC had still not demanded cuts, several more local authorities insisted on making their own decisions, prompted by the *Daily Mail* who had contacted each of these regional bodies in the UK. As that newspaper's adjectival sermonising and exhaustive rhetoric raged on, gradually more publications jumped to *Crash's* rescue, most notably the British Film Institute's *Sight and Sound* and the liberal paper the *Independent* (which published parts of the screenplay, albeit accompanied by an editor's piece that warned against the 'shocking' nature of the script). In March 1997 the BBFC decided not to demand cuts and issued the film with an 18 certificate. Only five local authorities used the powers granted to them under a 1912 act to ban *Crash*: Cardiff, Kirklees, North Lanarkshire, Walsall and the City of Westminster, which upheld its previous ban. When *Crash* eventually went on general release it got an indifferent, apathetic reception (see Andrews 1997; Malcolm 1997; Shone 1997).

According to Barker *et al.* an underlying reason for the controversy was the upcoming general election of 1997 in the United Kingdom, one in which family values and the moral view of bourgeois 'middle England' took centre stage, especially after the Conservative government of John Major had been rocked by a number of sex scandals (2001: 4). In that sense, the *Daily Mail's* campaign was an attempt to reinvigorate the Conservatives with a newfound moral backbone that would pull the middle-class voters together; opposing *Crash* was a rallying call. But there is also a wider cultural issue: that of the validity of offering moral judgements in general, and of proscribing what a population should be entitled to enjoy, and should be protected from. That is why the issue of censorship mattered so much. Throughout the 1990s films such as *Basic Instinct*, *Man Bites Dog* (Rémy Belvaux/André Bonzel/ Benoît Poelvoorde, 1992), *Child's Play III* (Jack Bender, 1993) and *Natural Born*

Killers (Oliver Stone, 1994) had been accused of corrupting minds, echoing in fact the 'Video Nasties' moral panic of the 1980s. Although in each case liberals, intellectuals and scholars had demonstrated the invalidity of claims that crimes or anti-social behaviour were directly linked to these films, by 1996 several press outlets were convinced there just had to be a connection. So, when *Crash* arrived, several reviewers of the Cannes screening saw the storm coming and warned it would be 'the next key exhibit in the screen violence debate' (Romney 1996: 8): 'David Cronenberg's latest film *Crash* is already being touted as the most depraved movie ever. [However] this stuff only works if you are already that way inclined. The effect of most imagery is that of reinforcement' (Moore 1996: 6). By the time *Crash* reached the shores of the UK such qualifications had largely disappeared, and it became easy prey for a press out to demonstrate the relevance of its moral value judgements, eager to hang the liberals out to dry.

Besides censorship and the bashing of 'depraved' intellectuals, an even bigger issue was that *Crash*'s 'coolness' fitted that of the times. Precisely because of its open-mindedness, and its appeal to like-minded audiences to find their own path through the symbols and metaphors, *Crash* offers itself as a 'hot pocket' on the battlefield of culture. By allowing multiple topics to fight for precedence, as it were, it makes it possible for commentators to see the film for what they want it to be. As Barker, Arthurs and Harindranath wrote:

> [Cronenberg] wanted what Ballard identified as an 'absence of a moral frame around the film'. Cronenberg positively *wanted* audience uncertainty and self-scrutiny. *Crash* declined to render a judgement on the characters and behaviours it showed. (2001: 5)

Not only does that cause confusion, it also exposes reviewers' motivations in terms of policy and ethics. Much of the British controversy around *Crash*, then, is one of critics struggling to either fit their agendas into reviews of the film, or keep those agendas away from it – of negotiation of alignment. Alexander Walker, the *Daily Mail* and its allies, as self-proclaimed defenders of such values, pitched themselves against what they saw as a film deconstructing human development ('the project of man') by portraying sex as play detached from procreation and disconnecting injury from disability, and invalidating the Protestant work ethic ('the project of profit') by painting labour, progress and transport as self-contained fetishes detached from efficiency and gain. For them, *Crash* was an attack on the foundations of the bourgeois public sphere and, hence, on them personally. As Walker stated in his 1997 review of the release:

> the word 'cool' has been one of the most bandied about by the defenders of David Cronenberg's film about a coven of degenerates who top up their fagged-out libidos with the thrill of car crashes. It's one of those words suggesting the users have freed themselves from most inhibitions – especially the elitist one of making moral judgements about other people. (1997a: n. p.)

And in a letter that responded to Kermode and Petley's criticism of his judgements, he added later:

> You find generous space to attack those newspapers whose critics write with passion and conviction against a film like *Crash* – as if passion and conviction were impermissible attributes in this 'cool' age when moral judgements on films are totally absent from the reviews which appear in your columns and elsewhere ... You should learn tolerance for critics whose views do not flatter your own refusal to pass judgement. (1997: 64)

'Cool' here means not just an aversion to pass judgement, but also, and especially in terms of the 'cool age', a reference to 'Cool Britannia', an attitude of hedonism and irony that immediately preceded the election of Tony Blair, who had opportunistically aligned himself with it through publicity appearances with some of its most popular proponents, such as Brit Pop bands and writers. At the level of the working class, the 'cool age' was exemplified by the 'I don't care' Generation-X (in less flattering and more gender specific terms also known as 'lad culture') that had been connected to films such *Clerks* (Kevin Smith, 1994), and *Trainspotting* (Danny Boyle, 1996) – which incidentally premiered together with *Crash* in Cannes, and with which the British press had far less of a quarrel. On a somewhat higher class echelon, the 'cool age' also referred to the boom of the dot.com era and what Andrew Ross (2004) called its 'no-collar employees' of 'industrialised bohemia', whose corporate amenities such as fancy cars, season tickets or chic sex – all of which *Crash* makes ample reference to via the designer clothes Catherine and James wear ('Victoria's Secret bras of frustrating gleam', one reviewer called them (Way 1996: 82)), the clanging and metallic guitar music soundtrack and the professions of the characters: all the jobs mentioned deal with technological transfer of information – commercials director, doctor at the immigration office, computer systems manager, chemical engineer, radiologist, pathologist, service manager and so forth.

The long-term reception of Crash
Inevitably, as the controversy in the UK continued, the press from other countries started reporting it, in most cases with a sense of bemusement about what was seen as a typically British tendency to get all worked up about an art movie supposedly derailing the island's morality. For instance, in Belgium, which saw *Crash* released in November 1996 to lukewarm reviews, the conservative newspaper *De Standaard* expressed similar concerns to the *Daily Mail* when stating that *Crash* was 'without moral values', but the stream of reports it published on the British controversy never showed any attempt to suppress *Crash* – although *De Standaard* used similar terms as the *Daily Mail* in the cultural concern it put forward in its reviews ('cultural pessimism') the aesthetic dislike of *Crash* did not warrant the leap towards an ideological or political campaign against 'depravity' and/or 'coolness' (Willemsen 1996: 12).[14]

In most European countries *Crash* had a limited but fairly successful run, with the Netherlands and Norway as territories where it did rather poorly (and critics did not like it much), and France and Italy as two countries where it did exceptionally well (undoubtedly helped by a favourable critical climate). In Canada, *Crash* was released in November 1996 and widely hailed as Cronenberg's best and most daring film. There was no blanket acclaim though. Bewildered by the critical praise *Crash* received, Canada's professional organisation of film scholars, the Film Studies Association of Canada (FSAC), published six short reports on the film in its autumn 1996 newsletter, one of which was positive (by Murray Pomerance), and five of which varied from bemused (Brian McIlroy) to 'intense dislike' (Bart Testa) (see Testa *et al.* 1996: 15–20). Cronenberg's peers, the Canadian film industry, seemed to side with the journalists: *Crash* won five Genie Awards (also in November) – though 'Best Film' was not among them. For once, the Canadian release was separate from the American one. In the United States, *Crash* was issued with an NC-17 certificate in June 1996, the first film to receive that label since *Showgirls* (Paul Verhoeven, 1995). It was also given a strong warning for its 'numerous explicit sex scenes' (Seiler 1996: 1D). Yet it took another nine months before the film was actually released. The main reason for that was the reluctance of Ted Turner, vice-chairman at Time-Warner, the parent company of distributor Fine Line Features, who took personal offence to the film, saying he had been 'appalled' by it (see Pener 1996; Dreyfus 1997). Turner only delayed procedures, however, and as the film was screened widely in Canada he vowed not to obstruct a March 1997 release. Ironically, European and Canadian publications, already reporting on the UK controversy, took Turner's objections more seriously than the British controversy (see Klein 1996). Even with the opposition of Turner, *Crash* managed to scoop some awards in the United States. The most eyebrow-raising was a laurel at the 1998 AVN Adult Entertainment Awards. Usually a competition reserved for hardcore pornography, '*Crash* came out of absolutely nowhere to win something called Award for Best Alternative Adult Feature', observed novelist David Foster Wallace, who covered the ceremony (2006: 46).

With all the attention it drew, *Crash* also fast became a feature in academic publications. In 1997 several British academics investigated the moral outrage surrounding the film, firmly pointing the finger at the *Daily Mail* for creating an atmosphere of hysteria.[15] *Screen* devoted a debate to the film in 1998. In it, Barbara Creed repositioned her views on Cronenberg, this time employing the ideas of Paul Virilio (about the philosophy of velocity) and Mark Seltzer (about 'wound and scar culture') to acknowledge *Crash* as a phallocentric' investigation of 'the nature of desire in the postindustrial and postmodern age' (1998: 175–6).

Cronenberg himself clearly felt frustrated that his active auteurship had, for once, failed. It left marks; years later, he would still return to the controversy with anger:

What I was exposed to in England was something beyond a reaction to a film. It got so personal to the extent that the press were attacking Jeremy Thomas and his children, trying to suggest he was some kind of Mafioso who did porno films. It got pretty sick and pretty bizarre and I was disappointed in the human condition as it's expressed in England, as opposed to anywhere else where it was not like that. And I really started to have a full appreciation for why the British press is derided and despised around the world, because they deserve it. I think every contemptible human bias is exemplified by the press, from hypocrisy to ... you name it ... I mean, it got really quite silly, to the point where people were making it a social issue in the weird way that it's done in England. It's sort of like an island mentality ... there's a sort of fortress mentality, the fear of being contaminated or infected or something. (In Hughes 2003: 113)

Taking exemption of the Cronenbergian reference to 'infection fear' as an insight into the British culture, it is useful to put Cronenberg's frustration with the 'island' or 'siege mentality' of the British Isles in contrast to what Northrop Frye has called the 'garrison mentality' of Canadian culture – an acute and chronic hyper-awareness of borders, or an 'edge-consciousness' as Bart Testa (1995) calls it. Although both mentalities to some extent rely on a sense of self as isolated from other areas of civilisation, and hence of necessary self-containment and self-governance (with rules designed to suit the emergency of the situation), the 'garrison mentality' assumes a less direct threat than the 'siege mentality' and, hence, less stringent and draconian measures for protection from harm by a direct threat. Cronenberg had spent years trying to unpeel Canada's 'garrison mentality' and his films had, in the process, become symbols of Canadian culture's negotiation of that anxiety. With *Crash* he had, unwittingly perhaps (but also quite topically in the case of the 'cool invasion'), put his finger on at least one of the UK's anxieties.

To be cool and to care

Throughout the reception of *Crash* runs the assumption that its characters are apathetic, disenfranchised and do not care for each other. As I have tried to show, however, they *do* care; in fact they love each other to bits.

Of all the reviews I have read of the film, only Roger Ebert (1997) sees this: 'When a college president makes dirty phone calls, when a movie star or TV preacher picks up a hooker in a red light district, we ask: what in the world were they thinking? The answer is: they are thinking (a) I want to do this, and (b) I can get away with it. *Crash* is a movie that understands that thinking.' Such compulsions are only a sign of a moral downfall if the characters are either totally detached from morality (amorality) or deliberately plotting to continue doing this out of some sort of revenge (immorality). In *Crash*, the characters are neither. As Ebert observes: 'Notice how they talk to each other: it is a point of pride to be cold and detached. That's not because they don't care. It's because they do. They are fascinated by each others minds, and by the tastes they share' (ibid.).

What has changed, however, is that the morality these characters – all of them 'damaged' – develop is a cynical reflection of the one society prescribes. It represents care without morality – without guilt. How could it not? The mid-1990s saw the West recover from the Cold War and economic crises, many countries eagerly joining the West's ideological system, only to find that procedures, organisations and corporations still obstructed their freedom; and that atrocities such as those in Rwanda and Bosnia, or smaller-scale ones such as the crimes of Marc Dutroux in Belgium, the political sex scandals in the UK, the shooting of first nations in Canada or the Rodney King trial and subsequent riots in Los Angeles, did still occur, in spite of moral righteousness. *Crash* does not promote a moral vacuum. The O. J. Simpson trial and the Monica Lewinsky affair do that. Instead, *Crash* posits a way of coping with the scars and wrecks that that leaves. The best strategy of defence against giving in to pessimism is to remove the blame-game from the morality of caring – to keep caring even if the means become absurd and the principles obscured. That is what *Crash* imagines.

CHAPTER NINE

Cues and Clues: *eXistenZ* and *Spider*

Only Cronenberg will grasp what is going on,
and only his core cult will care.

– *USA Today* (Snead 1999: 1D)

And I find it kind of funny, I find it kind of sad
These dreams in which I'm dying, are the best I've ever had
I find it hard to tell you, I find it hard to take
When people run in circles it's a very very … mad world.

– Tears for Fears, 'Mad World',
covered by Gary Jules as the theme from *Donnie Darko*

Oh no, what's this?
A spider web and I'm caught in the middle.

– Coldplay, 'Trouble'

Altamira and Rorschach

A sluggish brown smudge, shaped like a severed finger, extends across the screen. As the title 'A David Cronenberg Film' appears, the smear is replaced by a similarly vague figure. Gold dust spread over an uneven surface? Or the imprint of a head? Gradually, the screen fills with what appear to be brown superimposed images of cave walls inscribed with the most minimalist designs (a square, a few scratches) and fossil imprints of carbonised trees and leaves, then fish, and finally humans, before evapo-

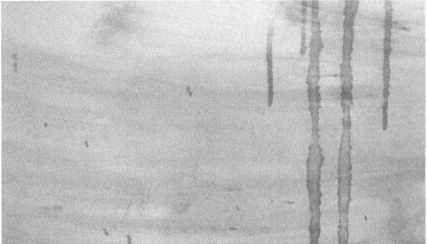

Cues and clues from art history in Cronenberg's credit sequences: cave wall painting references, or Anselm Kiefer, in *eXistenZ* (top); abstract expressionism, or Mark Rothko, in *Spider* (above)

rating to dust again, and fading to black. Thus proceeds the title sequence of *eXistenZ*. This solemn, abstract beginning evokes the process of evolution, a theme never far away in Cronenberg's oeuvre, and invites references to ancient prehistoric cave drawings such as the ones in Altamira or Lascaux. The linear and rudimentary summary of evolution also hints at the most basic attempts of storytelling and knowledge.

Another smear, this time on what looks like a worn white wall with yellow and brown wipes, like smoke stains. 'A David Cronenberg Film', says a title, and the image fades to black. It is replaced by a black and white Rorschach test, which dominates the screen until it too fades to black. Other Rorschach tests appear, in colour, and they too fade. One of the drawings' close details resembles a spider's head. This is the title sequence of *Spider*, Cronenberg's film following *eXistenZ*. At surface level, the sequence calls into mind sober introspection, attention to perception and psychology (the Rorschach blotches), and a state of mouldy degeneration; the state of mind of the film's main character, whose smoke-stained hands eagerly grasp at a past he cannot recall. Or as Cronenberg has it: 'the wallpaper is the lining of his skull'.[1]

Both title sequences are strikingly similar. Their design, tone and rhythm have the confident pacing and commanding elegance that comes with respected high art. They have an air of spontaneity, yet they simultaneously seem intensely controlled and self-contained. If printed, they would not look too out of place in an art gallery devoted to postwar Modernism. Both sequences are accompanied by musical scores that, while different in orchestration, radiate deliberation and clarity of purpose, at once ominous and relieving. Though *eXistenZ* and *Spider* contain stories *about* disintegration, chaos and ambiguity, the films themselves have a clear rationale and a determined solution. As the song over the titles of *Spider* observes, there are a lot of 'buried themes', in both films. The title sequences function as signs that in the end all will be solved, all will be clear – we *can* know the world, even in its complexities, and bend it to our understanding.

The Active Auteur

The title sequences of *eXistenZ* and *Spider*, and the affirmation of their stories, reflect Cronenberg's public status as an active auteur, a director in charge of his own frame of reference, in which he can intervene at will. After having established his reputation as a cultural hero with *Naked Lunch*, *M. Butterfly* and *Crash*, Cronenberg had reached that point in his career where, with nothing left to prove and on top of his game, he could allow himself to freely experiment and still be guaranteed visibility and, once funded, nice slots at festivals and critical praise.[2] No longer a man of the underground, or a Baron of Blood, merely a professional craftsman, uniquely a cult of horror icon; no longer someone who needed to be associated with the popular horror genre or use heavy literary references to add weight to his efforts; no longer the 'asset-stripper of the modernist cult-canon' as Iain Sinclair bitingly called him (1999: 12); Cronenberg was after *Crash* his own artistic and cultural point of reference; uniquely, and sometimes idiosyncratically, the centre of his own universe.

Inevitably, this had repercussions for how his work was received. As a taste leader, his suggestions and remarks about what inspired his work *would* be picked up by critics and press eager to 'unlock' the meaning of his films, and seen as significant cues and clues for making sense of them. I have suggested elsewhere that in the late 1990s the critical reception of Cronenberg reached a point where it became almost formulaic, both in its praise and in its use of critical markers (see Mathijs 2000: 487–501). Whatever project Cronenberg would embark upon, it would be channelled through the same networks of reception and interpretation, and be reconfirmed as a *Cronenberg Film*, which means reviewers would give it four out of five stars, be linked to contemporary and topical cultural developments either in the arts or cultural politics, and be praised for its consistent oddness and unwillingness to conform to commercialism (with a reference to one or two horrific shots to boost that claim).

Acutely and chronically aware of the prevailing critical attitudes towards his work, Cronenberg would not be Cronenberg if he would not be prepared to ambiguously appropriate and expose them at the same time – to offer the public the references it needs to compose their interpretations and hence get the reception he wants for his films (a few money shots here and there, a name or prop at well-chosen points), *and* to place a few traps that demonstrate to critics, reviewers and audiences he can still be unpredictable, creative, original. The way to achieve this is to intervene in the process of reception and to try and steer it without being seen as too intrusive – to become an active auteur.[3]

Cronenberg's play of allusion and collusion with critics described in chapter five shows that in a sense he had already been an active auteur for a while. But now the scope was considerably different: instead of conversing with critics, Cronenberg's active auteurship extended beyond the small and abstruse circle of critics into the entirety of his public presence. Partly, this was the result of Cronenberg's status, partly it was a sign of the times: the inevitable conjuncture of his oeuvre's reputation, his personality and the sensitivity of contemporary film audiences. The active auteur seemed a logical addition to what others would variously call intertextuality, postmodern mannerism or a cinema of allusions. Examples of this include the films of Quentin Tarantino, the Coen Brothers, the *Scream* trilogy (Wes Craven, 1996–2000), *The Matrix* trilogy (Wachowski Brothers, 1999–2003), *Fight Club* (David Fincher, 1999), *The Limey* (Steven Soderbergh, 1999), *American Psycho* (Mary Harron, 2000; a project Cronenberg was briefly associated with), or even isolated Canadian films like *Le Confessional* (Robert Lepage, 1995), *Cube* (Vincenzo Natali, 1997) and *Ginger Snaps*. These works, along with dozens of others, were smart and self-reflexive, and found themselves in tune with audiences ready to look for cues such as quotes, cameos, self-revealing clues or throwaway cultural references in the nooks and crannies of their styles and narratives that would help them see the subtext or implicit meaning therein.[4]

Because this perspective informs the films themselves as well as their public presence, the contexts within which the production and reception of *eXistenZ* and *Spider* occurred warrant careful attention, as does a discussion of the puzzle-structure of the narratives; themes such as the hazy make-up of personal and historical memories and the shaky shape of reality; and the clues through which stylistic and reflexive interventions address viewers.

Active actor: Last Night and Jason X
Since *Nightbreed*, Cronenberg had continued acting, mostly in Canadian films, so when he took a part in Don McKellar's *Last Night*, the fact he would be appearing in front of the camera was not really much of a surprise. Rather, the implication of this, and other, appearances tied in well with his active auteurship. The link with McKellar is interesting because he would be one of the major actors in *eXistenZ*, and Cronenberg had also appeared in McKellar's debut short *Blue* (1992), an appearance that raised a few eyebrows because of the film's interest in pornography (an issue Cronenberg had been dogged by; see chapter five). Following *Blue*, Cronenberg acted in four more Canadian films: the indie *Boozecan* (1994), directed by one of his veteran actors

David Cronenberg as actor (from left to right, top to bottom): a stoic project manager, in *Into the Night*; a psychotic doctor, in *Nightbreed*; a cheeky director, in *Trial by Jury*; a charming contract killer, in *To Die For*; an unperturbed postal supervisor, in *The Stupids*; a strict chair of a hospital board, in *Extreme Measures*; a phlegmatic administrator, in *Last Night*; a comforting priest, in *Resurrection*; a determined scientist, in *Jason X*.

Nicholas Campbell; the vampire movie *Blood and Donuts*, in which he plays alongside *Rabid*'s Frank Moore; the family story *Henry and Verlin* (1995), filmed by *Dead Ringers* electrician Gary Ledbetter as a tribute to his father (hence a family film in more than one sense); and the episodic gay film *The Grace of God* (1997), directed by actor Gérald L'Ecuyer. He also appeared in American productions: he was a director in the courtroom and mafia thriller *Trial by Jury* – a film from whose cast he would recruit Gabriel Byrne for *Spider*; a hitman in *To Die For*; a postal supervisor in the Tom Arnold comedy *The Stupids* (1996), directed by old buddy John Landis; a hospital lawyer in *Extreme Measures* (Michael Apted, 1996); and a detective in the television crime drama *The Judge* (2001), directed by another old pal – the former critic, distributor and *Masters of Horror* series producer Mick Garris. It does not take much to notice how Cronenberg's roles are endorsements more than indulgences. They are acts of support for friends and 'family' – the family of his oeuvre, the family of Canadian cinema, which he seemed to have started feeling some responsibility towards, and the family of old times – helping out chums such as Moore, Landis and Garris.[5]

For Adam Lowenstein, 'Cronenberg's acting roles tend to emphasise either murderous embodiment or bureaucratic disembodiment, often to reveal a combination of both' (2004). Indeed, Cronenberg is mostly cast as cold, methodic and rational, faculties the figures of the serial killer and the bureaucrat share (and which characterise the objectifying impersonal mode of address both are infamous for). For Lowenstein, these traits are 'Canadian', at least in comparison with Americans, hence he sees Cronenberg's parts as confirming 'the ostensibly bifurcated nature of Cronenberg's authorial signature: the director's identity as an icon of the horror film, on the one hand, and of Canadian national cinema, on the other' (ibid.). True, but the impact of Cronenberg's acting goes further than Lowenstein suggests. It relates not just to a nation or a genre, but to Cronenberg's position as a cultural hero or active auteur of international stature (in fact, Lowenstein employs the term 'author' here in much the same way I have used 'auteur'), whose very partaking in a film pushes that project several steps up the ladder of international recognition and visibility.

The quintessential film through which Cronenberg asserts his 'authorial signature' over Canadian cinema is, according to Lowenstein, *Last Night*. *Last Night* is set six hours before the world will end, on New Year's Eve 1999. People party, riot and try desperately to undertake some last substantial action that would testify to their values. Cronenberg's character, the meticulous gas company administrator Duncan, seems to refuse to accept that even if the world is coming to an end all meaning is lost. He calls all clients to thank them for their loyalty and custom and subsequently crosses them off the books with a pencil and ruler – via a neat, straight line. It may amount to nothing more than mannerisms and routine taking over at moments when no deeper meaning is available, but the meaning found in those very routines is not only comforting but significant in itself. It becomes a ritual through which cultural essence is communicated. Even Duncan does not escape the looters and rioters. When he opens his door to the noise outside, a young man with a shotgun aimed at him orders him to 'look at me'. Duncan's reply is one that steps beyond the boundaries of his character, into Cronenberg the cultural hero who has so often found himself defending filmic violence or the more edgy aspects of culture from 'copycat' or 'harmful effects' claims: 'I am not afraid,' he calmly states to the man as he backs into the shadows of his house's interior. 'I am not afraid of what you can do. You're the one who is afraid … You're the one who's afraid.' From the living room behind him comes a voice from the television set: a reporter commenting on the crowd's behaviour: 'There is a great deal of reality and forced play, still largely good natured, I understand,' the commentator's voice remarks. It seems Duncan has good faith he will not be harmed. As we discover at the end of the film, Duncan has been shot regardless, and it is tempting to see this resolution as a warning note that people who trust violence will not affect them might still get harmed or become victims, especially when, like Duncan/Cronenberg, they rely too much on the common sense of the inhabitants of the world they live in. But at the same time, Cronenberg's Duncan is an oasis of serenity, a beacon in what is otherwise a volcanic eruption of frustration and violence.

To McKellar, but also to the viewers most likely to see a Canadian film like *Last Night*, which did not easily reach audiences outside its native territory or beyond the festival circuit, the role of the nation's prime director Cronenberg is one of totemic mentorship, an endorsement of sizeable significance.[6] If one substitutes the framework of Canadian cinema for that of horror cinema, the same case can be argued with regard to Cronenberg's part in *Jason X*. Cronenberg's role in this film is so small it can almost be ignored, were it not for the generic references and intertextual play it evokes, and the consequences this has for how horror fans watch the film. *Jason X* is the tenth installment in the *Friday the 13th* series, a franchise that originated, in 1980, within the cult of horror that also catapulted Cronenberg to fame and infamy. As was explained in chapter four, a key characteristic of the cult of horror is the acknowledgement of its savvy audiences by offering them an 'early gruesome murder' that tests the audience's awareness of the genre, either by including knowing references, in the form of a cameo, or by an almost direct address of the audience (as in the exploding head shot in *Scanners*). True to its pedigree, *Jason X* offers exactly that, with Cronenberg doing the honours. After the credit sequence and an early scene which shows that the evil Jason Voorhees is about to be put on 'cryogenic suspension' in a research facility (a term loaded with Cronenbergian overtones of 'science gone mad'), Cronenberg's character, Doctor Wimmer, marches in at the head of a small posse of security agents, demanding to take the specimen. 'I want him soft,' he says. 'Are you willing to risk the deaths of innocent civilians?' asks his colleague. 'Yes,' answers Wimmer phlegmatically. Of course, before he even gets the chance to approach him Jason has already escaped, and after summarily killing the guards Jason impales Doctor Wimmer – he throws a pole straight through his body. There is no title credit for Cronenberg, nor is one needed. From the point of view of Cronenberg his part is perhaps only a favour to a friend who had supervised the special effects for *eXistenZ*. From the perspective of *Jason X*'s director Jim Isaac, however, Cronenberg is not just a friend and mentor, but an idol, a veteran of the cult of horror elevated into cultural icon. The cameo in *Jason X* reinforces Cronenberg's affiliation and continuous endorsement of the horror genre, and confirms his reputation as one of its most renowned directors – even if his own career has moved away from the genre entirely. Moments such as these demonstrate the extent to which Cronenberg's reputation is reconfirmed at every opportunity at this juncture in his career.[7]

Camera

Cronenberg's scattered screen appearances are not part of a careful career plan, far from it. Yet it is impossible not to notice his own awareness of how these intertextual and active interventions solidify his reputation as a touchstone of those segments of culture associated with Canada or the horror genre. Cronenberg further pressed this point with his own short film *Camera*, which he wrote and directed as part of a commissioned series, *Preludes*, celebrating the twenty-fifth anniversary of the Toronto International Film Festival.

Camera displays Cronenberg at his most confident and sanguine, and at his most senior, in this exploration of tropes such as retirement, anxiety and nostalgia. It is the story of an ageing actor, fittingly portrayed by Les Carlson, a veteran from the Canadian and American screen who had previously appeared in *Videodrome*, *The Dead Zone* and *The Fly*. Lamenting the state of his career, the actor claims to have grown anxious about the media and cameras. Because, after all, he argues, when looked at in the cold light, 'Photography is death. It's all about death. Memory and desire, ageing and death. For an actor in particular. These things are not abstractions. These things are as real as looking in the mirror.'

Continuing at a tangent, the actor recounts a dream of watching a movie with an audience, and suddenly becoming aware of an accelerated ageing process. In a determined Cronenbergian turn, the actor claims that the movie had given him 'some kind of disease'. 'And look at me now,' he continues as the camera takes his elderly face in extreme close-up, revealing every unkempt eyebrow hair and wrinkle. The actor is bothered by the fact some children brought in an old camera and were trying to convince him to 'act' for it. He warns this means recording 'the death of the moment'. 'Children and death are a bad combination, [that camera] will do irreparable damage to us all,' he adds, in an echo of decades of moral panics and media anxiety storms, many of which Cronenberg had had to weather. Gradually, however, the actor develops sympathy for the old camera: 'the camera itself had aged ... It had its own obsolescence and death to deal with ... gliding around like a clumsy, laughable, old ghost.' Maybe, he speculates, they were growing old together, like a 'bickering dotty, old couple', and that realisation replaces the anxiety and sadness with a 'taste of melancholy'. As he resigns to this cohabitation, we see the children become ever more active, lighting the room, blocking the scene and applying make-up to the actor's face. In the light of such 'pure and innocent fun, as far as those things can ever be innocent', the actor finally agrees to be filmed. 'Action,' one child directs.

Then, finally, after all the complaints and worries of the actor, we see, in the last shot of *Camera*, the magic of cinema at work. That last shot, in which the actor repeats the first lines of the film ('One day the kids brought home an old camera. I don't know where they found it, but they were very excited about it') is filmed with the very same 35mm camera the children had been gearing up. But the atmosphere has changed radically, indeed become more nostalgic. There is not just the acting performance that is different, with a wistful tear welling in the actor's eye. There is also the altered set-up, with the full use of lights, music, make-up and classical *mise-en-scène*: the actor is framed in widescreen, in one fluent shot that glides from a medium shot to a medium close-up (as opposed to the extreme close-ups of the digital video that had captured the preparation). The shot, and the film, end abruptly, with a rupture as if the reel breaks.

The contrast between the last shot and what precedes it generates mixed feelings. In hindsight, each line of dialogue from Carlson opens a veritable wave of intertextual references – obviously written with exactly that avalanche of allusions in mind. In that sense *Camera* is a bit self-indulgent. Beyond that, the film encapsulates an attitude of assuredness and accomplishment typical for the status of Cronenberg and his oeuvre. The film relies on the fact that those who will see it will know about Cronenberg's work and will smilingly acknowledge the numerous nods, winks and nudges to Cronenberg's career, to their own (previous and current) preoccupations as his audiences and to the neat and circular self-reflexivity of the narrative – folding onto itself.[8] The festival-goers witnessing the premiere of *Camera* are such an audience, as are the viewers perusing the extras on the Criterion Collection DVD release of *Videodrome*, the Cronenberg film in which Carlson had one of his most notable appearances. It is easy to dismiss *Camera* as mere *spielerei*, but it is nevertheless symptomatic of the state of Cronenberg's career as 'active auteur'.

In his astute analysis of *eXistenZ*, William Beard writes 'there are so many plot provocations, twists and sudden reversals, that the film passes right out of a "solvable" narrative paradigm, and right through one that parodies plot-solution movies, all the way to the condition of an unreadable enigma' (2005: 426). Similarly, Serge Grünberg has remarked that *eXistenZ* has no real ending or beginning, and is increasingly (and intentionally) confusing in its progress (2000: 166). Their assertions are correct, but their conclusions are not. *eXistenZ* does indeed challenge mainstream plot developments, and its attitude towards the parodic style so commonly employed in genre films of the time is dubious – at points it seems the film is parodying the parodies. But these convolutions do not create an 'unreadable enigma'. If one follows the clues spread throughout the narrative, displayed at well-chosen points, *eXistenZ* makes perfect sense, even in a linear way.

After the credit sequence, which has already crafted an atmosphere of tightly controlled puzzle-solving, the opening alerts the avid viewer to the fact that this is a film in which things are explained, and in which we will be taken for 'a wild ride'. In the first shot a public relations representative of a company (Christopher Eccleston) commences by explaining the title: 'eXistenZ. Written like this. Small e, capital X, capital Z. eXistenZ. It's new, it's from Antenna Research and it's here.' In a layout similar to *The Brood* and *Scanners*, the next shot reveals an auditorium with an audience – Cronenberg's by now stock way of addressing his viewers. The representative is addressing a focus group of invitees about to test the beta-version of a new computer game and game system, called eXistenZ. Leading the testing seminar, he announces, will be the 'game pod goddess herself', the creator of the game, the legendary but reclusive Allegra Geller (Jennifer Jason Leigh). In typical shy geek fashion, Allegra explains how her game, and its console, will revolutionise gaming. 'The world of games is in a kind of a trance,' she begins. 'People are programmed to accept so little but the possibilities are so great.' If taken as a clue, her remark warns the audience (the one in the movie as well as us) it needs to shape up and abandon its usual passivity if it wants to enjoy this story. Volunteers are handed game pods and enter a stage where they plug their pods into 'bioports' and await Allegra's sign to download the game into their nervous systems and experience eXistenZ. 'Now, I'm warning you. It's going to be a wild ride. But don't panic … no matter what happens, okay? All right, I'll see ya back here in no time at all.'

On cue, the music swells and we see Allegra fondle her pod, a squealing, flesh/rubber-like device that holds the middle somewhere between an oversized liver and a game console – a sign to the Cronenberg-trained audience that the 'real' movie is about to kick off. At this point, eight minutes into the film, a lot of explaining has occurred, even beyond the announcements and introductions offered by the public relations agent and Allegra, who can easily be seen as textual alter egos of the distributor/producer and director. Props such as surveillance devices, outré fashions and uncommon combinations of styles (the seminar room seems a mix between a church, a ski lodge and a cafeteria) tell audiences we are in the near future – recognisable enough to our eyes, but a little off. We are made aware gaming is a widespread pastime and popular form of entertainment. It is also a big business that warrants careful planning and protection – there are security measures, an unprecedented degree of secretive testing, seminars, previews and other hush-hush activities. Some of these seem a bit too much like self-promotion, and that is probably why the whole testing enclave has the feel of a fan convention. In other words, the first few minutes of the film are devoted to nothing else but explanations about what is happening and how it needs to be regarded. We are even given a full minute of repose to let all of that sink in, as the testers and Allegra slip into a trance, and the sound of squeaking consoles (and music) fills the auditorium. We also get a signal we can sit back and enjoy the show – 'back in no time at all'.

Immediately afterwards Allegra is shot with a gun made of flesh and bones by anti-gaming activist Noel Dichter (Kris Lemche), who also kills the PR officer at point blank range, before he himself is gunned down, receiving no less then eleven shots in the chest (a hyperbole not uncommon for games – no one just shoots once). Allegra is ushered away from the scene by marketing trainee Ted Pikul[9] (Jude Law), who is urged by the dying PR man to 'trust no one' (again a rhetorical device common for games – you are mostly all alone). They escape to the countryside. In order to help Allegra check the game system has not been damaged, the timid gaming novice Pikul has a bioport fitted into his spine by loyal Allegra fan and gas station operator Gas (Willem Dafoe). 'I have this phobia about having my body penetrated surgically,' explains Pikul, but then he has it done anyway, in a dirty garage no less, and aided by a dodgy stud finder. As if to remind his own loyal fans of his presence, this entire scene is rife with references to Cronenberg's themes, from sexual innuendo (the teasing between Gas and Pikul and Allegra's rubbing of his new orifice are overly sensual) through bodily deviation (with Allegra's mention of her 'decaying, fucking grotesque corpse' a line widely cheered at several genre festivals) to body mechanics, all culminating in Allegra showing her tongue to Pikul to demonstrate why bioports do not get infected, and defiantly asking the treacherous Gas (but it could be directed at us): 'Don't you ever go to the fucking movies'? 'I like your script,' Gas admits. 'I wanna be in it.' Then he is shot through the neck with the spine gun.

The next hour of the film follows the template of these first 25 minutes: brusque advances of the plot to uncover the conspiracy behind the assassination attempts on Allegra are frequently interrupted by the appearance of new characters (or their avatars) most of whom have foreign accents or accentuated speech patterns. These characters then offer clues and cues for Pikul and Allegra's quest into the mystery. Their odd behaviour also creates the opportunity for them to muse on the qualities of characters, screenwriting, props, emotional commitments or scene changes. Allegra's veteran colleague Kiri Vinokur (Ian Holm) and his aid Landry (James Kirchner) fix Allegra's pod and Pikul's port so they can move into the game world of eXistenZ – a transformation signalled by a distinctive change in their physical appearance that makes them look more alluring. Inside, the 'not very well drawn character' of shop-keeper D'arcy Nader (Cronenberg regular Robert Silverman) equips them with new pods. In the 'Trout Farm', a game factory filled with squealing little creatures being cut to pieces, they meet Yevgeni Nourish (Don McKellar) who tells them to have lunch at the 'Chinese Restaurant'. There, they argue about 'pausing the game' and the 'limited degree of free will a game allows'. They order the 'special', which turns out to be a dish with bones that can be used to assemble the gun that Allegra was shot with. Pikul shoots the waiter (Oscar Hsu) with it. A dog carries the gun away. Nourish appears to lead them to the next location, the 'Breeding Pools', where he reveals they are now regarded as part of the Realist underground that fights Cortical Systematics, owners of the Farm and Nader's shop. They return to Nader's shop where assistant Hugo Carlaw (Callum Keith Rennie) tells them Nourish and Nader (now dead) are double agents and the Chinese Waiter and himself are the real Realists. Nourish is the one they need to kill. They return to the Farm, eliminate Nourish and exit the game. There, they suspect Vinokur has infected Allegra's master game pod by inserting a faulty bioport into Pikul, 'introducing the theme of disease', Allegra remarks – another Cronenberg motif. Before they can do anything Carlaw, in full militia outfit, bursts into their chalet, shoots the pod and then tries to kill Allegra. Vinokur shows up and kills Carlaw, then urges them to join him and leave Antenna. Allegra kills him and also eliminates Pikul after he reveals he, too, is a mole. In true video game style we get killing after killing. Then, as Allegra shouts 'have I won?' she suddenly notices she is wearing a gaming hand- and headset.

'Are you all back?' asks Merle (Sarah Polley). Yes, they are all here, in the same seminar hall where the film began, all the characters of the scenes that happened since Allegra and Pikul fled that room. It appears the entire story up to now was a game in itself, called TransCendenZ ('capital C, capital Z'), by PilgrImage ('capital P, capital I'), designed by Yevgeni Nourish. All of the above-mentioned characters were just avatars of their real selves, now busily commenting on their achievements in the game (Gas laments being killed off so early, Carlaw complains about too many 'twists and turns at the end', Vinokur loathes his thick accent). As the gamers disperse, Pikul, Allegra and their dog approach Nourish and Merle, apparently to ask some questions. They assassinate them with exactly the same excessive number of gun shots Allegra and Dichter endured at the beginning. As they approach the exit, a security guard, begging for his life, asks, 'Tell me the truth. Are we still in the game?'

As a narrative, *eXistenZ* is incredibly tightly structured, not leaving any room for doubt at all. Essentially, there are three story worlds that fit into each other like a Russian doll: the story world (level 1), the world inside TransCendenZ inside that story world (level 2) and the world of eXistenZ inside TransCendenZ (level 3). These three worlds contain two styles of narration: the advancements of the plot, such as the killings or pieces of information shared between characters; and the intertextual allusions, the reflections upon the craft of making a movie and/or a game. Both the plot advancements and comments are propelled by numerous cues and clues, mentions and terms, quotes and observations that offer a solid navigating system through the film. Whenever the avatars or characters on level 3 are in doubt about what to do, cues from others offer solutions or progress. And whenever the function of what is happening in the film is unclear, allusions and asides remind us it is a Cronenberg horror/science fiction movie we are watching, and we need to adjust our expectations accordingly:

hard work when you're at it, but all will become clear at the end. At the start of the film we are on level 2, from where we enter level 3, which is where we are for most of the duration of the film. There is only one brief return to level 2, when Pikul and Allegra are at the restaurant and Pikul pauses the game because he feels 'disconnected'. During that pause Pikul expresses doubts about the conflation of the distinction between 'story reality' and 'game inside the story reality'. But there is no conflation – 'definitely not,' Allegra states. They re-enter and continue the game. When they finish their business on level 3 and return to level 2, the increasing confusion at that level – heightened by the appearance of level 3 avatars – only lasts a few minutes. After every avatar except Allegra is killed, we move to level 1, where everything is revealed and all loose ends are tied together. With TransCendenZ over and done, we are in the most basic of story worlds, the downright and plain diegetic fabula of *eXistenZ*.

Remembering Clues: Reading Spider

Spider's story also offers a closely controlled narrative that first appears to be laby-rinthine but which in the end makes perfect sense. From the start *Spider* announces itself as a man's quest into his own past. Dennis Cleg (Ralph Fiennes), a dishevelled-looking man in worn clothes, carrying an old suitcase, is the last person to step from a train at a station in London, England. Looking for an address on a crumpled piece of paper and muttering to himself he wanders around the more decrepit areas of East London (a canal, a factory, a looming gasworks tower, a boarded-up row of houses), picking up an old watch and some rubble – a man clearly looking for some-thing, but without much method to his search. Dennis arrives at Mrs Wilkinson's (Lynn Redgrave) old and mouldy halfway house, a monitored boarding hostel with stained wallpaper, ripped linoleum and cracked walls, for people recently released from care facilities who can reside there as they slowly get accustomed to society again (if ever). Dennis is as ill-kempt as he is ill at ease. Anxious, burdened by jerky body movements, he wears four soiled shirts, takes notes obsessively in a sort of runic handwriting as he mutters to himself (reciting addresses, places and people of the past – 'Kitchener Street, railway, my mum'). The hissing and roaring giant gasworks ominously towering over his window across the street does not alleviate his apprehen-siveness either. It quickly becomes clear Dennis is trying to remember things from the past, especially with regard to his mother, and though he only appears to be glimpsing fragments of that past and seems unable to trust his perceptions ('it is not real' he says when he views a picture of the countryside and imagines to be there with his fellow residents) he is nevertheless determined, clinging to each detail he recalls, jotting them down in tiny handwriting in his secret notebook. Each walk brings him more information. On his first, he visits a city/community garden (near a railway indeed) where he falls to the ground. 'Mummy, please,' he sobs. On his second, he finds a small brick house tucked away in a working-class neighbourhood and peers through the rear window into the kitchen.

Here, *Spider* shifts gear, and moves with its protagonist into the past. Young Dennis (Bradley Hall), aged about ten, is sitting at the table with his mother (Miranda Richardson). It is clear we are witnessing a moment the older Dennis remembers from his youth, and what we see are his interpretations of that past. Just so the viewer is aware of this subjectivity, the older Dennis is visually present in each of these 'flashbacks', and though his posture and facial expressions tell us he is 'reliving' those moments, and he occasionally mimics the conversations (repeating or whispering them in advance), he never attempts to intervene. He may be confused but he knows the past is gone for good and cannot be altered, only observed. Young Dennis is ordered by his mum to fetch his dad Bill (Gabriel Byrne) from the Dog and Beggar pub for dinner. In the pub, young Dennis is intimidated by a frank blonde woman (who flashes her breasts). Old Dennis sits in a corner of the pub and watches with a grave look on his face. Over dinner, the family of young Dennis is silent. From the glances we can tell young Dennis is 'mum's boy'. He adores her, greedily absorbing her stories about spider's eggs, dying spiders and spider webs (stories he must have taken to his heart as his room is filled with strings spun from one side to the other – like a web). He observes his dad much more reluctantly, as if he were an adversary.

Because it clarifies the film's title (it is also mother's nickname for the strange twine weaving hobby her son has), the metaphor of the web signals the viewer to pay attention from here on, as the rest of the story unfolds in a straightforward manner: in a way similar to the weaving of a spider's web we will keep switching between old Dennis's attempts to unravel his past (the web) and young Dennis's antics in that past (spinning that web), presumably leading to one defining moment that will explain how bright young Dennis became confused and traumatised old Dennis. Such a signal activates viewers' puzzle-solving abilities (the kind of 'Cluedo moment' that occurs when watching a detective story). All clues pivot around young Dennis's apprehension about his mother's sexuality, which is an issue he clearly has difficulties dealing with. He watches his parents flirt and cavort as they leave for an evening out. He imagines them sitting in the pub, his mum prudently powdering her nose and drinking a gin and tonic, while his dad casts a roving eye over at the corner where the 'looser' women sit. One of them is 'that fat tart Yvonne Wilkinson', the same blonde woman that flashed young Dennis earlier on. At this point viewers attuned to the story will raise an eyebrow: isn't 'Wilkinson' the name of old Dennis's stern matron? And hasn't the tart Wilkinson's posture and face changed to resemble that of his mother a little bit more? Surely this has to be a clue. The role of Yvonne is indeed also played by Richardson, though this is not necessarily known to viewers at this point (although those having read reviews on Richardson's 'multiple roles' will be aware of it), as the make-up and acting performance are quite different. In any case, old Dennis dutifully notes the name of 'Wilkinson' down in his notebook – thus demonstrating that not only does he visit the past he recalls, he also uses it, like the audience, to find clues himself. 'She made the first move,' he concludes.

Sadly, old Dennis confuses memory with conjecture. He could not have witnessed the pass Yvonne presumably made at his father, as he was not around. From this point on, *Spider* includes several more interpretations and fabrications about his father's sexual prowess that go beyond subjective memory, displaying activities young Dennis could not have witnessed: his father's visit to Yvonne to fix her plumbing (he is a plumber but the innuendo will not be lost to viewers), Bill picking up Yvonne in her fur coat for a walk (alongside the gasworks, with old Dennis peering at them from a bench) and having a few fast sex romps with her. These fabrications are fuelled by other memories, such as young Dennis inadvertently watching his mother in lingerie. In Cronenberg's own terms, the film takes on a tripartite structure:

> When adult Spider is present in a scene with the boy, you can assume it was something that actually happened. But there are moments when adult Spider is there but the boy is not, and you have to assume this is something he maybe imagined, but didn't actually witness. And then there's a third kind of reality, which we called infected memory, where he was hallucinating, basically. (In Said 2002: 23)

I would add that the 'imaginations' also protect old Dennis in that they prevent him from having to remember events that may be too painful to his conscience. At the halfway house the gasworks start 'getting' to old Dennis (as one resident puts it) and he imagines smelling gas everywhere, as he grows increasingly convinced of his father's infidelity in the past. In an elaborate reconstruction of the past (again one young Dennis could not have witnessed) he imagines his mother walking in on Bill and Yvonne having sex in their community garden's shed, and getting killed by Bill with a blow to the head. This crisis moment coincides with old Dennis looking on as another resident of the halfway house smashes a mirror and has to be restrained.

On his next walk, on one of the first sunny days in the film, old Dennis finally finds Kitchener Street, and the Dog and Beggar pub. He cannot make himself go inside, but sits on a bench outside. He recalls resisting Yvonne replacing his real mum, calling her a 'murderer' and getting punished by his dad. 'Why are you so angry with us?' he asks. 'You're making your mother very unhappy.' 'She's not my mother,' Dennis replies angrily. 'She's a tart!' By now, old Dennis is convinced his landlady is part of the conspiracy (her character too is now played by Richardson). Panicked by what he perceives to be her increasingly menacing and sexually intim- idating behaviour ('same woman,' he mutters) he barricades himself in his room, which he also adorns with twine and string. He observes young Dennis watching his dad and Yvonne go out to the pub and in their absence he sees his younger self wiring the house with strings, connecting it to the gas supply in the kitchen. Old Dennis steals his landlady's keys, breaks into her room and finds the fur coat Yvonne wore. At night, he sneaks up on her with a hammer and big screwdriver, ready to kill her, but then he hesitates. Young Dennis hears his dad and Yvonne returning from the pub and pulls the string that opens the gas. Bill is able to rescue young Dennis, but by the time he manages to drag Yvonne out of the house she is dead. 'You did this,' he yells at his son. 'You did your mum in. You killed your mother. You murdered your mum!' A horrified old Dennis watches on. With old Dennis still hesitantly bent over her, the landlady wakes up and asks, horrified, 'what have you done?'. The next day, Dennis is picked up by the people from the mental health institution. 'It was my mum,' he mutters as the car drives young Dennis away. The End.

Spider needs no epilogue. It was indeed Dennis who killed his mother, and there never was an Yvonne. In fact, as the clues about the apprehensiveness of Dennis towards his mother's sexuality indicate, Yvonne and 'mum' were both Dennis's projections of his perception of two sides of his mother: her caring self (the mother) and her sexual self (the wife). His father was not disloyal to her. They seemed instead to enjoy a largely happy marriage, the few rough spots of which were interpreted by Dennis as proof of his suspicions. His own psychosis did the rest, and the damage. In a sense, young Dennis represents an unaware audience, one that is easily shocked, thrown off-kilter by a flashed breast or an unexpected showing of lingerie – an audience perhaps, like young Dennis, in their early teens. Old Dennis is the thwarted result of the trauma young Dennis experienced. But in the same way that old Dennis is not representative of everyone whose youth includes traumatic experiences regarding parental sexuality, unaware viewers are not representative of Cronenberg's audience, especially at this point in his career.

Last lines and killing tools: meaning and smart audiences at the turn of the millennium
Labyrinths are only confusing when they contain errors, or to those who do not find the solution. Neither is the case in *eXistenZ* and *Spider*. Taken step by step, both narratives make perfect sense, as long as one carefully distinguishes between the levels of alternative realities offered, and follows the clues provided by the story. I have indicated above how much Cronenberg's public persona, and the reputation of his films, creates a certain attitude of intelligence and self-reflexivity. That attitude is also the one that typifies Cronenberg's audiences best at this time in his career. His films are viewed not only by the horror aficionados or gore geeks (in fact less so), but rather by the smart, self-reflexive audiences attracted to what Noël Carroll (1989) labelled labyrinthine enigmas such as *Citizen Kane* (Orson Welles, 1941), to what Jeffrey Sconce (2002) has called 'smart nerd cinema', and what Steven Schneider (2000) identified as 'reflexive neo-slasher': films filled with clues and cues that are approached cognitively and analytically; films that need dissection, not empathy.

There are several instances in *eXistenZ* and *Spider* that provide such opportunity for dissection. I have already pointed to the opening credits, and the way in which they prefigure an attitude of purpose, clarity and linearity, embellished with high-art (Altamira) and academic (Rorschach) references. There are also the last lines of both films. 'It was my mum', in *Spider*, articulates the whole plot at once. Once spoken, it confirms what most audiences have been working at throughout the film – fed by other clues such as the name Wilkinson, the prominence of the gasworks and the multiple performances of Richardson. In *eXistenZ*, the last line is somewhat of a conceit in the tight system of the film. It seems to cast doubt upon all that has happened before. It is in fact nothing more than a rhetorical epilogue device; a trick of the trade common to the genres of horror and science fiction – it is the hand from the grave in *Carrie*, or Jason's final rise out of the water in *Friday the 13th*. It is a generic mannerism that does not add to the understanding of the narrative. As Grünberg observes, it risks becoming a 'cult reply', a ritual void of actual meaning (2000: 166).

On 'the most pathetic level of reality' the cue to the mystery is gas: a gas station manned by 'Gas', in *eXistenZ* (left); the gasworks towering over the halfway house, in *Spider* (right)

Besides the beginnings and endings, I would like to single out one prevalent leit-motif in each film: the real and/or imaginary killing tools employed by the characters. In *eXistenZ*, that key motif is the 'gristle gun'. The plot is triggered, almost literally, by an assassination with a gun made up of fish bones and gristle (undetected by security devices). It is the same fish gun Pikul puts together from the special lunch he orders and which he uses to kill the Chinese waiter, and the same gun with which Vinokur kills Carlaw ('it was brought to me by my dog,' he explains). The gristle gun is at the centre of all the revolutionary talk the characters and factions in *eXistenZ* use to give their actions meaning. As such it is a key tool of rebellion and uprising. It is, as Nourish explains, even crafted out of the same mutant creatures that are used to manufacture the game pods, a subversive property which makes it totemic. But as the gun moves from person to person it is also an indication of the individual nature of the rebellion. In spite of all the talk of collectivity, each bearer of the gun uses it for his or her own purposes. Instead of a collective uprising, or resistance, it symbolises individual actions. As a result, reflections on its use become reflections on personal actions, not on ideologies. It is in this sense that *eXistenZ* is existentialist: in stressing the moral responsibility of the individual, *and* the impossibility of finding 'greater' knowledge outside oneself. In other words, the gristle gun explains better than all other talk the key philosophical message of the film.[10] Still, in the end, in the real world of level 1 only a real gun can kill. Allegra and Pikul shoot Nourish and Merle with traditional pistols. While the gristle gun carries the message, at the film's lethal moment it is nowhere to be found.

Spider* contains a similar dichotomy in its killing instruments, but in reverse. Dennis believes the blow to the head with the shovel killed his mother, whereas in reality it was his sophisticated web of strings (his spider web) that pulled open the gas handle. Instead of the fake killing tool (the shovel), *Spider* lets the real one, the gas, take centre stage throughout the film and deliver the message; that message is that all meaning, all significance in human existence is intangible, fleeting and fabricated. Like gas, it cannot be touched or visually observed (and is in fact often not worth hanging on to). Yet it is manufactured in large quantities and it seems to be everywhere. Even before we know who Dennis is, and where he is going, we have been shown the gasworks, dominating his walk from the train station, and these gasworks are omnipresent throughout the film, always looming in the background, occasionally emitting threatening noises. Dennis reacts to it instinctively, with revulsion, as we do when we smell something nasty (the gas metaphor pitches the 'irrational impulse' as a defence against 'constructing meanings'). Like gas, the meaning-making can be suffocating, and as fellow resident Terrence (John Neville) tells Dennis, it can 'get to you'. Of all the residents of the halfway house, and indeed of all the characters in the film, Terrence is the quintessential Beckettian figure, displaying physical resemblance to several characters of Beckett's plays, most prominently *Endgame*'s Clov. It is a reference (which I will return to further on) that was introduced by Cronenberg, Fiennes and novelist and screenwriter Patrick McGrath as an explanation for the location, mood and struggle for meaning over *Spider*.

Individualistic and essentially meaningless, these keywords for *eXistenZ* and *Spider* clash with the structure of the films as puzzle-solving, treasure-seeking narratives that, once the riddle is solved, offer one straight solution. As with sudoku or crossword puzzles, that single solution is indeed there, but it does not necessarily *mean* much – what indeed does a solved sudoku or crossword puzzle *mean*? The answers to the last lines in the films are, respectively: 'No, we're no longer in the game because people don't die in games', and 'Yes, it was your mum you killed because you couldn't cope with her being a sexual person.' The solutions to the key motives are: 'we are all alone, in our own moral universe', and 'all meaning is a construction of the mind; who really knows why we do things?' That does not get us very far.

Ironically enough, this meaninglessness and individualism fits much criticism directed at smart viewers, of the kind that make up the Cronenberg audience around the turn of the millennium. They offer answers to complex structures, but these answers are so self-contained they do not attempt to change the real world. It is criticism cognitivists such as David Bordwell have often had to hear, most prominently in a special issue of *Film Criticism* devoted to film interpretation. In it, Robin Wood and Robert Ray (1993) compared puzzle-solving to monarchs playing chess while a war rages: accepting of the status quo in culture, in fact profiting from it, assuming the act of interpretation is separated from prejudice and can be carried out in self-containment, without any repercussions for real life. Futile. In the end, nothing has changed. As Sconce (2002) indicated, and as I have pointed out in relation to certain viewers' attitudes towards cult films, smart audiences (like those Cronenberg's films attract) are often ironic and nihilistic in their interpretations, searching for answers without wishing these to become relevant to their lives (see Mathijs & Mendik 2008: 5–6). All that matters is the display of smartness. In an interview with Grünberg, Cronenberg hints at the fact that Spider's confusion of historical reality with faulty memory bears a parallel to the futility of film reviewing, since all interpretations are 'all equal, all of them not only plausible, but also sustainable' (in Grünberg 2002: 22). Hence nothing is ever wrong and only the cleverness of the structure counts. It may seem trite to blame the *fin de siècle* and its 'end of the future' sensibilities, or the shell shock of the immediate post-9/11 culture for this, but *eXistenZ* and *Spider* do cater extremely well to such an attitude.

Rushdie, video games and responsibility: the prefiguration of eXistenZ
With the reception of *eXistenZ* and *Spider* all these clues, relentless associations and the aforementioned 'active auteur' references function to create networks of meanings and discourses within which the cultural significance of a film can be placed. The public discourse of both films was illuminated by two conversations: the first one between Cronenberg and Salman Rushdie in 1995, and the second between Cronenberg and Patrick McGrath in 2003.

The first element in *eXistenZ*'s network of reception is Cronenberg himself, meaning his public reputation and his use of it. As mentioned before, Cronenberg actively intervenes in the reception of his films with the aim to facilitate (or forge) an interpretation that corresponds to the intentions he had when making the film. That was no different in the case of *eXistenZ*. Cronenberg presented it as a deliberation on issues of freedom of speech and the responsibilities of the artist to speak out. The key points of reference through which this issue was addressed in the prefiguration of *eXistenZ* were violence in video games and the fatwa against Salman Rushdie. The first reference is connected to the narrative of *eXistenZ*, and also a topic closely related to the censorship debates Cronenberg featured in during the 1980s. In that sense, there is a strong parallel with the debates surrounding *Videodrome* – both films are concerned with the moral responsibilities of the use of modern technology. Cronenberg's stance on the matter was that artists should have the freedom to explore the implications of potentially dangerous usage of technology, without the obligation to package their explorations as 'warnings'. With *eXistenZ*, that stance did not change, but a new element crept in, in the form of artists' responsibility towards the harm others can experience as a result of their explorations. As the narrative of *eXistenZ* shows, this element is very much at the core of the story: the first and the last shooting (and several in between) are accompanied by characters' declarations aimed at preventing either eXistenZ or TransCendenZ corrupting people's minds. There are several reasons why Cronenberg wanted to highlight this. The furore surrounding the reception of *Crash* in the US and the UK is one such reason. As Mark Kermode and Julian Petley's essay showed, he did feel personally affronted after the hostile attempts to ban his film (see chapter eight). Another reason might be Cronenberg's own children. As is prominently indicated on the sleeve of the graphic novelisation of *eXistenZ*, Cronenberg's children from his second marriage had entered their teenage years, and the mere fact that the graphic novel mentions this fact out of dozens of possible references demonstrates how much the concern of 'effect' and 'responsibility' is relevant to him. Or, as the sleeve puts it: 'Cronenberg has earned a reputation as a film director whose works are metaphors for larger social questions', immediately followed by: 'David Cronenberg lives in Toronto with his wife and teenage son and daughter' (Scoffield 1999).

The element of 'responsibility' also connects to the second reference Cronenberg consistently highlights in his active intervention in the reception of *eXistenZ*: Indo-

British novelist Salman Rushdie, and the religious death penalty (the fatwa) that was issued against him after the publication of his book *Satanic Verses* (1988), which reputedly insulted the Islamic religion. Issued in 1989, the fatwa urged all zealous Muslims to try and assassinate Rushdie. It caused him to spend most of the 1990s in hiding – a situation that was intensified after one of the Norwegian publishers of *Satanic Verses* was injured in a fudamentalist attack. Throughout the years, Rushdie received much support from the artistic community. In 1995, Cronenberg accepted the invitation of the Canadian magazine *Shift*, a publication with a declared interest in new media technology such as video games, to interview Rushdie.[11] Inevitably, responsibility became a topic of their conversation, introduced by Cronenberg from the outset when he expressed his upset at the negative press Rushdie received for being a 'parasite' on British society (first criticising it, now enjoying its security). After discussing religious fundamentalism, and recent films such as *Forrest Gump* (Robert Zemeckis, 1994) and *Pulp Fiction* (Quentin Tarantino, 1994) – judged too sentimental or too calculated in their use of violence respectively – and a few jabs at censorship, Cronenberg moved the subject to computers and interactive media:

> I'm very conscious that my films are always going to be seen by more people on tape or laser disc than in the cinema. Just what a film is has changed because you can have a library of videotapes and you can watch your favourite scenes and can choose not to watch others. (Cronenberg 1995: n. p.)

This 'change' in viewing is one that characterises the video generation's viewing strategies since *Scanners* and *Videodrome*. It is an observation Cronenberg made a number of times in the 1990s. To *Rolling Stone*'s David Breskin he formulated it like this:

> But video, once again, you can speed through the parts that don't interest you and hook up with the parts that do. Which is like rereading your favourite passages and scenes in a book, or skipping a chapter if you find it boring. It's really a toss-up, I think, as to whether that's more or less involving. It certainly is, as you say, taking control away from me, the filmmaker. I've got less control, there's no question. But maybe I'm more willing to give up that control than you are ... Maybe over ten years, twenty years, when you can have access to a film for twenty years because it's in your drawer, and you can take it out and look at it, ultimately, maybe there will be more involvement. And the abdication of some responsibility and some control by the director of the film will be balanced by the involvement over a long period of time by the person seeing the film. (In Breskin 1992: 236)

This is not just the anxiety of the auteur, worried that the loss of control he has over the meaning of his films will not be matched by a degree of viewer involvement that will almost certainly arrive at different conclusions on that meaning. For that kind of control, he can still intervene in the reception process, as he does so effectively in the case of *eXistenZ*. Rather, Cronenberg was ambiguous about how the 'involvement' viewers may find in their more individually managed access and exposure to media can ensure a viewing attitude that is actually not a genuinely harmful one. It is especially the-then fully emerging Internet and its 'interactive games' that Cronenberg worried about in his talk with Rushdie. After announcing that he has 'written a script for MGM about gaming,' he concurs with Rushdie that most of the stuff on the 'net' is 'junk'. 'Could there ever be a computer game that could truly be art,' he wonders. 'Could a game designer never be an artist?' (Cronenberg 1995: n. p.). Put differently, do artists bear a responsibility to society for the art they produce, or is the artist free to explore and the viewer, involved or not, limited in his reactions: either accept the experiment or resist it?

eXistenZ is specific about its inspirations: the phrase 'you are marked for death', referring to the fatwa concept, is repeated three times within a short time span, enough to ask viewers to ponder what it might refer to; a little further on Vinokur mentions the word 'fatwa' explicitly when he meets Allegra. For the clue-seeking audience surely this must trigger concerns similar to the ones Cronenberg vented in his conversation with Rushdie. However, to hammer home the point, as an active auteur would, Cronenberg employed them as rhetorical devices in the preparation for the reception of *eXistenZ*. He insisted the term fatwa was listed as one of several in an explanatory glossary in the press kit, and that the actors' relationships to computers and video games was one of its recurrent features. Still, it did not guarantee reviewers and audiences would apply them. Cronenberg therefore ensured he could intervene in the reception process by travelling with the film to its premiere venue, the Berlin International Film Festival.[12]

The Esoteric Network of Festivals: The Reception of eXistenZ

According to Jonathan Rosenbaum (1998), the film festival circuit in the late 1990s resembled that of an esoteric network, with critics and audiences rallying around the films and filmmakers that the regular distribution system tended to ignore, whether it is the Hollywood or the so-called indie circuit. At the same time, however, the festival network is one that ensures and rewards visibility. As pointed out in previous chapters, Cronenberg's films have fared well at festivals since his career went commercial. *Shivers* was awarded a prize at the Sitges festival, and ever since the director's films have done very well, not just at genre festivals in the early 1980s (see chapter five), but increasingly also at prestigious festivals such as Cannes, Berlin and Toronto. As a result, by the end of the 1990s Cronenberg was feeling very comfortable on the festival circuit, and well-placed enough to be able to intervene on behalf of his films.

eXistenZ was pitched to festivals in two ways: as an art-house movie, and as a horror/science fiction genre film. As the former, it played at the Berlin International Film Festival in 1999, where it was programmed alongside *Shakespeare in Love* (John Madden, 1998), *American History X* (Tony Kaye, 1998), *The Thin Red Line* (Terrence Malick, 1999) and *Aimée und Jaguar* (Max Färberböck, 1999) – none of them traditional genre films, all of them dealing, to varying degrees, with social issues, and each carrying some awareness of history and the past (beyond being set in the past). It was introduced as a film recounting Cronenberg's concern with issues of freedom of speech and the responsibility of the artist to speak out. Cronenberg's personal presence at the festival needs to be seen as an attempt to guide the interpretation of his film by critics and audiences. As he explained to Rushdie:

> Cronenberg: It never used to be a part of a movie's release that a director would go on the road with the picture. Maybe the stars.
> Salman Rushdie: But now, of course, the director is the star, or as big as the stars.
> Cronenberg: And if you want to achieve what I want, which is that you have a voice in your movie that's unique to you, then you're still the only one they want to speak to about what the movie is. (Cronenberg 1995: n. p.)

Dozens of interviews and hundreds of reviews appeared in the wake of *eXistenZ*'s world premiere in Berlin (on 16 February). Most of them dutifully mentioned the themes of the fatwa and video games, with publications devoting ample attention to how Cronenberg explained their significance in a 'relaxed and almost professorial' manner.[13] The Belgian paper *La Libre Belgique* even commented on Cronenberg's sense of humour in putting himself forward as 'auteur' in a manner similar to the ones hunted down in the film (see Pluijgers 1999). The only exceptions were the Canadian and British press. In the Canadian press, references to the fatwa and to video games were avoided in favour of references to 'Canadian' issues (with examples including the midtown Toronto accent of Jude Law and the presence of other Canadian films in Berlin – like *Emporte-moi* from Lea Pool). The second case is more complex. The British liberal press, including many film critics, made mention of the Rushdie reference in one way or another, but not so much to suggest how the 'fatwa' concept is essential to the meaning of the plot – as Cronenberg insisted – but rather to present Cronenberg the director (and his oeuvre) as culturally topical and relevant. The *Guardian* (Malcolm 1999) and the *Independent* (Anon. 1999b) both mentioned Rushdie and virtual-reality games, but only as rhetorical tools in a debate with other newspapers by framing *eXistenZ* in relation to the reception of *Crash*, several years before. *eXistenZ*'s connection to Rushdie offered the liberal press another means to get back at their right-wing counterparts, who had been hostile to *Crash* and had also campaigned against popular new media home entertainment such as videos or computer games ever since the 'Video Nasties' scandal in the early 1980s, and who had, as Cronenberg and Rushdie remarked during their conversation, depicted Rushdie as a 'fame hungry' arrogant attention seeker who 'has always criticised the police force' but is now only too happy to have them 'save his ass', 'Plus he's an immigrant .... He's got himself in trouble with his "own people"' (in Cronenberg 1995: n. p.). In *Sight and Sound*, Cronenberg revealed this tendency of the British tabloid press – which he of course also experienced with *Crash* – made him feel 'creepy' (in Rodley 1999: 8). At a Berlin press conference this weariness had led Cronenberg to compare British tabloid journalism to 'Frankenstein journalism' (in Freeman 1999: D1). As a result, the liberal British press did arrive at the point highlighted by Cronenberg's active intervention in the reception of *eXistenZ*, but for the wrong reasons: not to tout the film as worthy of cultural consideration, but to taunt the conservative press that had sided against Cronenberg, Rushdie and new media.[14] In the end, *eXistenZ* won a Silver Bear for artistic achievement, confirming the art-house reception Cronenberg wanted – the video games and Rushdie had paid off. In addition, the liberal press in the UK kept listing *eXistenZ* as one of the must-see films for months after its release.

The second way in which *eXistenZ* was presented was again through a festival channel, as a genre film. It was a logical choice to complement the art-house release, especially in territories where local genre festivals would enhance chances for successful distribution. After all, since *eXistenZ* was Cronenberg's first original script since *Videodrome*, comparisons between the two would be inevitable. In the run-up to the release several previews emphasised the generic pedigree of *eXistenZ*: *Starfix* called eXistenZ '*Videodrome 2.0*' (Thoret 1999). Kim Newman (1999) previewed it as part of a series of films dealing with virtual reality of which *Videodrome* was one of the first, and he compared the film to other VR-films such as *Total Recall* (once a Cronenberg project), *Brainstorm*, *Strange Days*, *Johnny Mnemonic* (Robert Longo, 1995) and *The Truman Show* (Peter Weir, 1998), as well as labyrinth films such as *Streetfighter* (Steven E. de Souza, 1994) and *Mortal Kombat* (Paul W. S. Anderson, 1995). In *Cinefantastique* too, the link with *Videodrome* was highlighted, as was the connection to the then fiercely hyped *The Matrix*. With festival screenings at the Brussels International Festival of Fantasy Film (the site of *Videodrome*'s European premiere in 1984), the Amsterdam Weekend of Terror (where it won the Silver Scream Award, selected by the audience) and the Dublin International Film Festival (not quite a genre fest but close), *eXistenZ* was released throughout Europe in a context perfectly equipped for genre references. Indeed, hardly any mentions to Rushdie occurred in the reviews of the European releases, with even the French press relatively mute on the subject of 'artistic responsibility'.[15] Tellingly, in its review, *Cahiers du cinéma* did not even use the opportunity of a review of the festival in Berlin, or news reports of *Natural Born Killers* attracting lawsuits, to build an association with the themes Cronenberg had forwarded (see Burdeau 1999; Lalanne 1999). If mentions of Rushdie appeared, they were usually from interviews conducted in Berlin. Instead, the self-referential, self-contained, clever and playful attitude of *eXistenZ* and its tone of genre pastiche became the central characteristic of this genre release, with ample discussions of the 'look' and 'attitude' of the film, described as a 'ludic' and 'amusing' 'knowing comedy' and 'puzzle', and a 'fabulously barmy', 'higher kitsch', 'nerd-cool infatuation' of a 'dirty mind', 'terrifying but not to be taken seriously'.[16]

In North America, the reception of *eXistenZ* was equally genre-dominated, but also peculiarly business-related. Most reviews emphasised the science fiction and thriller elements of the story, and Canadian publications had devoted at least as much attention to the international fame their native son had acquired (see Kirkland 1999; Saunders 1999). Even in these largely laudatory reviews remarks were prevalent about how Cronenberg continued to encounter resistance from Hollywood. In the American press, such remarks became a structuring element for the 'subversiveness' of *eXistenZ*. For some reviewers, it made Cronenberg an *auteur par excellence*; for others just a difficulty. When the *San Francisco Chronicle* exclaimed that *eXistenZ* made '*The Matrix* look like

Child's Play' it meant that it was outside most of the audience's reach in as much as it challenged viewers. The *New York Times* review mocked the title's pronunciation, spelling it 'eggs is tense' (Maslin 1999: E21). Even the Rushdie reference was upstaged by the perceived antagonism to Hollywood. As the *Washington Post* reviewer put it:

> [*ExistenZ*] was ostensibly inspired by the plight of author Salman Rushdie
> ... but the movie also seems to be a parable about Hollywood, as it makes
> disparaging remarks about good virtual games (like *eXistenZ* of course) and
> bad ones, which have cheaply created characters. (Howe 1999: N49)

This unfavourable comparison to Hollywood was repeated in nearly all American reviews, with stories about how the screenplay was refused further development by MGM, and references to Jennifer Jason Leigh's intensity and edginess becoming major features of the film's supposed alternative credentials. Cronenberg was even compared to Philip K. Dick and Stanley Kubrick, all three jostling for the 'top-weirdo' spot.[17] Even when the generic references were placed in a cultural perspective, and the issue of gaming was considered more broadly, the conclusion was that Cronenberg needed to make audiences care more about his characters – that he was too un-Hollywood. As if to confirm this impression of smart irrelevance, the first academic essay on *eXistenZ* framed it as an 'elevator film', a film woven of conceits the viewer has to be eager to enter, for the sake of it (Pomerance 2003).

Cronenberg's personal interventions in the second type of release may seem less explicit, but they are not less successful: aware of how well the majority of horror and science fiction fans know his oeuvre, and adore *Videodrome*, a few references to his previous work in interviews and a couple of reassurances that there will be the obligatory violence (the shootings are excessive) and gory moments (with the scenes at the Chinese restaurant satisfying every gourmand) sufficed. The momentum of the well-established network in which Cronenberg is a household name did the rest. Combined, the art-house and genre releases demonstrated how Cronenberg could release a film on two platforms, almost simultaneously, and receive differing receptions (though not differing evaluations!) by inserting the right references into the networks that regulated their premieres: social and artistic responsibilities for Berlin, markers such as violence and effects for the genre audiences.

As an afterthought to the reception of *eXistenZ*, Cronenberg's presidency of the jury at the 1999 Cannes festival reinforced the argument that, throughout the release trajectories of *eXistenZ*, the Baron-of-Blood-cum-Cultural Hero himself was the most significant point of reference. The controversy surrounding, and Cronenberg's defence of, the emotional severity and realistic harshness of prize-winning films at Cannes, such as *Rosetta* (Dardenne Brothers, 1999) and *L'humanité* (*Humanity*, Bruno Dumont, 1999), guaranteed *eXistenZ* a longer screen-life in Europe than in other regions. Added to that, events such as Cronenberg throwing the ceremonial first pitch of the baseball season, his inclusion in Canada's Walk of Fame (alongside hockey legend Maurice Richard and rock band Rush), ongoing speculation on his next films and abandoned projects (*Red Cars, Crimes of the Future, Basic Instinct II,*

Painkillers), as well as an exhibition of Cronenberg's creatures and mad machinery in Paris, gave his persona an even broader aura.

Baron of Blood Meets Beckett: The Reception of Spider

The prefiguration of *Spider*'s reception was characterised by one key reference: Samuel Beckett. By and large, this reference plays the same role in the reception of *Spider* as the Rushdie one in that of *eXistenZ*: it is a heavyweight reference that critics will eagerly pick up, and the one through which Cronenberg can assert his own view of the film in the process of reception. But the way in which Beckett ended up becoming that key reference was less the result of active auteurship, and more of a set of circumstances at play in the contemporary discourse of the esoteric network of festivals. The first time the link between Beckett and Cronenberg was made was by the director himself, in an interview nearly twenty years before *Spider* (see Beard & Handling 1983: 164), when he mentioned the name next to his favourite writers Nabokov and Burroughs (see chapter seven). When Burroughs took over as the most dominant literary reference in the reception of Cronenberg, Beckett's influence became dormant, until the 25th anniversary of the Toronto International Film Festival in 2000. As well as the screening of *Camera*, the festival premiered a series of short films, part of a project to put Beckett's plays on film.[18] Two of these films were directed by Canadian directors: Atom Egoyan's *Krapp's Last Tape* (2000) and Patricia Rozema's *Happy Days* (2000). Together with the other Canadian entries for the Preludes celebratory shorts, and the hugely popular *Ginger Snaps*, it gave that year of the Toronto International Film Festival a homely feel and local buzz. It invited pundits to muse about what Canada and Beckett would have in common ('darkness' mostly). And in the margin of such considerations, comparisons between Beckett and Cronenberg could easily bloom, even within the director's own mind.[19] When a year later journalists visited the set of *Spider*, Beckett was omnipresent: in the austere North London location, in Ralph Fiennes' apparel, in the eerie resemblance between John Neville's Terrence and David Thewlis's portrayal of Clov in *Endgame* (Conor McPherson, 2000; also screened at the Toronto International Film Festival), but especially as a stubbornly returning mantra in Cronenberg's explanation of the film: 'From the first page of *Spider*, I had thought of Samuel Beckett. *Spider, c'est Beckett et Freud à la fois'* (in Poirier 2001: 28). Another journalist noticed that 'while it is obvious Cronenberg has a Beckett obsession, it was not always so. In fact, it was not until recently that the director says he really began to appreciate such authors as Beckett, Dostoyevsky and Kafka' (Bouw 2001: R13). Dostyevsky would become a major influence on *Eastern Promises*. Beckett became the major point of reference for *Spider*.

> 'I'm starting to look more like the old Sam Beckett every day', the 58-year old Canadian director, once dubbed the 'baron of blood' says with a boyish grin. That Cronenberg is seeing Beckett in his own image these days is no accident. ... Cronenberg again reverts to Beckett as the inspiration for the kind of atmosphere he tried to build on set. 'Not his plays, but novels like *Molloy*, whose characters are very much like *Spider*' Cronenberg says'. (Ibid.)

Besides an auteur sharing his thoughts about art, the world and age with journalists, these mentions constructed a frame of reference for the film's reception, equipping it with the kind of weighty ballast reviewers enjoy delving into. For one, it offered Cronenberg a way of claiming ownership over the project. When asked whether he considered his film version of the story different from the sensibilities the novel's author (and screenwriter) Patrick McGrath had injected into it, he replied:

> He writes sort of modern gothic novels – and I absolutely don't do gothic. Although we are very interested in extremes ... I wouldn't say we are on the same plane stylistically ... Of course this is my own arrogance [but] I have to think this movie is pretty unique with the mixing of Patrick's sensibility and my own. (In ibid.)

With the Beckett reference in place, *Spider* began a reception trajectory that spanned ten months of regional releases. It premiered at the Cannes festival in May 2002. At the first press conference, the Beckett reference was reintroduced: 'Cronenberg presided over a subdued and intelligent press conference, one in which references to Beckett, Kafka and Freud were common' (Anon. 2002: D05). The French and European press eagerly picked up on these references (though Freud and Kafka received far fewer mentions subsequently), up to the point where Beckett became a 'predictable' influence. Yet, its presence was not all-encompassing, with mentions of Dickens, the premiere party and the issue of violence in cinema (not in Cronenberg's films this time but in Gaspar Noë's *Irreversible*) attracting more attention.

Over the course of the next months, however, the Beckett reference gradually sedimented, and reviewers increasingly used it to discuss the film. At the festival in Toronto there were still relatively few references to Beckett, perhaps because it was too highbrow a reference for a mainstream North American festival without too much of a competition element. Since Beckett's name was no longer being pushed by a series of films directed by Canadians he had lost his topicality in that arena. Still, for Toronto Cronenberg did not need topicality – he *is* the story. The question was not whether Cronenberg's film would receive adequate press attention, but rather was the programme slot appropriate for the interest it was guaranteed to attract. In this case, the prestigious opening gala slot went to Egoyan's *Ararat* (2002), like Cronenberg, one of the 'hometown guys ... with an international reputation – one might even say cult' (Knelman 2002: D02). *Spider* won one of the top prizes. At the festivals of Ghent and Sitges, both of which Cronenberg attended, the Beckett reference became gradually more entrenched, as the film garnered momentum as one of the autumn's major art-house releases.[20] Screenings at the Raindance Film Festival in London, touted as the UK's premiere independent festival, ensured even more credibility: Beckett fits grainy, rainy London better than sunny, classy Cannes or glamorous Toronto. By the time of the British and American releases, Beckett had become a fixture in most reviews. Even the formerly hostile Alexander Walker, who had hated *Crash* and *eXistenZ*, gave *Spider* a mildly positive evaluation (2003: 34).

At this point, Cronenberg's active auteurship also caused slight fatigue with reviewers, especially with his constant use of philosophical and literary references – as if the active auteur himself was perhaps too overly didactic: 'I think you can see Beckett in *Spider*,' said Cronenberg to critic Jonathan Romney, before also mentioning Schopenhauer, Nietzsche, Heidegger and Sartre (see Romney 2003: 8–11). In the *Daily Telegraph* this became: 'He will refer to philosophers such as Heidegger, Schopenhauer and Kant, to say nothing of Freud, Proust and Beckett' (Said 2002: 23). And that quickly turned into: 'David Cronenberg, not the most modest of veteran auteurs, describes *Spider* as having "the feel of Samuel Beckett confronting Sigmund Freud" (confronting him about what? The mind boggles)' (Shoard 2003: 7).

Generally free of irony, the North American reception employed the Beckett reference without cynicism, encouraged by Cronenberg's lifetime award from *Fangoria* and the Genie Award for Best Direction in Canada. As the reviewer for *Salon.com* put it:

> Sitting in a room with him and talking about Vladimir Nabokov's conception of memory, or Samuel Beckett as the iconic existential hero, as I recently did, might sound, in the abstract, unbelievably precious and pretentious. In fact it was a totally relaxed and good-humoured conversation with an elegantly dressed, grey-maned artist. (O'Hehir 2003: n. p.)

Similarly, when Cronenberg playfully attempted to rob McGrath of his contribution to the film, the *Village Voice* refrained from any comments. Cronenberg: 'This is the perfect fusion. I can't actually remember what you did, Patrick, so I will take all the credit for it' (in Hoberman 2003: n. p.). When the conversation moved to Beckett, and McGrath mentioned his idea for the figure playing Spider was a 'lanky, sort of tall' person like Samuel Beckett, Cronenberg reacted immediately:

> DC: 'You actually thought of Samuel Beckett?'
> PM: 'Oh, very much'
> DC: 'Because, it's not in your novel, obviously. And Beckett became our touchstone. I didn't know that you had had him in mind'. (In ibid.)

This conversation settled the active auteurship of Cronenberg: it demonstrates how central Beckett was to the project, as a point of reference, but also how essential the term 'Beckett' was to the channelling of the reception of *Spider*. It gave *Spider* critical gravitas, and it gave reviewers and audiences something to hang on to that channelled their interpretations. If that active auteurship eventually displayed some strain, it is worth remembering, as the reviewer of the *Jerusalem Post* did in a unique confessional encounter with Cronenberg, that even at the top of his art, even when manufacturing the tight, delightful puzzles that *eXistenZ* and *Spider* are, even when revered by audiences and showered with awards, Cronenberg remained anxious, 'a genuine auteur who has often said he was afraid he could end up with "an audience of one, namely myself"' (in Teitelbaum 2003: 42).

Where to go from here? *eXistenZ* and *Spider* are among Cronenberg's best tailored productions, and they demonstrate his talent for filmmaking and storytelling in every scene. In fact, they are so well crafted they were seen as too hermetic for 'normal' audiences. One had to be in the know, part of the esoteric network, in order to appreciate the puns, allusions and references to the rest of 'active auteur' Cronenberg's oeuvre. And therein lies the flaw in both films. Beyond their symptomatic representativeness for smart audience attitudes at the turn of the millennium, where is their relevance, their input into culture? Cronenberg really only answered that question with his next two films, *A History of Violence* and *Eastern Promises*, which placed core cultural elements such as family, legacy and immigration at the front of their narratives. Some signs pointing towards that road back to relevance were visible in embryonic form in *eXistenZ* and *Spider*.

The first sign concerns gender roles. Like other Cronenberg protagonists, Ted Pikul and Dennis Cleg are not the most savvy or potent of men. They are fallible and seem to stumble through the story instead of mastering the proceedings. It is difficult to root for them; they do not immediately attract sympathy. Though American reviewers loathed *eXistenZ* for this detachment, such male impotence enabled Cronenberg to foreground the story, the structure and several cues and clues he wanted viewers to note. But, strikingly, the fallible male was never replaced, or even balanced, by a strong heroine – a criticism Cronenberg had often received, and one that here too seems to hold. Admittedly, Allegra and mum/Yvonne are strong-willed characters, brimming with life. But they are also portrayed as dangerous and threatening, edgy and intense, especially when they display any desire to be sexually active. The moment Allegra becomes attracted to Pikul, he starts to suspect her, and she becomes less trustworthy. In the case of mum/Yvonne a display of sexuality even costs her her life. It is the reason Dennis kills her. The suggestion seems that only when women are asexual can we be assured of their allegiance. Yet Cronenberg, almost wickedly, fills his narratives with moments, props and tools that make avoiding sex altogether impossible. In *eXistenZ*, the bioports, Gas's gas station, and Nader's Emporium overflow with sexual tension. In *Spider*, the sexual tension starts at the pub and continues in the parents' bedroom, but as Dennis's encounter with his landlady shows, it spreads to the rest of the story as well. Cronenberg would explore such atmospheres of sexual tension further in *A History of Violence* and *Eastern Promises* in order to equip these films with a cultural relevance to gender roles within a 'family' context.

The second sign concerns technology. As Beard writes, 'near the beginning of his career, Cronenberg had some moments with *shiny technology*, but even as early as *The Brood* he was moving in a different direction – towards a darker and more organic environment for scientific invention and its human products' (2005: 445; emphasis added). With *eXistenZ* and *Spider* Cronenberg continues that direction. To be true, *eXistenZ* does contain some shiny technology, especially in the creation of one of the mutant bugs, whose movements were enhanced through digital imagery (by Toybox, to be precise). Yet, even the digital effects are, as Dennis Berardi of Toybox explains, completely different from regular uses of the technology:

What we're doing is more impressive [than fast-moving images] because in one beauty shot of the creature we're focused on him in close-up for something like 15 seconds, and the camera tracks, he's in full light, and he's crawling up a pump. (In Tillson 1999: 119)

In the larger scheme of *eXistenZ*, such effects remain a detail. By and large, Cronenberg's idea was to make the actual technology look old, and have it *be* old. He insisted on banning a long list of small appliances and gadgets usually associated with science fiction and futuristic designs from each shot: no computer screens, watches, television sets, telephones (the Pink Phone is one exception), not even futuristic fashion accessories or colourful or radiant outfits (too *Star Trek* perhaps). The gristle gun is decidedly organic and while it looks ingenious it is a fairly rudimentary device; a far cry from the sophisticated machinery in *Scanners*, *Videodrome* and *The Fly*. The game consoles and pods too are organically fuelled. Vinokur compares the surgery on Allegra's pod to pet care by 'glorified veterinarians', and when Pikul asks 'where the batteries go', Allegra answers: '*You* are the power source. Your body, your nervous system, your metabolism, your energy.'

In *Spider*, any technology is old – there is not one electronic appliance in the film (even Dennis's clock is mechanical). Gas is the highest form of technology. If one considers Cronenberg's whole oeuvre, a trend emerges: consistently and gradually he has been downsizing and regressing the technological qualities of his major tools and instruments until he arrived at the bare essentials of technology: bones, sticks and natural resources like gas. It feels almost like an attempt to liberate himself from the cyberpunk and science fiction burden that had been so strong at the time of *Scanners* and *Videodrome*, or the medical and automotive technologies dominating *Dead Ringers* and *Crash*. In *A History of Violence* and *Eastern Promises* Cronenberg would finally be able to empty the concept of technology of its 'cool' overtones and employ it for its essential applicability: guns for killing and cars and bikes for transport, with both frequently malfunctioning.[21]

Following *Crash*, *eXistenZ* and *Spider* both demonstrated that cultural hero Cronenberg had nothing left to prove; that he could go on making films and be confident about his skills and reputation, and the films' reception. Given that, Cronenberg could still not resist the urge to steer the reception of his films. That urge resembles Allegra's unease when she nervously inquires at the end of the game 'have I won'? Of course she won. Of course Cronenberg won over audiences again. There is no need for anxieties. Because the public frame of reference for Cronenberg's films was well-established, critics would go to great lengths to see any of his films as culturally relevant, even when they are so hermetically self-involved they seem, like *Spider*'s Dennis, to be talking mostly to themselves. For Beard, *eXistenZ* is near to self-parody, and *Spider* is testimony of what he calls Cronenberg's 'hard time' in settling. Put positively, *eXistenZ* reaffirms Cronenberg's skill as a writer, and *Spider* his talents for taking on someone else's work and still making 'a film that is powerful and aesthetically assured' (2005: 503). For Beard, *Spider* is Cronenberg *à la* Robert Bresson – austere and stoic.

At the start of this chapter I compared Cronenberg's status to that of being at the centre of his own universe. That universe is also that of cinema. Cronenberg had 'arrived' at one of the highest levels of respect and relevance a director can achieve: a totem for Canadian cinema, which he casually endorses; a hero and mentor for the horror genre; and a master in crafting any kind of film story. There are no more regrets about projects that failed to come through (*Red Cars*, *American Psycho*, *Painkillers* or *Basic Instinct II*),[22] no more risks to be taken – Cronenberg repeatedly declared that he no longer worried about projects and would henceforth only pursue those he would feel completely comfortable with. But Cronenberg's next films would testify that futures and legacies are never secure.

CHAPTER TEN

Family Affairs: *A History of Violence* and *Eastern Promises*

You're living the American Dream. You really bought into it, didn't you?

Richie Cusack (William Hurt) in *A History of Violence*

Whenever the tragic deed, however, is done within the family –
when murder or the like is done or mediated by brother on brother,
by son on father, by mother on son, or son on mother –
these are the situations the poet should seek after.

Aristotle, *Poetics*, 13–15

What will habit not do to a man?

Fyodor Dostoyevsky, *Demons* (1872: 8)

Viggo and David at the Head of the Table

If one speaks of legacy, one speaks of family and traditions, of values becoming habits and routines. In one of his least remarkable acting performances, as a film director in *Trial by Jury*, Cronenberg turns to Rusty (Armand Assante), head of a mafia family recently cleared by a corrupt jury, and says roguishly, as he escorts a glamour girl out of a night club, 'I wanna make a movie about your life.' It is an off the cuff remark, the

It's lonely as the head of the family: Viggo Mortensen at the head of the table in the closing shots of *A History of Violence* (top) and *Eastern Promises* (above)

routinely friendly exchange one would have with an acquaintance or family member before one realises what crime that person has *actually* committed, and before reassessing the relationship becomes necessary – before one is faced with the responsibility of breaking the ritual of habit and re-evaluating the values the relationship inhabits. About a decade after *Trial by Jury*, Cronenberg fulfilled his on-screen promise with *A History of Violence*. In it, he gave the part of the villainous head of a mafia family to William Hurt, who had played a vicious mobster in *Trial by Jury*. Two years later, he followed through with *Eastern Promises*, another film about mafia and family and about reassessing values embedded in family traditions and habits.

A History of Violence and *Eastern Promises* both conclude with images of Viggo Mortensen as a *pater familias*, a patriarch sitting at the head of a dinner table. In both cases he is victorious: he has overcome formidable opposition, vanquished his adversaries and safeguarded the mother/child bond that forms the core of the nuclear family. In both cases he is also alone – emotionally abandoned and physically isolated. His victory has come with the price of never being able to return to a 'normal' family and always having the moral implications and social consequences of the violence he has used restrain his further life – shackle him as it were. What was broken can be fixed, but never truly healed or made undone. Both scenes are extremely powerful in their contemplative resignation, reinstating ambiguity into narratives that only seconds before seemed to end happily.

In its discussion of Cronenberg's two most recent films, this chapter puts three perspectives forward: the films' portrayal of family lives under siege; their (and Cronenberg's own) position towards the role of families in the construction and maintenance of civilisation and cultural legacy; and their political and cultural relevance as evidenced in their reception. The overarching argument is that Cronenberg, now in his sixties, injected these films with an awareness previously only marginally represented in his work: an interest in the habits, rituals and traditions that help sustain family functions (of whatever kind) beyond their biological and/or socio-economic roles as reproducers of genes, values or capital. Such awareness pushes issues such as 'romance', 'love' or 'belonging', which had hitherto been underrepresented, to the fore of Cronenberg's oeuvre, exactly at a time when, as a cultural hero and totem of independent, liberal filmmaking, a father of three adult children and the head of a small 'family' business, he finds himself in a position not unlike that of Mortensen's characters: pondering his place at the head of the table.

Family (and) politics

A History of Violence and *Eastern Promises* take their cues from earlier Cronenberg films' considerations of family (see chapter six) and widen the lens through which these issues are addressed. They move the representation of family from the margins to the centre of their narratives. Moreover, they place those families in specifically identifiable situations, in cities and towns with particular socio-economic profiles (both 'paradises' that lose their innocence), making them recognisable as metaphors. In relating those recognisable situations to wider political concerns, both global and local, they imbue those representations with cultural significance and political relevance. *A History of Violence* and *Eastern Promises* reveal how contemporary family life – in a society fuelled by anxieties, marred by gender wars, bullied by real and fabricated fears and constantly on edge – consists of a constant, tense negotiation between an image of idealised, romantic family life and the harsh practicalities of survival. In both films the permanent threat to family happiness exposes its underlying foundations, based on sex, power, abuse and politics. By deconstructing 'family' the films also formulate a damning criticism of the difference between the rhetoric surrounding the 'happy nuclear family' in Western society, especially its use in a certain version of the American Dream, and the actual place of the family, under constant threat of dissolution. In doing so, the two films suggest a much more pragmatic view on family life, one that simultaneously surpasses and eradicates the 'romantic ideal' and acknowledges the forces that tear that ideal apart. The topicality of these forces in American society makes both films cultural markers of our time.

Two perspectives matter here; the first is politics. As observed in chapter five Cronenberg has often denied his films deal with politics in any direct way. He has often maintained they reflect human conditions, not ideological ones. This time, too, Cronenberg resisted having his films discussed along political lines, but the scope is decidedly different. Instead of the more abstract politics of gender or cultural representation, *A History of Violence* and *Eastern Promises* evoked comparisons with political praxis, in particular American president George W. Bush's policies in Iraq and the defence of 'family' as America's cultural backbone, and policies concerning organised crime, immigration, diaspora and human trafficking, respectively.

The second perspective is that of the different kinds of family. Both *A History of Violence* and *Eastern Promises* show not just one type of family; instead there are representations of the traditional nuclear family (man, wife, children), of one-parent families, of biological and adopted children and siblings, of large families that include countless cousins, aunts and uncles, of family as criminal brotherhood (most notably represented through the mafia), of American families and Russian families, families rooted in communities for ages and newly-immigrant families, rich and poor families, and rural and urban family situations. Through tropes and motifs commonly associated with family, from the historical 'legacy', 'roots' and 'tradition', to the institutional 'respect' and 'responsibility', and from the intimate 'romantic love' to the creepy 'one of us' a complex variety of configurations of family become possible. Several of these invite links with the political discourses mentioned above.

A History of Violence

Most viewers of *A History of Violence* will have been aware of Cronenberg's practices and routines. They know a happy family is not part of that. But even for viewers unaware of Cronenberg's reputation there is much in the opening minutes of the film that creates unease, and that makes viewers speculate on exactly what kind of threat, and what kind of family, they are being presented with.[1]

The first three segments of the film put family life at the centre of the narrative. The first is dominated by a slow, deliberate four-minute opening shot. Starting from a fairly low-key framing (a door, a plastic chair outside, the sun shining), two adults, Billy (Greg Bryk) and Leland (Stephen McHattie) drag themselves lazily, like bad, hung-over villains in westerns do, to their car, have a short argument about who is driving and make their way to what turns out to be the front office of a row of motel rooms. When they find they need water for their ride, the younger man goes inside. Once inside we discover his companion has killed the clerk and left him in a pool of blood. The young man seems unfazed, even bored, and starts filling his can of water. He is interrupted by a distressed young girl. He shushes her ... and shoots her.

The moment the gun goes off we cut to the second segment, to another girl (blonde, this time), screaming at the top of her lungs. It is Sarah (Heidi Hayes), the youngest daughter of the Stall family, and she is having a nightmare. Daddy Tom (Viggo Mortensen) walks in and comforts her; her brother Jack (Ashton Holmes) shows up as well, and he makes her smile; even mummy Edie (Maria Bello) comes to make sure everything is well. It is funny to observe how the mother seems less bothered by her screaming child than the males – they are so quick to react they must have been on guard, or sleeping uneasy. Perhaps her worry is less that of an external threat and more one of internal discomfort, an upset stomach, a small fever, but not a monster. The Stall family seems a perfect display of the all-American nuclear family, caring and loving: two understanding parents, an older son, a younger daughter. Their voices are hushed and soothing; they call each other 'baby' and 'kiddo'; they hug and kiss (a kiss against the monsters, a kiss for the mum, a kiss good morning). At the cosily set breakfast, with orange juice, coffee, cereal and a newspaper – the mum standing up in charge of the household, the dad sharing moments with daughter and son – the impression of happiness continues. No worse worries than playing outfield in gym baseball and dad's pick-up truck that won't start.

In the third segment, after a brief interlude that sees Edie and Tom drive into the sunrise in their minivan, Edie drops Tom off on her way to work and they kiss, again, twice, while saying sweet words (they even make a naughty 'pick me up' reference). Underneath the clock of the post office Tom posts the mail. Though it is early morning, the dial of the clock is stubbornly stuck on 1.15 – a town where time literally stands still. Before entering his business, a diner, Tom picks up litter from the street and throws it in the garbage – what a responsible citizen, what a peaceful life.

The perfection of the second and third segment surely fools no one; the brutality of the violent eruption in the first has alerted everyone. At this point there can be no doubt in any viewer's mind that the paths of the killers and the Stalls will cross and that the family happiness will be invaded. Given the classic composition of the Stall family and the romantic bond between Edie and Tom, the father of the house will be the one who has to stand up and defend his kin. Can he do that? The gut answer is yes: the family seems so strong they will weather the storm; and they will stand by him. But there are little cracks. Audiences, aware of – and maybe still recovering from – the brutal child-killing in the credit sequence, aware of Cronenberg's previous films and his reputation, know this exposition means that the family is under threat; and because they anticipate that, they no longer just see the Stall family as peaceful. As a Cronenberg creation, there must also be tensions, dysfunctions – they are simply too perfect. Their overbearing love and care betrays insecurity. Which household sees *everyone* get up in the middle of the night for one kid's bad dream? They seem anxious all of a sudden.

Indeed, it quickly becomes clear that things are not all nice with the Stalls. Even before the killers from the opening segment show up in Tom's town, there are signs, clearer than the inferences and associations so far, that the confrontation is not going to be all black and white. There is a secret undermining the Stall family, at the heart of which lies an inability to deeply connect at a romantic level. As the narrative develops, it turns out that Tom is a retired gunfighter, a mobster inadvertently coaxed out of seclusion by the professional way in which he eliminates the two killers when they rob his diner. His lethal skills draw the attention of a former enemy, Carl Fogarty (Ed Harris) who bullies Tom's family until he reveals his previous career and is led to violence, igniting a quest to battle his past demons and adversaries.

But *A History of Violence* takes its time leading to those developments. A good three-quarters of the film is dedicated to the slow breakdown of trust in the Stall household. And that breakdown reveals, even before the audience is given the official reason for the distrust, their happiness to be a charade, and their anxieties to run deeper than Tom's lies about his previous life. At the core is the sexual and romantic relationship between Edie and Tom. The first impression we get is that, like so many couples with growing kids, they have sidelined their romantic feelings in favour of an alliance to raise a family; they have exchanged their passion for security, and the habits and rituals that come with that. When Edie asks Tom if he wants to be picked up after work, he replies: 'Yeah. And then we can go to the drive-in and make out tonight.' Edie's flat reply is: 'There hasn't been a drive-in here since the early seventies, but…'. Tom kisses Edie, as if comforting her, and tells her he loves her. 'I love you too,' she responds, but when she tries to caress his cheek he turns his face away ever so slightly, not quite the cold shoulder but close, and we can see the glimpse of disappointment on her face.

Still, they seem to be doing much better than most at keeping their sex life alive. That night, Edie has arranged for them to be home alone, in an attempt to 'fix' the fact they 'never got to be teenagers together' as she puts it. She commands him into their bedroom. When she briefly excuses herself to the bathroom, Tom hurriedly cleans the bed, rids it of kids' toys, uncomfortable about what is to come, his composure almost reluctant. He prudently dims the light. Edie appears, donning a cheerleader outfit, lifting her skirt teasingly. She makes a few stripper moves, rips Tom's clothes off, mounts him and they engage in athletic sexual intercourse. It is unclear afterwards if the fixing was successful, but their first exchange is:

Edie: What is it?
Tom: Huh? (pause)I remember the moment I knew you were in love with me.
    I saw it in your eyes. I can still see it.
Edie: Of course you can. (She turns towards him) I still love you.
(pause)
Tom: I am the luckiest son of a bitch alive.

By the usual standards of bed conversations this is fairly romantic, but with the knowledge of a missing past and the ambiguity of the anxious attempts to pursue an active sex life within a domestic (and domesticated) setting, it becomes uncomfortable. Why the continuous verbal reassurance? What might be revealed or unleashed? Why is it presented as important they did not know each other as teenagers? Does it explain their current hunger for sex and romance? Why is it important to make us privy to that information?

The answer comes about one hour into the film, when *A History of Violence* shifts from being a film about problems in a romantic relationship to a film offering a post-romantic critique of family life. Fogarty's insistent harassments and allusions to Tom's past as a gangster have caused a gradual breakdown of trust in the family. Jack has got into a fight at school and when Tom reprimands him saying that 'in this family we do not solve our problems by hitting people' he retorts: 'No, in this family, we shoot them.' In reaction, Tom slaps his son in the face. Soon afterwards, Fogarty shows up on the Stalls' front lawn and a standoff follows. Tom is forced to use violence. He shoots Fogarty's henchmen before Jack kills Fogarty – right after Tom finally admits to Fogarty: 'I should have killed you when I had the chance in Phillie.'

Two confrontations: the 'family name' and 'rape'

The secret is now out in the open, at least within the family circle: Tom is Joey Cusack, a former mafia killer – quite another kind of family. At this point, most other stories would abandon the family context in favour of Tom's inevitable encounter with the bandits and his struggle to restore the lost balance; but not *A History of Violence*. Instead, the narrative remains focused on the Stalls for another twenty minutes, in a move to demonstrate how much of the breakdown cannot solely be blamed on Fogarty and Tom's professional past, but also on the now obvious lies in the family life of Tom and Edie.

Two confrontations between the couple illustrate this. The first takes place in that most Cronenbergian of settings, a hospital room, where Tom recovers from injuries sustained in his fight with Fogarty. In the midst of a bitter discussion, Edie suddenly stops, prompted by a realisation:

> Edie: And our name. Jesus Christ, my name. Jack's name. Sarah's name. Stall? Tom Stall? Did you just make that up? Where did that name come from?
>
> Tom: I mean … it was available.
>
> Edie: Yeah … I guess I was available too.

There is more at stake here than a mere moniker. For Edie, the name Stall was a symbol of their family union; she took on the name to solidify that bond, and their children's names are a symbol of it as well. If the name is a fake the bond falls apart. And Stall is not just a name; it is an omen. In a sense, his name describes his situation: Stall is just stalling – his life is parked in a seemingly happy lane, but it is going to have to move out of there soon. But Tom Stall, and Jack, Sarah and Edie are also uncharacteristically plain names for Cronenberg characters. In fact, only in *The Dead Zone* do similarly old-fashioned, common names occur (Johnny Smith and Sarah Bracknell).[2]

The second confrontation also connects with Cronenberg's oeuvre, in that it equates a supposedly romantic, loving relationship with a sexual struggle. After Tom has returned home, the local sheriff (Peter MacNeill – Seagrave from *Crash*), whose suspicions about Tom's past have been raised by Fogarty's death, asks to interrogate him. Edie turns up and much to Tom's surprise she backs up his denials of involvement. Moving herself from in between the two men (the sheriff standing, Tom sitting) to side with her husband she wonders if the 'family hasn't suffered enough', and asks the sheriff to leave them in peace. But the moment he has left she runs away, and when Tom tries to stop her she fights him off. He grabs her by the throat. Their mutual frustrations escalate into a struggle – domestic violence – but also to passion, and they have rough sex – a quasi rape – on the staircase. If it is unclear to what extent Edie is a consenting partner in this aggressive act of sex (they both seem passionate), her role as victim is emphasised after the act. When Tom finally pulls back she runs upstairs, tearing herself away from him. Tom spends the night on the couch. That night we see Edie alone in bed, crying in the dark, the wound on her back – some sort of bruise – clearly visible, reminding the viewer how much she has been stabbed in the back. Edie's dreams of a family life have been shattered, her romantic ideals betrayed.

These two confrontations are crucial, because they demonstrate how the romantic efforts of Tom and Edie were always doomed to fail. Tom's history of violence creeps up on them and becomes inescapable. Triggered by violence towards him, Tom in turn becomes violent, in an increasingly nasty way, first slapping his son, then virtually molesting his wife. In itself, this is a struggle not uncommon to portrayals of family in film, even in its extreme depiction (we stay with the sex/rape for at least two full, uncomfortable minutes). What is uncommon, however, is how the film does not move away from the troubled family. At the point of the second confrontation the film has been with the Stalls for more than an hour, showing only their point of view. By refusing to leave the household, and instead staying to detail the escalation, *A History of Violence* suggests that external causes (Fogarty, Tom's past) can only partly be blamed for the violence in the family. The crooks may have been the catalyst, but the potential for violence was already present, in the form of the fake, forced romance between Tom and Edie.

True to generic traditions, the film finds a narrative resolution in Tom's revenge. Prompted by his brother Richie (William Hurt), he travels to Philadelphia, confronts his past (and his 'real' family) and eliminates it by killing his brother. He rids himself of evidence at a nearby lake, cleanses himself there and returns home. This all happens swiftly. The actual time spent away from home occupies less than 17 minutes of the total screen time.

With the erasure of the past, nothing seems to stand in the way of the Stalls' happiness. But near the end *A History of Violence* reinserts a fresh dose of ambiguity. When Tom pulls up to his home there is no one to greet him. It is quite a change from the rally around little Sarah in the beginning. The indoor lights flicker on his face as we see his distress: is he able to go back inside and resume a life that was not his to begin with? Not a single word is uttered in the last four-and-a-half minutes of the film (the last sentence is Tom's adieu to his brother, his true family). The last two minutes, when Tom enters his home and slowly, reluctantly, reclaims his place at the head of the family, are incredibly tense. The setting is sparsely lit, highlighting the austerity of the interior (a kitchen). The music is elegiac in tone; there is no hint of triumph. Edie is serving dinner (a traditional American meal: corn, carrots, meatloaf, mashed potatoes) to Sarah and Jack when Tom enters through the back door. Tom and Edie cannot look each other in the eye and bow their heads, her hands folded in a prayer, his look forlorn. After a while, Sarah gets up and gets her dad a dinner plate. Tom sits at the head of the table (it is actually a square table but Tom's position facing the camera presents him as head). Another few tense seconds later, Jack offers his father the meatloaf. It is here that the ambiguity of *A History of Violence* is at its clearest. Sarah's and Jack's formal gestures reinstate Tom as head of the family, and while the future may look grim for the Stalls we can assume that the hierarchy of the family unit is saved from immediate disintegration. But when Tom and Edie finally face each other it becomes clear that the romantic foundation of the family is lost. Edie's face is carved with hurt; Tom's is fraught with despair. There is no solace, no happy ever after. Instead of cementing their romantic relationship by regaining, as Edie had attempted, an idealised past of teenage dates, the couple have now irretrievably moved beyond romance, into a present and future that is all too realistically recognisable in its compromise. The family may remain and the violence is gone, but their love is lost.[3]

The American Dream: The Reception of A History of Violence

From its earliest presence on the public stage A History of Violence was seen as revolving around violence and family. On the film's official website and in the press book it was presented as a 'family drama' as well as a thriller, an unusual choice for Cronenberg. The sexuality at the core of the relationship between the main characters was stressed at every opportunity, and the violence was frequently described as 'rooted' within 'the nuclear family'.[4] The film's first public screening was on 16 May 2005 at the Cannes Film Festival, where it was announced as a 'twisted look at family' (Anon. 2005b) with Cronenberg stating that he wanted to emphasise 'the sexual component in violence and [the] violent component in sexuality' (in Anon. 2005c).

Immediately reviewers and critics added to that the idea that A History of Violence provided a criticism of violence as embedded in the most general and respected type of 'family' available, namely civilisation.[5] This link unexpectedly turned the reception of the film into a politically coloured one. Initially, much of this had to do with the particulars of the 2005 Cannes Film Festival. For most reviewers there, A History of Violence was bound to be tied in with political arguments because it was screened in competition or conjunction with overtly political pictures such as the critique of America, Manderlay (Lars Von Trier), the thriller about the surveillance of an Arab scientist, Schläfer (Sleeper, Benjamin Heisenberg), the documentary about global terror, The Power of Nightmares (Adam Curtis) and the film about dictatorship and suppression during the Iraq/Iran war, Kilometre Zero (Hiner Saleem). Add to that a carryover from the highly politicised 2004 festival that saw Fahrenheit 9/11 (Michael Moore) take the top prize, and the recurrent unease about the confrontation between small and independent yet relevant auteur films (such as a later winner, Jean-Pierre and Luc Dardenne's L'Enfant (The Child, 2005)) and American blockbusters void of obvious cultural significance (such as the final Star Wars episode Revenge of the Sith (George Lucas, 2005)), and Cronenberg's film was inescapably associated with a political discourse.[6] That discourse quickly became a partisan one. When A History of Violence was released widely in the autumn of 2005, numerous European reviews eagerly pushed its political tenor into an antagonistic view of 'American violence', portraying the film as nothing short of an 'ideological tract' that forged a sharp critique of 'American mythology'.[7]

Traditionally, American reviewers have exempted themselves from such debates, emphasising aesthetics instead of ideology. However, in this particular case they not only shared the urge to bind *A History of Violence* to politics, in their reviews following the film's North American release (in the wake of a screening at the Toronto International Film Festival) they went even further: they regarded the film as a metaphor for a number of predicaments in American society and a solid critique of 'American values'. In an unusually charged surge of politically inspired interpretations, hundreds of American newspapers and periodicals from diverse plumage (though usually liberal in ideology) saw Tom Stall's deceptive father whose violent past isolates him from, and effectively destroys, his *fabricated* family 'idyll' as a representation of the violence hidden in the *fabric* of the America's family values.[8] This observation gave reviewers the opportunity to articulate a number of frustrations about some of America's pressing cultural issues such as domestic violence, self-defence or gun culture.[9] But it also allowed them to treat a film they saw as 'littered with dialogue that suggest affinities between Tom and President Bush' as a criticism of the American government's policies, most notably the 'mishandled' riposte to the 11 September 2001 attacks on the World Trade Center, President Bush's rhetoric of an eye-for-an-eye (quite a literal metaphor in the case of Fogarty, who has only one eye left – the other one was removed by Tom years ago), the administration's secretive and misleading 'regime of fear' to fund a sinister 'war on terror', and the mismanaged invasion of Iraq.[10] As a result, the film's theme of 'family' was pressed into an interpretive framework that presented it as exposing the root cause of America's troubled relationship with violence: a family can only unite around a shared cause; such a cause is the result of a perceived threat that creates the need for protection, and such protection can only be offered through blunt, repressive hostility – violence as inherited in the family system.

Cronenberg's position as a Canadian director, and indeed the status of *A History of Violence* as a Canadian film, led a number of reviewers to broaden the scope of their arguments beyond their topical impatience with the current political situation in the United States (one year after fiercely contested elections). This was obviously the case with a lot of Canadian publications, though several of them behaved very much like American reviews in seeing *A History of Violence* as a critique of American politics, albeit from a 'Canadian' perspective.[11] *Maclean's* suggested that the film referred to the United States 'as a country that reveals its dark side when provoked by an outside menace' (Johnson 2005: n. p.), and it quoted local liberal politicians who expressed concern the menace might not just be Arab terrorists, but perhaps also Canada. In American reviews, the Canadian identity of *A History of Violence* (often expressed through remarks on its Ontario locations standing in for Middle America) urged critics across the political spectrum to address wider ideological issues as well: 'Mr Cronenberg could care less about scoring cheap shots off the red states from his vantage point in liberal Toronto', wrote the *New York Times*, who called the film 'foreign' (Dargis 2005b: 37). More conservative papers admitted this 'liberal, tree-hugging Canadian' slammed American values in such a credible way it forced one to adjust perspectives, an opinion, incidentally, shared by *Variety* (Herrington 2005; McCarthy 2005).

As before, Cronenberg himself did not remain mute, insisting his film rose above topical considerations. As *Salon.com* put it 'despite his reputation as a gore-monger, Cronenberg is too meticulous and thoughtful an artist to be boxed into some narrow political critique' (O'Hehir 2005). Cronenberg's interventions started at the film's premiere in Cannes:

> Cronenberg shrugs off such interpretations as, for the most part, wrong. 'At the Cannes press conference, a couple of journalists wanted to turn it into an attack on the US,' Cronenberg says. 'Being the contrarian that I am, I said, look, there's not a nation in the world that was not founded on violence of some kind, and the suppression of native peoples or whoever happened to own the territory before. So, if you want to get philosophical about it, we're talking about the human condition, rather than just a particular US kind of focus.' (Strauss 2005: U11)

By and large, Cronenberg's attempt to defuse the politicising of his film's reception failed. Most North American critics, and indeed many European ones, seemed bent on seeing *A History of Violence* as a political statement. It invited parallels with *The Dead Zone*, the difference being that *The Dead Zone* contained unrevealed political foresight, and *A History of Violence* unrevealed hindsight.

Even though, in numerous interviews, Cronenberg repeatedly emphasised how *A History of Violence* presented violence as a founding aspect of all cultures (a general facet, not a topical one), and eventually some of that persistence did trickle through in the reception, it was frequently turned around to fit a political interpretation. It invariably did so in three steps. The first was a comparison between the film's small-town America of Millbrook and the kind of micro-culture traditionally at the centre of westerns. Cronenberg had frequently referred to westerns as a source of inspiration for *A History of Violence* (see below for speculation on how both this film and *Eastern Promises* problematise the model of the western family). In step two, most reviewers agreed that both *A History of Violence* and westerns presented violence as embedded in the American Dream. It enabled reviewers to discuss in detail the several violent acts in *A History of Violence*, such as the splitting of the skull of Fogarty's henchman Charlie (Aidan Devine); but also the heavy-handed school fight in which son Jack harasses Bobby (Kyle Schmid), the boy who bullied him. It led some to complain about the bursts of unnecessarily detailed gore, and others to celebrate such vintage Cronenberg shots, amidst general consensus about how such actions exposed the innate emotional impulse for violence in each individual, and by extension in American society.[12] Finally, in step three, that innate impulse was broadened to include the rape-like sex scene between Edie and Tom. This scene was, together with the abovementioned bursts of violence, one of the key moments in the film that provided reviewers with a particular action they could either object to, or highlight the audience impact of.[13] These discussions ultimately brought most interpretations back to arguing about issues such as self-defence, domestic violence, gun culture, misogyny and the role of the traditional North American nuclear family; all implicated in the western and *A History of Violence*, but also relevant to debates about distinctions between red states (conservative) and blue states (liberal) in the crisis of trust that was tearing the US apart – a worldwide concern of the time that suddenly gave *A History of Violence* a pressing cultural relevance.

'Selling out' and Scene 44

Regardless of the political debate that engulfed it, *A History of Violence* proved very popular. It became the second best-grossing Cronenberg film after *The Fly*. In usual independent cinema fashion it had a staggered release triggered by festival screenings in Toronto, the Netherlands and Bulgaria, from the end of September 2005 onwards (the last region to receive the film was the Asian Pacific Rim, in early 2006). The film's reception testified to Cronenberg's unique position in the market. It was no killer opening, yet neither was it the sleeper that keeps attracting consistent numbers of viewers months after its initial release. Instead, it managed to continuously do well in the middle term. In its first three weeks in the United States the film earned roughly $20 million at the box office, reaching a plateau of $30 million by the end of the year. Similar patterns occurred in the UK, continental Europe and Australia. The total worldwide gross was $60 million – ten times as much as *Spider*, making it one of the most successful R-rated films of the year. Even more remarkable was the fifty-fifty split between American and other earnings. Cronenberg's previous films *Crash*, *eXistenZ* and *Spider* had relied heavily on European receipts (more than two thirds of their gross).[14] That had now changed – with *A History of Violence*, Cronenberg gained a sizeable American audience.

One main reason for that was the impression that *A History of Violence* was Cronenberg's most accessible film since *The Fly*. It was ostensibly less demanding in its narrative and formal arrangements than previous films, and backed by a studio (New Line Cinema) whose wide distribution and promotion networks made it physically accessible to audiences. But Cronenberg himself also contributed to the wide access, declaring publicly how this had started as a 'contract film', offered to him by the studio, and joking about how this project had finally allowed him to 'sell out': 'I've been waiting for years to sell out,' he said in Cannes, 'it's just that nobody offered me anything before now' (in Dee 2005: n. p.). Coming from a notoriously uncompromising director, such remarks certainly worked to the film's advantage. The mix of Viggo Mortensen, a thriller/action movie (which is how New Line marketed it) and Cronenberg's promise to ease up, led to *A History of Violence* eventually drawing a mass audience of neophites to the theatres, on top of the usual Cronenberg crowd of fans and cinephiles.

At the same time, there was concern this accessibility might alienate Cronenberg from his 'hyperdevoted fan base'. The first Cronenberg film to be caught up in the accelerated process of reception that the Internet propels, *A History of Violence* provoked an abundance of rumours across fan sites that it might only be 'Cronenberg-lite'.[15] Cronenberg's grasp of his fans' sensitivities, something he had been carefully aware of since *The Brood* and *Scanners* (see chapter four), ultimately calmed such alarm. By ensuring there was a fair amount of explicit gore in the film, fans received the message it would be vintage Cronenberg. The close-ups of the bleeding and splattered heads of Leland, Bobby, Charlie and Richie's aides are reminiscent of Cronenberg's imagery from more explicit horror fare, and the intimate connection of such violence with kinetic sex would reassure any worried fan. Furthermore, the DVD of *A History of Violence* offered a deleted scene, Scene 44, which easily withstands comparison with some of the most gruesome effects from *Videodrome* or *The Fly*, as a gourmet addition for hardcore fans. In the scene Tom has a dream about blowing Fogarty away with a rifle in his diner, only for Fogarty to devilishly snigger from the smoking pool of blood and guts that is his torso, raise his gun and kill Tom. The featurette built around Scene 44, and Cronenberg's commentary that he shot the scene knowing it would not end up in the theatrical version, also demonstrate his appreciation of the fact his films were now experiencing multiple reception trajectories in which a theatrical version would no longer necessarily be the 'final' version – indeed, imagining Scene 44 to be part of the theatrical version of *A History of Violence* would make quite a different film.

In a sense, Scene 44 illustrates how much *A History of Violence* was part of a profound change in the reception of cinema. Alternative versions were fast becoming a fixture of DVD releases, and the fact they frequently altered key understandings of narratives and themes challenged any attempt to pin a film's 'final moment' (its final appearance as a finished product before an audience) down to its theatrical version. As extended DVD versions, director's cuts and alternative edits demonstrated, films had become texts whose meaning was dispersed across different versions and platforms.[16] When Cronenberg remarked how careful he had to be to announce anything these days – be it new projects or attitudes towards projects (like calling *A History of Violence* 'selling out') – it confirmed how his oeuvre no longer only consisted of the films he actually made, but to some degree also of the projects he had aborted, been offered or had only been associated with through rumours. It turned mentions of the long-abandoned *Red Cars* project (see chapter three), once-affiliated projects such as *American Psycho* or *Basic Instinct 2*, works-in-progress such as *Painkillers*, the Martin Amis adaptation *London Fields* or the adaptation of Christopher Hampton's play *The Talking Cure* (about Sabina Spielrein, a patient of both Sigmund Freud and Carl-Gustav Jung, which would re-unite Cronenberg with producer Jeremy Thomas) and even never-existing projects such as *I Kill*, into integral parts of the oeuvre.[17]

Eastern Promises

Echoing the opening of *A History of Violence*, *Eastern Promises* starts with a brutal and explicit act of violence. Inside a barber's shop in London, the young Ekrem (Josef Altin) follows his elder's orders and slits a customer's throat with a razor. Not only do we get to see the full size of the slit (and the slitting) in a close-up, but also a profile shot of the blood squirting from his throat – vintage Cronenberg a minute into the film. This gruesome act is immediately followed by one whose visceral impact is even higher. At a pharmacy the distressed, barefoot and pregnant 14 year-old drug addict Tatiana (Sarah Jeanne Labrosse) suddenly starts bleeding heavily and collapses. She is rushed to hospital where her baby is delivered via a caesarean section. Sadly, Tatiana does not survive the birth. It is 20 December, just after eleven at night, the darkest day of the year.

Darkness prevails throughout *Eastern Promises*. The first sound we hear is heavy rain falling on dark streets. It rains throughout the film, and all the streets and interiors seem grimy or damp – unwelcoming. There are only two single rays of sunlight in the entire film. The first one we see at the beginning, when Anna Khitrova (Naomi Watts), the midwife who delivered Tatiana's baby, drives her motorcycle across conspicuously empty London streets. The second offers hope in the penultimate shot, when Anna, who has now adopted Tatiana's baby, sits with the child in the small walled garden of her London townhouse, dressed in a traditionally 'mumsy' flowery dress. The idyll of the scene stands in sharp contrast with Anna's usually stressed-strained face, the depressing and menacing tones of the black leather biker-wear she dons throughout the story and the grey and rainy atmosphere of inner-city London – the cold and inhospitable cafeterias, river banks and back alleys that make up most of the locations in the film.

In between the death of Tatiana and that ray of light on Anna's newfound happiness stands a grim story of family violence and betrayal – a biblical allegory of the anxiety of contemporary cultures in an era of the breakdown of the classical family unit, desperate diasporas, attempts to 'control' immigration streams, human trafficking and wars between crime syndicates. *Eastern Promises* does not obfuscate its interest in the uses and functions of violence to protect family life, like *A History of Violence* did. Instead of a nice middle-class family in a perfectly normal small town filled with nice people who care for each other, we get the nitty-gritty struggle for survival that typifies the urban angst and squalor of the contemporary metropolis – portrayed as grey, with streets that seem void of human contact except for snarling passers-by not interested in each other; where no one lives because they want to, and everyone is looking to get away from; a place where the obstacles on the way to the ideal of the classical 'family' clash with the opportunities to develop alternative family formations.

The narrative of *Eastern Promises* revolves around three types of family relationships and their accidental, and violent, interactions. The first family is Anna's. She is just coming out of an unsuccessful relationship and is trying to get back on her feet. Of Russian descent through her father, she lives with her mother Helen (Sinéad Cusack). The only other family member is quaint and grumpy uncle Stepan (Polish director Jerzy Skolimowski), ex-KGB bureaucrat emigrated from Russia, a man visibly disappointed by the fake promises of life in the 'Free West' who expresses loyalty to his home culture through a staunch devotion to ceremonial culinary habits. His disappointment also leads him to curtly dismiss 'modern' values – 'it's not natural to mix race and race' comments Stepan when Anna and Helen briefly discuss her miscarriage and failed relationship with her previous, black, boyfriend Oliver; he adds that 'black men always run away'. As their humble home shows, Anna's family is not well off ('we are ordinary people,' insists Helen), and they look lost in a society that does not regard them as economically productive. But for all their idiosyncrasies and flaws they get along well enough and, importantly, they stick up for each other. Not once do they refuse each other support, thus exhibiting a solidarity and altruistic caring that does not fit with hawkish views on welfare. With Stepan as ersatz-father to 'carve the meat' they are the closest thing to a traditional family *Eastern Promises* has.

Anna's discovery of Tatiana's diary in the maternity ward, and her insistence on finding some answers about the girl's past, sets off a narrative that contrasts her family with that of Semyon (Armin Mueller-Stahl). An old-style patriarch, Semyon heads his family's branch of the Russian mafia syndicate, the Vory V Zakone. Officially, he is the owner and manager of the plush Trans-Siberian Restaurant. But in reality he is involved with smuggling, the drug-trade, human trafficking, prostitution and extortion. The man killed at the beginning of the film is in fact Soyka (Aleksander Mikic), a member of a rival gang of Chechens whom one of Semyon's associates, Azim (Mina E. Mina), ordered to be killed. The elimination ignites a war between the rival mafia families, which Semyon has difficulty controlling because of the erratic behaviour of his son, Kirill (Vincent Cassel). Kirill is supposed to be preparing to inherit the family leadership from Semyon, but his unreliability and dissolution make it increasingly impossible to rein him in, especially when the Chechens reciprocate by slitting Ekrem's throat in broad daylight in Brompton cemetery – in one of the most casually shocking scenes of the film. It follows after a football game between London teams Arsenal, traditionally associated with working-class labour, and Chelsea, associated with wealthy West London, and owned by Russian oligarch Roman Abramovich – freewheeling connections not to be missed.

Into this situation walks Anna with Tatiana's diary. Ignoring her uncle's call for caution, as he slowly translates the diary she traces Tatiana's whereabouts to the Trans-Siberian Restaurant, where Semyon shows too much eagerness to help her out. As he charms Anna and piques her interest in her own cultural roots with his tales of old-style Russian traditions (everything from borscht to folk songs) he tries to pry the diary from her, eventually threatening to harm the baby if the original is not delivered to him. There is a personal reason for Semyon's threat. As Stepan's readings of the diary confirm soon after, Semyon was not only behind the trafficking of Tatiana from Russia to London, where she was dumped into the sex trade, but the diary also reveals he has raped Tatiana and the baby is most likely his illegitimate child (and the genetic proof of his involvement in the sex trade). Ironically, at the same time that Semyon's power at the head of the mafia is consolidated through a sumptuous ritual family party for an elderly Russian lady (her hundredth birthday is celebrated in a fashion reminiscent of *The Godfather* (Francis Ford Coppola, 1972) – with extensive attention to the respect accorded to elderly guests who embody traditional customs), the arrival of new life in the form of the baby initiates the downfall of his empire.

At this point, the third family relationship enters the story – Kirill's trustworthy driver and bodyguard Nikolai Luzhin (Viggo Mortensen; the character's last name pays homage to a Nabokov novel), a man hired by Semyon to guard Kirill as much as protect him, and occasionally take care of some nasty business. The bond between Kirill and Nikolai is a peculiar one. Although Kirill displays a lot of affection towards him, treating him as his 'brother', he occasionally commands Nikolai to commit, and submit to, humiliating acts. To avoid having to admit his confusion about his own sexual feelings towards Nikolai, Kirill loses himself in sex orgies which leave him increasingly dissatisfied. When Nikolai does not readily join him in such excesses, Kirill orders him to have sex with a prostitute to prove he is no 'fucking queer'. Nikolai complies and has sex with the prostitute while facing the watching Kirill. The homoerotic S&M play between Kirill and Nikolai parallels some of the situations Cronenberg had previously explored in *M. Butterfly* and *Crash*, with Nikolai, like Gallimard and James, not wholly uninterested or victimised.[18]

Nikolai is ordered to collect the diary from Anna. Semyon does not know, however, that Nikolai and Anna have already met, just outside the door of the restaurant, first when he and Kirill mockingly admire her looks, and a second time when he helps Anna out when her motorcycle, an old Russian Ural bike, refuses to start – another nod to a staple Cronenberg motif not to be missed by seasoned fans, and one which Cronenberg had much pleasure in planting in the film (see Keough 2007). On these occasions, and mostly channelled via comments about Anna's bike, Nikolai expresses some fondness for her, though his reluctant posture and silence do not suggest to her just how much. As loners, Anna and Nikolai have a lot in common: their detachment from a 'root culture', their obsession with finding a path for themselves and their professionalism as a shield against loneliness, an element Roger Ebert singled out:

> The story puts their characters to a test: they can be true to their job descriptions within a hermetically sealed world where everyone shares the same values and expectations, and where outsiders are by definition the prey. But what happens when their cocoon is broached? Do they still possess fugitive feelings instilled by a long-forgotten babushka? And what if they do? (2007: n. p.)

With Nikolai's loyalties tested, however, there is at this point no time for any mutual attraction to develop. Nikolai does as he is ordered and even though Anna's family show fierce disgust at his affiliations with the mafia (Stepan spits in his face), they nevertheless comply and hand over the diary. At first, Nikolai's loyalty seems to pay off. Apparently choosing him over his own son, Semyon offers to induce Nikolai into the inner circle of the Vory V Zakone family. In an elaborate, Gnostic initiation ritual bathed in deep red and black tones, Nikolai repudiates his past: 'I am dead already,' he says. 'I died when I was fifteen.' After the leaders of the clan satisfy themselves of his loyalty by reading the numerous tattoos on Nikolai's body – the story of his flesh's path into crime that tells of teenage gang membership, Gulag hardship, army training and prison time – the star tattoos of the Vory are carved in his chest. But Nikolai's reward goes only skin deep. When faced with a crisis after the killing of Ekrem and threats to Azim's life, Semyon offers Kirill's life as a peace offering to the Chechens. However, instead of his blood son he sends his 'new son', the freshly tattooed Nikolai, to the place of his execution, an old-fashioned brick bathhouse. In the sauna, Azim identifies the naked Nikolai as Kirill to two knife-wielding musclemen. After a fierce struggle (which is discussed in detail below) Nikolai escapes. As he recovers from his injuries it becomes clear he is no ordinary driver, but a highly trained Russian undercover agent working with the London police to expose and destroy the Vory. With his knowledge of the diary Nikolai is able to have Semyon arrested for statutory rape if they get his DNA matched to that of the baby. 'For poetic reasons, I suggest you take his blood,' he instructs the police.

Through this gesture, Nikolai not only clears London of Semyon, he also liberates Kirill from his father's homophobia. After his blood has been taken and before he becomes aware of his arrest, Semyon complains to Kirill the needle used will have probably given him the 'fucking queer disease'. It is the last in a series of remarks that has Semyon railing against a 'city of whores and queers' in which 'it never snows'. He confides to Nikolai that he thinks 'London is to blame for what Kirill is.' It is ironic, then, that it is Kirill's buddy Nikolai who has him arrested, leaving gay Kirill *de facto* in charge of the family Semyon tried so hard to keep 'queer-free'. The 'queer disease', the last words Semyon speaks in the film, may well relate to his opinion on Nikolai and Kirill taking over his empire.

'Family is important to you people, isn't it?': class, religion, language
The precise position *Eastern Promises* takes towards the concept of 'family' in its three appearances is not difficult to ascertain. It asks us to consider, besides the 'traditional' nuclear family (husband, wife, children), the larger and constantly changing 'cultural family' that one shares certain conditions and common roots with in terms of race, religion, sexuality, language and class: the family we have not by choice but by chance.

There are three conditions that inspire such 'alternative' family constellations. The first is class consciousness. A firm realisation of their economic situation is a common factor in the conditions many of the characters' ancestors and siblings have had to endure, and have, at least to varying degrees, managed to escape. It inspires and explains many actions of Anna's family, and of Nikolai and Tatiana. Each of them is trying for a better life; and because they recognise the struggle in each other, they are all imbued with an instinctive respect for, and reflex to, survival. Tatiana did not make it because the odds were stacked against her, but with each opportunity Anna and Nikolai scramble to make it one more step up the ladder. Anna's character borders on the obsessive, as if her quest is a compensation for the 'loss' of her miscarried baby. Similarly, Nikolai's sphinx-like inscrutable posture hides an extreme ambition and – as it turns out – ruthlessness. But the obsession and ambition are vehicles in an attempt to have a simple, decent life, even in the case of Nikolai. He may tell Anna he does not care for her and Tatiana, that 'slaves give birth to slaves', but the very fact he uses the phrase shows his class-consciousness, his awareness of the similarity of their positions. That is why he is reluctant to kill Stepan, and why he saves the prostitute he is forced to rape, sending both of them into exile instead of death (an 'old school' solution he calls it). It also explains why he appears to dislike Kirill's family – Kirill repeatedly and arrogantly reminds this 'fucking Siberian' that his status as 'prince' of the family is his 'birthright'. As Anna gradually becomes aware of this their allegiance grows. Together they manage to convince an already wavering Kirill to hand over the baby – who is his half-sister after all – after he has kidnapped her from the hospital.

While it runs deep, the common class background of Anna and Nikolai does not permit them to extend their relationship beyond this one collaboration. When Anna asks Nikolai why he has helped 'us' (not just her, but her family), he replies: 'How can I become king if king is still in place?' His reply may harbour an underlying plan (saving the baby means condemning Semyon, which would hasten his path to the top of the mafia, perhaps in partnership with Kirill). But Nikolai's real ambition is not to be king of the crime syndicate. The phrasing of 'kingship' poignantly references the plight of one of Mortensen's earlier screen kings, Aragorn in *The Lord of the Rings* trilogy (Peter Jackson, 2001–2003): to accept only reluctantly.[19] What he really wants is what Anna is getting, to be king of the home, to have a family of his own. The situation he is in does not allow that. So in spite of this recognition of their common backgrounds, he and Anna kiss goodbye.

Another basis for family in *Eastern Promises* is religion, and its moral component in particular. *Eastern Promises* abounds with religious references. The entire story takes place between 20 December and New Year, in what is surely a biblical reference. A Christmas story as it were, in a city poor Tatiana saw as 'a place in the bible', with a newborn baby, a mother who thought she could not have a child, a *deus ex machina* with 'stars over his heart' who is at least a spiritual father to the baby (appropriately named Christine), and an old motorcycle as the mule – the Ural bike with its sentimental value figures prominently in the foreground when Anna and Nikolai comfort the rescued baby. In contrast with this small family unit built on love stand two big religiously inspired families for whom love is inconsequential when it comes to what constitutes a family: the influence of the Russian Christian Orthodox Church, whose ornamental symbols adorn much of the restaurant, and whose views on patriarchy are reflected in Semyon's, Azim's and Kirill's actions; and the semi-cultish congregation of the Vory V Zakone – most visibly in the form of the tattoos on Nikolai's chest – that relies on brutal abuse of power to hold a family together (Semyon's kicking of Kirill is just one example). Yet, no matter how different the religious dogmas and rituals are, when combined these three constellations make up a troika of moralities that, ultimately, all veer towards one principle, exclaimed by Nikolai: 'We don't kill babies.' All subsequent family structures are of secondary importance.

The third condition is language, an important indicator of family and cultural belonging in *Eastern Promises* – more than in any previous Cronenberg film, with only the intercultural communications of diplomatic conversation in *M. Butterfly*, the accents in *eXistenZ* and the inner mumblings of *Spider* giving much consideration to the spoken word in its linguistic variations. Beyond the voices and accents of the on-screen characters the significance of the texture and tone of language as a cultural marker is embodied by the voice-over from the diary, as for the first time since *Crimes of the Future* Cronenberg has made substantial use of a voice-over.[20] The feel of language matters, in the frail and naïve, choked up and broken voice of Tatiana (an undervalued vocal performance by Tatiana Maslany), revealed at the speed of Stepan's laborious translations dictated to Helen. It creates an atmosphere of desperation and exhaustion. According to Maslany, Cronenberg was meticulous in his instructions to give the texture of the language and the accents as authentic a feel as possible. 'I am Ukrainian, and many of the Russian sounds are similar to those I heard in my grandparents' house growing up, and that was crucial to Cronenberg.'[21] The same comment was repeatedly made by reviewers with regard to the rest of the cast. In an interview Cronenberg explained how Mortensen's 'musical ear and grasp of other languages' were vital in helping him nail the Russian lines in the script, 'something Mueller-Stahl, a German, and Cassel, a Frenchman, had to do as well' (in Ahearn 2007: n. p.). To this international mixture are added the British-born Australian Watts, Polish Skolimowski, Irish Cusack, French-Canadian Labrosse, poly-ethnic Canadian Mina and a score of smaller parts such as the Welsh Scotland Yard officer (Rhodri Miles), Indian doctor Aziz (Raza Jaffrey) and the customers of the pharmacy conversing in Hindi (Latita Ahmed and Badi Uzzaman). Anyone in the film with substantial dialogue comes from outside the narrow English/American ethnic pool usually (though, in reality, increasingly less so) associated with 'normalcy' in English-language cinema. The observation puts into perspective the few criticisms complaining that *Eastern Promises* came across as 'clunky and inauthentic-sounding' (Bradshaw 2007: n. p.) in its sketch of cultural surroundings. For most reviewers, the 'international diversity' of languages and ethnicities added to the 'disturbing aura of authenticity' of the film (McCarthy 2007: n. p.; Knight 2007: n. p.).

Language also appears in non-audible form. When first confronted with Tatiana's diary, before we have heard any voice-over, Stepan suggest they 'bury her secrets with her bodies'. Anna corrects him: 'Body,' she says, 'singular.' But Stepan made no mistake. In *Eastern Promises*, multiple bodies carry multiple stories. In Tatiana's case, the genes of her baby's body carry a story that points, via his semen, to Semyon's body, and implicates him in her death through their DNA. Other bodies carry similar stories: the mix of bruises and make-up on the skin of the prostitutes Kirill hangs out with, or the wrinkles on the faces of the elderly guests in Semyon's restaurant. Most impressive, however, is the story tattoos tell. Following a tradition of prison and military tattoos, each member of the Russian crime families has their story inked onto their body. The stars on the knees of Soyka's corpse meant he never kneeled for anybody. When Nikolai is inducted into the Vory V Zakone, Semyon and his associates read his story, that of his former life, and that of his loyalty to their family, from his exposed body – he is standing naked in front of them, to be judged then baptised into their cult. The scene in which the 'reading' occurs fits perfectly Cronenberg's fascination with the way the human body develops its own history, which he previously explored in terms of its viruses, fevers, scars and wounds. It also directly mirrors Vaughan's tattoo scene in *Crash*: his were a design for a future body, Nikolai's tell the tale of the past. The actual tattoos used in the film, developed by Stephan Dupuis and David Stoneman, were based on Danzig Baldaev's *Russian Criminal Tattoo Encyclopedia* (2004), and also on Alix Lambert's documentary *Mark of Cain* (2000), which paints the Russian tattoos as an 'incredibly detailed, rapidly evolving language'. Both Mortensen and Cronenberg acknowledged *Mark of Cain* as a profound influence.[22] Beyond that, the initiation scene of Nikolai also links neatly with a history of tattoos in cinema, from Robert Mitchum's religiously-inspired knuckle tattoos in *Night of the Hunter* (Charles Laughton, 1955), via Tim Curry's sexualised pop culture tattoos in *The Rocky Horror Picture Show* (especially the 'BOSS' and '4711' inscriptions),[23] the mad avenger tattoos of Robert De Niro in *Cape Fear* (Martin Scorsese, 1991) and the artful and sensual tattoo tapestries Ewan McGregor dons in *The Pillow Book* (Peter Greenaway, 1996), to the dirty, prophetic tattoos of Elias Koteas in *Crash* (see chapter eight). Nikolai's tattoos combine the functions of fanatic determination and dedication with the subversive subtext they (still) have in society. Even to those unaware what the signs on Nikolai's body stand for it is clear they are not embellishments – they command respect.

With its multitude of communities – religious, linguistic, ethnic and class-based – the London of *Eastern Promises* becomes an exemplar for the Babel that contemporary society and families are facing (a topic screenwriter Steve Knight had also explored in *Dirty Pretty Things* (Stephen Frears, 2002)). No one in the film has just one root, though most of them pretend to, or prefer to, and no one can readily assume the people they address speak the same language or share the same understandings. No borscht or squeaky violin, nor the insistence with which Nikolai and Semyon call her Anna Ivanovna (her father's name was Ivan) can commit Anna to her Russian family background if she does not speak the language and has no concept of the culture – in the end she does answer Nikolai in Russian with the last words she says to him ('Do svidaniya', 'goodbye'). It shows that with effort one can come close, although in reality everyone ends up halfway. The confusion such multitudes cause when pressed into a framework that only accepts straight lineages – such as the purity Semyon strives for – make one thing blatantly clear: in this world of subcultures (mafia, cults and so forth), mixed backgrounds and relentless immigration streams they are no longer valid. 'Family is important to you people isn't it?' says Anna at one point to Kirill. 'You people?' he asks incredulously. He is right. The question is meaningless in its simple distinction between two groups of people. Family is as important for Anna as it is for Kirill, and their cultural backgrounds make no difference in what they want: 'a better life'.

The last shot of *Eastern Promises*, seamlessly glued to the scene of family happiness at Anna's house via Tatiana's voice from the grave, is of Nikolai sitting in the Trans-Siberian restaurant, motionless, in a contemplative pose, his hand clutching his paternoster. There is ambiguity as to what Nikolai is doing there: has he defected from the police force and become head of the mafia family? But regardless of the visual ambiguity, the message the accompanying voice-over delivers is not to be misunderstood. It is the eternal lament of emigrants, delivered, for the second time in the film, with a near broken voice by the diary: 'My name is Tatiana, my father died in the mines in my village, so he was already buried when he died. We were all buried there. Buried under the soil of Russia. That is why I left. To find a better life.' 'To find a better life' – the phrase has, for centuries, inspired the millions that travelled across the world to escape abject misery and build family homes and find happiness. It is a phrase worth remembering in a time when shutting borders and violently denying people uprooted by a global economy seems to have become the norm.

Muses and inspirations are tough tools, both during the creative process and throughout its public reception. In *Henry and June*, the screen biography of bohemian authors Henry Miller and Anaïs Nin (see chapter seven), the massive figure of Fyodor Dostoyevsky hovers over the writers like a Damoclean sword: words are only worth writing if they live up to Dostoyevsky's prose. After proofreading one of Miller's manuscripts his wife June (Uma Thurman) softly complains 'I wanted ... Dostoyevsky.' It sparks a furious reaction from Miller (Fred Ward), who trashes the room, shouting 'with you, Dostoyevsky is impossible!' A few scenes on, however, June takes charge of negotiations with a potential publisher about that very manuscript, dismissing a five per cent royalties offer with the remark that she poured her 'heart and soul to make it into some kind of Dostoyevsky'. From a creative tool, 'Dostoyevsky' became a critical and marketing tool – something that could be used to present a book to the public.

Few wield muses and inspirations better than Cronenberg. As pointed out in previous chapters, the reception of his films has frequently incurred literary references in much the same way Dostoyevsky hovered over the reception of *Henry and June*. Dostoyevsky was also part of the inspiration for *Eastern Promises*, motivating Cronenberg to give the film a moody, old-world Czarist atmosphere, soaked in *schmerz* about the downfall of legacies, rituals and families. Yet, for once, Cronenberg seemed to forego the opportunity to showcase his literacy during the reception trajectory, not going further than a bland admission of the inspiration, even when pressed on the topic:

> PK: No Dostoyevsky references, even though I guess both of you have read *The Possessed*.
> DC: Yes, well, we read the version called *The Demons*. I phoned Viggo and said, maybe you should be reading this new translation of *The Possessed* which is called *The Demons* and he said, 'I've just finished it.' (In Keough 2007: n. p.)

Although pushed about further references (the use of the name Luzhin, a character called Nabokov), Cronenberg consistently downplayed these and he did not volunteer various other Dostoyevsky connections (the references to princes and kings, Stepan's name derived from Stipanovich and so forth). The reason is that Dostoyevsky is not as essential a reference to the reception of *Eastern Promises* as Rushdie and Beckett were for *eXistenZ* and *Spider*. Cronenberg's literary affiliations were well-known by the time of *Eastern Promises*, at least to those who would care about them, and explicit mentions of Dostoyevsky in the reception of *Spider* meant there was no need to reintroduce the reference or publicise it. Dostoyevsky may be neglected in Mark Browning's (2007) overview of Cronenberg's literary inspirations, but he fits the lineage of Nabokov, via Beckett, back into Modernism's questioning of the origins of culture that Cronenberg's recent films embarked upon. In other words,

Dostoyevsky was already present. And why become your own competition? *A History of Violence* went without literary references to become a big financial success, so audiences do not depend on Cronenberg waving about his literary credentials. Moreover, this avoidance of introducing canonical literary references in the receptions of his last two films prevented any immediate comparisons with figures like Dostoyevsky when news broke of Cronenberg's own entry into the literary world. In November 2007 he signed a contract for his first novel (see Anon. 2007d).

Not that there is not a wide range of references to other works or events in the reception of *Eastern Promises*. Since the film's world premiere at the Toronto International Film Festival in September 2007, and its European premieres at the festivals of San Sebastian and London, in late September and October respectively, virtually every review contained numerous little facts and asides regarding either Cronenberg's earlier work or that of the cast.[24] It was as if each reviewer and blogger felt compelled to illustrate their affinity with one of cinema's most accomplished auteurs and his widening popularity. Among them are tales about the shared history of Cronenberg and the festival in Toronto, the appearance of the fetishistic Ural motorcycle in the film, the coincidence of Watt's pregnancy during the shooting and the presence of her baby Sasha (of part Ukrainian heritage through her father, actor-director Liev Schreiber)[25] at the Toronto premiere, and of Cronenberg's lifetime achievement award at the Cannes Film Festival earlier that year – little factoids mixing the esteemed with the popular.

But one argument stood out across the reception trajectory of *Eastern Promises*: the meaning of the violence. The two detailed throat slittings and the bathhouse scene constructed what one festival programme called a 'palatable physicality', and most reviewers and commentators spent much of their allotted space discussing the functions and effects of that violence (see Hebron 2007). Most attention went to the bathhouse scene. In it, a naked Nikolai is attacked by two leather-clad Chechen heavyweights with scythe-shaped linoleum knives (a grim reaper allusion if ever there was one).[26] In three full minutes, without music, with only punches, crushing bones, knives slicing and grunts and animalistic screams audible, Nikolai's nude body is severely cut and beaten, his blood smeared all around the sauna. In its visceral impact, shock value, style and metaphors (the combination of cleansing off sin with water, the punishment for previous 'bad' behaviour, slashed bodies and the sexual component of nudity), the bathhouse scene has a lot in common with the shower scene in *Psycho*. Except, Nikolai survives. He manages to kill his assailants, pressing one's head through his own knife and planting another knife straight into the right eye of the other – the most shocking eye-puncturing since a razor slit a woman's eye in *Un chien andalou* and, in the sounds and position of the body receiving the stab, reminiscent of the killing of Barry Convex in *Videodrome*, his eyes popping out of his head as he lies amidst the quotes 'love comes in at the eye' and 'the eye is the window of the soul' (see chapter five). In a reversal of the scene in *Un chien andalou*, where the eye-slicing opened the viewer to the bizarre surreal tableaux that followed it, the eye-stabbing in *Eastern Promises* rips Nikolai, and us, out of the belief he was 'just a driver', revealing his true identity as a cop.

Prompted by its forcefulness, reviewers invariably put the bathhouse scene at the centre of their arguments, whatever they were. For some, the nudity in the scene emphasised the homoerotic undertones of the film. For others, it stressed a point Cronenberg had been trying to refute in his interventions in the reception of *Eastern Promises*: the brutal violence of the bathhouse fight is so typically Cronenberg in its emphasis on the dissection and vulnerability of the human body that it is in danger of being seen as 'played for knowing, if grisly, laughs rather than for its capacity to disturb' (Fisher 2007: 57). To some extent, such remarks are a staple feature of horror film criticism. It is the same argument that Linda Williams (1994) made about the shower scene in *Psycho*, with which the bathhouse scene bears so many resemblances. For Williams, the shower scene not only shocked audiences, it also provided fun. After all, viewers knew with the reputation of Hitchcock as 'master of suspense', and the publicity and prefiguration of the film, there were thrills to be administered, and the shower scene fulfilled those expectations, albeit in a novel manner. It remains to be seen which status the bathhouse scene will eventually obtain in the long-term reception of *Eastern Promises*, but it does seem clear that no matter how shocking the scene in itself is, the comparisons to *Psycho*, *Un chien andalou* and Cronenberg's career themes, as well as his reputation, favour a consideration of its self-contained, playful aesthetics.[27] For those familiar with Cronenberg's oeuvre it is therefore a nod to the history of disturbing cinema rather than a disturbance itself. For some, the violence of the bathhouse scene blocked any real discussion of the film's cultural relevance:

> violence is, in [Cronenberg's] movies, as punch line is to joke: a source of glee to his fans, although with every year I find it less amusing ... Cronenberg overplays his hand, with a shot of a sickle blade slicing into an eye; the balance is tipped, and the scene is spoiled. Why go that far? Must he cling to his schlocky reputation at all costs? (Lane 2007: n. p.)

But others considered it an element that contributed to what one reviewer called an 'almost subliminal sheen of menace' (Knight 2007: n. p.). With so many commentators writing about an extremely violent scene it seemed only a matter of time before one of them would take offence, as had been the case so often in Cronenberg's career. But not this time. Besides a half-hearted whine by the *Evening Standard* (the paper that started the *Crash* controversy – see chapter eight) about the fact the film went uncut by the BBFC, no real controversy emerged – though several publications eagerly referred to one in anticipation.[28]

In what is an acknowledgement of the global acceptance of Cronenberg, there are hardly any regional variations in the reception of *Eastern Promises*. Nearly all American and Canadian critics gave the film a glowing review, honouring it with some of the most elaborate praise for a Cronenberg film ever. In the *Village Voice*, J. Hoberman asserted: 'David Cronenberg is the most provocative, original and consistently excellent North American director of his generation' (2007: n. p.). The American-dominated compilation site of film reviews, Rotten Tomatoes, registered an impressive 88 per cent overall approval rating. In its blogsphere, too, the violence in *Eastern*

Promises became the marker of division between those appreciating the film and those disliking it. As one poster complained: 'Why are people who enjoyed the movie only allowed to enjoy it if they are turned on by the "gore and inhumanity of the mob?"'[29] In continental Europe, the successful screening of the film at the San Sebastian International Film Festival carried over into well-received regional receptions. Here, too, the violence took front stage, with *Le Monde* suggesting the bathhouse scene should not be discussed out of context as it is so much more meaningful within the framework of the entire film (see Sotinel 2007), and the *Frankfurter Allgemeine* asserting its violence is 'schlock free' (Lueken 2007: 41). The very positive French and German receptions were paralleled in most other European countries, even in the Netherlands, a region whose critics remained hitherto impervious to Cronenberg's qualities. The most interesting regional variation is the British reception. In spite of having enjoyed the film as the opener of the London Film Festival many reviewers only gave it a lukewarm appreciation, with traditionally Cronenberg-friendly publications such as *Sight and Sound* and the *Guardian* expressing disappointment in what they perceived as a 'lack of depth' and several other reviews remaining cautious (see Bradshaw 2007; Fisher 2007). It almost seems that the co-financing by the BBC, the British screenplay, the location shooting in London, the partly British cast and the London Film Festival premiere gave it too much proximity – made it too close for comfort, as it were, for British critics.

In the end *Eastern Promises* earned about $40 million at the box office, 45 per cent of which was earned in the US – a confirmation that much of *A History of Violence*'s American audience had stuck around. Like *A History of Violence*, the film also successfully captured nominations and prizes at awards ceremonies, gaining three Golden Globe nominations (drama, actor and score). Beyond the prizes, however, and largely left unmentioned in most comments, lies the cultural relevance of *Eastern Promises*. Bridging a gap between contemporary diaspora and root-culture parables such as *Once* (John Carney, 2006), *Children of Men* (Alfonso Cuarón, 2006) or *Everything is Illuminated* (Liev Schreiber, 2006), and near-apocalyptic anxiety stories such as *The Departed* (Martin Scorsese, 2006) or *No Country for Old Men* (Joel Coen/Ethan Coen, 2007) and unashamedly internationalist in its appearance, *Eastern Promises* put Cronenberg once more in the position of the physician taking society's pulse. This time he shows us that no matter how blinkered cultures and families anywhere become in their search for cosiness and security, they exist in a world constantly on the move, and in order to survive that frantic transition, strategies of coping and adaptation are needed – *not* insularity or insolence. Our reactions to violence may give some clues as to where to find such strategies.

Reluctance and Restraint: The Regulation of Violence that Makes Culture

At the time of the release of *Eastern Promises*, Cronenberg startled musical artist and writer Jian Ghomeshi during an interview on national Canadian radio by coldly offering to kill him, right there and then. 'I could kill you right now. I know how to do it,' he said, obviously unsettling Ghomeshi, 'but I won't.'[30]

The anecdote catches a key aspect of how Cronenberg's films relate to violence. Most of them have a violent component, some abounding with acts many viewers would deem extremely brutal. Yet they never just offer gratuitous violence, or let the viewer off the hook for the emotions released while experiencing the violence. As Cronenberg put it: 'I don't want to do a *Bourne*-type film … where you don't have to pay a penalty for that violence as an audience.'[31] Nor does he preach against violence by offering it in hyperbolic overdoses. As Cronenberg said at the Cannes press conference for *A History of Violence*:

> I'm not surprised that the audience would applaud the violence because I wanted them to be complicit in it. I wanted them to be involved in it. I guess you have to ask them after the movie's over how they feel about their complicity in those violent acts, because if it's done in such a way that the audience is repulsed and held outside the movie then I've actually lost the opportunity to deliver to them the paradox of enjoying something that morally they find reprehensible.[32]

Some of the tumult at the Cannes press screening of *A History of Violence* related to a loud quarrel between viewers assuming Cronenberg's depictions of violence were ironic, hence 'knowingly laughing' at them (as Mark Kermode would have it; see chapter four), and others taking the cool and distanced tone as 'too dry to be ironic and too scary to register to be absurd' (Hoberman 2005b: 56). All of Cronenberg's films oscillate between warning and indulgence – between a pointed finger and a cheer, they demand the viewer negotiate their own position towards the mayhem on the screen. This has frequently led to confusion with critics. As the Ghomeshi moment shows, the small furore that followed the violence in *Eastern Promises* demonstrates this approach continues to puzzle critics.

But *A History of Violence* and *Eastern Promises* exceed Cronenberg's earlier discussions of violence. Beyond sustaining ambiguity they suggest an attitude that might prevent violence and, failing that, they advocate an approach that helps understand it. With both films Cronenberg moved beyond the defeatist arguments about violence which insinuate 'it is just there' and 'it is all of the same kind', in favour of a close dissection of its history, function and its distinguishing components. Ever since *Shivers*, Cronenberg's films have explored the popular idea that violence is innate to humans and that its regulation is a foundational aspect of human culture – what René Girard calls the beginning of culture (see chapter two). As discussed in relation to *Rabid*'s Rose, Girard sees the figure of the martyr, the uniquely *bénéfique* suffering figure whose heroic self-sacrifice exposes violence and offers humans the ability to surpass it, as the only way out of the cycle of violence that engulfs a 'human condition' in which people are eternal adversaries in a struggle over property – territories designed to fence off enemies, gain advantage and protect the homestead, the family. Cronenberg's films do not believe in catharsis, they are consistently '*jenseits von Gut und Böse*' (Blokker 1990: 7). In an essay that emphasises how such struggles rely completely on how self-effacing Cronenberg's characters become, and that speculates how deep they can submerge themselves without losing their identity altogether, Patricia Canino (2008) singles out the 'animal instinct' for survival in Cronenberg's most recent films. The suicides and self-executions of Cronenberg's characters from Max in *Videodrome* to Gallimard in *M. Butterfly* may be intended as such, but the ways in which they self-destruct becomes less cathartic with each step, up to the point where the sacrifices in *eXistenZ* and *Spider* became meaningless and interchangeable.

Throughout the history of culture, religions and ideologies have championed families as strongholds against violence and the dissolution of culture. Do the ties that bind siblings together exempt them from the mimetic violence, and save them from succumbing to violence? Not in the films of Cronenberg: in *The Brood*, Frank Carveth fails to protect his family unit as much as the ferocious Nola does – she dies, he remains impotent, unable to save their daughter; in *Scanners*, the innocent Cameron and the megalomaniac Revok cancel each other out in a Homeric duel; *The Dead Zone's* tragic Johnny Smith comes perhaps closest to resisting the urge to execute violence but he has not even a family to save – only a dream of having once had the chance to have one. In *A History of Violence* and *Eastern Promises* the family unit is saved, but at the cost of abandonment and isolation – exactly what a family is supposed to be a refuge from.

Is there no hope to avoid violence, then, in Cronenberg's films? Not even in the close comfort of the family environment? Maybe there is. If one studies closely the details of the violent acts, the characters' actions and the generic templates against which the narrative unfolds in *A History of Violence* and *Eastern Promises*, an attitude emerges that offers a potential solution for these destructions and implosions: zeal or sacrifice are replaced by *reluctance*, a disinclination and hesitation to engage fully in violence, a restraint that keeps lethal skills or aggressive outbursts in check.[33] At the smallest level this is visible in the very controlled way *A History of Violence* and *Eastern Promises* portray small violent acts: even though audiences are treated to close-ups of bloodied faces and severed body parts, the actions and effects are portrayed as minute: there are no roaring charges, only muted sounds of impacts, low-key performances, matter-of-fact observations, subdued cutting and cinematography, no glorious music or slow motion – a far cry from the bombast of blockbuster action. The violent act itself is usually over in a flash of a second (or a few slashes in the case of *Eastern Promises'* bathroom fight). What stands out instead is the intimacy of the violence, the proximity between the adversaries, smelling each other as it were. In Cronenberg's words:

> The emphasis is always on getting close ... You should be able to smell the guy that's attacking you; you should feel his sweat. The idea is to get really close, which is not a normal person's response. You want to back away from the gun, the knife, the guy, whatever. That was very intriguing as a technique and very intriguing cinematically. It was the intimacy that was important. (In Anderson 2005: 15)

Reluctance to engage pervades characters' attitudes in *A History of Violence* and *Eastern Promises*. In the latter, Nikolai's multiple efforts to keep Kirill from lashing out in anger, and his refusal to immediately execute orders to eliminate Anna form a pattern through the narrative that ultimately culminates in Kirill's hesitance to drown the baby. In *A History of Violence*, Tom's reluctance is of course driven by his desire to keep the secret of his past life from becoming common knowledge. Still, he has to be drawn out at every occasion, pushed until he *has* to intervene. The best example of this reluctance is Jack Stall. He is involved in four of the film's seven violent scenes, and although with the exception of the showdown on the Stalls' lawn in which Jack kills Fogarty, they are not nearly as lethal or vicious as the ones his father gets involved in, they do stand out. In the first scene, Jack is taunted by Bobby after gym class, who shoves him and challenges him to a fight:

Bobby: C'mon chickenshit. Let's do this.
Jack: What's the point? I mean you win you win you win. You've established your alpha-male standing. You've established my unworthiness. But doing violence to me just seems – ahem – pointless and cruel, don't you think?
Bobby: Let's do this you punk bitch.
Jack: Shouldn't that be little punk ass chickenshit faggot bitch?

Bobby shoves Jack again but then backs off in frustration. Jack's reluctance worked – humour saved him. In a subsequent scene, however, after Tom has shot the two villains in his diner, Jack reacts differently. After being challenged again he steps down, then steps up to Bobby, only to step down again. Surrounded and ridiculed he suddenly lashes out, punches Bobby, slams him into a locker, kicks him down and hits him as he is on the floor. Something has changed in Jack after Tom has been violent. Immediately afterwards Tom confronts Jack and tells him off. As Jack smart-mouths his father, Tom – in an uncharacteristic move – slaps him in the face. Jack, hurt, runs away. In these scenes we see Jack starting to negotiate different situations and how to handle them, with violence an option in each of them. While we can assume the one time he abandons his policy of withdrawal and beats up Bobby is one that was provoked, it is also possible to see it as an assertive statement: Jack is learning to judge in each case if it is worth engaging or not, and he is increasingly gaining control over himself, to come to such decisions with a clear mind, not being provoked unless he sees a valid reason to allow himself to be engaged. It is easy to say that what Jack did to Bobby was wrong (of course it was), and that what he did to Fogarty was right (it saved his father's life). But from Jack's own perspective, standing up to Bobby mattered much, and the fact he did not just instinctively do it, but instead sourced a newly-found inspiration (his father) in a way that is both conscious and genetic. It is never only instinctive – 'we have a consciousness that supersedes that'.[34]

Beyond genes, the reluctance of Nikolai, Tom and others fits a generic ancestry: the gangster film and the western. In a string of references to *Hop-Along Cassidy* (Howard Bretherton, 1935), *Shane* (George Stevens, 1953), *Scarface* (Brian De Palma, 1983), *The Sopranos* (1999–2007), the Fritz Lang of *Western Union* (1941) and *Rancho Notorious* (1952), *Unforgiven* (Clint Eastwood, 1992) and *The Godfather* trilogy (Francis Ford Coppola, 1972–1990), Cronenberg exceptionally acknowledged the cinematic roots of *A History of Violence* and *Eastern Promises* in these two genres, in which reluctance also plays a crucial role – perhaps best captured in Al Pacino's cry: 'Just when I thought I was out, they pull me back in!' in *The Godfather III* (1990). The generic affiliation also gives us an understanding of the formalistic relationship between reluctance and violence. Robert Warshow explained in his seminal essay from 1954, 'The Westerner', how the gunfighter in westerns is drawn into violence reluctantly, using it carefully, measured, and only in defence. He has to be enticed, forced out of his complacency. But violence is inevitable: 'The gun tells us that [the hero] lives in a world of violence, and even that he believes in violence' (2004: 716). But the drama is one of self-restraint: the moment of violence must come in its own time and according to its special laws, or else it is 'valueless', falling outside culture (ibid.). These 'special laws' are regulations, 'rules of the game' and conventions. They include the 'duel', the 'provocation', the 'revenge' and so forth. By forcing violence to fit a system of conventions (like genres such as the western, the gangster film, the horror film and others), it becomes possible to explain key mechanisms of the connection between culture and violence without forcing us to think through the ultimate consequences of its presence – that it kills. When Aristotle states that the violence in the family is the deed the poet should seek out, he means it is the one whose shocking potential of 'turning on one's own' is in most need of conventionalisation. Portraying violence in the family through fiction as something that has 'rules' and occurs at certain 'moments', or answers to 'taboos', and demands 'sacrifices' or 'scapegoats', makes it possible to prevent and avoid it, or to postpone and deflect its most ruthless consequences. It turns it into a 'play', shocking nonetheless but less threatening to the cultural order. Formalising things makes them bearable.

The best framework for conventionalisation is through the representation of cultural systems alternative to 'normal' culture that resonate strongly in society; such alternatives are more likely to occur in the wake of the collapse of stable systems.[35] One could argue the cultural coherence of the town of Millbrook in *A History of Violence* had already started disintegrating with the late-night antics of Bobby and his 'gang' and the high-school bullying in the gym, and simply accelerated with Tom's killing of the two thugs when they entered town. Similarly, the rise of *Eastern Promises'* Vory V Zakone comes on the back of the fall of the Soviet Union's cohesion, and the breakdown of classical immigration waves. If we look at Cronenberg's earlier films, the cultural system most often used as an alternative to the 'normal' family is the conspiratorial cultist congregation. In *A History of Violence* and *Eastern Promises* we do not find such cults. Rather we find the 'family' of the mafia and the codes and conducts of organised crime that form alternatives to 'real' families and family values: the Irish East Coast mafia that Tom/Joey and his brother Richie stem from, and the Russian crime syndicate of the Vory V Zakone governed by Semyon and his son Kirill (the twist here of course is that 'real' refers to the family values considered proper in 'normal' culture, and not to the blood bond between siblings). The extremely violent ways of operating of both mafias (most poignantly represented by the despicable figures of Richie and Kirill) threaten 'normal' culture. Yet understanding those ways creates the opportunity of beating them at their own game, as Tom and Nikolai prove. And reluctance and self-restraint are key techniques in coming to, and exercising, that understanding. It comes with the heavy price of isolation, but it still beats getting killed.[36]

A History of Violence and *Eastern Promises* form the culmination of Cronenberg's long investigation into the causes and appearances of violence, from omnivorous dedication to aloof reluctance. They also represent a break with it. They are his first films that end not with the demise of the protagonist but with his formal victory over the opposition. As such, they aptly analyse the conditions, appearances and functions of violence, and the ways violence can be avoided or overcome without leading to self-destruction. They offer a map to survival. As victories void of catharsis they also beg an understanding of what exactly is the cost of such a survival.

Conclusion: The Last Auteur at the End of the World

A small short film made on the occasion of the sixtieth anniversary of the Cannes Film Festival forms the perfect conclusion to this chapter and this book. It also demonstrates that Cronenberg's concern for family goes wider than relatives and ancestors; it embraces the value of culture itself.

At the Suicide of the Last Jew in the World in the Last Cinema in the World (2007) lasts three-and-a-half minutes and consists of one shot: a dishevelled and distraught Cronenberg in the men's bathroom of the last remaining cinema in the world. Cronenberg inspects a range of bullets, selects one, loads it in a gun and holds the gun against his head, pressing it against his ear, poking it into his eye, wrapping his lips around the muzzle, apparently trying to commit suicide. He first holds the gun behind his ear, then against his eye (the two senses most directly activated via film) and finally puts it in his mouth. The film ends before he pulls the trigger. The shot is set up as

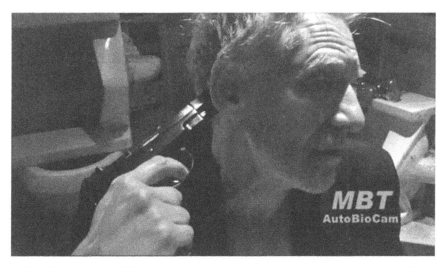

A Cultural Hero threatens to kill himself: *At the Suicide of the Last Jew in the World in the Last Cinema in the World*

if it were a surveillance camera or home video camera: a wide-angle lens framing the action from one top corner of the room. It even has a little logo in the lower right corner of the frame stating it is an 'MBT AutoBioCam' – a name decidedly Cronen- bergian in its combined reference to technology and the body. The beginning and end of the film are punctuated by two musical soundbites. They are the theme tune for a television news show but their symphonic and triumphant style also resembles the tunes for classic Hollywood studios (most like that of 20th Century Fox). The music brackets a continuous voice-over by two newscasters, Rob (voiced by Jesse Collins) and Sherry (voice of Gina Clayton), who discuss, live on the air, what happens, as it happens. Their broadcast chatter gives us the bare bones of the wider story: that the person we see has taken refuge in the last cinema in the world, and that he is in the men's room because the rest of the theatre is trashed; that it is a good thing that these theatres are now finally going to disappear, because cinema was such a horrifying failure ('Everybody will breathe a sigh of relief when this thing is blown to bits,' says Sherry); that the man inside (whose name the newscasters cannot seem to remember) used to work in film; that he is a Jew; that he is a Hungarian Jew; that he is the last Jew ever; that he was offered the option of execution but he chose suicide ('typical, to be expected,' adds Rob); and that they are not sure he is actually going to carry out his suicide. But, concludes Sherry, 'We won't blink, we won't turn away. We'll be right here until the end.' Cue the music again – probably to announce a commercial break – and the film ends.

While there is narrative progress in the film, there is no string of cause and effect events moving from plot point to plot point and ending in a climax. The story and its background are presented pretty much in the manner indicated above: the images observe Cronenberg trying different positions for the gun against his head (and there is no telling if anything will actually happen); the sound presents a diluted, frag- mented stream of contentions, comments, allegations, asides, *faits divers*, personal opinions and *aplombs*, guesswork and general phatic communication. There is lots of talk, but no real insight. We never hear the real truth behind the demise of cinema, or indeed that of the extinction of the Jews. Instead, Sherry and Rob bombard their viewers with numerous unchecked and incomplete claims, their discourse abundantly peppered with qualifiers such as 'apparently', 'might', 'I'm told', 'I'm not certain of this', 'somehow', 'somewhere'. Nevertheless, they follow up such qualifiers with blunt apertures and conjectures none of which are credited with any source. Tellingly, Rob and Sherry only quote an anonymous 'they' in their link between cinema and Jews:

> Sherry: He's the last Jew in the world, *I'm told*. And he is inside this place, the last cinema in the world.
> Rob: Wow, that is perfect, Sherry, given that, you know, *they say* Jews invented movies, and we know the horrific cost of that whole creation.
> Sherry: Well, *they really say* the Jews invented Hollywood, *but you know...*
> Rob: Same thing, isn't it?
> Sherry: Same thing.
> Rob: Same thing.

From suggestion and contention to agreed truth in less than ten seconds. In addition to these unfounded allegations, Sherry and Rob's news show also fails to illustrate anything of what is happening, robbing it completely of its context by delaying or ejecting visual evidence. They promise to check up on how the last cinema came to be 'exposed', but never do; they tell us they will show us the exterior of the building ('We'll have that for you as soon as we can'), but Sherry quickly moves on, asking us not to bother; they promise they will have the explosion of the cinema 'a little bit later on tonight', and that they 'won't turn away' and will be 'right here until the end' – then they abruptly cut for commercials.

Together, the conjectures and apertures, the delaying of evidence, the fragmented storyline and the contrast with the deliberate yet undetermined actions of the image form an indictment of contemporary television in its most incessantly 'real' formats: the news show and the reality-TV show, and the culture of egocentrism and narcissism it encapsulates. In that sense the qualifier 'to my way of thinking' Sherry uses also stands as a confirmation of herself as authority: it is true because she says so and she has the authority to say so because she is on television. Instead of being interested in the 'character' on display (the suicidal Jew), like a cinematic story would ask us to do, and engage with it, perhaps even see its point of view (even morally, as Cronenberg has so often remarked to critics who chide him for the actions of his characters), Sherry cheerfully interrupts Rob's semi-nostalgia for the lost era of cinema by remarking that 'we'll be a lot better off without it, we're in a better place right now and we don't need them. We have better things now.' 'Well said, Sherry,' Rob immediately replies, 'we have *us* don't we, that is … what you mean?' 'It is exactly what I mean,' chirps Sherry .

The film's criticism of television is also a warning against scapegoating, against the persecution of outsiders for the state the world is in. The film implies the filmmaker is convicted of a crime (he could have chosen execution, but he chose suicide), but it remains unclear whether the crime was being a Jew or being a filmmaker. The lack of distinction is significant, as it allows viewers to speculate on comparisons between Jews and cinema (as Sherry and Rob do) and the persecution of Jews and the persecution of cinema (in which they tellingly do not engage).[37] No wonder Cronenberg looks so unkempt and distressed: it is the look of a persecuted man, a man put in a camp. With perhaps the exception of one 'vision' in *The Dead Zone*, in which Doctor Weizak is forced to remember his wartime escape from a hellish Polish ghetto, and the comparison of his eviction from his rented home in the mid-1970s to the plight of 'the seer, the prophet, the Jew, the alien' (see chapter two), Cronenberg has kept any references to his Jewish legacy to an absolute minimum – though he has recently said that 'circumstances have forced it [his Jewishness] a little more out in the open' (in Taubin 2007b).[38] That is also why its use in *At the Suicide of the Last Jew in the World in the Last Cinema in the World* is so powerful. It explains Cronenberg's personal philosophy towards filmmaking, and art in general: he is the eternal outsider. That is why he is alone in the film, all alone, as the last auteur, the last defender of the art of cinema.

Concurrent with the warning against scapegoating the film asks us not to be too aloof in our detachments – random blaming and misinformed judgements should not be replaced with the blunt refusal to care at any cost that Sherry and Rob display. I have argued above that Cronenberg's most recent feature films favour reluctance and restraint, leading to an appreciation of formal arrangements over getting carried away. As far as such an attitude prevents (the escalation of) violence, it makes perfect sense. But Sherry and Rob's snubbing of Cronenberg's on-screen character shows that the formal arrangement of reality TV and the extreme disengagement of the bland, careless observation of news events (as seen in 24-hour news shows) can lead to an inability to care when it matters, an inability to connect the dots and have them make sense. Their disinclination to engage is understandable: the visceral ferociousness and 'in-your-face' visuals of *At the Suicide of the Last Jew in the World in the Last Cinema in the World*'s acts seem to make it impossible to unpack the event and analyse it without employing ready-made moral judgements. So they revert to irony and *je m'en foutisme*. Sherry cannot appreciate cinema because she has no idea what it was, and both of them are beyond caring for the fate of Jews because it is too embedded in history. When history is overrun by formal arrangements – by formats – nothing matters anymore.

In the twenty-first century, legacies seem to matter much to Cronenberg, and he is increasingly concerned with histories, family trees and roots. This includes of course his real family (son Brandon and wife Carolyn are explicitly thanked on the end credits of *At the Last Suicide of the Last Jew in the World in the Last Cinema in the World*); it also incorporates the professional families of his crew, Canadian cinema and the horror genre (which I feel he defends eloquently here by painting news shows and reality TV as mindless self-involved demagogy – hence the real garbage); and ultimately, it contains the heritage of cinema itself. *At the Last Suicide of the Last Jew in the World in the Last Cinema in the World* invites us to see cinema as an addition to cultural diversity – as diversity *itself* even, when compared to the tightly controlled commodity that is television. That diversity makes it dangerous, as Cronenberg's films of the past have so often demonstrated. Because films such as *Shivers*, *The Brood*, *Videodrome* and *Crash* showcased alternatives and differing points of view, and promoted critical awareness, they attracted angry reactions from those invested in the status quo. In times when Hollywood reigns, 'other cinema' is the scapegoat. Eliminating that cinema, and its history, means eliminating part of culture. As Sherry puts it in *At the Last Suicide of the Last Jew in the World in the Last Cinema in the World*: 'It's a significant moment in world history. Or at least I guess some kind of history of some culture.' For many, that kind of culture means the world.

NOTES

INTRODUCTION

1   Amassing cues and quotes and linking them to the public sphere requires evidence. I have tried to be as thorough as possible. More than ten thousand reviews were consulted for this study, from twelve countries, in an attempt to make the overview as internationally complete as possible. Only the ones that are directly referenced are listed in the notes and bibliography.

2   I have argued against such isolation on a number of occasions; see Mathijs (2002; 2003a; 2003b).

3   The main principle of this concept is that any person in this world can be connected to anyone else via no more than six steps (a step being a person knowing another one). The concept was popularised by American playwright John Guare. It was later playfully applied to the dense network of cinema through the so-called 'Six Degrees of Kevin Bacon' – a game that challenged players to connect any other film actor to Kevin Bacon via no more than six steps. Cronenberg has a Bacon number of two: Bacon worked with Holly Hunter in *End of the Line* (Jay Russell, 1987); she appeared in Cronenberg's *Crash*. But closer to my argument about the public presence of film in culture is Bacon's appearance in *Friday the 13th* (Sean S. Cunningham, 1980), a franchise that was, like Cronenberg's films, at the centre of the cult of horror in the early 1980s. See Guare (1990); also Plunka (2005).

4   For elaborations on the tensions between the 'private' and the 'public', see Jancovich (2002); Staiger (2005).

5   The term was first used in a seminar on Alternative Cinema in the Department of Theatre, Film and Television Studies at Aberystwyth University. I thank the students (and especially Matt Ross) for their valuable contributions and suggestions. Several of the essays from the seminar were published in *Kinoeye*: see http://www.kinoeye.org/index_04_03.php (accessed 28 November 2007).

6   William Beard calls him a 'card-carrying existentialist' (2005: ix).

7   Active auteur to the fullest extent, Cronenberg jokingly invokes a major theme in his films to criticise Prime Minister Stephen Harper: 'I had a look at the press release and when I read they were trimming fat and refocusing the spending on the priorities of Canadians, it made me crazy [...] There is always this idea that the arts are superficial, kind of frivolous. The notion that they are fat to be trimmed from the body politic makes me nuts. And, well, as you know, I'm always sensitive to the body metaphors.' See MacDonald (2006).

CHAPTER ONE

1   These collegiate institutes sit in between regular high schools and college education – comparable to Gymnasiums, Atheneums, or Sixth Form Colleges.

2   The quote is from Cronenberg's interview with Katherine Govier (1979). The death of Cronenberg's father is considered of high importance to his work by both Morris (1994: 58) and Rodley (1997: 1).

3   In the yearbook, Cronenberg's entry is followed by an editor's note, which says: 'The above article is a sample of David Cronenberg's writing ability. "GOOD LUCK!".' I thank Katherine Spring and her mother, who attended Harbord, for this information.

4   See Allinson (2002). Several others who graduated from Harbord mention Cronenberg as famous alumnus; see Bow (2004).

5· A paper that goes some way in exploring this, though it loses track of its own premise halfway through, is Fothergill (1977).

6   For overviews of the wider cultural sphere, see Dean (1968); Porter (1984a; 1984b).

7   The link between *Stereo* and vampirism is also observed, albeit impressionistically, by Lia Gangitano, who comments on it in her discussion of the Spectacular Optical exhibition (1998: 66).

8   Marshall McLuhan's Wikipedia site is the most prominent one featuring the claim: http://en.wikipedia.org/wiki/Marshall_McLuhan (accessed 14 March 2008).

9   In 1998, a Norwegian film called *Thirst – Crimes of the Future* (Rapp, Frogner, Warsinski) was released, based on three stories by Knut Hamsun.

10 For a timing of the shooting of *Crimes of the Future*, see Knelman (1969: 15).

11 For an elaboration of the Stanford Prison Experiment, see note 19 in chapter four.

12 The attendance was 75 people for *Stereo* and 67 for *Crimes of the Future*. I would like to thank Philip Delvosalle of the Belgian Royal Film Archives for the information on the screenings.

13 It is a link also noted by Pompon & Véronneau (2003: 34).

14 Hofsess gives a first-hand account of the trial (1970).

15 Though still acutely under-researched, this shift has received some attention recently; see Hawkins 2000; Betz 2003; Mathijs 2005.

CHAPTER TWO

1   For overviews of Cinépix's softcore enterprises, see Delaney (1969); and Desbarats (1970).

2   The story of the trip to Los Angeles to meet Roger Corman is recounted endearingly by Cronenberg's friend, writer Norman Snider. It is also a touching account of the surreal business practices of B-movie production and development, including rude secretaries, shady connections, red Mustangs, Quaaludes and being frisked by the LAPD; see Snider (1974).

3   Cronenberg interview included on the *Shivers* DVD (Image Entertainment/Lionsgate, 1998).

4 The story is told in detail in Rodley 1997: 50

5 If we press the pun of Emil Hobbes' name a little bit further, we might also wonder if his first name is not a reference to Jean-Jacques Rousseau's *Emile, ou de l'éducation*, a well-known work of the eighteenth century, in which the French philosopher discussed the nature/nurture dilemma in terms of its use for education. See, for instance, Sanjek (1996).

6 See, for instance, Ardrey (1967; 1970); Lorenz (1967); Morris (1967; 1969); Tinbergen (1968). For an excellent interpretation of how these works influenced films and filmmakers, see Barker (2004b).

7 The symbol of the Arc in *Shivers* is one particularly preferred by Italian critics Marcello Pecchioli (1994) and Paolo Vernaglione (1995).

8 In itself the Montreal street scenes are unique in documenting the by-then gradually disappearing combination of sleazy and middle-class entertainment within the same quarter, the area of Rue St Catherine.

9 Cronenberg, in the director's commentary for *Rabid*, spends at least five minutes elaborating the topic, including his own attitude towards the Crisis (he was in Paris at the time and learned of it via the French newspaper *Le Monde*).

10 Cronenberg in the DVD Director's Commentary, chapter 4.

11 Cronenberg in the DVD's Director's Commentary, chapter 11.

12 Girard's theories have often been associated with Catholic lines of reasoning. It is very fitting then that *Rabid* is largely set in Montreal, and the province of Québec, thresholds of Catholicism in North America, where theories concerning guilt and sacrifice have a distinct presence in cultural discourse. See Marchand (2005: 60–2).

13 For examples of how such distribution and exhibition networks operated, see Hawkins (2000); Betz (2003); Heffernan (2004).

14 Among the earliest overviews of these characteristics are Robin Wood's essays 'Return of the Repressed' (1978b) and 'Gods and Monsters' (1978c) in *Film Comment*, later adapted and reprinted in Andrew Britton, Robin Wood, Richard Lippe & Tony Williams (eds) *The American Nightmare*. Subsequent overviews include: Kristeva (1982); Grant (1984); Hogan (1986); Tudor (1989); Jancovich (1992); Badley (1995); Halberstam (1995); Grant (1996); Benshoff (1997); Humphries (2002); Lowenstein (2005); Schneider & Wiliams (2005).

15 I am leaving *The Reincarnate* (Don Haldane, 1971) out of my account, as it was released nearly half a decade before *Shivers*. Cronenberg did go on to use the film's main actor, Jack Creley, for a memorable role as Professor Brian O'Blivion in *Videodrome*.

16 Cronenberg directed *The Lie Chair* between August and October 1975, after finishing *Shivers* but before that film's release. It aired on 12 February 1976, when *Shivers* was gradually being released around the world. It was produced for the Canadian Broadcasting Company and featured as the second of three episodes in the series *Peepshows*. *The Lie Chair* tells the story of Carol (Susan Hogan) and Neil Croft (Richard Monette), whose car breaks down in the middle of the countryside during a terrible storm. They find refuge in Mrs Rogers' (Doris Petrie) old country house, occupied only by herself and her live-in housekeeper, Mildred (Amelia Hall). Since they have to stay overnight, they are invited to pass for Mrs Rogers' long lost grandson Robert and his wife Sylvia, with Mrs Rogers claiming it is for poor Mildred's benefit and Mildred telling them it would please Mrs Rogers. During the night they hear a boy's voice, go downstairs and find Mildred in a chair – the lie chair. She tells them Robert and Sylvia committed suicide long ago, when they discovered the 'lie chair' would not protect them from the evil world outside. Entranced, Neil walks to Mildred, kneels and hugs her. Carol flees the house in panic, finds their car and discovers herself and Neil inside it – dead. The next morning, at breakfast, they *are* Robert and Sylvia.

17 I have discussed Wood's aversion for *Shivers* in detail elsewhere (Mathijs 2003b), and I will elaborate on his reasons for disliking Cronenberg's films in chapter four.

18 See Knelman (1975; 1977); Lanken (1975a; 1975b); Schupp (1976); Shuster (1976).

19 See reviews in *The New Statesman* (1976), *Sight and Sound* (1976), *Monthly Film Bulletin* (Combs 1976), *The Observer* (Davies 1976), *The Sunday Times* (Powell 1976) and *Films Illustrated* (Whitman 1976).

20 Interview with Kim Newman, 8 December 2007. My sincerest thanks to Russ Hunter for relaying the questions and answers.

21 Author's translation. For a detailed elaboration on how reviewers used *Shivers* to position themselves against such trends, see Mathijs (2003b).

22 See Garris (1977); Overbey (1977); Rolfe (1977).

23 I would like to thank Philip Delvosalle of the Belgian Royal Film Archive for this information. For a review of the grindhouse re-releases, see a review in the Flemish newspaper *Het Volk* (4 August 1978).

24 The screening was highlighted in the programme listings of *Andere Sinema* (1979: 42)

25 For a symptomatic example see Kelly Parks http://www.feoamante.com/Movies/STU/shivers.html (accessed 16 March 2008).

26 See the references to Cronenberg in reviews of these films in Schneider (2007: 18, 67–8, 182, 213).

CHAPTER THREE

1 Cronenberg gives an interesting insight into Lonnie's discomfort when he reveals in the audio commentary to the DVD that Smith usually portrayed a 'bad guy', and felt uneasy in his role as a good character – it is tempting to see this discomfort transposing itself into the unease of Lonnie with his popularity.

2 It is worth emphasising here how frequently dialogue (or opportunities for dialogue) are replaced by car engine noise – a clear sign of Cronenberg's preference for exploring the technology of car racing over telling the tale of Lonnie and his crew.

3 One might even include the bunnies in this professional attitude. As true professional star-chasers (donned in the obligatory cut-off jeans), they shun PJ (who is only a mechanic) and prefer Billy (the driver). A scene mirroring this attitude is the one where Candy is first introduced to Billy. Only after he has assured her that he is not Lonnie's mechanic does she start showing him some affection.

4 Like *Fast Company*, *The Italian Machine* has been unavailable for a long time. At the time of writing, the episode was freely available as a streamed video via the British broadcaster Channel Four at: http://www.channel4.com/film/reviews/film.jsp?id=128191. There is also a Japanese DVD release, which also includes *The Lie Chair*.

5 As the record tells us, the sound we hear is that of a Norton motorcycle, the same motorcycle that Rose and Hart drive in the beginning of *Rabid*.

6 Bernard Thomas calls *The Italian Machine* Kenneth Anger-esque (1984: 41).

7 There is very little material on *The Italian Machine*, and what exists is usually written – like my own interpretation – years after the original screening. As Paul Taylor warns, this risks creating 'inappropriate criteria of evaluation, [...] doing both the work and the worker a disservice' (1984: 43–4).

8 For in-depth explorations of these films, see Osgerby (2005; 2007).

9 For those keen on emphasising the distinctions between European and North American professional racing I would like to stress how much the late 1970s were a time of convergence and crossover attention, perhaps best embodied by the legendary Mario Andretti, winner of both North American and European prime championships. Ronnie Peterson was Andretti's teammate with Lotus – and second in

the overall standings – when he died in 1978, the year Andretti became world champion. Niki Lauder was the defending F1 world champion when his car crashed and caught fire on the German Nurburg-ring in 1976. In 1977 he returned to racing and became world champion for a second time. He drove Cronenberg's favourite car: a Ferrari.

10 Jonathan Rayner makes a convincing case for these illegal race films as metaphors for the ambivalence attached to the fusion of 'mobility', 'transport' and 'progress'; see Rayner (2000: 223–33).

11 For the *Monthly Film Bulletin* reviewer this scene forms the only highlight of the film; see Taylor (1984b: 188).

12 Author's conversation with him at the Cine-Excess Cult Cinema Conference, in London, 3–5 May 2007.

13 Cronenberg was now living with Carolyn Zeifman, who had been a production assistant on *Rabid*, and was synch editor on *Fast Company*. She would later become an assistant editor on *The Brood*. She became the second Mrs Cronenberg.

14 Other sources add other types of cars and motorcycles to Cronenberg's collection. According to Noah James, he owned at the time 'a Lancia, a 1969-model Dino Ferrari and two Desmo Ducati motorbikes' (1979: 7). In 1983, the same magazine (*Maclean's*) printed that Cronenberg 'now owns a Porsche 930 Turbo, and four exotic Italian motorcycles … He also owns and races a 1962 Ferrari' (Czarnecki 1983: 62).

15 Author's interview with Nicholas Campbell, 5 July 2007.

16. When Robert Silverman, who is in more Cronenberg films than any other actor, had an accident and needed caring company during his long recovery, Cronenberg was one of the people who spent a lot of time at his side.

17 The addition of the emphasis will be explained in the note accompanying the next Pevere & Dymond quote (see note 17).

18 I hope readers see the connection to the emphasised *professionals* in the previous quote from *Mondo Canuck*: the tax shelter system and the need for (and move towards) professionalism went hand-in-hand.

19 One of the most visible portals is http://www.canuxploitation.com (accessed 15 March 2008) but there are numerous others.

20 See http://www.canuxploitation.com/review/fastcompany.html (accessed 10 July 2007).

21 See http://www.dvdmaniacs.net/Reviews/E-H/fast_company.html (accessed 10 July 2007).

22 See http://www.dvdverdict.com/reviews/fastcompanyle.php (accessed 10 July 2007).

23 It is fascinating to hear Cronenberg explain the details of the Norton motorcycle Rose and Hart ride during the credit sequence of *Rabid* (he spends several minutes on the topic in the director's commen-tary on the DVD). The sound, he explains, is that of his own Ducati 750, because it would make for a more reliable soundscape, without slipping clutches or any other disturbing side noises.

24 See Cronenberg's (2005) introduction to *Red Cars*. Turin: Edizioni Voluminata. Also available online at http://www.redcars.it/index2.htm (accessed 11 July 2007).

CHAPTER FOUR

1 A representative grab from four different countries includes Andrews (1981); Bastian (1981); Beer-ekamp (1981); Butstraen (1981); Duynslaegher (1981).

2 See Arnopp (2004: 48–51). The top ten is further made up of: *Day of the Dead* (George A. Romero, 1985), *The Omen, Hellraiser* (Clive Barker, 1987), *Zombie Flesh Eaters* (Lucio Fulci, 1979), *Cannibal Ferox* (Umberto Lenzi, 1981), *The Beyond* (Lucio Fulci, 1981), *City of the Living Dead* (Lucio Fulci, 1980), *Tenebrae* (Dario Argento, 1982) and *Cut and Run* (Ruggero Deodato, 1985).

3　For a range of reviews of the film, see Andrews (1980); Ramasse (1980); Whitman (1980); Anon. (2007e).

4　It was actually around the time of the release of *The Brood* and *Scanners*, and in the early 1980s, that the *Shivers* cult became established; see Mathijs (2003b).

5　See, respectively, McCarthy (1979); Conlogue (1979); James (1979).

6　For a range of reviews and articles, see Tesson (1979); Arnold (1981a); Feineman (1981); Testa (1981); Rickey (1983).

7　Among the dozens accessible via Google and IMDb, two of the most insightful are Shingle (2005) and Scheib (2005).

8　The German popular magazine *Der Spiegel* devotes some specific attention to how trailers of horror films lure audiences into theatres on 'false pretenses', but admits there is now a generation of film living up to the expectations; see Urs (1981).

9　Although Cronenberg also asserts he made considerable changes to the script that pulled it away from its real-life context, he still maintains that it contains 'words that were really spoken' (in Chute 1980: 39).

10　The earliest quotable source of the comparison with *The Brood* I could find is from January 1980, when Stephen Schiff described *The Brood* as a 'distorted mirror image' of *Kramer vs. Kramer* in his review in *The Boston Phoenix* (15 January) (reprinted in Schiff 1984).

11　A good example is the polemic between several Belgian film magazines that started with a review of *Kramer vs. Kramer* in *Film en Televisie* and ended, almost a full pregnancy later, with a laudation of Cronenberg's oeuvre in *Andere Sinema*, a magazine of an opposing ideological affiliation (see Mathijs 2000: 198–9; Gobbers 1980).

12　See, for instance: Conlogue (1979); Fox (1979); Guérif (1979); O'Toole (1979a); Rabourdin (1979).

13　Both Creed's and Beard's ideas have gone through substantial sedimentation: Creed introduced her ideas in a 1986 essay in *Screen*, and elaborated on them in a 1993 book; Beard first expressed his ideas in an edited book on Cronenberg, and reworked them for his excellent monograph nearly twenty years later. For further details, see Beard (1983; 2005); Creed (1986; 1993).

14　At the time, the few reviews that pointed to *The Brood*'s 'brooding' confusions and complications, such as Andrew Dowler's review for *Cinema Canada* and Tim Lucas's essay in *Cinefantastique*, were largely overlooked. Both find flaws in *The Brood*, but their assertions that the film 'works on the head and the heart' (Dowler 1979: 33) and 'shifts blame from science to conscience' (Lucas 1979: 42) are closer to the mark than many other judgements.

15　See, for example, Wood (1978b; 1978c; 1979a); Holthof (1980a; 1980b).

16　Plans for release also included Mexico and most of the Pacific Rim. There was a mention of *Scanners* in the form of its working title 'The Sensitives' even as *The Brood* was still in post-production, when the start of production company Filmplan was announced, in March 1979; see Scott (1979a).

17　In several interviews, Cronenberg fulminates against New World's treatment of *The Brood*; see Braun (1981); Harkness (1981); Polinien (1981).

18　Philip Zimbardo's infamous Stanford Prison Experiment of the early 1970s, which, though abruptly terminated before it could reach its conclusion, seemed to demonstrate the willingness of 'torturers' to exceed their peers' and superiors' commands and see incitement where there was none. Moral advocates (including lawyers, preachers, local school boards) connected it to the 'appeal' of on-screen torture to claim causal effects; see Zimbardo *et al.* (1973); Milgram (1974); Zimbardo (1985).

19　Illustrative examples are: Auty & Woolley (1981); Quinlan (1981).

20　For an indicative list of German *Scanners* reviews, see www.davidcronenberg.de (and follow the link to case studies and *Scanners*; accessed 17 March 2008).

21 The release was backed by a $2,750,000 promotion and public interest campaign. For details, see Kaminsky (1981). For an example of an ad, see the *New York Times*, 11 January 1981, page D14; the gun firing in the New York theatre was recounted by Québec poet Bill Furey (1981: 6).

22 See, for instance, Arnold (1981b); Canby (1981); Scott (1981).

23 Several critics have since mentioned *Newsweek*'s article as the big public breakthrough of Cronenberg. Katherine Monk writes: 'the film gained much critical attention and *Newsweek* even called him the next heir to the horror throne' (2001: 235).

24 Incidentally, several reviewers used the opportunity of *Scanners*' success to pull Cronenberg's earlier films, and Canada's other tax shelter horror films, into the limelight. *Cinema Canada* rehabilitated *Shivers*, and *Prom Night* and *My Bloody Valentine* were also allowed to bask in the glory of *Scanners*; see Kroll 1981; Testa 1981; Mathijs 2003.

25 It is fascinating to see Cronenberg's moniker evolve from 'king of schlock horror' over 'king of blood' before it settles on 'baron of blood'; see Rolfe (1977: 26); Testa (1978); Maronie (1981).

26 See, for instance, Anon. (1981a); Beaufays (1981); Beerekamp (1981); Braun (1981).

27 The fan press was not alone in giving an overview of Cronenberg's career. The regular press also made similar efforts.

28 The story was recounted with much affection by John Landis during his talk at the Cine-Excess Cult Cinema Conference, in London, 3–5 May 2007. Cronenberg's own version is reprinted in Monk (2001: 238).

29 Added to that was some confusion as to who did what. Different accounts of degrees of involvement created a huge debate among fans and audiences – often played out in letter pages and at conventions more than in official discourse. This debate quickly became a myth, and effects artists nowhere near the actual production began to be associated with it by proxy. *Variety* listed one Henry Piercig (a noble unknown) with effects work, and at times even Rick Baker was named as a contributor (probably a mix-up with his work on Cronenberg's next film, *Videodrome*).

30 See also Freedman (1983); Anon. (1989); Salem (1991); Anon. (1992).

31 As Conrich (2000) reminds us, we have to bear in mind that this early wave of video consumption mostly concerns rentals. In other words, it is a form of consumption with a particular relationship to 'repeat viewing' routines.

32 It is not that Zeller did not have a company; he did (Zeller International: www.zeller-int.com/zeller-main.htm). His efforts were so eclectically spread over a range of enterprises (the US Army Corps of Engineers and Cirque du Soleil among them) that from a film business point of view he seemed elusive.

33 See Grünberg (1992: 103); Rodley (1997: 91). Obviously, Arnopp (1994: 48) also carries it.

34 See the DVD review on *DVD Outsider* (http://www.dvdoutsider.co.uk/; accessed 18 August 2007).

35 See the review on *Motherfucking Masterpieces* (http://www.forbisthemighty.com/acidlogic/mother-fucking_masterpieces.htm; accessed 18 August 2007).

36 In fact, Cronenberg intended the exploding head scene to come even earlier on in *Scanners*. It was intended to be the first scene, with the explosion coming about two to three minutes into the film. After a test screening he decided 'to move the shot ten minutes into the film' (quoted in the 'Fear on Film' panel included as an extra on the Criterion edition of *Videodrome*).

37 The similarity between *Scanners* and *Psycho* is underscored by the simultaneous release, in several territories, of *Scanners* with *Psycho III* (Anthony Perkins, 1986).

38 'Cronenberg has learned director's diplomacy,' writes Ray Conlogue (1978), in a report on a set visit to *The Brood*.

1 For overviews of these developments, see Schneider (2003; 2007); Schneider & Williams (2005); Hantke (2006).

2 Staiger's insistence on seeing cult viewing practices merely as fandom limits it to small-scale networks of exhibition and reception. But the 1980s development of the cult of horror surpasses that. See, for instance, Van Extergem (2004). Staiger's quote is from her otherwise excellent study of reception (2005: 125).

3 See Jancovich (1992); Humphries (2002). The one work contradicting this parallel is Wood (1986).

4 There are dozens of ways in which these four films embody so much of what the 1980s stand for, and then push it into new meanings. I can only deal with a few of them here. For alternative considerations, which inevitably have some overlap with mine, I gladly refer to the excellent discussions of *Videodrome*, *The Dead Zone*, *The Fly* and *Dead Ringers* in Beard (2005: 125–276).

5 It is not often emphasised enough how much Cronenberg featured in academic scholarship's first attempts to theorise the functions of horror cinema in society: see the special issues that the journals *Camera Obscura* (in the US) and *Screen* (in the UK) devoted to the genre in 1986.

6 The earliest mention of *Videodrome* occurs amidst the reception of *Scanners*, in February 1981; see Anon. (1981a)

7 Lennick got his own acknowledgements when he was singled out among the crew working on *Video-drome.*; see MacRae (1982).

8 See Chute (1982); Devos & Holthof (1982); McKinnon (1982); Zoller (1982). Cronenberg later commented on how some of the extras involved in torture scenes did seem to get some kind of kick out of the shoot, and kept returning to hang around the set (in Rodley 1997: 97–8).

9 It also fitted Lucas's own, self-confessed fascination with the inspirations he felt he and Cronenberg shared: Nabokov, Pynchon and the fantastic; see Lucas (1981; 1982).

10 Cronenberg quoted in 'Fear on Film', on the Criterion edition of *Videodrome*.

11 Cronenberg refers to this endorsement in several interviews; the earliest reference is in Danvers (1984b). I would like to thank Philip Auslander for his helpful observations regarding the origin of this quote.

12 Cronenberg, quoted in 'Fear on Film', on the Criterion edition of *Videodrome*.

13 Cronenberg, Mark Irwin and a small crew actually shot a full five-minute segment of *Samurai Dreams* for *Videodrome*. It is included as an extra on the Criterion DVD edition. In it, we discover that the two samurai are an Asian man and a black woman who engage the geisha in a threesome. Mark Irwin, who, together with regular Cronenberg crew member Jock Brandis, had started his career as a cameraman for soft porn (*Diary of a Sinner*, Ed Hunt, 1975), referred to the shot of the samurai ganging up on the geisha as his 'Kurosawa shot'; quoted in Lucas (2004: 19).

14 For an overview of Pynchon's work, see Cowart (1980); Berressem (1993); Mathijs (2001).

15 The Pittsburgh reference is an intriguing one, not only because the word is repeated four times in a few seconds. Geographically, Pittsburgh is a convenient location near enough to the Canadian border, big enough to possibly harbour such an operation (and with the ready technological know-how available). But it also has a special resonance with horror fans as the home base of George A. Romero (who set most of his films there, including the then highly popular *Dawn of the Dead*) and it is of course the hometown of Andy Warhol.

16 I am not counting the short films *The Boogeyman* (Jeffrey C. Schiro, 1982) and *The Woman in the Room* (Frank Darabont, 1983), as these had only very limited public distribution at the time, even within the short film-hungry circuit of film festivals.

17 For elaborations on this trope, see Mathijs (2007b).

18 One of the most important concerns regarding media concentration was embodied by the MacBride commission of UNESCO, which attempted a report on the fair distribution and ownership of information in Third World countries. The net result was that the US and the UK left UNESCO, effectively drying up much of its funding.

19 Other examples include *The Thing, Under Fire* (Roger Spottiswoode, 1983), *Brainstorm, Enigma* (Jeannot Szwarc, 1983), *The Osterman Weekend* (Sam Peckinpah, 1983), *Daniel* (Sidney Lumet, 1983), *Liquid Sky* (Slava Tsukerman, 1983), *The Keep* (Michael Mann, 1983), *The Hunger* and *The Terminator* (James Cameron, 1984).

20 For elaborations on these themes, see Sterling (1986); Jameson (1992); Young (2002); Grace (2003).

21 A few of these aspects are also analysed in Testa (1989).

22 I am not the first to notice the Renaissance motif in *Videodrome*. It is briefly explored in Lucas (1983).

23 For these pieces, see Hogan (1983) and Lucas (1983b); Lofficier and Randy (1983a); McDonnell (1983); Robinson (1983); Stathis (1984).

24 These can be found in Klady (1983); Taylor (1983); Tuchman (1983).

25 For a range of commentary see Ansen (1983); Arnold (1983); Hoberman (1983); Maslin (1983); Rickey (1983); Tesson (1983).

26 See, for example, articles by Czarnecki (1983); Harkness (1983); Scott (1983).

27 See Andrews (1983); Peachment (1983); Pulleine (1983); Wood (1983).

28 Originally intended for the Toronto International Film Festival, from which it was pulled at the last minute because Paramount wanted to avoid premature coverage, *The Dead Zone* had its North American release in October 1983. It was unanimously praised, and did exceptionally well at the box office, topping *Scanners*. It was released in other territories in the spring of 1984.

29 For an overview of the European reception of *Videodrome*, see Mathijs (2000: 382–3, 427–32); see also Danvers (1984a); De Kock (1984); Tesson (1984a).

30 The full list is published as an appendix to Drew (1984).

31 I am excluding here the very short book essay on *Dead Ringers*; see Grant (1997).

32 See Lucas (2007); the Criterion DVD contains another lengthy essay by Lucas: 'Medium Cruel: Reflections on *Videodrome*' (2004).

33 I use the term 'admiration' here in the sense Martin Barker employs it as an evaluative term critics use to express appreciation without having to agree with the moral or aesthetic texture of a film; see Barker, Arthurs & Harindranath (2001).

34 Consider this comment from Cronenberg about *Scanners* the release of *Scanners* in New York: 'In New York [*Scanners*] was considered by the *Village Voice* and *Rolling Stone* in very political terms, very much so. Which maybe says more about the New York and slightly underground press than about the film. *Soho Weekly News* actually put me down for being so blatantly and overtly political – with the anti-corporate thing, and the thalidomide reference, and the core of paranoia about military-industrial complexes'; quoted in Auty & Woolley (1981).

35 Cronenberg speaks at length on the Ontario censorship board in a panel conversation included as an extra feature entitled 'Fear on Film', on the Criterion edition of *Videodrome*, and in McGreal (1984).

36 For two excellent analyses of the 'Video Nasties' controversy, see Barker (1984); Egan (2007).

37 Another such occasion was an interview with Cronenberg in *Cinema Canada*; see Ayscough (1983).

38 For further details, see Cronenberg, Burroughs *et al.* (1984: 5); Siren (1984); also see Scott (1984a; 1984b).

39 This 'film' is most likely a re-edit of previous films of Jack Smith, accompanied by a stage performance. Since it was not screened or performed, the film is not considered to be in official existence, though it was explicitly mentioned as part of the programme, and thus became part of the controversy. It is not unusual for Smith's work to be mislabelled. Mark Kermode and Julian Petley notice how in the midst of the *Crash* controversy, Smith's best-known film *Flaming Creatures* was called 'Flaming Anger' in the *Daily Mail* – a combination of the title and the name of fellow avant-garde filmmaker Kenneth Anger (1997: 17). For a discussion of Smith's elusive performances, see Banes (1998: 279).

40 The decisions stated the Board was illegally acting because it overstepped its brief by pretending to uphold community standards 'as prescribed by law'. The law only related to obscenity, which could already be dealt with under federal criminal law procedures (which most imported video porn would encounter if it broke a law). So if the Board wanted to impose 'other' standards, it would be acting illegally. Moreover, the jurisdiction did not include videotapes, only prints of film; see Fraser (1984b).

41 For more on this, see Downey (1987); Lacey (1987); Hurst (1989).

42 See Landsberg (1989); for a reaction that also brings in the wider scope of feminist censorship, see Allemang (1989).

43 For Cronenberg's reaction, see Breskin (1997: 256).

44 Further details can be found at 'Critics Slam Plan to Limit Funds for 'Offensive' Films', CTV News website, at: http://www.ctv.ca/servlet/ArticleNews/story/CTVNews/20080229/film_censorship_0802 29/20080229?hub=CTVNewsAt11 (accessed 29 February 2008).

45 See, for instance, Ayscough (1983).

46 The Renaissance theme was later also discussed by Christopher Sharrett (1986).

CHAPTER SIX

1 Landis gave small parts to about two dozen directors, musicians and industry people in *Into the Night*, an approach he also used in *The Blues Brothers* (1980) and *Trading Places* (1983). Among them are Jonathan Demme, Carl Perkins, David Bowie, Amy Heckerling, Paul Bartel, Rick Baker, Paul Mazursky, Don Siegel, Jim Henson, Jack Arnold, Roger Vadim and Lawrence Kasdan.

2 *The Fly* and *Dead Ringers* do not go as far as *Videodrome*, in which the unreliability and unaccountability of Max is so far-reaching his reality becomes a permanent hallucination. In that respect it is not so much *Wall Street* that proves to be the proper point of reference, but *American Psycho* (the 1991 novel by Bret Easton Ellis, made into a film by Mary Harron in 2000), a more sinister parable of the excesses of greed, in which the paranoid unreliability of Wall Street advisor Patrick Bateman is complemented by an obsession with violent videos, sadism and sex so extreme it verges on satire. The parallel is noted in Browning (2007: 72–3) and Kaufmann (1998).

3 For Jim Leach, this opening sequence sets up *The Fly* as a Canadian film, with references to Canada that are further reinforced throughout the film. In fact, Leach claims, this Canadian emphasis is also present in the original *The Fly* (Kurt Neumann, 1958); see Leach (2006: 68).

4 The changes in voice pitch accompany Seth's increasingly agitated mindset, as it becomes clear his newfound abilities come with a price. For an elaboration on sound in *The Fly*, see Theberge (2004: 136).

5 It would be reinforced by the fact that soon afterwards Cronenberg directed one episode of the televion series based on *Friday the 13th*, called 'Faith Healer' (1988).

6 The figure is from Box Office Mojo and is not adjusted for inflation.

7 The project was first mentioned at the time of *Videodrome*; see Lucas (1982c).

8 Rodley notes the bitterness of Cronenberg at Irwin's absence (1997: 143).

9   Several dozen reviews make these, and similar comments; see James (1986); Van Tongeren (1986).

10   I believe it is indicative of Cronenberg's removal from the heart of the horror genre that he would gradually be seen more as a mentor and inspiration rather than a fellow combatant; see Barker (1987).

11   For more on these views of Cronenberg, see Kirkland (1986; 1987); Timpone (1986); Lucas (1987); Lucas & FAL (1987).

12   Most fan magazines only published short, late reviews, or just video reviews of *Dead Ringers*. The exception was the fiercely loyal *L'Écran fantastique;* see Cognard (1989); Doherty (1989); Karani & Schlockoff (1989); Kimber (1989).

13   See, for example, Bergstrom, Lyon & Penley (1986); Boss (1986); Brophy (1986); Penley (1986).

14   I have discussed this connection in detail elsewhere; see Mathijs (2003a).

15   Harkness's remark was invited by Wood's own public address of his homosexuality; see Wood (1978c).

16   These concerns included attention to the relationships between AIDS and pornography, scapegoating, activism, media responsibility and the ideological aspects of news production. Several of these concerns were echoed in book publications written around 1986; see Watney (1987); Crimp (1988); Sontag (1988). By 1986, these concerns were widely published in articles, and also resonated in cultural products, art production, writing and other activities; see Pastore (1993). These works focus on the US. For a focus on the cultural representation and negotiation of AIDS in the UK, see Miller & Williams (1994); Miller, Kitzinger, Williams & Beharrell (1998).

17   Many reviewers use quotes from the film's dialogue as evidence for their AIDS interpretation, mentioning lines such as 'it's showing itself as a bizarre form of cancer', or 'it's general cellular chaos', or 'I wasn't pure'. Also, the scenes in which Veronica has a dream about giving birth to a deformed foetus, and the sexual relationship between Brundle and a prostitute, are often singled out as evidence for the AIDS metaphor.

18   It is by no means incidental that both these reviews appear in New York-based publications. As is sufficiently pointed out in several essays on the representation of AIDS, New York played a major role in introducing the process of making cultural meaning of the AIDS epidemic. Some of the first cultural artefacts dealing with AIDS were produced in New York, such as the plays *As Is* (William M. Hoffman, 1985), *The Normal Heart* (Larry Kramer, 1985) or several novels published by New York publishers; see Reed (1993: 92–3).

19   Cronenberg would later repeat this observation in Rodley (1997: 127–8) and Grunberg (2000: 91).

20   For an astute overview of the rhetorical techniques used in the reception of *Dead Ringers*, see Klevan (2000).

21   See, for instance, Tesson (1989); Tesson, Katsahnias & Ostria (1989).

22   For more on this subject, see Knee (1992); Snowden (1992); Ramsay (1999).

23   See, for example, Charity (2001; 2007). It was also mentioned on the website of the theatrical release of *Eastern Promises*: www.focusfeatures.com/easternpromises/ (accessed 24 October 2007).

24   See, for instance, Siclier (1998).

25   See De Vos, Schwarz & Stam (1989); Van den Tempel (1989); Robbins (1993); Beard (1996a).

26   Quoted on the extra features of the *The Fly* and *The Fly 2* DVD (20th Century Fox).

CHAPTER SEVEN

1   The term 'end of history' refers to Francis Fukuyama's (1992) appropriation of the phrase, borrowed from Marx and Hegel.

2   The term Generation X was coined by Canadian novelist Douglas Coupland, who first used it in September 1987. It reached a wide audience with his 1991 novel *Generation X: Tales for an Accelerated Culture*.

3   This terminology owes much to feminist film criticism, especially to Laura Mulvey (1975).

4   William Beard devotes a few pages to discussing Cronenberg as a 'self-conscious artist' in his chapter on *Naked Lunch* (2005: 285–7).

5   See, for instance, Garsault (1991); Grünberg (1991); Parra & Ross (1991); Rouyer (1991).

6   According to Rodley, Cronenberg directed four segments, between 15 and 30 seconds in length. Several flashes (between 5 and 15 seconds) are available on the website You Tube; see http://www.youtube.com/watch?v=8en2-fVyVxg (accessed 22 December 2007).

7   These rallies and social occasions demonstrate the extent to which Cronenberg has become a public figure in Toronto. They include neighbourhood rallies to raise money for infrastructure, charity work and even racing cars; see Anon. (1990); Hume (1990); Shotton (1990); Wilson (1991).

8   See, for instance, the 1991 essay on *Dead Ringers* by Marcie Frank, a seventeenth- and eighteenth-century literary criticism specialist, in the *Publications of the Modern Language Association* (*PMLA*).

9   George Langelaan was the original writer of the story of *The Fly*; James Clavell was the screenwriter of the 1958 film adaptation.

10   See, for instance, comments in Overbey (1977); Sammon (1981); Rodley (1997: 22–3).

11   For early references to Kafka, see Silverman (1984: 32) and Tesson (1984b).

12   Remember that Roger Corman's AIP had organised the distribution of *Rabid* in North America; that Scorsese famously endorsed Cronenberg's films on several occasions; and that several of Cronenberg's films had been compared to the immensely popular *Alien* films. See chapters two, four and five.

13   First mentions of *Naked Lunch* appeared as *Dead Ringers* was being released; see Malcolm (1988); Warren (1988). Derek Malcolm's article also mentions the Japanese and Dutch roots of the financing of *Naked Lunch*.

14   For some of these responses, see Duncan (1992a; 1992b); French (1992).

15   See, for example, Lyons (1992); Palmer (1992); Snowden (1992); Vice (1993).

16   See, for instance, Béhar (1992); Gorlier (1992).

17   One form of evidence of Cronenberg's college crowd reputation was the number of German-language books on him and his work that appeared in the years around the release of *Naked Lunch*. Most of them were collections that had originated as student projects; see Robnik & Palm (1992); Gaschler & Vollmar (1993); Oetjen & Wacker (1993).

18   See, for example, Malcolm (1992); O'Pray (1992); Taubin (1992); Thompson (1992).

19   The phrase is from *Videodrome*: when Max Renn evaluates pilot tapes of Japanese soft porn with his co-executives, one of them suggests Oriental sex will always sell well to Western audiences.

20   An excellent overview of the different ways in which the *Butterfly*-myth has spread across different texts can be found in Wisenthal *et al.* (2006).

21   An interesting case to see *M. Butterfly* as a horror film is made by Asuman Suner (1998).

22   For Cronenberg's comments on the comparison, see Rodley (1997: 180–3). For a critical approach to the two films, see Grist (2003).

23   For more, see Béhar (1993); Duynslaegher (1993); Messias (1993); Norcen (1994).

CHAPTER EIGHT

1   I will return to this again near the end of the chapter, but for clarity I would like to quote the only review that picks up on this theme, by Roger Ebert (1997). He writes: 'Notice how they talk to each other: it is a point of pride to be cold and detached. That's not because they don't care. It's because they do. They are fascinated by each others minds, and by the tastes they share'. Available online at www.rogerebert.suntimes.com (accessed 12 October 2007).

2   *Crash*'s Catherine is one of a few recent Cronenberg heroines, like Edie in *A History of Violence* and Anna in *Eastern Promises* who would warrant comparisons to Hitchcock's late career obsessions with icy blondes. The reference to 'immaculate cleanliness' is from the novel; see Ballard (1995: 112).

3   See Cronenberg's elaboration on how cars have changed sexuality, in Rodley (1997: 199–200).

4   I am using the concept of fetishism here as defined by poststructuralist and feminist scholars such as Claudia Springer (1996) and Constance Penley (1997a; 1997b).

5   I have elaborated on Cronenberg's oeuvre and its link to the concept of the 'cinéma de la cruauté' elsewhere; see Mathijs (1993; 1998).

6   I have shown *Crash* to my students in classes every year since 1997 and the film always leads to more polarised and opinionated arguments than other films (with the exception of *Irréversible* (Gaspar Noé, 2002)). Interestingly, a research project investigating audience reactions to a stage adaptation of *Crash* in Aberystwyth, Wales, in 2001 (directed by David Rabey), revealed audiences were more upset and shocked by the film version than by the theatre version – drama and performance's reputation of being more valuable cultural vehicles succeeds in demanding audiences try harder in accepting the narrative's point of view instead of their own predispositions; see Barker (2003).

7   *Post Script* published a special issue on Cronenberg in 1996, only months after it had published one on Canadian cinema, and there were books in Italian, German and French abut his films; see Grunberg (1992); Robnik & Palm (1992); Pecchioli (1994); Canosa (1995); Vernaglione (1995); Yates (1995); Haas (1996).

8   Several jury members abstained in the vote for the award for *Crash*. The Palme d'Or that year went to Mike Leigh's *Secrets and Lies*; see McCarthy & Klady (1996: 14).

9   See, in the order mentioned, McCarthy (1996); Maslin (1996); Romney (1996); Dwyer (1996); Galvin (1996); Mérigeau (1996); Lefort (1996); Queva (1996); Butstraen (1996); Caprara (1996); Gerstel (1996).

10 Much of the controversy has been brilliantly dissected by Martin Barker's research team in a project analysing the reception of *Crash*; see Barker, Arthurs & Harindranath (2001).

11 Further to this, an example of the *Daily Mail*'s campaign is Poulter (1996: 22). Barker *et al.* (2001: 3) provide chilling details of how one specialist examiner, Dr Paul Britton, was vilified – and the moment he changed his position and called for a ban the *Daily Mail* started quoting him as a 'leading scientist'. The *Daily Mail*'s sister publication, the *Evening Standard*, focused on two all-night 'underground' programmes at the Institute for the Contemporary Arts (ICA) which supposedly featured 'sexual practices even more extreme than the controversial movie *Crash*'. According to the paper one of the films was entitled *Flaming Anger* (sic). The report was accompanied in the same edition with a review of *Crash*: the paper later had to admit the writer had not even seen the film but but had read 'most of the script'; see Kermode & Petley (1997: 17).

12 One such example is Leslie Dick's (1997) review of *Crash*, which insisted on its metaphorical meanings; for Dick, the film *only* makes sense as a metaphor. Unfortunately, this review only appeared at the tail end of the campaign.

13 A good example of this is an article in the conservative *Daily Telegraph* (Reynolds 1996). While agreeing that *Crash* is 'disgusting, depraved and debauched', the reviewer states it is not more dangerous than *The English Patient* (Anthony Minghella, 1996) which is equally capable of instigating euthanasia, treachery, adultery, or setting the individual above the greater cause.

14 Further reports appeared in the editions of 22 November and 24 December.

15 The first project, by Mark Kermode and Julian Petley, was initiated through a complaint to the Press Complaints Commission. The second, led by Barker, was funded by the Economic and Social Research Council (ESRC); see Kermode & Petley (1997: 16–18); Barker *et al.* (2001).

1   According to Cronenberg, the 'dampness, peeling wallpaper bubbling with stuff underneath' resemble 'Spider's head'; see Romney (2003: 8–11).

2   Being an active auteur or cultural hero did not give Cronenberg the reputation of a 'safe investment'. Though his movies had always made money, fundraising for *Spider* in particular was so difficult that the crew had to work on a promise of being paid for quite some time, and Cronenberg had to personally get involved in active money-seeking during the shooting. He also forfeited his own salary (worth two years of work); see Abraham (2003: 25).

3   In note 4 of chapter seven I refer to how William Beard identifies Cronenberg's active auteurship as 'Cronenberg the self-conscious artist' (see 2005: 285–7). I think the term I am employing here indicates, more than Beard's, how much I see this self-conscious positioning as not just an accompaniment to the films, but part of the struggle of what they are really about – part of the films' public meaning, part of their existence, even part of the films themselves if one wants to put it as strongly as that. It is a different philosophical perspective.

4   On a theoretical level, Cronenberg's activity, attitude and reputation, and his films of that period fit an approach to storytelling and perception that was quite in vogue in film scholarship at the time; approaches that stress how films are clever and smart, and reliant on detective work by an audience aware of how the world outside the film, including the world of filmmaking, can be inferred within the narrative. The two main perspectives through which this approach was exercised were a school of cognitivist film viewing that links comprehension to puzzle-solving (exemplified by David Bordwell), and a school that studied film genre from a syntactic/semantic approach (exemplified by Rick Altman) that claims that films fit genres not just because they are produced as part of a series, franchise, cycle or recurrent production system, but also because they are *presented and received* as part of a cycle, an oeuvre, a tendency or an era; see Bordwell (1989); Altman (1999).

5   One more example is *I'm Losing You* (Bruce Wagner, 1998). This time Cronenberg is not an actor but the executive producer, most likely in an effort to support this project of old comrades John Dunning and Andre Link (formerly of Cinépix, which had become part of Lionsgate), two producers who had put their faith in him when he tried to get *Shivers* off the ground.

6   McKellar repaid the favour generously by writing a glowing video review of *The Brood*; see McKellar (1999: 58–9).

7   Take the part in *Resurrection* as a final example of just how far this can go. Cronenberg plays the friendly Catholic priest Father Roussell in what is basically a *Frankenstein* story about a serial killer compiling a body from the parts of bodies of others, with the only major difference that the body here is supposed to be Christ and it is supposed to be brought to life at Easter. The theme of *Frankenstein* has always been associated with Cronenberg, ever since the fan press started touting the story that he had been offered the chance to direct his own version of it in the early 1980s. If we exempt the ones Cronenberg adapted for the screen, *Frankenstein* is, in fact, the single most mentioned book/story in the critical reception of Cronenberg since then, appearing in about one out of every ten Cronenberg reviews between the early 1980s and the late 1990s – a favourite reference point for critics, and one that Cronenberg could probably not resist inviting even more associations with.

8   Indeed this was very much the reception the film enjoyed at the annual Film Studies Association of Canada conference in May 2001 (University of Laval, Quebec), where Liz Czach introduced a screening of the film.

9 Pikul asks Allegra: 'How do you know my name?' She replies: 'You're labelled.' To us, too, Pikul comes labelled.

10 In that sense it fulfils largely the same function as Kung-Fu in *The Matrix* (Wachowski Brothers, 1999), a film with which *eXistenZ* was often compared upon its release. In *The Matrix*, Kung-Fu is the skill through which the main characters can rebel against oppression. But it is an individual skill, a talent impossible to transfer onto others almost – which is why the one who excels in it, Neo, is 'The One', the only saviour. Kung-Fu explains the near-religious tone in *The Matrix*, evidenced more clearly in the sequels; see Mathijs (1999).

11 As Cronenberg put it, the interest of *Shift* 'is in media, and the effect of media on culture and all of that'; Cronenberg (1995: n. p.).

12 For news on Cronenberg's decision to attend, or be invited, as the protocol stipulates, see Foreman (1999: 5).

13 For a representative overview, see Freeman (1999); Frodon (1999); Johnston (1999); Lefort (1999); Pede (1999); Stratton (1999).

14 As if to ensure it did not matter much, the conservative press had kept on bashing Cronenberg's films, with Alexander Walker (1999) naming it one of the worst films of the century.

15 The only exceptions to that were some reviews in the left-wing and liberal papers *De Morgen* (Belgium), *Libération*, *Le Matin* and the magazine *Les Inrockuptibles* (France).

16 The quotes are from a selection of reviews; see Blumenfeld (1999); Bradshaw (1999); Carels (1999); Carriere (1999); Christopher (1999); De Bruyn (1999); Hoyle (1999); Tirard (1999); Van De Popeliere (1999); Wignesan (1999).

17 For more on this, see Hoberman (1999); Persall (1999); Rea (1999); Taubin (1999).

18 The total series contains 19 films, one for each play, but only 16 had been shot by the time of the 2000 Toronto festival. Subsequently, all the films were released in a DVD box set *Beckett on Film* (Blue Angel Films, RTE, Channel Four, 2001).

19 At this point, Cronenberg more or less 'shared' the Beckett reference with Atom Egoyan, who had appropriated Beckett in several projects: as the director of *Krapp's Last Tape*, and as the executor of a London project called *Steenbeckett* (in which that film was suspended from a ceiling over a Steenbeck editing machine). Cronenberg later acknowledged *Krapp's Last Tape* as a source of inspiration for *Spider*: 'when you think of *Krapp's Last Tape*, I think of *Spider*. Krapp is living in this vagrant hovel, playing tapes of memories' (in Kaufman 2003: n. p.). See also Dwyer (2000); McCarthy (2000); O'Connell (2002).

20 See, for instance Cendros (2002); Jobin (2002); Temmerman (2002); Tranchant (2002).

21 In this line of argument it would have been particularly fascinating to see Cronenberg's *Painkillers* project come to fruition. It was to be a film about 'performance artists of the future', who would use their bodies as weapons of resistance.

22 Cronenberg goes into detail about his unfinished projects in an interview in the British magazine *Empire*, where he discusses *Red Cars*, *Total Recall*, *Basic Instinct II* and *Painkillers*; see Hughes (2003: 110–11).

CHAPTER TEN

1 As Cronenberg commented: 'the opening scene of the movie ... contaminates, in a sense, all the scenes that follow. That tells you in no uncertain terms to be a little nervous, however nice and stable things seem to be. There are things that are not so nice and not so stable, lurking under the surface' (in O'Hehir 2005).

2　Much can be said about Cronenberg's character names and the actions they imply: In *Scanners*, Darryl Revok revokes; in *Videodrome*, Brian O'Blivion causes oblivion; in *Dead Ringers*, Claire Niveau levels the Mantle twins; and in *eXistenZ*, Gas is a gas attendant.

3　The presence of Christian symbols at key points in *A History of Violence* is remarkable: when Edie confronts Tom she calls to Jesus, and during the sex/rape scene she calls out 'Oh my God'; the final exchange between Tom and Richie is 'Jesus Joey' – 'Jesus Richie' (it is actually the last piece of dialogue in the film); and when Tom cleans himself in the lake after he has killed his brother (an act of absolution if ever there was one) we see a silver cross prominently dangling from a necklace. But that is not what critics, reviewers, journalists and the people involved in the promotion of the film chose to highlight. After all, the redemptive aspect is largely missing from the film's coda. The only critic picking up on it is a staff writer from *Christian Spotlight on the Movies*, and he mentions it because the vain use of the name of the Lord offends him; see Monroe (2005).

4　The quote is from Viggo Mortensen; see www.historyofviolence.com (accessed 10 October 2006).

5　See, for instance, Bruce Kirkland in his short report for the *Toronto Sun*, where he uses references to 'sexual violence', 'glamourised violence', 'extreme violence', 'cinematic violence', 'promotion of violence' and 'responsible violence' to draw distinctions between the kinds of images portrayed on-screen (2005a: 42). The story also ran, in slightly different versions (with the longer ones elaborating on the sex scenes) in the *London Free Press* and the *Edmonton Sun* on the same day. The American press showed no substantial differences; see Hoberman (2005a: 50).

6　See, for instance, the editorials and articles in leading magazines and papers such as *Der Spiegel* (9 May), *Le Figaro* (11 May), *Belfast Telegraph* (11 May), *El Pais* (17 May), *La Tribune* (17 May), *Guardian* (21 May).

7　See, for instance, Ballard (2005); Cameron-Wilson (2005); Fuller (2005); Mestdach (2005); Stockman (2005).

8　See Dargis (2005a); Lee (2005a); Taubin (2005a).

9　Carrie Rickey of *The Philadelphia Inquirer* quotes figures about gun culture to prove how domestic use of lethal violence is embedded in family life in the US: 'Canada has roughly one-tenth the population of the United States (32 million versus 295 million in 2002) and roughly three one-hundredths of its gun deaths (816 to 30,242). To Canadian eyes, Americans are gun-crazy. And when they watch American movies something comes between us that's a lot wider than the 49th parallel' (2005: n. p.)

10　The quotes are from, respectively, Dargis (2005a); Lee (2005b); Alexander (2005); Thomson (2005); Lim (2005); Adams (2005); Granat (2005).

11　See, for instance, Anderson (2005); Kirkland (2005b).

12　Going perhaps furthest in this is Roger Ebert (2007) who, in a syndicated review that was carried by dozens of papers and publications, argued how the violence of the film illustrated Richard Dawkins' theory of 'selfish genes' – the innate impulse as a biological feature of mankind towards survival that happens to affect culture; see Dawkins (1976). It is worth remembering that Dawkins was a student of Tinbergen, whose thoughts on evolution and violence are referred to in chapter two, and whose thoughts influenced Dawkins' theories.

13　In her review for *Film Comment*, Amy Taubin writes of the sex scenes that every time she watches the film, she feels 'the audience change in these scenes, coming together like one mesmerized body' (2005: 26).

14　See the Internet box office reporting service and online journal Box Office Mojo for the exact figures: www.boxofficemojo.com.

15 It was campus- and student-affiliated sites in particular that carried this worry: see, for instance, Watson (2005). This concern was also expressed by some reviewers, especially British ones. See Andrews (2005); Barber (2005); Landesman (2005); McGill (2005).

16 For an elaboration on the 'final moment' concept, see Austin (2002); Barker (2004a); Mathijs (2005; 2006b).

17 See, for instance, Hughes (2003); Anon. (2005); Franklin (2006). In an unsurprising twist, rumours apparently also affected *A History of Violence*'s chances at the Academy Awards. In early 2006 the film received a number of prestigious awards from film critics' circles. But it 'only' collected two Academy Award nominations: for adapted screenplay and supporting actor (William Hurt). The gossip that Cronenberg had reportedly performed real sex acts with his wife in order to stimulate the actors for the sex scenes in *A History of Violence* will surely have handicapped the film's chances as much as its perceived political stance on American culture; see Dargis (2006); Hoberman (2006).

18 In several interviews Cronenberg makes explicit mention of the homoerotic tension between Kirill and Nikolai as an intentional subtext that provides extra layers to the relationship between the family successor and his servant.

19 *The Lord of the Rings* trilogy also explores the theme of family bonds and cultural allegiances; see Mathijs (2006b).

20 I make exception of two instances. The first is in *Videodrome*, about thirty minutes into the film, when Max's increasing sense of intoxication by the torture show 'Videodrome' is highlighted through a few spoken words in an echoed voice-over. The second occurs ninety minutes into *The Dead Zone*, when Johnny's voice-over tells us the content of his farewell letter to Sarah. In both cases, the voice-over only lasts about a minute.

21 Email interview with Tatiana Maslany, 27 November 2007.

22 See the official site for *Eastern Promises*: www.focusfeatures.com/easternpromises/ (accessed 1 December 2007).

23 For an elaboration of the use of tattoos in cult cinema, see Weinstock (2007).

24 See, for example, Anon. (2007b); Hebron (2007).

25 Only few journalists pushed this a bit further, to include the fact that Schreiber had only recently made his directorial debut with *Everything is Illuminated* (2006), a film that explores the issue of Eastern European roots and family background extensively, from the perspective of Schreiber and the novelist Jonathan Safran Foer; see Monk (2007).

26 In an interview with Amy Taubin (2007a) for *Film Comment*, Cronenberg explains the details of the knife fight in *Eastern Promises*, including the nakedness of Mortensen, the shape of the knives and the choreography.

27 See, for instance, Ahearn (2007).

28 See Curtis (2007). The concern is also voiced on the Internet Movie Database (IMDbPro), which carries an article about the BBFC's unwillingness to cut *Eastern Promises*; see Anon. (2007c).

29 See numerous threads at www.rottentomatoes.com (key word: eastern promises) (accessed 14 December 2007).

30 The interview is available as a podcast from http://origin.www.cbc.ca/podcasting/. Many thanks to film librarian Richard Payment of the University of British Columbia's Centre for Cinema Studies for the recording and careful archiving of the interview.

31 The reference is to the successful trilogy of films, starring Matt Damon, adapted from the *Bourne* novels by Robert Ludlum: *The Bourne Identity* (Doug Liman, 2002), *The Bourne Supremacy* (Paul Greengrass, 2004) and *The Bourne Ultimatum* (Paul Greengrass, 2007); see Anon. (2007b).

32. Parts of the Cannes press conference are documented as a special feature of the DVD of *A History of Violence*. The segment is called *Too Commercial for Cannes*.

33 I hasten to add there may be several more synonyms that apply, such as 'withdrawal', 'resistance', 'reservation', 'delay', 'prudence' or 'disinterestedness' – one need not think too far to see how these tools can not only help family life, but might also find use in governance and policy; or sex life. Suiting Cronenberg's adage that sex and violence go together like bacon and eggs, the reluctance to engage in violence parallels a lack of sexual enthusiasm. Nikolai has to be ordered to have sex with a prostitute, and still only reluctantly obliges; and with the Stalls it is Edie who initiates the two sex scenes we are privy to. Instead of solidifying the Stalls' family bond, sex jeopardises it. Sex leads to violence. The anxieties surrounding the sex lives of Nikolai and Tom predate the downfall of the families they are involved with (symbolised by Kirill and Edie respectively) – the sex suggestively pre-empting the violence, opening the door for the violence *against* the family to become violence *in* the family.

34 Cronenberg frequently referred to this 'genetic impulse'; see Graham (2005).

35 In this sense I agree with William Beard (2005: vii) that Cronenberg's films are postmodern: they give a privileged place to cultural systems that exist outside 'normal' culture. But this does not mean the films themselves (the narratives, the themes and the resolutions) are postmodern.

36 The metaphor of sport makes this even clearer. Traditionally, sport in a Cronenberg film equals racing. In *Fast Company*, the near-violent antagonism between adversaries is transferred to the racetrack, where excellence in professionalism (biding one's time, choosing the right moment, following rules) determines the winner. Given the involvement of mechanics in *Fast Company*, that professionalism is often seen as a mastery over technology. But if we strip sport from its technological setting, we see the real issue. *A History of Violence* and *Eastern Promises* are the only Cronenberg films in which any sport besides racing plays a role of any significance, and their brief treatment of these sports helps us comprehend the importance of reluctance in regulating, formalising and containing violence. In *A History of Violence*, the beginning of Jack's confrontation (not its cause I would argue, that lies probably further back) happens when he manages to catch a ball in the outfield during a baseball game in gym, thus eliminating a furious Bobby. While Jack is not portrayed as interested in sport, he nevertheless concentrates when the ball comes towards him so he can make the best possible catch. If he were really terrified of Bobby, Jack would have let the ball hit the ground and allow Bobby his glory. But he knows that the rules of the game allow him to make the catch and hence 'beat' Bobby – fair and square, at the jock's own game and in a way that would make any response from Bobby seem inappropriate. That gives him an advantage, and probably the guts to ridicule Bobby. There is no reason for *A History of Violence* to have a scene with Jack intently catching the ball if it were not to demonstrate how fairly and squarely the reluctant Jack outperforms Bobby and can thus gain the upper hand in any subsequent violent confrontation. Or, as they say: it's the team that scores that wins, not the team that fights. As if to show how blurry the lines between cultural systems are when extending into culture, one of the most chillingly violent scenes in *Eastern Promises* occurs when, after a football game, Ekrem is assaulted and his throat is slit – not by hooligans of the opposing side (who taunt and shout but do not touch him), but by the Chechen mafia. In other words: once outside the heavily codified world of professional sport, and the shady codes of football hooliganism, anything goes and there is no way to predict, comprehend or knowingly avoid the violence that lurks around each corner. At that point, not being restrained and disinterested verges on stupidity. It is, in that respect, fascinating to note how the extra features of *A History of Violence* include a telling reference to Canada's national sport: ice hockey – a sport torn between thuggish brawls and elegant expertise. There is a scene in which much is made of the fact that Viggo Mortensen was a huge fan of the Montreal Canadiens team, and sported their

colours several times during the shoot (according to him to spark some antagonism). At the end of the shoot the largely Toronto crew gave him a present: a shirt of their own favourite team – the Toronto Maple Leafs, arch rivals of the Canadiens.

37 Of course, *At the Suicide of the Last Jew in the World in the Last Cinema in the World* talks about one kind of cinema only: independent cinema, cinema at the margins of multinational corporate control, cinema like that of Cronenberg (let us not forget he produced this short for a festival, not a major distributor).

38 After *At the Suicide of the Last Jew in the World in the Last Cinema in the World* was screened in New York, and the DVD became readily available, more comments were published, especially on the Internet. Cronenberg has offered this on the subject: 'My parents were secular. I was never bar mitzvahed. At a very early age, I decided I was an atheist, and I still am. I don't feel the need to involve myself with the traditions of Judaism. In fact, I'm rather anti-religious … I wasn't hiding my Jewishness. It just never seemed to be an issue. But when I started to make this little short, suddenly, it was. It was provoked by what's going on in the world right now. The pronouncements of various Islamic leaders about how nice it would be to kill all the Jews in the world—you know, like the Hezbollah leader. I thought, "Well, what if that would happen? How would that happen?"' (in Klawans 2008: n. p.). Cronenberg also gives more and longer comments on the matter in Taubin (2007b).

FILMOGRAPHY

Transfer (1966)
Short film, 7 minutes
Direction, production, screenplay,
    cinematography, editing: David Cronenberg
Sound: Margaret Hindson, Stefan Nosko
Cast: Mort Ritts, Rafe Macpherson, Stefan Nosko

From the Drain (1967)
Short film, 14 minutes (Emergent Films)
Direction, screenplay, cinematography, editing:
    David Cronenberg
Production: Stefan Nosko, Mort Ritts
Sound: Margaret Hindson
Cast: Mort Ritts, Stefan Nosko

Stereo (1969)
Feature film, 65 minutes (Emergent Films)
Direction, production, screenplay,
    cinematography, editing: David Cronenberg
Production aids: Stefan Nosko, Pedro
    McCormick, Janet G. M. Good
Cast: Ron Mlodzik, Iain Ewing, Jack Messinger,
    Clara Mayer, Paul Mulholland, Arlene Mlodzik,
    Glenn McCauley

Crimes of the Future (1970)
Feature film, 70 minutes (Emergent Films)
Direction, production, screenplay,
    cinematography, editing: David Cronenberg
Production assistant: Stefan Nosko
Title design: Jon Lidolt
Cast: Ron Mlodzik (Adrian Tripod), John Lidolt,
    Tania Zolty, Jack Messinger, Iain Ewing,
    William Haslam, Rafe Macpherson, Willem
    Poolman, Don Owen, Ray Woodley, Norman
    Snider, Stefen Czernecki, Kaspars Dzeguze,
    Bruce Martin, Brian Linehan, Paul Mulholland,
    Leland Richard, Stephen Zeifman, William
    Wine, Udo Kasumets, Sheldon Cohen, George
    Gibbons, Count Aus Von Blicke

Letter From Michelangelo (1971)
TV filler
Direction, production, screenplay,
    cinematography, editing: David Cronenberg
Cast: Paul Mulholland (voice-over)

Tourettes (1971)
TV filler
Direction, production, screenplay,
    cinematography, editing: David Cronenberg

Jim Ritchie Sculptor (1971)
TV filler
Direction, production, screenplay,
    cinematography, editing: David Cronenberg
Cast: Jim Ritchie (himself)

Winter Garden (1972)
TV filler
Direction, production, screenplay,
    cinematography, editing: David Cronenberg

Fort York (1972)
TV filler
Direction, production, screenplay,
    cinematography, editing: David Cronenberg

Don Valley (1972)
TV filler
Direction, production, screenplay,
    cinematography, editing: David Cronenberg

Lakeshore (1972)
TV filler
Direction, production, screenplay,
    cinematography, editing: David Cronenberg

Scarborough Bluffs (1972)
TV filler
Direction, production, screenplay,
    cinematography, editing: David Cronenberg

In the Dirt (1972)
TV filler
Direction, production, screenplay,
    cinematography, editing: David Cronenberg

Secret Weapons (1972)
TV episode in the series *Programme X*, 30 minutes
    (Canadian Broadcast Corporation, Emergent
    Films)
Direction: David Cronenberg
Screenplay: Norman Snider
Production: Paddy Sampson, George Jonas
Cast: Charles Oberdorf (himself as host),
    Lister Sinclair (voice-over), Barbara O'Kelly
    (motorcycle gang leader), Norman Snider (wise
    man), Vernon Chapman (bureaucrat), Ron
    Mlodzik, Bruce Martin, Tom Skudra, Moses
    Smith, Michael Spencer, G. Chalmers Adams

Shivers (1975)
Feature film, 87 minutes (Cinepix, Canadian Film
    Development Company, DAL Productions)
Direction, screenplay: David Cronenberg
Production: Ivan Reitman, John Dunning, André
    Link, Alfred Pariser, Peter James
Cinematography: Robert Saad
Editing: Patrick Dodd
Art Direction: Erla Gliserman
Sound: Michael Higgs
Music: Ivan Reitman
Special effects and make-up effects: Joe Blasco
Cast: Paul Hampton (Roger St Luc), Joe Silver (Rollo
    Linsky), Lynn Lowry (Nurse Forsythe), Allan
    Migicovsky (Nicholas Tudor), Susan Petrie (Janine
    Tudor), Barbara Steele (Betts), Ron Mlodzik
    (Merrick), Barrie Baldero (Detective Heller),
    Camille Ducharme (Mr Guibault), Hanka
    Posnanka (Mrs Guibault), Vlasta Vrana (Kresimer
    Sviben), Fred Doederlein (Emil Hobbes)

The Victim (1975)
TV episode in the series *Peep Show*, 30 minutes
    (Canadian Broadcast Corporation)
Direction: David Cronenberg
Production: Deborah Peaker, George Bloomfield,
    Gerald Mayer
Screenplay: Ty Haller
Cinematography: Eamonn Beglan, Ron Manson,
    John Halenda, Dave Doherty, Peter Brimson
Editing: Gary Fisher
Art Direction: Niloai Solovyov
Costume Design: Suzanne Mess
Sound: Brian Radford, Bill Dunn
Cast: Janet Wright (Lucy), Jonathan Welsh
    (Donald), Cedric Smith (man in the park)

The Lie Chair (1975)
TV episode in the series *Peep Show*, 30 minutes
    (Canadian Broadcast Corporation)
Direction: David Cronenberg
Production: Eoin Sprott, George Bloomfield,
    Gerald Mayer
Screenplay: David Cole
Cinematography: Eamonn Beglan, George
    Clemens, Tom Farquarson, Peter Brimson
Sound: Roland Huebsche, Bill Dunn
Sets: Rudi Dorn
Cast: Richard Monette (Neil), Susan Hogan
    (Carol), Amelia Hall (Mildred), Doris Petrie
    (Mrs Rogers)

The Italian Machine (1976)
TV episode in the series *Teleplay*, 30 minutes
(Canadian Broadcast Corporation)
Direction, screenplay: David Cronenberg
Production: Stephen Patrick
Cinematography: Nicholas Evdemon
Editing: David Denovan
Sound: Tom Bilenkey
Art Direction: Peter Douet
Costume Design: Hilary Corbett
Music: Patrick Russell
Cast: Gary McKeehan (Lionel), Frank Moore
(Fred), Hardee Lineham (Bug), Chuck Shamata
(Reinhardt), Louis Negin (Mouette), Toby
Tarnow (Lana), Géza Kovács (Ricardo), Cedric
Smith (Luke)

Rabid (1977)
Feature film, 91 minutes (Cinepix, Canadian Film
Development Company, DAL Productions)
Direction, screenplay: David Cronenberg
Production: Ivan Reitman, John Dunning, André
Link, Danny Goldberg, Don Carmody
Cinematography: René Verzier
Editing: Jean Lafleur
Art Direction: Claude Marchand
Costume Design: Erla Gliserman
Sound: Richard Lightstone, Danny Goldberg
Music: Ivan Reitman
Special effects and make-up effects: Joe Blasco, Joe
Elsner, Al Griswold
Casting: Sharon Wall
Cast: Marilyn Chambers (Rose), Frank Moore
(Hart Read), Joe Silver (Murray Cypher),
Howard Ryshpan (Dan Keloid), Patricia Gage
(Roxanne Keloid), Susan Roman (Mindy
Kent), Roger Periard (Lloyd Walsh), Lynne
Deragon (Nurse Louise), Terry Schonblum
(Judy Glasberg), Victor Désy (Claude
LaPointe), Julie Anna (Nurse Rita), Gary
McKeehan (Smooth Eddy), Terence Ross
(farmer), Miguel Fernandes (man in cinema),
Vlasta Vrana (cop at clinic), Jack Messinger
(policeman on highway), Robert Silverman
(man in hospital), Ron Mlodzik (male patient),
Louis Negin (Maxim), Richard W. Farrell
(camper man), Peter MacNeill (loader)

Fast Company (1979)
Feature film, 91 minutes (Michael Lebowitz Inc.,
Canadian Film Development Corporation,
Quadrant Films)
Direction: David Cronenberg
Production: Michael Lebowitz, Peter O'Brian,
Courtney Smith
Screenplay: Phil Savath, Courtney Smith, David
Cronenberg (story: Alan Treen)
Cinematography: Mark Irwin
Editing: Ronald Sanders
Art Direction: Carol Spier
Costume: Delphine White
Sound: Bryan Day
Music: Fred Mollin
Special Effects: Tom Fisher
Casting: Gail Carr
Cast: William Smith (Lonnie Johnson),
Claudia Jennings (Sammy), John Saxon (Phil
Adamson), Nicholas Campbell (Billy 'the
Kid' Brocker), Cedric Smith (Gary Black),
Judy Foster (Candy), George Buza (Meatball),
Robert Haley (P. J.), David Graham (Stoner),
David Petersen (Slezak)

The Brood (1979)
Feature film, 92 minutes (Victor Solnicki
Productions, Elgin International Films,
Canadian Film Development Corporation,
Mutual Productions)
Direction, screenplay: David Cronenberg
Production: Claude Heroux, Pierre David, Victor
Solnicki
Cinematography: Mark Irwin
Editing: Alan Collins
Art Direction: Carol Spier
Costume Design: Delphine White
Sound: Bryan Day
Music: Howard Shore
Special Effects: Alan Kotter, Dennis Pike
Cast: Oliver Reed (Hal Raglan), Samantha Eggar
(Nola Carveth), Art Hindle (Frank Carveth),
Cindy Hinds (Candice Carveth), Henry
Beckman (Barton Kelly), Nuala Fitzgerald
(Juliana Kelly), Susan Hogan (Ruth Mayer),
Michael Magee (inspector), Joseph Shaw
(coroner), Gary McKeehan (Mike Trellan),
Nicholas Campbell (Chris), Robert Silverman
(Jan Hartog), Reiner Schwartz (Doctor Birkin)

Scanners (1981)
Feature film, 103 minutes (Victor Solnicki
    Productions, Filmplan, Canadian Film
    Development Corporation)
Direction, screenplay: David Cronenberg
Production: Claude Heroux, Pierre David, Victor
    Solnicki
Cinematography: Mark Irwin
Editing: Ronald Sanders
Art Direction: Carol Spier
Costume Design: Delphine White
Sound: Don Cohen
Music: Howard Shore
Special Effects: Chris Walas, Gary Zeller, Stephan
    Dupuis, Tom Schwartz, Dick Smith, Dennis
    Pike
Cast: Jennifer O'Neill (Kim Obrist), Stephen
    Lack (Cameron Vale), Patrick McGoohan
    (Doctor Paul Ruth), Lawrence Z. Dane
    (Braedon Keller), Michael Ironside (Darryl
    Revok), Robert Silverman (Benjamin Pierce),
    Adam Ludwig (Arno Crostic), Mavor Moore
    (Trevellyan), Fred Doederlein (Dieter Tautz),
    Sony Forbes (killer in attic), Géza Kovács
    (killer in record store), Victor Désy (Doctor
    Gatineau), Louis Del Grande (first scanner),
    Jack Messinger (scanner at door), Murray
    Cruchley (programmer 1)

Videodrome (1983)
Feature film, 87 minutes (Victor Solnicki
    Productions, Filmplan, Canadian Film
    Development Corporation)
Direction, screenplay: David Cronenberg
Production: Claude Heroux, Pierre David, Victor
    Solnicki, Lawrence Nesis
Cinematography: Mark Irwin
Editing: Ronald Sanders
Art Direction: Carol Spier
Costume Design: Delphine White
Sound: Bryan Day
Music: Howard Shore
Special Effects: Rick Baker, Mark Shostrom,
    Michael Lennick
Cast: James Woods (Max Renn), Deborah Harry
    (Nicki Brand), Sonja Smits (Bianca O'Blivion),
    Peter Dvorsky (Harlan), Les Carlson (Barry
    Convex), Jack Creley (Brian O'Blivion), Lynne
    Gorman (Masha), Julie Khaner (Bridey), Reiner
    Schwartz (Moses), David Bolt (Raphael), Lally
    Cadeau (Rena King)

The Dead Zone (1983)
Feature film, 103 minutes (Dino De Laurentiis
    Company, Lorimar Film Entertainment)
Direction: David Cronenberg
Production: Debra Hill, Dino De Laurentiis,
    Jeffrey Chernov
Screenplay: Jeffrey Boam (novel: Stephen King)
Cinematography: Mark Irwin
Editing: Ronald Sanders
Production Design: Carol Spier
Costume Design: Olga Dimitrov, Denise
    Cronenberg
Sound: Bryan Day
Music: Michael Kamen
Special Effects: John Belyeu, Michael Lennick
Casting: Deirdre Bowen
Cast: Christopher Walken (Johnny Smith),
    Brooke Adams (Sarah Bracknell), Martin Sheen
    (Greg Stillson), Herbert Lom (Doctor Sam
    Weizak), Tom Skerritt (Sheriff Bannerman),
    Anthony Zerbe (Roger Stuart), Nicholas
    Campbell (Frank Dodd), Colleen Dewhurst
    (Henrietta Dodd), Sean Sullivan (Herb
    Smith), Jackie Burroughs (Vera Smith), Géza
    Kovács (Sonny Elliman), Roberta Weiss (Alma
    Frechette), Peter Dvorsky (Dardis), Simon
    Craig (Chris Stuart), Julie-Ann Heathwood
    (Amy), Barry Flatman (Walt), Jack Messinger
    (therapist), Cindy Hinds (Natalie), Les Carlson
    (Brenner), Hardee Lineham (deputy), William
    B. Davis (ambulance driver)

The Fly (1986)
Feature film, 95 minutes (Brooksfilms)
Direction: David Cronenberg
Production: Stuart Cornfeld, Marc Boyman, Kip
    Ohman
Screenplay: Charles Edward Pogue, David
    Cronenberg (short story: George Langelaan;
    original screenplay: James Clavell)
Cinematography: Mark Irwin
Editing: Ronald Sanders
Production Design: Carol Spier
Costume Design: Denise Cronenberg
Sound: Bryan Day, Wayne Griffin, David Evans
Music: Howard Shore
Special Effects: Chris Walas, Hoyt Yeatman,
    Lee Wilson, Jim Isaac (consultant: Michael
    Lennick)
Casting: Deirdre Bowen
Cast: Jeff Goldblum (Seth Brundle), Geena Davis
    (Veronica Quaife), John Getz (Stathis Borans),

Joy Boushel (Tawny), Les Carlson (Doctor Brent Cheevers), George Chuvalo (Marky), Michael Coperman (2nd man in bar), David Cronenberg (gynaecologist), Carol Lazare (nurse), Shawn Hewitt (clerk)

Faith Healer (1988)
TV episode in the series *Friday the 13th*, 26 minutes (Hometown Films, Paramount Television)
Direction: David Cronenberg
Production: Frank Mancuso, J. Miles Dale, Iain Paterson, Ronald Sanders
Screenplay: Christine Cornish
Cinematography: Rodney Charters
Editing: Gary L. Smith
Production Design: Stephen Roloff
Sound: Nolan Roberts
Music: Fred Mollin
Special Effects: Randy Daudlin, Megan Hope-Ross
Casting: Pamela Basker, Deirdre Bowen
Cast: John D. LeMay (Ryan Dallion), Louise Robey (Micki Foster), Chris Wiggins (Jack Marshak), Miguel Fernandes (Stewart Fishoff), Robert Silverman (Jerry Scott), John Bethune (man in wheelchair), Lynne Gorman (Sylvia), Robert King (faith healer)

Dead Ringers (1988)
Feature film, 115 minutes (Mantle Clinic II, Morgan Creek Productions, Telefilm Canada)
Direction: David Cronenberg
Production: Carol Baum, John Board, Marc Boyman, David Cronenberg, Sylvio Tabet, James G. Robinson, Joe Roth
Screenplay: Norman Snider, David Cronenberg (book: Bari Wood and Jack Geasland)
Cinematography: Peter Suschitzky
Editing: Ronald Sanders
Production Design: Carol Spier
Costume Design: Denise Cronenberg
Sound: Bryan Day, Wayne Griffin, John Laing, David Evans
Music: Howard Shore
Special Effects: Lee Wilson
Casting: Deirdre Bowen
Cast: Jeremy Irons (Beverly Mantle, Elliot Mantle), Geneviève (Claire Niveau), Heidi Von Palleske (Cary), Barbara Gordon (Danuta), Shirley Douglas (Laura), Stephen Lack (Anders

Wolleck), Nick Nichols (Leo), Lynn Cormack (Arlene), Damir Andrei (Birchall), Miriam Newhouse (Mrs Bookman), Richard W. Farrell (Dean of Medicine), Jill Hennessy (Mimsy), Murray Cruchley (assisting surgeon), David Cronenberg (obstetrician)

Hot Showers (1989)
Commercial advertisement, 30 seconds
Direction: David Cronenberg
Client: Ontario Hydro, for the energy conservation campaign
Agency: Burghardt Wolowich Crunkhorn
Production Company: The Partners' Film Company

Laundry (1989)
Commercial advertisement, 30 seconds
Direction: David Cronenberg
Client: Ontario Hydro, for the energy conservation campaign
Agency: Burghardt Wolowich Crunkhorn
Production Company: The Partners' Film Company

Cleaners (1989)
Commercial advertisement, 30 seconds
Direction: David Cronenberg
Client: Ontario Hydro, for the energy conservation campaign
Agency: Burghardt Wolowich Crunkhorn
Production Company: The Partners' Film Company

Timers (1989)
Commercial advertisement, 30 seconds
Direction: David Cronenberg
Client: Ontario Hydro, for the energy conservation campaign
Agency: Burghardt Wolowich Crunkhorn
Production Company: The Partners' Film Company

Bistro (1990)
Commercial advertisement, 30 seconds
Direction: David Cronenberg
Client: William Neilson Ltd, Cadbury, for their product Caramilk
Agency: Scali McCabe Sloves
Production Company: The Partners' Film Company

Surveillance (1990)
Commercial advertisement, 30 seconds
Direction: David Cronenberg
Client: William Neilson Ltd, Cadbury, for their
  product Caramilk
Agency: Scali McCabe Sloves
Production Company: The Partners' Film Company

Transformation (1990)
Commercial advertisement, 30 seconds
Direction: David Cronenberg
Client: Nike International
Agency: Wieden and Kennedy
Production Company: The Partners' Film Company

Regina versus Horvath (1990)
TV episode in the series *Scales of Justice*, 48
  minutes (Canadian Broadcasting Corporation)
Direction: David Cronenberg
Production: Carol Reynolds, George Jonas
Screenplay: Maichael Tait, George Jonas
Cinematography: Rodney Charters
Editing: Ronald Sanders
Production Design: Carol Spier
Sound: Bryan Day
Music: Howard Shore
Cast: Justin Louis (John Horvath), Les Carlson
  (Larry Proke), Len Doncheff (John Molnar),
  Kurt Reis (Mr Justice Gould), Michael Caruana
  (Mr R. D. Schantz)

Regina versus Logan (1990)
TV episode in the series *Scales of Justice*, 48
  minutes (Canadian Broadcasting Corporation)
Direction: David Cronenberg
Production: Carol Reynolds, George Jonas
Screenplay: Maichael Tait, George Jonas
Cinematography: Rodney Charters
Editing: Ronald Sanders
Production Design: Carol Spier
Sound: Bryan Day
Music: Howard Shore
Cast: Barbara Turnbull (herself), Richard
  Yearwood (Cliff), Desmond Campbell (Hugh),
  Mark Ferguson (Warren)

Naked Lunch (1991)
Feature film, 115 minutes (Film Trustees,
  Nippon Film Development, Recorded Picture
  Company, Ontario Film Development
  Corporation, Telefilm Canada)
Direction: David Cronenberg
Production: Jeremy Thomas, Gabriella Martinelli
Screenplay: David Cronenberg (novel: William
  Burroughs)
Cinematography: Peter Suschitzky
Editing: Ronald Sanders
Production Design: Carol Spier
Costume Design: Denise Cronenberg
Sound: Bryan Day, Wayne Griffin, David Evans
Music: Howard Shore, Ornette Coleman
Special Effects: Chris Walas, Jim Isaac
Casting: Deirdre Bowen
Cast: Peter Weller (Bill Lee), Judy Davis (Joan
  Lee, Joan Frost), Roy Scheider (Doctor
  Benway), Ian Holm (Tom Frost), Julian Sands
  (Yves Cloquet), Michael Zelniker (Martin),
  Nicholas Campbell (Hank), Monique Mercure
  (Fadela), Joseph Scorsiani (Kiki), Robert
  Silverman (Hans), Yuval Daniel (Hafid),
  John Friesen (Hauser), Michael Caruana
  (pawnbroker)

M. Butterfly (1993)
Feature film, 101 minutes (Geffen Pictures,
  Miranda Productions)
Direction: David Cronenberg
Production: David Henry Hwang, Gabriela
  Martinelli, Philip Sandhaus
Screenplay: David Henry Hwang (play: David
  Henry Hwang)
Cinematography: Peter Suschitzky
Editing: Ronald Sanders
Production Design: Carol Spier
Costume Design: Denise Cronenberg
Sound: Bryan Day, Wayne Griffin, John Laing,
  David Evans
Music: Howard Shore
Special Effects: Georges Demétrau
Casting: Deirdre Bowen
Cast: Jeremy Irons (René Gallimard), John
  Lone (Song Liling), Barbara Sukowa (Jeanne
  Gallimard), Ian Richardson (Ambassador
  Toulon), Annabelle Leventon (Frau Baden),
  Shizuko Hoshi (Comrade Chin), Richard
  McMillan (embassy colleague), Vernon
  Dobtcheff (Agent Etancelin), David Hemblen
  (intelligence officer), Damir Andrei (intelligence
  officer), Tristam Jellinek (defence attorney),
  Philip McGough (prosecution attorney), David
  Neal (judge), George Jonas (mall trustee),
  Michael Mehlmann (drunk in Paris bar)

Crash (1996)
Feature film, 100 minutes (Alliance Atlantis Communications, The Movie Network, Recorded Picture Company, Telefilm Canada)
Direction: David Cronenberg
Production: Jeremy Thomas, David Cronenberg, Andras Hamori, Chris Auty, Robert Lantos, Stephane Reichel, Marilyn Stonehouse
Screenplay: David Cronenberg (novel: J. G. Ballard)
Cinematography: Peter Suschitzky
Editing: Ronald Sanders
Production Design: Carol Spier
Costume Design: Denise Cronenberg
Sound: David Lee, Wayne Griffin, John Laing, David Evans
Music: Howard Shore
Special Effects: Stephan Dupuis
Casting: Deirdre Bowen
Cast: James Spader (James Ballard), Holly Hunter (Helen Remington), Elias Koteas (Vaughan), Deborah Unger (Catherine Ballard), Rosanna Arquette (Gabrielle), Peter MacNeill (Colin Seagrave), Yolande Julian (airport hooker), Cheryl Swarts (Vera Seagrave), Judah Katz (salesman), Nicky Guadagni (tattooist), Alice Poon (camera girl), Markus Parilo (man in hangar)

eXistenZ (1999)
Feature film, 97 minutes (Alliance Atlantis Communications, Canadian Television Fund, Harold Greenberg Fund, The Movie Network, Natural Nylon Entertainment, Serendipity Point Films, Union General Cinematographique, Telefilm Canada)
Direction, screenplay: David Cronenberg
Production: David Cronenberg, Andras Hamori, Robert Lantos, Sandra Tucker, Michael MacDonald, Damon Bryant, Bradley Adams
Cinematography: Peter Suschitzky
Editing: Ronald Sanders
Production Design: Carol Spier
Costume Design: Denise Cronenberg
Sound: Glen Gauthier, Wayne Griffin, John Laing, David Evans
Music: Howard Shore
Special Effects: Jim Isaac, Stephan Dupuis
Casting: Deirdre Bowen
Cast: Jennifer Jason Leigh (Allegra Geller), Jude Law (Ted Pikul), Ian Holm (Kiri Vinokur),

Don McKellar (Yevgeni Nourish), Willem Dafoe (Gas), Callum Keith Rennie (Hugo Carlaw), Christopher Eccleston (seminar leader), Sarah Polley (Merle), Robert Silverman (D'Arcy Nader), Oscar Hsu (Chinese waiter), Kris Lemche (Noel Dichter)

Camera (2000)
Short film, 6 minutes (part of the series *Preludes* for the Toronto International Film Festival, 25th anniversary)
Direction, screenplay: David Cronenberg
Production: Niv Fichman, Jody Shapiro, Jennifer Weiss
Cinematography: Andre Pienaar
Editing: Ronald Sanders
Production Design: Carol Spier
Costume Design: Denise Cronenberg
Sound: John Laing, David Evans
Music: Howard Shore
Cast: Les Carlson (the actor), Marc Donato (lead), Harrison Kane (lead), Kyle Kass (lead), Natasha La Force, Katie Lai, Daniel Magder (director), Chloe Randle-Reis, Stephanie Sams, Camille Schniffer (lead).

Spider (2002)
Feature film, 98 minutes (Capitol Films, Artists Independent Productions, Odeon Films, Media Suits, Catherine Bailey Ltd, Grosvenor Park Productions, David Films, Metropolitan Films, Red Pictures, Telefilm Canada)
Direction: David Cronenberg
Production: David Cronenberg, Maria Aitken, Catherine Bailey, Sanjay Burman, Sara Giles, Samuel Hadida
Screenplay: Patrick McGrath (novel: Patrick McGrath)
Cinematography: Peter Suschitzky
Editing: Ronald Sanders
Production Design: Carol Spier
Costume Design: Denise Cronenberg
Sound: John Midgley, Glen Gauthier, David Evans, Wayne Griffin
Music: Howard Shore
Special Effects: Stephan Dupuis, Alan Senior
Casting: Suzanne Smith, Deirdre Bowen
Cast: Ralph Fiennes (Spider, Dennis Cleg), Miranda Richardson (Yvonne, Mrs Cleg) , Gabriel Byrne (Bill Cleg), Lynn Redgrave (Mrs Wilkinson), John Neville (Terrence),

Bradley Hall (Spider, Dennis Cleg as a child), Gary Reineke (Freddy), Philip Craig (John), Cliff Saunders (Bob), Tara Ellis (Nora), Sara Stockbridge (Gladys)

A History of Violence (2005)
Feature film, 96 minutes (New Line Productions, BenderSpink, Media I Filmproduktion Munchen and Company)
Direction: David Cronenberg
Production: Chris Bender, J. C. Spink, Jake Weiner, Roger Kass, Toby Emmerich
Screenplay: Josh Olson (graphic novel: John Wagner and Vince Locke)
Cinematography: Peter Suschitzky
Editing: Ronald Sanders
Production Design: Carol Spier
Costume Design: Denise Cronenberg
Sound: Glen Gauthier, Wayne Griffin
Music: Howard Shore
Special Effects: Stephan Dupuis, Neil Trifunovich, Dennis Berardi
Casting: Deirdre Bowen
Cast: Viggo Mortensen (Tom Stall, Joey Cusack), Maria Bello (Edie Stall), Ed Harris (Carl Fogarty), William Hurt (Richie Cusack), Ashton Holmes (Jack Stall), Heidi Hayes (Sarah Stall), Peter MacNeill (Sheriff Sam Carney), Stephen McHattie (Leland), Greg Bryk (Billy), Kyle Schmid (Bobby), Sumela Kay (Judy Danvers), Gerry Quigley (Mick), Deborah Drakeford (Charlotte), Aidan Devine (Charlie Roarke), April Mullen (kid in diner)

At the Suicide of the Last Jew in the World in the Last Cinema in the World (2007)
Short film, 4 minutes (Cannes Film Festival 60th anniversary)
Direction, screenplay: David Cronenberg
Collaborators: Brandon Cronenberg, Carolyn Zeifman, John Bannister
Music: Howard Shore
Casting: Deirdre Bowen
Cast: David Cronenberg (Last Jew), Jesse Collins (Rob), Gina Clayton (Sherry)

Eastern Promises (2007)
Feature film, 100 minutes (Serendipity Point Films, Astral Media, BBC Films, Corus Entertainment, Focus Features, Kudos Film and Television, Scion Films, Telefilm Canada)
Direction: David Cronenberg
Production: Paul Webster, Robert Lantos, Tracy Seaward, David M. Thompson, Stephen Garrett, Julia Blackman, Jeff Abberley
Screenplay: Steve Knight
Cinematography: Peter Suschitzky
Editing: Ronald Sanders
Production Design: Carol Spier
Costume Design: Denise Cronenberg
Sound: Wayne Griffin, Michael O'Farrell, Stuart Wilson
Music: Howard Shore
Special Effects: Manex Efrem, Stephan Dupuis
Casting: Deirdre Bowen, Nina Gold
Cast: Viggo Mortensen (Nikolai Luzhin), Naomi Watts (Anna Khitrova), Vincent Cassel (Kirill), Armin Mueller-Stahl (Semyon), Mina E. Mina (Azim), Sinéad Cusack (Helen), Jerzy Skolimowski (Stepan), Sarah-Jeanne Labrosse (Tatiana), Aleksander Mikic (Soyka), Josef Altin (Ekrem), Rhodri Wyn Miles (senior officer), Raza Jaffrey (Doctor Aziz), Dona Croll (nurse), Badi Uzzaman (chemist), Latita Ahmed (customer), Tatiana Maslany (Tatiana's voice)

BIBLIOGRAPHY

Abraham, Brad (2003) 'The Amazing Spider Men', *Dreamwatch*, 101, February, 25.

Adams, Sam (2005) 'Way to Big-City Bloodbath in *A History of Violence*', *Philadelphia City Paper*, 29 September.

Adilman, Sid (1979) '*Fast Company*', *Variety*, 295, 23 May, 24.

Ahearn, Victoria (2007) 'Cronenberg likens *Eastern Promises* bathhouse scene to *Psycho* shower scene', *Maclean's*, 7 September, available online at: http://www.macleans.ca/article.jsp?content=e090759A (accessed 27 November 2007).

Albertazzi, Silvia (1995) 'Letteratura e cinema: David Cronenberg dagli incubi del gotico inglese ai disagi dell'eta postcoloniale', *Problemi: Periodico Quadrimestrale di Cultura*, 103, 234–41.

Alexander, Al (2005) '*History* a Riveting Look at America and Murder', *Patriot Ledger*, 23 September, 13.

Alioff, Maurie (2005) 'Double Identity: David Cronenberg's *A History of Violence*', *Take One*, 14, 51, 8.

Allemang, John (1989) 'Violence and Anger', *Globe and Mail*, 9 December.

Allinson, Ashley (2002) 'David Cronenberg', *Senses of Cinema*, http://www.sensesofcinema.com/contents/directors/02/cronenberg.html (accessed 2 September 2007).

Altman, Rick (1999) *Film/Genre*. London: British Film Institute.

Alvarez, Marisol (2000) 'Flesh that Matters: David Cronenberg's *Crash*', *European Journal for Semiotic Studies*, 12, 4, 617–30.

Amis, Martin (1996) 'Cronenberg's Monster', *Independent on Sunday*, 10 November, 8–21.

Anderson, Jason (2005) 'A Comedy of Terrors', *Eye*, 22 September, 15.

Andrews, Nigel (1980) 'Black Comedy', *Financial Times*, 7 March.

____ (1981) 'It's an ill wind', *Financial Times*, 24 April.

____ (1983) 'Eaten by the video nasties', *Financial Times*, 25 November, 17.

____ (1997) 'Watch out, here comes *Crash*', *Financial Times*, 29 May.

____ (2005) 'The Lure of Innocence is a Wicked Tease', *Financial Times*, 29 September, 15.

Anon. (1963) 'Bitter Ash to Challenge the Censors', *Ubyssey*, 15, 16 October, 1.

____ (1970) 'Film Making in Canada', *Film*, 58, 27–28.

____ (1979a) 'Filmplan unveils three new films', *Globe and Mail*, 7 August.

____ (1979b) 'David Cronenberg's films may not make the critics happy but they sure do please his backers', *Financial Post*, 13 October, 85–8.

____ (1979c) 'You Can't Join, You're a Star', *Globe and Mail*, 20 October.

____ (1981a) 'Studio Announces New Courses', *Globe and Mail*, 23 February.

___ (1981b) 'Scanners', Copie Zéro, 10, 40.

___ (1983a), 'Censor Defends Ban on Uncut Horror Flick', Globe and Mail, 14 September.

___ (1983b), 'Minneapolis Asked to Attack Pornography as Rights Issue', New York Times, 18 December, 1, 44.

___ (1984a) 'Stereo', Variety, 22 August, 17.

___ (1984b) 'Cronenberg Visits Rome', Cinema Canada, 107, 3–4.

___ (1989) 'Chromosome 3 (TV)', La Dernière Heure, 1 September.

___ (1990) 'Getting in on the Joke', Toronto Star, 1 April, V20.

___ (1992) 'Chromosome 3', Vers l'Avenir, 20 April.

___ (1996) 'Ban This Car Crash Sex Film', Daily Mail, 9 November, 1.

___ (1999a) 'Rushdie Inspires Cult Sci-Fi Thriller', Canberra Times, 20 February, A19.

___ (1999b) 'Rushdie Inspires Sci-Fi', Independent, 21 February, 2.

___ (1999c) 'Two Canadian Films vie for Berlin Bear', Toronto Star, 21 February.

___ (2002) 'Denial Comes First, Detail Comes Last at Press Scrums', Toronto Star, 22 May, D05.

___ (2005a) 'Cronenberg takes on Painkillers', Hollywood Reporter, 16 May.

___ (2005b) 'Viggo Mortensen Brings Violent Film To Cannes', AP Press Release, 16 May, available online at: http://msnbc.msn.com/id/7876543/ (accessed 8 October 2006).

___ (2005c) 'Cronenberg's Film Full Of Violence, Sex', AP Press Release, 16 May, available online at http://movies.yahoo.com/mv/cannes/news/apc/20050516 (accessed 8 October 2006).

___ (2007a) 'Spanish Fest to Offer Worldly Fare', Vancouver Sun, 25 August, F11.

___ (2007b) 'Cronenberg Describes His Latest Film as a Homoerotic Thriller About the Mob', CBC Arts, 7 September, available online at: http://www.cbc.ca/arts/tiff/story/2007/09/07/cronenberg-promises-erotic.html#skip300x250 (accessed 2 December 2007).

___ (2007c) 'Censors Slammed for Release of Eastern Promises', IMDbPro, 22 October, available online at: http://pro.imdb.com/news/wenn/2007-10-22/celeb/7 (accessed 30 December 2007).

___ (2007d) 'Canadian film auteur Cronenberg to pen first novel', CBC Arts, 27 November, available online at: http://www.cbc.ca/arts/film/story/2007/11/27/cronenberg-book.html (accessed 3 December 2007).

___ (2007e) 'The Brood', Terror Trap, available online at: http://www.terrortrap.com/thebrood/ (accessed 20 July 2007).

___ (2008a) 'The Buzz on The Fly', Star, 7 July, available online at: http://www.thestar.com/entertainment/article/455484 (accessed 24 July 2008).

___ (2008b) 'French Critics, even Snootier than Expected, Pan Cronenberg Opera', New York Magazine, 7 July, available online at: http://nymag.com/daily/entertainment/2008/07/ (accessed 24 July 2008).

Ansen, David (1983) 'TV or Not to Be', Newsweek, 14 February, 85, 87.

Ardrey, Robert (1967) The Territorial Imperative: A Personal Inquiry into the Animal Origins of Property and Nations. New York: Dell Publishing.

___ (1970) The Social Contract: A Personal Inquiry into the Evolutionary Sources of Order and Disorder. New York: Dell Publishing.

Arnold, Gary (1969) 'Science Fiction Review', Washington Post, 30 July, B8.

___ (1981a) 'Film Notes', Washington Post, 1 January 1981, B9.

___ (1981b) 'The Powers That See', Washington Post, 14 January, B1.

___ (1983) 'The Jumbled Signal of Videodrome', Washington Post, 9 February, F11.

Arnopp, Jason (2004) 'Ouch, that'll smart in the Morning: Horrible Film Deaths', SFX Horror Special Collector's Edition, 48–51.

Austin, Thomas (2002) Hollywood, Hype and Audiences. Manchester: Manchester University Press.

Auty, Chris and Steve Woolley (1981) 'A Terror so Complete That It's Almost a Kind of Peace', Time Out, 1 May.

Ayscough, Susan (1983) 'Sex, Porn, Censorship, Art, Politics and other Terms; Interview with David Cronenberg', Cinema Canada, 102, 15–18.

Badley, Linda (1995) Film, Horror, and the Body Fantastic. Westport: Greenwood Press.

Ballard, J. G. (1995) Crash. London: Vintage.

___ (1997) 'Set for Collision', Index on Censorship, 3, 97.

___ (2005) 'The Killer Inside', Guardian, 23 September, 5.

Banes, Sally (1998) Subversive Expectations. Ann Arbor: University of Michigan Press.

Barber, Nicholas (2005) 'Waiter, There's a Bullet in my Soup', Independent on Sunday, 2 October, 8.

Barker, Clive (1987) 'The Fly', American Film, 12, 10, 65.

Barker, Martin (1984) The Video Nasties: Freedom and Censorship in the Media. London: Pluto Press.

___ (2003) 'Crash: Theatre Audiences and the Idea of Liveness', Studies in Theatre and Performance, 23, 1, 21–39.

_____ (2004a) 'News, Reviews, Clues, Interviews, and other Ancillary Materials: A Critique and Research Proposal', *Scope, Online Journal of Film Studies* (February), available at: http://www.nottingham.ac.uk/film/journal/ (accessed 22 November 2007).

_____ (2004b) 'Violence Redux', in Steven Jay Schneider (ed) *New Hollywood Violence.* Manchester: Manchester University Press, 57–79.

Barker, Martin, Jane Arthurs and Ramaswami Harindranath (2001) *The Crash Controversy: Censorship Campaigns and Film Reception.* London: Wallflower Press.

Barratt, A. J. (1997) 'The Effects Debate 2: Letter', *Sight and Sound*, 7, 2, 71.

Bastian, Günther (1981) *'Scanners – Ihre Gedänken können töten'*, *Filmdienst*, 34, 6, 24 March, 19 (file 22852).

Beard, William (1979) *'Fast Company'*, *Cinema Canada*, 58, 32–3.

_____ (1983) 'The Visceral Mind: The Major Films of David Cronenberg', in Piers Handling (ed.) *The Shape of Rage: The Films of David Cronenberg.* Toronto: General Publishing, 1–79.

_____ (1993) 'An Anatomy of Melancholy: Cronenberg's *Dead Zone, Journal of Canadian Studies*, 27, 4, Winter, 169–78.

_____ (1994a) 'The Canadianess of David Cronenberg', *Mosaic*, 27, 2, June, 113–33.

_____ (1994b) 'Cronenberg, Flyness and the Other-self', *Cinémas*, 4, 2, Winter, 153–73. .

_____ (1995) 'Book Review: Peter Morris' "Cronenberg"', *Canadian Journal of Film Studies*, 4, 1, 81–5.

_____ (1996a) 'Lost and Gone Forever: Cronenberg's *Dead Ringers'*, *Post Script*, 15, 2, 11–28.

_____ (1996b) 'Insect Poetics: Cronenberg's Naked Lunch', *Canadian Review of Comparative Literature*, 23, 3, 823–52.

_____ (2005) *The Artist as Monster: The Cinema of David Cronenberg.* Toronto: University of Toronto Press.

Beard, William and Piers Handling (1983) 'Interview with David Cronenberg', in Piers Handling (ed.) *The Shape of Rage: The Films of David Cronenberg.* Toronto: General Publishing, 159–98.

Beard, William, Piers Handling and Pierre Véronneau (1990) 'Interview avec David Cronenberg', in Piers Handling and Pierre Véronneau (eds) *L' horreur intérieure: les films de David Cronenberg.* Parijs-Montréal: Editions du Cerf-La cinémathèque Québécoise, 11–55.

Beaufays, Yves (1981) *'Scanners'*, *Grand Angle*, 46, July, 58.

Beerekamp, Hans (1981) 'Bloed en vuur: *Scanners'*, *NRC Handelsblad*, 4 September.

Béhar, Henri (1992) 'Au début était le livre', *Le Monde*, 14 March.

_____ (1993) 'Le parfait mensonge', *Le Monde*, 12 September.

Beker, Marylin (1989) 'David Cronenberg', *Expression*, March–April, 148–56.

Benjamin, Walter (1969) 'The Work of Art in the Age of Mechanical Reproduction', in *Illuminations.* London: Fontana, 217–251.

Benshoff, Harry (1997) *Monsters in the Closet: Homosexuality and the Horror Film.* Manchester: Manchester University Press.

Bergstrom, Janet, Elizabeth Lyon and Constance Penley (1986) 'Science Fiction and Sexual Difference: Editorial', *Camera Obscura*, 15, 4–5.

Berressem, Hanjo (1993) *Pynchon's Poetics: Interfacing Theory and Text.* Chicago: University of Illinois Press.

Bettelli, Fabrizio (1987) 'Et in Arcadia ego: la mosca', *Filmcritica*, 38, 372, March, 109–12.

Betz, Mark (2003) 'Art, Exploitation, Underground', in Mark Jancovich, Antonio Lazaro-Reboll, Julian Stringer and Andy Willis (eds) *Defining Cult Movies: The Cultural Politics of Oppositional Taste.* Manchester: Manchester University Press, 202–22.

Billson, Anne (1989) 'Cronenberg on Cronenberg: A Career In Stereo', *Monthly Film Bulletin*, 56, 660, 4–6.

Biltereyst, Daniel, Ernest Mathijs and Philippe Meers (2007) 'An Avalanche of Attention: The Prefiguration and Reception of *The Lord of the Rings'*, in Martin Barker and Ernest Mathijs (eds) *Watching the Lord of the Rings: Tolkien's World Audiences.* New York: Peter Lang, 37–59.

Blakesley, David (1998) 'Eviscerating David Cronenberg', *Enculturation*, 2, 1, 8.

Blokker, Jan (1990) 'Inleiding', in Marc Moorman (ed.) *David Cronenberg. Transformatie van een horrorfilmer.* Rotterdam: Filmfestival Rotterdam, 7–10.

Blumenfeld, Samuel (1999) 'Le Playstation est l'avenir d l'homme', *Le Monde*, 15 April.

Bordwell, David (1989) *Making Meaning: Inference and Rhetoric in the Interpretation of Cinema.* Cambridge, MA: Harvard University Press.

Borràs Castanyer, Laura (2003) eXistenZ, de David Cronenberg: ciberficciones para la posthumanidad', *Digithum*, 5, available online at: http://www.uoc.edu/humfil/articles/esp/borras0303/borras0303.html (accessed 23 January 2008).

Boss, Pete (1986) 'Vile Bodies and Bad Medicine', *Screen*, 27, 1, 14–24.

Bouruet-Aubertot, Veronique (2000) 'David
Cronenberg: le prophete du gore', *Beaux Arts
Magazine*, 198, 56–9.

Bouw, Brenda (2001) 'Baron of Blood meets Beckett',
Globe and Mail, 29 September, R13.

Bow, James (2004) 'Brace For Impact', *Journal of
James Bow & His Writing*, http://bowjamesbow.
ca/2004/03/22/brace-for-impac.shtml (accessed 2
September 2007).

Bradshaw, Peter (1999) 'Game for Anything',
Guardian Weekly, 9 May, 27.

____ (2007) 'Eastern Promises', *Guardian*, 26
October, available online at: http://film.guardian.
co.uk/ (accessed 3 December 2007).

Braun, Eric (1981) 'The Gentle Art of Mind
Boggling', *Films*, 1, 7, June, 22–5.

Breskin, David (1992) 'Interview with David
Cronenberg', in *Inner Views: Filmmakers in
Conversation*. New York: Da Capo Press, 201–66.

Brigg, Peter (1971) '*Crimes*', *Take One*, 2, 6, July–
August, 21.

Britton, Andrew, Robin Wood, Richard Lippe and
Tony Williams (eds) (1979) *The American
Nightmare: Essays on the Horror Film*. Toronto:
Festival of Festivals.

Bronfen, Elisabeth (1998) 'A Womb of One's Own,
or the Strange Case of David Cronenberg', in
The Knotted Subject: Hysteria and its Discontents.
Princeton, NJ: Princeton University Press,
381–407.

Brophy, Philip (1984) 'Tales of Terror: The Horror
Films You Think You Know', *Cinema Papers*, 49,
400–7.

____ (1986) 'Horrality: The Textuality of
Contemporary Horror Films', *Screen*, 27, 1,
2–13.

Brottman, Mikita and Christopher Sharrett (2002)
'The End of the Road: David Cronenberg's *Crash*
and the Fading of the West', *Literature/Film
Quarterly*, 30, 2, 126–32.

Brown, Geoff (1996) 'A Vintage Year for Aficionados',
Times, 21 May.

Browning, Mark (2003) '"Thou, the player of the
game, art God": Nabokovian game-playing in
Cronenberg's *eXistenZ*', *Canadian Journal of Film
Studies*, 12, 1, 57–69.

____ (2007) *David Cronenberg: Author or Filmmaker?*
London: Intellect Books.

Bruno, Marcello Walter (1989) 'Effetto Giorno',
Segnocinema, 9, 39, September, 2–5.

Bukatman, Scott (1990) 'Who Programs You? The
Science Fiction of the Spectacle', in Annette
Kuhn (ed.) *Alien Zone: Cultural Theory and
Contemporary Science Fiction Cinema*. London:
Verso, 196–213.

Burdeau, Emmanuel (1999) 'La difference entre
Cronenberg', *Cahiers du cinéma*, 534, April, 66.

Burroughs, William (1962) *Naked Lunch*. New York:
Grove Press.

____ (1992) 'Introduction', in Ira Silverberg (ed.)
*Everything Is Permitted: The Making of Naked
Lunch*. New York: Grove Weidenfeld, 13–16.

Butstraen, Raf (1981) '*Scanners*: denken en doden', *De
Standaard*, 12 June.

____ (1987) '*The Fly*: een vlieg in de boter', *De
Standaard*, 23 January.

____ (1996) 'Filmfestival Cannes eindigt zonder
glans', *De Standaard*, 20 May, 5.

Calvin, Ritch (2004) 'The Real *eXistenZ*: TransCendz
the Irreal', *Extrapolation: A Journal of Science
Fiction and Fantasy*, 45, 3, 276–93.

Camblor, Manuel (1999) 'Death Drive's Joy Ride:
David Cronenberg's *Crash*', *Other Voices:
E-Journal of Cultural Criticism*, 1, 3, available
online at: http://www.othervoices.org/1.3/
mcamblor/crash.html (accessed 23 January
2008).

Cameron-Wilson, James (2005) '*A History of Violence*',
Film Review Special, 60, September, 109.

Campbell, Mary B. (1984) 'Biochemical Alchemy and
the Films of David Cronenberg', in Barry Keith
Grant (ed.) *Planks of Reason: Essays on the Horror
Film*. Metuchen: Scarecrow Press, 307–20.

Canby, Vincent (1976) 'They Came From Within',
New York Times, 7 July, 46, 4.

____ (1981) '*Scanners*', *New York Times*, 14 January,
C21, 5.

____ (1986) 'Stuart Gordons from Beyond', *New York
Times*, 24 October, C18.

Canino, Patricia (2008) 'Dubbelspel en dubbelspion:
de netwerkenoorlog in *Eastern Promises* van
Cronenberg', *Rekto:Verso*, 30, July/August,
available online at: http://www.rektoverso.be/
content/view/778/15/ (accessed 24 July 2008).

Canosa, Michele (ed.) (1995) *La bellezza interiore; il
cinema de David Cronenberg*. Recco: Le Mani.

Caprara, Fulvia (1996) 'Divento Bunon per Enzo
Ferrari', *La Stampa*, 18 May, 24.

Carels, Edwin (1996) '*Crash*: Sex Drive', *Andere
Sinema*, 134, December, 42–5.

____ (1999) 'We leren om te spelen', *Financieel
Economische Tijd*, 19 May, 2.

Carriere, Christophe (1999) '*eXistenZ*', *Premiere*, 266,
May, 58.

Carroll, Michael Thomas (1993) 'The Bloody
Spectacle: Mishima, The Sacred Heart, Hogarth,
Cronenberg, and the Entrails of Culture', *Studies
in Popular Culture*, 15, 2, 43–56.

Carroll, Noël (1982) 'The Future of Allusions',
October, 2, 51–81.

_____ (1985) 'Film', in Steven Trachtenberg (ed.) *The Postmodern Moment*. Westport: Greenwood Press, 100–33.

_____ (1989) 'Interpreting *Citizen Kane*', *Persistence of Vision*, 7, 51–62.

Celeste, Reni (2005) 'In the web with David Cronenberg: *Spider* and the new auteurism', *CineAction*, 65, 2, 4.

Cendros, Teresa (2002) 'David Cronenberg: Director de Cine Hollywood Esta Maleducando al Publico', *El Pais*, 7 October, 44.

Charity, Tom (2001) 'Come Fly with Me', *Starlog* (UK edition), December, 78.

_____ (2007) '100 Greatest DVDs: *The Fly*', *Vancouver Sun*, 8 September.

Charlot, Alain and Marc Toullec (1989) 'Dossier David Cronenberg', *Mad Movies*, 58, 42–9.

Charney, Mark (1996) 'Creating a New Reality: Cronenberg on Cronenberg', *Post Script*, 15, 2, 70–4.

Chesley, Steven (1975) 'It'll Bug You: on *Shivers*', *Cinema Canada*, 22, 22–5.

Childs, Mike and Alan Jones (1980) '*Scanners*', *Cinefantastique*, 10, 1, 35.

Christopher, James (1999) 'Cronenberg's Tricks of the Light', *Times*, 29 April.

Chute, David (1980) 'He Came from Within', *Film Comment*, 16, 2, 36–9, 42.

_____ (1982) 'Twelve New Movies: The Latest from Cronenberg and Venice', *Film Comment*, 18, 1, 2, 4.

Cielo, Silvana and Bruno, Edoardo (1986) '*Videodrome*', *Filmcritica*, 37, 368, October, 495–6.

Ciment, Michel (1989) 'Entretien avec David Cronenberg', *Positif*, 337, 33–43.

Ciment, Michel and Laurent Vachaud (1999) 'Entretien: David Cronenberg', *Positif*, 458, 15–20.

Clark, Mike (1990) 'Almost Paradiso', *USA Today*, 2 March, 4D.

_____ (1991) '*Naked Lunch* not for the Finicky', *USA Today*, 30 December, 4D.

_____ (1993) 'Middling Malice; Small-Change Money', *USA Today*, 1 October, 8D.

Clarke, Frederick (1981) 'Editorial', *Cinefantastique*, 10, 4, 3.

Cloutier, Jacques (1981) '*Scanners* fit fureur à New York', *La Presse*, 16 January, B2.

Clover, Carol (1992) 'The Eye of Horror', in *Men, Women and Chainsaws: Gender in the Modern Horror Film*. London: British Film Institute, 191–205.

Coe, Jonathan (1997) 'There is no Paedophilia or Sexual Humiliation in *Crash*', *New Statesman*, 6 June.

Cognard, François (1989) 'Faux Semblants', *Starfix*, 77, 91.

Collins, Michael J. (1996) 'Medicine, Lust, Surrealism, and Death: Three Early Films by David Cronenberg', *Post Script*, 15, 2, 62–9.

Combs, Richard (1976) '*Shivers*', *Monthly Film Bulletin*, 43, 506, March, 62.

Conlogue, Ray (1978), 'King of Horror Keeps Brood Under Wraps', *Globe and Mail*, 28 December.

_____ (1979) '*The Brood* a Grotesque Family Thriller', *Globe and Mail* (4 June).

Conrich, Ian (2000) 'An Aesthetic Sense: Cronenberg and Neo-Horror Film Culture', in Michael Grant (ed.) *The Modern Fantastic: The Films of David Cronenberg*. Trowbridge: Flicks Books, 35–50.

Contenti, Fulvio (1986) 'I migliori film del 1985: *Videodrome*', *Filmcritica*, 37, 361, January, 32.

Cook, Pam (1987) '*The Fly*', *Monthly Film Bulletin*, 54, 636, January, 45–6.

_____ (1989) '*Dead Ringers*', *Monthly Film Bulletin*, 56, 660, January, 3–4.

Cornea, Christine (2003) 'David Cronenberg's *Crash* and Performing Cyborgs', *Velvet Light Trap*, 52, 4–14.

Costello, John (2000) *David Cronenberg*. Harpenden: Pocket Essentials.

Coupland, Douglas (1987) 'Generation X', *Vancouver*, September, 164–9, 194.

Cowart, David (1980) *Thomas Pynchon: The Art of Allusion*. Carbondale: Southern Illinois University Press.

Craven, Jill (2000) 'Ironic Empathy in Cronenberg's *Crash*: The Psychodynamics of Postmodern Displacement from a Tenuous Reality', *Quarterly Review of Film and Video*, 17, 3, 187–209.

Creed, Barbara (1986) 'Horror and the Monstrous Feminine: an Imaginary Abjection', *Screen*, 27, 1, 44–71.

_____ (1987) 'From Here to Modernity: Postmodernism and Feminism', *Screen*, 28, 2, 47–67.

_____ (1990) 'Phallic Panic: Male Hysteria and *Dead Ringers*', *Screen*, 31, 125–46.

_____ (1993) 'Woman as Monstrous Womb: *The Brood*', in *The Monstrous Feminine; Film, Feminism, Psychoanalysis*. London: Routledge, 43–58.

_____ (1998) 'Anal Wounds, Metallic Kisses: *Crash*', *Screen*, 39, 2, 175–9.

Crimp, Douglas (ed.) (1988) *AIDS: Cultural Analysis, Cultural Activism*. Cambridge, MA: MIT Press.

Cristalli, Paola (1995) 'Dei miraggi ingannatori, *M. Butterfly*', in Michele Canosa (ed.) *La bellezza interiore: il cinema de David Cronenberg*. Recco: Le Mani, 130–41.

Cronenberg, David (1967) 'Cinethon', *Globe and Mail*, 21 June.

_____ (1975a) 'Film Criticism', *Globe and Mail*, 4 October, 7.

_____ (1975b) 'Letter to Delaney', *Saturday Night*, 90, 6, 3560, November, 6.

_____ (1977) 'The Night Attila met the anti-Christ, she was shocked and he was outraged', *Globe and Mail*, 14 May, 6.

_____ (1984) '"Festival of Festivals": 1983 Science-Fiction Retrospective', in Wayne Drew (ed.) *David Cronenberg*. London: British Film Institute, 57.

_____ (1995) 'Cronenberg meets Rushdie', *Shift Magazine*, 3, 4, June.

_____ (2002) *Collected Screenplays 1*. London: Faber and Faber.

_____ (2006) 'Introduction', *Red Cars*. Turin: Edizioni Volumina, available online at: http://www.redcars.it/index2.htm (accessed 11 July 2007).

Cronenberg, David, Jackie Burroughs *et al.* (1984) 'Porn Policy Protest', *Cinema Canada*, 106, 5.

Curtis, Nick (2007) 'I Want People to See what Violence Does', *Evening Standard*, 26 October, available online at: http://www.thisislondon.co.uk/ (accessed 14 December 2007).

Czarnecki, Mark (1983) 'A Vivid Obsession with Sex and Death', *Maclean's*, 14 February, 62.

D. L. (1986) '*The Dead Zone*', *Le Soir*, 13 October.

Dale, Stephen (1982) 'Reiner Schwarz: Odysseus of the Air Waves', *Globe and Mail*, 3 April.

Danvers, Louis (1984a) 'La chair et le câble', *Visions*, 19, 12.

_____ (1984b) 'Dans la 'Zone' avec Cronenberg', *Le Vif/L' Express*, 17 May, 122–23.

Dargis, Manohla (2005a) 'Revisiting the Past By Way of Cannes', *New York Times*, 20 May, E1.

_____ (2005b) 'A Nice Place To Film, But Heavens Not To Live', *New York Times*, 11 September, 37.

_____ (2006) 'Dark Truths of a Killing Love', *New York Times*, 15 January, 2A–1.

Daviau, Allen and Peter Elmes (1997) 'Auto Erotic: Interview with Peter Suschitzky', *American Cinematographer*, 78, 4, April, 36–42.

Davies, Russell (1976) 'Superstar Newsmen', *Observer Review*, 2 May, 28.

Dawkins, Richard (1976) *The Selfish Gene*. Oxford: Oxford University Press.

De Bruyn, Olivier (1999) '*eXistenZ*: Jeu est un autre', *Positif*, 458, 12–14.

De Kock, Ivo (1984) 'David Cronenberg: Body and Mind', *Andere Sinema*, 60, July–August, 4–10.

De Lauretis, Teresa (1999) 'Popular Culture, Public and Private Fantasies: Femininity and Fetishism in David Cronenberg's *M. Butterfly*', *Signs*, 24, 2, 303–34.

_____ (2003) 'Becoming Inorganic', *Critical Inquiry*, 29, 4, 547–70.

De Vos, Erik E., Hans Schwarz and Huib Stam (1989) '*Dead Ringers*: Ijzingwekkende horror zonder bloed', *Skoop*, 25, 4, April, 38.

Dean, William (1968) 'Criticism and the Underground Film', *Take One*, 1, 12–14.

Dee, Jonathan (2005) 'David Cronenberg's Body Language', *New York Times*, 18 September.

Delaney, Marshall (1967) '48 Hours with the Underground', *Saturday Night*, 82, 8, 3471, August, 26–9.

_____ (1969) 'Movies: *Valérie*', *Saturday Night*, 84, 9, 3466, September, 40–1.

_____ (1970a) 'Canada Can't Make Big Movies Yet, But Personal Cinema Is Alive', *Saturday Night*, 85, 2, 3500, 34–7.

_____ (1970b) 'What We Needed: Perfect Bad Taste', *Saturday Night*, 85, 10, 36–8.

_____ (1975) 'You Should Know How Bad This Film Is. After All, You Paid For It', *Saturday Night*, 90, 4, 83–5.

Denton, Herbert (1987) 'Canada's Vision Quest: Hollywood Finds the Climate Chilly in the Great North', *Washington Post*, 14 June, F1.

Desbarats, Peter (1970) 'The Walt Disney of Sexploitation', *Saturday Night*, 85, 11, 3509, 29–30.

Devos, Luc and Marc Holthof (1982) *De explosieve charme van de fantastische film*. Antwerpen: Exa.

Dick, Leslie (1997) 'Crash', *Sight and Sound*, 7, 6, 48–9.

Doherty, Thomas (1987) '*The Fly*', *Film Quarterly*, 40, 1, 38–41.

_____ (1989) 'David Cronenberg's *Dead Ringers*', *Cinefantastique*, 19, 3, 38–9.

Dostoyevsky, Fyodor (2000) *Demons*, trans. Richard Pevear and Larissa Volokhonsky. New York: Everyman Library.

Douglas, Mary (1966) *Purity and Danger: An Analysis of Concepts of Pollution and Taboo*. London: Routledge.

Douglas, Dave (1996) 'Exile on Hastings & Main Street: The Vancouver Films of Larry Kent', *Canadian Journal of Film Studies*, 5, 2.

Dowler, Andrew (1979) '*The Brood*', *Cinema Canada*, 58, 33–4.

Downey, Donn (1987) 'Library Doors Closed as Porn Bill Ridiculed', *Globe and Mail*, 11 December.

Downing, David and Kim Kerbis (1998) 'Exterminate all rational thought: David Cronenberg's filmic vision of William S. Burroughs's *Naked Lunch*', *Psychoanalytic Review*, 85, 5, 775–92.

Drew, Wayne (ed.) (1984) *David Cronenberg: BFI Dossier 21*. London: British Film Institute.

Dreyfus, Louis (1997) 'Ted Turner censure *Crash*', *Première*, 238, January, 47.

Duncan, Jody (1992a) 'Borrowed Flesh: Special Effects in *Naked Lunch*', in Ira Silverberg (ed.) *Everything Is Permitted: The Making of Naked Lunch*. New York: Grove Weidenfeld, 89–110.

____ (1992b) 'Borrowed Flesh: *Naked Lunch*', *Cinefex*, 49, 24–38.

Dupont, Joan (1993) 'From Baron of Gore to Cultural Hero', *International Herald Tribune*, 20 September, 18.

Duynslaegher, Patrick (1981) 'De bizarre horrorkunstjes van David Cronenberg', *Knack Magazine*, 22 April, 76.

____ (1993) 'Chinezen overzee; het filmfestival van Toronto', *Knack Magazine*, 39, 29 September, 90–2.

Dworkin, Andrea (1981) *Pornography: Men Possessing Women*. New York: Putnam.

Dwyer, Michael (1996) 'Collision Course at Cannes', *Irish Times*, 24 May, 13.

____ (2000) 'Trawling for Mystic Nuggets', *Irish Times*, 23 September, 65.

Dzeguze, Kaspars (1969) 'Happy Film Images and Money to Boot', *Globe and Mail*, 18 October, 4.

Eagleton, Terry (1984) *The Functions of Criticism*. London: Verso.

Ebert, Roger (1979) '*The Brood*', *Chicago Sun-Times*, 5 June 1979, available online at: http://rogerebert. suntimes.com/ (accessed 21 July 2007).

____ (1997) '*Crash*', *Chicago Sun-Times*, 21 March, available online at: http://www.rogerebert. suntimes.com (accessed 12 October 2007).

____ (2007) '*Eastern Promises*', *Chicago Sun-Times*, 14 September, available online at: http://rogerebert. suntimes.com/ (accessed 14 December 2007).

Edwards, Natalie (1975) 'The Parasite Murders', *Cinema Canada*, 22, 44–5.

Egan, Kate (2007) *Trash or Treasure?: Censorship and the Changing Meanings of the Video Nasties*. Manchester: Manchester University Press.

Everman, Welch (1993) *Cult Horror Films*. New York: Citadel Press.

Feineman, Neil (1981) 'Cronenberg Views Horror from a New Perspective', *L.A. Herald Examiner*, 19 January, B1–B4.

Fisher, Mark (2007) '*Eastern Promises*', *Sight and Sound*, 17, 11, 57.

Florence, Bill (1991) '*Total Recall*: The Bizarre Mars of David Cronenberg', *Cinefantastique*, 21, 5, 42–4.

Foreman, Liza (1999) 'Boffo Berlin Blast: High-Profile Helmers Eyed for 49th Film Fest', *Variety*, 11 January, 5.

Forman, Murray (2001) 'Boys Will Be Boys: David Cronenberg's Crash Course in Heavy Mettle', in

Murray Pomerance (ed.) *Ladies and Gentlemen, Boys and Girls: Gender in Film at the End of the 20th Century*. New York: State University of New York Press, 109–27.

Fothergill, Robert (1977) 'A Place Like Home', in Seth Feldman and Joyce Nelson (eds) *The Canadian Film Reader*. Toronto: Peter Martin Associates, 347–63.

Foucault, Michel (1991) 'Complete and Austere Institutions', in *Discipline and Punish: The Birth of the Prison*. London: Penguin, 231–56.

Fox, Jordan (1979) '*The Brood*', *Cinefantastique*, 8, 4, 23.

Frank, Arthur (1992) 'Twin Nightmares of the Medical Simulacrum: Jean Baudrillard and David Cronenberg', in William Stearns and William Chaloupka (eds) *Jean Baudrillard: The Disappearance of Art and Politics*. New York: St. Martin's and Macmillan, 82–97.

Frank, Marcie (1991) 'The Camera and the Speculum: David Cronenberg's *Dead Ringers*', *Publications of the Modern Language Association of America*, 106, 3, 459–70.

Franklin, Garth (2006) 'Cronenberg Gives Lowdown on Next Films', *Dark Horizons*, available online at http://www.darkhorizons.com/news06/060329n. php (accessed 22 November 2007).

Fraser, Matthew (1984a) 'Anti-Censorship Tide on the Rise', *Globe and Mail*, 13 October.

____ (1984b) 'Censor Board Bans Jean Genet Film', *Globe and Mail*, 18 October.

Freeland, Cynthia A. (1996) 'Feminist Frameworks for Horror Film', in David Bordwell and Noël Carroll (eds) *Post-Theory: Reconstructing Film Studies*. Madison: University of Wisconsin Press, 195–218.

Freeman, Alan (1999) '*eXistenZ* draws Crowds in Berlin World Premiere: Cronenberg Says Movie Not Extreme', *Globe and Mail*, 17 February, D1.

Freedman, Adele (1983) 'Censor Defends Ban of Uncut Horror Flic', *Globe and Mail*, 14 September, 16.

French, Karl and Philip French (1999) *Cult Movies*. London: Pavilion Books, 51–2.

French, Lawrence (1992) 'Special Effects in *Naked Lunch*', *Cinefantastique*, 22, 5, 15–17.

French, Philip (2003) 'Oh What a Tangled Web we Weave...', *Observer*, 5 January, 12.

Frodon, Jean-Michel (1999) 'Le Festival de Berlin à l'heure de la question kurde', *Le Monde*, 21 February.

Fukuyama, Francis (1992) *The End of History*. London: Free Press.

Fulford, Robert (1978) '*Shivers*', *Globe and Mail*, 5 June, 6.

Fuller, Graham (2005) 'Good Guy, Bad Guy', *Sight and Sound*, 15, 10, 12–16.

Furey, Bill (1981) '*Scanners* Shoot Out in NYC', *Cinema Canada*, 73, 6.

Galvin, Peter (1996) 'Take One', *Sydney Morning Herald* , 23 May, 14.

Gangitano, Lia (1998) 'Blue Data', in Sandra Antlo-Suarz and Michael Madore (eds) *Spectacular Optical*. New York: Trans/Arts, Cultures, Media: Thread Wading Space, 66.

Garnier, Philippe (1989) 'Le fil du rasoir: faux semblants', *Première*, 143, February, 66–71.

Garofalo, Marcello (1993) 'Naked Film: la realta nova del pasto nudo', *Segnocinema*, 13, 60, 10–12.

Garris, Mick (1977) '*Rabid*', *Cinefantastique*, 6, 2, 28.

Garsault, Alain (1991) 'Corps: substance solide et palpable', *Positif*, 359, 26–30.

Gaschler, Thomas and Eckhard Vollmar (1993) *Dark Stars. Zehn Regisseure im Gespräch*. Munich: Belleville.

Gasher, Mike (2002) *Hollywood North*. Vancouver: University of British Columbia Press.

Geasland, Jack and Bari Wood (1974) *Twins*. New York: Signet.

Gerstel, Judy (1996) 'And You Can See the Skid Marks Left by the Perplexed After Their First Glimpse', *Toronto Star (Metro Edition)*, 17 May, C1.

Gibson, William (1984) *Neuromancer*. New York: Ace Science Fiction.

Girard, René (1977) *Violence and the Sacred*. Baltimore: Johns Hopkins University Press.

____ (1986) *The Scapegoat*. Baltimore: Johns Hopkins University Press.

____ (1987) *Things Hidden Since the Foundation of the World*. Stanford: Stanford University Press.

Gleiberman, Owen (1988) 'Cronenberg's Double Meanings', *American Film*, 14, 1, October, 38–43.

Gobbers, Eric (1980) 'It's Alive: David Cronenberg', *Andere Sinema*, 22, October, 19–21.

Goddard, Peter (1990) 'Life After Sex and Lies for Steven Soderbergh', *Toronto Star*, 5 May, G2.

Godin, Marc (1994) 'David Cronenberg', in *Gore: autopsie d' un cinéma*. Paris: Editions du collectioneur, 110–13.

Goffman, Erving (1961) 'On the Characteristics of Total Institutions', in *Asylums. Essays on the Social Situation of Mental Patients and Other Inmates*. New York: Doubleday, 15–24.

Gorlier, Claudio (1992) 'Il Libro Culto', *La Stampa*, 17 February, 13.

Govier, Katherine (1979) 'Middle-class Shivers', *Toronto Life*, July, 50–1, 56–8, 61–2.

Grace, Dominick (2003) 'From *Videodrome* to *Virtual Light*: David Cronenberg and William Gibson', *Extrapolation*, 44, 3, 344–55.

Graham, Jamie (2005) 'Making Movies About Death Is a Positive Act: Interview With David Cronenberg', *Total Film*, October, 124–8.

Granat, Aaron (2005) '*History of Violence* Tackles Important Social Issues', *Badger Herald* (University of Wisconsin), 5 October.

Grant, Barry Keith (ed.) (1984) *Planks of Reason: Essays on the Horror Film*. Metuchen, NJ: Scarecrow Press.

____ (ed.) (1996) *The Dread of Difference: Gender and the Horror Film*. Austin: University of Texas Press.

Grant, Kieran (1999) 'Canuck Walk of Fame just got a little longer: Legends including Cronenberg, Rush Honoured', *Toronto Sun*, 28 May, 77.

Grant, Michael (1998) 'Crimes of the Future: on *Crash*', *Screen*, 39, 2, 180–5.

____ (1997) *Dead Ringers*. London: Flicks Books.

Gressard, G. (1976) 'Parasite Murders', *Mad Movies*, 13, October, 34.

Grist, Leighton (2003) '"It's Only a Piece of Meat": Gender Ambiguity, Sexuality, and Politics in *The Crying Game* and *M. Butterfly*', *Cinema Journal*, 42, 4, 3–28.

Groen, Rick (2003) 'Mind Games', *Globe and Mail*, 28 February, R1.

Grossberg, Lawrence (1996) 'Identity and Cultural Studies – Is That All There Is?', in Stuart Hall and Paul Du Gay (eds) *Cultural Identity*. London: Sage, 87–107.

Grünberg, Serge (1991) 'Sur les terres de Cronenberg', *Cahiers du cinéma*, 446, 34–42.

____ (1992) *David Cronenberg*. Paris: Cahiers du cinéma.

____ (2000) *Entretiens avec David Cronenberg*. Paris: Cahiers du cinéma.

____ (2002) '*Spider*, c'est moi', *Cahiers du cinéma*, 568, May, 22.

Grundmann, Roy (1997) 'Plight of the Crash Fest Mummies', *Cineaste*, 22, 4, 24–7.

Guare, John (1990) *Six Degrees of Separation*. New York: Vintage.

Guérif, François (1979) 'Chromosome 3', *La revue du cinéma/ Image et Son*, 345, December, 119.

Guerrero, Edward (1990) 'AIDS as Monster in Science Fiction and Horror Films', *Journal of Popular Film and Television*, 18, 3, 86–93.

Haas, Lynda and Mary Pharr (1996) 'Somatic Ideas: Cronenberg and the Feminine', *Post Script*, 15, 2, 29–39.

Haas, Robert (1996) 'Introduction: The Cronenberg Project: Literature, Science, Psychology, and the Monster in Cinema', *Post Script*, 15, 2, 3–10.

Halberstam, Judith (1995) *Skin Shows: Gothic Horror and the Technology of Monsters*. Durham and London: Duke University Press.

Hall, Stuart (1990) 'Cultural Identity and Diaspora', in Jonathan Rutherford (ed.) *Identity: Community, Culture, Difference*. London: Lawrence and Wishart, 223–7.

Ham, Martin (2004) 'Excess and Resistance in Feminised Bodies: David Cronenberg's *Videodrome* and Jean Baudrillard's *Seduction*', *Senses of Cinema*, 30, http://www.sensesofcinema. com/ (accessed 23 January 2008).

Hampton, Howard (1993) 'When in *Videodrome*: Travels in the New Flesh', *Artforum*, 31, February, 70–3, 113.

Handling, Piers (1983) (ed.) *The Shape of Rage: The Films of David Cronenberg*. Toronto: General Publishing.

Handling, Piers and Pierre Véronneau (eds) (1990) *L' horreur intérieure: les films de David Cronenberg*. Parijs-Montréal: Editions du Cerf-La cinémathèque Québécoise.

Hantke, Steffen (2004) 'Spectacular Optics: The Deployment of Special Effects in David Cronenberg's Films', *Film Criticism*, 29, 2, 34–52.

____ (ed.) (2006) *Caligari's Heirs: German Cinema of Fear after 1945*. Lanham, MD: Scarecrow Press.

____ (2007a) 'Genre and Authorship in David Cronenberg's *Naked Lunch*', in R. Barton Palmer (ed.) *Twentieth-Century American Fiction on Screen*. Cambridge: Cambridge University Press, 164–77.

____ (2007b) 'Out From the Realist Underground; or, the Baron of Blood Visits Cannes: Recursive and Self-reflexive patterns in David Cronenberg's *Videodrome* and *eXistenZ*', in Richard J. Hand and Jay McRoy (eds) *Monstrous Adaptations: Generic and Thematic Mutations in Horror Film*. Manchester: Manchester University Press, 67–81.

Harkness, John (1981) 'David Cronenberg: Brilliantly Bizarre', *Cinema Canada*, 72, 17.

____ (1983) 'The Word, the Flesh and the Films of David Cronenberg', *Cinema Canada*, 97, 23–5.

____ (1994) '*M. Butterfly*', *Sight and Sound*, 4, 5, 44–5.

Harpold, Terry (1997) 'Dry Leatherette: Cronenberg's *Crash*', *Postmodern Culture*, 7, 3.

Harrington, Richard (1981) '"It's a Conspiracy of Darkness": Horror Director David Cronenberg', *Washington Post*, 18 January, H1.

Hawkins, Joan (2000) *Cutting Edge: Art Horror and the Horrific Avant-Garde*. Minneapolis: University of Minnesota Press.

Hebron, Sandra (2007) '*Eastern Promises* Gala Opening', *British Film Institute Website*, http://www.bfi.org.uk/whatson/lff/film_programme/ (accessed 27 November 2007).

Heffernan, Kevin (2004) 'The Family Monsters and Urban Matinees: Continental Distributing and *Night of the Living Dead*', in *Ghouls, Gimmicks and Gold: Horror Films and the American Movie Business, 1953–1968*. Durham: Duke University Press, 202–19.

Heldreth, Leonard G. (1996) 'Festering in Thebes: Elements of Tragedy and Myth in Cronenberg's Films', *Post Script*, 15, 2, 46–61.

Herrington, Chris (2005) 'It Comes From Within', *Memphis Flyer*, 30 September.

Herzogenrath, Bernd (2003) 'Brundlefly For President: Cronenberg, Kafka and the Fiction of Insect Politics', in Matthew Sweeney and Michal Peprník (eds) *[Mis]understanding Postmodernism: Fiction of Politics and Politics of Fiction*. Olomouc: Univerzita Palackého v Olomouci, 273–90.

Hickenlooper, George (1989) 'The Primal Energies of the Horror Film (interview with David Cronenberg)', *Cinéaste*, 17, 2, 4–7.

____ (1991) 'David Cronenberg: Nothing to Fear', in *Reel Conversations: Candid Interviews with Film's Foremost Directors and Critics*. New York: Citadel Press, 314–28.

Hoberman, J. (1983) 'Tech It or Leave It', *Village Voice*, 15 February, 50.

____ (1999) 'Trip Teases', *Village Voice*, 27 April, 131.

____ (2003) 'Along Came A Spider', *Village Voice*, 26 February, available online at: http://www.villagevoice.com/news/0309,hoberman2,42134,1.html (accessed 26 October 2007).

____ (2005a) 'Historical Oversight. Desensitized to Cronenberg's *Violence*, jury anoints Dardennes over Jarmusch and von Trier', *Village Voice*, 24 May.

____ (2005b) 'The Last Action Hero', *Village Voice*, 26 September, 56.

____ (2006) 'Violent Reaction', *Village Voice*, 3 January, 26.

____ (2007) 'Still Cronenberg', *Village Voice*, 11 September, available online at: http://www.villagevoice.com/film/0737,hoberman,77750,20.html (accessed 14 December 2007).

Hoberman, J. and Jonathan Rosenbaum (1983) *Midnight Movies*. New York: Da Capo Press.

Hofsess, John (1970) 'The Witchcraft of Obscenity', *Saturday Night*, 85, 8, 3506, 11–16.

____ (1975) 'Quick Ma, the Penicillin', *Maclean's*, 88, 10, 6 October, 90.

____ (1977) 'Fear and Loathing to Order', in Seth Feldman and Joyce Nelson (eds) *The Canadian Film Reader*. Toronto: Peter Martin Associates, 274–8.

____ (1978) '*Shivers*', *Globe and Mail*, 8 June, 6.

Hogan, David (1983) '*Videodrome*', *Cinefantastique*, 13, 4, 61.

____ (1986) *Dark Romance: Sexuality in the Horror Film*. Jefferson, NC: McFarland.

Holthof, Marc (1976) '*Shivers*', *Film en Televisie*, 230–231, 36–37.

____ (1980a) 'Off-Hollywood', *Andere Sinema*, 18, March, 24–31.

____ (1980b) 'It's Alive', *Andere Sinema*, 21, September, 14–17.

Hookey, Robert (1977) 'Backtalk ... with David Cronenberg', *Motion*, 6, 4–5, 16.

Hotchkiss, L. M. (2003) '"Still in the Game": Cybertransformations of the "New Flesh" in David Cronenberg's *eXistenZ*', *Velvet Light Trap*, 52, Fall, 15–32.

Howe, Desson (1999) 'Heightened *eXistenZ*', *Washington Post*, 23 April, N49.

Hoyle, Martin (1999) 'Dragged into the Realms of Higher Kitsch', *Financial Times*, 29 April.

Hughes, Don (2003) 'David Cronenberg: Hall of Fame – the Maverick Series', *Empire*, 164, February, 110–11.

Hultkrans, Andrew (1997) 'Body Works: Andrew Hultkrans talks with J. G. Ballard and David Cronenberg', *Artforum*, 36, 7, 76–81, 118.

Hume, Christopher (1990) 'Battle Lines Drawn at Harbourfront', *Toronto Star*, 20 December, B6.

Humm, Maggie (1997) 'Cronenberg's Films and Feminist Theory', in *Feminism and Film*. Edinburgh: Edinburgh University Press, 58–89.

Humphries, Reynold (2002) *The American Horror Film: An Introduction*. Edinburgh: Edinburgh University Press.

Hurley, Kelly (1995) 'Reading like an Alien: Posthuman Identity in Ridley Scott's *Alien* and David Cronenberg's *Rabid*', in Judith Halberstam and Ira Livingston (eds) *Posthuman Bodies*. Bloomington: Indiana University Press, 203–24.

Hurst, Linda (1989) 'Is Controversial Porn Bill Dead or Slumbering?', *Toronto Star*, 11 May, A26.

Hwang, David Henry (1993) *M. Butterfly*. New York: Plume.

____ (2003) 'Afterword to *M. Butterfly*',in Carl Klaus, Miriam Gilbert and Bradford Field (eds) *Stages of Drama: Classical to Contemporary Theatre*, fifth edition. New York: Bedford St. Martins, 1404–6.

Irving, Joan (1977) 'David Cronenberg's *Rabid*', *Cinema Canada*, 37, 57.

Jacobowitz, Florence and Richard Lippe (1989) '*Dead Ringers*: The Joke's On Us', *CineAction!*, 16, May, 64–8.

Jaehne, Karen (1988) 'Double Trouble: *Dead Ringers*', *Film Comment*, 24/5, 20–7.

____ (1992) 'David Cronenberg on William Burroughs: Dead ringers do *Naked Lunch*', *Film Quarterly*, 45, 3, Spring, 2–6.

James, Caryn (1986) '*The Fly*', *New York Times*, 15 August, C18.

James, Nick (2003) 'The Right Trousers', *Sight and Sound*, 13, 1, 14.

James, Noah (1979) 'The Horrifying David Cronenberg', *Maclean's*, 9 July, 7.

Jameson, Fredric (1992) *The Geopolitical Aesthetic: Cinema and Space in the World System*. London: British Film Institute, 22.

Jancovich, Mark (1992) *Horror*. London: Batsford.

____ (2002) 'Cult Fictions: Cult Movies, Subcultural Capital and the Production of Cultural Distinctions', *Cultural Studies*, 16, 2, 306–22.

Jobin, Thierry (2002) '*Spider*, l'effrayant diagnostic du docteur David Cronenberg', *Le Temps*, 14 November.

Johnson, Brian (1986) 'Creepy Capers from a Master of Horror', *Maclean's*, 25 August, 41.

____ (2005) 'Violence hits home', *Maclean's*, 14 October.

Johnston, Sheila (1999) '*eXistenZ*', *Screen International*, 1197, 26 February, 31.

Jones, Alan (1996) '*Crash*: David Cronenberg turns S&M injury to S. F. metaphor', *Cinefantastique*, 28, 3, 8–9, 61.

____ (1999a) '*Crimes of the Future/Red Cars*', *Cinefantastique*, 31, 8, 7.

____ (1999b) '*eXistenZ*: Video-gaming Cronenberg Style', *Cinefantastique*, 31, 5, 7.

Jones, Kent (2005) 'Stay Away Closer', *Cinemascope*, 23, Summer, 44–6.

Jones, Martha (1978) 'Cronenberg on Wheels', *Cinema Canada*, 49/50, 17.

Jourd'hui, Gérard (1985) 'Les effets secondaires de la migraine', *Le nouvel Observateur*, 19 July.

Kael, Pauline (1986) '*The Fly*', in *Hooked*. New York: E. P. Dutton, 209–12.

Kaminsky, Ralph (1981) 'AVEM Launches *Scanners* in 450 Sites with Big Ad/Pub $$', *Film Journal*, 84, 1, 10–11.

Karani, Cathy and Alain Schlockoff (1989) 'Faux semblants', *L'Écran fantastique*, 101, 20–5.

Kareda, Urjo (1967) 'Cinethon: A Bewildering Madness', *Globe and Mail*, 19 June, 14.

Kaufman, Anthony (2003) 'David Cronenberg on *Spider*: Reality is What You Make Of It', *indieWIRE*, January, available online at: http://www.indiewire.com/people/ people_030228cronen.html (accessed 26 November 2007).

Kaufmann, Linda (1998) David Cronenberg's Surreal Abjection', in *Bad Girls and Sick Boys: Fantasies in Contemporary Art and Culture*. Berkeley: University of California Press, 115–45.

Keane, S. (2002) 'From Hardware to Fleshware: Plugging into David Cronenberg's *eXistenZ*', in Geoff King and Tania Krzywinska (eds) *Screenplay: Cinema/Videogames/Interfaces*. London: Wallflower Press, 145–56.

Kellner, Douglas (1989) 'David Cronenberg: Panic Horror and the Postmodern Body', *Canadian Journal of Political and Social Theory*, 13, 3, 89–101.

Keough, Peter (2007) 'Promises Fulfilled at TIFF: Cronenberg III', *The Phoenix.com*, 16 September, available online at: http://www.thephoenix. com/OutsideTheFrame/ (accessed 10 December 2007).

Kerekes, David and David Slater (2000) *See No Evil: Banned Films and Video Controversy*. Manchester: HeadPress, 65–7.

Kermode, Mark (1992) 'Interview with David Cronenberg', *Sight and Sound*, 1, 11, 10–13.

____ (1997) 'Crash Course 1: letter', *Sight and Sound*, 7, 9, 64.

____ (2001) 'I was a Teenage Horror Fan: or, "How I Learned To Stop Worrying and Love Linda Blair"', in Martin Barker and Julian Petley (eds) *Ill Effects: The Media/Violence Debate*, second edition. London: Routledge, 126–34.

Kermode, Mark and Julian Petley (1997) 'Road Rage: Cronenberg's *Crash* and its would-be censors', *Sight and Sound*, 7, 6, 16–18.

Kimber, Gary (1989) David Cronenberg on *Dead Ringers*', *Cinefantastique*, 19, 1–2, 86–7, 120.

King, Stephen (1979) *The Dead Zone*. New York: Viking Press.

____ (1981) *Danse Macabre*. New York: Everest House.

Kirkland, Bruce (1986) '*The Fly*', *Cinefantastique*, 16, 3, 15, 60.

____ (1987) 'After a lengthy, forced hiatus, *The Fly* marks Cronenberg's return to directing', *Cinefantastique*, 17, 1, 47.

____ (1999) 'Original Cronenberg: Filmmaker goes against Hollywood Grain again with Sci-Fi Thriller', *Toronto Sun*, 18 April, S3.

____ (2005a) 'At Cannes, Canadian David Cronenberg's Provocative Film Shocks Festival', *Toronto Sun*, 17 May, 42.

____ (2005b) 'History Lesson', *Toronto Sun*, 4 September, S14.

Klady, Leonard (1983) '*Videodrome*', *Variety*, 2 February, 18.

Klawans, Stuart (2008) 'Endgame: David Cronenberg's *At the Suicide of the Last Jew in the World*', *Nextbook: A New Read on Jewish Culture*, 20 March, available online at: http:// www.nextbook.org/cultural/feature.html?id=803 (accessed 24 July 2008).

Klein, Naomi (1996) 'Let's Stop Tolerating Corporate Censorship', *Toronto Star*, 25 November, A17.

Klevan, Andrew (2000) 'The Mysterious Disappearance of Style: Some Critical Notes About the Writing on *Dead Ringers*', in Michael Grant (ed.) *The Modern Fantastic: The Films of David Cronenberg*. Trowbridge: Flicks Books, 148–67.

Knee, Adam (1992) 'The Metamorphosis of *The Fly*', *Wide Angle*, 14, 1, 20–34.

Knelman, Martin (1969) 'Three Shoot on a Shoestring', *Globe and Mail*, 27 October, 15.

____ (1975) 'Trash, Not Better Movies, May Be the Product of the Quota System', *Globe and Mail*, 6 September, 33.

____ (1977) *This Is Where We Came In: The Career and Character of Canadian Film*. Toronto: McClelland and Stewart.

____ (2002) 'Egoyan and Cronenberg Face Off', *Toronto Star*, 30 June, D02.

Knight, Chris (2007) 'Review: *Eastern Promises*', *National Post/Vancouver Sun*, 14 September, available online at: http://www.canwest.com (accessed 27 November 2007).

Köhne, Julia (2005) 'Männliche Schwangerschaft und weibliche Penetration: Transmutationen, Shifts und die Figur des Dritten in David Cronenbergs *Shivers*', in Julia Köhne, Ralph Kuschke and Arno Meteling (eds) *Splatter Movies*. Berlin: Bertz & Fischer, 68–88.

Kraglund, John (1970) 'Synergetic Theatre: Gong, Song, Slides and Sermon', *Globe and Mail*, 2 April, 11.

Kristeva, Julia (1982) *Powers of Horror: An Essay on Abjection*, trans. Leon Roudiez. New York: Columbia University Press.

Kroll, Jack (1981) 'The Beauty of Horror', *Newsweek*, 9 March, 73, 75.

Kuhn, Annette (1999) '*Crash* and Film Censorship in the UK', *Screen*, 40, 4, 446–50.

Kuhn, Thomas (1962) *The Structure of Scientific Revolutions*. Chicago: Chicago University Press.

Lacey, Liam (1987) 'Book Industry Groups Protest Anti-Porn Bill', *Globe and Mail*, 17 September.

Lahde, Maurice (2006) 'Den Wahn erlebbar machen. Zur Inszenierung von Halluzinationen in Ron Howard's *A Beautiful Mind* und David Cronenberg's *Spider*', in Jörg Helbig (ed.) *Camera Doesn't Lie*. Trier: WVT, 43–7.

Lalanne, Jean-Marc (1999) 'Cinéma Chromosome', *Cahiers du cinéma*, 534, April, 63–5.

Landesman, Cosmo (2005) '*A History of Violence*', *Sunday Times*, 2 October, 14.

Landsberg, Michele (1989) 'Killer's Rage Familiar for Many Canadians', *Toronto Star*, 8 December, A1.

Lane, Anthony (2007) 'Space Cases', *New Yorker*, 17 September, available online at: http://www. newyorker.com (accessed 3 December 2007).

Lanken, Dane (1975a) 'Writer-Director David Cronenberg Protests the Maniac Tag', *Montreal Gazette*, 11 October, 19.

___ (1975b) '*The Parasite Murders* Is Horrible', *Montreal Gazette*, 11 October, 19.

Larue, Johanne (1993) 'Le Canada selon David Cronenberg', *Séquences*, 167, November–December, 53–6.

Latham, Rob (1997) 'Screening Desire: Posthuman Couplings in Atom Egoyan's *Speaking Parts* and David Cronenberg's *Videodrome*', in Michael A. Morrison (ed.) *Trajectories of the Fantastic*. New York: Greenwood Press, 171–82.

Laurence Pastore, Judith (ed.) (1993) *Confronting AIDS Through Literature: The Responsibilities of Representation*. Urbana: University of Illinois Press.

Lauwaert, Dirk (1990) *David Cronenberg: Tekst en Beeldessay*. Leuven: Stuc publikatie.

Lavery, David (2001) 'From Cinespace to Cyberspace: Zionists and Agents, Realists and Gamers in *The Matrix* and *eXistenZ*', *Journal of Popular Film and Television*, 28, 4, 150–7.

Leach, Jim (2006) *Film in Canada*. Oxford: Oxford University Press.

Leayman, Charles (1976) 'They Came from Within', *Cinefantastique*, 5, 3, 22–3.

Lee, Nathan (2005a) 'A Very American Story', *New York Sun*, 18 May, 14.

___ (2005b) 'Simply Smashing', *New York Sun*, 23 September, 13.

Lefort, Gérard (1996) 'Conduite en état d'ivresse sexuelle', *Libération*, 18 May, 28.

___ (1999) 'Belles questions eXistenZielles', *Libération*, 18 February.

Levin, Charles (2003) 'The Body of the Imagination in David Cronenberg's *Naked Lunch*', *Canadian Journal of Psychoanalysis*, 11, 523–36.

___ (2004) 'Sexuality as Masquerade: Reflections on David Cronenberg's *M. Butterfly*', *Canadian Journal of Psychoanalysis*, 12, 115–27.

Lewis, Brent (1987) 'Nightmare Man: Interview with David Cronenberg', *Films and Filming*, 389, 17.

Lidolt, Jon (2007) 'Working With Cronenberg on *Crimes*', *DVD Savant*, available online at: http://www.dvdtalk.com/dvdsavant/s1830cron.html (accessed 3 September 2007).

Lim, Dennis (2002) 'Under My Skin: The Films of David Cronenberg at Anthology Film Archives', *Village Voice*, 10–16 July, available online at: http://www.villagevoice.com/film/0228,lim,36368,20.html (accessed 4 September 2007).

___ (2005) 'The way of the Gun', *Village Voice*, 27 September, 34.

Link, André (1975) 'Delaney's Dreary Denigration', *Cinema Canada*, 22, 24.

Liptay, Fabienne (2006) 'Sinn es noch einmal, *Spider!* Ambiguität als Voraussetzung für die doppelte Filmlektüre am Beispiel von David Cronenbergs *Spider*', in Jörg Helbig (ed.) *Camera Doesn't Lie.* Trier: WVT, 189–223.

Littau, Karin (1999) 'Adaptation, Teleportation and Mutation from Langelaan's to Cronenberg's *The Fly*', in Deborah Cartmell, I. Q. Hunter, Heidi Kaye and Imelda Whelehan (eds) *Alien Identities: Exploring Differences in Film and Fiction*. London: Pluto Press, 141–55.

Livingston, Ira (1993) 'The Traffic in Leeches: David Cronenberg's *Rabid* and the Semiotics of Parasitism', *American Imago: Studies in Psychoanalysis and Culture*, 50, 4, 515–33.

Lofficier, Jean-Marc and Randy (1983a) '*Videodrome*: entretien avec David Cronenberg', *L'Écran fantastique*, 35, 18–23.

___ (1983b) '*The Dead Zone*: entretien avec David Cronenberg', *L'Écran fantastique*, 39, 50–7.

Lorenz, Konrad (1967) *On Aggression*. New York: Bantam.

Lowenstein, Adam (1999) 'Canadian Horror Made Flesh: Contextualizing David Cronenberg', *Post Script*, 18, 2, 37–51.

___ (2004) 'David Cronenberg and the Face of National Authorship', *Kinokultura*, 6, available online at: http://www.kinokultura.com/articles/oct04-natcine-lowenstein.html (accessed 10 October 2007).

___ (2005) *Shocking Representation: Historical Trauma, National Cinemas and the Modern Horror Film*. New York: Columbia University Press, 145–75.

Lucas, Tim (1979) '*The Brood*', *Cinefantastique*, 9, 1, 42.

___ (1981) 'David Cronenberg: A Post Script', *The Vladimir Nabokov Research Newsletter*, 7, Fall, 10–15.

___ (1982a) '*Videodrome*: Cronenberg's Wild Weird Attack on TV', *Cinefantastique*, 12, 1.

___ (1982b) '*Videodrome*', *Cinefantastique*, 12, 2–3, 4–7.

___ (1982c) '*Videodrome*', *Cinefantastique*, 12, 5–6, 6–7.

_____ (1982d) 'Dead Zone', Cinefantastique, 13, 2–3, 10.

_____ (1983a) 'The Image as Virus: Filming Videodrome', in Piers Handling (ed.) The Shape of Rage: The Films of David Cronenberg. Toronto: General Publishing, 149–58.

_____ (1983b) 'Videodrome', Cinefantastique, 13, 4, 4–5.

_____ (1986a) 'The Fly: New Buzz on an Old Theme', American Cinematographer, 67, 9, 60–7.

_____ (1986b) 'The Fly-papers', Cinefex, 28, 4–29.

_____ (1987) 'Le choc des images', L'Écran fantastique, 76, January, 23–6.

_____ (2004) 'Medium Cruel: Reflections on Videodrome', Videodrome Criterion DVD Booklet, 15–31.

_____ (2008) Videodrome. London: Millipede Press.

Lucas, Tim and FAL (1987) 'La mouche', Starfix, 44, January, 27–31, 80.

Lueken, Verena (2007) 'Aus dem Tagebuch der Toten', Frankfurter Allgemeine Zeitung, 20 September, 41.

Lyons, Donald (1992) 'Lubricating the Muse', Film Comment, 28, 1, 14–16.

McM, M. (1969) '…While Cronenberg Takes a Weird Look at Life', Globe and Mail, 1 March, 22.

MacDonald, Gayle (2006) 'Cronenberg sees Red as Harper Trims "Fat"', Globe and Mail, 1 November, R1.

MacInnis, Craig (1993) 'This Butterfly Never Leaves the Ground', Toronto Star, 1 October, C3.

MacKinnon, Kenneth (2005) 'The Mainstream AIDS Movie Prior to the 1990s', in Graeme Harper and Andrew Moor (eds) Signs of Life: Medicine and Cinema. London: Wallflower Press, 33–44.

MacMillan, Robert (1981) 'Shivers … Makes Your Flesh Creep!', Cinema Canada, 72, 11–15.

MacRae, Paul (1982) 'Video Machines End the Tyranny of the Tube', Globe and Mail, 16 October.

Magid, Ron (1986) 'More about The Fly', American Cinematographer, 67, 9, 68–76.

Magistrale, Tony (1996) 'Cronenberg's Only Really Human Movie', Post Script, 15, 2, 40–5.

Maher, Janemaree (2002) '"We don't do babies": Reproduction in David Cronenberg's Dead Ringers', Journal of Gender Studies, 11, 2, 119–28.

Malcolm, Derek (1988) 'British Film Man in 70 Million Pounds Production Deal', Guardian, 4 November.

_____ (1992) 'Diet of demons', Guardian Weekly, 3 May.

_____ (1997) 'On a freeway to sex, death and nihilism', Guardian Weekly, 15 June, 27.

_____ (1999) 'SFX on the Brain: Derek Malcolm in Berlin feels like pulling the Plug on David Cronenberg', Guardian, 18 February, 11.

Marchand, Philip (2005) Ghost Empire: How the French Almost Conquered North America. Toronto: McClelland and Stewart.

Marchetti, Gina (2004) 'From Fu Manchu to M. Butterfly and Irma Vep: Cinematic Incarnations of Chinese Villainy', in Murray Pomerance (ed.) Bad: Infamy, Darkness, Evil, and Slime on Screen. Albany, NY: State University of New York Press, 187–200.

Marcuse, Herbert (1964) One-Dimensional Man. Boston: Beacon Press.

_____ (1966) Eros and Civilization. Boston: Beacon Press.

Maronie, Sam (1981) 'Interview with David Cronenberg: Scanners', Starlog, 43, 24–8.

Martin, Bruce (1969) 'For $10.000 He's Making Canada's Most Controversial Movie', Toronto Star, 13 September, 29.

Martin, Jack (1983) Videodrome. London: New English Library.

Martin, Judith (1981) 'Sick Scanners', Washington Post, 16 January, 23.

Martin, Robert (1976) 'A Canadian Movie Wins at Box Office with a Bloody Tale of Wormy Parasites', Globe and Mail, 29 June, 29.

Maslin, Janet (1983) 'Videodrome: Is This What's Next?', New York Times, 4 February, C9:1

_____ (1991) 'Drifting in and out of a Kafka-esque Reality', New York Times, 27 December, C1.

_____ (1993) 'Seduction and the Impossible Dream', New York Times, 1 October, C3.

_____ (1996) 'At Cannes, the Star was Quality', New York Times, 26 May, 11.

_____ (1999) 'In a Grisly Virtual Game, Flesh and Blood Are Not', New York Times, 23 April, E21.

Mathijs, Ernest (1993) 'Moraliteit en hedendaagse film: David Cronenberg'. Nieuw Tijdschrift van de VUB, 6, 3, 201–12.

_____ (1998) 'David Cronenberg en de horrorfilm', Nieuw Tijdschrift van de VUB, February, 92–106.

_____ (1999) 'Kung-Fu and Fish: The Story Worlds of eXistenZ and The Matrix', Cinemagie, 229, 53–7.

_____ (2000) 'Referentiekaders van Filmkritiek; een onderzoek naar de interpretatie en evaluatie van Cronenberg', unpublished PhD dissertation, Free University of Brussels.

_____ (2001) 'Reel to Real: Film History in Pynchon's Vineland', Literature/Film Quarterly, 29, 1, 62–70.

_____ (2002) 'Controverse en Censuur in Film: de Receptie van Crash in Groot-Brittannie', Nieuw Tijdschrift van de VUB, 15, 4, 93–109.

_____ (2003a) 'AIDS References in the Critical Reception of David Cronenberg: It May Not Be Such a Bad Disease After All', Cinema Journal, 42, 4, 29–45.

____ (2003b) 'The Making of a Cult Reputation: Topicality and Controversy in the Critical Reception of *Shivers*', in Mark Jancovich, Antonio Lazaro-Reboll, Julian Stringer and Andy Willis (eds) *Defining Cult Movies: The Cultural Politics of Oppositional Taste*. Manchester: Manchester University Press, 109–26.

____ (2005) 'Bad Reputations: The Reception of Trash Cinema', *Screen*, 46, 4, 451–72.

____ (2006a) 'The Critical Reception of *The Lord of the Rings* in the United Kingdom' in Ernest Mathijs (ed.) *The Lord of the Rings: Popular Culture in Global Context*. London: Wallflower Press, 119–42.

____ (2006b) '*The Lord of the Rings* and Family: A View on Text and Reception', in Ernest Mathijs and Murray Pomerance (eds) *From Hobbits to Hollywood: Essays on Peter Jackson's Lord of the Rings*. New York and Amsterdam: Rodopi Editions, 41–63.

____ (2007a) 'David Cronenberg', in Steven Jay Schneider (ed.) *501 Movie Directors*. Haupauge, NY: Barron's Entertainment, 470–1.

____ (2007b) 'Tijd, Cultcinema en de jaren Tachtig: *Back to the Future* en *Peggy Sue Got Married* via *Donnie Darko* en *It's a Wonderful Life*', in Daniel Biltereyst and Christel Stalpaert (eds) *Filmsporen, Opstellen over film, Verleden en Geheugen*. Ghent: Academia Press, 180–98.

Mathijs, Ernest and Bert Mosselmans (2000) 'Mimesis and the Representation of Reality: A Historical World View', *Foundations of Science*, 5, 1, 61–102.

Mathijs, Ernest and Xavier Mendik (2008) 'What is Cult Cinema?', in Ernest Mathijs and Xavier Mendik (eds) *The Cult Film Reader*. London: Open University Press/McGraw-Hill, 1–11.

McCarthy, Todd (1979) '*The Brood*', *Variety*, 295/5, 6 June, 20.

____ (1981a) 'Cronenberg Likes Freedom Found in Canadian Filming', *Variety*, 7 January, 18.

____ (1981b) '*Scanners*', *Variety*, 21 January, 26.

____ (1993) '*M. Butterfly*', *Variety*, 10 September.

____ (1996) '*Crash*', *Variety*, 17 May, 30.

____ (2000) 'Leftovers, Launches Feed Toronto Festgoers', *Variety*, 18 September, 22.

____ (2005) '*A History of Violence*', *Variety*, 16 May.

____ (2007) '*Eastern Promises*', *Variety*, 8 September, available online at: http://www.variety.com (accessed 27 November 2007).

McCarthy, Todd and Leonard Klady (1996) '*Secrets* takes top spot', *Variety*, 27 May, 14.

McCarty, John (1981) *Splatter Movies: Breaking the Last Taboo*. Albany, NY: FantaCo Enterprises.

McDonnell, David (1983) 'Films of Fantasy, Fear and Flying: Videodrome', *Starlog*, 76, 91.

McGill, Hannah (2005) 'The Brutal Truth', *Glasgow Herald*, 29 September, 8.

McGrath, Patrick (1991) *Spider*. New York: Vintage.

McGreal, Jill (1984) 'Interview with David Cronenberg', in Wayne Drew (ed.) *David Cronenberg: BFI Dossier 21*. London: British Film Institute, 3–15.

McGregor, Gaile (1992) 'Grounding the Countertext: David Cronenberg and the Ethnospecificity of Horror', *Canadian Journal of Film Studies*, 2, 1, 43–62.

McKellar, Don (1999) 'Children of Canada', *Sight and Sound*, 9, 7, 58–9.

McKinnon, John (1982) '*Videodrome*: Insidious Effects of High Tech', *Cinema Canada*, 81, 32.

McLarty, Lianne (1996) 'Beyond the Veil of the Flesh: Cronenberg and the Disembodiment of Horror', in Barry Keith Grant (ed.) *The Dread of Difference: Gender and the Horror Film*. Austin: University of Texas Press, 231–52.

McLuhan, Marshall (1964) *Understanding Media: The Extensions of Man*. New York: McGraw-Hill.

McLuhan, Marshall with Quentin Fiore (1967) *The Medium is the Message: An Inventory of Effects*. New York: Random House.

Medjuck, Joe (1969) '*Stereo*', *Take One*, 2, 3, 22.

Meininger, Sylvestre (1998) 'Faux-semblants: masochisme masculin et politique des auteurs', *Iris*, 26, 65–81.

Melnyk, George (2004) *One Hundred Years of Canadian Cinema*. Toronto: University of Toronto Press.

Mérigeau, Pascal (1996) 'Sujet 'sale' pour un film propre', *Le Monde*, 19 May, 20.

Messias, Hans (1992) 'Die Schuld der Opfer: die neuen Filme von David Cronenberg', *Filmdienst*, 45, 10, 4–7.

____ (1993) '*M. Butterfly*', *Filmdienst*, 46, 24, 24.

Mestdach, Dave (2005) 'Geweldig, geweldig: *A History of Violence*', *Focus Knack*, 2 November, 76.

Milgram, Stanley (1974) *Obedience to Authority*. New York: Harper & Row.

Miller, David and Greg Philo (1996) 'Against Orthodoxy: The Media Do Influence Us', *Sight and Sound*, 6, 12, 18–20.

Miller, David and Kevin Williams (1994) 'Negotiating HIV/AIDS Information: Agendas, Media Strategies and the News', in John Eldridge (ed.) *Getting the Message: News, Truth and Power*. London: Routledge, 126–42.

Miller, David, Jenny Kitzinger, Kevin Williams and Peter Beharrell (1998) *The Circuit of Mass Communication: Media Strategies, Representation, and Audience Reception in the AIDS Crisis*. London: Sage.

Modleski, Tania (1986) 'The Terror of Pleasure: the Contemporary Horror Film and Postmodern Theory', in *Studies in Entertainment: Critical Approaches to Mass Culture*. Bloomington: Indiana University Press, 155–66.

Monk, Katherine (2001) *Weird Sex and Snowshoes, and Other Canadian Film Phenomena*. Vancouver: Raincoast Books, 235–8.

____ (2007) 'Star of *Eastern Promises* Finds a Connection Between Motherhood and her Latest Film', *Vancouver Sun*, 14 September, H3.

Monroe, Chris (2005) '*A History of Violence*', *Christian Spotlight on the Movies*, 23 September, available online at: http://www.christiananswers.net (accessed 12 October 2006).

Moore, Suzanne (1996) 'Mooreover: our Bodies, our Texts', *Guardian*, 8 June, 6.

Morris, Desmond (1967) *The Naked Ape*. New York: McGraw-Hill.

____ (1969) *The Human Zoo*. New York: McGraw-Hill.

Morris, Peter (1994) *David Cronenberg: A Delicate Balance*. Toronto: ECW Press.

Mulvey, Laura (1975) 'Visual Pleasure and Narrative Cinema', *Screen*, 16, 3, 6–18.

Murphy, Kathleen and Richard Jameson (1993) 'Scented memories, whiffs of bad faith', *Film Comment*, 29, 6, 66–7.

Murphy, Marsh (2006) '*Nobody Waved Goodbye*', in Jerry White (ed) *The Cinema of Canada*. London: Wallflower Press, 53–62.

Nelmes, Jill (ed.) (2003) *An Introduction to Film Studies*, third edition. London: Routledge.

Newman, Kim (1984) '*Fast Company*: The Machine Movie', in Wayne Drew (ed.) *David Cronenberg: BFI Dossier 21*. London: British Film Institute, 45–7.

____ (1999) 'Time Machines', *Sight and Sound*, 9, 4, 11.

Nguyen, Dan Thu (1990) 'The "Projectile" Movie Revisited: The Female Body in *Track 29* and *Dead Ringers*', *Film Criticism*, 14, 3, 39–54.

Nicholas, Joe and John Price (1998) *Advanced Studies in Media*. Cheltenham: Thomas Nelson and Sons.

Norcen, Luca (1994) '*M. Butterfly*', *Segnocinema*, 14, 65, 36–7.

Nutman, Philip (1992) 'The Exploding Family', in Christopher Golden (ed.) *Cut! Horror Writers on Horror Film*. New York: Berkeley Books, 171–82.

O'Connell, Alex (2002) 'Geek Bares his Gifts', *Times*, 4 February.

O'Day, Mark (2002) 'David Cronenberg', in Yvonne Tasker (ed.) *Fifty Contemporary Filmmakers*. London: Routledge, 126–35.

O'Hehir, Andrew (2003) 'The Baron of Blood does Bergman', *Salon.com*, 28 February, available online at: http://www.salon.com/topics/david_cronenberg/ (accessed 26 October 2007).

____ (2005) 'Beyond the Multiplex', *Salon.com*, 22 September, available online at: http://www.salon.com (accessed 20 November 2007).

O'Pray, Michael (1992) 'Fatal Knowledge', *Sight and Sound*, 1, 11, 9–10.

O'Toole, Lawrence (1979a) 'Growing Bumps in the Night', *Maclean's*, 11 June, 50.

____ (1979b) 'The Cult of Horror', *Maclean's*, 16 July, 46–7, 49–50.

____ (2008) 'The Cult of Horror', in Ernest Mathijs and Xavier Mendik (eds) *The Cult Film Reader*. London: Open University Press/McGraw-Hill, 257–62.

Oetjen, Almut and Holger Wacker (1993) *Organischer Horror: Die Filme des David Cronenberg*. Meitingen: Corian-Verlag.

Oren, Michel (1998) 'The Grotesque in the Films of David Cronenberg', *Exposure*, 31, 3/4, 5–12.

Osgerby, Bill (2005) *Biker: Style and Subculture on Hell's Highway*. Guildford, CT: Lyons Press.

____ (2007) *Full Throttle Cinema: Hollywood, Subculture and the Biker Mythology – A Study in Cultural History*. London: I. B. Tauris.

Oster, Corinne (1999) '*Dead Ringers*: A Case of Psychosis in Twins', *American Imago*, 56, 2, 181–202.

Overbey, David (1977) 'David Cronenberg: quand le Canada frissonne', *L'Écran fantastique*, 2, 32–9.

Palmer, Robert (1992) 'The Novelist, the Director and the Mugwumps', *American Film*, January–February, 32–7.

Pao, Angela (1992) 'The Critic And The Butterfly, Sociocultural Contexts And The Reception Of David Henry Hwang's *M. Butterfly*', *Amerasia Journal*, 18, 3, 1–16.

Parker, Andrew (1993) 'Grafting David Cronenberg; Monstrosity, AIDS Media, National/Sexual Difference', in Marjorie Garber, Jann Mattlock and Rebecca Walkowitz (eds) *Media Spectacles*. New York: Routledge, 209–31.

Parra, Danièle and Philippe Ross (1991) 'David Cronenberg: les tréfonds de l'âme et de la chair', *La revue du cinéma*, 472, 57–64.

Pastor, Andrea (1992) 'Un anomalo tradimento', *Filmcritica*, 43, 430, 535–44.

Pastore, Judith Laurence (ed.) (1993) *Confronting AIDS Through Literature: The Responsibilities of Representation*. Urbana: University of Illinois Press.

Paul, William (1994) 'Revolting Bodies', in *Laughing Screaming: Modern Hollywood Horror and Comedy*. New York: Columbia University Press, 353–4, 368–80, 396–400.

Peachment, Chris (1983) '*Videodrome*', *Time Out*, 24 November.

Peary, Danny (1981) *Cult Movies*. New York: Delta Books.

____ (1991) *Cult Movie Stars*. New York: Simon and Shuster.

Pecchioli, Marcello (1994) *Effetto Cronenberg: Metacritica per un cinema delle mutazione*. Bologna: Edizione Pendragon.

Pede, Ronnie (1999) 'Berlinale 1999', *Film en Televisie*, 491, April, 10–12.

Pener, Degen (1996) 'Ted's Civil War', *Entertainment Weekly*, 354, 22 November, 19–24.

Penley, Constance (1986) 'Time Travel, Primal Scene and the Critical Dystopia', *Camera Obscura*, 15, 67–86.

____ (1997a) *NASA/Trek: Popular Science and Sex in America*. London: Verso.

____ (1997b) *The Visible Woman: Imaging Technologies, Gender and Science*. London: Verso.

Persall, Steve (1999) 'The Marriage of Self and Technology', *St. Petersburg Times*, 23 April, 8.

Petit, A. (1975) 'Parasite Murders', *Vampirella*, 20, 41–2.

Petley, Julian (1997) 'Crash Course 2: letter', *Sight and Sound*, 7, 9, 64.

Petley, Julian and Martin Barker (1997) 'The "Effects" Debate: Letter', *Sight and Sound*, 7, 2, 70–1.

Pevere, Geoff (1992) 'Letter From Canada', *Film Comment*, 28, 2, 61–5.

Pevere, Geoff and Creig Dymond (1996) *Mondo Canuck*. Scarborough, Ont: Prentice-Hall.

Pizzello, Stephen (1997) 'Driver's Side: interview with David Cronenberg', *American Cinematographer*, 78, 4, 43–7.

Pluijgers, Jean-François (1999) '*eXistenZ*, un Cronenberg de sErieB', *La Libre Belgique*, 18 February.

Plunka, Gene A. (2005) 'John Guare and the Popular Culture Hype of Celebrity Status', in David Krasner (ed.) *A Companion to Twentieth-Century American Drama*. Oxford: Blackwell, 352–69.

Poirier, Agnes Catherine (2001) 'L'enfer Cronenberg en formation', *Libération*, 29 August, 28.

Polinien, Gilles (1981) '*Scanners*: entretien avec David Cronenberg', *L'Écran fantastique*, 19, July, 72–4.

Pomerance, Murray (2003) 'Neither Here Nor There: *eXistenZ* as "Elevator Film"', *Quarterly Review of Film and Video*, 20, 1–14.

Pompon, Géraldine and Pierre Véronneau (2003) *David Cronenberg: la beauté du chaos*. Paris: Cerf-Corlet.

Pope, Alexander (1711) *Essay on Criticism*, available online at: http://poetry.eserver.org/essay-on-criticism.html (accessed 11 March 2008).

Porter, John (1984a) 'Artists Discovering Film/ Post-War Toronto', *Vanguard*, June–August, 24–6.

____ (1984b) 'Consolidating Film Activity/Toronto in the '60s', *Vanguard*, June–August, 26–9.

Portman, Jamie (1976) '*Shivers* Generates Industry Shock Waves', *Ottawa Citizen*, 18 March, 74.

Porton, Richard (1999) 'The Film Director as Philosopher: An Interview with David Cronenberg', *Cineaste*, 24, 4, 4 9.

Pospíšil, Tomáš (2004) 'Films by David Cronenberg and the Fantastic Postmodern Body', in Franková Coelsh-Foisner (ed.) *The Human Figure in (Post-) Modern Fantastic Literature and Film*. Brno: Masarykova univerzita, 99–107.

Poulter, Sean (1996) 'Sony Determined to make Cash from *Crash*: Japanese Giant Ignores Outcry over Move to Show Depraved Sex and Wrecks Film in British Cinemas', *Daily Mail*, 9 December, 22.

Powell, Dilys (1976) 'In Jugular Vein', *Sunday Times*, 9 May, 35.

Prédal, René (1992) 'Comptes rendus: L' horreur intérieure: les films de David Cronenberg', *Cinémas*, 2, 2–3, 237–41.

Pringle, Douglas (1970) 'New Film in Toronto', *Artscanada*, 142–3, 50–4.

Pulleine, Tim (1983) '*Videodrome*', *Films and Filming*, 350, 43.

Queva, Marie (1996) 'L'orgasme auto-motive', *Les Echos*, 16 July.

Quinlan, David (1981) '*Scanners*', *Films Illustrated*, 10, 116, May, 287.

Rabey, David Ian (2003) 'Staging *Crash*: The sexualising of language in action', *Studies in Theatre and Performance*, 23, 1, 41–54.

Rabourdin, Dominique (1979) '*Chromosome 3*', *Cinéma*, 252, November, 88.

Rafferty, Terrence (1987) 'Out of the Blue', *Sight and Sound*, 56, 1, 30–3.

Ramasse, François (1980) '*Chromosome 3*', *Positif*, 227, 88–9.

____ (1989) 'La chair dans l' âme: Faux semblants', *Positif*, 337, 28–32.

Ramsay, Christine (1999) 'Dead Queers: One Legacy of the Trope of "Mind over Matter" in the Films of David Cronenberg', *Canadian Journal of Film Studies*, 8, 1, 53.

Ray, Robert (1993) Film Studies/Crisis/ Experimentation', *Film Criticism*, 17, 2–3, 56–78.

Rayner, Jonathan (2000) 'The Cult Film, Roger Corman, and the Cars that Ate Paris', in Xavier Mendik and Graeme Harper (eds) *Unruly Pleasures: The Cult Film and Its Critics*. Guildford: FAB Press, 223–33.

Rayns, Tony (1971a) 'Stereo', Monthly Film Bulletin, 38, 453, 204.

_____ (1971b) 'Crimes of the Future', Monthly Film Bulletin, 38, 454, 217–18.

Rea, Steven (1999) 'A Virtual Reality Game is at the Heart of eXistenZ', Philadelphia Enquirer, 23 April, 3.

Redfern, Nick (2004) 'Information and Entropy: The Disintegration of Narrative in Cronenberg's Videodrome', EnterText, 4, 3, 6–24.

Reed, Paul (1993) 'Early AIDS Fiction', in Judith Laurence Pastore (ed.) Confronting AIDS Through Literature: The Responsibilities of Representation. Urbana: University of Illinois Press, 91–4.

Reynolds, Nigel (1996) 'Violent, nasty, and morally vacuous', Daily Telegraph, 9 November.

Rickey, Carrie (1983) 'Make Mine Cronenberg', Village Voice, 1 February, 62–5.

_____ (2005) 'In Director's Hands, Sex and Violence are not the same-old same-old', Philadelphia Inquirer, 26 September.

Riepe, Manfred (1994) 'Das Fieber im Kopf: David Cronenbergs Filme', Blimp, 27–8, 44–54.

_____ (2002) Bildgeschwüre: Körper und Fremdkörper im Kino David Cronenbergs. Bielefeld: Transcript Verlag.

Robbins, Helen W. (1993) 'More Human Than I Am Alone: Womb Envy in David Cronenberg's The Fly and Dead Ringers', in Steven Cohan and Ina Rae Hark (eds) Screening the Male: Exploring Masculinities in Hollywood Cinema. London: Routledge, 134–47.

Robey, Tim (2003) 'A Haunting Exploration of Mental Breakdown: Masterpiece of Intricacy', Daily Telegraph, 3 January, 23.

Robinson, David (1980) 'A wasted Titanic and some titanic minnows', Times, 7 March.

Robinson, Lisa (1983) 'Videodrome: Interview with Deborah Harry', Starlog, 70, May, 50–1.

Robnik, Drehli and Michael Palm (eds) (1992) Und das Wort ist Fleisch geworden: Texte über Filme von David Cronenberg. Vienna: PVS Verlag.

Roche, David (2004) 'David Cronenberg's having to make the word be flesh', Post Script, 23, 2, 72–87.

Rodley, Chris (1992) 'So Deep in My Heart, That You're Really a Part of Me', in Ira Silverberg (ed.) Everything Is Permitted: The Making of Naked Lunch. New York: Grove Weidenfeld, 111–18.

_____ (1996) 'Crash: Interview with David Cronenberg', Sight and Sound, 6, 6,7–11.

_____ (ed.) (1997) Cronenberg on Cronenberg, second edition. London: Faber and Faber.

_____ (1999) 'Game Boy', Sight and Sound, 9, 4, 8.

Rolfe, Lee (1977) 'David Cronenberg on Rabid', Cinefantastique, 6, 3, 26.

Romney, Jonathan (1996) 'Shock Value', Guardian, 20 May, 8.

_____ (2003) 'He Calls Himself the Baron of Blood but Colleagues Say He's Just a "Split Personality": Interview with David Cronenberg', Independent on Sunday, 12 January, 8–11.

Roodnat, Joyce (1985) 'In de video-hel', NRC Handelsblad, 16 August.

Rooney, David (2002) 'Spider', Variety, 27 May.

Rosenbaum, Jonathan (1998) 'Criticism', in John Boorman and Walter Donahue (eds) Projections 8: Filmmakers on Filmmaking. London: Faber and Faber, 48–50.

_____ (2000) 'Two forms of Adaptation: Housekeeping and Naked Lunch', in James Naremore (ed.) Film Adaptation. New Brunswick, NJ: Rutgers University Press, 206–20.

_____ (2005) 'A Depth in the Family', Chicago Reader, 30 September, available online at: http://www.chicagoreader.com (accessed 10 October 2006).

Ross, Andrew (2004) No-Collar. Philadelphia: Temple University Press.

Roth, Marty (2000) 'Twice Two: The Fly and Invasion of the Body Snatchers', Discourse, 22, 1, 103–16.

Rouyer, Philip (1991) 'Incubation: les premiers films de David Cronenberg', Positif, 359, 23–5.

Royer, Carl (2005) 'The darkness is not the devil: atheism and "the death of affect" in the films of David Cronenberg', in The Spectacle of Isolation in Horror Films: Dark Parades. New York: Haworth Press, 53–75.

Russo, Mary (1994) 'Twins and Mutant Women: David Cronenberg's Dead Ringers', in The Female Grotesque. New York and London: Routledge, 107–27.

Sachs, Loyd (1976) 'They Came from Within', Variety, 282, 7, 24 March, 21.

Sage, Victor (2000) 'The Gothic, the Body, and the Failed Homeopathy Argument', in Xavier Mendik and Graeme Harper (eds) Unruly Pleasures: the Cult Film and Its Critics. Guildford: FAB Press, 137–53.

Said, Edward (1978) Orientalism. London: Routledge.

Said, S. F. (2002) 'After The Fly comes Spider', Daily Telegraph, 20 December, 23.

Salem, Rob (1991), 'Madness Series Gives Offbeat Gems Brief Shot at Big-Screen Exposure', Toronto Star, 6 September, D8.

Sammon, Paul (1981) 'David Cronenberg', Cinefantastique, 10, 4, 20–34.

Sanchez-Biosca, Vicente (1996) 'Entre le corps évanescent et le corps supplicié: Videodrome et les fantaisies postmodernes', Cinémas, 7, 1–2, 73–88.

Sanjek, David (1996) 'Dr. Hobbes's Parasites: Victims, Victimization, and Gender in David Cronenberg's *Shivers*', *Cinema Journal*, 36, 1, 55–74.

Sarris, Andrew (1983) 'Media Politics and other Potpourri', *Village Voice*, 28, 45, 8 November, 43.

____ (1986) 'Winged Victory: *The Fly*', *Village Voice*, 19 August, 47.

Sartor, Freddy (1984) '*Videodrome*: in the flesh', *Film en Televisie*, 329, October, 45.

Saunders, Doug (1999) 'Cronenberg Mines his Own *eXistenZ*', *Globe and Mail*, 17 April, C4.

Scheib, Richard (2005) '*The Brood*', in *Moria, The Science Fiction, Fantasy and Horror Review*, available online at: http://www.moria.co.nz/ horror/brood.htm (accessed 20 July 2007).

Schiff, Stephen (1984) '*The Brood*', in Wayne Drew (ed.) *David Cronenberg: BFI Dossier 21*. London: British Film Institute, 28–30.

Schlockoff, Alain (1975) 'Fantastique du monde entier: Festival de Cannes 1975', *Cinéma d'aujourd'hui*, 3, 3, Summer, 122–3.

Schneider, Steven Jay (2000) 'Kevin Williamson and the Rise of the Neo-Stalker', *Post Script: Essays in Film and the Humanities*, 19, 2, 73–87.

____ (ed.) (2003) *Fear Without Frontiers: Horror Cinema Across the Globe*. Guildford: FAB Press.

____ (ed.) (2007) *100 European Horror Films*. London: British Film Institute.

Schneider, Steven Jay and Tony Wiliams (eds) (2005) *Horror International*. Detroit: Wayne State University Press.

Schreger, C. (1977) '*Rabid*', *Variety*, 288, 8, 29 June, 28.

Schupp, Patrick (1976) 'Frissons', *Séquences*, 83, January, 35.

____ (1979) 'Les monstres de l'été', *Séquences*, 98, October, 27–32.

Scoffield, Sean (1999) *David Cronenberg's eXistenZ. A Graphic Novel*. Toronto: Keyporter Books.

Sconce, Jeffrey (2002) 'Irony Nihilism, and the New American "Smart" Film', *Screen*, 43, 4, 349–69.

Scorsese, Martin (1984) 'Internal Metaphors, External Horrors', in Wayne Drew (ed.) *David Cronenberg: BFI Dossier 21*. London: British Film Institute, 54.

Scott, Jay (1979a) 'New Canadian Company Plans 14 Films', *Globe and Mail*, 7 March.

____ (1979b) 'Higher Canadian Profile at Cannes in Future', *Globe and Mail*, 18 May.

____ (1979c) 'All the Monsters You've ever Had Nightmares About', *Globe and Mail*, 1 September.

____ (1979d) 'Jigsaw falls to pieces, and *Fast Company* isn't', *Globe and Mail*, 3 October.

____ (1981) '*Scanners*: High-Gloss Gore', *Globe and Mail*, 19 January, 17.

____ (1983) 'Cronenberg Bright, Gentle, Master of Gore', *Globe and Mail*, 1 February.

____ (1984a) 'ACTRA Porn Policy Meets Resistance', *Globe and Mail*, 21 March.

____ (1984b) 'Actors Protest ACTRA Porn Policy', *Globe and Mail*, 27 March.

____ (1986) '*The Fly*: David Cronenberg elevates *The Fly* to art without pulling his punches', *Globe and Mail*, 15 August.

____ (1992) '*Naked Lunch*', *Globe and Mail*, 10 January.

Seiler, Andy (1996) '*Crash* lands NC-17 Rating: "this is not a film for children"', *USA Today*, 3 June, 1D.

Shale, Tom (1982) 'The Ghostly Grab: One Mote Potshot at TV', *Washington Post*, 30 May, G1.

Sharrett, Christopher (1983) 'Apocalypticism in the Contemporary Horror Film', unpublished PhD dissertation, New York University.

____ (1986) 'Myth and Ritual in the Post-Industrial Landscape: the Horror Films of David Cronenberg', *Persistence of Vision*, 3, 4, 111–30.

Shaviro, Steven (1993) *The Cinematic Body*. Minneapolis: University of Minnesota Press.

Shaw, D. B. (2002) '"The Video Word Made Flesh": Spectacular Transgressions in David Cronenberg's *Videodrome*', *Foundation*, 84, 22–35.

Shepard, Richard (1969) 'Going Out Guide: Flicks', *New York Times*, 7 December, 32.

Shingle, Bryan (2005) '*Scanners*', *Motherfucking Masterpieces*, 1 May, available online at: http:// www.forbisthemighty.com/acidlogic/mm_ scanners.htm (accessed 17 July 2007).

Shoard, Catherine (2003) 'Breakneck Shots from the Slums Cinema', *Sunday Telegraph*, 5 January, 7.

Shone, Tom (1997) 'Crashing bore not auto erotica', *Sunday Times*, 8 June, 11.

Shotton, Sheila (1990) 'Swell Party for Metro's most talented', *Toronto Star*, 11 October, D6.

Shuster, Nat (1976) '*Shivers*', *Motion*, 5, 3, 47–8.

Siclier, Jacques (1998) 'Jeremy Irons sous le scalpel de David Cronenberg (TV)', *Le Monde*, 16 February, 22.

Siegel, Lois (1980) 'Artists of Illusion', *Cinema Canada*, 63, 20–7.

Silverman, Michael (1984) 'A Post-Modern Cronenberg', in Wayne Drew (ed.) *David Cronenberg: BFI Dossier 21*. London: British Film Institute, 31–4.

Sinclair, Iain (1999) *Crash*. London: British Film Institute.

Siren, Paul (1984) 'Censorship and Pornography: ACTRA replies to dissidents', *Cinema Canada*, 107, 6.

Skloot R. (1990) 'Breaking The Butterfly – The Politics of Henry David Hwang', *Modern Drama*, 33, 1, 59–66.

Slotkin, Richard (1973) *Regeneration Through Violence: The Mythology of the American Frontier.* Middletown: Wesleyan University Press.

Smith, Gavin (1997) 'David Cronenberg: interviewed', *Film Comment*, 33, 2, 14–29.

Smith, Marq (1999) 'Wound Envy: Touching Cronenberg's *Crash*', *Screen*, 40, 2, 193–202.

Smith, Murray (2000) '(A)moral Monstrosity', in Michael Grant (ed.) *The Modern Fantastic: The Films of David Cronenberg.* Trowbridge: Flicks Books, 69–73.

Snead, Elizabeth (1999) 'Virtual Certainty: Films Reflect Computer Fears', *USA Today*, 21 April, 1D.

Snider, Norman (1974) 'Just Two Innocent Canadian Boys in Wicked Hollywood', *Saturday Night*, 89, 7, July, 17–22.

____ (1980) 'Pop Goes the Culture Once Again', *Globe and Mail*, 8 March.

____ (1983) 'Temporarily Out of Vogue but the Beats Go On', *Globe and Mail*, 5 March.

____ (1984) 'Some Slings and Arrows from Outraged Lilliputians', *Globe and Mail*, 29 September.

Snowden, Lynn (1992) 'Which is the Fly and Which is the Human?', *Esquire*, February, 112–16.

Sontag, Susan (1988) *AIDS and Its Metaphors.* New York: Farrar, Straus and Giroux.

Sotinel, Thomas (2007) 'Excellent: Cronenberg toujours plus fort', *Le Monde*, 7 November, 23.

Spenser, Michael (1975) 'In Defence of the CDFC', *Saturday Night*, 90, 7, December, 4–6.

Springer, Claudia (1996) *Electronic Eros: Bodies and Desire in the Postindustrial Age.* Austin: University of Texas Press.

Staiger, Janet (2000) 'Hitchcock in Texas', in *Perverse Spectators: The Practices of Film Reception.* New York: New York University Press, 179–87.

____ (2005) *Media Reception Studies.* New York: New York University Press.

Stanbrook, Alan (1989) 'Cronenbergs Creative Cancers', *Sight and Sound*, 58, 1, 54–6.

Stathis, Lou (1984) 'It Comes From Within: Probing the Twisted (But Not Very Paranoid) Mind of David Cronenberg', *Heavy Metal*, 8, 6, 70–4.

Steele, Daria (1986) 'Epure pour les durs: *Scanners* (TV)', *Libération*, 2 January.

Stein, Elliott (1982) 'Have Horror Films Gone Too Far?', *New York Times*, 20 June, 2, 1.

Sterling, Bruce (ed) (1986) *Mirrorshades: Cyberpunk Anthology.* New York: Ace Books.

Sterritt, David (1981) 'Recalling Hollywood at the Height of the Cold War', *Christian Science Monitor*, January, 18.

Stockman, Eric (2005) '*A History of Violence*', *HUMO*, 3400/44, 31 October, 60.

Stolnitz, Jerome (1960) *Aesthetics and the Philosophy of Criticism.* Boston: Riverside Press.

Stratton, David (1999) '*eXistenZ*', *Variety*, 22 February, 56.

Strauss, Bob (2005) 'Hurts So Good', *Daily News of Los Angeles*, 26 September, U11.

Suner, Asuman (1998) 'Postmodern Double Cross: Reading David Cronenberg's *M. Butterfly* as a Horror Story', *Cinema Journal*, 37, 2, 49–64.

Sutton, Martin (1982) 'Schlock! Horror! The Films of David Cronenberg', *Films and Filming*, 337, October, 15–21.

Taubin, Amy (1988) 'Body Double: *Dead Ringers*', *Village Voice*, 33, 39, 27 September, 68.

____ (1992) 'The Wrong Body: Cronenberg and Burroughs', *Sight and Sound*, 1, 11, 8–9.

____ (1999) 'He Got Game', *Village Voice*, 7 April, 136.

____ (2005a) 'Kings But No Queens', *Film Comment*, 41, 4, 54.

____ (2005b) 'Model Citizens', *Film Comment*, 41, 5, 26.

____ (2007a) 'David Cronenberg: The Director of *Eastern Promises* on Muslim Extremism, the Russian Mob, and a Certain Naked Knife Fight', *Film Comment*, 43, 5, 52–5.

____ (2007b) 'Foreign Affairs', *Film Comment*, September/October, available online at: http://www.filmlinc.com/fcm/so07/cronenberg.htm (accessed 24 July 2008).

Taylor, Paul (1981) '*Scanners*', *Monthly Film Bulletin*, 48, 567, 78.

____ (1983) '*Videodrome*', *Monthly Film Bulletin*, 50, 598, November, 310–11.

____ (1984a) 'Cronenberg's Television Work', in Wayne Drew (ed.) *David Cronenberg: BFI Dossier 21.* London: British Film Institute, 43–4.

____ (1984b) '*Fast Company*', *Monthly Film Bulletin*, 51, 605, 188.

Teitelbaum, Sheli (2003) 'A Beautiful Twisted Mind', *Jerusalem Report*, 27 January, 42.

Temmerman, Jan (1989) 'Na de baby's nu de tweelingen', *De Morgen*, 9 January, 19.

____ (1990) 'Cronenberg en Kubrick in Het Stuc', *De Morgen*, 27 March, 28.

____ (2002) 'Aki Kaurismaaki wint filmfestival van Gent', *De Morgen*, 19 October.

Tesson, Charles (1979) 'Chromosome 3', *Cahiers du cinéma*, 306, December, 58.

____ (1981) 'Caïn et Abel, version S.F.: *Scanners*', *Cahiers du cinéma*, 322, April, 57–8.

____ (1983) 'Violence et voyeurisme', *Le Monde diplomatique*, 349, April, 26.

____ (1984a) 'À vos cassettes (*Videodrome*)', *Cahiers du cinéma*, 360–1, February, 108–9.

____ (1984b) 'Main, trop humain (*The Dead Zone*)', *Cahiers du cinéma*, 357, March, 50–1.

____ (1987) 'Les yeux plus gros que le ventre: *The Fly* de David Cronenberg', *Cahiers du cinéma*, 391, January, 25–7.

____ (1989) 'Voyage au bout de l'envers: *Dead Ringers* de David Cronenberg', *Cahiers du cinéma*, 419, February, 9 12.

____ (1999) 'L'Aventure Intérieure: Entretien avec David Cronenberg', *Cahiers du cinéma*, 534, April, 69.

Tesson, Charles and Thierry Cazals (1987) 'Quelque chose qui n'a jamais existé: entretien avec David Cronenberg', *Cahiers du cinéma*, 391, January, 28–30.

Tesson, Charles, Iannis Katsahnias and Vincent Ostria (1989) 'Entretien avec David Cronenberg', *Cahiers du cinéma*, 419, February, 12–13 and 62–4.

Testa, Bart (1978) 'The King of Blood', *Globe and Mail*, 31 May, F11.

____ (1980) 'New Wave is a New Style: "it's cool"', *Globe and Mail*, 16 February.

____ (1981) 'No Thrills or Chills', *MacLean's*, 2 February, 51.

____ (1983) 'Homage to a Master of Horror', *Globe and Mail*, 10 September.

____ (1989) 'Panic Pornography: *Videodrome* from Production to Seduction', *Canadian Journal of Political and Social Theory*, 13, 1–2, 56–72.

____ (1995) 'Technology's Body: Cronenberg, Genre, and the Canadian Ethos', *Post Script*, 15, 1, 38–56.

Testa, Bart, Brian McIlroy, Barry Grant, William Wees, Gene Walz and Murray Pomerance (1996) '*Crash* (and Burn?): FSAC Members Collide with Cronenberg', *FSAC/ACEC Newsletter*, 21, 1, 15–20.

Theberge, Paul (2004) 'These Are My Nightmares: Music and Sound in the Films of David Cronenberg', in Philip Hayward (ed.) *Off the Planet: Music, Sound, and Science-Fiction Cinema*. Eastleigh: John Libbey, 129–48.

Thomas, Bernard (1984) 'The Victim: New Rules For an Old Game', in Wayne Drew (ed.) *David Cronenberg: BFI Dossier 21*. London: British Film Institute, 41–2.

Thompson, David (1992) '*Naked Lunch*', *Sight and Sound*, 2, 1, 56–7.

Thompson, Kristin (2007) 'Cronenberg's Violent Reversals', available online at: http://www.davidbordwell.net/blog/?p=1412 (accessed 23 January 2008).

Thomson, Desson (2005) 'Likeable Face of Violence', *Washington Post*, 23 September, C04.

Thoret, Jean-Baptiste (1999) '*eXistenZ: Videodrome* 2.0', *Starfix*, 5, March–April, 22–7.

Tillson, Tamsen (1999) 'Feature Creature Captures Cronenberg', *Variety*, 4 January, 119.

Timpone, Anthony (1986) 'Geena Davis: The Birds, the Bees, and *The Fly*', *Starlog*, 110, September, 37–40.

Tinbergen, Niko (1968) 'On War and Peace in Animals and Men', *Science*, 160, 1411–18.

Tirard, Laurent (1999) 'La leçon de cinéma', *Studio Magazine*, 144, 92–5.

Tobin, Yann (1996) 'Qu'est-ce qu'ils entendent par pornographie? Entretien avec David Cronenberg', *Positif*, 425/6, 88–94.

Tookey, Chris (1996a) 'Ban This Car Crash Sex Film', *Daily Mail*, 9 November, 1.

____ (1996b) 'Morality Dies in the Twisted Wreckage', *Daily Mail*, 9 November, 6.

Tranchant, Marie-Noelle (2002) '*Spider* de David Cronenberg', *Le Figaro*, 13 November.

Tuchman, Mitch (1983) 'From the Lake of Niagara, Ontario', *Film Comment*, 19, 3, 9–10.

Tudor, Andrew (1989) *Monsters and Mad Scientists*. Oxford: Blackwell.

Urs, Jenny (1981) 'Nun killt mal schön', *Der Spiegel*, 11, 9 March.

Van de Popeliere, Bernard (1999) 'Is filmmaker David Cronenberg een vies ventje?', *P Magazine*, 12 May, 112–14.

Van den Tempel, Mark (1989) 'Horror: de ondergang van een genre', *Skoop*, 25, 6, June, 8–11.

Van Extergem, Dirk (2004) 'A Report on the Brussels International Festival of Fantastic Film', in Ernest Mathijs and Xavier Mendik (eds) *Alternative Europe: Eurotrash and Exploitation Cinema Since 1945*. London: Wallflower Press, 216–27.

Van Tongeren, Phil (1986) 'Ouvreuse, mag ik een teiltje: de body-horror van David Cronenberg', *Skoop*, 22, 9–10, 18–21.

Varga, Darrell (2003) 'The Deleuzean Experience of Cronenberg's *Crash* and Wenders' *The End of Violence*', in Mark Shiel and Tony Fitzmaurice (eds) *Screening the City*. London: Verso, 262–83.

Vatnsdal, Caelum (2004) *They Came From Within: A History of Canadian Horror Cinema*. Winnipeg: Arbeiters Ring.

Vernaglione, Paolo (1987) 'Cronenberg: veux-tu venir chez moi après la peste?', *Filmcritica*, 38, 372, 101–5.

____ (1989) 'Conversazione con David Cronenberg', *Filmcritica*, 40, 393, 162–9.

____ (1995) *David Cronenberg*. Naples: Edizione Scientifiche Italiane.

Vice, Sue (1993) 'Hallucinatory Reality in David Cronenberg's *Naked Lunch*', *Dionysos: The Literature and Addiction TriQuarterly*, 4, 3, 43–7.

Viviani, Christian (1975) 'The Parasite Murders', *Positif*, 171/172, July/August, 68.

Walker, Alexander (1996) 'A Movie beyond the Bounds of Depravity', *Evening Standard*, 3 June.

____ (1997a) 'Porn goes into Overdrive', *Evening Standard*, 6 June.

____ (1997b) 'Teaching Tolerance', *Sight and Sound*, 7, 8, 64.

____ (1999) 'The 99 Worst Things this Century Part II', *Evening Standard*, 12 January, 23–4.

____ (2003) 'Web of an Invisible Man', *Evening Standard*, 2 January, 34.

Wallace, David Foster (2006) 'Big Red Son', in *Consider the Lobster and Other Essays*. New York: Little Brown, 3–50.

Wardle, Paul (1997) 'The 50 Most Important People in Science Fiction: No. 47: David Cronenberg', *Cinefantastique*, 28, 12, 44.

Warren, Ina (1988) 'Film Notes: *Dead Ringers* Creeps its Way to Success in US Cinemas', *Globe and Mail*, 1 November.

Warshow, Robert (2004 [1954]) 'Movie Chronicle: The Westerner', in Leo Braudy and Marshall Cohen (eds) *Film Theory and Criticism*. Oxford: Oxford University Press, 654–67.

Watney, Simon (1987) *Policing Desire: Pornography, AIDS, and the Media*. Minneapolis: University of Minnesota Press.

Watson, Glen (2005) 'A History of Violence', *Daily Info, Oxford*, 2 October, available online at: http://www.dailyinfo.co.uk (accessed 22 November 2007).

Way, Ben (1996) 'David Cronenberg *Crash* sur la Croisette', *Studio Magazine* (Cannes Special), 112, June, 81–2.

Weiler, A. H. (1969) 'Museum Will Offer Science (Non)Fiction Film Series', *New York Times*, 22 July, 32.

Weinstock, Jeffrey (2007) *The Rocky Horror Picture Show*. London: Wallflower Press.

Whitman, Marc (1976) 'Shivers', *Films Illustrated*, 5, 57, 330.

____ (1980) 'The Brood', *Films Illustrated*, 9, 103, 254.

Wiater, Stan (1992) 'Interview with David Cronenberg', in *Dark Visions: Conversations with the Masters of the Horror Film*. New York: Avon Books, 59–65.

Wiegmann, Mira (2003) *The Staging and Transformation of Gender Archetypes in A Midsummer Night's Dream, M. Butterfly, and Kiss of the Spider Woman*. Lewiston, NY: Edwin Mellen Press.

Wignesan, Nachiketas (1999) 'Dossier Cronenberg', *Repérages*, 6, May–June, 5–19.

Willemsen, Paul (1996) '*Crash*, of de kick van de frontale botsing', *De Standaard*, 30 October, 12.

Williams, Christian (1982) 'Aaagghh! The Power of the Gory: Grisly Cinema Slithers into a High-Tech Golden Age', *Washington Post*, 27 May, D1.

Williams, Linda (1994) 'Learning to Scream', *Sight and Sound*, 4, 12, 14–17.

Williams, Linda Ruth (1993) 'Movie Nightmares: A Virus is Only Doing Its Job', *Sight and Sound*, 3, 5, 30–3.

____ (1999) 'The Inside-out of Masculinity: David Cronenberg's Visceral Pleasures', in Michele Aaron (ed.) *The Body's Perilous Pleasures: Dangerous Desires and Contemporary Culture*. Edinburgh: Edinburgh University Press, 30–48.

Williams, Tony (1996) *Hearths of Darkness: The Family in the American Horror Film*. Fairleigh: Dickinson University Press.

Wilson, Ian (1991) 'Oscar Winner to race rare cars at Speedweeks', *Toronto Star*, 8 June, K3.

Wilson, Scott and Fred Botting (1998) 'Automatic Lover: *Crash*', *Screen*, 39, 2, 186–92.

Wisenthal, Jonathan, Sherrill Grace, Melinda Boyd, Brian McIlroy and Vera Micznik (eds) (2006) *A Vision of the Orient: Texts, Intertexts, and Contexts of Madame Butterfly*. Toronto: University of Toronto Press.

Wood, Robin (1975) 'New Cinema at Edinburgh', *Film Comment*, 11, 6, 25–9.

____ (1978a) 'Responsibilities of a Gay Film Critic', *Film Comment*, 14, 1, 12–17.

____ (1978b) 'Return of the Repressed', *Film Comment*, 14, 4, 24–32.

____ (1978c) 'Gods and Monsters', *Film Comment*, 14, 5, 19–25.

____ (1979a) 'An Introduction to the American Horror Film', in Andrew Britton, Robin Wood, Richard Lippe and Tony Williams (eds) *The American Nightmare: Essays on the Horror Film*. Toronto: Festival of Festivals, 1–24.

____ (1979b) 'Apocalypse Now: Notes on the Living Dead', in Andrew Britton, Robin Wood, Richard Lippe and Tony Williams (eds) *The American Nightmare: Essays on the Horror Film*. Toronto: Festival of Festivals, 91–7.

____ (1980) 'Neglected Nightmares', *Film Comment*, 16, 2, 28.

____ (1983) 'Cronenberg: A Dissenting View', in Piers Handling (ed.) *The Shape of Rage: The Films of David Cronenberg*. Toronto: General Publishing, 115–35.

____ (1986) *Hollywood From Vietnam to Reagan*. New York: Columbia University Press.

____ (1993) 'Critical Positions and the End of Civilization; or, a Refusal to Join the Club', *Film Criticism*, 17, 2–3, 79–92.

Yacowar, Maurice (1977) 'You Shiver Because It's Good', *Cinema Canada*, 34/35, 54–5.

Yates, James (1995) 'David Cronenberg as Mythmaker: An Archetypical Interpretation of his Films, 1975 to 1991', unpublished PhD dissertation, Oklahoma State University.

Young, Suzie (2002) 'Forget Baudrillard: The Horrors of "Pleasure" and the Pleasures of "Horror" in David Cronenberg's *Videodrome*', in Eugene Waltz (ed.) *Canada's Best Features: Critical Essays on 15 Canadian Films*. Amsterdam and New York: Rodopi, 147–74.

Zimbardo, Philip (1985) *Cults Go To High School: A Theoretical and Empirical Analysis of the Initial Stage in the Recruitment Process*. American Family Foundation.

Zimbardo, Philip, Craig Haney, W. Curtis Banks and David Jaffe (1973) 'The Mind is a Formidable Jailer: A Pirandellian Prison', *New York Times Magazine*, 8 April, Section 6, 38.

Zoller, Stephen (1982), 'Videodrome', *Mediascene Prevue*, January.

Zurbrugg, Nicholas (1999) 'Will Hollywood Never Learn? David Cronenberg's *Naked Lunch*', in Deborah Cartmell and Imelda Whelehan (eds) *Adaptations: from Text to Screen, Screen to Text*. London: Routledge, 98–112.

INDEX

1984 (1984) 118–19

9/11 (11 September 2001) 2, 213, 233

A History of Violence (2005) 2, 6, 69–70, 115, 154, 171, 222–37, 246, 248–53

Adams, Brooke 114–15

After Hours (1985) 141

AIDS 2, 102, 104, 122, 132, 147–52

Aimée und Jaguar (1999) 216

Alberta 63–4

Alien (1979) 83, 96, 107, 114, 161

Aliens (1986) 100, 146, 170

All the President's Men (1975) 47, 88

Alliance of Canadian Cinema, Television, and Radio Artists (ACTRA) 54, 126

Altin, Josef 237

Amant, L' (1992) 175

American Graffiti (1973) 62

American History X (1998) 216

American Psycho (2000) 156, 199, 224

American Werewolf in London, An (1981) 93, 96, 105

Amis, Martin 237

Amityville II (1982) 98

Andrews, Julie 125

Anger, Kenneth 13, 16, 25–6, 50–1, 124

Anthrax 146

Apocalypse Now (1979) 84

Argento, Dario 43, 89, 94, 103

Arquette, Rosanna 182

At the Suicide of the Last Jew in the World in the Last Cinema in the World (2007) 7, 253, 255–6

Atame! (1990) 157

Atlantic City (1980) 67

Atwood, Margaret 36, 127, 162

Avco-Embassy 84, 95

Avoriaz Film Festival 47, 103, 113, 122, 127, 144–5

Ayscough, Susan 128, 162

Baker, Rick 105–6

Ballard, J. G. 8, 102, 162, 180–1, 187–8, 191

Barker, Martin 181, 189–91

Barrymore, Drew 113

Bartel, Paul 45, 62

Barton Fink (1991) 169

Basic Instinct (1992) 175, 191

Basic Instinct II (2006) 219, 224, 237

Baudrillard, Jean 124

Bava, Mario 30, 33, 52, 84, 103

Bazin, André 187

Beard, William 18, 21, 25, 32, 54, 57, 75, 81–2, 87, 140, 186, 204, 219, 223–4

Beckett, Samuel 8, 13, 162, 219–21, 245

Beckman, Henry 77

Bello, Maria 228

Benjamin, Walter 120

Bertolucci, Bernardo 126, 169

Beverly Hills Cop (1984) 142

Beyond the Darkness (1979) 52

Bill C-10 127

Bill C-54 127

Black Rider 160

Black Robe (1991) 142

Blade Runner (1982) 118

Blair, Tony 192

Blasco, Joe 33, 38, 63

Blondie 85, 106

Blood and Donuts (1995) 188, 200

Bloodsucking Freaks (1982) 125
Blow Out (1981) 118
Blue (1992) 199–200
Boam, Jeffrey 113
Board, John 101, 145
Body Double (1984) 118
Bonin, Gordie 57
Boogeyman, The (1980) 125
Boozecan (1994) 200
Bordwell, David 3, 128, 212
Borges, Jorge Luis 161–2
Bowie, David 119, 156
Boxcar Bertha (1972) 45
Boyman, Marc 145
Boys from Brazil, The (1978)
    88
Brain Damage (1988) 146
Braindead (1992) 170
Brainstorm (1983) 89, 114,
    217
Brault, Michel 40, 45
Brazil (1984) 118
Breton, Andre 95
British Board of Film
    Classification (BBFC) 125,
    189–90, 247
Brood, The (1979) 2–3, 5–6,
    49–50, 69–97, 100–1, 104,
    126, 154–5, 188, 204, 223,
    236, 250, 256
Brooks, Mel 144
Brophy, Philip 106–7
Brussels International Festival of
    Fantastic Film 170, 217
Bryant, Anita 149
Bryk, Greg 228
Bujold, Genevieve 131
Buñuel, Luis 123
Burroughs, Jackie 115, 126
Burroughs, William 8, 11, 95,
    117, 160, 162–4, 166–71,
    218–19
Byrne, Gabriel 200, 208

Campbell, Nicholas 4, 55, 63,
    65, 73, 77, 101, 114, 116,
    165, 200
Camus, Albert 183
Canadian Broadcast Corporation
    (CBC) 24–5, 59
Canadian Film Development
    Corporation (CFDC) 25,
    32, 38, 46, 49
Canadian Tire 60–1

Cannes Film Festival 8, 25,
    45, 49, 54, 59, 188, 191–2,
    215, 218–21, 233–6, 246,
    249, 253
Cannibal Holocaust (1979) 111,
    125
Canonball (1976) 62
Canonball Run (1981) 62
Cape Fear (1991) 244
Capture of Bigfoot, The (1979)
    98
Car, The (1977) 62
Carlson, Les 44, 112, 114, 120,
    160, 202–4
Carpenter, John 24, 43, 83–5,
    89, 94, 96, 98, 103, 107,
    113, 123, 151
Carrie (1976) 40, 43, 94, 107,
    113, 211
Carroll, Noël 128, 210
Casablanca (1942) 167, 169
Cassel, Vincent 239, 243
Cat People (1982) 106–7
Cats 103
Censorship 2, 97, 104, 122,
    124–7, 162, 166, 189, 191,
    213–14
Chambers, Marilyn 38, 40,
    42, 64
Changeling, The (1980) 66, 84
Chant d'amour, Un (1950) 126
Chien andalou (1928) 123,
    246–7
Child's Play III (1993) 191, 218
Children of Men (2006) 248
Children of the Corn (1984) 113
Christine (1983) 113
Christmas Story, A (1983) 67
Chute, David 85–6, 97
Cinéfantastique 8, 48–9, 72, 85,
    94–8, 103, 106, 122, 128,
    146, 148, 170, 217
Cinema Canada 47–9, 51, 97
Cinépix 32–3, 38, 40, 43–6
Citizen Kane (1941) 210
City of the Living Dead (1980)
    24, 30, 32, 43, 45, 47–8,
    50–1, 83, 94, 100, 146
Clark, Bob 44, 67, 84, 160,
    169, 175
Clavell, James 144, 161
Clerks (1994) 192
Clockwork Orange, A (1971)
    107, 123

Coen Brothers 169, 199, 248
Cohen, Larry 43, 84, 93, 103
Coleman, Ornette 164
Columbus of Sex, The (1969) 25
Conan the Barbarian (1982)
    114
Confessional, Le (1995) 199
Conrich, Ian 92, 97
Conversation, The (1974) 88
Convoy (1977) 62
Cook, The Thief, His Wife and
    Her Lover, The (1989) 157
Coppola, Francis Ford 84, 88,
    147, 188, 239, 252
Corman, Roger 33, 46, 49,
    61–2, 161–2
Cornfeld, Stuart 144
Coscarelli, Don 84
Costello, John 150
Crash (1996) 2–5, 51, 69–70,
    102, 134, 154–5, 162,
    179–81, 184–95, 216–17,
    221, 223, 236, 240, 243–4,
    247, 256
Craven, Wes 43, 50, 84, 89, 93,
    98, 103, 199
Crazy Mama (1975) 45
Creed, Barbara 81–2, 91, 138,
    146, 151, 153, 193
Creepshow (1982) 113
Creley, Jack 109
Crimes of the Future (1971) 2,
    6, 9, 18–26, 30–2, 40, 56,
    65, 68–9, 123, 154–5, 161,
    219, 242
Crying Game, The (1993) 175
Crying of Lot 49, The 118
Cube (1997) 199
Cujo (1983) 113
Curtis, Jamie Lee 94
Cusack, Sinéad 238

Dafoe, Willem 205
Dali, Salvador 95
Danse Macabre 75, 113
Dante, Joe 94, 98, 103, 170
David, Pierre 92, 100–1, 105,
    142
Davis, Geena 131, 153
Davis, Judy 157, 166, 169
Dawn of the Dead (1978) 32,
    75, 83, 93, 96–7, 107
Day of the Dead (1985) 103
Day, Bryan 65, 101

De Laurentiis, Dino 113–14, 142–4
De Niro, Robert 244
De Palma, Brian 40, 84, 89, 94, 118, 156, 251
Dead Ringers (1988) 2, 7, 11, 26, 69–70, 101, 104, 129–32, 135, 138–46, 150–4, 161–3, 169–72, 200, 223
Dead Zone, The (1983) 2, 4–5, 8, 21, 26, 69–70, 88, 100–4, 113–18, 120–8, 142, 144, 154, 159–63, 172, 202, 231, 235, 250, 255
Dead Zone, The (television series (2002-) 2, 4–5, 8, 21, 26, 69–70, 88, 100–4, 113–28, 131, 142, 144, 154, 159–63, 172, 231, 235, 250, 255
Dean, James 70, 182
Death Race 2000 (1975) 45, 62
Deathsport (1978) 62
Dekalog (1987–89) 150
Del Grande, Louis 73
Delaney, Marshall 13, 23, 46, 62
Demme, Jonathan 32, 45, 114
Demons (1985) 52
Departed, The (2006) 248
Descartes, René 95, 124, 162
Desy, Victor 101
Devine, Aidan 235
Dewhurst, Colleen 116
Dick, Philip K. 142, 218
Dimension Films 100
Dirty Pretty Things (2002) 244
Doederlein, Fred 34, 86, 101
Dostoyevksy, Fyodor 8, 219, 225, 245–6
Douglas, Michael 131
Drag Racer (1971) 62
Dragonslayer (1981) 98
Dreyfuss, Richard 143
Driller Killer (1979) 125
Drugstore Cowboy (1990) 169
Ducati 60, 70
Dune (1984) 118
Dupuis, Stephan 96, 98, 101, 144, 243
Dvorsky, Peter 109, 114–15
Dymond, Greig 66–7, 99–100

Eastern Promises (2007) 2, 6, 69–70, 154, 179, 219, 222–8, 235, 237–53

Easy Rider (1969) 39, 61
Ebert, Roger 76, 194, 240
Eccleston, Christopher 204
Edinburgh International Film Festival 45, 47
Edmonton 54, 57, 64, 67
Eggar, Samantha 64, 77, 79–80, 208–9
Egoyan, Atom 127, 152, 188, 219–20
El Topo (1970) 26, 50
Ellis, Brett Easton 156
Emmanuelle (1973) 50
Empire of the Sun (1987) 188
Empire Strikes Back, The (1981) 145
Emporte-moi (1999) 216
Endgame (2000) 212, 219
Equinox (1970) 50
Eraserhead (1977) 50–1, 75
Everman, Welch 75
Everything is Illuminated (2006) 248
Evil Dead, The (1983) 98, 125
eXistenZ (1999) 2, 11, 69–70, 154–5, 173, 196–9, 202, 204–7, 210–24, 236, 245, 250
Extreme Measures (1996) 200

Faces of Death (1979) 98, 124
Fahrenheit 9/11 (2004) 233
Family Viewing (1987) 152
Fangoria 8, 94, 97–8, 103, 146, 221
Fantasporto Festival 144–5, 170
Farewell to My Concubine (1993) 175
Fast Company (1979) 2, 26, 53–71, 79, 84, 101, 155, 171, 186
Faulkner, William 169
Ferrari 53, 60, 64, 69, 189
Fiennes, Ralph 207, 212, 219
Fight Club (1999) 199
Film Comment 81, 84–5, 96, 150
Film festivals 8, 25, 45, 47, 49, 51, 80, 84, 94, 97, 103, 123, 126–7, 144–5, 160, 170, 174–5, 188–90, 202, 215, 217, 219, 221, 233–4, 246, 248, 253
Firestarter (1984) 113

First Blood (1982) 67
Flaming Creatures (1963) 126
Flashdance (1984) 142
Flaubert, Gustave 162
Fly II, The (1990) 100
Fly, The (1986) 2, 4, 6, 8, 11, 21, 51, 69–70, 100, 104, 129–54, 171, 188, 202, 223, 236
Fly, The (opera) (2008) 179
Fog, The (1980) 94
Fonda, Jane 64
Forbes, Sonny 101
Forbidden Planet (1956) 10, 23, 80
Formula One 62, 69
Forrest Gump (1994) 214
Foster, Judy 55
Francks, Don 55
Freaks (1932) 50, 75, 125
Freud, Sigmund 39, 90–1, 109, 162, 220–1, 237
Friday the 13th (1980) 103, 106, 211
Friday the 13th franchise (1980–) 146, 160, 202
Friday the 13th TV series (1987–90) 160, 202
Frightmare (1974) 43
From Beyond (1986) 146
Frye, Northrop 194
Fulci, Lucio 84, 89, 94, 103
Fulford, Robert 46, 49, 51
Fury on Wheels (1971) 62

Gang, Pierre 188
Garris, Mick 49, 95, 200
Geasland, Jack 161, 163
Genet, Jean 126
Getz, John 133
Ghomeshi, Jian 248–9
Giacometti, Alberto 91
Gibson, William 108, 118
Ginger Snaps (2000) 127, 199, 219
Ginsberg, Allen 165
Girard, René 30–1, 37, 41, 123, 249
Globe and Mail 13, 23, 46, 49, 75, 85, 148, 161, 163, 170
Godfather III, The (1990) 252
Goldberg, Daniel 12, 25, 33
Goldblum, Jeff 130–1, 153, 161

Gorman, Lynne 110
Grace of God, The (1997) 200
Grand Prix (1966) 61
Grand Theft Auto (1977) 62
Grant, Barry Keith 123
Gravity's Rainbow 118
Greenaway, Peter 150, 157, 161, 169, 244
Gremlins (1984) 98
Gremlins II (1990) 170
Grünberg, Serge 7, 54, 87, 204
Guardian, The 189, 216, 248
Guare, John 4
Guerrero, Ed 151
Gumball Rally, The (1976) 62

Haley, Jonathan 135
Haley, Nicholas 135
Haley, Robert 55
Halloween (1978) 83, 94, 100, 103, 114, 146
Halloween III (1982) 107
Hampton, Christopher 237
Hamsun, Knut 18
Harcourt, Peter 46
Harder They Come, The (1972) 50
Harkness, John 53, 79, 147–9
Harris, Ed 229
Harry, Deborah 64, 106, 109
Hayes, Heidi 228
Hedley, Tom 142
Hell's Angels on Wheels (1967) 61
Hellraiser (1987) 146
Henry and June (1990) 157, 169, 245
Henry and Verlin (1995) 200
Heroux, Claude 101, 105
Herrmann, Bernard 89
Higher Learning (1995) 157
Hill, Debra 113
Hill, Terrence 98
Hills Have Eyes, The (1977) 50, 93
Hinckley, John 124
Hindle, Art 44, 77, 79, 88, 95
Hinds, Cindy 77, 101
Hitchcock, Alfred 37, 89, 179, 247
Hitler, Adolf 121, 127
Hobbes, Thomas 6, 34–6
Hogan, David 153
Hogan, Susan 78, 101

Holm, Ian 167, 205
Holmes, Ashton 228
Hop-Along Cassidy (1935) 251
Howling, The (1980) 94
Huillet, Daniele 45
Hunger, The (1984) 146
Hunter, Holly 181

I've Heard the Mermaids Singing (1987) 152
In a Lonely Place (1950) 128
Indiana Jones and the Temple of Doom (1984) 98
Indochine (1992) 175
Inferno (1980) 47, 94
Internet 26, 51, 67, 99, 215, 236
Into the Night (1985) 7, 130, 200
Invasion of the Body Snatchers (1956) 23, 30
Invasion of the Body Snatchers (1978) 45, 47–8, 83, 88, 114
Invocation of my Demon Brother (1969) 26, 50
Irons, Jeremy 131, 136, 145, 158, 161, 169, 171
Ironside, Michael 86, 88
Irwin, Mark 5, 57, 59, 65, 68, 101, 144–5
It Happened Here (1965) 145
It Lives Again (1978) 93
It's Alive (1974) 43, 93
It's Alive III (1985) 103
Italian Machine, The (1976) 7, 26, 38, 53, 56, 59–63, 101

Jason X (2001) 7, 199–200, 202
Jennings, Claudia 54–5, 57, 62, 64–5
Johnny Mnemonic (1995) 217
Jones, Martha 54, 64
Joy Luck Club, The (1993) 176
Judge, The (2001) 200
Jung, Carl-Gustav 237
Jungle Fever (1991) 157

Kael, Pauline 148
Kafka (1991) 169
Kafka, Franz 8, 134, 161–2, 166, 219–20
Kamen, Michael 113
Kelly, Grace 183

Kennedy, John F. 173, 180, 183
Kerouac, Jack 165
Khaner, Julie 108
Killing of America, The (1981) 125
Kilometre Zero (2005) 233
King, Stephen 8, 75, 83, 97, 103–4, 113, 124, 161
Kiss 83
Kissed (1996) 127
Klee, Paul 124
Knelman, Martin 46, 220
Knight, Steve 243–4, 247
Knightriders (1981) 103
Koteas, Elias 181, 244
Kovács, Géza 60, 101, 114, 120
Kramer vs. Kramer (1979) 79–80
Krishna, Srinivas 188
Kroll, Jack 93
Kubrick, Stanley 23, 113, 160, 169, 218
Kümel, Harry 25–6, 42, 103

L'Enfant (2005) 233
L'humanité (1999) 219
Labrosse, Sarah Jeanne 237, 243
Lacan Jacques 91
Lack, Stephen 86, 101, 137
Laing, R. D. 91
LaMarsh, Judy 46
Landis, John 7–8, 63, 89, 93, 96, 103, 200
Lang, Fritz 23, 251
Langelaan, George 144, 161
Last Dragon, The (1985) 98
Last Embrace (1979) 114
Last Night (1998) 7, 199–201
Law, Jude 205, 216
Le boucher (1970) 48
Le Mans (1971) 61
Leach, Jim 12, 67, 158
Lebowitz, Michael 63–5
Lee, Bruce 98
Legend of Sleepy Hollow, The 115
Leigh, Jennifer Jason 204, 218
Lemche, Kris 205
Lennick, Michael 105
Lenny (1974) 51
Lepage, Robert 188, 199
Les Ordres (1974) 40, 45
Letterman, David 123

Leventon, Annabel 158
Lie Chair, The (1976) 7, 44, 69–70, 101
Limey, The (1999) 199
Lineham, Hardee 60
Lom, Herbert 114–15
Lone, John 173, 175
Love at First Bite (1979) 83
Lowenstein, Adam 36, 200–1
Lowry, Lynn 33–4, 42
Lucas, George 1, 5, 8, 24, 62, 233
Lucas, Tim 7, 106, 113, 123, 128, 144
Luna (1979) 126
Lynch, David 50, 118, 160–1, 176

M. Butterfly (1993) 2, 51, 69–70, 154–9, 163, 171–8, 198, 242, 250
MacGoohan, Patrick 64
MacKinnon, Kenneth 149
Maclean's 47, 75, 234
Mad Max (1980) 62, 118
Mafia 7, 200, 225–6, 228, 231, 239–40, 242, 244, 252–3
Makaveyev, Dusan 126
Man bites Dog (1992) 191
Manderlay (2005) 233
Mansfield, Jayne 183–4, 187
Marcuse, Herbert 17, 31–2
Mark of Cain (2000) 243
Mark of the Devil (1970) 114
Martin (1977) 93
Masala (1996) 188
Maslany, Tatiana 242
Matrix trilogy (1999–2003) 199
Matrix, The (1999) 217–18
Mauvais sang (Bad Blood) (1987) 147
McDonald, Bruce 152
McGoohan, Patrick 86–7
McGrath, Patrick 8, 212–13, 220–1
McHattie, Stephen 228
McIlroy, Brian 193
McKellar, Don 7, 199, 201, 206
McLuhan, Marshall 17, 124, 162–3
McQueen, Steve 61–2
Meat Loaf 83

Meatballs (1979) 66–7
Medea (1969) 51
Melnyk, George 12, 66–7
Mercure, Monique 168
Messinger, Jack 12, 114
Midnight movie 26, 45, 50–1, 76, 83, 104
Mikic, Aleksander 239
Miller, Henry 169, 245
Mina, Mina E. 239
Mitchum, Robert 243
Mlodzik, Ron 14, 25, 33–4, 38, 65
Mollin, Fred 66
Monde, Le 23, 189, 248
Mondo Cane (1962) 110
Monk, Katherine 99
Monkey Shines (1988) 103
Monthly Film Bulletin 23, 92
Moonshine Highway (1996) 188
Moore, Brian 142, 191
Moore, Frank 38, 60, 200
Moreau, Marsha 135
Morris, Peter 10–12, 16, 24–6, 43, 54
Mortal Kombat (1995) 217
Mortensen, Viggo 226–8, 238–9, 242–3
Moses und Aaron (1975) 45
MTV 102, 108
Mueller-Stahl, Armin 239
My Bloody Valentine (1981) 67

Nabokov, Vladimir 245
Naked Lunch (1991) 2, 4, 51, 69–70, 104, 142, 154, 156–78, 198
National Film Board (NFB) 11, 16, 46, 68
Natural Born Killers (1994) 191, 217
Negin, Louis 60
Nelmes, Jill 153
Neumann, Kurt 144
Neuromancer 108, 118
Neville, John 212, 219
New Line Cinema 125, 236
New World Pictures 49
New York Times 170, 189, 218, 234
Newman, Arnold 91
Newman, Kim 47, 57, 64, 217
Newsweek 93, 117
Nicholson, Jack 64, 88

Night of the Hunter (1955) 243
Night of the Living Dead (1968) 24, 30, 32, 43, 45, 47–8, 50–1, 83, 94, 100, 146
Nightbreed (1990) 7, 160, 188, 199–200
Nightmare on Elm Street (1984) 98, 100, 103, 146
Nin, Anaïs 169, 245
Nine and a Half Weeks (1986) 141
No Country for Old Men (2007) 248
North by Northwest (1959) 89

O' Bannon, Dan 100, 142
O'Brian, Peter 63
O'Neill, Jennifer 87, 94
Odets, Clifford 169
Omen, The (1976) 50
Once (2006) 248
One Flew Over the Cuckoo's Nest (1975) 88
Ontario 2, 25, 44, 46, 64, 113, 125–6, 160, 174, 179, 234
Orientalism 159, 175, 177, 179
Ottawa 18, 23

Pac Man 102
Papirnick, Bob 57
Parallax View, The (1974) 88
Peary, Danny 65, 74–5, 83, 90, 100
Peggy Sue got Married (1986) 147
Peterson, Ronnie 62
Pevere, Geoff 66–7, 99–100
Pike, Dennis 96, 101
Pillow Book, The (1996) 244
Pink Flamingos (1972) 50
Piranha (1978) 94
Plan 9 From Outer Space (1959) 75
Pleasence, Donald 89
Poe, Edgar Allen 114
Pogue, Charles Edward 144
Polley, Sarah 206
Poltergeist (1982) 98, 103, 107
Pomerance, Murray 193, 218
Pool, Lea 216
Porky's (1981) 67
Porsche 182–3, 185
Power of Nightmares, The (2005) 233

Premonition, The (1975) 47
Prisoner, The (1967) 88
Prom Night (1980) 66–7
Prospero's Books (1991) 169
Psychic, The (1977) 94
Psycho (1960) 37, 48, 91, 99,
  153, 156, 199, 224, 237,
  246–7
Psychoanalysis 90–1, 136
Puccini, Giacomo 8, 158, 173,
  178
Pulp Fiction (1994) 214
Puppetmaster, The (1993) 175
Pynchon, Thomas 109, 118,
  162

Q, the Winged Serpent (1982) 103
Québec 2, 33, 39–41, 44,
  46, 64

Rabid (1977) 2, 6, 21, 23,
  28–30, 32, 37–44, 48–52,
  59, 61, 63, 65–6, 68, 70, 84,
  90–1, 101, 110, 149, 188,
  200, 249
Race with the Devil (1975) 47
Raiders of the Lost Ark (1981) 98
Rameau's Nephew (1982) 126
Ramsay, Christine 151
Rancho Notorious (1952) 252
Raven, The 114
Ray, Nicholas 128
Ray, Robert 212
Rayns, Tony 24, 161
Reagan, Ronald 102, 114, 118,
  124, 146, 149
Re-Animator (1985) 146
Red Cars 7, 68, 71, 189, 219,
  224, 237
Redford, Robert 88
Redgrave, Lynn 207
Reed, Oliver 64, 73
Reitman, Ivan 12, 25, 32–3,
  38, 44, 46, 63, 65–7
Rennie, Callum Keith 206
Repulsion (1965) 24, 48
Resurrection (1999) 7, 40, 200
Return of the Jedi (1983) 98
Return of the Living Dead (1985)
  100, 146
Revenge of the Sith (2005) 233
Reversal of Fortune (1990) 145
Rice, Anne 83
Richardson, Miranda 208–10

Roadkill (1989) 152
Robards, Jason 64
Rocky Horror Picture Show, The
  (1975) 43–4, 46–7, 50, 83,
  145, 158, 244
Rodley, Chris 5, 10, 16, 18,
  21, 38, 44, 54, 65–6, 79–80,
  91, 100, 108, 122, 129,
  142, 144, 162–3, 174, 177,
  184, 217
Rollin, Jean 42, 103
Rosemary's Baby (1968) 24,
  44, 153
Rosetta (1999) 219
Rothman, Stephanie 84, 103,
  125
Rourke, Mickey 141
Rozema, Patricia 152, 188, 219
Ruby (1977) 50
Rushdie, Salman 3, 8, 213–19,
  245

Sanders, Ronald 65, 101
Sands, Julian 168
Sarris, Andrew 123, 148
Saturday Night 46
Savath, Phil 63
Savini, Tom 74, 96, 98
Saw (2004) 100
Saxon, John 44, 55, 57, 64–5
Scanner Cop (1994) 100
Scanner Cop II (1995) 100
Scanners (1981) 2–4, 8, 49–51,
  69–77, 84–9, 91–101,
  104–5, 122, 124–6, 142,
  155, 162, 182, 188, 202,
  204, 214, 223, 236, 250
Scanners II: the New Order
  (1991) 100
Scanners III: the Take Over
  (1992) 100
Scarface (1983) 251
Scheider, Roy 167
Schlock (1973) 93
Schlöndorff, Volker 126
Schmid, Kyle 235
Schneider, Steven Jay 210
Schreiber, Liev 246, 248
Schwartz, Tom 96
Schwarzenegger, Arnold 143
Sconce, Jeffrey 210, 2112
Scorsese, Martin 8, 45, 63,
  89, 123, 128, 141, 161–2,
  244, 248

Scorsiani, Joseph 157
Scott, Jay 51, 54, 80, 84, 93,
  126, 148, 152, 163, 170
Scream trilogy (1996–2000)
  199
Secret Weapons (1972) 7, 24–6
Serpent and the Rainbow, The
  (1987) 103
Seven Year Itch, The (1955) 164
Shakespeare in Love (1999) 215
Shakespeare, William 162, 169
Shamata, Chuck 60
Shane (1953) 251
Shape of Rage, The 123, 128,
  147, 160
Sharrett, Christopher 123
She's Having a Baby (1988) 147
She-Devils on Wheels (1968) 61
Sheen, Charlie 131
Sheen, Martin 116
Sheltering Sky, The (1990) 169
Shining, The (1980) 113
Shivers (1975) 2–3, 6, 21,
  28–30, 32–52, 61, 63, 65–6,
  68–70, 75, 80, 101, 108,
  147, 154–5, 188, 215, 249,
  256
Shore, Howard 66, 101, 113,
  179
Shostrom, Mark 105
Showgirls (1995) 193
Shwarz, Reiner 101, 108
Siegel, Don 23, 30, 89, 97
Silverman, Robert 77, 86, 101,
  157, 206
Sitges Festival 47, 215, 220
Skerritt, Tom 114–15
Skolimowski, Jerzy 238, 243
Slayer 146
Sleeper (2005) 233
Slow Learner 118
Smith, Courtney 63
Smith, Dick 96, 98, 106
Smith, Jack 51, 126
Smith, William 55, 57, 62, 64
Smits, Sonja 111
Smokey and the Bandit (1977)
  62
Snider, Norman 18, 25, 32, 85,
  142, 144, 163
Snow, Michael 12–13, 16, 126
Snuff (1976) 111
Soderbergh, Steven 169, 199
Solnicki, Victor 101, 105

Sopranos, The (1999–2007) 251
Sous-sol (1996) 188
Spader, James 180–1
Spasms (1983) 98
Spenser, Michael 46
Spider (2002) 2, 5, 69–70, 154–5, 196–213, 219–24, 236, 242, 245, 250
Spielberg, Steven 42, 98, 103, 188
Spier, Carol 65, 101
Springsteen, Bruce 65
Starlog 94, 103, 122, 146
Steele, Barbara 29, 32–5, 37, 64
Stein, Chris 85
Stereo (1969) 2, 9, 13–14, 16–26, 30, 32, 40, 46, 56, 65, 68–9, 123, 154
Stopkevitch, Lynne 127
Strange Days (1995) 89, 217
Strange Invaders (1983) 98
Straub, Jean-Marie 45
Streetfighter (1995) 217
Stupids, The (1995) 200
Sukowa, Barbara 173
Sullivan, Sean 115
Suschitzky, Peter 140, 145
Suspiria (1977) 43, 50, 94
Sweet Movie (1974) 126

Tarantino, Quentin 199, 214
Taxi Driver (1976) 89, 123–4
Taylor, Paul 92
Teague, Lewis 113
Telefon (1977) 89
Terminal Island (1973) 125
Testa, Bart 85, 92, 123, 193–4
Texas Chainsaw Massacre, The (1974) 32, 43, 47, 50, 83, 98, 124
Thatcher, Margaret 102, 146, 149
They Live (1988) 103
Thin Red Line, The (1999) 216
Thing, The (1982) 98, 107, 151
Thomas, Jeremy 163, 171, 189, 194, 237
Three Days of the Condor (1975) 88
Three Men and a Baby (1987) 147, 153
Thurman, Uma 245
Tin Drum, The (1981) 126

To Die For (1995) 7, 200
Top Gun (1986) 142
Toronto 2, 8–13, 16–18, 21, 23–4, 26, 49–51, 54, 66, 80, 94, 97, 108, 123, 126, 135–6, 145, 152, 161, 164, 172, 174–5, 181, 202, 214–16, 219–21, 234, 246
Toronto International Film Festival 51, 80, 84, 94, 97, 123, 126, 145, 174–5, 202, 219, 234, 246
Total Recall (1990) 7, 142–4, 217
Tout va bien (1972) 51
Towering Inferno, The (1974) 47
Trainspotting (1996) 192
Treen, Alan 63
Trial by Jury (1994) 7, 200, 225–6
Trouble Every Day (2001) 52
Truffaut, François 187
Truman Show, The (1998) 217
Turner, Ted 193
Twin Peaks (1990) 160
Two-Lane Blacktop (1971) 62

Un monde sans pitié (1989) 150
Unger, Deborah Kara 181

Van Sant, Gus 7, 169
Vancouver 11, 63, 66, 152
Variety 26, 59, 65, 75, 93, 125, 171, 188, 234
VCR 98, 102, 110–11
Verhoeven, Paul 7, 143, 175, 193
Véronneau, Pierre 54, 160
Vertigo (1958) 89
Video Nasties 107, 125, 191, 216
Videodrome (1983) 2, 4, 6, 9, 11, 21, 26, 51, 69–70, 88, 101–24, 126–8, 131, 138, 142, 154, 159–61, 165–6, 202–3, 213–14, 217–18, 223, 237, 246, 250, 256
Village of the Damned (1960) 153
Village Voice, The 26, 148, 221, 247
Vineland (1990) 118
Vipco Video 103, 125

Virilio, Paul 193
Von Palleske, Heidi 136

Waits, Tom 160
Walas, Chris 8, 96, 98, 100–1, 144, 170
Walken, Christopher 114, 161
Walker, Alexander 189, 191, 221
Wall Street (1987) 131–2
Wallace, David Foster 107, 193
War Game, The (1965) 145
Ward, Fred 245
Warhol, Andy 13, 23, 26, 95, 107, 123, 179
Warshow, Robert 252
Watergate 43, 88
Watts, Naomi 238, 243
Wedding Banquet, The (1993) 157, 175
Weird Science (1986) 147
Weller, Peter 157, 164
Western Union (1941) 251
Whitehouse, Mary 125, 149
Wild Angels, The (1966) 61
Wild at Heart (1990) 160
Wilder, Billy 164, 183, 193
Williams, Tony 99, 106, 125, 153, 178, 247
Wilson, Bob 160
Wings of Desire (1987) 150
Winning (1969) 61
Witkin, Joel Peter 150
Witness (1985) 142
Wizard Video 125
Wolfe, Tom 156
Wood, Bari 161
Wood, Robin 45, 80, 94, 123, 128, 147, 151, 212
Woods, James 108, 123, 161
Working Girl (1988) 147

X-Files, The (1993–2002) 89, 175

Young Racers, The (1964) 61

Zeller, Gary 96–8
Zelniker, Michael 165
Zemeckis, Robert 214
Zerbe, Anthony 120
Zéro de conduite (1933) 123

www.ingramcontent.com/pod-product-compliance
Ingram Content Group UK Ltd.
Pitfield, Milton Keynes, MK11 3LW, UK
UKHW032309030325
455810UK00003B/153